Resources for

THE BEDFORD ANTHOLOGY OF WORLD LITERATURE

Package A

Beginnings–1650

General Editor: Mary Rooks
Lock Haven University

Book 1, The Ancient World

Brainard Cowan, *Louisiana State University*

Fidel Fajardo-Acosta, *Creighton University*

Ana Galjanic, *Harvard University*

David Johnson, *University of New Mexico*

Bryce Sady, *Harvard University*

Book 2, The Middle Period

Gabriel Gryffyn, *The University of Minnesota*

Margaret Wald, *Rutgers State University*

Book 3, The Early Modern World

Shari Evans, *University of New Mexico*

Dan Reese

Susan Reese, *University of New Mexico*

Mary Rooks, *Lock Haven University*

BEDFORD/ST. MARTIN'S   BOSTON ◆ NEW YORK

Copyright © 2004 by Bedford/St. Martin's

All rights reserved.

Manufactured in the United States of America.

6   5   4   3   2
f   e   d   c   b   a

For information, write: Bedford/St. Martin's, 75 Arlington Street, Boston, MA 02116
(617-399-4000)

ISBN: 0–312–40268–6

Instructors who have adopted *The Bedford Anthology of World Literature* as a textbook for a course are authorized to duplicate portions of this manual for their students.

Preface

In *The Bedford Anthology of World Literature*, we hope to present a fresh approach to world literature — one that is truly global in scope and that truly addresses the challenges inherent in teaching such an incredible range of materials. Every piece of the anthology has been put together with these aims in mind — but obviously the tools we provide *outside* the anthology to help instructors are crucial to our success. The help we provide in these two manuals — to accompany Package A and Package B, respectively — is far more coherent and comprehensive than any other resource we've seen for this course. Together with the anthology and *World Literature Online*, we've tried to assemble a pedagogical package that makes teaching and taking the world literature course a truly enjoyable experience — one with less emphasis on research and more emphasis on teaching.

Resources for Teaching THE BEDFORD ANTHOLOGY OF WORLD LITERATURE include layered discussions of each text, author, culture, and context, as well as additional connections, writing and discussion prompts, and annotated lists of resources for further reading. There are also entries for each thematic *In the World* and *In the Tradition* cluster. Each entry in the Instructor's Manual looks something like this:

General Introduction — A brief overview about the author and the text builds on the introduction in the anthology and addresses key issues students may face when reading and discussing the work.

Text & Context — Highlighting central historical, social, cultural, philosophical, and literary issues, these discussions open up multiple ways to approach each text.

In the Classroom — A variety of lecture topics with associated discussion questions, informal, in-class writing prompts, and connections questions.

Beyond the Classroom — This series of assignments focuses on traditional research papers or less traditional, creative projects.

Further Reading and Media Resources — Bibliographies provide suggestions for print, audio, and visual resources for further research.

Sample syllabi at the end of each package suggest thematic and generic ways to structure courses around each book and each pack — we realized, as we put these together, that the anthology contains the materials for hundreds of different possibilities!

WORLD LITERATURE ONLINE

Also be sure to keep in mind yet another teaching support available—Bedford/ St. Martin's *World Literature Online*, the book's companion Web site, found at www. bedfordstmartins.com/worldlit. The Web site is coordinated with this instructor's manual through marginal notes (designated with a www) that will remind the instructor when there is additional content available for use in preparing lectures, tests, and class assignments.

VIDEO LIBRARY

Selected videos of plays or works represented in the anthology are available from the Bedford/St. Martin's video library to qualified adopters.

It is our hope that the time, energy, and efforts that went into creating and carefully coordinating this full package — the text, instructor's manual, and Web site — will assist in providing the richest and most enjoyable teaching and learning experience possible for you and your students.

ACKNOWLEDGMENTS

Resources for Teaching THE BEDFORD ANTHOLOGY OF WORLD LITERATURE is a truly collaborative result of the contributions of many thoughtful, creative teachers. Expertly developed, edited, and assembled by Mary Rooks and Julie Berrisford, the entries were written by many people with different expertise. We thank all the contributors — and hope you find the results useful as you prepare to teach world literature.

Paul Davis
Gary Harrison
David M. Johnson
Patricia Clark Smith
John F. Crawford

Contents

Japan: Birth of a Culture   396

BOOK 3: THE EARLY MODERN WORLD, 1450–1650

Africa: Epic and Empire in Mali   425

Europe: Renaissance and Reformation   432

The Americas: Aztec Empire and New Spain   531

THE BEDFORD ANTHOLOGY OF WORLD LITERATURE

Package A
Beginnings–1650

Book 1
The Ancient World
Beginnings–100 C.E.

MESOPOTAMIA: THE FORMATION OF CITIES AND THE EARLIEST LITERATURES

The Descent of Inanna (p. 23)

WWW   For a quiz on *The Descent of Inanna,* see *World Literature Online* at bedfordstmartins.com/worldlit.

The most obvious observation to make about *The Descent of Inanna* is that it is the first and oldest story in this anthology, and probably, therefore, the oldest extant written story in the world. Undoubtedly, there are many stories whose oral roots stretch backwards in time to some indefinite, obscure period before the advent of writing, but we can actually locate *The Descent of Inanna* in the urban culture of Sumer, which can be dated c. 3500 B.C.E. Since Sumer developed a written language c. 3200 B.C.E., at about the same time as Egypt, we think of Mesopotamia and Egypt as having the oldest written literature. There is obviously a challenge to making these distant dates relevant to students. A second important point about *The Descent of Inanna* is that it is primarily about women — an earthly goddess and her underworld sister (also an immortal). Students might have encountered goddesses like Athena, Hera, and Aphrodite in Greek and Roman literature, but they are typically portrayed as intervening in mortal affairs and as subordinate deities who are ultimately subject to the rule of a patriarchal male like Zeus or Jove. Students are less likely to have dealt with goddess-heroes like Inanna, who has adventures and performs mighty deeds in her own right, or with a ritual, oral text that was very likely used in ceremonies honoring the goddess and celebrating the seasonal cycles of growth, death, and renewal. Because of its oral roots and its use in religious ceremony, we highly recommend beginning the study of Inanna and her stories with the wonderful videotape *Epic of Inanna,* by the master storyteller and performer Diane Wolkstein (available from Cloudstone, New York City).

Although we do not know about the exact cultural uses of Inanna and Ereshkigal, we can surmise that they played central, religious roles. Inanna was Queen of heaven, the ruler of light and love, fertility and fruitfulness. Ereshkigal was the Queen of the netherworld, in control of darkness and sorrow, death and rebirth. We should probably view these two powerful female figures as two halves of a whole, since the provinces of both deities taken together make up our earthly existence, akin to the agricultural cycle, from birth in the spring to harvest and death in the autumn. Planted under the earth, the seed emerges from the earth as a green plant only to return to the underworld after the harvest. A passage in Genesis (Hebrew Scriptures) connects the plant cycle to humans: "You shall gain your bread by the sweat of your brow / until you return to the ground; / for from it you were taken. / Dust you are, to dust you shall return" (Gen. 3:19). At an early stage of human history, this agricultural cycle was the domain of goddesses and women. Both Inanna and Ereshkigal — the light and the dark, the earth and the underworld — are necessary parts of the life cycle.

From a contemporary point of view, Inanna's story is one of ultimate testing; no worldly power, no wealth or beauty or protection, no human concept of what is just or fair can make us immune to physical death. Similarly, most of us must go through life-changing experiences in which we suffer some sort of death of a part of ourselves. The inexorable way

1

in which Inanna is stripped, one by one, of all of her adornments and tokens of rank is dramatic and devastating. With luck, like Inanna, we will at least have friends to stand by us. One of the most moving aspects of this spare story is her helper Ninshubur's unwavering loyalty even in the face of death; he will not rest until Inanna is restored.

TEXT & CONTEXT

ORAL LITERATURE & CULT

The narrative of Inanna's descent contains a number of catalogues, such as the lists of Inanna's domains, her allies, and the adornments and objects that symbolize her personal power. The narrative also relies heavily on repetition, as when Inanna is told time and again not to question the rites of the netherworld. We know from scholarly discussions of epics such as *The Odyssey* that repetition and catalogues provide mnemonic aids for the poet or reciter who is expected to memorize thousands of poetic lines and recite them at religious gatherings or festivals. These aids were important for the audience as well, who needed reminders about the sequence or meaning of events. But the story and form of Inanna's descent also suggests that it had a cultic use — that is, it was used in religious worship or ritual.

Recognizing that literature, and especially drama, has its roots in religious practice, there is some debate about which came first, the myth or the rite. Was there originally a collection of stories about the Goddess Inanna, which led to the development of religious ceremony involving her? Or was there some practice, like a ritual, that celebrated the passage of winter into spring, around which stories of Inanna's descent arose? Unfortunately, we cannot answer these questions, but anthropologists argue that myth and ritual arise out of crises confronting the traditional community. A myth, for example, might be performed at critical points in the seasonal cycle, or at time of catastrophe such as a flood, famine, or drought. Rebirth rituals in the spring, which involve a descent into the underworld and the awakening of the earth, are common throughout the Middle East and Mediterranean regions — the Babylonian Ishtar and Tammuz, the Syrian Astarte and Adonis, the Egyptian Isis and Osiris, the Canaanite Anat and Baal, and the Greek Demeter and Persephone. The Christian story of the death and resurrection of Jesus in the spring is also indebted to this tradition.

FROM MATRIARCHY TO PATRIARCHY

In 1861, J. J. Bachofen, a Swiss legal historian, published an extraordinary book in Germany, *Mother Right: An Investigation of the Religious and Juridical Character of Matriarchy in the Ancient World*. The underlying thesis of Bachofen's book is that before the advent of male rule (patriarchy) in human history there was an earlier period characterized by female rule and goddesses. In a lengthy transition from one to the other, men defeated, subdued, and dominated women and created a hierarchy of male priests and rulers and made male deities supreme. L. H. Morgan (1818–1881), an American anthropologist, found evidence of matriarchal principles in the kinship system of Native Americans and compared them with the native peoples of Asia, Africa, and Australia. In the meantime, Bachofen was largely discredited. Outside of a few isolated cultures in which women play a predominant role, there is no evidence of a period in history in the ancient world in which women ruled in the same way that we find evidence of patriarchy. Understanding this, Robert Briffault in *The Mothers* (1927) refines the idea of matriarchy: He does not argue for Bachofen's political rule by women or for a widespread system of inheritance through the maternal line. Instead, Briffault provides evidence of cultures in which women were socially respected and even predominant in certain roles.

Arguments about the role of women in history are being bandied about down to the present day. Feminist scholars point to the evidence of women's prominence, if not dominance, in ancient archeological sites in Turkey (c. 8000 B.C.E.). Some male scholars, caught up in their own biases, argue for the subservience of women and condemn them to minor roles in history. Interestingly enough, Bachofen's writings are still in print, largely because he pointed to varied roles in the social development of men and women. The following is a tribute he paid to women: "The relationship which stands at the origin of all culture, of every virtue, of every nobler aspect of existence, is that between mother and child; it operates in a world of violence as the divine principle of love, of union, of peace. Raising her young, the woman learns earlier than the man to extend her loving care beyond the limits of ego to another creature, and to direct whatever gift of invention she possesses to the preservation and improvement of this other's existence. Woman at this stage is the repository of all culture, of all benevolence, of all devotion, of all concern for the living and grief for the dead. . . . Whereas the paternal principle is inherently restrictive, the maternal principle is universal; the paternal principle implies limitation to definite groups, but the maternal principle, like the life of nature, knows no barriers. The idea of motherhood produces a sense of universal fraternity among all men, which dies with the development of paternity."

IN THE CLASSROOM

I. THE MEANING OF INANNA'S JOURNEY

There are several layers of meaning surrounding Inanna's descent or journey into the underworld. Inanna has a mission. The passage itself involves seven gates; the number "7" carries magical properties and was probably related to the moon or menstrual cycle of the goddess and was the basis for developing a monthly calendar. The stripping away of Inanna's attire suggests something about the condition with which individuals inevitably enter the underworld. In addition to releasing the life force from the grasp of death so that spring might once again take place, the descent is also interpreted in personal, psychological terms. Scholars often remark that in confronting her sister Ereshkigal, Inanna is symbolically coming to terms with the most negative and frightening parts of herself. Joseph Campbell's *Hero with a Thousand Faces* is invaluable for interpreting the basic ingredients of the journey.

Discussion

1. Think of the ways a journey can become a learning experience. Discuss the reasons for Inanna's descent, how she prepares for it, and whether the preparations assist her in her journey. There is also the question of the significance of a woman descending into the darkness and whether women or goddesses are uniquely equipped for such an adventure. The relationship between Inanna and Ereshkigal involves the feminine dimension of fertility and the shadow side of death. The end of the story involves the substitution of Dumuzi for Inanna; Dumuzi then becomes the dying-and-rising god symbolizing spring and the emergence of plant life.

Connections

1. The ancient world is filled with journeys. It is instructive to first compare Inanna's descent to the Mesopotamian hero Gilgamesh (p. 55), who also travels to the end of the world to gain either power or knowledge. Both of them must overcome trials and tests to reach their destinations. Inanna and Gilgamesh create paradigms for the quest that are used by later writers and mythmakers.

2. Odysseus in *The Odyssey* (p. 421) and Aeneas in *The Aeneid* (p. 1181) undertake two other very famous journeys into the underworld. Does the motivation for Inanna's descent seem different from the motives of Odysseus or Aeneas for their underworld journeys?

3. The most famous Christian journey into the underworld is found in Dante's *The Inferno* (Book 2).

Groups

1. After a discussion of the nature of the descent into the underworld, the journey might be divided into segments or parts. The parts of the external, physical journey might be correlated to an internal spiritual or psychological journey. Each group might be assigned to a part, which is then researched and shared with the class.

Writing

Ask students to write a short paper in response to one or more of the following:

1. Inanna makes preparations for her descent. Do any of these preparations assist her in her journey?

2. Lists and repetitions are devices we often love when we are children but don't encounter much in contemporary literature. How do these lists and repetitions in *The Descent of Inanna* add to or detract from the story for you?

3. What does Inanna gain from her journey? How does the journey enhance her role as the queen of heaven and earth?

II. THE NATURE OF THE UNDERWORLD AND THE CONCEPT OF IMMORTALITY

One of the most fascinating topics that arises from the study of this story is the nature of the underworld and the concept of immortality or life after death. It would be advisable, however, to supplement the description of the underworld in Inanna's story with materials from *The Epic of Gilgamesh* (p. 55). Ereshkigal's domain appears to be a shadowy imitation of a kingdom above the earth, just as the realm of Hades in Greek myth represents a locus of power similar to that of Zeus or Poseidon. The Mesopotamian underworld — like the Greek Hades — is not evil, as it will later become in the Christian myth of hell. In fact, it is the source of life and the place to which the dead return. The Mesopotamian version of immortality appears to be rather boring, since the dead simply repose in the dust. The story does mention Annuna, the judges of the underworld, who make a judgment against Inanna. Apparently, the Annuna were originally chthonic deities associated with fertility. A comparison with the Egyptian underworld is instructive, since the Egyptians put a great deal of effort into describing a process whereby the souls of humans are weighed and judged, then rewarded or punished. A similar process was followed by the Zoroastrians in Persia (c. 1200 B.C.E.). Both the Egyptian and Persian underworlds become the basis for the Christian version. If time permits, it is interesting to follow the evolution of the underworld to the Jewish ideas of Sheol and Gehenna and then later to the Christian concept.

Discussion

1. Ask students to consider why the ancient Mesopotamians and Greeks (Persephone was queen of Hades) connected the underworld to women. Consider the main characteristics of Ereshkigal.

2. Ask students to consider the possible origins of different conceptions of the underworld. How might the ideas of rewards and punishments have come to be linked to the underworld? What seem to be the roles of the kugarra and the galatur?

Connections

1. Students may be interested in comparing this story to other versions of underworlds and the various means of entering and escaping from them. This anthology contains

underworlds in Homer's *The Odyssey* (p. 421), Virgil's *The Aeneid* (p. 1181), Ovid's account of Orpheus and Euridyce in the *Metamorphoses* (p. 1270), Dante's *The Inferno* (Book 2), and, in a manner of speaking, in Plato's Allegory of the Cave (p. 1111).

Groups

1. Different groups might investigate individual cultural traditions surrounding the underworld. The underworld might be divided into individual parts, like the location, the entrance, judges, and underworld conditions.

Writing

Ask students to write a short paper in response to one or more of the following:

1. When Dante and Virgil enter hell in *The Inferno*, they see engraved over the gate the words "Abandon Hope, All Ye Who Enter Here." Is Inanna's netherworld hopeless? Which of the underworlds that you have encountered in literature seems most truly hopeless?

2. Ancient peoples believed that there were certain places on earth where the world above the earth touched the lower world. These were called thresholds and usually involved depressions in the earth like caves or canyons. Mountains were a similar threshold connecting earthly life to the heavens. How does one enter and emerge from other underworlds in literature? What are the issues involved with moving from one dimension or spiritual realm to another?

3. Most underworlds' guidelines forbid an ordinary mortal from visiting the underworld without special permission. It is also forbidden for someone to return to ordinary reality from the underworld. What are the reasons for this condition or rule?

BEYOND THE CLASSROOM

RESEARCH & WRITING

1. It is probable that individual students have gone through a testing experience similar to Inanna's descent into the netherworld. Have students write an account of this personal ordeal. It may either be a poetic account modeled on the Inanna story or simply a description of the experience in a prose voice. A comparison with Inanna's journey might add meaning to the account.

2. A complicated topic involves research into the evolution of the underworld from Mesopotamia to Israel. Does this history involve a transition from physical punishment to psychological punishment akin to twentieth-century writer Jean-Paul Sartre's statement "Hell is other people!" found in his *No Exit*?

3. Students interested in psychology might be encouraged to research and write about the connections between the underworld and the unconscious in the individual. What are the implications for the descent into self-knowledge if the underworld is turned into hell as it was in the Western Middle Ages?

Projects

1. Role models in religion and literature are important for girls as well as boys. Has popular culture (comics, novels, cartoons, movies, video games) provided more and better female heroes? Have students identified with any of them? Who are the heroic women -- real or fictional — to whom students turn to emulate?

2. Assume the "descent" represents early ritual rooted in a crisis involving the awakening of life or fertility in the natural world. The theme might also point to the slow death in society from something like video games or television. Devise a modern-day ritual or play with this theme.

FURTHER READING

Eisler, Riane. *The Chalice and the Blade: Our History, Our Future.* 1988.

Gimbutas, Marija. *The Goddesses and Gods of Old Europe: Myths and Cult Images.* 1989.

Harding, M. Esther. *Woman's Mysteries: Ancient and Modern.* 1971.

Neumann, Erich. *The Great Mother: An Analysis of the Archetype.* 1974.

Sjoo, Monica, and Barbara Mor. *The Great Cosmic Mother: Rediscovering the Religion of the Earth.* 1987.

Stone, Merlin. *When God Was a Woman.* 1976.

Thompson, William Irwin. *The Time Falling Bodies Take to Light: Mythology, Sexuality, and the Origins of Culture.* 1981.

Walker, Barbara. *The Woman's Encyclopedia of Myths and Secrets.* 1983.

MEDIA RESOURCES

VIDEO

Epic of Inanna
49 min., 1988 (Cloudstone, New York City)
This is a video of the epic of Inanna by the master storyteller and performer Diane Wolkstein.

WEB SITES

Ancient Near East Sacred Texts
www.sacred-texts.com/ane/index.htm
This site contains electronic texts of a number of key sacred texts of the Near East and links to sites answering frequently asked questions (FAQs) on the religion and mythology of the region.

The Descent of Inanna
www.jelder.com/mythology/inanna.html
A very interesting site developed by John Elder, this site provides an overview of the Inanna myth, commentary, and bibliography for further study.

The Epic of Creation (p. 40)

WWW   For a quiz on *The Epic of Creation,* see *World Literature Online* at bedfordstmartins.com/worldit.

A mythology is a collection of stories about the nature of the cosmos that represents the fundamental vision or worldview of a particular people or culture. All groups old enough and large enough to have created a picture of the universe (or cosmogony) have also created a mythology to support and transmit this view. Myths, then, tend to be those stories that explain the origins of the world and of society, and explain the relationships between humans, deities, nature, and the cosmos. As sacred stories, they tend to recreate a primordial age before written history and provide a narrative context for religious rituals and beliefs. In this context, the word *myth* does not mean "fiction" or "falsehood," as the word is sometimes used today. The ancient Greeks, for example, used mythos for the English "myth" and came to mean "stories," which may or may not contain important truths. Insofar as most religions have stories about the relation of deities to humans, we speak in this anthology of Egyptian, Jewish, Christian, or Hindu myths, among others. Myths use symbolic patterns called "archetypes," which are repeated in stories around the world. The earliest sky deities, for example, often were originally weather gods. The garden paradise in Genesis, with its trees, serpents, and fruit, has its antecedents in Babylonian and Persian gardens. The underworld is associated with goddesses. Flood stories are told around the world. Heroes, both East and West, go on remarkably similar journeys (see Joseph Campbell's *Hero with a Thousand Faces*). Because similar archetypes can be found in different bodies of mythology, it has been proposed that mythologies have either spread through actual cultural contact or are the result of the basic structure of the human unconscious and its dream life.

The first task of a creation myth such as the Babylonian "Epic of Creation" is to deal with its origins: the transformation of chaos into cosmos; the creation of earth, sky, and an under-the-earth three-tiered world; the relationship of the three domains; the creation of the first humans, plants, and animals and how they fit into the cosmic scheme of things; and the origin of death and the end of the world. The process used for creating the world reflects the basic worldview of the culture. The principle involved is "what is above is also below, and vice versa." Suppose, for example, that a particular culture lived close to nature, modeled itself after the plant cycle, and, in general, adopted an organic view of the world. The people's deities — goddesses as well as gods — would be associated with fertility, procreation, and health. Their creation story would most likely be modeled after childbirth with the mating of a god and goddess or the autogenetic act of the goddess alone. A more urbanized culture that had developed a significant body of law might have a very different worldview and believe that the world functions according to fixed laws of right and wrong; that good is rewarded and evil is punished — if not in this lifetime, then in the next world. This culture might posit a patriarchal deity in the heavens who is associated with orderly rule and justice. The creation story appropriate in this case might involve hierarchical distinctions, transcendent authority, and obedience.

Mesopotamia became famous for the creation of a militaristic society, especially with the successors to the Sumerians — the Akkadians, Babylonians, and Assyrians. They developed the infantry phalanx, the use of chariots, leather-plaited armor, shields, and spears. The defeated populace — men, women, and children — were either killed or taken into slavery. Rape was used as an instrument of terror. Captives were blinded for work in the orchards; an inscription of Shalmaneser (c. 1250 B.C.E.) states that 14,400 captives had their eyes put out. Castration was used for servants in the harem or temples. The Akkadian Sargon the Great, who displayed a defeated king wearing a dog collar, ruled enemy cities by destroying their walls and setting up an army garrison to rule. It is not strange, then, that the Babylonian creation story reflects the pattern of warfare and combat common in the culture.

When early peoples believed that the essential pattern of life was conflict or combat, they conceived of the cosmos itself in terms of a dramatic struggle between chaos and order, light and dark, day and night, drought and rainfall. Each day involved the powers of light overcoming the powers of darkness; each season pitted the god or goddess of green plants against powers of death and infertility. Annually, the year was reborn with the recitation of the creation story and the ritual reenactment of the primordial battle that would set the stage for the rest of their history. The Mesopotamians developed a highly organized religious system in which gods and goddesses controlled the various aspects of the cosmos and were represented in the political courts of the different city-states. Nevertheless, two conditions contributed to a sense of insecurity and an awareness that the forces of chaos might cause the disintegration of the kingdom: They had to contend with the forces of nature — drought, flooding, sandstorms — and they were subject to invasions from outside enemies, especially from the east.

TEXT & CONTEXT

ZIGGURAT

Located in the sacred center of each Mesopotamian city was a central tower called a ziggurat (from Assyrian *ziqquratu*, "summit, mountain top," and from *zaqaru*, "to be high"). A ziggurat resembles the Egyptian terraced or stepped pyramid with successively receding stories and a temple on top. Usually there were seven stories corresponding to the seven planetary bodies in the heavens. On the top of the ziggurat was a temple in which the patron deity of the city resided. Daily, the deity was cared for and worshipped. The ziggurat was the earthly residence of the god or gods as well as the place where rulers — reflecting a divine pantheon of deities — regulated the course of civic and social life as well as "controlling" events in nature. Such a structure rising above the alluvial plain suggests that the founding peoples originally came from mountains to the north. The Tower of Babel described in Genesis (Hebrew Scriptures) was probably a ziggurat. Although ziggurats are characteristic of ancient Babylonian and Assyrian architecture, they were also built by the Maya of ancient Mesoamerica and are found in Yucatán and Guatemala.

The first ziggurat was built by the Sumerians as early as c. 3500 B.C.E. The ziggurat in Babylon became a major edifice under Hammurabi (c. eighteenth century B.C.E.). Destroyed by enemies, it was rebuilt by Nebuchadnezzar (c. 600 B.C.E.) into an incredible sanctuary. Each side was 288 feet long, and the overall height was 288 feet. The first of the series of stages or tiers was 106 feet high, and the second was 58 feet high. Then, there were four levels of 19 feet each. On top was the temple of Marduk, called Esagila ("house with the lofty top"), also known as "the palace of heaven and earth." Its walls were 48 feet high, plated with gold and blue enameled bricks. The sun's reflection could be seen throughout the city. Inside the temple was a gold statue of Marduk. The Greek historian Herodotus (fifth century B.C.E.) visited this temple in Babylon and maintained that the statue and other accessories of pure gold weighed 26 tons. One can imagine the priests ascending the stairway and reaching the summit of the universe, the sacred precinct where the ceremonial marriage provided the climax of the New Year's Festival.

ASTROLOGY, DIVINATION, AND TABLETS OF DESTINY

On the eleventh day of the Babylonian New Year's Festival (the Akitu), the gods gathered in the ziggurat to participate in a Festival of the Fates, a ceremony in which omens were determined for each of the upcoming twelve months. This festival was determined by the creation epic when Marduk seized the Tablets of Destiny from Qingu and then created the ritual calendar by ordering the constellations, dividing the year into twelve months, and assigning appropriate stars to each. The systematic observations of the heavens by astronomers and mathematicians led to astrologer-priests who studied the heavens and harmonized celestial movements with the passage of seasons, the agricultural cycle, and society. This led to the creation of a calendar and a liturgical schedule recording the significant festivals of the year. By around 2000 B.C.E., Mesopotamians settled down to a calendar of 360 days divided into 12 months. The day was divided in hours, minutes, and seconds. The Babylonians were famous for their astrologers. Each major temple had a library of astronomical and astrological literature, useful for divination. Besides interpreting the zodiac, priest-diviners examined the patterns of oil on water and the condition of the livers of animals. Dream interpretation was important, since they believed that the gods literally appeared in dreams with instruction or wisdom. Divination, after all, provided a sense of control in the face of fate — the unpredictability of desert storms and floods and of disease and catastrophe.

IN THE CLASSROOM

I. THE RELATIONSHIP BETWEEN MYTHIC STORY AND WORLDVIEW

The fundamental issue about a creation myth is not whether the ancient Mesopotamians actually believed that a primordial struggle between Marduk and Tiamat took place in some distant past. Rather, the most important question is how did they actually use the myth in their everyday lives, assuming that creation myths provided a kind of blueprint for both cosmos and society? As city-states began to impinge on each other economically and compete for available resources, warfare and the warrior-class took center stage in society. *The Epic of Creation* validated militarism and aggression toward neighbors.

Discussion

1. The relation between mythic story and worldview is the core issue here. How do the actions of the gods and the struggle between Marduk and Tiamat provide a system of values for human beings? What goes on above goes on below and vice versa. It is certainly appropriate to discuss the basic American myths that have provided a framework for social values and foreign policy in the United States — like the myth of the immigrant coming to the Promised Land, the myth of Manifest Destiny, the myth of the West and the Frontier, the myth of the Founding Fathers, and the myth of the Protestant Ethic. Students probably have to be reminded about the use of the word *myth* in this discussion, not as falsehood or fantasy but as those stories that connect human beings to some kind of larger purpose or cosmic model.

Connections

1. It is easiest first to make connections with creation stories that are similar: the Egyptian "Creating the World and Defeating Apophis: A Ritual Hymn" (p. 109) and the Indian "Indra Slays the Dragon Vritra" (p. 1338). These stories provide a dramatic conflict between chaos and creation.

2. A comparison with Genesis (Hebrew Scriptures) provides similarities and differences. The creation story in chapter one of Genesis was composed much later in history and is more abstract and intellectual. Although the primordial condition is water, the serpent Tiamat has evolved into *tehom*, the Hebrew word for the "abyss," in Genesis 1:2. Order is achieved through speech.

Groups

1. Different groups might investigate the different parts of Mesopotamian society that would be affected by a militaristic worldview. Gerda Lerner's *The Creation of Patriarchy* and the books by Rick Fields and Shannon E. French are very helpful in this area.

2. Groups also might be assigned to research the nature of warfare in different periods and different countries of the ancient world. Two ancient societies famous for warfare are Assyria and Rome.

Writing

Ask students to write a short paper in response to one or more of the following:

1. Given the location of Mesopotamia and its geography, why might conflict or battle be appropriate metaphors for creation? What aspects of ordinary life correspond to battle?

2. What accounts for the importance of the warrior in ancient society? A comparison with Achilles and Hektor in Homer's *The Iliad* (p. 288) might be useful. A comparison with the hero status of the soldier in modern society is also relevant.

3. Why is it difficult for a person of peace or a religious person to become famous or heroic?

II. HUMAN-LIKE QUALITIES OF THE MESOPOTAMIAN GODS

Marduk and Tiamat have cosmic, god-like roles, but they also are portrayed with human qualities and are therefore analogous to human beings. This correspondence allowed for the dramatic presentation of the mythic story, whereby the various roles in the story could be played by humans. But as important as the ritual drama was the fact that humans could identify with these deities and emulate and learn from them. Marduk was the ideal warrior-king, while Tiamat was the force of chaos and disorder. In addition, there were different generations of gods and an evolutionary movement from the most basic or primitive deities to the more modern assembly of deities that promoted Marduk and his concept of the new world order. The first generations of the gods quarreled and acted very much like the different generations in a human family.

Discussion

1. Discuss the origin of the conflict in the quarrelsome relationship between the generations of the gods. The class might speculate as to why the ancient Mesopotamians included a family quarrel as motivation for a cosmic battle. Next, the discussion might deal with the preparations for the battle and how Marduk and Tiamat are equipped in very different ways. How is the battle itself easily adaptable to dramatic ritual?

2. After conquering Tiamat, Marduk establishes his control over the cosmos. Discussion here might focus on the ways in which this control is manifested in the workings of the universe and the lives of the people.

Connections

1. The Mesopotamian conflict between generations is similar to the generational conflict in the stories found in *Theogony* by the Greek Hesiod (p. 263). There is also generational conflict in Sophocles' *Oedipus Rex* (p. 899).

2. A very different concept of warfare can be found in India's Bhagavad Gita (p. 1492), in which the spiritual qualities of the warrior are emphasized — his place in the universe and his inner preparation for death.

3. Tiamat as serpent can be related to the serpent in the Garden of Eden (Genesis, Hebrew Scriptures).

Groups

1. Groups can be assigned to bring in information about the ancestries of the figures of Marduk and Tiamat. Early civilizations deliberately created deities in human form (anthropomorphic) so that they could be recognized and imitated. Marduk is often pictured with wings and carrying arrows. What are the meanings of the visual attire? Tiamat is pictured as a serpent. Investigations might focus on the connections between serpent and chaos as well as the relation between serpent and goddess.

2. Another line of inquiry might be to have groups compare the anthropomorphic qualities of Mesopotamian deities with the anthropomorphic deities in Egypt, India, or the Judeo-Christian tradition.

Writing

Ask students to write a short paper in response to one or more of the following:

1. What are the particular strengths of Tiamat and her allies? Are they appropriate for a woman or goddess?

2. The figure of Tiamat seems to exemplify a long-held fear of serpents and snakes. What lies behind the fear of snakes? Why are snakes associated with the underworld?

3. Why is it appropriate for the world to be created out of Tiamat's body?

BEYOND THE CLASSROOM

RESEARCH & WRITING

1. The association of women with the chaotic forces of nature, such as hurricanes, lies behind the figure of Tiamat. Stereotypes have linked men to rational order and women to emotional, unpredictable disorder. Is there a relationship to the two sides of the brain, right and left? There are traditions associated with the right and left hands and right and left sides of the body. Witches are left-handed. The first recognition that baby might be a saint was his or her refusal of the left breast. Throughout antiquity, it was believed that boys were products of the right testicle and that girls were the product of the left. Of course there is much more on this to be uncovered, along with the influence on contemporary attitudes toward the sexes.

2. A problem that plagued ancient societies was the transformation of militarism into civil society. How should subject peoples be treated? What do you do with soldiers when they return home from a war? How does a country transform the passions of warfare after the war is over? Once militaristic values are elevated in a society, it is a challenge to provide men and women with incentives toward peace and harmony. Ancient Greece provides a graphic example of the problem: the values exemplified by the Trojan War (c. 1200 B.C.E.) were slowly transformed into the Golden Age of art and philosophy in the fifth century B.C.E. only to be undermined by the Peloponnesian War (431–404 B.C.E.). This research topic stretches therefore from antiquity to the present day. After the twentieth century, which has been portrayed as the bloodiest century in history, the question has again been raised as to whether warfare can ever lead to the peaceful coexistence of nations.

3. The examination of the structure of *The Epic of Creation* will reveal its usefulness as a script for dramatizing a New Year's ceremony in which the new year triumphs over the old.

Projects

1. Students might investigate how America's major holidays reflect the American myths that lie behind them.

2. Ask students to use the tools of the Internet as well as interviews of local citizens and politicians to ascertain the worldviews to which modern Americans actually ascribe. Do people believe that we live in a "dog-eat-dog" world? Do we live in a world of abundance and plenty? Is the world run by justice and love? This project involves digging below what people might publicly espouse about their worldviews to the fundamental paradigms by which they actually live. Somebody's peace and love might turn out to be "survival of the fittest."

FURTHER READING

Campbell, Joseph. *The Masks of God: Occidental Mythology.* 1964.

Ceram, C. W. *Gods, Graves and Scholars: The Story of Archaeology.* 1976.

Fields, Rick. *The Code of the Warrior in History, Myth, and Everyday Life.* 1991.

French, Shannon E. *The Code of the Warrior: Exploring Warrior Values Past and Present.* 2003.

Gaster, Theodor H. *The Oldest Stories in the World.* 1952.

Hetherington, Norriss S., ed. *Cosmology: Historical, Literary, Philosophical, Religious, and Scientific Perspectives.* 1993.

Jacobsen, Thorkild. *Toward the Image of Tammuz and Other Essays on Mesopotamian History and Culture.* 1976.

Kramer, Samuel Noah. *History Begins at Sumer.* 1959.

Mumford, Lewis. *The Transformations of Man.* 1956.

MEDIA RESOURCES

WEB SITES

Ancient Near East Sacred Texts
www.sacred-texts.com/ane/index.htm
This site contains e-texts of a number of key sacred texts of the Near East and links to sites answering frequently asked questions on the religion and mythology of the region.

The Babylonian Creation Epic
saturn.sron.nl/~jheise/akkadian/enuma1_expl.html
This site provides a helpful subsection of John Heise's "Akkadian language," Chapter 3 (cuneiform texts) about the Babylonian creation epic, in which the cuneiform text is given, and there is discussion on the work's literary style and an explanation of the first few lines.

The Epic of Gilgamesh (p. 55)

WWW   For a quiz on *The Epic of Gilgamesh,* see *World Literature Online* at bedfordstmartins.com/worldlit.

The Epic of Gilgamesh is classic epic material, the same stuff that makes movies like *Rambo* and books like Bronte's *Jane Eyre.* It is about self-discovery, beating the odds, friendship, and adventure. Almost unbelievably, it came to us among 22,000 clay tablets of cuneiform writing from modern-day Iraq. The story originates from a king who lived in Uruk, about 150 miles south of Baghdad, sometime between 2800 and 2500 B.C.E. Uruk would have been a city of perhaps 50,000 people, with large walls (which Gilgamesh is supposed to have built) and a large temple. Some of the old city remains even today. Among the many accomplishments of this civilization, called the "Sumerian" civilization, is likely the invention of beer, which plays an important role in the rite of passage of Enkidu (one of the main characters in *The Epic of Gilgamesh;* note that *wine* is the word used in this translation).

What is perhaps most amazing about *The Epic of Gilgamesh* is its own story. Like the Greek epics attributed to Homer, *The Iliad* and *The Odyssey, Gilgamesh* began by being part of an oral culture, that is a culture where oral storytelling passes important cultural information down from generation to generation without the need for writing. Although the civilization that the ancient king Gilgamesh lived in did have writing, it was not used for literary purposes. It was the Akkadian king, Ashurbanipal, who had it written down and stored away some time during the eighth century B.C.E. It was subsequently lost until 1839, when A. H. Layard found them. It survives in Akkadian (a relative of Hebrew, the language of the Old Testament) as well as Hittite and Hurrian (ancient languages of Asia Minor). Because the characters used to write down the epic were cuneiform, and not a more modern, alphabet-like form of Akkadian, it wasn't until 1872 that George Smith translated them into English. Recently, it has become one of the most popular epics read in modern times. There are eighty translations into English alone, as well as several novels, movies, plays, and musicals based on the legend. On the Web, there is almost a cult presence of individuals inspired by *The Epic of Gilgamesh* to resurrect the world of Mesopotamia. What was once the province of Assyriologists and intellectuals interested in puzzles became an essential text for biblical scholars and, now, a popular text. Recently, the fall of Saddam Hussein's regime in Iraq brought the world's attention to Iraq's museums, which were looted in the days following Baghdad's defeat. Among the items stolen were objects that date from the same period as the story of Gilgamesh.

The epic begins with a description of Gilgamesh's accomplishments. Besides being the handsomest of all kings, he is strong and probably quite romantic (he honored the goddess of love). The narrator introduces us to the old city of Uruk, welcoming the foreign listener. It turns out that Gilgamesh is an overindulgent king, however. He sleeps with all the virgins before they sleep with their lovers, and he divides fathers from sons. The people complain to Anu, the local god, who responds by making Enkidu, a young man who can match Gilgamesh. Enkidu is something like Gilgamesh's id: He is an animal who requires to be civilized. He goes to Gilgamesh, awed by his reputation, and is awarded a temple prostitute. The Mesopotamian culture was quite different from our own. Whereas many sexual taboos are reinforced by our religious systems of beliefs, ancient cultures regarded sex as a rite and thus incorporated priestesses of sex into their temples. Unfortunately, in present-day India, similar practices remain, much to the detriment of young girls in these areas.

Enkidu is civilized by a ritual orgy of six days and seven nights, after which he can no longer be part of the animal world. Gilgamesh realizes that Enkidu now poses a challenge because he dreams about it. In this way, it seems that Enkidu is now fully incorporated into Gilgamesh's subconscious. When he has learned about Gilgamesh's bad treatment of the people of Uruk, he attempts to challenge him. While Gilgamesh goes out to claim "first night" (a royal's privilege of sleeping with the bride before the husband does), Enkidu stops him. A wrestling match ensues and Gilgamesh beats Enkidu, who immediately compliments him and they become friends. There is no mention as to what happens to the bride.

Gilgamesh longs to possess some of the lumber of Enlil's forest, up the Euphrates River. But, in order to do so, he must kill the Humbaba, a monster that guards the forest. Enkidu and the council of elders do not believe he should go, but Gilgamesh obtains protection from the sun-god, Utu. Ninsun, Gilgamesh's priestess mother, knowing that her son was born a mortal (his father was a god), adopts Enkidu and bids him to accompany Gilgamesh on the trip to help him return safely. Their journey — which should have taken months to complete — takes three days, including nightly rests. At the gate to the forest, Enkidu tries to convince Gilgamesh not to go into the forest, but Gilgamesh is not persuaded. In the forest are beautiful cedars (that might give the location of the place away as Lebanon or Syria), which he wants for Uruk. The god Shamash travels with them in the form of a wild bull. When Gilgamesh fells a tree, Humbaba's anger is roused, but Shamash is there to protect them. Our hero decides this is a good time to sleep, which he does for a long time until he has regained his strength. When he rises again, he is like a bull himself, and he begins to cut down trees. For each tree he cuts, Humbaba comes out against Gilgamesh but is lashed by fire from Shamash. Finally, Humbaba offers to give Gilgamesh the whole forest if only he will spare his life. But Enkidu persuades Gilgamesh to kill Humbaba.

Gilgamesh's next adventure starts when Ishtar, the goddess of grain (the same goddess as Inanna in *The Descent of Inanna* (p. 23), proposes to be his wife and to make love to him. He responds with a litany of complaints about her previous exploits and her reputation for being a poor wife. Insulted, Ishtar goes to her father, Anu, and asks for the Bull of Heaven with which to destroy Gilgamesh. Anu grants Ishtar the bull, which Enkidu and Gilgamesh kill, dedicating its heart to Shamash. Ishtar is even more inflamed, but Enkidu only insults her further. He then dreams that the gods have decreed that either he or Gilgamesh must die for having killed the Bull and Humbaba. Enkidu curses the gate made of the cedar he stole and then the woman who brought him to civilization. But Anu reminds Enkidu how good the woman was and Enkidu retracts the oath. Enkidu then can only take comfort in speaking his terrifying dreams to Gilgamesh, who watches him die. Gilgamesh creates a song worthy in itself for its epic qualities, mourning over Enkidu.

Alone, Gilgamesh begins to wander the earth, genuinely afraid of what death, which has come to his adopted brother Enkidu, has in store for him. He travels eastward toward the mountain of Mashu (perhaps in Iran or Kashmir?), killing lions and wearing their hide, until he meets dangerous scorpion-men, who ask him about his quest. He responds that he is looking for Utnapishtim, a mortal who became a god, in order to find a way to everlasting life. After they let him pass, he goes into something like a tunnel and reemerges on the other side in the land of the gods. He meets a veiled bar maid for the gods, who at first is somewhat afraid of him. This woman, Siduri, doesn't believe that Gilgamesh is the man standing before her. All the mourning for Enkidu and long travel has made him haggard and emaciated. Siduri tries to encourage him, revealing one of the great paradoxes of divinity: If men are mortal, then they can at least enjoy life, for it is rare and special. Gods, on the other hand, have no need to fear death, and life is nothing to them, one enjoyment after the other, all the same and none spectacular. Gilgamesh asks Siduri for the route to Utnapishtim. There is a forest, and beyond the forest there is a mooring by which the mysterious boatman, Urshnabi, stands.

Gilgamesh follows these directions with hope that he might be able to cross the sea to Utnapishtim. But Gilgamesh is angry when he sees the boat, and he smashes a box on the boat. Urshnabi discovers Gilgamesh and asks him what is wrong. When Gilgamesh tells him that he is afraid of death and wants to cross the sea in search of Utnapishtim, he responds that they cannot cross because Gilgamesh has destroyed part of the cargo of the ship that protects the ship when crossing the sea of death. Gilgamesh must supply the ship with poles, painted with tar, with which he will pole the boat across the sea. Utnapishtim is quite surprised to see Gilgamesh arrive on the shores of his island. They have a conversation much like the conversation that Gilgamesh had with Siduri and Urshnabi. Utnapishtim then tells him, like Shelley in his poem "Ozymandias," that nothing lasts forever and that there is no such thing as "permanence." But Gilgamesh wants to know how it is that Utnapishtim, who once was a mortal, came to be among the gods.

Utnapishtim responds with the story of the flood, a story that resonates in many creation myths, but in particular, in the story of Noah and the ark in the Old Testament. Long, long ago, men were too loud and the gods could not sleep. The god Enlil decided to exterminate the race of men by means of a huge flood. But the god Ea commanded Utnapishtim to tear down his house and build instead a large boat and fill it with the male and female of every species. Utnapishtim followed these orders and then it began to rain violently for six days and nights. When he comes out from the ship's hold, Utnapishtim releases birds to see if they will come back, having looked in vain for land. When the birds finally do not come back, he opens his holds to the winds and makes sacrifices. All the gods, starved from so many days without sacrifices, gather around. They forbid Enlil from coming to take part in the sacrifice. Enlil, enraged, wants to know who let out the secret about the flood. Ea doesn't quite admit to it, but he sings a song about finding the appropriate punishment for the crime. Enlil exiles Utnapishtim from other mortals, making him and his wife immortal but alone.

It is now time for Gilgamesh to return to the land of the living, but Utnapishtim offers him a test: Stay awake for six days and seven nights, and he might become immortal. Gilgamesh fails before he even begins. Just as in the episode with Humbaba, he does not know the proper time for work and the proper time for rest. He falls asleep. Utnapishtim's wife believes that they should wake him, but Utnapishtim tells her that he will trick them. Instead, they devise to bake a loaf for each day and to lay that loaf next to his bed. When he wakes up, the condition of the loaves tell him how many days he has slept — seven. Utnapishtim banishes Urshnabi, the ferryman, for having brought Gilgamesh and tells Gilgamesh to take a bath and put on new clothes. Gilgamesh's new clothes, given to him by Utnapishtim, will be forever new-looking. Utnapishtim's wife wants a sendoff present for Gilgamesh. The old man rewards him by telling him about a plant that grants immortal life and grows at the bottom of the sea. Gilgamesh dives down with rocks tied to his feet in order to harvest the plant. He does not eat it right away, but, rather, says that he will give it to the old men of Uruk to eat. This sacrifice is meant to show he is a good king at last. Gilgamesh and Urshnabi travel together, and, when stopping for a bath at a pool, a snake steals the plant from them. Gilgamesh arrives as a hero in Uruk, where he engraves his life's story on stones. In an epilogue written long after the formation of the epic (the so-called "Twelfth Tablet"), Gilgamesh dies, granted immortality only through the monuments he has built and the poem that we read. The people praise his deeds and the greatness of their king.

TEXT & CONTEXT

The key features of *The Epic of Gilgamesh* lie in what earlier critics may have called its "primitive" origins. As a product of a traditional society, it contains highly symbolic features. Although strict Jungian interpretations of literary works are no longer popular, the Jungian method of identifying symbols and archetypes is a useful way to have students engage in the deeper meaning of a text. Unlike *The Iliad* or *The Odyssey*, the plot of *The Epic of Gilgamesh* is entirely self-contained and thus relatively easy to understand. What is more difficult to understand are the wider symbols and their relationship to literature in general. Why, for example, is it that a snake eats a plant that grants everlasting life? Likewise, in Antoine de Saint-Exupéry's *The Little Prince*, it is the snake who deprives the prince of returning to his planet. The snake, which sheds its skin, is clearly a symbol of rebirth and renewal, but the story is turning toward Gilgamesh's death. Students might try to grapple with the interpretation of this symbol. Other symbols abound that are common in epic. Gilgamesh's voyage across the sea and even beneath the sea are common themes of many epics (*The Aeneid* or *The Odyssey*, for example). Freud might say that this is a journey through the subconscious. The subconscious plays a significant role in this epic. Many plots and schemes are revealed in dreams as well as future or simultaneous events occurring elsewhere.

What *The Epic of Gilgamesh* has in common with other epics will also provide ample material for discussion. In many ways, Gilgamesh's quest has much in common with the quest in Tolkien's *Lord of the Rings*. Although immortality is not the goal, many of the tests and trials are similar in character. Even more similarities lie between the *The Epic of Gilgamesh* epic and *Beowulf* (Book 2). The combination of commonalities with other epics and certain universal symbols makes the genre of epic recognizable to the modern and ancient audience alike. Students should explore in discussion what goes into making a story of epic proportions. As in baking a cake, a certain recipe is required: a quest, magic stones, a hero who is part divine, a long voyage, a great battle, horrible monsters, and so on. Students will recognize these elements from other things they have read or seen, such as the story of

Christ in the New Testament or even the epic *Star Wars.* As always, although it may seem a bit outdated, Jung's *Man and His Symbols,* which attempts to show the universality of such themes, may be helpful. Since this course may be the beginning of students' adventures in literary landscapes, it is a good time to begin some free-response exercises in which students try to identify certain universals. For example, what are the meanings of certain colors? How do students feel about green, or black, or blue? What about certain animals? What do they mean? What can the snake symbolize in various cultures?

IN THE CLASSROOM

I. SYMBOLS AND SIMILARITIES: THE MAKING OF EPIC

A discussion of *The Epic of Gilgamesh* should begin with a brief outline of the key episodes in the epic and a discussion of what changes throughout the epic. From there, it will be profitable to offer a brief introduction to symbols and their use in literature. Numbers, symbols, character types (like old man, old woman, young man), animals, trees, and monsters (especially those that are half human) are all important "signs" in a piece of literature that are meant to stimulate those parts of our imagination profoundly influenced by our culture. The reaction we have to seeing the dragon in an icon of St. George is significantly different from the image of the dragon embroidered on the royal vestments of the Chinese emperor. However, both societies associate the sun with the source of life and darkness with death. We see similar properties at play in *The Epic of Gilgamesh.*

Some images to examine are earth and water (especially important in flood narratives), which represents both death and rebirth (note how Gilgamesh takes a bath in order to leave the world of the dead and then even plunges himself into the sea). The rising sun means birth, creation, or enlightenment, but the setting sun means death. The color red can be violence, passion, sacrifice, or power. Green can represent hope, fertility, youth, but also death and decay. Blue is associated with divinity and mystery as well as purity (the color of sky and water). Black is representative of evil, mystery, darkness, or some kind of ancient wisdom, whereas white can be either purity and goodness or terror and fright (the color of the truce or cease-fire flag and of Chinese funerals). Shapes and numbers are also significant. The circle represents wholeness or unity, rebirth and renovation, and thus the shape of the egg is also quite symbolic. The circle is born in such figures as the symbol of the snake eating its own tail or the Chinese yin-yang sign. The number four is associated with the four spatial directions, the four seasons, or four elements, whereas three is associated with temporal direction (past, present, and future) or the unity of the triangle (the Father, Son, and Holy Spirit). Seven is a combination of three and four and thus highly meaningful, as is ten, which means perfection, and nine, which is as close to perfection as we can come. There are also clues in the landscapes: Gardens are places of innocence and fertility, but trees can represent wisdom and tradition. A desert or open sea can represent hopelessness and emptiness. These symbols help to create certain types of archetypes: (1) the quest, in which the hero undertakes some long journey (spiritual or physical) in which impossible tasks must be performed, monsters must be dealt with, and even death overcome, upon which he may return and profit his country; (2) the initiation, in which the hero must be tested with excruciating tasks in order to pass from adolescence to adulthood, and (3) the scapegoat, in which the hero must die in order to save his country or people. These three plots, or combinations of them, form much of the content of epic, and it will be up to the students to seek out and find the connections that will help them recognize what is there.

Discussion

1. Of the archetypes given above (quest, initiation, scapegoat), which one best applies to *The Epic of Gilgamesh?* Why? Does Enkidu follow a different archetype from Gilgamesh?

2. What is the meaning of the snake in this epic? Why is it significant that he sheds his skin upon eating the plant? What about the plant? What do its thorns symbolize?

3. What is the meaning of the great flood? What similarities does this have with Enkidu's or Gilgamesh's having to take a bath at various points in the story? What are all the possible meanings of water in this story?

4. The "boar hunt" and the "bull hunt" in *The Epic of Gilgamesh* were traditional ways for adolescent men to show their prowess and manliness and thus were often tests of maturity. How has Gilgamesh been transformed by his journeys? In what ways has he matured? What about Enkidu?

Connections

1. After reading Apollodorus's story about Heracles, comment on the similarities between Heracles and Gilgamesh, their trials, what they wear, and the kind of hero they represent to their cultures. Also, you might try and compare the image of Gilgamesh (p. 57) with the image of Heracles (p. 1128).

2. In this work, there are many references to how immortality is achieved among men. In Book 1 (pp. 71 and 76), there is discussion of creating a poem or a city wall or some feat that becomes immortal. Read the following poem by Shelley, and discuss whether or not literature can be permanent or provide immortality.

    > Ozymandias
    > by Percy Bysshe Shelley (1817)
    >
    > I met a traveller from an antique land,
    > Who said — "Two vast and trunkless legs of stone
    > Stand in the desert. . . . Near them, on the sand,
    > Half sunk a shattered visage lies, whose frown,
    > And wrinkled lip, and sneer of cold command,
    > Tell that its sculptor well those passions read
    > Which yet survive, stamped on these lifeless things,
    > The hand that mocked them, the heart that fed;
    > And on the pedestal, these words appear:
    > My name is Ozymandias, King of Kings,
    > Look on my Works, ye Mighty, and despair!
    > Nothing beside remains. Round the decay
    > Of that colossal Wreck, boundless and bare
    > The lone and level sands stretch far away.

3. Compare the death of Enkidu with the death of Tom in Harriet Beecher Stowe's *Uncle Tom's Cabin* (Book 5). What roles are similar in the two works? Why does mourning take on this character? What do the characters have in common in terms of their relationship with death?

Groups

1. Break students up into small groups, assigning each group a set of symbols. Have students discuss what the symbols mean to them and come up with general meanings for each of the symbols. When the groups have finished this task, have them present their interpretations of the symbols. How much do they differ? What might influence how these symbols are perceived? Finally, how might these symbols apply to the story and meaning of *The Epic of Gilgamesh*?

2. Have students break up into small groups, and collectively draw one scene from *The Epic of Gilgamesh*. After they have finished their drawings, each group should present

the scene, explaining how they have incorporated various elements from the epic into their illustration and also drawing from their new knowledge of symbols to explain their interpretation of the meaning of the scene.

Writing

Ask students to write a short paper in response to one or more of the following:

1. Women play a particularly interesting role in the initiation of Enkidu and also in Gilgamesh's transformation from bad king to good. Describe the different types of women and what function they play in the epic.

2. Ring composition is when the subject at the beginning of a scene or an entire work resembles the subject at the end of the work, forming a ring or a cycle of events. In *The Epic of Gilgamesh*, are there any cycles or evidence of ring composition within the work? What about the work itself — is it composed according to the ring cycle convention? Perhaps if we remove the final section on his death, will it be ring composition? If so, what does this say about *The Epic of Gilgamesh?*

3. Gilgamesh's mother first describes Enkidu as an axe and a meteor, based on the dreams of Gilgamesh. Write a paper explaining which qualities of Enkidu are like an axe and a meteor and why she has chosen to describe him in this way.

BEYOND THE CLASSROOM

RESEARCH & WRITING

1. This epic is largely concerned with ideas of knowledge and self-understanding. At first, Enkidu knows things that Gilgamesh does not know, which causes him to be afraid. But then, Gilgamesh becomes afraid of what he does not know. Write an essay, citing material from the text, describing the role of knowledge in the culture *The Epic of Gilgamesh* represents.

2. Compare the description of the flood in the Old Testament (p. 145) with the flood in *The Epic of Gilgamesh*. Are the motivations the same? What about the results of the flood? In what ways might the story of Utnapishtim be a different interpretation of the same outcome as that in the Old Testament?

Projects

1. Many have called Mark Twain's *Huckleberry Finn* the American epic. In this story, Huckleberry makes friends with an African American, Jim, and they have many adventures together. *Huckleberry Finn* is narrated in such a way that it seems almost like universal myth. Although he begins his quest of a better society in ignorance and innocence, Huck grows up in the process and sacrifices himself so that Jim won't be turned over to the police as a runaway slave. Write a paper discussing the similarities and differences between *The Epic of Gilgamesh* and *Huckleberry Finn* in terms of their both being epics.

FURTHER READING

Best, Robert M. *Noah's Ark and the Ziusudra Epic: Sumerian Origins of the Flood Myth.* 1999.

Black, Jeremy, and Anthony Green. *Gods, Demons and Symbols of Ancient Mesopotamia: An Illustrated Dictionary.* 1992.

Cirlot, J. E. Trans. Jack Sage. *A Dictionary of Symbols.* 1962.

Frazer, James G. *The Golden Bough.* 1922.

Heidel, Alexander. *The Gilgamesh Epic and Old Testament Parallels.* 1963.

Jung, C. G. *Man and His Symbols.* 1964.

Maier, John, ed. *Gilgamesh: A Reader.* 1997.

Tigay, J. *The Evolution of the Gilgamesh Epic.* 1982.

MEDIA RESOURCES

WEB SITES

Ancient Near East Sacred Texts
www.sacred-texts.com/ane/index.htm
This site contains e-texts of a number of key sacred texts of the Near East and links to sites answering frequently asked questions on the religion and mythology of the region.

The Epic of Gilgamesh: An Outline with Bibliography and Links
www.hist.unt.edu/ane-09.htm
This site, developed by Lee Huddleston of the University of North Texas, is a phenomenal resource for the study of the Gilgamesh epic. Included here are an outline of the epic, a very complete bibliography, links to translations, links, and correlations.

Gilgamesh Summary
www.wsu.edu/~dee/MESO/GILG.HTM
Richard Hooker's page (of Washington State University) provides an excellent overview of the Gilgamesh epic with hotlinks to other interesting comparative or background sites.

GENERAL MEDIA RESOURCES

VIDEO

Ancient Religions of the Mediterranean
50 min., 1999 (Insight Media)
This video examines some of the ancient mythologies that have influenced the religions of the modern world. It explores the social, political, and cultural significance of the faiths and belief systems of Mesopotamia, Egypt, Greece, and Rome.

The Birth of Civilization (6000–2000 B.C.E.)
26 min., 1985 (Insight Media)
This program traces the birth of civilization in the fertile valleys of the Near East and China. It relates social structures to the growth of cities and discusses the development of the calendar, the wheel, and ceramic and metalworking techniques. It also discusses the invention of mathematics and a system of writing.

Civilization and Writing
23 min., 1998 (Insight Media)
This educational program explores the early river valley civilizations and traces the change from oral traditions to literature. Featuring dramatic readings and commentary by former Poet Laureate Robert Pinsky, the program explores the practical reasons for the development of writing in China, Egypt, Mesopotamia, and Phoenicia as well as its connection to religion, politics and economics. It covers the various literary forms found in ancient writings, including epics, lyrical poems, and sacred dramas and examines the universal themes found in these works.

First Storytellers
58 min., 1988 (PBS Video)
Joseph Campbell discusses the importance of accepting death as rebirth. In order to illustrate his point, Campbell uses the myth of the buffalo and the story of Christ, the rite of passage in primitive societies, the role of mystical shamans, and the decline of ritual in today's society. Part of the acclaimed *Power of Myth* PBS series hosted by Bill Moyer.

Great Religions of the World
33 min., 1995 (Insight Media)
This video explores the major beliefs, origins, and histories of Buddhism, Christianity, Judaism, Hinduism, Islam, and Taoism. It differentiates between ethnic and universalizing religions, discussing how each of the universalizing religions developed from an ethnic base and expanded past national boundaries.

The Hero's Adventure
58 min., 1988 (PBS Video)
Long before medieval knights charged off to slay dragons, tales of heroic adventures were an integral part of all world cultures in which Joseph Campbell challenges everyone to see the presence of a heroic journey in his or her own life.

Love and the Goddess
60 min., 1988 (PBS Video)
Joseph Campbell talks about romantic love, beginning with the twelfth-century troubadours. He also addresses questions about the image of woman as goddess, virgin, and Mother Earth.

Masks of Eternity
60 min., 1988 (PBS Video)
Joseph Campbell provides challenging insights into the concepts of God, religion, and eternity. He draws his insights from Christian teachings and the beliefs of Buddhists, Navajo Indians, Schopenhauer, Jung, and others.

Message of Myth
54 min., 1988 (PBS Video)
Joseph Campbell compares the creation story in Genesis with creation stories from around the world. As the world continues to change, religion has to be transformed and new mythologies created. People today are stuck with old metaphors and myths that don't fit their needs.

Sacrifice and Bliss
58 min., 1988 (PBS Video)
Joseph Campbell discusses the role of sacrifice in myth, which symbolizes the necessity for rebirth. He also talks about the significance of sacrifice, in particular, a mother's sacrifice for her child and the sacrifice of marriage. Campbell stresses the need for every one of us to find our sacred place in the midst of today's fast-paced technological world.

The World's Philosophies
60 min., 1994 (Insight Media)
In this video, Huston Smith defines three basic types of human relationships — with nature, with other people, and with one's self — and explains how these relationships correspond to the philosophical traditions of the West, of China, and of India.

WEB SITES

ABZU: A Guide to Information Related to the Study of the Ancient Near East on the Web
www.etana.org/abzu/
An excellent guide to ancient Near East resources, hosted by the Oriental Institute.

Ancient Adventures Cybermuseum
members.tripod.com/jaydambrosio/cybermus.html
A lavishly illustrated basic overview of ancient civilizations.

Ancient Africa in the Virtual Classroom
www.mrdowling.com/609ancafr.html
The Phoenicians and the Nok, trade and Timbuktu, and more.

Exploring Ancient World Cultures
eawc.evansville.edu/
The University of Evansville's site contains a nice collection of sites; very well presented.

Internet Ancient History Sourcebook
www.fordham.edu/halsall/ancient/asbook.html
The goal of the Ancient History Sourcebook is to provide and organize texts for use in classroom situations. Links to the larger online collections are provided for those who want to explore further. It also includes links to visual and aural material, since art and archeology are far more important for the periods in question than for later history. The emphasis remains on access to primary source texts for educational purposes.

Perseus Digital Library — Greek and Roman Materials
www.perseus.tufts.edu/
The Perseus Digital Library, a Web site created and maintained by the classics department at Tufts University, offers users a vast archive of ancient Greek and Roman images and e-texts.

Voice of the Shuttle: Classical Studies
www.qub.ac.uk/english/shuttle/classics.html
Alan Liu's humanities index of great breadth, the Classical Studies page is excellent, as is every one of thirty-plus subindices.

AUDIO

Great Speeches in History
2 tapes or 2 CDs, 2:38 hrs. (Naxos Audio)
From Socrates to Charles I, Danton to Lincoln — here are some of history's most significant figures with their most important speeches. Fighting for justice, for freedom of speech, and sometimes even for their own lives, these orators demonstrate the finest resources of language in the service of the most dramatic issues of their day.

The History of Theatre
3 tapes or 3 CDs, 5 hrs. (Naxos Audio)
This bold undertaking covers Western theater from ancient Greece to the present day. It traces the development of dramatic art through the miracle plays, the great Shakespearean period, Molière and Racine in France, and Goethe in Germany through the nineteenth century and the main movements in the twentieth century. It is illustrated by numerous examples of differing styles, with some historical recordings as well and excerpts from nearly fifty plays.

Living Biographies of Great Philosophers
7 tapes, 9:75 hrs. (Blackstone Audiobooks)
Included in this program are Plato and Socrates, Aristotle, Epicurus, Marcus Aurelius, Thomas Aquinas, Francis Bacon, Descartes, Spinoza, Locke, Hume, Voltaire, Kant, Hegel, Schopenhauer, Emerson, Spencer, Nietzsche, William James, Henri-Louis Bergson, and Santayana.

VIDEO

Iraq: Stairway to the Gods
27 min., 1977 (Insight Media)
Traveling back fifty centuries, this video explores the origins of human civilization in the region between the Tigris and Euphrates rivers, now modern Iraq. It examines archaeological finds that date to ancient Assyria and Sumer. It also discusses the development of cuneiform writing.

Mesopotamia
52 min., 1995 (Annenberg/CPB Video)
Settlements in the Fertile Crescent gave rise to the great river civilizations of the Middle East.

Mesopotamia: I Have Conquered the River
59 min., 2000 (Films for the Humanities & Sciences)
Literally "the land between the rivers," Mesopotamia was host to some of the world's earliest and most powerful civilizations. Shot on location, this program seeks to understand how the Sumerian city-states, cradled by the Tigris and Euphrates rivers, built a vibrant agricultural economy — and why, after centuries, the wheat crop suddenly failed. Commentary by Asli Ozdogan, of Istanbul University, and Kazuya Maekawa, of Kyoto University; discussion of cuneiform, the Code of Hammurabi, and *The Epic of Gilgamesh;* and a remarkable 3-D computer re-creation of a peopled street scene offer a glimpse of life in Lower Mesopotamia.

Mesopotamia: Return to Eden
36 min., 1995 (Time-Life)
Time-Life goes back to the great world traditions of the Christian, Jewish, and Muslim faiths and traces their roots to the river valleys of Mesopotamia's Fertile Crescent. Join archaeologists as they unearth physical clues to the truth behind the biblical stories of Noah and his ark, the great flood, the Tower of Babel and more in the country that today is known as Iraq.

WEB SITES

Collapse: Why Do Civilizations Fail?
www.learner.org/exhibits/collapse/mesopotamia.html
This Annenberg/CPB site explores the fall of civilizations through four examples: the ancient Maya, Mesopotamia, the Anasazi, and the medieval African empires of Mali and Songhai.

Internet Ancient History Sourcebook — Mesopotamia
www.fordham.edu/halsall/ancient/asbook03.html
The goal of the Ancient History Sourcebook is to provide and organize texts for use in classroom situations. Links to the larger online collections are provided for those who want to explore further. It also includes links to visual and aural material, since art and archeology are far more important for the periods in question than for later history. The emphasis remains on access to primary source texts for educational purposes.

Mesopotamia
www.wsu.edu:8080/~dee/MESO/MESO.HTM
Richard Hooker's page (of Washington State University) provides an excellent overview of Mesopotamia, including information on its history and peoples and culture, and many links to additional resources.

EGYPT: THE SEASONS OF THE NILE: PYRAMIDS, TOMBS, AND HIEROGLYPHICS

Hymns (p. 104)

WWW   For a quiz on Egyptian hymns, see *World Literature Online*
at bedfordstmartins.com/worldlit.

The literature and culture of ancient Egypt are often treated as exotic, colorful material that is notable for its antiquity and "difference" from our culture and way of life. The ubiquity of such perceptions, both in the scholarship and the popular imagination, speak of intense and thoroughgoing cultural labor in the definition of an Other that is supposed to stand in radical opposition to the (post)modern subject and its culture. Together with, and in many ways drawing from, serious historical scholarship, popular culture has done its share in the manufacturing of an image of ancient Egypt marked by profound differences measurable in terms of time and geographical distance as well as cultural practice. Mystery, the supernatural, and an alluring yet dangerous eroticism color popular conceptions of ancient Egypt. Hollywood has certainly played a major role in the crafting and dissemination of such perceptions with efforts such as *The Mummy* (1932), *Cleopatra* (1934), and the variety of later treatments of the same subjects, like the 1963 staging of Elizabeth Taylor as the Egyptian queen and the more recent *The Mummy* (1999) and *The Mummy Returns* (2001). Vigorously producing and promoting such imagery, our culture entertains and comforts itself with picturesque representations of a world that is simultaneously attractive and repellent, sophisticated and superstitious, buried in the sands of time and yet strangely alive — a world seemingly so unlike our own and yet so curiously unavoidable in the efforts by which we strive to understand ourselves.

As is the case with most aspects of popular culture, its products embody a measure of insight and of error. In the particular case of the historical and cultural realities of ancient Egypt, modern popular conceptions err in stressing their degree of difference with respect to our own world. In this, however, popular culture was only (mis)guided by the errors of cultural and historical scholarship itself. Traditional historicism, emphasizing the insulation of the cultural Other and its definition in its own terms, has for years been primarily responsible for the lack of a dynamic understanding of the relatedness and continuity of human cultures across time and space. The dusty and condescending positivism of what used to be called "orientalism" constitutes in effect a deadening of Egyptology's genuine heart and promise. Born of the exciting historical and cultural events of the Romantic era — including discoveries like that of the Rosetta stone, Champoillon's decipherment of the hieroglyphics, and the efforts of maverick archaeologists and adventurers like James Bruce and the Count de Volney — Egyptology has the potential to be a living practice, one capable of revealing the secrets of our own culture and its historical trajectory. Where popular culture, on the other hand, happily diverges from static forms of scholarship is in the suggestion that whatever ancient Egypt actually was is something alive and well, interacting with us, and waiting only to be freed from the veils that conceal its nature and identity. Staying true to the Romantic soul of Egyptology, a spirit preserved in part in the wild imaginings of our popular culture, is one of the challenges of an effective pedagogical practice — one that seeks to illuminate the relevance of the past to the passions, the living truths, and the problematics of the present. In the study of the literature and culture of ancient Egypt, the great promise, then, is that we may just come to realize that the face hidden in the sarcophagus, concealed by the bandages of time, may very well be our own.

TEXT & CONTEXT

The fundamental identity of Egypt's ancient past and its postmodern present is embodied in a variety of shared contextual features — a thriving economy, a hierarchical social structure, and a form of thought simultaneously earthly and transcendentalist. First of all, the cultural products of ancient Egypt need to be understood as emerging from the context of a prosperous and vigorous economy, one featuring substantial agricultural surpluses and trade as well as a sophisticated division of labor expressed in a rich set of crafts, professions, and industries. The foundation of such success was, as is often noted, the fertility of the lands adjacent to the Nile — in particular, the Delta. A surplus of food and the corresponding leisure to engage in other activities, and in trade, provided the conditions for the development of a truly advanced civilization. As is well known, ancient Egypt is notable for its having attained a remarkable degree of accomplishment in a variety of arts, crafts, and technologies, including construction and engineering, painting, sculpture, writing, copper works, cloth making, and the manufacturing of paper, jewelry, and cosmetics. The scale of production and the successes of the Egyptians in these and other areas of activity speak of the development of a complex economy of truly industrial proportions — one capable of supporting a large population and a high standard of living.

Life in ancient Egypt appears to have been marked by a wealth and well-being, which might have even trickled, to some extent, to those in the lower classes. Recent research in Egyptology (e.g., Zahi Hawass and Mark Lehner) has questioned the traditional image of ancient Egypt as a slave society, where a brutalized laboring class was forced to erect gigantic monuments to the egos of bloodthirsty and cruel tyrants. Rather than abject slavery, the reality of the pyramid builders seems to have been one of a relatively free and well-motivated labor force that took pride in its work and received some degree of payment in the form of meat, beer, and bread. Overall, the condition of the average Egyptian appears to have been one of substantial contentment and attachment to life — a situation where nearly all classes of society partook of and delighted in the dream of personal immortality, the idea of the indefinite prolongation and extension of what was perceived as a rather good life. Not wanting to overly idealize the matter of the living conditions of the Egyptian working classes, however, it may be necessary to note that happiness is, after all, a relative matter and often little more than the relief of bare survival — the oppressed human being thankful for the meager necessities that make the dawning of one more day possible. Whatever the case, the celebration of the power and fertility of life-sustaining nature, the idea of personal immortality, and the pursuit of eternal life were the fundamental aspects of Egyptian religion and the central themes of its literature. As if continuing and reflecting the successes and rewards of economic activity, ancient Egyptian literary work took material accomplishments and represented them in the realm of the spirit-allowing imaginative writing to celebrate, enhance, and further dream of the potential of what the economy made possible.

Perhaps most remarkable in the religious hymns of ancient Egypt is the attitude of reverence and awe toward natural forces and creatures — the sun, the river, the land, the human body. To the Egyptians, nature seemed to be rich, powerful, generous, and seemingly inexhaustible in its variety and vitality. Thus the hymns offer excellent opportunities for reflection on the specific ways in which human religion emerges from the sense that what sustains material life is sacred. An agricultural people depending in a fundamental way for their survival on water, land, sunlight, and the life cycle of vegetation naturally develops a religious cult where such phenomena are held in reverence. The religious cosmology of Egypt is clearly dominated by deities representing the various forces and elements of importance to the material survival of the people: the sun gods, Re and Aten; the vegetation deity, Osiris; Isis, a goddess of maternal fertility; Nun and Tefnut, associated with water and moisture; and Geb, a divinity of earth and land. Depicting the dramatic engagement and conflict of the beneficent gods against evil antagonists such as Seth, representing dryness and the desert heat, and Apophis, the serpent of darkness, the religion and literature of the ancient Egyptians represents effectively the drama of the human economic struggle for survival and the regeneration and continuation of life. As has often been noted, the Christ of Western cultures is a deity likely patterned on, or at least presenting remarkable analogies with, the Egyptian Osiris — an agricultural, vegetation god who is born, dies, and resurrects in synchrony with the solar cycle. One of the rewards of studying ancient Egyptian literature is therefore the possibility of coming to a better understanding of our own religious ideas — particularly the character of our deities and the notions of salvation and eternal life. Demystified and stripped of their obscure otherworldliness, such concepts can be brought down to earth and revealed as symbolic representations of the essential goals of the human economic process and embodiments of the human desire for continuity and permanence.

However much the fertility of the Nile valley and the sophisticated economy it spawned may have sustained a sizable and relatively satisfied population, the facts of social inequality, power, violence, and oppression in ancient Egyptian life cannot be ignored. The social hierarchies and the military and political systems of ancient Egypt must then be taken into account in any examination of its cultural products. Much of what speaks in texts like the religious hymns is, after all, the voice of power, the discourse of privileged individuals and social classes buttressing, justifying, and enhancing their own image through a rhetoric of self-divinization and the corresponding demonization of antagonists, both domestic and foreign. The patronage and production of literary and other works of art is a phenomenon that also needs to be firmly located as originating in and taking its motivation from the interests of the upper classes. Though other voices can and are indeed often heard in the ancient Egyptian texts, the picture they paint is one colored by the ideological perceptions of those in power. Given that situation, it may then be possible to understand why the picture of social life emerging from such texts is rather benign and suffused with a sense of harmony, happiness, order, and justice. The actual situation was necessarily a much more complex and ambiguous matter — the pictures of life promoted by the ruling elite not necessarily granting substantial representation to the oppressed members of the social body.

The ancient Egyptian hymns offer a unique opportunity for reflection on the character of literary works as a discourse of power and expressions of dominant political and other interests. Very notable in a hymn like "Creating the World and Defeating Apophis" is the effort at the characterization of the self as a supreme god and the justification of the violent suppression of a demonized antagonist, who can certainly be identified with the abstract powers of darkness but evidently also has a human identity. Religious mythology and poetic imaginations are in this case the vehicles of a partially suppressed and ideologically reworked human history. The overthrow, driving away, and annihilation of evil enemies in which the hymn delights are images with forgotten historical signifieds and constitute the continuation, on the ideological plane, of actual and evidently very bloody human confrontations and struggles for power: "He is one fallen to the flame, Apophis with a knife on his head . . . I have consumed his bones . . . I have cut his vertebrae at his neck, severed with a knife which hacked up his flesh and pierced into his hide." In the hymn, the speaking voice is quickly identified as that of the "All-Lord," Atum or Re, who asserts his own uncontested supremacy, as the origin and source of all life, and the subordination of everything to his powers of creation and destruction. The voice of the god seems conscious of a form of creation, a validation of being, which takes place as a speech act: "Many were the beings where came forth from my mouth. . . ." His words can give existence but they can also deny it, silencing the undesirable aspects of the past: "his name is no (more) in this land." As if aware of the ideological functions of language and discourse, the speaking "god" characterizes language as a sort of divine magic capable of annihilating an enemy: "When (these gods) rich in magic spoke, its was the (very) spirit of magic, for they were ordered to annihilate my enemies by the effective charms of their speech." Here, then, we observe a rhetoric of power grounded on and extending acts of physical violence — the deployment of a kind of verbal political magic that allows the speaker to characterize himself as the highest possible and most uncontestable of powers.

Akhenaten's invention of monotheism in the fourteenth century B.C.E. was evidently a religious development with political content — one corresponding to an absolutist understanding of his own authority and a rhetorical "naturalizing" of that authority, making it as unquestionable as the goodness of the sun and of life itself. Akhenaten's "Hymn to Aten" is one of the rhetorical speech acts involved in the articulation of a new religion whose explicit innovation is the idea of a single god and essential, inescapable content is the uncontested worship of one worldly ruler. A calm survey of all of existence, the hymn sings its way over created nature as the sun glides over the limpid sky, beholding and bringing to light the beauty and orderliness of the divine and the human realms. A masterly work marked by keen observation of the natural world and a shrewdly subtle interweaving of the religious, the economic, the scientific, and the political, the hymn stands as a monument to the powers of language to celebrate life and also, in the process, to suggest illegitimate associations. While the ancient Egyptians did not owe their crops, their fertile land, and the life-giving powers of the sun to Akhenaten, the hymn certainly strove to insinuate those connections and initiated the tradition of radical absolutism as a political form with supposedly natural and divine foundations. The absolutism of the French monarch Louis XIV and the idea of him as the "Sun King" are intriguing later offshoots of that tradition.

The route by which such ideas reached seventeenth-century France is of course primarily biblical. The lessons of the ancient Egyptians were indeed not wasted on Moses who, living among them, likely in the thirteenth century B.C.E., learned to use the magic of the Egyptian verbal arts in his own quest for absolute political power.

In ancient Egypt, we find the very ancestor of our culture and way of life. In both direct and indirect ways, the culture of Egypt has influenced, shaped, and informed our own. As we survey the panorama of modern capitalist cultures, with their primarily Christian working classes toiling in urban environments dominated by gigantic skyscrapers, what we observe is not essentially different from the lot of the ancient Egyptians building the pyramids, humbly submitting to the wills and egos of their godly rulers, and wishing for eternal life in the next world. Still believing in personal immortality and a literal afterlife; still worshiping the single God invented by the Egyptians, as well as his offspring, the deity that dies and resurrects; still patiently accepting domination and inequality as natural aspects of life; still fascinated with power and oppression as quasi-divine rights and prerogatives; still promoting self-sacrifice to the greater mission of the building of financial and other megaliths, the culture of the postmodern world bears the unmistakable mark of its ancient Egyptian ancestry. Those connections and continuities are not generally made explicit primarily because we have employed the culture of Egypt as a false Other against which to define our modernity. To recognize the analogies, on the other hand, is to question and put in doubt our identity as an advanced, rational culture constituted by free and autonomous individuals — to blur the lines between freedom and slavery, between reason and superstition. But however we choose to look at it, the half-decomposed face of the mummy turns out to be indeed our own — the hidden material referent of our values and beliefs; the fact of our identity with an ancient people who recognized their dependence on the powers of the sun, the river, and the land and made gods out of them; who fantasized of immortality and gullibly accepted the divinity of their masters; and who yielded to a kind of slavery not so much of chains and whips subjecting the body as of tales and stories acting on the mind.

IN THE CLASSROOM

Discussion

"Creating the World and Defeating Apophis: A Ritual Hymn"

1. What does Apophis represent? What may be its significance in terms of nature and natural forces? How are attitudes toward natural forces translated into moral terms?

2. Are we seeing in this hymn an illustration of the birth of morality and moral dualism? On what are they grounded? What constitute the earliest ways of judging between good and evil? What are the criteria of such judgments?

3. Is it significant that the speaking god in the hymn insists on the idea that he created the world all by himself? Why? What may be the underlying concerns behind such an idea? Does it have political significance? What does it exclude? What does it silence? To what or to whom does it deny credit?

4. What perceptions does this hymn seek to establish as real? Which ones does it seek to obscure or silence? Why does it consider it important that the name of the enemy be forgotten? What does it want for its audience to believe? What does that suggest regarding its possible motivations and political subtexts?

5. What about the violent imagery of the hacking to pieces and burning of the body of the enemy? Is this purely symbolic, or does it have historical significance? If history is in some way hinted at, is this a balanced or objective perception of that history?

6. What is the significance of the idea that the act of creation is related to speech, the words of the deity? What does that suggest regarding language? Is language in any way related to our perceptions of reality? Is reality somehow dependent on language? How is naming related to existence? Do things that have no name exist? In what sense? Can others' perceptions of reality be influenced by language and rhetoric? Is language in a way, as the hymn suggests, a kind of magic? How does it operate?

"Hymn to Osiris"

1. What does Osiris represent? Why is he so important in ancient Egyptian religion and literature? What did the Egyptians worship in the form of Osiris? Why is that so fundamental to the Egyptian way of life?

2. Is Osiris related to the Egyptian material and economic way of life? Is it important that he is allied with Nun, a water deity? What about his association with his sister Isis, a goddess of fertility, birth, and motherhood? Is it significant that Osiris's main antagonist is Seth, the god of dryness and desert heat?

3. Why is Osiris also a deity associated with mystery and even the underworld? Is it important that he dies and resurrects and that he offers immortality to his followers? How about the fact that Osiris presides over the judgment of the dead, who are then punished with eternal fire or rewarded with eternal bliss? What does that suggest?

4. Is it significant that Osiris has a "kindly face, on whom men love to look?" Why is he so much loved by his followers? Why is it said that "all people were happy, cheerful of mind, and with glad hearts; all men cried out for joy, and all people adored his goodness"?

"Hymn to Aten"

1. What was the ancient Egyptian attitude toward nature and life, as seen in this text? Do the observations on nature made in the hymn have a certain scientific validity? Is the sun the source of all life, as the hymn suggests? Are there other aspects of nature featured? What is said about them? What does that suggest regarding the state of development of ancient Egyptian understanding of the mechanics of the natural world?

2. Where is the boundary between religion, literature, and science? Do they have a common origin? What may be the relationship between the theological and philosophical ideas and images in the hymn and the political situation in the Egypt of Akhenaten's time?

3. How does Akhenaten portray his relationship to the divine? How is the religious monotheism of Akhenaten connected to his own political and social agendas?

4. Is it important that Akhenaten may have either authored or sponsored this hymn? Why? How does patronage affect the content of art? Is art independent of politics or the interests of those who craft or sponsor it?

Connections

1. Ask students to reflect on the similarities between ancient Egyptian religion and Judeo-Christianity, in particular monotheism as expressed in Akhenaten's "Hymn to Aten" and, for example, Psalm 104 (p. 205). Also of interest is the consideration of the similarities between Osiris and Christ.

2. Ask students to compare and contrast accounts of creation like those in "Creating the World and Defeating Apophis," the Babylonian *The Epic of Creation* (p. 40), and Genesis 1 (p. 140). For example, what are the main features of such stories of creation? What are the basic elements, materials, or situations out of which creation arises? What is the force that catalyzes the coming into being of the world? Is it significant that in some accounts the creation is enacted by one deity and in others a duality of forces is emphasized? What is the significance of those differences?

3. Based on a reading of the Egyptian hymns as well as the ancient Mexicans' creation stories and the myth of Quetzalcoatl, ask students to compare the cosmogonies and mythologies of these cultures. Are there significant similarities in the ideas and images featured in the literatures of these pyramid-building peoples? Are there analogues for aspects of the story of Quetzalcoatl (the plumed serpent) in Egyptian myth? Are there similarities, for example, between Quetzalcoatl and Osiris? How about the Aztecs' cult of the sun and their efforts, through human sacrifice, to ensure its return after the nighttime's journey? What may be some explanations for the intriguing analogies in the cultures of these ancient peoples?

Writing

Ask students to write a short paper in response to one or more of the following:

1. Throughout your reading of the ancient Egyptian hymns, keep a journal of personal reflections by tracking down your thoughts on the similarities or differences between

the ideas expressed in the texts and your own religious, ethical, or other values and beliefs.

2. Write a paper identifying and examining the references to language, names and naming, and the verbal arts in the ancient Egyptian hymns. What are the functions and implications of such references? Why do they seem to be so prominently featured in this literature?

3. Write a paper identifying and characterizing the references to nature and natural processes in the ancient Egyptian hymns. What attitudes are expressed in those references? How are they similar or different from contemporary ideas of the natural world?

4. Based on the textual evidence provided by the hymns, write a paper reflecting on the significance of the association between the ancient Egyptian gods and nature and natural processes. Why is nature sacred in ancient Egyptian literature? Do we observe similar characteristics in contemporary world religions, including Judeo-Christianity? What are the implications of such connections?

5. Write a paper assessing how economic and social life is portrayed in the ancient Egyptian hymns. Are such pictures accurate portrayals of historical realities? Do they constitute idealizations? What may be the motivation of such portrayals, and what are their implications?

BEYOND THE CLASSROOM

RESEARCH & WRITING

1. Undertake some research into the details and circumstances of the economic life of the ancient Egyptians. Then write a paper using your findings as evidence in a consideration of the ways in which economics and economic concerns and ideas seem to be expressed in the religion and literature of the ancient Egyptians.

2. Undertake some research into the social and political conditions of life in ancient Egypt. Then write a paper using your findings in a consideration of the ways in which the social structure and its political institutions are expressed and reflected in the religion and literature of the ancient Egyptians.

3. Based on research of the history of the respective periods, write a paper exploring the intriguing similarities between the political situation in Akhenaten's day and seventeenth-century French absolutism, as seen in the worship of Louis XIV as the "Sun King" and the idea of the monarch as a visible divinity. Are these similarities due to direct or indirect influence, circumstance-driven analogy, or other homology?

4. Modern theories of language often emphasize the notion that language plays a fundamental role in the construction of our sense of reality and the real (Sapir-Whorf Hypothesis; see, for example, Benjamin Whorf, *Language, Thought and Reality*, 1956; D. Mandelbaum, *Edward Sapir: Culture, Language, and Personality*, 1956; A. Bloom, *The Linguistic Shaping of Thought*, 1981). On the basis of research and reflection on that idea, consider the possible significance of images of the divine word or language as underlying the act of creation. Compare, for example, references in "Creating the World and Defeating Apophis" ("Many were the beings where came forth from my mouth . . ."), God's creation by verbal command in Genesis 1, and the Book of John ("In the beginning was the Word . . ."). Are ancient accounts of creation in some way early insights into the linguistic nature of reality?

Projects

1. Watch the films *The Mummy* (1999) and *The Mummy Returns* (2001), and consider the reasons why our culture continues to be fascinated by ancient Egyptian culture. What may be the significance of the idea of the mummy's return to life? What do the resurrected mummies want? What is their goal? What do the heroes seek? How does that create an engaging conflict for the audience? What contemporary cultural, social, or political issues do the films tackle via the imagery of evil mummies chasing heroic adventurers? How are other cultures, ancient and contemporary, represented in these films? What problems in our own perceptions do such films reveal? Are the films accurate representations of the historical past? If not, how does the modern world project and visualize its own concerns and problems in such representations?

FURTHER READING

Aldred, Cyril. *The Egyptians.* 1984.

Baines, John, and Jaromír Málek. *Cultural Atlas of Ancient Egypt.* 2000.

Hawass, Zahi. "Tombs of the Pyramid Builders." *Archaeology* (January/February 1997): 39–43.

Hawass, Zahi, and Mark Lehner. "Builders of the Pyramids." *Archaeology* (January/February 1997): 30–38.

Lehner, Mark. *The Complete Pyramids: Solving the Ancient Mysteries.* 1997.

Morell, Virginia, and Kenneth Garrett. "The Pyramid Builders." *National Geographic* (November 2001): 78–99.

Shaw, Ian, ed. *Oxford History of Ancient Egypt.* 2000.

Trigger, B. G., et al. *Ancient Egypt: A Social History.* 1983.

MEDIA RESOURCES

VIDEO

Cleopatra
192 min., 1963 (IMDB)
Starring Elizabeth Taylor and Richard Burton, this film is the historical and poetical drama of Queen Cleopatra of Egypt, who wants to stabilize her power by using the tensions in the Roman Empire. Julius Caesar as well as Marc Antony, his opponent, fall in love with her because of her beauty, but Cleopatra decides for the wrong side and loses all in the end.
Cleopatra
100 min., 1934 (IMDB)
In 48 B.C.E., Cleopatra, facing palace revolt in her kingdom of Egypt, welcomes the arrival of Julius Caesar as a way of solidifying her power under Rome. When Caesar, whom she has led astray, is killed, she transfers her affections to Marc Antony and dazzles him on a barge full of DeMillean splendor.

The Mummy
124 min., 1999 (IMDB)
Brendan Fraser stars as a French Foreign Legion soldier, who on an archaeological dig at the ancient city of Hamunaptra accidentally awakens the Mummy.

The Mummy Returns
130 min., 2001 (IMDB)

The story is set in 1933, ten years after the events of the first film. Rick O'Connell (Brendan Fraser) is now married to Evelyn (Rachel Weisz), and the couple has settled in London, where they are raising their eight-year-old son Alex. When a chain of events finds the corpse of Imhotep resurrected in the British Museum, the mummy Imhotep walks the earth once more, determined to fulfill his quest for immortality. But another force has also been set loose in the world — one born of the darkest rituals of ancient Egyptian mysticism and even more powerful than Imhotep. When these two forces clash, the fate of the world will hang in the balance, sending the O'Connells on a desperate race to save the world from unspeakable evil and to rescue their son before it is too late.

The Scorpion King
94 min., 2002 (IMDB)
A desert warrior rises up against the evil army that is destroying his homeland. He captures the enemy's key sorcerer, takes her deep into the desert, and prepares for a final showdown.

WEB SITES

Ancient Egypt Bibliography
www.ancient-egypt.org/bib/lit_translations.html
Though this site is commercial in that it is tied in with Amazon.com, it presents wonderful historical and cultural information on ancient Egypt through links on its navigation bar.

Ancient Egyptian Literature
mockingbird.creighton.edu/worldlit/works/egypt.htm
Dr. Fajardo-Acosta's (Creighton University) site on ancient Egyptian literature, which provides useful information on historical context, bibliography, and (soon) links.

The Sphinx and the Pyramids: 100 Years of American Archaeology at Giza
www.fas.harvard.edu/~semitic/hsm/GizaHomePage.htm
Curated by Mark Lehner and based at the Harvard Semitic Museum, this site provides an illustrated overview of information on the archaeology of the Sphinx and the Pyramids.

PBS: Pyramids—The Inside Story
www.pbs.org/wgbh/nova/pyramid/
PBS and Nova's site devoted to the Pyramids; includes wonderfully well-illustrated information on individual sites and resources such as maps.

The Plateau: The Official Web Site of Dr. Zahi Hawass
www.guardians.net/hawass/
This is the Web site of Egyptologist Dr. Zahi Hawass, which contains information on individual sites of the Pyramids as well as links to Egyptian history sites and pertinent articles.

Love Poems (p. 118)

WWW   For a quiz on Egyptian love poems, see *World Literature Online* at bedfordstmartins.com/worldlit.

To our culture, ancient Egypt is almost synonymous with a sensuous love tinged with both the most alluring and most dangerous sort of eroticism. The images of love and sexuality that modern popular imagination associates with ancient Egypt are pervasive, rich in sensuality, and powerful in their capacity to simultaneously entice and repel. Indeed, some of the pictures that might pop into our minds when thinking of ancient Egypt may very well be those of dark-eyed beauties performing stylized dances to the tune of exotic music — all with a backdrop of pyramids, palm trees, and, not very far away, sinuous serpents, scorpions, and other deadly creatures of the desert. The legends of the torrid love affairs of Cleopatra VII with the Roman rulers Caesar and Marc Antony and the Hollywood films on the subject — Cleopatra (1934) starring Claudette Colbert and the 1963 remake with Elizabeth Taylor — have been central to the shaping of these visions. The stories are well known: the daring Queen undressing and then having herself wrapped in a carpet and delivered to Caesar, her ambitions and meddling in court intrigues and international politics, her tragic amorous entanglement with Marc Antony, and her eventual suicide by placing an asp to her breast. Thus Cleopatra dominates and colors our perceptions of love in Egypt as a self-assertive, self-indulgent, fleshly, ambitious, sinister, dangerous, and, ultimately, deadly passion. If anything, the moral films and other popular elaborations on the subject that strongly urge on modern audiences is the idea that those who allow themselves to be lured by such unabashedly carnal beauty end up — well — clearly dead. The self-righteous Octavian — the eventual emperor Augustus and notorious crusader against sexual immorality — is clearly posited, in this narrative tradition, as the victor and the only legitimate ruler of the empire that resisted the seductions of and finally overcame Egypt.

Notwithstanding the fact that Cleopatra wasn't even Egyptian — she was a Macedonian Greek of the Ptolemaic dynasty — modern cultural work has created in her a potent signifier, manufacturing and exploiting images of ancient Egyptian love and sensuality, whose main function is the moral justification of imperial domination (Rome and modern superpowers are successors of this practice). Whether unwrapping mummies or undressing Cleopatra, our culture has indeed engaged in a clearly self-serving othering of the ancient Egyptian subject as an exotic semivillain whose curse and alluring charms are to be exorcised and resisted, with the implied promise that such disciplined, stoic self-control will result in imperial triumph and success in the treasure-hunting quest of the Western hero. Such representations are rather hypocritical in that, like Odysseus tied to the mast but willingly listening to the song of the Sirens, we relish the sight of Cleopatra's naked flesh — after all, that's what packs the movie houses — and yet have secured ourselves firmly to the seats of our solid Western values that condemn such filth and demand to see it perish in the flames of a divinely sanctioned cultural superiority. In that project of Western cultural self-assertion, love, pleasure, and the human body are obviously cast as demonic antagonists of the austere, hard-working, Christian European (or North American) pilgrim/explorer whose only goal is to redeem the gold (or other treasures/resources) that once so unrighteously belonged to self-indulgent pagans. Avoiding the lure of the seductive siren is no easy task though, as any action-packed film featuring orientalized villains clearly demonstrates. In his journey to victory, the hero must work hard, wage fierce battles, and overcome myriad traps and seductions (those of the flesh being the most insidious and difficult to master). Images of virtuous heroes overcoming the ambitious seductresses and decadent tyrants of outdated Eastern worlds are indeed a staple of our culture and certainly continue to do good work in the service of the worldwide expansion of Western interests.

It is with such baggage of peculiarly eschewed perceptions that a student is likely to attend her or his meeting with the love lyrics of the ancient Egyptians. The situation is both a curse and a blessing — a curse because it will take a good deal of ingenuity to get students to suspend the culturally conditioned and nearly automatic leap to moralizing judgment and a blessing because an interest in the subject matter of Egypt, however misguided, can almost be taken for granted. As with all educational endeavors in the postmodern classroom, however, activating the students' interest will require the proper hints and reminders. Showing or assigning a relevant film is highly advisable. Even the most recent and cheesiest cinematic monstrosities will do — *The Scorpion King* (2002), *The Mummy Returns* (2001), and the like.

Fortunately, all of them feature their version of Cleopatra, complete with seminudity and the hottest love encounters as well as the infamous tyrants who must be battled right back to the dust out of which they crawled. The challenge of the instructor will lie in the task of hinting at the subtle ways in which such representations speak not so much of the past as of our own concealed ambitions and desires. Like the films then, modern translations of ancient Egyptian poetry present us with unique opportunities, not for moralistic judgment but for self-discovery and, who knows, maybe even for moments of honest acknowledgment of our common carnality and humanity. However much maligned by those who would subject it for political or economic gain, the body has a language of its own, perhaps most closely articulated in the love lyric, speaking of cravings of the flesh that seem to be, after all, truly universal. Those cravings for the merging of self and other — the heart of love and desire — are quite the opposite of the colonialist/imperialist impulse which seeks to separate, dominate, and violently obliterate difference. Thus it is that the lasting beauty and power of love poetry are perhaps to be found in that it deals with and embraces the facts of naked desire — moments of passion when the human being sees what she or he truly wants and, throwing caution to the winds and recklessly forgetting itself, plunges into the abyss of the other.

TEXT & CONTEXT

Though love may well be a universally experienced emotion, we must not make the error of forgetting that its manifestations are ultimately always culturalized and played out in ways that are clearly context dependent. Part of what exaggerates our sense of love's universality is indeed only a homology or analogy of contextual circumstances. The classical topoi of love poetry then — the love sickness, love as healing medicine and nourishing food, the contradictions of a passion of sweet sorrows and delightful torments, the deification of the object of desire, the willing and inescapable servitude and slavery of the lover to the beloved — are aspects of a cultural phenomenon that emerges under specific social, political, and economic conditions. Whether we think of ancient Egypt, Ovidian Rome, medieval Arabic culture, the courtly love of the twelfth-century troubadours, or the modern and postmodern culturalizations of beauty and love, what we essentially see is a set of similar contexts: complex commercial economies, social distinctions, and privileged classes with the leisure and resources necessary to dress up and inaugurate a cult of beauty and love of high sophistication. Love, as we know it, is unthinkable in contexts of poverty, continuous necessity to labor, or social homogeneity. Love requires social boundaries, socially superior and forbidden objects, the art of cosmetics, and expensive, shimmering garments carefully designed to half cover, half reveal the body as well as the time and leisure to engage in complex games of teasing, enticement, evasion, and pursuit.

Though representations of love often insist otherwise, love is mostly not a natural but a cultural phenomenon. Thus nature imagery and the sexual character of love should not be allowed to obscure love's social, economic, and political significance. Love, in a very important sense, is certainly related to but also to be distinguished from animal reproductive urges. The pervasive presence of nature imagery in love poetry has to be carefully analyzed for its expression of the functions of love in the biological continuation of life and also for cultural and social significance in many ways transcending, and at times even denying, the biological telos. Images of plants and animals in love poetry reveal, then, a double motion toward affirmation of the natural and naturalization of the cultural — a tendency to blur the boundary between animal givens and socially imposed strictures. A commonplace of ideological representations, images of the natural speak, ironically, of the very artificiality of the constructs of love. Much like cosmetics and fancy dress, pictures of the natural world provide an unnatural framework against which a social reality and its conflicts are brought to consciousness and fixed as supposedly timeless representations. In the manner of Keats's Grecian urn turned "sylvan historian," the poetry of love is a manufactured human product pretending to encapsulate and finally express an eternal truth of nature — in the process revealing something not so much about nature as about an internal social situation marked by tragic limits and differentials that can only be overcome in imagination.

It may be said that the essential condition for the emergence of love is power; that is, a privileged socioeconomic and political situation which, through its very nature as a higher state, calls into being the creatures we call yearning and desire. Love then tends to manifest itself as an upwardly mobile emotion — it flows from those without power (the eager lovers) toward those with power (the often indifferent beloved), simultaneously a worship of and a desire for social superiority. The beloved is thus always a higher being, perceived as divine, all powerful, with the ability to — with a mere word or gesture — grant life or death to the pining and humble victim of desire. In love poetry, the beloved is often associated with a variety of privileged states and commodities generally available to the wealthy but lacking for others — clean and healthy bodies, food and wine, medicine and comfort, rest and play, beautiful garments, jewelry, and other alluring body decorations. The beloved is perceived as somewhat of a divinity, controlling and capable of granting a better life to the yearning lover. Such cult of the beloved is revealing of the socioeconomic and political content of the love passion but also of the functions of love and of love poetry as sanctions of an existing social order — one where the illusions created by cosmetics, luxurious clothing, and intoxicating words are an integral part of the ideological work by which the upper classes justify and per-petuate their social domination. Love then is always transgressive and, at the same time, pro-foundly conservative, as it affirms a gap/difference, but it also seeks to unite the two entities that are declared different and separated by social and other boundaries. And it is precisely in love's dualized and contradictory drive to cement and erase distinctions, reaching for and sighing away the socially elevated stars, that we find the reasons representations of desire are so often marked by contradictions, exaggerations, impossibilities, and hyperbolic language as well as images of intoxication, excess, and extravagance. Such features of love poetry play a significant role as representations of the antagonistic relationship between the privileged existence of the powerful and the dreamy aspirations of the subordinated — a situation where the actual satisfaction of desire is never quite something of this world.

The presence of women's voices in love poetry is not an historical accident. In terms of a theory of power and subjection as the preconditions of the love passion, the fact of female poets engaging in the crafting and singing of love lyrics may be understood as one of the symptoms of gender oppression. As a subordinated gender subclass, within the ruling Egyptian aristocracy as well as other strata of society, women had a primary reason for find-ing an ideal medium of expression in such lyrics — voicing in them a desire simultaneously sexual and political. The historical fact of women rulers like Hatshepsut (r. 1473–1458) and Cleopatra, on the other hand, also suggests the reality of the participation of women in power and their own dualized role as lovers and objects of desire. Cleopatra's situation in particular, yearning for the power of Rome and also inspiring similar passions in the Roman rulers, offers a significant illustration of the entanglements between and mutual determina-tions of love, wealth, and domination. In that sense, then, the Christian Western idea that taints love with the sense of the sinful, of weakness, and of death finds a partial justification in the recognition that to love is in a sense to acknowledge one's own inferiority and lack with respect to the desired object. What the death of Cleopatra dramatically embodies then is not evidence of the wages of carnal sin but of the destiny of the subordinated in a world ruled by power and force. Whether understood as an allegory of the subjection of women, of the physical body, or of all human beings for one reason or another crushed under the wheels of power, the story of Cleopatra and the history of love in general offer traces of an ongoing set of problems and contradictions in human society — problems of distribution that are manifest in all human groups where wealth has reached a substantial degree of development but where power keeps that wealth scarce and ever just out of the reach of the yearning masses of necessarily "loving" subjects.

What the love poetry of the ancient Egyptians can tell us, in the last analysis, has much to do not with the reality of a world of sensuous pleasure and self-indulgent frolicking but instead one of violent power, stern hierarchical divisions, and insurmountable social obstacles — a world where power divided people, and poets sang of the pains of separation and the pleasures of a paradise glimpsed only through the cracks in the walls of the royal baths and gardens. The shadows cast by towering pyramids and gigantic statues of the pharaohs, like the mirages of the desert, are rendered in the poetic texts in images of lovely gardens, glistening bodies emerging from limpid waters, and lovers kissing and embracing in the tantalizing landscapes of the unattainable. Such images are certainly very familiar to us, not so much through our much-neglected reading of ancient literature but through the ubiquitous influence and presence of advertising and other media content in our lives. What illusions the ancient Egyptians gleaned from the words of poets and the strains of their haunting melodies, we postmoderns prosaically acquire from television, film, and computer screens — merchandising mirages depicting love in paradise while peddling the junk that guarantees our subjection and dispossession. Why love remains the central theme, myth, and obsession of our contemporary postmodern culture is fully explainable in terms of the lessons learned from the historical experience and the cultural record of a people long lost and buried in the sands of time.

IN THE CLASSROOM

Discussion

"If I am [not] with you, where will you set your heart?"

1. Who is speaking is this poem? What are the implications of the fact that the beloved seems eager to leave and the lover is anxious about his impending absence and his activities while away from her?

2. How is the beloved characterized? Is it significant that he seems more interested in food than in her? What about the fact that she wears "stylish clothes"? What does that suggest regarding the relative social positions of the lover and the beloved? Are food and clothes in any way related to the love passion? Is social status a factor in this relationship?

3. How does the lover seek to entice the beloved? What does she offer? What does that suggest? Is her body a form of food? Why does she conclude that "better indeed is one day in your arms . . . / than a hundred thousand [anywhere] on earth"? What does that reveal regarding her view of herself and her own life relative to the beloved?

4. Why is love characterized, in this and other poems, as a desire to be desired? How is that related to other asymmetries, nonreciprocities, and disparities in the emotional, social, economic, political, and other conditions of the parties to a love situation? Can love ever be truly mutual and reciprocal?

"My love for you is mixed throughout my body"

1. Who is the speaker in this poem? What is the significance of her use of the salt-in-water, gum-in-medicine, and milk-in-water metaphors? What does that suggest regarding the material context of the lives of the poem's protagonists? What sorts of crafts may have been practiced in that context?

2. How does each of the metaphors characterize the love passion? Are different feelings involved? How complex is love? According to this poem, what does it feel like to be in love? Why is love depicted as a flame? Is it pleasant to be in love?

3. Why the use of the animal imagery, the stallion and falcon? Do these animals have anything in common? Why are they used to represent the beloved? According to those metaphors, how does the lover see herself in relation to her beloved?

"My heart is not yet happy with your love"

1. Why is the beloved here characterized as a "wolf cub"? Why is the lover inciting him to "be lascivious unto drunkenness"? What does she want? Is she satisfied with what he offers her?

2. Is the love depicted here obsessive? What images are used to characterize the intensity of the lover's attachment?

3. Is there equality/reciprocity in the emotions in this and other poems? Are the lovers generally loved back with the same fervor they express to their beloveds? Why or why not? What does that suggest about the nature of love? Is it a one-way street? In which direction does it point? Who tends to love whom?

"I sail downstream in the ferry by the pull of the current"

1. Who is the speaker in this poem? Do poems with male speakers differ from those where females are the main protagonists? Are the emotions or images different? How? What does that suggest regarding the possibly gendered nature of the expression of love in ancient Egypt?

2. What is the role of the gods in this poem? What do the gods represent? Is it important that the speaker is on his way to offer prayers and sacrifices to the gods? For what does he ask? Is the poem a form of prayer/sacrifice? How? What does that imply? Where is the boundary between the sacred and the profane for the ancient Egyptians?

3. What is the significance of the setting, the river, and other natural imagery employed in the poem? How do they contribute to the characterization of love and the love wish made by the lover? Are the gods associated with nature? What are the implications?

4. What about the references to and images of wine? Why is the sea portrayed as being wine? Why is wine characterized as an appropriate sacrifice to "the good-looking god"? What may be the role and significance of wine in religious worship and in love poetry?

"My god, my [lover . . .]"

1. Why is the beloved depicted as a god? What does that imply regarding the speaker's perception of herself relative to her lover? From such references and the setting, what may be inferred regarding his social status? Is he a powerful man? Who may she be? Are wealth and power relevant to the occurrence of love?

2. What is the lover offering the beloved? What is her attitude toward her own body?

3. Is it significant that she alludes to her swimsuit as a "garment of royal linen, wet [and clinging]"? How does she use the description of herself in such attire? What are her intentions? What is the role of luxurious clothing in love affairs?

4. What is the "red fish" to which she refers? Who is fishing here? Who is the fisherman, and who the fish? What is the bait?

"I embrace her"

1. Who is speaking here? How is love characterized? What images are employed to describe the experience of embracing and kissing the beloved?

2. How is paradise (Punt) described? How are drugs and alcohol employed in such descriptions? What is their significance, and what may be their implications regarding the experience of love?

3. Why is love seen as an escape from everyday reality? What does that suggest regarding the underlying significance of the love passion and the condition that it seeks to remedy?

"I wish I were her washerman"

1. Is it important that the speaker wishes to be the beloved's servant, her "washerman"? What are the implications of such characterizations? How are social class and economic issues relevant to love and the represented situation? What can we infer from the fact that she wears fancy clothing and anoints her body with expensive oils? What can we infer regarding his social position and his chances of approaching her?

2. Does the speaker consider himself worthy of the beloved? What exactly does he want? How is doing her laundry going to bring him close to her? What are the implications of the desire to handle her clothes and the oils that once touched her body? Are these signs of proximity or of distance?

3. Does this poem present a case of sexual fetishism? If so, how is it connected to a larger set of social problems? Do we witness here a society where wealth and power separate people? Is the fetishistic situation a symptom of that alienation?

"Seven days have passed, and I've not seen my lady love"

1. Why is love characterized as a sickness? What is the remedy for it? Can physicians and medicines cure it? What is the only solution for the lover's pain? What are the implications of these medical metaphors? In what sense is the beloved lady a cure and comfort to a painful illness? May there be underlying symbolic significance in the images of the illness and the cure? Are these ideas related to other social, economic, or political problems?

2. Is it significant that the lady's absence is precisely seven days? Is there implied significance in the time span specified?

"Please come quick to the lady love"

1. Why does the speaker characterize herself as a gazelle fleeing from the hunters? Who is the beloved in this case? Is he one of the hunters? What does that suggest?

2. Why does the speaker/gazelle promise that her beloved/hunter will find "her hideaway"? Does the fleeing gazelle actually mean to be captured and killed by the hunter? What are the implications of these images in the characterization of love? How can their contradictions and oddities be explained? Who is hunting whom?

3. Why is the deity of love characterized as the "Golden Goddess"? What does that imply? How is gold an issue in love and its representation? Are power and wealth factors in love?

Connections

1. Ask students to compare the dynamics of the love passion of Ishtar for Gilgamesh, in the *The Epic of Gilgamesh* (p. 55), with the situations depicted in the Egyptian love poetry. Are there similar motifs, emotions, or ideas invoked in the representations of love in these texts? Why is it that Gilgamesh does not reciprocate the love of the goddess? What does that suggest regarding issues of power and their relations to the realm of the affective?

2. Ask students to do textual comparisons of imagery and language involving the Hebrew Song of Songs (p. 208) and Egyptian love poems. Ask them to speculate as to the possibility of direct influence and to place their discussion in the wider context of the historical and cultural contacts between the Egyptian and the Hebrew peoples.

3. Ask students to do textual comparisons involving the representation of the love passion in ancient Egyptian poems and the poetry of Sappho (p. 791). Is it significant that some of the poetry of Sappho has survived because of papyrus fragments discovered in an Egyptian village? What cultural and historical contacts between the Egyptians and the Greeks are relevant to such situations?

4. Ask students to think about the points of contact between the poetry of Roman authors like Catullus (p. 1164) and Ovid (p. 1265), and the love poetry of the Egyptians. Which of the classical topoi of love poetry can be traced back to Egypt?

5. Ask students to consider possible analogies between medieval Arabic poetry, such as the works of Jalaloddin Rumi (Book 2) and the love lyrics of Muslim Spain, and ancient Egyptian poetry. In this context, ask students to reflect on the possible role of the Arabs in the transmission of the culture of archaic and classical antiquity to the European cultures of the high and late Middle Ages.

6. Ask students to compare the characterization of love in Egyptian poetry and in southern French lyrics of the twelfth and thirteenth centuries (e.g., Bernart de Ventadorn, the Countess of Dia, Castelloza in Book 2). An interesting reflection in this context involves the comparison of and distinction between poems featuring female and male speakers. As represented in the relevant literary texts, did ancient Egyptian women and men experience love in ways similar to those of their counterparts in medieval Europe?

Writing

Ask students to write a short paper in response to one or more of the following:

1. Analyze the use of animal imagery in ancient Egyptian poems. What animals tend to be featured in the poems? Why? What sorts of attributes or characteristics seem to be associated with the animals? How are those characteristics related to the representation of love? In what activities do the animals engage? Are animal interactions a form of symbolism? What aspects of the love passion do they represent?

2. Identify and analyze references to clothes, textiles, and fabrics in ancient Egyptian love poems. What is the role of such images in the love poetry? What economic or cultural contexts do the allusions to clothing suggest? Are clothes of certain sorts important to love and its representation in the literary art? Can love flourish in the absence of luxury commodities such as fashionable clothing?

3. Identify and analyze references to food and drink in ancient Egyptian love poetry. What is the role of eating and drinking as they are featured in the poems? How is this related to the love motif that the pining lover is often unable to eat, drink, or sleep in the

absence of the beloved? How about the idea of the beloved as a form of food or nourishment? Do these images have economic significance? Does love have economic significance?

BEYOND THE CLASSROOM

RESEARCH & WRITING

1. Ask students to pursue a research project investigating the similarities and possible connections between ancient Egyptian ideas of love and the European culture of courtly love and troubadour poetry in the twelfth and thirteenth centuries. Such a project can involve reading selections of Andreas Capellanus treatise *The Art of Courtly Love* (Book 2) as well as lyrics from the troubadours included in the anthology. Interesting questions to consider are those of the possible routes of influence and the continuities of those influences in modern culture and its courtship rituals and ideas of love.

2. Ask students to ponder and investigate the analogies of Egyptian and other love poetry and the language and ideas of religious, theological, and mystical works expressing the love of God. Have them examine the love lyrics of ancient Egypt and other cultures in conjunction with a variety of mystical/religious texts (both poetry and prose) and authors including Mirabai, Hafiz, Rumi, Hildegard of Bingen, Saint John of the Cross, Sor Juana Inés de la Cruz, Julian of Norwich, Saint Teresa of Ávila, and others.

Projects

1. Ask students to craft creative reconstructions of selected Egyptian love poems by introducing their own interpolations and elaborations in dealing with the gaps and problematic passages in the texts. The use of brackets, half brackets, and ellipses to indicate the translator's restorations and other emendations in the anthology will indicate to students which material to preserve and where to begin their own imaginative writing.

2. Ask students to compile a collection of contemporary song lyrics with love themes and to compare and contrast the images, ideas, and characterizations of love in those lyrics with the corresponding material in the ancient Egyptian texts.

3. Ask students to view some recent films with ancient Egyptian themes and to characterize the love relationships featured there. For example, in *The Mummy* (1999) and *The Mummy Returns* (2001), the ancient Egyptian priest Imhotep (Arnold Vosloo) has a love affair with the royal mistress Anck-Su-Namun (Patricia Velasquez). The film contrasts this love of lust and ambition with the supposedly much healthier but no less passionate relationship between the heroes of the story, the explorer Rick O'Connell (Brendan Fraser) and his Egyptologist wife Evelyn (Rachel Weisz). Ask students to speculate as to the reasons, motivations, and cultural functions of such portrayals.

FURTHER READING

Baines, John, and Jaromír Málek. *Cultural Atlas of Ancient Egypt.* 2000.

Foster, John L. *Love Songs of Ancient Egypt.* 1992.

Fowler, Barbara Hughes. *Love Lyrics of Ancient Egypt.* 1994.

Pound, Ezra, and Noel Stock. *Love Poems of Ancient Egypt.* 1962/1978.

Royster, Francesca. *Becoming Cleopatra: The Shifting Image of an Icon.* 2003

Shaw, Ian, ed. *Oxford History of Ancient Egypt.* 2000.

Trigger, B. G., et al. *Ancient Egypt: A Social History.* 1983.

MEDIA RESOURCES

VIDEO

Cleopatra
192 min., 1963 (IMDB)
Starring Elizabeth Taylor and Richard Burton, this film is the historical and poetical drama of Queen Cleopatra of Egypt, who wants to stabilize her power by using the tensions in the Roman Empire. Julius Caesar as well as Marc Antony, his opponent, fall in love with her because of her beauty, but Cleopatra decides for the wrong side and loses all in the end.

Cleopatra
100 min., 1934 (IMDB)
In 48 B.C.E., Cleopatra, facing palace revolt in her kingdom of Egypt, welcomes the arrival of Julius Caesar as a way of solidifying her power under Rome. When Caesar, whom she has led astray, is killed, she transfers her affections to Marc Antony and dazzles him on a barge full of DeMillean splendor.

The Mummy
124 min., 1999 (IMDB)
Brendan Fraser stars as a French Foreign Legion soldier, who on an archaeological dig at the ancient city of Hamunaptra accidentally awakens the Mummy.

The Mummy Returns
130 min., 2001 (IMDB)
The story is set in 1933, ten years after the events of the first film. Rick O'Connell (Brendan Fraser) is now married to Evelyn (Rachel Weisz), and the couple has settled in London, where they are raising their eight-year-old son Alex. When a chain of events finds the corpse of Imhotep resurrected in the British Museum, the mummy Imhotep walks the earth once more, determined to fulfill his quest for immortality. But another force has also been set loose in the world — one born of the darkest rituals of ancient Egyptian mysticism and even more powerful than Imhotep. When these two forces clash, the fate of the world will hang in the balance, sending the O'Connells on a desperate race to save the world from unspeakable evil and to rescue their son before it is too late.

The Scorpion King
94 min., 2002 (IMDB)
A desert warrior rises up against the evil army that is destroying his homeland. He captures the enemy's key sorcerer, takes her deep into the desert, and prepares for a final showdown.

WEB SITES

Ancient Egypt Bibliography
www.ancient-egypt.org/bib/lit_translations.html
Though this site is commercial in that it is tied in with Amazon.com, it presents wonderful historical and cultural information on ancient Egypt through links on its navigation bar.

The Ancient Egypt Site
www.ancient-egypt.org/
Jacques Kinnaer's site features guides to the history, monuments, and language of ancient Egypt.

Ancient Egyptian Literature
mockingbird.creighton.edu/worldlit/works/egypt.htm
Dr. Fidel Fajardo-Acosta's (Creighton University) site on ancient Egyptian literature provides useful information on the historical context of ancient Egyptian poetry and provides
a full bibliography and links to other sources.

Links to Ancient Egypt Online
www.swan.ac.uk/classics/egypt/goegypt.html
Kasia Szpakowska's portal provides access to information on daily life in ancient Egypt,
including many links to topics like love, marriage, women's life, clothing, jewelry, dancing,
drinking, games, agriculture, and animals in addition to general information on ancient
Egypt.

Love in the Arts
www.wsu.edu:8080/~brians/love-in-the-arts/
Created by Paul Brians (Washington State University), this site provides online resources
including study guides on ancient Egyptian poetry, the Song of Songs, Chinese and
Japanese love poetry, Classical Greek and Roman love poems, Medieval and Renaissance
love songs, mystical love poetry, and other topics.

Study Guide for "Love Poems from the New Kingdom of Ancient Egypt"
www.wsu.edu:8080/~brians/love-in-the-arts/egyptian.html
This is the portion of Paul Brians's site that is devoted specifically to Egyptian love poems.

GENERAL MEDIA RESOURCES

VIDEO

Ancient Egypt
47 min., 1997 (Films for the Humanities & Sciences)
For almost three thousand years, the pharaohs ruled a civilization that is arguably the
grandest of the ancient world. This program sheds new light on this enigmatic empire,
offering information on the god-kings, the construction of the Pyramids, religions and
cults, mummification and burial rites, the Rosetta stone, and the vast treasures of
Tutankhamen. Interviews with noted Egyptologists, a professor from Cairo University, the
chief inspector at the archaeological digs at Gaza, and the son of the guide who led
Howard Carter to the tomb of Tutankhamen in 1922 add valuable insights. Computer
graphics re-create pyramids, temples, and the sphinx in their original states.

The Ancient Egyptians
30 min., 1997 (Annenberg/CPB Videos)
Egyptian irrigation created one of the first great civilizations.

Cleopatra's World: Alexandria Revealed
100 min., 2001 (A&E Video)
The history of Alexandria's two most famous buildings — the Lighthouse at the island of
Pharos and the library — receive most attention. The proposed projects of a new library
and a lighthouse under the auspices of UNESCO also get a mention. Intertwined in the
story is the life of Cleopatra from before her birth until her death. The narration covers her
lineage, education, and ascent to power as well as her affairs with the two most powerful
men of the time — Julius Caesar and Marc Antony.

Egypt: The Quest for Immortality
36 min., 1995 (Time-Life)
Time-Life explores the allure of a culture in which everyone believed that eternal life was a natural right. Learn how archaeologists are penetrating Egypt's long-buried mysteries, from the science of preparing a mummy for eternity to the art of composing a love letter in hieroglyphs and beyond. Through computer graphics and ancient writings, experience the texture of past lives in a world where every death was a new beginning.

Egypt: The Sands of Time
41 min., 1998 (Films for the Humanities & Sciences)
The history of ancient Egypt is traced through the Old, Middle, and New Kingdoms, using location footage and maps. Topics include the importance of the Nile to life in Egypt from 3000 B.C.E. and the patterns of migration of early peoples from Asia Minor and North Africa as well as their various influences on Egyptian culture, including arts, crafts, and religion. Pharaonic ascendancy is examined, along with specific topics including religion, art, the Pyramids, Cleopatra's role in securing Roman territory for Egypt, and her relationship with Julius Caesar and Marc Antony. The discovery of the Rosetta stone and its importance to facilitating the study of Egyptian culture is discussed.

Egypt's Great Queen
50 min., 1997 (A&E Video)
Well over a thousand years before the rise of Cleopatra, another woman was at the helm of the Egyptian empire. A&E looks at Hatshepsut, a compelling and misunderstood figure who ruled the kingdom by the Nile for twenty years. After her death, traces of her reign were all but eliminated by those who followed. What could she have done to inspire such hatred? Examine the tumultuous life of Egypt's first queen.

Library of Alexandria
50 min., 1997 (A&E Video)
For over six hundred years, the Library of Alexandria stood as the ultimate collection of the world's wisdom. Then, in the third century C.E., a disastrous fire robbed the world of its riches. From its founding by Ptolemy the First to its fiery demise, learn the fabled history of this legendary library and why its destruction may have been the result of a brutal civil war.

Mysteries of Egypt
40 min., 1999 (National Geographic Videos)
Omar Sharif plays the role of a grandfather who takes his visiting granddaughter around the country in order to introduce her to the magic of ancient Egyptian civilization. Re-enactments show such events as the building of the Pyramids, the exploits of the pharaohs, and the discovery of Tutankhamun's tomb. Viewers are surrounded with images of colossal monuments and landscapes, and will witness brilliant architects, massive work teams, and gifted artisans as they create some of the world's greatest wonders.

Secrets of the Rosetta Stone
50 min., 1998 (A&E Video)
A&E recounts the fascinating saga of the Rosetta stone, the ancient basalt slab that helped unlock the mysterious language of Egyptian hieroglyphics. Trace the numerous attempts and dead-ends that stumped scholars, while leading historians discuss the life of Jean Francois Champollion, whose brilliant obsession with the stone helped crack its code.

The Sphinx of Egypt
50 min., 2000 (A&E Video)
From the mystery of its missing nose to the secrets of its construction, probe the enduring riddles of one of ancient Egypt's most recognizable monuments.

WEB SITES

Internet Ancient History Sourcebook –– Egypt
www.fordham.edu/halsall/ancient/asbook04.html
The goal of the Ancient History Sourcebook is to provide and organize texts for use in classroom situations. Links to the larger online collections are provided for those who want to explore further. It also includes links to visual and aural material, since art and archeology are far more important for the periods in question than for later history. The emphasis remains on access to primary source texts for educational purposes.

Egyptology Resources
www.newton.cam.ac.uk/egypt/index.html
Set up and maintained by Dr. Nigel Strudwick, a British Museum curator, Egyptology Resources has been serving the Egyptological community since 1994. As such, it is the longest-established — and one of the best-documented — portal sites on ancient Egypt.

Etana
www.etana.org/abzu/
This site is a guide to information related to the study of the ancient Near East on the Web.

Egyptology.com
www.egyptology.com/
This site bills itself as having the best Egypt links on the Web.

THE ANCIENT HEBREWS: THE PATH OF RIGHTEOUSNESS AND THE TEN COMMANDMENTS

Hebrew Scriptures (p. 134)

WWW   For a quiz on the Hebrew Scriptures, see *World Literature Online* at bedfordstmartins.com/worldlit.

Hebrew Scriptures simply means "the writings of the Hebrew people." The overarching story told by these writings is not unlike *The Epic of Gilgamesh* or *The Iliad*. However, instead of being about a particular individual, in this work a culture is the hero of the story. The story takes over a thousand years to transpire, and it happens in diverse locations; nonetheless, it tells the tale of a culture that profoundly shaped Western civilization. The Hebrew Scriptures are sometimes called the Old Testament, a term designated by Christians to refer (approximately) to writings from before the time of Christ. "Testament" is another word for "witness," which implies that the people who named it thus believed that it was a completely true story. "Hebrew Scriptures" is a more neutral usage, and it also demonstrates the origins and history of these writings as part of the sacred history of the Jewish people.

Many of the episodes contained in the Hebrew Scriptures have a basis in the oral and written histories of other civilizations, helping us to establish the date of their *actual* occurrence. Archeological expeditions have also confirmed certain events described by them. However, the work is not a simple annalistic account of the trials and successes of the Hebrews. It possesses deeply embedded codes for living, a description of the faith and culture that experienced those things described by the Hebrew Scriptures, and a mystical frankness about human nature. The history that unfolds reads like a Greek tragedy: murder, revenge, sex, and genocide are the main themes throughout. The picture it paints of human nature is by no means saintly and sacrificial but rather venomous and faithless.

Were the readers of such a work, then, supposed to believe in the same God — Yahweh — as its character? For more than three billion people around the world of Jewish, Muslim, and Christian faith, this is not only a great work of literature, it is also a sacred text. To work oneself through the whole text is supposed to confirm one's faith, not shake it. And yet, when we read of the Great Flood, the trials of the Hebrews in Egypt, or the suffering of Job, we cannot but wonder what kind of God the Hebrew God is. This is because the work is not a proselytizing allegory. It is not really a piece of cultural propaganda or a missionary work. It represents all of the cultural and religious debates present in the culture that produced the Hebrew Scriptures. The debate or dialectic (a method of asking questions in a logical fashion) that became institutionalized by the Talmud seeks not necessarily to come up with answers for the way things are but rather to involve the listener and speaker in a process that confirms faith, even with the presence of unanswerable mystery. The world in the Hebrew Scriptures is not a just one, it is a true one. For people of Jewish or Christian faith, the challenge was to reconcile the true world with a just God.

Like most cultural histories, this one begins with the creation of the world. The order in which God creates things is very interesting: first a division between heaven and earth, then

44

night and day, the sea and air, earth and water, upon which follows life, stars, and the first day of rest. But there is a second story that comes, revealing the oral-folk tradition underlying the entire work. It is a story somewhat full of contradictions. God makes everything, but there is nobody there to till the grounds. The seas aren't separated from the land but rather rise up out of it. Man is made of mud (which happens also to be the case in the Prometheus story as well as in Chinese mythology). God tells the man he is to till the land, but, in fact, all he does is eat things that grow in abundance without the use of agriculture. Woman comes along, tells him to eat a forbidden fruit (the fruit of knowledge), and then they are punished. God now *condemns* them to till the ground: "You shall gain your bread by the sweat of your brow until you return to the ground; for from it you were taken. Dust you are, to dust you shall return." We cannot be certain what happens next: They must wear clothes and leave "the garden of Eden to till the ground from which he had been taken." In the next generation, Cain kills his younger brother Abel, and the blood seeps into the ground. Cain is condemned to get nothing from tilling the ground. It is a story about the earthiness of the snake, of the men and women made from dust who till the dust, versus a being who jealously guards the fruit of knowledge and the fruit of life. This is a difficult way to encounter the religion that will be so fundamental throughout the work.

But that is what makes this such a good read. It is worthy of much debate to sort through the paradoxes left behind by the transparency of this work. There are references to other gods, other religions, and other peoples from the beginning. But there is only one race that is going to be saved — the Hebrew race. Only Noah is saved from the flood. The story is really identical to the story of the great flood sent by Enlil in *The Epic of Gilgamesh* (p. 86). Like Enlil, God learns from it only "never again [to] kill every living creature, as I have just done." God makes a covenant, or a promise. This promise begins a new relationship between mankind and God. All creatures will receive protection from God, and He will be present in all things.

But just as we are becoming accustomed to this new image of God who is sorry for having killed everyone, He is afraid of their accomplishments, lest they be too much. So He confuses everybody's speech so that they cannot understand one another. The Tower of Babel is left unbuilt and the workers scatter as if the bosses took off with their pay. But we are not the only people who are confused and cannot understand what God is doing. Rapidly, we can begin to identify with major characters in the drama that unfolds. They are the great families and patriarchs who obeyed their God with no more knowledge than have we, the readers. Unlike other epics, the heroes of the Hebrew Scriptures, even at their most knowledgeable, operate with less knowledge of the outcome than Achilles or Gilgamesh.

Parallels abound nonetheless. The great flood in *The Epic of Gilgamesh* and the episode of Noah and the ark are identical, and Abraham's near sacrifice of his son is perhaps similar to Agamemnon's sacrifice of Iphigenia before the beginning of the Trojan War (an event referred to in Aeschylus's *Agamemnon* [p. 806]). In some versions, Iphigenia is saved by being transported to a magical island and replaced by a deer on the altar. The guilt of Joseph's brothers when they say, "Why not sell him to the Ishmaelites? Let us do him no harm, for he is our brother, our own flesh and blood," is like that of Creon when he sets out the food for Antigone near the pit, just out of reach, in Sophocles' *Antigone* (p. 952). The story of Joseph and his master's wife seems a little like a variation of a Greek story about the Lydian Candaules and Gyges told by Herodotus in his *Histories*.

The mini-epic of Joseph's rise to the throne is somewhat emblematic of a more typical oral epic buried within. It is a rags-to-riches story very much like that of the immigrant who strikes good in a land of promise and learns to overcome the old order of his homeland. Joseph is sold into slavery by his brothers, taken for dead by his father because of this, and then thrown in prison when framed by his master's wife. But Joseph's ability to interpret dreams (a divine quality) gains him access to the Pharaoh, who lets him rule Egypt. When famine strikes, his brothers go unknowingly to Joseph to buy grain. Through an elaborate plot, Joseph reveals his identity as well as discovers his brothers. He supplies a caravan for his extended family to come to Egypt.

But there they are made slaves. The beginning of Exodus describes the bondage of the Israelites to the people of Egypt. It ends when Moses leads them out of Egypt into the "Promised Land." The Moses story is a classic archetype: It is the story of Romulus (described in Livy's *Ab Urbe Condita*) as well as Cyrus, king of Persia (in Herodotus's *Histories*). The orphaned Moses is adopted by the Pharaoh but knows his true identity as a Hebrew. When he sees that an Egyptian beats a Hebrew, he kills the Egyptian while nobody is looking. But the palace finds out, and he must flee. Now no longer a prince, he is approached by God in the form of a burning bush. The God of the Book of Exodus seems much more compassionate: He has seen the misery of the Hebrews and promises to save them. This is the founding moment of the faith of Judaism: God announces who he is — "I am that I am," — and operates through Moses to the Hebrews. God tells Moses *verbatim* what to say to the Hebrews and instructs him in what faith means, since this will be the prerequisite for surviving the journey to Israel. But the Pharaoh, despite God sending many plagues on Egypt, would not let the Hebrews leave. Only when the firstborn of all living things was killed did he permit them to go. Cultural information, akin to that found in Hesiod's *Works and Days* is passed down — the exact diet for Passover. A kind of preparation for a long voyage can be seen in the logic of the Passover meal. Furthermore, by leaving the mark of blood on the doorpost of each house, there begins to form a community that will leave Egypt together. "Signs" and "marks" are special cultural symbols that help to separate one tribe from another but also to give the feeling of allegiance among members of a tribe (think about how a pilot feels when he gets his "wings" or how strongly people felt about putting flags up in response to the tragedy of September 11, 2001).

The Exodus was not just a physical journey but a mental one. The Israelites prepare themselves by keeping awake the night before. The Hebrews must pass through "the wilderness," a wonderful metaphor for inner soul-searching and the attempt to clear out the bush and brambles that lead to sin or loss of faith. But the way that these families have chosen to come cannot be crossed alone. At the last moment, God must divide the sea into two parts in order to let them pass to Israel. The act is at once a great act of mercy for his own people but also one of great arrogance: God wants to pit his revenge against the army of the Pharaoh. Likewise, there are two readings about the Exodus: There were easier paths to follow than the one the Israelites took, but God chose the more difficult one. In the New Testament, it will be written that the path to heaven is not the easiest path open to someone. This concept of trial and initiation is common to most religions. But God has already tried to release the Israelites from Egypt. To make them pass through more hardships seems pointless. Is it only because he wants them to appreciate him more when they finally arrive in Israel? Is what we might consider to be "spiritual growth" only an elaborate form of indoctrination? The first commandments after Moses and the Hebrews leave Egypt are "Don't worship anyone but me. Don't worship carved idols. Don't worship anyone but me because I will even punish the children of a sinful father. Don't say my name with a bad meaning. Don't do anything but worship me on the seventh day of the week." And this from a dark cloud with lightning and the sound of trumpets.

This is, of course, precisely the debate going on in the Book of Job. God sits at a council of unnamed divine presences facing his adversary, Satan, who has scoured the earth. He challenges Satan with the faith of Job, who is but a pawn in this game. Why? If Job, even by

God's own admission at the beginning of the book, is the most faithful and righteous man on earth, then why test him? Why mess with what clearly works? The debate proceeds extremely logically. When Job has no children and no possessions, he says that he was "born naked and will return to nature naked" and thus he admits that his possessions and family are of less importance than his relationship with God. When he is attacked by disease and hunger, he responds only that if one is happy with the good that God brings, one needs also to be happy with the bad that God brings. He doesn't pause to think whether or not God *should*, in fact, be bringing anything bad. A series of speeches from Job's friends try to decipher his fate. The first wonders if it is possible that Job was too righteous, too faithful, so as even to challenge God, who, as we see from the first commandment, doesn't really like to be challenged. And, his friend adds, God is capable of everything and will sooner or later help him for having made him suffer — "Happy the man whom God rebukes!" is his message. Job responds that he has a good enough case for the court. This is a key mistake because he presumes to know that God's intention — to defeat Satan — is wrong. But Job only really wants to know what he has done wrong. Like an abused child, he cannot understand why he has been struck down without explanation.

Zophar, who is evidently quite wise, tells Job that it is impossible to know the will of God: If one could only be confident that God, if nobody else, knows what he is doing, then one will know that everything will be okay. Job again answers that he only wants to know what he has done wrong and that the relationship between the cause (his sins) and the effect (his misery) could be understood even by birds and cattle. Another speaker, Eliphaz, again accuses Job of trying to know the unknowable. Job cannot stand their speeches. He retorts that only God can be believed and that God can defend himself and his actions. His friends repeat their speeches to him, urging him not to complain too much. But Job continues, reminiscing about his days of prosperity. God's answer is almost as violent as Satan's attack on Job. He says absolutely nothing of his ability to be just or fair, only that he has created everything in all its complexity. Job's answer is one of resignation: "How can I argue with you? I'm of no consequence." God again speaks, boasting of his abilities. Job, who never denied it to begin with, says that he knows God is omnipotent and that he speaks of things he doesn't understand. He has so few words that we find ourselves rereading them several times, wondering why he has given up.

But the contradictions aren't over. God rewards Job for speaking well (he said almost nothing) and requires intercession on behalf of those who tried to speak on his behalf. If this is any indication of what is required of mortals, then everyone who has uttered the words "it was all God's plan" at the death of somebody's mother or father, is wrong. In fact, the story was taken throughout the Middle Ages by various people to mean that Job deserved the punishment, trial, and initiation he got. But, according to God himself, Job spoke and complained, "as [he] ought." The story is extremely disconcerting and confusing. The guiltlessness of Job is not brought into question in the end but rather are the complaints against God. God loses the lawsuit brought against him and pays back Job *double* what he took from him. Did the author of the Book of Job truly condone the idea of an imperfect God?

On the other hand, as Milton recognized in his epic poem *Paradise Lost*, the divine fight between Satan and God, like the various gods of *The Iliad*, have an effect on humans that cannot be clearly known to them. In the Psalms, which are probably of much older origin, we see poetry uncritical of God, displaying the world Job had taken from him, such as the words of Psalm 23, "Thou spreadest a table for me in the sight of my enemies; thou has richly bathed my head with oil, and my cup runs over." But these riches, the reader is meant to understand, are metaphorical. In Psalm 104, instead of God giving a list of his creative powers, the poet wonders at all the natural world in its beauty. Psalm 137 is not addressed to God (although he is clearly meant to be within earshot) but is a lament for the city of Jerusalem, destroyed by the Babylonians in 587 B.C.E. It ends alarmingly with the revengeful cry, "Happy is he who shall seize your children and dash them against the rock."

The sensual love poem of the Song of Songs, which is supposed to have been composed in the third or fourth century B.C.E., is a somewhat surprising discovery in a canon of literature where there are numerous occasions that men avoiding women or vice-versa is considered more than virtuous. It has usually been taken as a metaphor for the love of God, but the language is so explicit that it is hard to imagine that it doesn't at least derive from a tradition, as exists in many cultures, of wedding hymns, which are fairly detailed in their content (such as those of Sappho, p. 791). The encounter between Enkidu and the temple priestess is equally explicit in *The Epic of Gilgamesh* (p. 55). Early translations of the Song of Songs into Greek suggest that it was understood in a very literal sense as well as a theological one: The Greek translation makes no effort to hide the original sensuousness of the Hebrew — "Hurry like a young deer to the fragrant mountain."

TEXT & CONTEXT

The Hebrew Scriptures are a canon. That is to say, it is not a singular whole work conceived all at once but rather it has been assembled over a long history and contains certain chosen stories, and, with them, the implicit reality that other versions of those stories were rejected. This method has given us a fantastic overview of the subtle cultural and linguistic changes a society makes over time and how it perceives itself compared to those around it. The language of the Hebrew Scriptures is Hebrew, a Semitic language. There are few early written texts that can tell us when it was put together or by whom. It was most probably a process that lasted thousands of years. Besides subtle changes of style between different books, translations into other languages can help establish some of the history of this text. Around 285 B.C.E., during the reign of the Ptolemy Philadelphus, who was king of Egypt after Alexander the Great, the Hebrew Scriptures were translated into ancient Greek, a version known as the *Septuagint*. Nothing is known for sure of how this translation was performed, since it isn't even mentioned until the second century. Philo (p. 788), a Jew who lived among the Greeks, acknowledges the worthiness of this translation with quotation from it. However, ancient and modern scholars alike recognized that in some cases it was fundamentally different from the Hebrew version (sometimes called the Masoretic text, or MT), a text that was created *after* the *Septuagint*, between the first and tenth centuries C.E. However, the discovery of the Dead Sea Scrolls in 1947 (the earliest written version of the Bible, p. 242) has vindicated the *Septuagint* somewhat, which appears to accord frequently with passages in the Dead Sea Scrolls.

The *Septuagint* remained a popular translation of the Hebrew Scriptures and formed the basis of quotations from the Hebrew Scriptures in the Greek-language New Testament, which is the story of Christ, a Jew who taught philosophy in Roman times and who was put to death for his beliefs and teachings. Alongside the Hebrew version, it also became important in the Latin translation of the Bible, called the *Vulgate*, performed by Jerome in 382 C.E. The Latin text superseded the Greek and Hebrew ones in the West, but the *Septuagint* went on to have a life in Slavonic and Bulgarian translations of the same period. Growing discontent over the monopoly of the Latin version in the West drove John Wycliffe, an Oxford theologian, to translate the text into English in 1380, using the *Vulgate*. Erasmus, a polymath of the sixteenth century who had learned Greek from Byzantine teachers, started a flurry of interest in the Greek and Hebrew texts, and William Tyndale followed with an English translation from the Greek in 1525. Despite the church's attempt to confiscate and burn these

Bibles, they circulated widely. Finally, in 1611, a sanctioned English-language Bible combining both the Hebrew Scriptures and New Testament was published. This version, called the King James Version, has become the basis for almost every subsequent English translation and for the numerous allusions and quotations which abound in the history of English-language literature. The Bible remains the most translated work in history and is available in nearly every known language.

IN THE CLASSROOM

I. THE CULTURE REFLECTED BY THE HEBREW SCRIPTURES

The Hebrew Scriptures present a host of unanswerable questions that will spark a lot of debate in class. It is important to let the students voice their opinions but also to teach them to refer to the text at hand. These writings are about a specific culture at a specific point in time. It is true that they may well be about other things, but focusing on the meaning of the text for those who produced it will help bound the discussion somewhat and force the students to rely on reference to what they have read. It may be helpful to produce a small timeline of events covered by the Hebrew Scriptures as a handout for the students (or to have the students do a timeline exercise on the book companion Web site). From here we can begin to ask questions of characterization, plot, and setting. Students might try to approach the Hebrew Scriptures from a cultural critical point of view. One technical word they might find useful comes from a kind of German novel of the nineteenth century; it is called a *Bildungsroman*, which is a novel in which the hero is at odds with the society around him but learns to grow up. In the Hebrew Scriptures, it is the whole Jewish culture that is always afflicted by those around it and must learn to adapt and make the best of its situation.

The conclusion that the Hebrew Scriptures is a work exclusive to the Jews challenges its traditional universality. And yet, it will help if students can point out situations in which the work transparently regards itself as meant for the Hebrews. Students should try to identify scenes, such as the trial in Egypt, where Hebrews must find their identity and relationship to other tribes.

Discussion

1. How do the Hebrews see themselves in relation to their God? As a chosen people, how does this affect their narrative?

2. In what ways do the challenges the Hebrews face mirror the challenges that Job must face? Are the outcomes similar? Compare, for example, Psalm 137 (p. 207) with Job's complaint, or the scene of Moses in the wilderness with Job's miseries.

3. In what ways is Job portrayed like the early Israelite Patriarchs at the end of the Book of Job? Why is this effect chosen by the author? How does this validate the Book of Job?

4. Compare the Hebrew Scriptures to epics such as *The Epic of Gilgamesh* or *The Iliad* and *The Odyssey*. What makes the Hebrew Scriptures like an epic? How does it differ from these epics?

Connections

1. In what ways is the dialogue format of the Book of Job similar to the method of inquiry used by Socrates and Confucius? Do the Hebrew Scriptures also teach through questioning? What are the advantages of this method?

2. Compare the "Song of Songs" with other ancient love poetry such as the Egyptian love songs (p. 118), Sappho's love poetry (p. 791), Catullus's poetry (p. 1164), and the *Book*

of Songs (Shi jing) (p. 1573). What are the common features of these different works? What might be different or unique about the Song of Songs (p. 208)?

3. Compare Philo Judaeus's view of God in *On the Creation of the World* (p. 788) with that found in the Hebrew Scriptures. Is it possible to tell that his faith derives from the Hebrew Scriptures and that he shares his culture with the Hebrews, or does he seem more Hellenic (Greek) to you?

Groups

1. Break students up into small groups and have each group act out one section of the Hebrew Scriptures. For thousands of years, performance and oral reading of the Hebrew Scriptures was the main means of transmission. Does one's perception of a particular episode change when acting it out or watching it being acted out?

2. Have various groups prepare a presentation on a creation story from different cultures. Then, compare this story to the two creation stories offered in the Hebrew Scriptures. What features do these creation stories share in common? Why was it necessary to have two creation stories in the Book of Genesis?

Writing

Ask students to write a short paper in response to one or more of the following:

1. How might the Hebrew Scriptures be perceived as being universal instead of solely for the Hebrew people? Or is it not a universal work? What clues are there in the text that inform you of the identity of the work's audience?

2. A physical journey is often a metaphor for a spiritual journey. Some examples of this are represented in the movie *City Slickers* (1991) or in *The Epic of Gilgamesh*. In what way is the Book of Exodus a spiritual road trip, that is to say, what did the Hebrews learn in their flight from Egypt, and how did they change?

3. Compare the role of women in the Hebrew Scriptures (particularly in Genesis) with that in the Song of Songs. What, if anything, has changed?

4. Compare the different voices of the Psalms. In each Psalm, who is the singer? Is it a group or an individual? What are the circumstances of that individual?

II. HISTORY AND CANONICITY

The Chinese chose to write annalistic history. That is to say, at a given day of each season of each year, an appointed historian would preserve the important events of that year in writing. By the age of Sima Qian (145–90 B.C.E.), who is the Chinese "father of history," this method of fact keeping was remarkable, a singular event in the world. The Hebrews chose to compose their history much later and in a much different fashion. They chose various patriarchs and rulers as well as important figures to write about. In this way, they did not compose an entirely annalistic history (although the painstaking genealogies in the Bible show an attempt to show continuity). The history of the text of the Hebrew Scriptures shows many attempts to establish canonicity. They tried to make all the books in the Hebrew Scriptures consistent from an historical and theological point of view as well as to establish a cultural history through the selection of key texts from their oral and folk traditions.

Students should be introduced to the idea of a canon, and several examples should be listed: for example, the Daoist and Buddhist canons, the New Testament, or what is sometimes referred to as "The Canon," a collection of the most important works of Western literature. How useful are canons? Why and how do they change? It may help to discuss briefly the textual history of the Hebrew Scriptures as well as the New Testament (which suffers from similar problems of Apocryphal writings and variation among several accounts of one story). The relationship between canons and gender, canons and genre, and canons and political power are also very important. For example, how were the texts chosen for the anthology? What is the ideology which drives that choice?

Discussion

1. What are the key historical events the Hebrew Scriptures name, and how are they referred to?

2. Besides the extensive genealogies, what other attempts are made at establishing the authenticity of the text (e.g., its historicity)?

Connections

1. Read the excerpt from Apollodorus's *Bibliotheca* (p. 1129), which is a summary of certain myths about Heracles. What features of the Old Testament make it different from a retelling of myth? What attempts are made at establishing the authenticity of its account?

2. The *Shi jing* (p. 1573) and the Psalms (p. 204) are both collections of early poetry that have been made into a canon, the former by Confucius and Confucian scholars and the latter by Hebrew scholars. Describe some of the similarities and differences between these two collections. What may have driven the selection of pieces for the those works? How do they reveal the culture that produced them?

3. Compare Plato's *Republic*, the "Allegory of the Cave" (p. 1111), to the situation in the Book of Job (p. 169). Who in the cave most closely resembles Job? Who most closely resembles the wise men?

Groups

1. Using a map of the Mediterranean Sea and surrounding areas, chart the progress of the Hebrews. Relate each area to a specific spot in the text. How does the geographical certainty of the Hebrew Scriptures help its historicity? How does it differ in this respect from, say, *The Epic of Gilgamesh* or *The Odyssey*?

Writing

Ask students to write a short paper in response to one or more of the following:

1. It is often said that history repeats itself. In the Hebrew Scriptures, there are several patterns that recur many times (e.g., in the story of Cain and Abel and of Adam and Eve, there is some crime being hidden from God). What are these patterns? Describe events that seem to always recur.

2. One view of mythology, developed by Euhemerus (p. 783), is that myth is simply history distorted by time and primitive culture. Given the similarity between the earliest parts of the Hebrew Scriptures with mythology from nearby regions of the world (e.g., Noah's Ark ark and the Flood), is this a possible interpretation of the earlier books of the Hebrew Scriptures? Or, since the Hebrew Scriptures contains more than history, is the Euhemeristic point of view not applicable?

BEYOND THE CLASSROOM

RESEARCH & WRITING

1. The Hebrew Scriptures lend a code of ethics to their readers. What are these ethics, and how are they taught?

2. Read the selections from the New Testament in Book 2. How has the image of God changed in this work? In what ways is it influenced by the Hebrew Scriptures?

3. Read the selections from John Milton's *Paradise Lost* in Book 3. In what ways is this work influenced by the Hebrew Scriptures? What parts of the narrative are based on scenes from the Book of Job? What parts from the book of Genesis?

4. Read the selections from Goethe's *Faust* in Book 5. How has the image of God changed in this work? In what ways is it influenced by the Hebrew Scriptures?

Projects

1. Consider all the forms that God takes in this work, including in dreams and before his own people. Research the significance of these symbols and appearances and comment on the importance of these symbols in various cultures and how it helps to create a particular image of God.

2. Look at a movie or musical (such as Andrew Lloyd Weber's *Joseph and the Amazing Technicolor Dreamcoat*) based on a biblical theme. How does performance of a text affect your understanding of it?

FURTHER READING

Albright, W. F. *Yahweh and the Gods of Canaan.* 1968.

Barthes, R. Trans. Alfred Johnson. *Structural Analysis and Biblical Exegesis: Interpretational Essays.* 1974.

Davies, Philip. *Scribes and Schools: The Canonization of the Hebrew Scriptures.* 1998.

Freedman, David Noel, ed. *The Anchor Bible Dictionary.* 1992.

Friedman, R. E. *Who Wrote the Bible?* 1997.

Hackwell, W. J. *Signs, Letters, Words.* 1987.

Jaffee, Martin. *Early Judaism.* 1997.

Jellicoe, Sidney. *The Septuagint and Modern Study.* 1968.

Kraft, Robert A., and George W. E. Nickelsburg, eds. *Early Judaism and Its Modern Interpreters.* 1986.

Lance, H. D. *The Old Testament and the Archaeologist.* 1981.

Pritchard, J. B. *Atlas of the Bible.* 1987.

Sabo, Magne, ed. *Hebrew Bible/Old Testament: The History of Its Interpretation.* 1996.

Sandmel, Samuel. *Philo of Alexandria: An Introduction.* 1979.

Tov, Emanuel. *Textual Criticism of the Hebrew Bible.* 1992.

Watson, Wilfred G. E. *Classical Hebrew Poetry: A Guide to Its Techniques.* 1984.

MEDIA RESOURCES

VIDEO

Abraham
150 min., 1994 (Library Video Company)
Richard Harris and Barbara Hershey star in Turner Home Entertainment's production about the life of Abraham. The Old Testament story is depicted in which an ordinary shep-

herd is called on by God to show his abiding faith by leaving home and embarking on a dramatic odyssey through the desert to Canaan. Here, Abraham will become father of countless future generations.

Abraham: One Man, One God
50 min., 1999 (A&E Video)
The story of Abraham's unwavering faith has made him one of the holiest men in Judaism, Islam, and Christianity. His covenant with God led to the birth of Israel, and in the ultimate test of devotion, he was asked to sacrifice his son at the fabled Dome of the Rock.

Abraham: The First Hebrew
21 min., 1993 (Insight Media)
Presenting him as an introspective man of profound religious convictions, this program traces the course of Abraham's life and explores the roots of his monotheism. It also examines the history and legends of how he brought the idea of monotheism to a people and became the first patriarch of Israel.

The Bible: A Literary Heritage
27 min., 1970 (Zenger Media)
"All is vanity and a striving after wind." From Ecclesiastes to the Sermon on the Mount, Donald Pleasance and a professional cast recreate scenes from the Bible, showing this one book to be many books — history, short stories, poetry, songs, drama, social criticism, prophecy. Filmed on location in Israel, Pleasance and his actors illustrate the Bible's evolution from tribal origins to the ethical teachings of Jesus and relate its words to modern life. Scenes include Abraham and Isaac, Job's suffering, lovers in the Song of Solomon, vignettes from Psalms, and Jesus teaching to the multitudes.

The Bible as Literature: Part 1 — Saga and Story in the Old Testament
27 min., 1974 (Insight Media)
This program discusses the influence of the King James version of the Bible on literature, and reads through portions of the Old Testament from both a literary and an historical standpoint.

The Bible as Literature: Part 2 — History, Poetry and Drama in the Old Testament
24 min., 1974 (Insight Media)
This program examines Joshua, Samuel, and Kings as historical documents, the Book of Proverbs as lyric poetry, and the prophetical books as protest literature.

Christianity: The First Thousand Years
200 min., 1998 (Insight Media)
This video draws on ancient text and Scripture as it reviews the history of Christianity from the Crucifixion to the Crusades. It includes the commentary of historical scholars and theologians on the shaping of the New Testament. It also examines how pagan festivals were transformed into Christian holidays.

Dead Sea Scrolls, Early Christianity, and Judaism
4 tapes, 60 min. each, 2000 (Insight Media)
One of the most important Dead Sea Scrolls ever found, MMT spells out differences between the scrolls sect and mainstream Judaism in ancient times. This set discusses what current scroll research reveals about early Judaism, visits the caves of Qumran, and speculates on the nature and religious activities of the community at Qumran.

Great Figures of the Bible Collection
360 min., 2000 (Library Video Company)
Nobel Peace Prize winner Elie Wiesel looks at the moral and ethical dilemmas found in stories of legendary biblical heroes. Filmed on location in the Holy Land, the programs fea-

ture dramatic re-enactments of biblical stories. Episodes include Adam and Eve and After: The Story of Temptation; The Story of Cain and Abel: The First Murder; Abraham and the Binding of Isaac: About Fathers and Sons; The Story of Job: Suffering and Sacrifice; The Story of Moses: The Agony of Power; and The Story of David: Greatness and Passion.

Joseph
185 min., 1995 (Library Video Company)
Paul Mercurio, Ben Kingsley, Martin Landau, and Leslie Ann Warren star in Turner Home Entertainment's production about the life of Joseph, the favorite son of Jacob. Watch as he falls victim to the jealousy of his brothers and is sold to a powerful Egyptian landowner, only to face unbearable tests of cruelty and pain. Through his own cunning, Joseph eventually makes a place for himself in the land of Egypt.

Joseph: Master of Dreams
50 min., 1999 (A&E Video)
The story of Joseph is one of the Bible's most celebrated epics. Sold into slavery by his brothers because of his gift of prophecy, Joseph is finally rewarded with great political power when he uses his divine gift to help the pharaoh save Egypt from famine.

Moses
100 min., 1996 (A&E Video)
Moses was a complex man and a reluctant prophet. But when called on to save his people, he overcame his doubts and fears and defeated the most powerful empire on earth.

Moses
184 min., 1996 (Library Video Company)
Ben Kingsley, Frank Langella, and Christopher Lee star in Turner Home Entertainment's production about the amazing life of Moses. See how he was raised by the pharaoh's daughter and later followed God's command to lead the Israelites out of Egypt.

Moses, the Leader
24 min., 1995 (Insight Media)
This docudrama tells the story of Moses, the exodus from Egypt, and the revelation on Mt. Sinai.

The Old Testament
28 min., 1993 (Insight Media)
This program discusses the origins of the Bible, examining its authors, the structure of the Old Testament, and the importance of the Book of Genesis. Comparing the God depicted by the Old Testament with that of the New Testament, it also considers the role of the Ten Commandments in today's church and society.

Three Pillars: Confucius, Jesus, and Mohammed
53 min., 1998 (Insight Media)
This video studies the identities of the founders of three major religions — Confucianism, Christianity, and Islam. It looks at how Confucianism blended into the Chinese social and political structure; the significance of Jesus as a prophet for Muslims and as God incarnate for Christians; and the teachings of Mohammed and the Koran.

Voyage Through the Bible (2 CD-ROMs)
1996 (Insight Media)
These CD-ROMs explore the text and context of the Bible. The Old Testament features creation stories and the full text of the Books of Moses. It takes users on tours of ancient Egypt, Mesopotamia, and the Fertile Crescent. The New Testament travels to ancient Jerusalem and the Sea of Galilee, and includes modern footage of Israel and Egypt.

Who Wrote the Bible?
150 min., 1995 (A&E Video)
Part of an A&E network investigation into real-life mysteries. The Bible is the world's most widely read and revered book. It is regarded as the word of God by the faithful. Examine the facts behind the creation of this immortal text. Scientific research and theological insight combine to probe its most profound mysteries. Explore when, where, and by whom its books were written.

WEB SITES

The Ancient Hebrews
www.wsu.edu:8080/~dee/HEBREWS/HEBREWS.HTM
Richard Hooker's page (of Washington State University) provides an excellent overview of the ancient Hebrews, including information on its history, culture, and religion.

The Hebrew Scriptures
www.religioustolerance.org/chr_jf.htm
This is a very good site for an overview of information about the Old Testament.

Hebrew Scriptures
religion.rutgers.edu/vri/tanakh.html
This is an index site with wonderful links to all types of topics created by the religion department of Rutgers University.

Internet Ancient History Sourcebook — Israel
www.fordham.edu/halsall/ancient/asbook06.html
The goal of the Ancient History Sourcebook is to provide and organize texts for use in classroom situations. Links to the larger online collections are provided for those who want to explore further. It also includes links to visual and aural material, since art and archeology are far more important for the periods in question than for later history. The emphasis remains on access to primary source texts for educational purposes.

AUDIO

Abraham
(MyAudioBooks.com)
At a moment when the world is asking "Can the religions get along?," one man stands out as the shared ancestor of Jews, Christians, and Muslims. One man holds the key to our deepest fears — and our possible reconciliation. This man is Abraham. Bruce Feiler set out on a personal quest to better understand our common patriarch. Feiler uncovers fascinating, little-known details of the man who defines faith for half the world. Both immediate and timeless, Abraham is a powerful, universal story, the first-ever interfaith portrait of the man God chose to be his partner. Thoughtful and inspiring, it offers a rare vision of hope that will redefine what we think about our neighbors, our future, and ourselves.

The Book of Psalms
6:18 hrs. (Audio Literature)
The Psalms express the heart and essence of humanity, covering a wide range of emotions, and the lessons derived from them have had a far-reaching effect through the ages. They are a unique portion of the Old Testament — 150 songs and poems that include hymns of praise, thanksgiving, lament, wisdom, and liturgy. Written over a long period of time by multiple authors, the Psalms illustrate the theology and worship of the Israelites over the

centuries. This reading of Psalms uses the King James version of the Bible, a translation whose language is praised as some of the greatest poetry ever written. Michael York brings out the eloquence of this language in his beautiful narration.

The Essential King James Bible
4 tapes, 6 hrs. (AudioBooksToday.com)
Beginning with the story of creation, and culminating with an excerpt from Revelation, this anthology is a beautifully narrated treasure. Half of the stories are from the Old Testament, half from the New. The brilliant, sensitive readings are accessible to listeners of all ages. Each performer reads individual stories in their entirety.

Living Biographies of Religious Leaders
8 tapes, 11:25 hrs. (Blackstone Audiobooks)
This program presents the lives of twenty great founders and leading advocates of the world's foremost religions. Here are the historical facts and legends associated with these forceful personalities who have inspired and influenced humankind through the centuries. Presented are Jesus Christ, Moses, Isaiah, Zoroaster, Buddha, Confucius, John the Baptist, Paul, Muhammad, Francis of Assisi, John Huss, Luther, Loyola, Calvin, George Fox, Swedenborg, Wesley, Brigham Young, Mary Baker Eddy, and Gandhi.

The Old Testament
6 tapes or 6 CDs, 7:45 hrs. (Naxos Audio)
Here are the greatest and best-loved stories from the Old Testament, stories that can be read as much for their human, literary, and historical appeal as for their religious meaning. The selection ranges from childhood favorites like David and Goliath, to key moments in Jewish history (such as the Exodus) and also includes some of the finest poetry in the Old Testament (the Song of Solomon, for example).

A Poet's Bible
3 hrs. (Audio Literature)
Rediscover the voices of the original text of the Bible in this fresh retelling of its most powerful stories. The author introduces the listener to many new authors, reveals the imaginative power of the original verse, and heralds a new era in biblical scholarship. With vivid, accessible language and playful metaphor, A Poet's Bible revitalizes the living poetry at the core of biblical verse and allows the secular listener to grasp this great classic in modern terms.

In the World: **Creating Cosmogony** (p. 221)

When a society decides to establish civic order, it has some necessary choices to make. Any kind of order presumes that there is some system in place to ensure that the order is followed. It is not complicated to state a rule, but it is very difficult to enforce it. Because of this, the history of law is a fascinating subject. Many legal systems in the world and throughout history rely on a religious force to help enforce and give authenticity to laws and regulations. For example, a person in a court will be asked to swear an oath that the truth is being told while giving testimony. The right hand is raised or placed over a Bible while saying the words "so help me God." In some countries, a code of law called "Sharia" is followed, which is a form of law established by the Islamic faith based on principles derived from their religion. In the eighteen century, rulers espoused the idea of "Absolutism," which meant that their ability to rule was ordained by God. In *The Iliad* and *The Odyssey*, kings are given a scepter by Zeus, which marks their legitimacy to rule.

The relationship between an ordered heaven and an ordered earth was not difficult for our ancestors to admit. Watching the stars and planets in skies uncluttered with skyscrapers and mosquito traps, they could watch the regularity with which the moving bodies of light passed through various points. By day, they could see the cyclical nature of the passing of the seasons; the rise and the fall of rivers; the birth, death, and rebirth of vegetation; the migration of birds; and the ordered conduct by which lions chose their mates. A concerted effort was made by many ancient rulers, philosophers, and religious leaders to imitate the perfect patterns of nature among the more varied circumstance of men. We can see this from the Greek word for the universe, *cosmos*, which comes from the Greek verb *cosmeo*, "to put into order" and "to embellish or decorate." A girl who wore beautiful dresses was said to be in "good order," according the Greeks, as was a government that was well run. But the ideal of "good order," as the form of the word gives away, was Mother Nature herself. In this kind of society, the only valid legal code can be one sanctioned by the divine order, which ordains rulers among men. Thus it is Agamemnon in Homer's *The Iliad* who wields the most weight, even if he is not the mightiest, and it is Moses who comes down off the mountain holding the tablets.

So the modern notion of separation of Church and State is quite contrary to the ancient way of doing things. Even in democratic Athens, priests, priestesses, and seers were present at important ceremonies of state. In most countries of the world, a judge wears a special robe resembling the outfits of medieval religious clerics. While world leaders, even kings and queens, have no need to wear special uniforms, law enforcement and military personnel and judges and priests still wear robes as a mark of the office. We are not too far from the world in which the ancients lived; law must command an almost religious respect.

In the Pyramid Texts, we read of the sun-god, Re-Atum, choosing princes of heaven and the powers of the kings on earth. In a cyclical pattern, the dying king becomes the immortal Osiris, and the new king becomes Horus. Since Horus is born of Isis, a goddess, all Egyptian kings are divine, and his rules are an extension of the divine natural order. When Hammurabi lays down his Code, he mentions in his preface that Anu, the highest god, ordered Marduk to work out human law. Since Hammurabi is a human descendent of Marduk, his legal code has the stamp of approval of Anu and Anunnaki, the highest gods.

Other systems incorporate the whole of human society within the sphere of divine order. Humans are subject to simple laws that govern all of nature. For example, the "Golden Rule," which states that one should only do good if one expects to receive good and bad if one expects to receive bad. The Upanishads describe just such a system of cause and effect. Instead of saying that a ruler or judge is ordained by a god, social laws are made to seem more like physical laws. Karma describes not only an individual's actions in the world but also those actions he deserves against him. If he makes good karma then good karma will return to him just as lead will yield lead and gold will yield gold.

The Hebrew Scriptures employ a kind of combination of natural and divinely sanctioned law, in the form of the Ten Commandments, which derive from God through Moses — whom God appointed to be leader of the Hebrew race. However, the laws are there as part of a social contract. In return for following his Commandments, God will save his chosen race. So strongly did the descendents of these people believe that this set of laws were to be followed in return for divine protection, that the author of Deuteronomy — the fifth book of the Hebrew Scriptures — restated the passage from Exodus so that it would be again part of the legal code of his people. The Dead Sea Scrolls, produced by a similar culture in a later period, show influences of this contractual theory, whereby people must follow a divine rule in order to obtain benefit. In the selection of the Dead Sea Scrolls provided to the students, a prophecy assures adherents of a certain divinely ordained military policy that they will be victorious over all the rival tribes.

The Chinese philosopher Mengzi (Latinized to Mencius) also felt that natural order among men mirrored that in heaven: "[He] who fully understands man's true nature . . . understands Heaven." To be human, according to Mencius, is to be humane. The word for man, *ren* (sometimes spelled *jen* but pronounced *rhen*), sounds just like the word for humane, *ren.* Justice, or *yi* (pronounced *ee*), is the employment and expression of men. Mencius is somewhat unique in this respect because he holds the ruler responsible for being just at the penalty of being overthrown (whereas Confucius did not condone revolting against an unjust ruler). This innate humanity (*ren*) in human beings, expressed by justice (*yi*), was a mirror of the established order of heaven, *tian* (sometimes spelled *t'ien,* prononced *tyan*). Plato, the student of the great Greek philosopher Socrates, also believed that divine order applied not only to the heavens but also to the innate properties of man. He believed the soul was immortal and good from birth. While trapped in the prison of the body, it loses its purity, sullied by the mortality of the body with all its appetite and desires. Like Mencius, he believed that the process of study called *philosophia,* or "love of knowledge," would help the soul to retain its former purity and aid it in regaining the memory of all the knowledge it lost in transitioning from heaven, where the soul is born, to the body.

TEXT & CONTEXT

The Pyramid Texts are so named because they are inscribed on the stones of the interior of pyramids at modern-day Saqqara in Egypt. While not as big as the famous Great Pyramids at Giza, these smaller pyramids are so vast that it is easy to fill them with volumes of writing. The Pyramid from which this selection was taken is dedicated to Unas, the last king of the Fifth Dynasty. Just as the texts describe the order of heaven played out on earth, the ceiling of the rooms in which these texts were found is decorated with stars. Most of the texts dictate what food and drink offerings are to be given to the dead, including bread and beer, the staples of the Egyptian diet. Although the texts were discovered in the nineteenth century, they were translated into English by Samuel Mercer in 1952. In the year 2000, a new set of texts were discovered.

The text of The Code of Hammurabi is in Akkadian, a Semitic language distantly related to modern Arabic. It possesses many similarities with the code of law present in the Hebrew Scriptures and the culture of Mesopotamia. Although Hammurabi was the king of Babylon, the text does not come from Babylon. Later Persian conquerers were so impressed that they took this monument with them, and it was discovered in Iran in 1902; it is now housed in the Louvre in Paris. In total, there are 282 codes on everything from the price of rice to the punishment for murder.

The Upanishads, which literally mean "sitting down near," were written between the eighth and fourth centuries B.C.E. They begin with a discussion on creation and the inquisitive nature of man and proceed to explain certain doctrines meant to be taught and expounded by a spiritual teacher. As part of a larger group of religious texts, the Vedas, they form a more practice-oriented part of religious study.

Deuteronomy is the fifth book of the *Pentateuch,* or the first five books of the Hebrew Scriptures. It gets its name from the Greek words *deuteros,* "second," and *nomos,* "law" or "custom." This book was probably written in the mid seventh century and incorporated into the cannon of the Hebrew Scriptures soon thereafter. Its author is attempting to restore faith through the laws established under the patriarch Moses. It explains and interprets the concept of a contract between God and his people. By beginning with the assertion that Deuteronomy is a transcript of Moses' own speech, it gives legitimacy to its writings.

Plato was the student of the great Greek philosopher Socrates, who didn't write anything. The form of Plato's writings usually is the dialogue, in which Socrates debates with his students about the true nature of things using what is now called the "Socratic method," that is, asking questions about things in order to lead the students gradually to the true answers. Socrates did not believe that the democratic system established at Athens was good for the city, and he often argued for a panel of experts to rule the city instead. His study was largely devoted to understanding the relationship between the human soul and the world around it. Because of his beliefs and the challenges that he posed to certain officials, he was tried and put to death by an Athenian jury in 399 B.C.E. The *Timaeus* is a dialogue known for being one of the few documents that describes the lost city of Atlantis, a pre-Greek city in the Atlantic Ocean, which has been the obsession of many explorers ever since.

Mencius (Mengzi) lived in the Warring States Period in China. During this period, states fought with one another as well as suffered from civil strife. Meanwhile, China was buffeted by attacks from the Xiong-nu tribes to the northwest (believed to be the ancestors of the Huns) and other non-Chinese tribes on their borders. Ironically, during this time, a great deal of philosophy flourished, much of it political philosophy. Although there are no historical records about the life of Mencius, it is commonly believed that he was raised by his mother, who is revered in China as the model of motherhood.

The Dead Sea Scrolls were written by the Hebrew sect known as the Essenes, at Qumran, between the fourth and first centuries B.C.E. They are written in Hebrew, Aramaic (a local language), and Greek on sheep's skin and papyrus, stored in earthenware jars in a cave. They were not discovered until shepherds came across them in Palestine in 1947. Public interest was aroused by these controversial texts by an article published in the *New Yorker* in the same year. The countless fragmentary texts are housed in Jerusalem and at the Oriental Institute at the University of Chicago. Because of the division of Palestine in 1947 into Palestine and the state of Israel, and because of competing groups of scholars and states trying to gain access to the scrolls, scandal began to emerge out of efforts to translate and interpret the texts. Some scholars alleged that the texts might contain content that would discredit the Christian church. Until 1991, only a very few scholars had access to the complete set of texts, preserved by a set of photographs guarded by the Israeli government.

IN THE CLASSROOM

I. SCROLLS, TABLETS, AND CODES

Students need to know that many of the texts they are reading in this section are documents that were important at the time they were written. They do not always take on a literary form but are often very direct. And yet, while all the texts are quite didactic, they are also quite different in form, and they employ different strategies. It will be useful for students to try and analyze for what kind of audience these texts were written, what special value they held, and why they take on the form that they do. Some texts will be legal codes, others a guidebook for living, some interpretive works, and others more philosophical and theoretical.

Discussion

1. Of what does each text consist? Is it a list of things or more like a general theory? Describe the differences in strategy.

2. How would each text be stored? Imagine you are in an ancient city. Where would you have to go to consult this text? Would you even be allowed to see it? What difference does that make in the overall impression of authority and authenticity it gives?

3. How do texts that are not legal works, such as the selection of Mencius, give authority to their words? Since it does not receive divine sanction, nor is it part of the law of the land, what influence do these texts have?

4. Consider the effect of writing. In these examples, unlike epic or other forms of oral literature, they are all written texts. How does writing lend authenticity and make something appear authoritative? What is special about writing and the way in which writing developed? Consider also which texts may have had a more casual printing and which were specially cared for. Also consider whether the text was part of a canon or not. What effect would that have?

Groups

1. Divide students up into small groups. Have them practice reading the texts aloud to one another. Which texts lend themselves naturally to sounding legalistic, and which texts sound more philosophical? What words or kind of words or grammatical patterns persuade you of this?

2. Have each group of students give a ten-minute presentation on the archeological background of each text. What is the provenance (physical origin) of each text, what form did it take, how was it kept and preserved, and in what condition and circumstances was it found?

Writing

Ask students to write a short paper in response to one or more of the following:

1. Divine figures often operate through a human figure. Describe the different ways in which gods and goddesses use mortals to achieve their ends and what effect this has on the listener of the story.

2. Plato begins the *Timaeus* with an account of Solon, an Athenian sage, traveling to Egypt, where he found out about ancient society and ancient knowledge from a priest. How might this beginning affect the interpretation of the passage you read?

3. What is the difference between a code for living and a legal code? Which texts are more of a guide for living, and which seem to you like a standard set of laws? What features of the text inform you of this?

II. CONNECTIONS

Laws can also be an expression of a culture's values. Even subtle differences between countries play themselves out quite differently in legal terms. Whereas most people would agree that Canadians and Americans appear at least superficially similar, their laws are quite different. Marriages between people of the same gender are permitted in Canada but not in most of the United States, and immigration laws differ between the two countries even though they share a relatively open border. Some of this has to do with history and experience, but a lot has to do with the values of a particular society. The texts in our selection are similar to literature in exactly this way: They are products of complex civilizations and examples of the height of those civilizations.

Discussion

1. Some of these writings derive from a larger group of literature. What is it about these excerpts that make them belong to a legalistic genre? Is there anything else we have read that might also belong to this genre?

2. What are some of the differences between Unas Pyramid Text 217 and the description of Gilgamesh's (p. 55) divine origins and refusal of Ishtar (p. 74)?

3. How does the relationship between God and Moses in Deuteronomy differ from the relationship in Exodus between God and Moses or God and Abraham in Genesis?

4. How does what Plato says in the *Timaeus* accord with his vision of the soul in *The Republic* (p. 1111)?

Groups

1. Have each group of students pick one major work of literature (or, especially in the case of Egypt, a film) that has something to do with the culture that produced the texts they have read, and show how these ideals are incorporated in that work.

Writing

Ask students to write a short paper in response to one or more of the following:

1. How does history play a role in the presentation of these texts? Do they take historical events into account, or does history make the documents seem less "timeless"?

2. Compare Mencius (p. 239) with Confucius (p. 1591). How is the form of their writing the same? What about the content? Does it change? What genre would you say they shared?

3. Compare and contrast the form of the prophecy given in the selection from the Dead Sea Scrolls with the prophecies given in *The Epic of Gilgamesh* (p. 55) or the prophecies give to Aeneas in the underworld (p. 1240).

BEYOND THE CLASSROOM

RESEARCH & WRITING

1. What is the significance in the names the sons of *light* and sons of *dark*? What other kinds of imagery is used by the excerpts to denote polar opposites and different classes of people?

2. In many of the selections, there is reference made to birth and rebirth: For example, the soul enters a body that will define it, or a goddess becomes pregnant with a body she will define. Discuss the significance of all of these references.

3. One of the strong aspects in some of the texts we have read, such as Deuteronomy, the Dead Sea Scrolls, and The Code of Hammurabi is the notion of revenge. How might revenge be considered an extension of the way of nature?

Projects

1. Research the historical or personal conditions under which these documents were created. How has that influenced their production and preservation?

2. Many legal scholars point to The Code of Hammurabi as being the first legal system in the world. Read a set of modern codes (most city, state, provincial, and federal governments now put these online). What are the differences between The Code of Hammurabi and these modern codes in terms of breadth and the inclusion of fines and punishments?

FURTHER READING

Allen, James P. *Religion and Philosophy in Ancient Egypt.* 1989.

Allen, Thomas George. *Occurrences of Pyramid Texts, with Cross Indexes of These and Other Egyptian Mortuary Texts.* 1950.

Brisson, Luc. *Inventing the Universe: Plato's* Timaeus, *the Big Bang, and the Problem of Scientific Knowledge.* 1995.

Campbell, Jonathan G. *Deciphering the Dead Sea Scrolls.* 2002.

Chan, Alan Kam-leung. *Mencius: Contexts and Interpretations.* 2002.

Davies, Philip R. *The Complete World of the Dead Sea Scrolls.* 2002.

Faulkner, R. O. *The Ancient Egyptian Pyramid Texts.* 1969.

Gerbrandt, Gerald Eddie. *Kingship According to the Deuteronomistic History.* 1986.

Gotshalk, Richard. *The Beginnings of Philosophy in India.* 1998.

Johns, C. H. W. *Babylonian and Assyrian Laws, Contracts and Letters.* 1904.

Kupperman, Joel. *Classic Asian Philosophy: A Guide to the Essential Texts.* 2001.

McDonald, Lee Martin. *The Canon Debate.* 2002.

Noth, Martin. *The Deuteronomistic History.* 1981.

Pritchard, J. B., ed. *Ancient Near Eastern Texts Relating to the Old Testament.* 1969.

Radau, H. *Early Babylonian History.* 1900.

Sharples, R. W. *Ancient Approaches to Plato's* Timaeus. 2000.

GENERAL MEDIA RESOURCES

WEB SITES

The Catholic Encyclopedia
www.newadvent.org/cathen/
This online encyclopedia is a useful resource for biographical and historical information; it has the added benefit of embedded hotlinks as gateways to further information.

The Dead Sea Scrolls
www.abc.net.au/religion/features/scrolls/default.htm
With five engaging illustrated lectures by Jehon Grist, this online course provides background on key persons involved in the controversy surrounding the scrolls, the debate over the character of the settlement at Qumran, and excellent introductions to major scrolls including the Temple Scroll, Copper Scroll, War Rule, Community Rule, Damascus Covenant, Torah Precepts, and Messiah Apocalypse.

The Pyramid Text
www.touregypt.net/featurestories/pyramidtext.htm
This site gives an authoritative background on the Pyramid Texts accompanied by illustrations; the narrative also contains hotlinks that provide additional information.

Sacred Pyramid Texts
www.civilization.ca/civil/egypt/egcw03e.html
A brief background of the Pyramid Texts that contains important hotlinks, particularly to the complete text of the Book of the Dead.

Sacred Texts
www.sacred-texts.com/index.htm
This wonderful site provides complete versions of sacred texts from around the world. Under the Near East is found The Code of Hammurabi; under Confucianism, the works of Mencius; under Egypt, the Book of the Dead; and the Upanishads is found under Sacred Texts of the East.

Scrolls from the Dead Sea
www.loc.gov/exhibits/scrolls/toc.html
From the Library of Congress, this well-done site provides an introduction to the scrolls along with a well-narrated exhibit of scroll artifacts.

West Semitic Research Project: Dead Sea Scrolls
www.usc.edu/dept/LAS/wsrp/educational_site/dead_sea_scrolls/
Created at the University of Southern California, the site contains many low resolution images posted with commentary for educators; includes the discovery site, messianic testimonia, Rule of the Messianic Congregation, and the Copper Scroll.

GREECE:
THE GOLDEN AGE OF
LITERATURE AND PHILOSOPHY

HESIOD, from *Theogony* and *Work and Days* (p. 259)

WWW   For a quiz on *Work and Days*, see *World Literature Online*
       at bedfordstmartins.com/worldlit.

Most Greeks believed that the history of their literature was founded by two people: Hesiod and Homer. While Hesiod may seem obscure to the modern reader, he was usually mentioned right alongside Homer by Greek writers. This means that while many of the texts attributed to Hesiod survive, Homer was just too tough an act to follow; thus Hesiod did not have an afterlife in the form of countless literary allusions in Romantic and Contemporary literature. Recent scholarship (at least scholarship of the past two hundred years or so) has moved away from considering Homer to be an actual poet who produced complete works toward the concept of an oral tradition of literature (like the tradition that produced the earlier books of the Bible) codified at some point in time. Even to the Greeks, Homer was an abstract figure, and experts in his poetry who sang the uncodified episodes of his epics were called "Homeridae," or "Sons of Homer." Hesiod, on the other hand, speaks rather directly about himself in the poem, leaving behind not only personal details but a certain kind of person. Sometime in the eighth century B.C.E., Theogony and *Works and Days* were produced following the conventions of the oral school. Even though Hesiod claims authorship of the poems, their similarity to the oral style of Homer tell us the issue is probably more complex. Nevertheless, out of convenience, we refer to Homer as the author of *The Iliad* and *The Odyssey*, and Hesiod as the author of Theogony and *Works and Days*.

Theogony is a kind of creation story and an amalgam of many early Greek myths. *Theos* means "god," and *gonos* is a word for "offspring." Theogony, then, was originally meant to account for the genealogy of the Greek pantheon. It will help students tremendously to draw diagrams of the essential gods of the pantheon as they read different pieces of Greek literature. Not only does it help students to learn and remember the names, but it will give them insight on one of the fundamental characteristics of Greek myths: Whatever happens to one set of divinities is *bound* to happen to the next one. Gaia (Earth) and Ouranos (Heaven) gave birth to many children, among whom is Kronos (Time), who cuts the penis off of his father and thus dethrones him. Kronos and Rhea make children whom Kronos swallows (out of fear that he too will be dethroned). One of the children is Zeus, who escapes being swallowed, since Rhea gives Kronos a large stone wrapped in baby's clothes instead (nobody knows if Kronos asked Rhea why they had a boulder for a baby). Kronos gets sick, throws up the children, and Zeus, who was not swallowed, takes the opportunity to free all the gods and thus dethrones Kronos. Now Prometheus, Zeus's uncle, tried to trick Zeus by hiding meat from him, instead wrapping up huge ox bones in fat and giving the impression he was giving a lot of meat to Zeus. Zeus, however, knows what's going on and simply keeps his anger to himself. This reaches a crisis when Prometheus then steals fire away from Zeus inside of a fennel stalk. Prometheus gives the fire to humans (who evidently procreate without the need for women). Zeus enacts his revenge by making the perfect woman. At this point, we get to see what a horrible misogynist either Zeus, Hesiod, or both, were. After the woman is made, Hesiod basically says "can't live with 'em; can't live without 'em." If a man doesn't marry a

64

woman, he will be lonely in old age. If the man does marry her, she will go shopping every day until he is bankrupt. Thus Zeus ends the cycle of overthrowing gods by creating the ultimate weapon. These patterns of violence will reappear as the students read Greek tragedy and even as they learn the complicated background of the Trojan War while reading Homer.

The stories, being genealogies and essentially about creation, also describe some early perception about the origins of Greek thought. In the fight between Kronos and Ouronos, Kronos dethrones Ouronos by cutting off his father's penis. If students are familiar with Freud's Oedipus complex (in which the young boy envies his father's relationship with his mother) as well as the Greek story of Oedipus (who kills his father and marries his mother), they will immediately see a pattern. The blood falls to earth and becomes the divine embodiment of revenge (the Furies), which seems appropriate since it is revenge for Ouranos's treatment of Gaia that drives Kronos to emasculate him. The penis falls into the ocean (the seat of the unconscious, perhaps?), where it is surrounded by white foam that grows into Aphrodite (whose name derives from *aphros*, the Greek word for "foam"), the goddess of love. The connection between the penis, the dreamy sea water, and Aphrodite is a telling statement of Greek thoughts on love and desire (although it is hard to say what it is really meant by it all). The stories are highly symbolic and require a lot of decoding.

Students can try to identify what the various gods and pieces of the puzzle stand for and then reconstruct what was meant. Theogony is Archaic Greece's answer to Aristotle's *Physics* or the modern science textbook. It attempts to explain a lot of natural phenomena and their origins through complex stories of interactions between gods. One thing that is curious about the *Theogony* is that, unlike its sister work, *Works and Days*, it does not concern itself with ethics. Takeovers of heaven are invariably hostile, and even Zeus's rule seems harsh and undemocratic. The world that Hesiod tries to create is a barren, Cenozoic landscape of rough-hewn rocks, stormy seas, and skies full of fire and brimstone. It is the true archetype of the creation myth.

Both *Theogony* and *Works and Days* belong to an ancient genre that we call "wisdom literature." Other examples of such literature are the Indic Upanishads (p. 1346). These combine religious/mythic stories with explanations of physical and social phenomena as well as ethics in the form of a didactic poem meant to address a variety of audiences (usually a ruling class). *Works and Days* is ostensibly addressed to Perses, Hesiod's lazy, no-good brother. The poet tells us that when it came time to divide their father's inheritance, Perses ran off with most of it by bribing the officials who were dividing the property. Apparently, Perses squandered the money because he was now begging on Hesiod's doorstep. Hesiod thus completed this guide for him (some aspects of this story seem similar to the parable of the prodigal son in the New Testament). Hesiod's poem, however, also addresses the kings, whom he considers it his duty to advise (and their duty, he says, to listen).

Most of *Works and Days* is an agricultural how-to book. From this point of view, it is a fantastic source of knowledge on how Greeks farmed, but it also includes a great deal of information that is less historically useful, like the advice he gives "never urinate facing the sun," and "don't defecate in the drinking water." Other pieces of advice are moral snippets common to this brand of literature, "Love who loves you, meet who meets you; give to the giver, but don't give to the one who doesn't give. To give is good, to grab is not. The grabber's gift is death." *Works and Days* also includes an almanac with helpful advice on when to plant grain and slyly coded warnings about personal conduct. Although the landscape of *Works and Days* is not as desolate and harsh as that in *Theogony*, the language and syntax of *Works and Days* is frank and scatological. It is a very human, but also somewhat embittered, look at society. Sometimes, its honesty is as brutal as the violence of *Theogony*.

The first excerpt included from *Works and Days* is an interesting retelling of the story of Prometheus and Pandora also told in *Theogony*. This time it is told more from the human perspective. The second excerpt is about the ages of man, which is a further attempt to show how humans must work for their bread. The story will later become a political trope during the Roman Empire: Each time a new great emperor was about to be enthroned, they thought it to be the dawn of the golden age, when (and there are long Roman poems about it) milk and honey run out of the ground, and the grape vines turn into wine without any work. According to Hesiod, people lived long lives in leisure, but because of the jealousy or anger of gods, they are "hidden in the ground," a euphemism for death. Each generation lives in an inferior manner for fewer years until the fifth age — that of iron — in which Hesiod lives. He has nothing good to say about the Iron Age, and his criticisms doubtlessly stem from his personal experience. In another sense, though, that personal experience forms the foundation of these two great works of literature. Some have viewed them as rant spoken in meter (perhaps even a very early predecessor to urban hip-hop?). It has always been the artist's province to complain about the social and environmental condition of his time as being uniquely bad, and Hesiod was no different in this respect.

TEXT & CONTEXT

The story of an ancient text is a precarious one. It is handed down first by word of mouth from one person to another, sometimes for generations. After many versions are written down, they are compared, edited, and sometimes thrown away. Even if a canonical form is chosen, it will be copied thousands and thousands of times, each time introducing new errors into the manuscript as well as corrupting and confusing the text, prompting scholars to do further compilations, comparisons, and editing. If a text survived to the invention of the printing press in the fifteenth century, its chances of survival were greatly increased. Even then, though, texts might fight a losing battle for longevity, since few people read the ancient language and, of those that were read, only a few may have been found to be of contemporary interest. Some authors, however, have always sparked interest.

Because anthologists of the Byzantine era were interested in making things uniform, they most commonly made copies of just two of Hesiod's works, *Theogony* and *Works and Days*, though there is actually a group of fragments and a long list of other pieces of literature attributed to Hesiod (but this is less certain than the attribution of *Theogony* and *Works and Days*). Thus only these works survive at this time. Since they are oral literature, their written record — and thus the canonical form we read today — was probably established after their creation in the eighth century B.C.E. The earliest scraps of the manuscript of Hesiod are from a relatively more recent period, the third century B.C.E. However, there are quotations and references to the text from as early as the sixth century.

Hesiod was probably at the height of his career around 700 B.C.E., during which time the earliest use of alphabetic writing by Greeks is documented. Whether or not Hesiod availed himself to this tool is unknown. Hesiod did not live in a democratic, cosmopolitan Athens. His world was the beginning of the Archaic Age, when trade was picking up between the Greek islands after a prolonged period of economic inactivity. At some point early in his life, he migrated from Cume to the poor community of Ascra. The governments of this area were evidently quite corrupt. There were judges and kings who held inordinate power. It was a slave-owning society but otherwise not very delineated in class or citizenship. Hesiod cared deeply about farming and the land, a sentiment probably the result of his ideologies rather than any virtue in agricultural work. To be "of the land" and to possess land indicated that one was native and, if not native, wealthy. Although it was possible to get rich by trading on the seas, this was regarded as a kind of stateless existence, where lack of rule of law might lead to other excesses that would be punished by the gods in the form of a capsized ship or lost cargo.

IN THE CLASSROOM

I. The Battle of the Gods and the Battle against Nature

Begin a lecture by briefly introducing, or asking the students to brainstorm, elements of the archaic society in which Hesiod lived. What is it about his style or tone that gives away the genre in which he is writing? It may be helpful to ask students to come up with different examples of wisdom literature and to name its characteristics. This could be followed by a brief discussion of symbols and the use of symbols in literature. Some symbols and archetypes have already been given in this book under the entry for *The Epic of Gilgamesh*. This may be particularly useful for discussing certain highly charged episodes, such as the fight between Ouranos and Kronos. It may also be used in determining the simple relationship of metals to the ages of men and the meaning of the Prometheus story. A discussion about gender can also take place, since the Pandora story, in both forms, reveals some attitudes toward women in this period. Looking past some of the outwardly misogynist comments also reveals interesting perceptions on the role women *did* take in society, which was not necessarily a bad one, and was often, in fact, a simultaneously artistic and managerial one.

Discussion

1. What is the difference between Love (Eros), at the beginning of the excerpt on "The Castration of Uranus," and Aphrodite?

2. Which gods are born through a sexual process, and which are born without divine intercourse? How does this affect the nature and character of these gods? How do Athena and Night, for example, differ from Zeus and Iapetus?

3. Describe the physical appearance of Pandora. Does it give any warning as to how she might be used against men by Zeus?

4. What are the major differences in the two accounts of Pandora in *Theogony* and *Works and Days*? From whose point of view are they told, respectively? How might this affect the telling of the story?

Groups

1. Have students break up into groups and draw the genealogies of the gods described in *Theogony*. Which gods seem not to have families? Which are firmly part of the main genealogical tree? What part and aspects of the universe and social world are represented by these gods?

Connections

1. Compare and contrast the myth-telling method of Hesiod with that of Apollodorus, a much later collector of myths who retold many of the same myths in the *Biblioteca* (p. 1129).

2. In both the Book of Genesis (p. 140) in the Hebrew Scriptures and *Works and Days*, humans are obliged to till the land in order to survive. Describe the similarities in the situations by which humans came to this fate in these two works. What do the two descriptions of the "Ages of Man" have in common?

3. Compare and contrast Euhemerus's view (p. 783) that the origins of the gods were just a garbled view of history with Hesiod's view. Is there a possibility that Hesiod may be writing about gods who behaved as though they were humans in a primitive society?

Writing

Ask students to write a short paper in response to one or more of the following:

1. Describe the role of mothers in *Theogony*. What do female gods typically do? How do the mothers of Zeus and Kronos determine their fate?

2. Sometimes Hesiod tries to explain how a god or goddess got his or her name. What are some examples of this, and what are the different strategies he uses for establishing the reason that a god or goddess has a certain name?

3. Why does the circle of sons overthrowing their fathers end with Zeus? What does Zeus do to ensure his rule? Is Zeus more political than his predecessors? How so?

4. What is the point of the story that Hesiod tells after the description of his own age, about the hawk and the nightingale? What does the hawk represent? What about the nightingale?

BEYOND THE CLASSROOM

RESEARCH & WRITING

1. Compare the description of Pandora to other descriptions of women from ancient literature (such as *The Epic of Gilgamesh* or the Hebrew Scriptures). How is the beauty or cleverness of a woman qualified? What is the overall attitude toward women in these societies? Use quotations from the text to support your point.

2. What are the differences between humans in the *Theogony* and humans in *Works and Days*? How have their roles and status changed?

3. What leads to the procession of ages in "The Ages of Man"? Are the five unconnected examples of human existence? What does Hesiod want us to notice, and, in particular, how did things become so bad in the Age of Iron?

Projects

1. Look at various portraits of the gods as described in *Theogony* (such as Botticelli's *Venus* or Goya's *Saturn Eating his Children*, which can be searched for and downloaded at http://www.artchive.com). How well or how differently do these paintings portray Hesiod's account of the myth?

WWW   For additional information on Hesiod and annotated Web links, see *World Literature Online* at bedfordstmartins.com/worldlit.

FURTHER READING

Adkins, Arthur. *Merit and Responsibility: A Study in Greek Values.* 1975.
Autsin, M. M., and P. Vidal-Naquet. *Economic and Social History of Ancient Greece.* 1977.
Burford, Alison. *Land and Labor in the Greek World.* 1993.
Hanson, Victor Davis. *The Other Greeks.* 1995.
Janko, Richard. *Homer, Hesiod and the Hymns: Diachronic Development in Epic Diction.* 1982.

Lincoln, Bruce. *Myth, Cosmos, and Society: Indo-European Themes of Creation and Destruction.* 1986.

Nagy, Gregory. *Poetry as Performance: Homer and Beyond.* 1996.

Nelson, Stephanie. *God and the Land.* 1998.

Pucci, Pietro. *Hesiod and the Language of Poetry.* 1977.

Rowe, C. J. *Essential Hesiod.* 1978.

Tandy, David, and Walter Neale. *Hesiod's "Works and Days": A Translation and Commentary for the Social Sciences.* 1996.

MEDIA RESOURCES

WEB SITES

Greek Mythology.com: Hesiod — Theogony
www.greekmythology.com/Books/Hesiod-Theogony/hesiod-Theogony.html
Find an outline of *Theogony* as well as a complete e-text at this site.

Hesiod, the Homeric Hymns, and Homerica
Sunsite.berkeley.edu/OMACL/Hesiod/
This page from the Berkeley Digital Library includes e-text translations of a number of Hesiod's works, including *Theogony* and *Works and Days*. It also offers hymns, epigrams, and fragments by Homer and several post-Homeric cycles and fragments.

Malaspina Great Books — Hesiod
www.malaspina.com/site/person_635.asp
A wonderful site to visit for background information on Hesiod, this site includes a biography of the poet as well as a number of links to useful research sites.

HOMER, *The Iliad* and *The Odyssey* (p. 277)

WWW   For a quiz on the *The Iliad*, see *World Literature Online* at bedfordstmartins.com/worldlit.

Students will often find it a daunting task to read through either of Homer's epics, *The Iliad* and *The Odyssey*. Not only are there many characters who are called by various names and have complex relationships to one another, but there are many events and crises separated by minor, almost meaningless episodes. Then, there is that repetitive language and difficult translation style. It will be essential for students to know first the plots and the characters before they even sit down to read these works. Not only are they the two fundamental pieces of Western literature, but a firm grasp of them is necessary for understanding subsequent Greek literature. We recommend that you draw up a chart with the names of the families and their relationships on the board. This will help students concentrate more on the plots, which are full of love stories, bloody retribution, sexy goddesses, wars and war protests, drug addicts, and everything else essential to the modern soap opera.

The Iliad reads very much like a Sopranos episode: Loyalties are broken and regained and common enemies are crushed, but Achilles spends good deal of his time in therapy, crying before his mother and his friend while outwardly refusing to cooperate with the other Greeks. Meanwhile, the rival Trojans gain on the divided Greeks, culminating in a great crisis that backfires, leaving the Trojans without a hero. Despite the familiarity of the themes, the problem with understanding these epics is that Homer's audience not only already knew the story before they heard it, they also already knew all of the characters, their attitudes and dispositions, and what was going to happen to them. The audience was not entertained by hearing new and fresh material but rather by hearing it presented in a new way, with fascinating commentary on divine backstabbing and unexpected moments of crisis: The audience knew *what* was going to happen, but not *when* or *how*. This compares easily with what most horror films try to accomplish today.

It should also be made clear to students from the outset that we do not know who Homer was, if he existed, and whether or not these were works composed by him. *The Iliad* and *The Odyssey* should be regarded not as a modern authoritative text but rather like a traditional text with a diachronic history, for example, in the same way as the Old Testament. Although people use the name "Homer" to speak of the poet of the epics, it is merely a convention for describing a monumental tradition of story-telling, perhaps thousands of years old, which was probably not written down until the sixth century B.C.E. Despite not really having an author, however, the epics still have many characteristics of the modern novel: They have setting (time, place), characters (female, male, gods, monsters, semidivine creatures, talking horses), and action (romantic, violent, tragic, comic). Students should always try to be aware of these simple questions: *Who? Where? When? What? Why?* For every episode, there is a cause that the poet tries to explain, and the ordering of the episodes — strung together like pearls — affects the outcome of the whole. Students should feel comfortable asking and answering the most basic questions about the plot and structure. Also, because of the relatively unfamiliar format of the epic to the modern reader, students should constantly be trying to relate to the story as modern reader would to a novel or television series. They should not be afraid to ask, "Was Agamemnon wrong to take Brieis?" "Is Helen a traitor or has she been forced to live in the Trojan city?" One goal of these epics is to give students a grounding for subsequent reading and to look at how cultures identify their values. But a further goal is to enhance their interest in reading in general and learning to ask questions informed by clues in the text.

HOMER'S WORLD OR A LOST CIVILIZATION?

So who are the people that *The Iliad* talks about? In 1822, Heinrich Schliemann, a wealthy trader and businessman, discovered bronze and gold treasures near Hissarlik, on the northwest coast of Turkey. A civilization emerged out of deep burial chambers and mountain citadels. Today, this site is believed to be where Troy stood at the end of the second millennium B.C.E. This city and its wealthy inhabitants found themselves on the border between Europe and Asia and were influenced by cultures from all over the Mediterranean. The economic might of Troy must have been substantial because of its prime location. Sometime around the year 1200 B.C.E., attacks from a rival civilization — perhaps based in Knossos, on Crete, or Mycenae, on the Peloponnese — must have had a devastating impact on Asia Minor. All of the trade in gold and iron slowed to a trickle after this period. What civilization could have been so powerful as to have destroyed Troy, and yet so vulnerable as to itself have been destroyed? Around 1900, Sir Arthur Evans discovered documents from Knossos written on lead tablets in unknown scripts. Only in 1953 did the young engineer Michael Ventris, with the help of John Chadwick, decipher the mysterious language, called "Linear B," the earliest written form of Greek. It is widely believed that this civilization, the Myceneans, exhausted their resources in decimating Troy. Could these two competing civilizations be the infamous Trojans and Greeks of Homer's *The Iliad*?

By contrast, vases recovered from the period in which it is assumed this poem was created are simple and without decoration (hence the name "Geometric Age" given to this period). Furthermore, these early Greeks, unlike the earlier Myceneans, had no writing system. In the four centuries intervening between the Trojan War and the rise of Greek civilization, nearly all memory of the previous "Heroic Age" would have vanished. Indeed, some of the weapons and cities described in *The Iliad* are anachronistic. The action of *The Iliad* may very well belong to the mysterious generation of Priam and Achilles, but whose culture is reflected in the text? Do we really see the worldview of all but vanished civilizations, or are we witnessing the development of new Greek ideals and even the Greek city-state? This epic, after all, is not only part of the grand narrative of the Trojan saga, but it will become the primary source of all Greek education and learning for over two thousand years. As well, it will be the source for countless allusions right down to the twenty-first century. Contained in this work are recipes for food, hymns, other myths about older heroes and the gods, a geography and ethnography of the known world, instructions for holding marriages and funerals, how to race a chariot, and even advice on how to give a speech. Recitations of the epics occurred nearly annually, and kings had scholars go around the Mediterranean recording these recitations in order to acquire "authoritative" versions of it.

THE MYSTERY OF HOMER

And yet, nothing is known about the supposed author, Homer. Tradition tells us he was blind and from Chios, an island off the coast of Turkey in the Aegean Sea. In the song of Demodocus (*The Odyssey*, Book Eight; see p. 279), there is the tentative identification of the poet. Although he is credited with many epics, only *The Iliad* and *The Odyssey* survive. Even in antiquity, there was doubt that Homer ever existed, or, if he had existed, that he wrote both works. In 1795, Friedrich Wolf wrote an essay, *Prolegomena ad Homerum*, which sparked the modern debate on Homer: Did Homer write both epics (the unitarian position), or did something else happen (the analyst position)? In the nineteenth century, several practical considerations were examined: If there really was a poet named Homer from this period, he would have had no alphabet in which to write, only his voice to pass the story on to the next generation. Could he have remembered such long poems? Were the poems accretive (a skeleton story by Homer and then subsequently added to by various other bards)? Nobody knows conclusively the answer to these questions.

THE STYLE OF HOMER AND FORMULAIC COMPOSITION

A certain style of composition exists in *The Iliad* and *The Odyssey* that suggests the epics come from a tradition of "oral poetry," that is, poetry composed within highly controlled conventions about set subjects and orally passed on from master bard to apprentice. Some evidence suggests that the Greeks also knew about this process of composing poetry. Finally, in the 1930s, Milman Parry and his student, Albert Lord, began recording epics in Yugoslavia that possess similar language devices, and they drew conclusions about the poetry of Homer.

What are these defining characteristics of the Homeric style? Just as the letter is the base unit of an English word or the word the base unit of the sentence, the "formula" is the base unit of the Greek epic style. The reader might notice that the diction is often repetitive. For instance, when a character speaks he always "answers with wingéd words" and dawn always rises with "rosy fingers." Every sacrifice or meal contains lines that are the same. Sometimes a god tells a character something that character repeats *verbatim* only a few lines later. All of these are "formulae." In addition, characters come with stock epithets, such as "shining-helmet Hektor," which may vary, usually depending on how long of a formula is needed to put together lines. These formulae or pieces of the line are stitched together like a quilt to form the language of Homer. Although this can be hard to bring out in translation, one example suffices to explain how this works. When Homer wants to say "and then spoke," it only takes up a third of the line, so he needs a longer epithet to finish the line, thus "and then spoke Agamemnon, the lord of men" and "and then spoke great Ajax, the son of Telemon." But when Homer wants to say "spoke answering with wingéd words," he will use a shorter epithet, "powerful Agamemnon spoke, answering with wingéd words" or "Ajax, son of Telemon spoke, answering with wingéd words." All of these epithets are set, and therefore the poet must draw from these pieces of the line to compose his verse, just as a prose writer would draw from the available words in the English language.

The repetition of these stock formulae and epithets are all parts of a rhythmic construct that underlies the whole poem. Every line is in a so-called "dactylic hexameter" — a long pattern of syllables with a break in the middle. In Fitzgerald's text, this is represented by roughly two lines of the translation per every line of Greek. The rhythm is very fast, and it is believed that the combination of this rhythm and the use of formulae helped the performer to compose the text according to strict tradition, patching together his memory of different stories and texts around the received framework of the plot. Below is printed the tenth line of *The Iliad* in transliterated Greek and the rhythm to which it would have been performed:

> BUH-duhduh BUH-duhduh BUH-duhduh BUH-duhduh BUH-duhduh BUH-BUH
> NOOzon anA STRaton ORSe kakAEN olekONTo de LA-OI
> *[He] conjured up an evil plague and the people began to die /*

Although this may have helped the oral composition of the story and may have sounded pleasant to the ancient audience, this system is often found to be repetitive and overly artificial for the modern reader. We recommend that some time be set aside to appreciate the formula system. Have students find certain formulae or epithets in the text and show different combinations of the formulae. There are some older recordings available of people reciting epics that may be used. However, in general, any attempt to reproduce the original feel or sound of the Greek will be difficult to appreciate. We suggest instead letting the students explore the English translation. This may be a good opportunity to talk about the difficulties of translation. Perhaps you might bring in different translations of *The Iliad*, such as prose translations or the early English translations by Alexander Pope. What should be the goals of the translator — to reproduce the feeling of the original text or to reproduce the story and feelings in that text that motivates a non-native audience to share in the emotions of that text?

The Iliad (p. 288)

TEXT & CONTEXT

The Iliad begins *in medias res* and with the conflict among the Greek leadership in the tenth year of the war against Troy. The first word, *mênin*, "anger," talks about the subject of the epic: The young and brash Achilles, a more tragic version of Shakespeare's Romeo, is enraged because King Agamemnon has taken away his girlfriend, Briseus. When the action unfolds, Apollo has unleashed a deadly plague in response to Agamemnon taking Chyses, the daughter of a nearby prophet of Apollo. When Agamemnon returns Chryses in order to appease the god and release the army from the plague, he says "everyone must pay me back for this," and he asks Achilles for Briseus. By the end of Book One, Agamemnon has Briseus, and Achilles and his army have withdrawn from the Greek coalition. The rest of the epic is consumed with the disastrous effects of Achilles' withdrawal and with the efforts to appease him without Agamemnon losing face. This very personal and frequently emotional conflict takes place on a stage of much greater proportions: The Greeks have been in Troy for ten years and have been entrenched in a war they cannot win. The men no longer want to be there and doubt that the cause of the war is justified. At one point Achilles says "I will not fight over another man's faithless wife (i.e., Helen)." The reason for the war is that Agamemnon's brother, Meneláos, had a wife, Helen, who was stolen away by Paris, a Trojan prince. In *The Iliad*, even though Aphrodite is responsible, Helen blames herself continually for the war, but she seems otherwise to be a good woman. Since Paris refuses to return Helen to Meneláos, Agamemnon launches the Greek coalition to bring her back.

All of this action transpires before *The Iliad* opens. We get a number of glimpses of Paris and his personality in Books Three and Six: Unlike his brother, Hektor, he is somewhat effeminate, interested largely in his sexual but childless relationship with Helen. Hektor, on the other hand, the Trojan hero, enjoys an honorable status among Priam's children and is characterized partially by a poignant scene in Book Six, where he consoles his wife, Andromache, and his child, Astyanax, who is frightened at the sight of his military uniform. Meanwhile, in heaven, the gods are divided over the outcome of the war. Zeus cannot decide who will win, since he has interests on both sides of the battle line. The other gods, particularly Apollo, Hêra, Athêna, and Aphrodite fight it out bitterly, sometimes taking over the bodies and voices of the heroes. The sea-goddess Thetis, Achilles' mother, tries to intercede on her son's behalf as early as the Book One, asking Zeus to make Agamemnon suffer for having offended Achilles. The Greeks do suffer in battle after battle, sometimes due to Agamemnon's incompetence. In a desperate move, they build a wall, really a wooden fence, to protect their camps and the ships, which, if torched by the Trojans, will eliminate any chance of their returning home. An embassy is sent by Agamemnon to Achilles, promising great rewards if he returns to the coalition. Achilles receives the eloquent speakers hospitably but refuses to cooperate (Book Nine). Finally, after the Trojans set fire to some ships, Achilles is persuaded that the situation has become too grave for him to ignore. Convinced by his best friend, Patróklos, Achilles lets him fight with the Greeks, dressed in his own (Achilles') armor (Book Sixteen). Hektor, who is having a good day on the battlefield, what in Greek is called an *aristeia*, destroys Patróklos, and, at that moment, he is condemned to death by Zeus. The Trojans make off with Achilles' armor and the Greeks rescue the dead body of Patróklos. Achilles grieves for days, and we begin to understand how deeply emotional he is. Again, Thetis tries to help him, acquiring a new magical set of armor from Hephaistus. We get a break in the action as the poet describes scenes from everyday life, sometimes strikingly violent, at other times beautifully peaceful, all etched masterfully onto Achilles' shield (Book Eighteen).

Before Achilles can take revenge on Hektor, Agamemnon must give all the gifts he promised Achilles in Book Nine and return Briseus, whom Agamemnon insists he has not touched (Book Nineteen). When Achilles finally launches into battle, he is unstoppable, killing an astounding number of Trojans. Finally, in Book Twenty-two, after two books on Achilles' *aristeia*, Achilles and Hektor meet as if two gods on the battlefield. Hektor suddenly realizes that he is alone and begins to run away. With his parents, Priam and Hecuba, watching from the city walls, he turns to take on Achilles, but is caught instead. He begs Achilles to treat his body fairly and return it to Priam. Instead, Achilles kills Hektor and desecrates the body repeatedly (Books Twenty-two through Twenty-four). With Hektor dead, Achilles can bury Patróklos properly by holding games in his honor (Book Twenty-three), a small break in the action before the next crisis. But even here, Achilles is dangerously reckless: He builds a bonfire of Trojan princes (Book Twenty-two). Meanwhile, Troy is in turmoil, and Priam, having lost confidence in his remaining children, leaves the city to meet Achilles. He is accompanied by Hêrmes who is in disguise as a young man. When he arrives undetected at the camps of the Greeks, he is taken to Achilles' tent. Priam reminds the young hero of his own father, Peleus, in Phthia: "Have pity on me and remember your own father, Achilles. I have done what nobody could bring themselves to do: I've put my mouth on the hands that killed my child." Achilles weeps at the thought of his father and then relents. He rushes out of the door and tells his servants to clean the body and shroud it in elegant garments. When he returns, he prepares dinner for Priam and they eat together. In the morning, Achilles asks Priam how many days of truce he requires to bury Hektor. Nine days are given. When Hektor returns to the Trojan camp, all the women mourn over the body, and a nervous funeral is held outside the city walls for Hektor. When the action of The Iliad ends, the city already knows that it is only a matter of time before they fall.

IN THE CLASSROOM

I. THE GODS AND RELIGION IN HOMER'S EPIC

Throughout Greek literature, several reasons are given for the Trojan War. Herodotus claims that the Trojans stole Helen because the Greeks (through Jason) had already kidnapped Medea, all as part of an elaborate chain of kidnapped wives and revenge stories. In his drama, *Helen*, Euripides writes that Zeus wanted to make the weight of people less oppressive on his mother, Earth, and therefore he held a great war to control the population. In the epic cycle, the gods are to blame. Hêra, Aphrodite, and Athêna all want to be called "most beautiful," and Zeus chooses Paris, the Trojan prince, to decide. Paris's choice of Aphrodite and his reward, Helen, begins the conflict. Sometimes, the behavior of the gods, compared with human mortality, appears frivolous and petty. At the end of Book One, they hold a banquet that seems comic in comparison to the tragedy occurring at the Greek camp. It will be important for the students to know what each god represents: like Arês is the god of war and Aphrodite the goddess of love. It may be useful to review the gods and their relationships just as you review the main characters and their relationships. Not all students will be familiar with the Greek names of the gods that otherwise they might know about (Hêphaistos for the Roman Vulcan, for example).

Discussion

1. Have students outline the various conflicts: Greek-Trojan, Achilles-Agamemnon, Hêra-Zeus. How are these conflicts characterized? On whose side do the various gods fall? Are gods always to blame for the conflicts, or do men also cause conflicts? Whose fault is it that they are fighting? Is it really "about another man's wife"?

2. Have students generate a list of gods who are involved in the plot in one way or another, such as Thetis, Zeus, Apollo, Hêphaistos. What are the characteristics of those gods? To whom are they married? What role do they play in the action?

Connections

1. The world presented in Hesiod (p. 259) is much more sparse and violent than that in Homer. What are the inconsistencies? Are the gods any less violent than the older deities described in Hesiod?

2. What would you describe as the main difference between the Hebrew god and the Greek polytheistic system? Are there any similarities? Is Zeus a benevolent god? Consider Achilles' speech to Priam about the urns of Zeus in Book Twenty-four. What about the "Parable of the Litai" or the description of Prayer, daughters of Zeus, and Ruin in Phoenix's speech in Book Nine. Of what does this remind you?

Groups

1. Throughout the epic, and in particular in Books Nine and Twenty-four, there are smaller stories, such as the Calydonian boar hunt, told by the various characters. Identify these smaller stories and try to discover (a) of what the stories attempt to persuade their listeners, and (b) whether they are persuasive or relevant.

Writing

Ask students to write a short paper in response to one or more of the following:

1. At the beginning of *The Iliad*, we are told that "the will of Zeus was done." What is the will of Zeus? Was it in fact completed? Is it the same at the beginning of the epic as at the end?

2. In Book Twenty-four, Achilles knows that Priam has arrived at his tent with the help of a god, since otherwise he would have been detected. Where else in the epic does a mortal recognize that a god is present or is helping some other mortal? What effect does that have on that character?

II. MORTALS

In *The Iliad* there are kings (Priam, Agamemnon), heroes (Achilles, Hektor), wives (Andromache, Helen), fathers (Priam, Peleus), and mothers (Thetis, Hecuba), among other mortals. Many times they behave in ways that may seem irrational to us but are part of an elaborate culture of honor, such as Agamemnon's decision to take Briseus away from Achilles. This forms part of the cultural world of *The Iliad*. You may want to bring in some modern examples here. What are certain conventions and cultural expectations of which we are familiar? In Japan, for example, people are expected to bow and to present business cards with both hands. In the United States, however, casually handing over a business card with one hand and shaking hands with the other is perfectly acceptable. There are also other conventions, such as what to say when one is speaking to a minister or congressman. What actions do we take before swearing an oath or saying a prayer that lets everyone else around us know what we are about to do? The Greeks had these movements as well, and students can find them repeated throughout the text. You might stimulate discussion by asking them what kind of cultural conflicts they have encountered and then ask them to describe familiar or unfamiliar cultural aspects of *The Iliad*.

Discussion

1. Why does Agamemnon feel justified in taking Briseus? Is he right in doing so? What about Achilles' response? Is it appropriate to what Agamemnon has done to him? What really bothers Achilles?

2. What are the women of *The Iliad* like? Consider Andromache in Book Six and descriptions of Helen elsewhere. Are women just objects for men to steal (Helen, Chyses, Briseus), or do they play a more elaborate role? Consider Helen, Hecuba, and Andromache. What about the goddesses? How do human women and goddesses compare?

Connections

1. In Hesiod's "The Ages of Man," different generations are spoken of as being of different qualities, just like metals. Can you perceive a similar division of the generations in Homer's *The Iliad*?

2. Mencius (p. 1526) says that men are born good but society corrupts them. Consider some aspects of the society presented in *The Iliad*. Are these men essentially of a good nature but corrupted by the circumstances surrounding their society, or do they have to learn to be good? Does Achilles learn anything from his initial refusal to return the body of Hektor?

Groups

1. Anthropologists sometimes try to find certain patterns that constitute a cultural behavior. Certain such patterns become clear as one reads the epic. For example, each time someone comes to visit Achilles, he makes dinner for that person. Are there other conventions that are part of this culture? Brainstorm different passages in which identical or similar behavior takes place.

Writing

Ask students to write a short paper in response to one or more of the following:

1. The gods are nearly completely absent from the description of Achilles' shield in Book Eighteen. What are the scenes shown on the shield? Are these men similar to the characters of the outer epic, or do they represent something else?

2. Do the Trojans and Greeks behave differently or alike? Are they essentially similar cultures, or can you distinguish between the two of them?

III. THE EPIC AND ITS WORLD

Several features make up the epic besides the lines, formulae, and epithets. There is a distinct setting and time frame for the action. The poet frequently compresses space and time to serve his purpose. He uses metaphors and long similes to "slow down" certain motions as well as extensive geographic descriptions. These are all part of the arsenal of tools the poet has at his disposal to create anticipation and suspense. Students should be aware that epic has a "cinematographic" aspect to it. In many ways, the movie director uses techniques similar to the poet to speed up or slow down the action of a scene. Compare various scenes from *The Iliad* to contemporary action films. What are the similarities in technique? It will be important to make sure that the students understand the background to the crises and how the poet has worked up to the climax. There are also other episodes that seem disconnected or not attached to the narrative as a whole. Ask the students to propose theories as to why these unrelated episodes (for example, the battle with Aeneas in Book Twenty) are placed in there. What do they accomplish? How might they have been "added" to the epic?

Discussion

1. Have students draw a map of Homer's Troy. Where were the ships? There are certain trees, gates, city walls, fences, camps, plains, and rivers that are all part of the narrative. Have the students brainstorm various events and describe the geography in which the battle takes place. Many of these geographical features are described at the height of action between Achilles and Hektor, such as certain trees and the two springs. Why is that?

2. How long is *The Iliad*? Most of the days that pass are waiting for the gods to get back from Ethiopia in the first book. How is the rest of the action divided? What battles take the longest to fight, and which are relatively short?

3. Try to reconstruct the shield of Achilles on the blackboard. What are the various scenes, and how are they represented? What is missing from the shield? What world does it portray?

Connections

1. The poems of Hesiod (p. 259) and Homer (p. 277) are both assumed to derive from the "oral tradition." What features of style do they have in common? Even in translation, many aspects of their method of composition should be apparent.

Groups

1. Christa Wolf wrote a novel entitled *Cassandra* in 1983 that describes the Trojan War entirely from the Trojan Princess Cassandra's point of view, beginning with the abduction of Helen and ending with Cassandra's own murder by Clytemnestra, Agamemnon's wife. Consider various points of view in *The Iliad*. Does the author take any particular side? Try to reconstruct the events from a particular character's point of view.

Writing

Ask students to write a short paper in response to one or more of the following:

1. When a hero has his *aristeia*, what changes in the style of the epic?

2. Translating *The Iliad* means not only translating the individual ancient Greek words but also trying to recreate the feel of the original language and text. What are the challenges of translating this work into English? What are some of the problems that a contemporary audience faces when it tries to read the translation?

BEYOND THE CLASSROOM

RESEARCH & WRITING

1. Some critics in the past have said that *The Iliad* is an accretive text. This means that there was originally a skeleton version of *The Iliad* plot and that various later poets added and embellished different episodes to make the lengthier epic that we have today. Write an essay arguing for or against this position.

2. The speeches in Book Nine are often marked out as great examples of eloquence. Compare the styles and strategies of each of the speakers. How are they similar or different? Who is the most persuasive? Why? Use quotes from the text to prove your argument.

3. Throughout Greek literature, *The Iliad* is sometimes described as being antiwar because of the descriptions of brutality and violence and the unwillingness of some of the heroes to fight (at the beginning of Book Two, the Greek soldiers threaten to leave). Others consider it to be a description of the virtues of heroes and not against war *per se*. Some later authors, such as Thucydides, were highly skeptical about the piece and considered it propaganda. Which seems most likely? Are there other modern narratives — books or movies — that have an equally ambiguous interpretation?

4. The *aristeia* of Achilles and Hektor are both central to the climax of the story of *The Iliad*. However, it seems like Hektor's reputation may be larger than his ability. His *aristeia* is much smaller and less significant than Achilles: His only major victim is Patróklos. Otherwise, he runs from Achilles, he is beaten by Ajax, and thrown off by Diomedes. Does the poet set Hektor up to be defeated by Achilles easily, or does he create an equal match for Achilles? What do their respective *aristeia* say about their characters?

5. After Troy is taken, Achilles will be killed with a poisoned arrow to his ankle. Although he is the son of a goddess and a great warrior, Achilles is imperfect in many ways. Some critics call him the "tragic hero," since he possesses a "tragic flaw" that acts to his demise. What is wrong with Achilles? Does he improve in time, or is his quick anger ever present, even in the final moments with Priam? Why did the poet create such a vulnerable hero, who cries before his mother and becomes angry so easily?

Projects

1. Schliemann's "discovery of Troy" has been much problematized since 1822. Not only are there different "levels" of Troy, but there is also evidence that many of the weapons described in Homer do not belong to the period of the historical Trojan War. Research various recent discoveries about the historical Troy, and relate them to the text of Homer in an annotated bibliography.

2. *The Iliad* has had a great influence in Western art. Not only did the Greeks display it on their vases and on the sides of their public buildings, such as the Parthenon in Athens,

but the Roman as well as European societies frequently showed scenes from the epic. Investigate some of these paintings. What are the most common scenes portrayed? During which periods of history was *The Iliad* most popular?

WWW   For additional information on Homer and annotated Web links, see *World Literature Online* at bedfordstmartins.com.

FURTHER READING

Bowra, C. M. *Tradition and Design in the* Iliad. 1930.
Kirk, G. S. *The Songs of Homer.* 1962.
Latacz, J. *Homer, His Art, and His World.* 1995.
Redfield, J. M. *Nature and Culture in the* Iliad. 1975.

WWW   See *World Literature in the 21st Century* at bedfordstmartins.com/worldlit for information on the relevance of Homer to today's world.

MEDIA RESOURCES

VIDEO

Helen of Troy
141 min., 1955 (Library Video Company)
Rosanna Podesta and Jack Sernas star in the story of Homer's *The Iliad*, where the Greeks bring a treacherous gift to conquer the Trojans. Discover this story of the mammoth wooden horse that secretly houses Greek fighting men, and learn how it is gotten inside the walls of Troy. Robert Wise directs this epic capturing some 30,000 people on screen, among them Sir Cedric Hardwicke and Brigitte Bardot.

The Iliad
360 min., 1998 (Library Video Company)
Roger Rees performs an abridged recording based on Homer's epic that is set against the backdrop of the final days of the Trojan War. Tells the story of Achilles, a retired Greek warrior, who is called back into battle following the death of his friend, Patróklos. Achilles sets out to avenge his friend's death and bring the city of Troy to ruins.

The Iliad and the Trojan War
79 min., 1996 (Educational Video Network)
Homer's *The Iliad* and the accompanying epics about Troy have survived in classical culture for more than 1,500 years. Heroes and gods strive toward glory.

WEB SITES

The Homer Homepage
www.dc.peachnet.edu/~shale/humanities/literature/world_literature/homer.html
A fantastic resource, this site provides users with links to e-texts of *The Iliad, The Odyssey*, and the Homeric Hymns as well as an audio recording of a reading from *The Iliad*. It also offers links to a large number of Web sites devoted to Homer and the Homeric world, teacher's guides, maps of ancient Greece, literary criticism, images, and various works of art and culture with connections and allusions to Homer.

Homer's *The Iliad* and *The Odyssey*
Library.thinkquest.org/19300/data/homer.htm
Created by students, this site contains links to the complete e-texts of Homer's works.
Users will also find here links to historical information on Homer and his world and background on the myths in Homer's works as well as a study guide to *The Odyssey*.

AUDIO

The Iliad
9 tapes, 12:75 hrs. (Blackstone Audiobooks)
The terrible and long-drawn-out siege of Troy remains among one of the classic campaigns, and the heroism and treachery of the combatants have been unmatched in song and story.

The Iliad
3 tapes or 3 CDs, 3:56 hrs. (Naxos Audio)
Perhaps the greatest poem of the Western world, *The Iliad* tells the story of fifty critical days toward the end of the Trojan war. Achilles has quarreled with Agamemnon and sulks in his tent, while Hektor brings his Trojans to the brink of victory; but fate will have the last word.

The Iliad
1 hr. (Caedmon Audio)
Heroism. Love. Rage. Despair. Such is the stuff of legend. In this retelling of one of the greatest epics in all of human history, veteran stage actor Anthony Quayle brings the ancient tale to life. Hear the story of the Greeks and Trojans battling over Helen of Troy, the blind arrogance of Agamemnon, the anger of Achilles, and the heroic death of Hektor in an elemental tale of jealousy, war, hubris, and sadness that has endured for over 2,000 years.

The Odyssey (p. 421)

WWW   For a quiz on the *The Odyssey*, see *World Literature Online*
at bedfordstmartins.com/worldlit.

THE EPIC CYCLE

The two epics discussed in this book are actually part of a larger group of epics, called the "Epic Cycle." Some of these epics were later credited to or written down by other authors, but only *The Iliad* and *The Odyssey* survive in full form today. The first epic, *Cypria* — another name for Aphrodite — covers everything from the decision of the gods to cause the Trojan War down to the events of *The Iliad*, which is the next epic of the cycle, its main theme being the argument between Achilles and Agamemnon. The *Aethiopis* follows directly upon *The Iliad*, and it concerns the coming of the Amazons, fierce warrior women who fought on the side of Troy, and the "Choice of Arms," in which the armor of Achilles is given to Odysseus by Athena, and Ajax, going mad, kills himself. This episode is recounted also briefly in *The Odyssey* (Book Eleven). The *Little Iliad* discusses the fall of Troy in more detail, in particular the death of Achilles. The *Sack of Troy* is where the episode of the wooden horse is described: A wooden horse is built by the Greeks and offered to the Trojans, but, inside the horse, there are Greek soldiers hidden who will attack the city once the horse has been let inside. This epic also discusses the rape of Cassandra, the death of Priam, and the throwing of Astyanax from the city walls. The evil deeds of the Greeks are not without retribution, however. In the *Nostoi*, or *Returns*, gods wreck the ships at sea, and only a few heroes return home. Even they, however, are killed by sons and wives, or they discover their families altered after ten years. Meneláos wanders around Egypt with Helen for many years before returning to his home in Sparta, and Agamemnon comes home to an angry wife who kills him and his new mistress, the Trojan princess Cassandra. *The Odyssey* follows this epic and focuses largely on the wanderings of Odysseus. However, unlike the other Greek kings and generals, he finally returns and is happily reunited with his wife. There may also have been other epics that follow *The Odyssey* and speak about the generation of Telemachus and the eventual death of Odysseus.

COMPARING *THE ILIAD* AND *THE ODYSSEY*

The Iliad and *The Odyssey* were compared throughout antiquity, different genres of later literature emanating from them. *The Odyssey* became the archetype for the travel narrative and thus the foundation for the Greek novel, developed in the third century B.C.E. and beyond. *The Iliad*, on the other hand, was sometimes seen to be the forerunner to Greek tragedy. While *The Odyssey* has a happy reunion as its ending, *The Iliad* describes an endless battle of revenge, and it sets the stage for the eventual destruction of Troy. *The Iliad* has one setting, but *The Odyssey* has many. While the narrative of *The Iliad* is more or less linear, *The Odyssey* is actually composed of stories within stories, sometimes shifting scenes without shifting time, like Penelope's situation at home versus Odysseus's time among the Phaeacians. The men of *The Iliad* are brave and daring, sometimes more so than their leaders. The men of *The Odyssey* are, as the poet tells us in the opening lines, "fools." *The Odyssey* contains relatively simpler language with fewer metaphors and similes, although the same system of formulae is used as was used in *The Iliad*. The major gods do not play as large a role in *The Odyssey*; scenes that take place in heaven common in *The Iliad* are relatively rare in *The Odyssey*. Although *The Odyssey* is called *Odysseia*, or "poetry about Odysseus" in Greek, *The Iliad* means "Tale of Troy," and yet it is more specifically about Achilles and his *aristeia* than about Troy.

TEXT & CONTEXT

A TALE OF TWO CITIES: HUMANITY AND GEOGRAPHY

As our hero wanders throughout the Mediterranean, he first encounters civilizations like his own. However, as he gets farther and farther away from Ithaca and his home, the civilizations that he runs into are full of increasingly inhospitable monsters. As he begins his journey back to Ithaca, he meets civilizations that are more and more human in nature and, at times, the poet does not conceal the fact that some civilizations, such as the Phaeacians, are more civilized than the situation back home in Ithaca.

SYNOPSIS

While Odysseus has been gone, ten years for the war and ten years wandering the Mediterranean, Penelope has had to fight off a continual train of men who want to marry her and get Odysseus's wealth. Penelope is a model woman in many respects, trying to stay faithful but managing the monsters that have invaded her home. She is clever, a wife that all the heroes whom Odysseus meets in the underworld only wish they could have. Telemachus, Odysseus's son, has come of age and wants to go off to seek his father before all of Penelope's suitors have squandered her wealth. This is the situation when the epic opens. Athena urges Telemachus to leave in search of his father, a sort of rite of passage for a generation that was too young to fight at Troy. The poet describes the difficult situation with which Penelope is presented. In Book Two, Telemachus tries unsuccessfully to persuade the suitors to leave. Instead, he and Athena must secretly leave Ithaca; otherwise, he will be killed. Telemachus's journeys in Books Three and Four take him to the houses of the famous Greek leadership: Nestor in Pylos and Meneláos and Helen in Sparta. It is at Meneláos' house that Telemachus learns that Odysseus has been shipwrecked on the island of Calypso (a seductive witch who lives off the coast of Italy). Meanwhile, on Ithaca, the suitors plot to kill Telemachus when he returns. Finally, in Book Five, we catch a glimpse of the main hero. The god Hêrmes tells Calypso to let Odysseus, who has essentially been her sex slave, go. Poseidon, angry that Odysseus should be allowed to return home, wrecks his ship, and he lands on Scheria. When Odysseus washes ashore, he has nothing and appears merely a shipwreck. Nausikaa, princess of the Phaeacians, takes him in as guest and provides him with clothes. In Book Seven, a reception is held by King Alcinoe and queen Arete, during which Odysseus hears a tale very much like *The Iliad* being sung. The Phaeacians hold a set of games, during which it becomes apparent that Odysseus is no ordinary shipwreck. Seeing the potential relationship develop between Nausikaa and Odysseus, Alcinoe asks Odysseus to tell his name and story.

Books Nine through Twelve are a story within a story, a Chinese-box strategy that helps to delay the final conflict between Odysseus and the suitors and the safe reunion of Telemachus, Odysseus, and Penelope. Odysseus's first deed after the end of the Trojan War is to raid the Zirconia's. The crew of his ships ignores his orders to leave, choosing instead to get drunk. They are ambushed the next morning and Odysseus just escapes with some of his crew. From here, he meets progressively stranger people. First, he arrives at the land of the Lotus-Eaters, who are drug addicts. Predictably, his crew gets caught up in the local produce, and many choose not to leave. Next, Odysseus meets Cyclops, a one-eyed monster who knows nothing of laws or gods, named Polyphemus. Odysseus tricks the monster through various tools of language, saying he is "Nobody," instead of giving his real name. In Greek, the word for "Nobody," (*me tis*), sounds like the word for "clever," (*metis*). The monster eats Odysseus's companions but is unfamiliar with the effects of wine. Odysseus stabs out his eye after putting him to sleep with a barrel of wine. The hero and his surviving companions make way for Aeolus, who controls the winds. He helps provide wind to send them home, but the companions, nearly having reached Ithaca, open the bag to look for gold and let out all the winds, blowing the ship back off course. After a few days, they arrive at the land of the Laestrigonians and their huge matron (as big as a mountain), Artacie. The Laestrigonians turn out to be cannibals, so Odysseus flees with his men and ends up on Circe's island. Circe is also a powerful witch who transforms Odysseus's sailors into pigs. The god Hêrmes tells Odysseus to sleep with Circe in order to release his companions, and he gives Odysseus a kind of herb to prevent Circe from casting a spell over him. Odysseus spends a year with Circe, feasting, dining, and enjoying Circe's bed. But the companions long to leave. Circe directs Odysseus to get advice from the underworld, where the dead souls lie. Book Eleven is consumed with the stories that Odysseus hears from the dead, many of which serve as lessons for his own return home. In Book Twelve, Odysseus encounters the horrible sea-monster Scylla and the whirlpool Charybdis. The men arrive at Thrinacia, where the sun god, Helios, keeps his cattle. When the men eat the cattle instead of taking Circe's earlier advice to avoid it, the entire crew is destroyed, and Odysseus alone escapes to Calypso's island.

Now that Alcinoe and Arete know Odysseus's story, they set about returning him to Ithaca. Odysseus is asleep when they arrive, and the next morning he wakes up to Athena, whom he doesn't recognize. He lies to her and claims to be an exile, making up an elaborate story. Athena calls him a liar but informs him of the situation in Ithaca and disguises him as an old man. In Book Fourteen, Odysseus meets his old swineherd, Eumaius, and tells him a terrifically complicated lie that Eumaius only barely believes. In Book Fifteen, the action begins to pick up again. Telemachus is informed by Athena that the time to return is now, and he returns home with many gifts from Meneláos. In order to get home, however, Telemachus must master cunning tricks, which rival only that of his father. In Book Sixteen, father and son are reunited in secret and plot their revenge against the suitors. The personality and treachery of the suitors is briefly revealed. In Book Seventeen, Odysseus makes his way, still in disguise, to Penelope's house, where most of the rest of the action will unfold. The dog, Argos, recognizes Odysseus but dies out of excitement. In Book Eighteen, the situation becomes tense between Odysseus, who is begging at the house, and the suitors. However, the poet still must hold off the final duel between him and the suitors. In Book Nineteen, Odysseus finally meets Penelope but does not reveal himself to her, although he comforts her and says that Odysseus is nearing home. Penelope treats this mysterious beggar well but doubts his prediction. The nurse, Eurycleia, recognizes a scar on Odysseus while she is bathing him, but Odysseus silences her. Penelope and Odysseus plan a contest: Whoever can string Odysseus's bow and fire an arrow through the holes of twelve axes will win her. In Book Twenty, the suitors begin to arrive, teasing Telemachus. Book Twenty-one is concerned with the competition. None of the suitors can string the bow or fire the arrows. Odysseus asks if he can try. Penelope lets him, despite the protests of the other suitors. Naturally, he accomplishes the task. In Book Twenty-two, Odysseus loses his disguise and kills all the suitors. Penelope pretends not to recognize Odysseus, giving him one last test, a trick that only the true Odysseus will realize. When Odysseus passes this final trial, Penelope and Odysseus embrace, and the hero recounts his stories to her. In Book Twenty-four, they go visit Odysseus's father, Laertes. The suitors plan a revenge, but it is foiled by Odysseus and Athena.

IN THE CLASSROOM

I. GENRE

Many students find the story of *The Odyssey* more compelling than that of *The Iliad*. The hero travels to many lands and meets many monsters. *The Iliad*, on the other hand, is more personal and full of hostile revenge scenarios and endless bloody battle scenes. Therefore, *The Odyssey* has enjoyed a rich modern reception, from Virgil's *The Aeneid* in ancient times to Dante's *Inferno* in the Middle Ages to James Joyce's *Ulysses* in the twentieth century to countless movies, such as *O Brother, Where Art Thou?* (2001). Also, some of the scenes in *The Odyssey* are very comical, almost parodies or caricatures of the more serious *The Iliad*. In relation to the "unitarian" versus "analyst" position, the differences between these works are not trivial. But there are also important implications for what "genre" these works belong to: for example, tragedy, comedy, the novel, or romance. Several things for students to consider will be (a) why has *The Odyssey* received a greater reception than *The Iliad*; (b) what elements of *The Odyssey* make it more humorous than *The Iliad*, even if there are still violent scenes of cannibalism and homicide; (c) consider the time frame of *The Iliad*, which is about two-months' worth of action, versus *The Odyssey*, which contains ten years of narrative; and (d) the portrayal of men and gods seem reversed in *The Odyssey* (that is, now the gods seem more reserved and less trivial, while the men seem to act foolishly and selfishly).

Discussion

1. Have students list differences between *The Iliad* and *The Odyssey* as well as similarities. Take certain passages, such as ritual sacrifices or the preparation of food, which are the same in both works, and compare them.

2. Also look at the portrayal of Odysseus in *The Iliad*, and compare it with his portrayal in *The Odyssey*. Are they similar or different? What about the other heroes? Ajax and Agamemnon seem changed in the underworld, not like their *Iliad* selves. What have they learned? Is this also a lesson for Odysseus, or does he continue to make mistakes after he meets these souls in the underworld?

Connections

1. Both *The Iliad* and *The Odyssey* contain stories within stories. Odysseus tells a number of lies that comprise longer stories about nonexistent heroes, or he is told about the heroes at the house of Alcinoe. Telamachus also hears stories at the houses of Nestor and Meneláos. Compare these stories. How does the act of storytelling differ? Why is there so much attention paid to lying and tricking in *The Odyssey*, which is less prevalent in *The Iliad*?

2. Compare Odysseus with Job in the Hebrew Scriptures (p. 169). Why must these men face trials and tests? What is the nature of their religious structure that compels them to obey or be destroyed? What might be the purpose of these stories? What are the similarities and differences between the fate of Job and that of Odysseus?

Groups

1. *The Iliad* and *The Odyssey* are structured similarly in that they both begin with an unsatisfactory situation: a disagreement between Greek leaders and the encroachment of suitors on Penelope and Telemachus. The reader must nearly finish a very long epic before a climax is reached. In *The Iliad*, this is accomplished through long battle scenes but also through metaphors and similes. In *The Odyssey*, there are other methods of delaying the climax. For example, there are frequently lengthy descriptions of natural phenomena. In groups, discuss other strategies that the poet employs in delaying the crisis of the work.

Writing

Ask students to write a short paper in response to one or more of the following:

1. Many of the episodes, such as the death of Odysseus's dog or Odysseus's conversations with Polyphemus, are clearly humorous. Choose one of these episodes, and discuss what is unexpected or unusual about these episodes that make them funny. Use citations from the text to support your argument.

2. Odysseus meets many people in the underworld who want to give him advice or tell him their story. Whose story is the most convincing and persuasive? Why? How different or similar are these stories to the speeches in Book Nine of *The Iliad*? Do they play the same role in the overall work?

II. GENDER

The women of *The Odyssey* are clearly quite different from those of *The Iliad*. Penelope is the paragon of a great wife, who manages to even outwit her husband at the end of the work. Helen and Meneláos have reunited without argument, and it seems as if Helen has learned a few magical potions from the Egyptians. Clytemnestra kills Agamemnon on his return from Troy. Even the divine and semidivine females are unusual. Circe and Calypso are seductive witches who easily master Odysseus (note that Odysseus is not reluctant to just stay in the arms of Circe). There are also horrible female monsters, like Scylla and Charybidis. Nausikaa is an interesting figure, and her relationship with Odysseus might show that Odysseus is maturing and learning how to resist his temptations. It may be useful at first to contrast these women against those found in *The Iliad*, like the Iliadic Helen or Hecuba, Andromache, and the "spear-brides" Chryseis and Briseis. But eventually, it will be necessary to see what kinds of gender patterns emerge. Often, the women outsmart the men or have more knowledge, such as Eurycleia, Odysseus's nurse, compared with Eumaius, his old swineherd. Also, there are number of witches or women who know magical or semimagical things. Discuss the characterization of various women and what significance this has on the larger spectrum of "gender roles," that is, specific tasks or stereotypes assigned to specific genders.

Discussion

1. Athena plays a prominent role in assisting Odysseus in this work. Describe how that role differs or is similar to the role she plays in helping the heroes of *The Iliad*.

2. In addition to killing the suitors, Odysseus and Telamachus punish the maids for inviting in and sleeping with the suitors. This scene is stands out somewhat from the rest. As Penelope sleeps, what does Odysseus do to the maids? What do you suppose the purpose is of the simile in this description? How would you characterize this scene? Are there others like it in *The Odyssey*?

3. Describe the relationship that Odysseus has with Nausikaa. After sleeping with Circe and Calypso, how does this relationship prepare him for his homecoming? What does it say about the culture of the Phaeacians and that of Odysseus?

Connections

1. Hesiod in *Works and Days* (p. 272) makes women out to be monsters in his description of Pandora. What does Homer accomplish in his description of the women of *The Odyssey*? Keep in mind that there are female monsters and witches in the *The Odyssey*, alongside the admirable and beautiful Penelope.

Groups

1. Homer switches the point of view (that is, whose thoughts are the most prominent) at different times during the narrative. This is particularly evident during the Nausikaa episode (Book Six). Often, attention is shifted from Odysseus to one of the characters reacting to him. In groups, discuss how this is done and how this helps to characterize the different individuals who Odysseus and Telemachus meet.

2. There may be similarities in the behavior between Odysseus's men and the suitors of Penelope. In groups, identify some of these similarities. What are episodes in which one group of men reminds you of the other? What happens to each group of men?

Writing

Ask students to write a short paper in response to one or more of the following:

1. In the literature we have read so far, what are some of the positive role models for women? Why have those texts attempted to create them? Does this mean that we can assume there was a female audience to listen to these role models?

2. Some people have speculated that the author of *The Odyssey* might be a woman. Write an essay in support of or against this speculation. Be sure to support your ideas with evidence from the text.

BEYOND THE CLASSROOM

RESEARCH & WRITING

1. When Telemachus goes in search of his father, his mother bids him to find him. Some have read this as a metaphor for Telemachus to try to achieve the same level of heroism as his father. What does Telemachus learn on his voyage? In what way does he become worthy of his father by the end of *The Odyssey*? If you disagree with this theory, state why and support your reasons with examples from the text.

2. *The Odyssey* has been recognized as the earliest travel narrative of Western literature. Find another example of a travel narrative, such as *Gulliver's Travels* by Jonathan Swift (Book 4) or Wu Chengen's *Journey to the West*. What are the main goals of travel narratives? What are their common features? Why are they so popular?

3. Some people have said that the different monsters that Odysseus meets are all examples of different kinds of human behavior and that they are metaphors for the human condition. In *The Odyssey*, there are drug addicts, cannibals, violent criminals, liars, and noble kings. What aspect of human nature does each of these civilizations that Odysseus encounters represent?

4. Death is every bit as common in *The Iliad* as it is in *The Odyssey*. Describe some of the deaths of *The Iliad* versus those in *The Odyssey*. What are the essential differences? Are the deaths less tragic in *The Odyssey*? Why might it be easier to laugh at a monster eating human beings but not at deaths in war? What are the circumstances of most deaths in *The Odyssey* ? Compare the funeral of Hektor in *The Iliad* Book Twenty-four with that of Elpenor in *The Odyssey* Book Twelve.

5. What are the characteristics of Greek epic? Are they all formal (the use of formulae, meter, oral composition), or are there structural conventions? Compare the structure of *The Iliad* and *The Odyssey*. Many aspects might be similar, like opening in the middle of the action, delaying the action at the end, having a book of denouement, or a book of speeches and stories in the middle (Odysseus in the underworld or the embassy sent to Achilles) of the work. Develop your thesis around specific episodes and examples in the text of *The Iliad* and *The Odyssey*.

PROJECTS

1. The plot of *The Odyssey* has been used for many other travel narratives in films, television series, novels, and other epics such as Virgil's *The Aeneid* and Dante's *Divine Comedy*. Choose one work that has been influenced by *The Odyssey*, and make a chart that relates episodes of *The Odyssey* to episodes of your chosen text. In what ways do other authors make their story more relevant to their contemporaries?

2. Odysseus tells several lies after returning to Ithaca. Is there anything in these lies that could be construed as being true? Show how the lie may be a manipulation of facts rather than a new story. Are the stories and fates familiar of the people he pretends to be? In a chart, compare each fact of a specific story with facts from the true account of Odysseus's wanderings.

WWW   For additional information on Homer and annotated Web links, see *World Literature Online* at bedfordstmartins.com.

FURTHER READING

Hyde, W. W. *Ancient Greek Mariners.* 1947.
Mondro, D. B. *Homer's Odyssey.* 1901.
Pucci, P. Odysseus Polutropos: *Intertextual Readings in the* Odyssey *and the* Iliad. 1987.
Stanford, W. B. *The Ulysses Theme.* 1954.

WWW   See *World Literature in the 21st Century* at bedfordstmartins.com/worldlit for information on the relevance of Homer to today's world.

MEDIA RESOURCES

VIDEO

A Critical Guide to the Odyssey
31 min., 1999 (Films for the Humanities & Sciences)
It is said that every road movie and novel about a defining journey owes a debt to *The Odyssey*. This imaginative program uses the poem's division into groupings of books as a framework to allow Dr. Tom Winnifrith, of Warwick University; Dr. Douglas Cairns, of Leeds University; and Ken Dowden, senior lecturer at Birmingham University, to analyze the oral tradition and key elements of the story line. Readings and dramatizations from *The Odyssey* enhance the discussion of recurrent themes, characterization, relationships, morals, and the cumulative effect of the ten-year journey in shaping and seasoning Odysseus.

The Perilous Voyage: Homer's Odyssey
90 min., 1997 (Films for the Humanities & Sciences)
A brilliant and warm, easily accessible and classically correct introduction to — or review of — what has been called, variously, the first novel or the first comedy. Sir Michael Hordern, dressed as Homer, speaks the beautifully translated text, sometimes facing the camera as the bard reciting his epic, most often as the narrator of the wonderful illustrations that heighten comprehension of the action as well as of those poetic touches, like the wine-dark sea, that characterize Homer. The six programs cover all the main episodes; each is fifteen-minutes long. The series includes The One-Eyed Cyclops, Circe the Sorceress, Scylla and Charybdis, The Country of the Dead, The Homecoming, and The Slaying of the Suitors.

Ulysses
104 min., 1954 (IMDB)
This adaptation of Homer's *The Odyssey* stars Kirk Douglas as the seafaring hero Ulysses. Doomed to journey aimlessly across the sea after the Trojan War, Ulysses battles many adversaries on his way home from war to his wife Penelope, where he must meet and master a final challenge.

The Odyssey
32 min., 1989 (Educational Video Network)
Retrace the steps of Odysseus to the sites of his adventures and gain insights about Homer's epic as we explore the world of Greek heroes.

The Odyssey
173 min., 1997 (Library Video Company)
Homer's classic epic poem about the travels of Odysseus after his conquest of Troy is brought to the small screen. This is a made-for-TV production starring Armand Assante, Greta Scacchi, and Isabella Rosellini.

O Brother, Where Art Thou?
106 min., 2000 (IMDB)
Loosely based on *The Odyssey,* this movie deals with the adventures of Everett Ulysses McGill and his companions Delmar and Pete in 1930s Mississippi and stars George Clooney, John Turturro, and Tim Blake Nelson.

WEB SITES

The Homer Homepage
www.dc.peachnet.edu/~shale/humanities/literature/world_literature/homer.html
A fantastic resource, this site provides users with links to e-texts of *The Iliad*, *The Odyssey*, and the Homeric Hymns as well as an audio recording of a reading from *The Iliad*. It also offers links to a large number of Web sites devoted to Homer and the Homeric world, teacher's guides, maps of ancient Greece, literary criticism, images, and various works of art and culture with connections and allusions to Homer.

Homer's The Iliad and The Odyssey
Library.thinkquest.org/19300/data/homer.htm
Created by students, this site contains links to the complete e-texts of Homer's works. Users will also find links to historical information on Homer and his world and background on the myths in Homer's works as well as a study guide to *The Odyssey*.

Homer's The Odyssey Resources on the Web
www.robotwisdom.com/jaj/homer/odyssey.html
This site includes summaries of the episodes in *The Odyssey*. It also provides several translations of Homer's tale for comparative study. Other helpful elements include a guide to pronunciation and several links to Homer sites.

AUDIO

The Odyssey
2:45 hrs. (Caedmon Audio)
There is nothing else in Western literature quite like *The Odyssey*. Possibly the first and most influential literary work ever recorded, it is the epic tale of one man's incredible courage and perseverance against all odds. Gifted British actor Anthony Quayle brings Odysseus and his adventures to vivid life.

The Odyssey
8 tapes, 11:25 hrs. (Blackstone Audiobooks)
So much has been written about Homer that the legendary blind bard might just as well himself be included among the great pantheon of Greek gods about whom he wrote so well. *The Odyssey* is concerned with Odysseus's difficulties in returning home after the Trojan War, which was won by the Greeks. It is unquestionably one of the great epic masterpieces of Western literature and a storehouse of Greek folklore and myth. With its wise and always magnificent hero and its romantic theme, it has established itself as perhaps the greatest adventure story of all time.

In the World: Changing Gods: From Religion to Philosophy (p. 769)

In this section, students will be reading short texts wherein content has been compressed by the editors. Their understanding of the arguments presented by each of these texts will be crucial. Ask them to summarize each text in a sentence or two before discussion so that all of the students can understand why these particular passages were chosen and what their significance is in relation to the transformation from religious beliefs to philosophical practice. Also, because these texts are from varying regions and backgrounds, it will be very helpful, even if it may seem obvious to some students, to review the origin of each passage and author and when it was written. It may be a good exercise to have students name other authors from the same time period and region in order to test their overall comprehension of the texts they have read so far.

Since this section deals mostly with a shift in thinking from the religiously inspired or myth-based to the rational or philosophical-based, students should be encouraged to brainstorm the consequences of such a transformation. Since kings and rulers in a religious system can be appointed by gods and goddesses, rulers who have come to power during a period of rational inquiry must find alternative ways of authenticating their mandate to rule. It is likely that students will notice that political changes accompany changes in religious belief. Furthermore, economic and social changes will both cause rational inquiry (like during the Age of Exploration or in Hellenistic Greece) and be the result of new progress in philosophy (like during the Arab invasion of Western Europe). Not all transformations will be complete, however. For example, Socrates still makes use of obscure myth in order to prove philosophical points. Many philosophers continue to believe that the soul is divine even if they refute the idea or the origins of the gods. Other systems, such as Buddhism, refuse to speculate on divine subjects but rather focus on the human condition. Many texts are concerned with answers for human suffering. Students should be encouraged to research contemporaneous events in India and China that led to dialogues about misery. Finally, students might want to consider the birth of religions after this period of philosophical inquiry, such as Islam and Christianity, and how they were influenced by the work of pagan intellectuals.

TEXT & CONTEXT

The initial text is from the Rig Veda, the earliest of the selected passages and one of the earliest completely expressed religious doctrines. They are written over a span of 2,500 years (from 1000 B.C.E. to 1500 C.E.). Students should outline each of the numbered arguments, beginning with the first section, on questions of being. Note that, despite being the poetic format of a hymn (like the Proverbs), it does not address any gods. Furthermore, although the Indian pantheon was full of many deities, this passage addresses a unique Oneness, something students will see present in many of the texts.

The *Majjhima Nikaya* or "Medium-length Discourses" were written largely in the sixth century B.C.E. It is the second *nikaya* in a larger canon of Buddhist literature, the *Pali Canon*. It consists of 152 discourses on Buddha and the nature of religion. The practice of Buddhism involves studying many of these sutras, or short passages intended to illustrate problems facing the novice. As the passage in the book (Sutra 63) shows, the religion is highly practical. Instead of being concerned with various theogonies and superstitious practices, it outlines a method for living, meant to relieve the practitioner from suffering and misery.

All that survives of Heraclitus is a collection of aphorisms in the format of highly condensed and often paradoxical sentiments. It has been theorized that this is the original format of Heraclitus's teachings, since, from the earliest reference, he is known as "the dark one" for the impenetrability of his statements. Students should concern themselves with trying to understand the consequences of each statement. In either Greek or English, these aphorisms are linguistically easy to comprehend. However, it is less clear what is intended. For example, "You cannot step twice into the same river, for other waters and yet others go ever flowing on" (no. 21) sounds like a description of a physical phenomenon. However, it could also be a comment on human behavior, or natural phenomena beyond water.

Sextus Empiricus (160–210 C.E.) was a Greek physician who lived in most of the major Mediterranean cities of his time: Rome, Athens, and Alexandria. His main work is the *Hypotyposes*, or "*Outlines*," which sets out to defend the skeptic position and attack the dogmatic position. The school of the skeptics was founded by Pyrrho of Elis (c. 375–260 B.C.E.), about the time of Alexander the Great's death. The skeptics believed that old creeds and superstitions could not support people living in the politically tumultuous world following the end of Alexander's empire. Instead, they thought that humans should try to achieve *atarxia*, or "unshakeability." Ataraxia was not happiness or pleasure or freedom from misery but rather a kind of apathy toward all things good or bad. To the skeptics, it was preferable to desire nothing than to desire something good and not achieve it. The dogmatic philosophies, on the other hand, were concerned with a moral path that disciples would have to follow in order to achieve some kind of happiness. Many competing philosophies fell under this rubric, including the nonbelieving Xenophanes and Heraclitus as well as Socrates. Aristotle (384–322 B.C.E.) studied largely physical phenomena. The majority of his works attempt to describe the world around him in a schematic fashion, by labeling and categorizing species of animal and even human personality types. He had numerous scientific and philosophical beliefs, but it is important to recognize that his ethical beliefs stressed the virtue of the "the Mean," or trying not to go to either of two extremes. He also believed that bodily goods (health, money, pleasure) were part of the human goal or happiness. In Sextus Empiricus's work, *Hypotyposes*, the last two books (called *Adversus Dogmaticos*) — which were against the dogmatic philosophies — contain summaries of those philosophies, including that of Aristotle on the origins of religion. Aristotle says that religion explains either (1) events that affect the soul or (2) natural phenomena. Students should be encouraged to discuss differences between these two causes of religion and whether or not Aristotle was oversimplifying or overcomplicating the reasons for religion — is (1) the same as (2) or are there even more causes of religion?

Euhemerus (c. 340–280 B.C.E.) wrote a travel novel, *Sacred History*, which has been summarized by Diodorus Siculus and Eusebius. In it, he describes an imaginary voyage to a group of islands in the Indian Ocean, particularly Panchaea, where such great gods as Zeus had been real human rulers. Earlier authors had written of similarly imaginary utopias, including Homer, who wrote of the Phaeacians in *The Odyssey*. It is difficult to interpret Euhemerus's purpose. On one hand, he may have believed, like others before him, such as Heraclitus, that there were no gods to obey and that myth was distorted history. On the other hand, the rulers of his lifetime received worship for their services and were turned into gods upon their deaths. Therefore, the work could be read as an atheist and rationalizing account of the Greek pantheon or as support for ruler-cults of his time. As always, students should be aware that literature is often affected by changes in the political climate. Quotes and summaries of Euhemerus survive, curiously, through the work of early Christian writers and church historians such as Eusebius, John Malalas, and Eustathius. The early Christians, unable to reject many of the philosophical tenets of the pagans, tried to explain how the Greeks and the Romans may have strayed from the orthodox monotheism of Judeo-Christianity.

Lucretius, whose strict atheism was anathema to the Christians, was a materialist philosopher. Cicero, the famous Latin orator, called this book "most learned." His only surviving work *On the Nature of Things (De rerum natura)* is in six books. The first book introduces his main principle: that nothing is born from nothing, and thus the universe is both eternal and can never be born again. The second book describes the construction of the universe and the nature and movement of atoms, which are the unbreakable (*a-temno* means "not-to-break") and basic unit of all matter. This book also describes *clinamen*, or the slight variation on motion that leads to random behavior of atoms. The third book describes the human soul and the nature of the soul (*anima*) and the mind (*animus*). In the fourth book, the human passions are discussed. All bodies emit thin atomic outlines of themselves, which he calls *simulacra*, and these cause sight, hearing, and smell. When the simulacra penetrate other bodies, they can arouse the emotion of love but also can lead to sensations in dreams. The fifth and sixth books describe the world and the evolution of language and society. The book ends with a description of meteorological phenomena and a description of the plague based on an account in the Greek historian Thucydides' work, *History of the Peloponnesian War*. Like the skeptics, Lucretius believed that men feared death and, for this reason, were led to immoral behavior or passions. He tried to teach men not to fear death and thus only to live honestly and healthily until death came instead of trying to avoid it by becoming rich or powerful. In the third book, he gives a description of the underworld, making each prominent horrible monster a metaphor for a real human behavior in his world. As a result, he paints an interesting picture of Roman life at the beginning of the first century B.C.E.

Philo Judaeus (20 B.C.E.–41 C.E.) lived between three worlds: the classical Greek one in which he was educated, the political and economic prominence of Caesar Augustus's Rome at the turn of the millenium, and the traditions of his Jewish faith. He is part of the same tradition that translated the Old Testament into Greek (called the *Septuagint*), and he wrote a commentary on the first five books of the Old Testament. Always seeking to describe the Jewish faith in Greek philosophical terms, he turned often to the natural philosophers, such as Pythagoras, in order to make his work seem more "scientific." But like others in his generation, he looked up to the work of Plato. The Neoplatonists were interested in resurrecting Socrates' ideas that the soul was immortal and that there was but one divinity (i.e., the idea of Oneness). To many Christian, Islamic, and Jewish theologians, Socrates' teachings seemed to prophecy the philosophy and nature of their own religions. In the Renaissance, Dante was inspired by Neoplatonic thought, which mixed Socrates' philosophy with Pythagoreanism and other philosophical systems. Students may want to read ahead to the extracts from Plato to get a better idea of his work and to compare them to the passages of Philo quoted in the text.

IN THE CLASSROOM

HISTORY

Have a student read the quote of Lewis Mumford (p. 772) aloud. When Mumford says "With this [change of religion to philosophy] a new kind of person and a new kind of community took form," he appears to see this transformation as the cause for the subsequent centuries: the rise and fall of Athens, the Roman Empire, and the advent of Christianity and Islam. However, he does not place much emphasis on the historical cycles that might have led to this shift in beliefs. It will be useful to look at a comparative timeline of world history during these periods. Confucius, who lived in the "Spring and Autumn" period of Chinese history, saw his country fragmented into tiny states, each state full of factions at war with each other. The historian Herodotus notes not only the rise and prominence of Athens during the Persian War (in which the dramatic poet Aeschylus fought and that Heraclitus saw) but also the beginning of its strife with rival Sparta. The war between Athens and Sparta, according to Thucydides, was the largest ever fought, both sides coming near to disaster many times. The Athenians lost their great general Pericles, put to death the philosopher Socrates, suffered under a great plague (described later by Thucydides and Lucretius), and were eventually taken over by Philip of Macedon and his son Alexander the Great. It is difficult for us to imagine, but, in these extremely trying times, many schools of philosophy were developed in Athens, and literature — especially the great tragedies and comedies — was strong. Lucretius lived during a time of internal struggle in Rome and described many battle scenes full of gore. Philo Judaeus saw his world transformed by the strong Roman rule of the East. It seems that just as this transformation from religious to philosophical systems changed the course of history, so also did the then current events in history and the development of empires help to cause this transformation in the first place.

Discussion

1. Historiography, or writing about history, like philosophy, often tries to point to the causes of things. Many of our texts (e.g., Lucretius, the Rig Veda, Philo) discuss the creation of the world. Why is this of such fundamental importance? What historical events might drive a search for answers about creation?

2. How does a change in governance also change a traditional religious system? Have students think of modern nation-states that have a strong religious component. Why is religion valued so highly in strongly democratic states, such as the United States? What changed in the political landscape of the world these authors lived in that caused philosophy to come about?

3. The story of the arrow in our extract from the Majjhima Nikaya comes to the conclusion that religious life does not depend on the immortal life. Instead, it focuses on ever-present human suffering. Thinking of other philosophical systems, such as Daoism or Christian philosophy, discuss why religion would be concerned with the human condition. What does Heraclitus mean when he says that without suffering there would be neither gods nor men (no. 27)? How does this paradox manifest itself in an atheist philosophical system?

4. According to Sextus Empiricus, Aristotle describes two reasons for religion: to explain events that affect the soul and to explain natural phenomena. Does this imply that the soul is necessary in order to have religion? If so, can philosophy satisfactorily explain the nature of the soul? What is unsuitable about natural philosophy (i.e., science) that it cannot address the human condition? Or can it?

Groups

1. Have pairs of students introduce each of the texts for ten minutes, making a handout or PowerPoint presentation with key words and philosophical concepts as well as giving an overview of the historical and geographic context of that passage.

2. In groups, have students create a comparative timeline showing progress in art, music, literature, and historical events for the texts in this section and the regions and time periods in which they were written.

Writing

Ask students to write a short paper in response to one or more of the following:

1. At the end of the selection of Lucretius's Book Four, he describes some aspects of Roman life. What tone does he use? Does he speak approvingly of the rich man who owns a country mansion and a town house? What kind of picture does he paint about Roman life? Do any of the other texts describe the world in which they were written? How critical are they?

2. What other major historical events have led to a change in religious or philosophical beliefs? How was this shift similar to or different from what we read about in the selected passages?

Connections

Many of the passages we are dealing with are concerned with some kind of Oneness. While it is mathematically and physically convenient to speak of a unique divinity with special and irreproducible characteristics (which ostensibly explains why we don't see any of them), it is significantly different from the polytheistic systems of Hesiod or traditional societies. Students should be encouraged to search for connections along the line of this Oneness as expressed in sections 2–4 of the Rig Veda, Heraclitus (19 and 120), and Philo, as opposed to the strict atheism of Lucretius and possibly Euhemerus. Other similarities and differences can be found in the forms of writing used to express the philosophical tenets, some of which are surprisingly conservative while others, such as the dialogue, are novel.

Discussion

1. Is monotheism innately more prone to philosophical inquiry than polytheism? Are the philosophical systems of traditional cultures that believe in animism — that all things are endowed with a divine spirit — any less valid than those that believe there is only one divine spirit? What might be the natural philosophical consequences of a monotheistic system?

2. Many of the texts we are concerned with express language in a paradoxical fashion (consider, for instance, the first line of the Dao De Jing [Tao Te Ching], "The Tao [Dao] that can be told is not the eternal Tao. The name that can be named is not the eternal name" [p. 772]). What is the relationship between language and reality? Keep in mind that many of the Athenian philosophical schools began as a means to train young lawyers who wanted to learn how to speak in clever ways (like the Sophists). Why do you suppose that the word for *reason, story, explanation*, and *word* is the same (*logos*) in Greek? What does this mean for our texts?

3. Different works take different forms. Some, like Lucretius and the Rig Veda, take the traditional form of a hymn. Lucretius even addresses the goddess of love and beauty, Venus, in his poem. However, his work states that there are no divinities in the world. Both Plato and the Majjhima Nikaya take the form of dialogues. Euhemerus wrote a novel. Why did these authors choose the form that they did for expressing their philosophical systems?

Groups

1. Have students set out to classify the texts into various categories of thinking, much as Sextus Empiricus does in his work. Students may add to these lists with suggestions of their own. It may also help students to learn the various philosophical schools of the time and how they are distinct. Review terms like *materialism, natural philosophy*, and *euhemerism* beforehand.

Writing

Ask students to write a short paper in response to one or more of the following:

1. Xenophanes, Heraclitus, and Euhemerus, among others, recognize that people tend to make gods anthropomorphic, that is, in the shape of mankind. Even Philo speculates on this. Is this a purely Western phenomenon? Students might consider looking at visual evidence from traditional societies that believe in animism. Are their gods also anthropomorphic? What do our non-Western texts say about this?

BEYOND THE CLASSROOM

RESEARCH & WRITING

1. Euhemerus sets his text far away on an imaginary island near Sri Lanka. Lucan, Shakespeare, Montesquieu, and C. S. Lewis also employed this technique to criticize their native lands. What is the effect in the case of Euhemerus? What do you suppose his purpose was in creating Panachea?

2. Besides changes in economy and governance, what other historical events may lead a culture to change from religious to philosophical systems?

Project

1. Natural philosophy is essential ancient science. Writers such as Aristotle were interested in describing the natural world, as was Lucretius. What are the consequences of advances in science? Use the Archimedes Project Web site listed under Further Readings to do additional research on the history of science.

FURTHER READING

Archimedes Project. Harvard University, the Natural Science Foundation and the Deutsche Forschungsgemeinschaft. 2002. http:// archimedes.fas.harvard.edu.

Barnes, J. A. *The Presocratic Philosophers.* 1979.

Blackburn, Simon. *Oxford Dictionary of Philosophy.* 2000.

Burnyeat, M., ed. *The Skeptical Tradition.* 1983.

Edgerton, Franklin. *The Beginnings of Indian Philosophy: Selections from the Rig Veda, Atharva Veda, Upanisads, and Mahabharata.* 1965.

Ergardt, Jan T. *Faith and Knowledge in Early Buddhism: An Analysis of the Contextual Structures of an Arahant-Formula in the Majjhima-Nikay.* 1977.

Sambursky, S. *The Physical World of the Greeks.* 1956.

Sandmel, F. *Philo of Alexandria: An Introduction.* 1979.

Vernant, J. P. *The Origins of Greek Thought.* 1962.

MEDIA RESOURCES

WEB SITES

The Catholic Encyclopedia
www.newadvent.org/cathen/
This online encyclopedia is a useful resource for biographical and historical information; it has the added benefit of embedded hotlinks as gateways to further information.

Cosmos of the Ancients
www.stenudd.com/myth/
This interesting site discusses the ancient's view on myth and cosmology; in addition it provides background information on Euhemerus, Plato, and Aristotle.

Internet Encyclopedia of Philosophy
www.utm.edu/research/iep/
This is a very useful online reference that provides in-depth information on philosophies and individual philosophers. Check here for more information on Euhemerus, Lucretius, Philo Judeas, Aristotle, and Plato.

The Rig Veda
campus.northpark.edu/history/WebChron/India/RigVeda.html
This page, created at North Park University, looks at the Rig Veda in its historical context.

Sacred Texts
www.sacred-texts.com/index.htm
This wonderful site provides complete versions of sacred texts from around the world. Under Hinduism is found the Rig Veda; there are also many Buddhist texts and resources available here.

SAPPHO (p. 791)

WWW   For a quiz on the poetry of Sappho, see *World Literature Online* at bedfordstmartins.com/worldlit.

There are many Sapphos. There is Sappho the bookish schoolmistress, her pupils collected about her. There is Sappho the twentieth-century lesbian and feminist figurehead (not in the geographical sense). There is Sappho the beautiful and tragic and the Byzantine Sappho who is dark and ugly. There is Sappho the author of banned books and Sappho the muse. There is Sappho the inspiration of philosophers and Sappho the inspiration of pornographers. The myths about Sappho outweigh the facts. One myth about her (being a married woman) has her throwing herself off a cliff for the love of Phaon, a young man; another is that she looked rather masculine and was fiercely jealous; and yet another is about all the love affairs she had with her female students. Anacreon, Plato, Ovid, Byzantine clerics and Catholic popes (who banned her), Swinburne, Lawrence Durrell, Rossetti, Peter Green, among others, all had a tale about Sappho. But the sum of these stories is mostly a testament to the lasting beauty of her poetry, in whatever fragmentary fashion it has been left to us today.

Sappho lived in the last half of the seventh century B.C.E. on the Greek island of Lesbos, which is in the Aegean Sea, only a short ferry's ride from Asia Minor (Turkey). She probably lived in the capital, Mytilene, which was ruled by an unpopular tyrant who was killed in her lifetime. Little else is known about contemporary events she may have witnessed. Lesbos was obviously an important trading island, a kind of Singapore-like stopover for ships from Egypt and Asia Minor on their way to the Greek mainland. Archeological evidence points to a bustling and wealthy international community with a genuine appreciation for the arts. The government was a tyranny, which can best be compared to rule by mob boss. A sole individual held sway on the island in all decisions, and his word was enforced by loyal thugs and family members. At his death, there would be a struggle for power and, really, at any moment, coups d'état were a possibility. This was the world in which much of seventh-century Greece lived. Athens and Sparta were still not powerhouses, and Asia did not yet present a major threat to Greece. Artists of the time were firmly grounded in Homer and Hesiod and probably Archilochus, the first Greek lyric poet, who lived about fifty years before Sappho. The earliest records indicate that Sappho was married; her daughter Cleis, her brother (who works in Egypt), and her mother play prominent roles in her poems. In fifth-century comedy, she was usually paired with unlikely male lovers. Since a large part of her poems have to do with love and marriage, it is no wonder that stories about Sappho center on her love affairs with both men and women. There is a tendency to romanticize female authors; male authors might idealize and fall in love with the muse, objectify her somewhat, and spin a story compatible with their own erotic desires.

The debate about Sappho derives from a poem by Anacreon, from the generation after her, who wrote poems of a variety of genres, often about the *symposium*, a cultural institution something like a soiree, where a prominent person invites his good friends along for some wine and music and, hopefully, a night with high-class prostitutes. In this poem he writes:

> But this girl from that splendid island,
> Lesbos — she's got beautiful skin —
> She doesn't want to be my girl.
> Instead, she gapes at another
> Girl. (Anacreon fr. 5D)

Standing next to the poems of Sappho in which she swoons before her female companions, it is easy to suppose that Anacreon is making reference to Sappho. Who else could be from Lesbos? Furthermore, in order to be clever and sophisticated, literature of the symposium, when not talking about itself, talks about other pieces of literature. So begins the interpretation of Sappho as a lesbian, something that the post-Classical world — despite Ovid's retelling of her love affair with Phaon, a young man of Lesbos — took for fact.

But Sappho's world, and the women in it, was rather different from our own. After reading Hesiod's portrayal of Pandora, we imagine that women had no world at all and that they were locked indoors, weaving all day. While this may be true, it turns out that women existed in a very social world, a world often devoid of men until the moment of marriage and sometimes even after marriage. Contemporary scholars have shown that for all the formal ceremonies a man might have to mark stages of his life, women had similar ceremonies, many of them held outside of urban centers or in certain temples, such as the temple of Aphrodite, the goddess of love. These were social spaces in which women shared stories and shared physical bonds and sympathies unavailable to them in the male space. Sappho gives us insight on the language of this world. There is no reason to totally discredit a homoerotic reading of the poetry, only a reason to discredit that homoeroticism as a perversion. The Greeks did not have our hang-ups about same-sex affairs. Homoerotic relationships were encouraged among socially elite males, and some scholars have posited that what we would call "lesbianism" would have been the norm among women as well.

It is more complicated than that, of course. Sappho's poetry was evidently popular enough to leave the enclave of female listeners and was sung in the presence of men. The wedding hymns, for example, "It's no use," and others would have been told in the presence of men. It is no wonder, then, that these are couched in terms that may appear to the reader to be written with such sexually longing language. The complex jealousy of the rival lover in "He is more than a hero" seems just as easily a male sentiment as one from a female. This has to do with the problem of voice in Greek poetry. We are so used to reading experiential poetry from the Romantic Period that we read the "I" and "me" of Greek poetry as emanating from the authors themselves. Greek poetry, though, was really more of a predecessor to the dramatic convention, where we know, as the audience, that when the actor says "I *blah blah blah*" or "*blah blah blah* me," we know that they are speaking in character. Do we *know* whether or not Sappho was speaking in character or in person? No, but we get a picture of archaic poetry as being a mixture of these. There were popular themes. Like country music, the abandoned lover and unlucky guy — fictitious or real — were both hits. If we had a chance to interview Sappho, she might very well say that she was "inspired by her own life story" or that she simply followed the right conventions. It is undeniable, however, that the unsurpassed beauty of her language and her simple, transparent descriptions and tormented emotions are a persuasive song for the reader.

In "Don't ask me what to wear," Sappho tries to console her daughter, Cleis, because she doesn't have a nice headdress for her to wear. This segues into a description of what her mother wore and then back to the subject of her daughter, whose hair is too light for a headdress but is just right for flowers. It is a poem written in circular style, about three generations of women. In this sense, it may be a classic example of poetry intended for a purely female audience, since it speaks of traditions being passed down from mother to daughter. This quality gives it a sentimental touch, somewhat like the movie *How to Make an American Quilt* (1995). Cleis is also the subject of "Sleep, darling" but not the addressee. Again, the value of a daughter is not something we find in the male poets, so we can presume this to be something unique. The fact it was preserved, however, means that the quality of the poem was perceived to be no less than the *epithalamiums*, or wedding hymns, such as "Lament for a Maidenhead." "It's no use" is a poem addressed to her mother that is very similar to another poem by Sappho addressed to the goddess of love, perhaps on the same issue of unrequited love.

"You know the place: then" is one of the oldest surviving bits of Sappho's poetry to survive. It was inscribed on a pot from the third century B.C.E. and is one of the hymns that Sappho had written to Aphrodite. The audience of the hymns and their relevance to genuine religious worship is uncertain. However, it has the traditional form of the Greek hymn. The first line is missing, which should have addressed the goddess and explained her genealogy (in Hesiod, she is born out of the sea-foam formed from the cut-off penis of Ouranos, the sky god, that was floating in the water, although there are other accounts of how she was born). The next lines list the usual haunts of the goddess, Crete and Cyprus, and then invite Aphrodite to join the poet and her companions at a holy grove dedicated to the goddess. The description of and the invitation to the grove, however, mirror invitations that poets give to companions and other artists to join them for mutual inspiration and music making.

"Lament for a Maidenhead" and "I have had not one word from her" are both part of the genre of wedding hymns. Rather than belonging to a wedding union ceremony, as we might suppose, they may have belonged to other rituals related to the main wedding ceremony. Dances that were set to music, during which girls sang (or one particular girl sang), were common, and several examples have survived besides these poems by Sappho. Essentially, these poems are the words to songs that were danced to, in which maidens declare the beauty (often in erotic terms) of the lead girl, and then, after she is led away, how much they miss her. It is also possible that the girls performed the dance after she had already been led away to be married or after she would be simply too old to be part of that group of girls anymore. Some of the feelings of "He is more than a hero" seem to be part of a similar genre, but the individualistic aspect of it, as opposed to the references to groups in the other poems, make it unique.

"He is more than a hero" is probably Sappho's most famous poem. Catullus produced a Latin translation of it (see p. 1172) that toyed with some of its ideas. One ancient Greek literary critic (perhaps Longinus in a work entitled *On the Sublime*) wrote, "Is it not wonderful, how she summons at the same time soul, body, hearing, tongue, sight, color, all as though they had wandered off apart from herself? She feels contradictory sensations, freezes and burns, thinks unreasonably. . . . She wants to display not a single emotion, but a whole congress of emotions." A lot of affects, unfortunately, don't translate. For example, in the Greek, the gender of the people she is looking at is kept quite vague — not that we don't know that it is a man and a woman, but we cannot tell who she says she sees, the man talking to the woman, the woman, the man. The Greek, translated literally, begins "seems like a hero, that one, whoever opposite you, sits, and to you full sweetly talking he listens closely, laughing, passionately, *that* makes — ah — my heart below my breasts beat fast." The problem is that, in English, the "you" is quite transparent; in Greek it isn't. Another interesting effect is that when Sappho says she cannot speak when seeing her, she uses words that have all vowels, something never done in Greek poetry, producing a broken effect, sounding something like the stuttering "*ioloss-A E A YI E*." The word that Sappho uses for the rumbling in her ears is sounds like *rrrrrumble*. Sappho thus transforms the physical symptoms of love into the sounds and syllables of Greek poetry and music.

TEXT & CONTEXT

There were four hundred years between Sappho's lifetime and the compilation of her works into nine books (completed in the third century, probably), which we know were obtainable in the first century B.C.E. (Cicero, the great Roman orator and statesman pur-chased a copy). Theoretically, she would have continued to be a school text, would have been extracted into anthologies, and should have survived to the ninth century C.E., at which point either she would have been kept in the format of nine books, or perhaps a "best of" volume would have been produced, which would survive to us today. That is the usual story for poems in ancient Greece but not for Sappho's work. It is remarkable that she survived intact in nine books (that is, nine rolls of papyrus or approximately one-third of *The Iliad*) for so long, and it means that her poetry was immensely popular. Most of what survives of Sappho's works dates from this collection period, since Sappho survives in fragments of papyrus on which they are written. The majority of these pieces of papyrus come from Egypt sometime after the death of Alexander the Great.

What happened afterwards was twofold: Anything that survived into a durable format was burned in the fourth century C.E. at Constantinople by Christians who interpreted her poetry as being pornography and homosexual (which went against Church tenets). What poetry survived apparently made it beyond the ninth- and tenth-century process of copying the old texts into the sturdy Byzantine format that most Greek writing went into. The reason we can tell this is because of late reference to her, and, also, her books were again ordered to be burnt in the eleventh century C.E. by Pope Gregory VII, probably about the time they were gaining revival. Sappho is again silent until the sixteenth century, though there was so little of her work by this time that people wrote poems and attributed them to her. Not until the nineteenth and twentieth century did a renewed effort begin in reconstructing the writings of Sappho. She has since become a spokeswoman for many causes — from feminism to gay and lesbian literature to efforts against book banning and book burning.

IN THE CLASSROOM

I. POET OF HER TIMES

Since poetry is such an aural experience, students should spend some time reading the poems aloud, experimenting with reading methods, and even rewriting the poems in their own words (sometimes the job of the translator) to try to make sense of them. Sappho's imagery is particularly vivid. It is worthwhile to resort to the five senses: what is she smelling, seeing, tasting, touching, and hearing? Mary Barnard's poetry also tries to capture the speed of Sappho's poems — her rapid changes of emotions and how Sappho loses her way some-times and changes the subject. Another useful avenue for discussion will be the issue of gen-der and desire and how students interpret the poems in light of the productive forces behind them, which are usually love and women.

Discussion

1. What are Sappho's feelings about motherhood? What kind of mother does she think she is? In "Don't ask me what to wear," how does she compare the relationship between her and her daughter with that between her and her mother?

2. What might the meaning of the trampled hyacinth in "Lament for a Maidenhead"? What about the quince-apple? About whom are the speakers talking?

3. Sappho often compares things to plants. What are the characteristics she uses most? What is particular about plants and nature that makes her think of love?

Connections

1. Refer to Homer's *The Iliad*, Book Eighteen (p. 363) on the ancient Greek wedding cere-mony portrayed on the shield of Achilles. Does this help you to understand the cir-

cumstances under which Sappho's wedding hymns were performed? Describe the ancient Greek wedding, and imagine how Sappho's works might be employed in the rituals.

2. Look at Catullus's "He is changed to a god he who looks on her" (p. 1172). What does Catullus alter in the translation? What effect does that have? Does knowing that Catullus is a man change the way this poem is read, or does it change your impressions of Sappho's poem?

3. Read Li Bai's "Ch'ang-Kan Village Song" (Book 2), and contrast and compare the point of view, emotions, and sense of anticipation between this piece and Sappho's wedding hymns.

Groups

1. Have students break up into small groups and try to rewrite the poems of Sappho in their own words. This is often a difficult task. Tell them to concentrate on reproducing Sappho's descriptions and reactions to her environment.

Writing

Ask students to write a short paper in response to one or more of the following:

1. Sappho's reaction to love in many of her poems is very physical. Citing the text, show in what ways her response to passion evokes a response in her body.

2. Compare and contrast "Lament for a Maidenhead" with "In the wilds there is a dead doe" from the *Book of Songs* (p. 1579). Even though these poems are separated by time and region, does reading "In the wilds" help your understanding or give you a different interpretation of "Lament for a Maidenhead"? How?

3. What are the differences and similarities between Sappho's impression of women and Hesiod's in the Pandora episodes (pp. 269 and 272)? How might Hesiod have interpreted Sappho's view of the world of women?

BEYOND THE CLASSROOM

RESEARCH & WRITING

1. Why is Sappho's sexual orientation such an issue for modern readers? How do her poems differ, in terms of addressee, from other poems of the Greek world? Who is missing in her poems? Does that affect the way we read her poetry?

2. Read Aristophanes' *Lysistrata* (p. 1049). What is Aristophanes' impression of a community of women, and how does he make their situation comic? In what ways does this differ from Sappho's more sentimental view?

Project

1. There were several female poets of ancient Greece, and much of their poetry survives (for example, that of Corinna, Myrtis, Telesilla, Anyte, Praxilla and Erinna). Research and find translations of their poems (the book by Snyder in the bibliography will help). Why, perhaps, was Sappho considered superior to these poets? What might they share in common? What are some differences?

WWW For additional information on Sappho and annotated Web links, see *World Literature Online* at bedfordstmartins.com/worldlit.

FURTHER READING

Bremmer, J. *From Sappho to de Sade.* 1989.
Burnett, Anne Pippin. *Three Archaic Poets: Archilochus, Alcaeus, Sappho.* 1983.
DeJean, Joan E. *Fictions of Sappho, 1546–1937.* 1989.
Duban, Jeffrey M. *Ancient and Modern Images of Sappho: Translations and Studies in Archaic Greek Love Lyric.* 1983.
Page, D. L. *Sappho and Alcaeus.* 1955.
Rayor, Diane J. *Sappho's Lyre: Archaic Lyric and Women Poets of Ancient Greece.* 1991.
Rissman, Leah. *Love as War: Homeric Allusion in the Poetry of Sappho.* 1983.
Segal, Charles. *Aglaia: The Poetry of Alcman, Sappho, Pindar, Bacchylides, and Corinna.* 1998.
Snyder, Jane. *The Woman and the Lyre: Women Writers in Classical Greece and Rome.* 1989.
Williamson, M. *Sappho's Immortal Daughters.* 1995.

MEDIA RESOURCES

VIDEO

Greek Lyric Poetry
31 min., 1962 (Insight Media)
An examination of the rhythm and poetic imagery characteristic of Greek lyric poetry, this video features a dramatization of a lyric chorus led by actor John Neville. It explores the works of Callimachus, Sappho, Simonides, Pindar, and Aeschylus.

WEB SITES

The Academy of American Poets — Sappho
www.poets.org/poets/poets.cfm?prmID+327
Read a brief biography of the poet at this site.

The Divine Sappho
Classicpersuasion.org/pw/sappho/
This user-friendly site includes a first-line index and e-texts of Sappho's poems in translation. Also provided are a biography of the poet and links to several secondary works.

Sappho
www.temple.edu/classics/sappho.html
Part of the Temple University Classics Home Page, this site offers a helpful selection of links to background material on Sappho and her age. Included are images, a bibliography of works by and about Sappho, biographical information, and links to pages about Aphrodite, a major figure in Sappho's poetry.

Tufts Hellenic Society — Sappho
www.tufts.edu/org/hellenic/kazazis/Sappho.html
Read a short biography of Sappho at this site.

AESCHYLUS, *Agamemnon* and *The Eumenides* (p. 798)

WWW   For a quiz on *The Oresteia*, see *World Literature Online*
        at bedfordstmartins.com/worldlit.

One of the most unique legacies of Greece is its tragedies, the main tradition being associated most closely with Athens in the fifth century B.C.E. The tragic stage was not paralleled by Rome. Other genres, like the novel, became of critical importance and eclipsed classical Greek tragedy. Before your students can delve into the text — not only one of the hardest things to read in Greek but also challenging to read in English — they will need to know a few things about the ancient Greek theater. First, there were set dates on which the dramas were to be performed, either the "Greater Dionysia" or the "Lenaia," both festivals in honor of the god Dionysus. During the festival, some women might have carried phalluses on their head, and a giant statue of Dionysus would be set up in the theater. Very little is actually known about the theater itself. Later stone theaters survive — one such famous example is in Ephesis — but the theaters in which the plays of Aeschylus and Euripides were performed were made out of wood and intended to be used only twice a year. Apparently, people were required to attend the theater, and not everybody enjoyed it. Prominent political persons were placed up front, women (if they went at all) were in the back. It is not clear exactly how much one might be able to hear. There was just a flute that played along with the singing actor. The stage was sparse at best. A set of doors existed (this is certainly true for *Agamemnon*), and there were passages for the chorus to enter and exit on either side of the stage. In front of the stage was either a rectangular or circular area where a chorus danced and sang the chorus parts. Above the stage may have been a balcony where gods stood when they spoke.

We know so little of the visual and aural aspect of the play, however, that it may be best to focus on a few formal features. There were three actors in total. This meant that only three characters could be on the stage at once and that some of the actors would have to play more than one part. Women were played by men, but since everybody wore somber masks and long robes (as opposed to the giant penises and wool leggings of the satyr plays), it really didn't matter. Tragedy attempts to catch the moment of disaster, so in consequence of that, it only covers a day at most in its dramatic action. To show previous events or foreshadow future events, the chorus could give a long narrative or the actor a long monologue, but the actions itself were confined to a small part. There are three basic types of speech in tragedy. First, there is the monologue, called a *rhesis*, where the speaker gives a long speech. Then, there is the rapid conversation known as *stychomuthia*, literally "one-liners," where lines are traded back and forth between characters. Then, there is whatever goes in between. The chorus can take part in *stychomuthia* with an actor, or it can perform an *ode*, or "song." The formal features of the ode are complicated, but essentially there are three parts to the ode. The makeup of the chorus determines the character of the play. In *Agamemnon*, they are helpless old men; in *The Eumenides*, they are awful revening witch-demons. In the drama itself, there are five parts (1) a *prologue*, a summary of the events leading up to the present moment, (2) *parados*, the entrance of the chorus onto the scene, and then (3) the *episode*, in which characters debate or the crisis begins to unfold. Episodes have intervening (4) *stasimon*, "singing in place," where the choir sings its odes. Finally, at the end of the play there is (5) an *exodus*. There are a number of other formal features scholars have observed among all the plays. One of them is that there is no violence on the stage. (It is interesting to note that the word *obscene* derives from the Greek theater's convention of not showing violence overtly but, rather, having it take place *ob skene*, offstage). When violence does occur, a messenger will come in and report what has just happened. Of course, there are usually screams offstage, as there aren't many tragedies in which nobody dies.

Producing a drama was a little like getting your screenwriting to air on network television. An author like Aeschylus would be paid (after having submitted samples) by a producer to enter the dramatic competition of the Greater Dionysia. The playwright would author a trilogy (three tragedies, like *The Oresteia* by Aeschylus) or a tetralogy (three tragedies and a satyr play concerning a related subject, and about which we know less than we know about tragedy). Then, for six months, a *choregos*, choir trainer, would prepare the dancers and singers to put on the play. The producer paid for everything, and if his drama won, he received — for his 3600 drachma investment — some leaves to put in his hair. After a day of musical competitions, the audience would wake up early in the morning and watch three tragedies, then a satyr play, take a nap, and then watch some comedy. Sometime during that day, they would show everybody the treasury, wheeled out in carts, and they would also parade orphans from the ongoing war with Sparta. One comical writer, Aristophanes, writes that it would have been nice to have been a bird so that you could fly off and get something to eat, find a mistress, or at least go to the bathroom, and then come back whenever you wanted to.

That isn't to say that your students should find the plays equally uninteresting. The mainstream elite in Athens considered the two dramatic festivals to be important social occasions. The study of tragedy was very important to the later history of intellectual development in Greece, and there are many commentaries on them. In particular, later authors modeled the passion of Christ on the tragic victim. Students will need to realize that the experience of watching a tragedy was coupled with the religious overtones of the festival and the important political and national duty that each citizen had to take part in that festival. It is furthermore a great testament to Athenian democracy that the plays that were critical of the government (some tragedies can be thus interpreted) were still allowed to be performed.

TEXT & CONTEXT

Aeschylus (c. 525–456 B.C.E.) was probably born near Eleusis, a district (*deme*) near Athens. Because he fought at Marathon against the Persian invasion, he was considered first a soldier and then a playwright. He composed between seventy and ninety plays, among which were thirteen for which he received first prize at the drama festivals. Aeschylus wrote connected tetralogies. The playwright was innovative in his use of tragic conventions, often employing the latest technology in his productions, like cranes to hold flying actors or gods. More so than his main competitors, Sophocles and Euripides, he believed in the ultimate justice of the gods. His plays attempt to show that human suffering is profound, the gods implacable, and many of them end with a final justice imposed from a divine source.

Agamemnon (p. 806)

The *Oresteia* is the name given to the only complete surviving tragic trilogy. Although the three "Theban plays" by Sophocles, *Oedipus Rex, Oedipus at Colonus*, and *Antigone* are often coupled together in modern performance, they were originally composed and performed in different years. The events of *The Oresteia* begin after the after the fall of Troy, sometime during the end of Odysseus's wanderings. You will no doubt remember that Agamemnon, the king of Argos, is one of the people who Odysseus meets in the underworld. Agamemnon already then speaks of Clytemnestra's brutal murder of himself and Cassandra.

After the fall of Troy, Agamemnon and the other Greek captains divide up the spoils. Cassandra, the princess of Troy who plays but a minor role in *The Iliad* (although Homer calls her the most beautiful of Priam's daughters), falls to Agamemnon. Cassandra was raped by the god Apollo when she was young and then was given the gift of prophecy. However, she was also cursed that nobody would believe anything she says, even if true. A number of legends surround the figure of Cassandra, including a poem from the third century, a long, tragic monologue in her voice, called the *Alexandra* by Lycophron.

When the play opens, Agamemnon is about to return home. The watchman, who is getting tired not only of his watch but of being ruled by Clytemnestra, suddenly spots a beacon light that tells him Agamemnon is returning home after ten years of fighting at Troy. The chorus then launches into a long choral ode and explains what went on before the battle at Troy. When Agamemnon is getting ready to set sail for Troy, the goddess Artemis silences all the winds out of anger for some misdeed of Agamemnon and Meneláos. In order to make the goddess happy, Agamemnon is required to sacrifice one of his daughters, Iphigenia, on the altar. Instead of telling Clytemnestra that he is going to kill their daughter, he tells her to send Iphigenia to be married to Achilles. Agamemnon does the deed and sails to Troy (note that these details are not included in *The Iliad* or *The Odyssey*). Aegisthus, who happens to be Agamemnon's nephew, is left behind and begins to associate with Clytemnestra in Agamemnon's absence. In the course of this strange relationship, Clytemnestra — the more masculine and strong character — takes over and the emasculated and weak Aegisthus (he didn't, after all, go to Troy) plays the part of Clytemnestra's lover and henchman. Together, they plot Agamemnon's murder. The entire play rests on this single action. Agamemnon finally arrives home after the chorus has sung, along with his new mistress, Cassandra. Clytemnestra offers purple carpets for Agamemnon to walk on. The king refuses, knowing that he would appear as being hubristic in the eyes of the gods. But Clytemnestra insists and the king relents, marching to his sure death within the house. It is interesting to view such a powerful man controlled so absolutely by Clytemnestra. Cassandra begins to prophecy Agamemnon's destruction, much to the amazement of the chorus. When Clytemnestra returns, she invites Cassandra in. The young Trojan knows she will die alongside Agamemnon, but she enters in nevertheless. When Aegisthus and Clytemnestra come back out again, their hands bloodied with gore, the chorus cries out in alarm. Although the two rulers believe they have acted justly, the choir claims that there has been a breach of civil liberties, and they do not believe that the murders are over. It is on this note that the play ends.

The middle play, which is not printed in this anthology, is *The Libation Bearers*. The play is given this name because it revolves around a scene of paying honor to the grave of Agamemnon. The action of this play involves the next step of the trilogy. Agamemnon's son, Orestes, and daughter, Electra, take vengeance against their mother and Aegisthus. The cycle of murder does not stop here, however. Clytemnestra's ghost summons up horrible demons, the Eumenides, who avenge matricide by driving the perpetrator insane. *The Eumenides* will be concerned with finding an agreeable and just solution for Orestes.

IN THE CLASSROOM

I. THE PERILS OF RETRIBUTION IN TRAGEDY

After explaining the basic conventions of Greek drama, students should first review the names and places that were important for *The Iliad*, adding to this list Clytemnestra (Agamemnon's wife), Orestes, Iphigenia and Electra (Agamemnon's children), Aegisthus (Clytemnestra's lover, son of Thyestes), Atreus (Agamemnon and Meneláos' father), and Thyestes (Atreus's brother, Aegishtus's father). Be sure and review the plot after the students have read the play so that they understand the main points of crisis: (1) whether it was right for Agamemnon to kill his daughter and obey the goddess, (2) whether it was right for Clytemnestra and Aegisthus to kill Agamemnon and Cassandra, (3) whether or not it was right for Agamemnon to have stepped on the purple carpet, (4) whether or not it was right for Agamemnon to have brought Cassandra home from Troy. Some of these will provide good material for debate and perhaps bring insight into ancient Greek culture. For example, the Greek audience might not find it shocking that Agamemnon brought Cassandra back from Troy, but they did find the fact that Ajax raped Cassandra very alarming (particularly, since — according to various sources — it occurred in a temple of Athene).

Discussion

1. What are the main crises of the play? Does the chorus refer to other crises? How do they view the Trojan War — positively or negatively?

2. How well does this play relate to the events of *The Iliad*? Are there any points at which they diverge?

3. The presence of a chorus differs significantly from how modern plays are written and also from screenplays and movie-script characters. What, if anything, has replaced the presence of the chorus? What role does the chorus serve? Are they mere commentary, the voice of the author, or a separate personality on the stage? Ask students to imagine how the chorus might stand in relation to Clytemnestra or Agamemnon and to demonstrate their role with citations from the text.

4. What does the play say about free choice? Did Agamemnon choose his fate, or did the gods decide for him? If he has no free choice, then what moral lesson can we obtain from this kind of text?

Connections

1. Compare the discussion of Agamemnon's death in *The Odyssey* (Books Four and Eleven) to the events of Aeschylus's *Agamemnon*. Which one is stronger? Does point of view influence the description?

2. In this play, there are descriptions of two human sacrifices: Iphigenia and Agamemnon. Even in *The Odyssey* (Books Four and Eleven), Agamemnon speaks of his murder like a sacrificial victim. What words or phrases remind you of typical sacrifice scenes in *The Iliad*? Are the descriptions of Agamemnon and Iphigenia's deaths in *Agamemnon* similar?

Groups

1. In the opening choral ode, the beacon is passed from place to place across the Mediterranean Sea. Research the names of these places, and draw a map showing how the beacon of light was passed. What is the effect of having such a long choral ode at the beginning of *Agamemnon*?

Writing

Ask students to write a short paper in response to one or more of the following:

1. Since the Greek audience would have seen this play early in the morning, the beam of light described in the first lines of the play would have been experienced simultaneously by the audience and the actor. As the sun comes up, the sun acts as a prop for the play, a beacon for the watchman. Describe the character of the watchman. Where are his loyalties or mistrusts? How does he set the tone for the play?

2. How would you characterize the old men who make up the chorus? Are they simply the audience of the drama, or do they also contribute to the action? How do they change through the course of the play?

3. What are Clytemnestra's stated reasons for killing Agamemnon? Did it have to do entirely with Iphigenia, or for having brought home his mistress, or for having abandoned her for ten years? What about Aegisthus? What are his reasons? Is he just "going along" with Clytemnestra, or does he have his own motives?

BEYOND THE CLASSROOM

RESEARCH & WRITING

1. In Christa Wolf's novel *Cassandra* (1983), a different point of view is described in the final scenes in order to characterize the Greek men and Clytemnestra as opposed to Aeschylus's point of view, in which Cassandra is the foreign woman in a Greek society. How influenced, then, is *Cassandra* by Aeschylus's play?

2. In many ways, Clytemnestra appears to be the most powerful person in the play, often playing the role of a typical Greek man. Aegisthus and Agamemnon, on the other hand, are often emasculated. Citing examples from the text, show how this is so. If you do not agree, then use examples from the text to make an argument against this statement.

Project

1. Aeschylus is said to have used different kinds of props in his play. One of these was the *skene*, a painted backdrop — usually very simple — containing a doorway in the exact center and passages on either side from which the chorus enters and exits. Another device was the *ekkyklyma*, a flat cart with wheels that rolled out from the doors of the *skene* to present a scene from within the house or palace. The third device would have been the *mechane*, which was a crane from which actors hung if they had to fly or if they were goddesses coming down from heaven. Which of these devices would have been used in *Agamemnon*? Build a diorama, or write a detailed explanation of how a scene might employ one or more of these devices.

The Eumenides (p. 858)

Agamemnon will have to be a prerequisite for reading *The Eumenides*, even more so than *The Iliad* is for *Agamemnon*. In *The Libation Bearers*, the play between *Agamemnon* and *The Eumenides*, Orestes returns home from Phocis, where he has been exiled by his mother. Ostensibly, Orestes is exiled for his own safety, but the more likely explanation is that Clytemnestra wants him out of the way so that he cannot take the throne from her when he comes of age. Unexpectedly, Clytemenstra bids Electra to pour a libation on her father's (Agamemnon's) grave. Here, she meets Orestes, whom she does not recognize at first. When she realizes it is her brother, the two plot the murder of their mother, Clytemnestra. In the course of their deliberations, they arouse the ghost of Agamemnon himself to gain his support for their plans. Orestes enters the palace with the news of his own death for his mother and thus tricks her. The chorus, a group of women helping Electra, tells the nurse (who knows Orestes) to fetch Aegisthus without his bodyguard. Orestes kills them both but, in the last moments of the play, realizes that the Furies (later called the Eumenides) are chasing him and revenging Clytemnestra's death.

In *The Eumenides*, Orestes goes to the Temple of Apollo at Delphi in order to be purified. Apollo purifies Orestes through the standard Greek practice — by cutting open a suckling pig over his head and letting the blood drip on him. The Furies, however, do not believe that he should be left alone, and they continue to pursue him. The play begins with a gruesome description of the Furies by the Pythia, a priestess of Apollo. Apollo promises to help Orestes and urges him to take his case to Athens. The ghost of Clytemnestra, on the other hand, continues to urge on the Furies. The Furies are actually in their right; they are to pursue those who kill their own kin, regardless of purification. At Athens, Athene questions the Furies, who are afraid that their authority is being undermined by the more powerful gods and goddesses. Apollo acts as Orestes' councilor, with Athene playing the role of judge. The god argues on various grounds: (1) his superior rank over the Furies, regardless of their age, (2) the idea that Clytemnestra, as a mother, does not count as Orestes' kin. Athene votes with Orestes, and the civilian jury at Athens is divided on whether or not Orestes' murder of Clytemnestra is justified, thus acquitting him of the murder. The Furies are enraged, of course, but Athene pacifies them by promising them special honors at the Areopagus and in Athens. They then lead a triumphant dance praising the greatness of the city.

TEXT & CONTEXT

Three years before Aeschylus would have produced the play, the Areopagus court played a central role in an issue that threatened to take the city into civil war. Before that time, the Areopagus had permission to rule certain laws passed by the Athenian council as "unconstitutional." Ephialtes, the democratically elected leader of the time, along with Pericles, revoked the privilege of the Areopagus. When the city was on the brink of an uncontrollable conflict, Ephialtes was assassinated, and his murderers, who would have been tried at the Areopagus, were never found. The Areopagus, which means "crag of Ares," served as a kind of international law court for cases of homicide throughout the Greek world. Aeschylus's choice to attach this myth to the court of Areopagus is probably an attempt to justify its continued existence. However, the diplomatic fashion with which the Furies are treated is significant. It must be remembered by students that Greek drama was produced and performed by a country at war. After driving off the Persians, divisions in the Greek world began what were known as the Peloponnesian War, or the war between Sparta and Athens. The war was so devastating to the city of Athens that its democratic institutions, famed civil liberties, and judicial system were under constant threat. The Areopagus is also the site of St. Paul's speech about the Unknown God in Acts.

IN THE CLASSROOM

I. RELATING THE MYTHICAL PAST TO THE ATHENIAN PRESENT

Because students will be more accustomed to the conventions of Greek tragedy at this point, the content of the tragedy can be dealt with more seriously. Unlike *Agamemnon*, in which the common cultural taboo of murder is the main crisis (e.g., the murder of Iphigenia or Agamemnon), the conflicts of *The Eumenides* are more complex. It will be important to explain to students the significance of bringing the homicide trial to Athens. In a way, the Athenian conflict of 462 and 461 B.C.E. is a conflict between democracy and constitutional tradition, between rule by the people and rule by the elite few that are part of the Areopagus. Within *The Eumenides*, these conflicts are characterized by whether the Furies should receive proper respect or whether Apollo's oracles should be fulfilled. Gods who make prophecies must have them come true in order to retain the faith of those who use the prophecies, but gods who have to fulfill certain duties must be given the powers to carry out those duties. The trial itself is a fascinating scene in that a trial would have been familiar to most Greek males. All trials were public, including the famous trial of Socrates in 401 B.C.E., which can be read about in *Apology* (p. 1089).

Discussion

1. We now see that the Greek tragedies had contemporary relevance for the viewing audience. Although the play is about the mythical past, its setting and dramatic action hint

at the present situation. Perhaps, this is the intent of the playwright. If this is the case, then these plays may well be relevant to our own world and experiences. Let students brainstorm different contemporary situations similar to the conflicts of *The Eumenides*. Gradually segue back into the Greek drama by asking students to describe the outcome of the plot and the rationality of the arguments that have been presented by Apollo, the Chorus, and Athene.

2. Students should recognize that the religious system is the same in Greek tragedy as it is in Homer, essentially polytheistic and deterministic. How does the involvement of these minor goddesses change the impression of Greek religion that one might obtain from Homer? How does the fulfillment of Apollo's oracle differ from the determinism in *The Iliad* and *The Odyssey*?

3. Some writers have seen *The Eumenides* to be a conflict between Violence (the Age of Homer) and Reason (the Age of Aeschylus). How is that conflict embodied? What is necessary in order to make the proper transition?

Connections

1. Review the Ten Commandments, The Code of Hammurabi, and Deuteronomy 6–7:25. Comparing the court situation that occurs in *The Eumenides* with the strict written word of the law, how much does legal precedent matter in the ancient world? Can you think of exceptions for, say, the Ten Commandments? Why are courts necessary?

2. Courtroom drama has become a prominent feature of our modern culture. Not only are there many television series, like *Ally McBeal*, which glamorize the legal profession, but there are countless movies and increased coverage of celebrity trials. What features does *The Eumenides* share with these modern examples? Why are courtroom dramas so popular?

Groups

1. Organize a small group of students into two parts: the defense (Orestes) and the prosecution (the Furies). Using the text of *The Eumenides* as their starting point, encourage students to argue on behalf of their respective clients, developing the arguments present in *The Eumenides*. How successful are the arguments? Did Apollo win by good argumentation or by other means? Was Athene fair in her judgment?

Writing

Ask students to write a short paper in response to one or more of the following:

1. How does Aeschylus characterize the Furies? How do they change throughout the course of the play? In the final scene, how do they overcome their appearance and position? Concentrate in particular on the Second Stasimon of *The Eumenides* (pp. 868–71) as well as the last ode.

2. Since Greek tragedy was a religious and civil obligation for the audience as well as a form of entertainment, describe what the audience was supposed to get or learn from *The Eumenides*. Take into account how frightening the Furies are and the relevance of the Areopagus.

BEYOND THE CLASSROOM

RESEARCH & WRITING

1. Adrienne Munich says, "How many of us . . . were taught that *The Oresteia* is about the establishment of justice for Western civilization, rather than that it is a great act of

mythopoeia [mythmaking] in which politics are sexualized and where the idea of justice becomes defined as 'masculine.'" (p. 804). Comment on this statement, taking into consideration both *Agamemnon* and *The Euripides*. You may also want to consult translations of *The Libation Bearers*.

2. In many traditional cultures, certain rituals appear to be strange and even inappropriate for the circumstances. What is the ritual in *The Eumenides* that seems so strange? Can you think of examples outside of the play that are similar? What might be a reason that traditional societies follow such rituals? [Students should be looking at the ritual of killing a pig over the homicide's head; advanced students may also want to examine ritual "binding," or Clytemnestra's attempt to cast a spell over Orestes.]

Project

1. Actors and producers use "blocking" to create scenes of action on the stage. What characters are doing while other characters are speaking as well as how different characters speak are extremely important for communicating the nature of the action that transpires on the dramatic stage. Pick a scene from *The Eumenides*, and describe the blocking in detail. Who speaks when, and what is each character doing during each speech? Are there any pauses?

WWW   For additional information on Aeschylus and annotated Web links, see *World Literature Online* at bedfordstmartins.com/worldlit.

FURTHER READING

Goldhill, S. *Reading Greek Tragedy*. 1986.
Green, R., and Handley, R. *Images of the Greek Theater*. 1995.
Hall, E. *Inventing the Barbarian: Greek Self-Definition through Tragedy*. 1989.
Jones, Hugh-Lloyd. *The Oresteia*. 1979.
Lebeck, Anne. *The Oresteia: A Study in Language and Structure*. 1971.
Podlecki, A. J. *The Political Background of Aeschylean Tragedy*. 1967.
Scodel, R. *Theater and Society in the Classical World*. 1993.
Taplin, O. *The Stagecraft of Aeschylus*. 1977.
———. *Greek Tragedy in Action*. 1978.
Winnington-Ingram, R. P. *Studies in Aeschylus*. 1983.

MEDIA RESOURCES

VIDEO

Aeschylus: The Oresteia
3 tapes, 230 min., 1989 (Films for the Humanities & Social Sciences)
The National Theatre of Great Britain's production of the trilogy. English version by Tony Harrison, directed by Peter Hall, video production by Channel 4, London. It was the objective of Britain's National Theatre not to pay homage to *The Oresteia* but to make it stirring and entertaining; to meet the hard concepts of masks and chorus and poetic language head-on and overcome the difficulties of time and place by the sheer force of art.

Justice or Vengeance
26 min., 1998 (Films for the Humanities & Social Sciences)
The program examines the continuing resonance of this issue through the ages, from the House of Atreus to Sicilian and Sardinian blood feuds to contemporary film.

Mourning Becomes Electra
290 min., 1986 (Library Video Company)
Bruce Davison and Joan Hackett star in Eugene O'Neill's classic drama of love, revenge, murder, and suicide. Set against the backdrop of a small New England town in the post-Civil War era, O'Neill's saga of family discord fueled by psychological undercurrents is from Aeschylus's *The Oresteia.*

WEB SITES

The Internet Classics Archive — Aeschylus
classics.mit.edu/Browse/browse-Aeschylus.html
Read the complete e-texts of Aeschylus's plays at this wonderful site.

Poetry Archive — Aeschylus
www.poetry-archive.com/a/aeschylus.html
This page provides e-texts of Aeschylus's poems as well as links to several other relevant sites.

Theatre Database — Aeschylus
www.theatredatabase.com/ancient/aeschylus_001.html
This is a useful biographical site with some links to interesting pages pertaining to the life and works of Aeschylus.

Theatre History.com — Aeschylus and His Tragedies
www.theatrehistory.com/ancient/aeschylus001.html
This is the site to visit for background information on the life of Aeschylus as well as links to several other relevant pages.

SOPHOCLES, *Oedipus Rex* and *Antigone* (p. 891)

WWW   For a quiz on *Oedipus Rex*, see *World Literature Online*
at bedfordstmartins.com/worldlit.

The Greek playwright Sophocles wrote more than any of the other great Greek tragedians (Aeschylus and Euripides). Of his more than 120 plays, twenty-four of which were awarded first prize at the drama festivals, only seven survive to the present day. He first competed against Aeschylus in 468 B.C.E. and competed the last time, with himself and his choir dressed in mourning clothes for the recently dead Euripides, in 406 B.C.E. He died a few months later. Whereas Aeschylus was formerly in the military service during the Persian Wars (500–479 B.C.E.) and subsequently retired from political life, Sophocles was always engaged in the political life at Athens, even during its decline. He served as a priest and devotee to the god Asclepius and the healing deity Halon, erecting a monumental snake in his home in their honor. Following the political crisis when democracy was nearly abandoned in 413 B.C.E. (the year the Athenian armada was destroyed at Syracuse), he was part of an appointed advisory council of ten people.

We do not know the dates of either play that has been selected for the book. *Antigone* probably came first and won the first prize; *Oedipus Rex,* presented at a later date, was defeated at the festival. Sophocles' style was said by later authors to be between the austere and Wagnerian Aeschylus and the lighter Euripides. He thus emerged as a playwright between the two. However, his plays are as equally as violent as any Aeschylus or Euripides play, and he treats situations as discomforting as any proposed by the other dramatists. His plays take advantage of certain objects and actions that mark a character. Often, recognition — which is central to the design of tragedy — occurs by means of a simple prop. In *Oedipus Tyrannus*, for example, there are a series of small signs, like the pierced foot or the place where three roads meet. The entry and exit of characters is always highly marked and sparks a new direction in the plot. The final entry of the main character, Oedipus in *Oedipus Rex* and Creon in *Antigone*, is often accompanied by gore and many dead bodies.

Sophocles' language is always very formal and controlled. Only a few characters withdraw from this formal language. The private conversations initiated by Iocaste with Oedipus are an example of more natural and quiet speech. The effect eerily reminds the viewer of the play that the normal formal separation between parent and child has been severed and replaced with an uncomfortable intimacy. The elaborate structure of *Oedipus Rex* was complimented by Aristotle in his *Poetics*, but the play never was recognized at the festival. *Antigone*, on the other hand, won first prize but possesses a more puzzling structure.

TEXT & CONTEXT

Students will find Sophocles a much easier read than Aeschylus because there is more dialogue and because the plot requires less foreknowledge. The *Theban Cycle* describes the history of the city of Thebes, which seems to have been perpetually struck by disaster. It is an interesting coincidence that Thebes was one of the cities not aligned with the Delian league (an alliance led by Athens of all the Greek states) against the Persian invasions (550–479 B.C.E.). But the Theban plays might also serve as a dislocation of events so as not to criticize Athens directly. (It is interesting that plays that seem to come to a hopeful conclusion, such as Aeschylus's *The Eumenides* and Sophocles' *Oedipus at Colonus* occur at or have something to do with Athens).

The city is founded by Cadmus (by sowing dragon's teeth into the ground), who is married to Harmonia, who gave birth to a son, Polydorus, and four daughters, one of which, Semele, was raped by Zeus and gave birth to the god Dionysus (who is also the god of Tragedy). One of the daughters, Agave, gave birth to Pentheus, whom she destroyed in a fit of revelry in the Dionysiac cult. Pentheus's son, Menoeceus, gave birth to Creon and Iocasta and Polydorus to Labdacus, who subsequently had a son, Laius. Iocasta and Laius are Oedipus's parents. Creon's children are Menoeceus II and Haemon. Oedipus kills his father and marries his mother, Iocasta, and gives birth to children Eteocles, Polyneices, Antigone, and Ismene. When Oedipus was thrown out of Thebes, his two sons, Eteocles and Polyneices, asserted their right to the throne. Eteocles succeeded, expelling Polyneices to Argos. Polyneices collects six Argives and makes an attack on Thebes. The young Menoecues II, Creon's child, sacrifices himself for Theban victory. In the end, all are killed but one of the Argives who flees to Athens. This leaves Creon still in power. He issues a proclamation forbidding Polyneices's burial, which the dead man's sister, Antigone, disobeys. When Creon imprisons and effectively drives to death Antigone for breaking his law, his own son Haemon, Antigone's lover, kills himself. At Haemon's death, Creon's wife also destroys herself. Adrastus raises an army at Athens to avenge his countrymen's death. Since Oedipus has died at Athens, the city has special powers, and, consequently, Thebes is utterly destroyed.

If students are curious what the relationship is between the house of Thebes and the house of Atreus (from which Agamemnon descends), they all are related to Agenor, Cadmus's father, and are all descendents of Zeus. The Theban family arises from Zeus's rape of Io, and the Atreus family from Tantalus, a son of Zeus. The *Theban Cycle* must be older than the events of the *Trojan Cycle*, since parts of the story are already known in *The Iliad* and in Hesiod. However, according to the genealogy, the events are nearly simultaneous. Nothing survives in epic format to tell us the complete *Theban Cycle*.

The title of the play, *Oedipus Rex*, is a Latin translation of *Oedipus Tyrannus*. The word *tyrannos* in Greek is where the English word *tyrant* comes from but only has the meaning of "dictator," without any of the overtones of being a bad leader. However, already by the time of Sophocles, the word *tyrannos* had come to mean a bad leader as opposed to a democratic system of government. *Oedipus Rex* means "Oedipus the King," which is not an entirely correct translation, since a king (*basileus* in Greek) inherits the throne, which Oedipus does not. Although he is the rightful prince of Thebes, he gains the throne by marriage to the queen of Thebes (unwittingly his own mother), Iocasta. The reason he is allowed to serve as king instead of Creon is that he answers the famous riddle of the Sphinx. The Sphinx asks, "What creature walks on four legs in the morning, two at midday, and three in the evening?" The question is a double metaphor, since neither "legs" nor the time of day is literal. The answer, of course, is "man." Oedipus was a man without home or country at the time he answered the question. Little did he know that his saving the Theban people from the Sphinx would have such dire consequences for himself. In *Oedipus Rex*, he attempts to remove a plague that has been bothering the Theban people. He believes that if he could solve the puzzle of the Sphinx, he will be able to do likewise for the plague. When he recognizes that the solution lies in his own exile, he comes to the shocking conclusion that the fate he has been trying to avoid — killing his father and marrying his mother (who he believes to be King Polybus and Queen Merope of Corinth) — is his fate. Likewise, Iocaste, who has been trying to avoid this same fate, discovers that the man she has married, Oedipus, is both her son and her husband's murderer.

IN THE CLASSROOM

If students aren't familiar with the structure and outlay of Greek drama and tragedy in particular at this point, provide a quick background for them. Again, reproduction of the Greek experience is almost futile, and effort should be spent on the moral and ethical dilemmas raised by the plays. Unlike Aeschylus, in which the gods control much of the destiny of human actors, Sophocles endows his characters with some degree of choice. Ismene does not behave like her sister in *Antigone*, purely out of her own choice to obey Creon. On the other hand, the gods are not completely absent, as they are in some plays by Euripides. Oedipus continually makes reasonable choices but cannot see that the consequence of those choices brings about his downfall. One of the possible discussion topics to present to students is the issue of free choice and conflicting interests. Oedipus's responsibility is to his own people, a responsibility that he, as a good ruler, carries out diligently. When the play opens, we see that he cares for his adopted country, but, as the play develops, Oedipus's treatment of Creon and Tiresias and his hot temper cloud his ability to make decisions. If we are to believe Aristotle, this temperament is his "tragic flaw" or *hamartia*. The idea of a tragic flaw, however, seems to conclude that characters have a choice in their behavior that will lead them to devastating or good conclusions.

Another avenue for discussion may lay in the way that Sophocles creates the relationship between Oedipus and Iocaste. Their conversations often follow difficult episodes for Oedipus. He appears to seek her advice and confide in her like a son to a mother, but Iocaste responds more intimately as though a wife. Governance and control also play a central role in this work. While these plays were being produced, Athenians were beginning to question whether or not replacing the aristocracy with a democratic government was a good decision. Many crises of government ensued during the Peloponnesian War (between Athens and Sparta, 431–404 B.C.E.), during which Sophocles served as an adviser. While Oedipus appears to care for the well-being of his citizens (particularly at the opening of the play, where his words display a self-sacrificial quality), he is suspicious of other rulers. For example, when he learns of how Laius dies, he assumes that it must be a rival political faction that paid someone to kill Laius (ll. 127–30). Oedipus's mistrust of Tiresias is couched in the language of treason. He then turns against Creon, whom he assumes wants to take the crown from him (ll. 366 ff.). Creon's final lines after he has assumed rule of Thebes critique Oedipus's governance, "Think no longer / That you are in command here, but rather think / How, when we were, you served your own destruction" (ll. 1466–68). Students should think back on this question if they have read *Antigone*, since similar questions will come up concerning Creon's rule and the conflict between human legal codes and divine law.

Students might also notice that there is a recurring metaphor of sight, blindness, and vision throughout the play. They should be encouraged to search out phrases and words related to this metaphor and to judge how they are used in an ironic sense or in an alarmingly truthful sense. Since tragedy, particularly *Oedipus Rex*, revolves around the Greek notion of recognition (*anagnorisis*), the characters require special vision to recognize their defeat. This is true more so in Sophocles than in any other tragedian.

Discussion

1. If we are to believe Aristotle, the cause of Oedipus's downfall is his tragic flaw. If this is true, then the characters must have free choice (which brings about the flaw) in order to bring about their fate. Otherwise, it is simply the revenge of gods that has brought down Oedipus. No matter how good he is or tries to be, he is destroyed by the gods. Students should debate the merits and problems with Aristotle's interpretation of this play in relation to free choice. One puzzling statement comes from Oedipus's own mouth: "But no man in the world / Can make the gods do more than the gods will" (ll. 267–68). Could Oedipus have known his own limit in making choices?

2. Describe the relationship between Oedipus and Iocaste. What are the techniques of language that the author uses to create tension (or lack of tension) between them? Do they have a parent-child relationship or a husband-wife relationship? Does either of them say something that could be ironically interpreted? Be sure that the students understand the meaning of irony and how it applies to drama (i.e., the audience knows what the characters do not know).

3. What does this play say about democracy versus rule by an individual? Consider what Creon says about only good rulers having the right to rule (l. 598) and how exactly Oedipus came to power. It may also be useful to think about the naming of the play and Oedipus's assumptions about Tiresias.

Connections

1. Both *Oedipus Rex* and Aeschylus's *The Eumenides* (p. 858) are concerned with children killing their parents and the idea of "pollution" (in Greek, *miasma*). What do these plays have in common in terms of their treating the concept of pollution? For example, what will happen to Oedipus's children? What evidence could someone use to show that these plays come from the same culture?

2. Both *Agamemnon* (p. 806) of Aeschylus and *Oedipus Rex* are about a powerful king who returns home only to be destroyed. Agamemnon is killed by his wife Clytemnestra, but he makes certain decisions, such as killing his daughter, bringing his mistress Cassandra home, and stepping on the purple carpet, which lead to his downfall. How similar or different are these actions from those of Oedipus in *Oedipus Rex*? What moral or value is being shown by these plays? Why would a culture explain a story in this way (i.e., a king comes home only to be destroyed)?

Groups

1. Ask each group to outline the structure of the drama. How much time is devoted to each conversation? How are the conversations related to one another? The students should break up the play into several scenes.

2. The play works in the same way as a detective novel. Although we know the answer (who the murderer is), the detective (Oedipus) does not. Several clues are given over the course of the play, some of which Oedipus correctly interprets, some of which he does not. Have the students make a list of these clues and Oedipus's reactions to each of them. How does he handle each piece of information? What "blinds" him or prevents him from perceiving the truth? Often Oedipus repeats information to himself (e.g., ll. 731ff) that is false. Why does he do this?

Writing

Ask students to write a short paper in response to one or more of the following:

1. Although Oedipus claims to respect the oracles of the gods, he does not listen to any of these oracles. What are the oracles and prophecies that are contained in *Oedipus Rex*? How does he treat each of them? What are his reasons for dismissing them or misinterpreting them?

2. Aristotle says that good tragedy should produce a *katharsis* or "cleansing of the soul." This requires that the viewers see some aspect of themselves in the principle characters of the drama. At what level would members of an audience share something in common with Oedipus, who has killed his father and married his mother?

BEYOND THE CLASSROOM

RESEARCH & WRITING

1. Metaphors concerned with sight and blindness occur throughout the play. In the end, Oedipus chooses not to kill himself like Iocaste but rather to blind himself. Does this make him more pitiable? How does this mirror his position of being metaphorically blind throughout the rest of his play? How does the author play with these terms of seeing and blindness?

2. Oedipus spends most of the play trying to find out his true identity. Why do you suppose tragedy should be so concerned with identity? If it is the gods that make one do what one does, behavior cannot make one what one is; instead something else must substitute for identity. What is that something else?

Project

1. Read Sophocles' *Oedipus at Colonus*, the last work written by Sophocles. How does the characterization of Oedipus and Creon differ from what we read in *Oedipus Rex*?

WWW   For additional information on Sophocles and annotated Web links, see *World Literature Online* at bedfordstmartins.com/worldlit.

FURTHER READING

Anouilh, Jean. *Antigone.* 1942.
Bowra, C. M. *Sophoclean Tragedy.* 1944.
Goheen, R. F. *The Imagery of Sophocles'* Antigone. 1951.

Jones, J. *On Aristotle and Greek Tragedy*. 1962.
Knox, B. M. W. *Oedipus at Thebes*. 1957.
———. *The Heroic Temper*. 1964.
Reinhardt, K. *Sophocles*. 1979.
Segal, C. *Tragedy and Civilization*. 1982.
Winnington-Ingram, R. P. *Sophocles: An Interpretation*. 1980.

WWW   See *World Literature in the 21st Century* at bedfordstmartins.com/worldlit
for information on the relevance of Sophocles in today's world.

MEDIA RESOURCES

VIDEO

Oedipus at Colonus
120 min., 1986 (Films for the Humanities & Sciences)
Bearer of an almost unspeakable, immutable fate, Oedipus yet feels that he is a man chosen
— favored — by the gods. Now an old man, blind and outcast, Oedipus wanders through
Greece guided by his daughter Antigone until he comes to Colonus, where he knows he
will die. With Anthony Quayle as Oedipus, John Shrapnel as Creon, Juliet Stevenson as
Antigone, and Kenneth Haigh as Polynices.

Oedipus Rex
90 min., 1957 (Insight Media)
Directed by Sir Tyrone Guthrie, this version of the play adds a different stroke — the actors
wear masks, thus performing their roles just as the Greeks did in Sophocles' time.

Oedipus the King
120 min., 1995 (Films for the Humanities & Sciences)
Sophocles often won the leading prize at the Dionysia, the principal dramatic festival of
Athens, but *Oedipus the King* was a runner-up, winner of the second prize. Posterity, however, considers the play second to none. The play tells the beginning of the Oedipus saga,
setting the stage and creating the characters who will continue the story to its conclusion
in *Antigone*. With Michael Pennington, John Gielgud, and Claire Bloom.

Oedipus Tyrannus
60 min., 1977 (Insight Media)
This excerpted version of Sophocles' classic tragedy, which begins with the entrance of the
Corinthian shepherd, avoids archaic language while preserving the dignity and the clarity
of the text. The documentary section of the program shows scenes of Greek theaters and
examines Aristotle's definition of tragedy.

WEB SITES

The Internet Classics Archive — Sophocles
Classics.mit.edu/Browse/browse-Sophocles.html
Read the complete e-texts of Sophocles' plays at this site.

Poetry Archive — Poems by Sophocles
www.poetry-archive.com/s/sophocles.html
At this site, users will find several poems by Sophocles as well as links to other sites about
the author and his works.

Sophocles
www.imagi-nation.com/moonstruck/clsc1.htm
Visit this site for background on the life of Sophocles as well as links to other useful pages.

Sophocles Links
www.vroma.org/~riley/sophocles/portrait_links.html
Providing users with numerous links, this site is a good place to begin research on Sophocles. Find links to images, biographies of the writer, pages about ancient Greek culture and art in general, secondary sources, and information about contemporary performances of plays by Sophocles and other ancient Greek dramatists.

AUDIO

Oedipus Rex
2 tapes or 2 CDs, 2 hrs. (Naxos Audio)
This new translation of the great classic of ancient Greece starts a cycle of drama recordings by Naxos AudioBooks. The anguished tale of Oedipus — who having solved the riddle of the Sphinx and becomes king of Thebes gradually realizes the crimes he has unwittingly committed — remains a drama of unremitting power 2,500 years after it was written.

Antigone (p. 952)

WWW   For a quiz on *Antigone*, see *World Literature Online*
at bedfordstmartins.com/worldlit.

If *Oedipus Rex* is clearly about Oedipus and his fate, *Antigone* presents a great puzzle. She is gone about two-thirds of the way through the drama and thus it is the fate of Creon, and, ultimately, Thebes, that become the concern of the play. Whereas students can identify wrongs done in *Oedipus Rex* and see that Oedipus, while suffering unjustly, is likewise no perfect man, *Antigone* presents a conflict that on the surface seems easy to comprehend. Creon kills Antigone for burying her brother. Even though Creon has issued an edict, the law seems to be unjust. But on close inspection, how do we expect leaders to treat the enemy? After September 11, 2001, the United States government detained hundreds of people captured in Afghanistan at Guantanamo Bay in Cuba. These detainees had relatives who depended on them and on whom they depended. Human rights groups have claimed that the legal category the U.S. government invented — unlawful combatants — does not adequately provide protections for these people's rights. And yet, a country must defend itself and its territory from those who would harm it. The trials of those arrested in the search for terror cells following the disasters in New York City, Pennsylvania, and at the Pentagon were difficult to make fair: Some witnesses who might help the defendants in the American legal system might also undermine the security of the country. Although Creon is by no means a likeable character, his behavior is in the interest of his own state. Polynices and his allies from Argos committed treason against the government of Eteocles and Athens posed an imminent threat to the fate of Thebes. As Creon says, "These are my principles. Never at my hands / will the traitor be honored above the patriot. / But whoever proves his loyalty to the state — / I'll prize that man in death as well as life" (ll. 232–35).

Antigone, on the other hand, must obey her traditions. Imagine for a moment that she is a young veiled American Muslim whose brother, upon whom she depends for her livelihood because she is a single woman, has been detained on suspicion of terrorist activities. Even if her brother is guilty, how will she view the government? Will she feel that its laws, which seem so arbitrary and imposed only to the benefit of those in power, are worth obeying? Antigone thus follows her traditions, and, against the orders of her government, buries her brother. We cannot even say that she buries her brother. She throws some dirt and wine on the rotting and bloated corpse — "did the rites," as the messenger reports. She tells Creon that her religion is obviously of more weight than man-made laws: "Nor did I think your edict had such force / that you, a mere mortal, could override the gods, / the great unwritten, unshakable traditions" (ll. 503–5). But perhaps Antigone exaggerates or goes too far. At the beginning of the play, she asks Ismene for help: "you're either with me or against me." But Ismene refuses, thinking that it is best for women to obey stronger men. She even believes that the laws are ordained with reasonable thinking and that they are like divine covenants (ll. 70–77). Ismene neither buries her brother (although she tries to take credit for it later to save her sister) nor does she defy the laws of state. Of all the characters, she alone survives.

The characters, besides the strong-willed Antigone and Creon, are also very interesting components of the drama. Ismene is the voice of reason, always trying to do her best for her family without violating any laws. She has a much better coping strategy than her brothers or sisters, although she recognizes the blight from which her family suffers. Haemon, who is Creon's son and Antigone's lover, appears quite late in the drama. In fact, because of this, it is almost certain that the actor who plays the part of Ismene later plays the part of Haemon. The two characters are quite similar. Haemon tries to persuade his father to rescue Antigone before it is too late. He tries to show his father that rulership cannot be cold and iron-like but requires flexibility. His father dismisses all his criticisms as the sentiments of an insubordinate youth.

The seer Tiresias tries to be honest, but by now he is used to hot-headed leaders who do not listen to him. Creon assumes that he is just trying to get rich. When he leaves, the chorus notes that Tiresias has never lied. Creon is instantly changed and, for the first time in the play, asks for advice. The choir is composed of Theban citizens and their leader. They try very hard to be loyal to Creon, supporting him in his debate with Haemon. They are somewhat sympathetic toward Antigone but blame her fall on her blind passion, a theme they repeat throughout her final ode. They are older men and reflect on the world with a great deal of experience. More than in any other tragedy, the choral odes are extremely poignant reminders of the fragile human condition, the role of chance, and the danger that lies in freedom of choice. They praise the efforts and accomplishments of man and unambiguously praise the person who is not too daring or reckless (ll. 375ff.). The sentry who first sees the newly buried corpse is a figure out of comedy. In a play full of Creon's explosive outbursts and Antigone's passionate speeches, the sentry, on the other hand, speaks in a simple drawl, rambling along, and then is unable to properly express what has happened to the body (the syntax is just garbled "body . . . buried . . . dust . . ."). When Creon says that he hates listening to him, the sentry answers, "Where does it hurt you, in the ears or in the heart?" (l. 359). A few lines later, when the sentry enters with Antigone, he exclaims with glee that he has found the perpetrator.

TEXT & CONTEXT

As early as the time of Solon, one of the ancient founders of the Athenian system of government (in the sixth century B.C.E.), limits were placed on the number and nature of the mourners in a Greek funeral. Traditionally, all the women from the community would carry out the rites in honor of the dead. We can see how this was very central to a woman's duties from the prominence it plays in so many tragedies — *The Libation Bearers* by Aeschylus (part of *The Oresteia*), and in the *Electra* of Sophocles and of Euripides as well as others. In the reforms of Cleisthenes, many of these kinds of laws were changed in favor of the more democratic system with which he is credited. By contrast, Creon's government is not at all democratic. "And is Thebes about to tell me how to rule?" "The city *is* the king — that's the law!," he retorts.

IN THE CLASSROOM

I. THEMES IN *ANTIGONE*

Like *Oedipus Rex*, this play is greatly concerned with government (probably even more so). Creon is unreasonably hot-tempered. His city has been attacked, and there are threats mounting in Athens. Like a true tyrant, he suspects everyone around him of plotting against him, accusing everyone, including his own son, of not only failing to be loyal but also of treason. Some of his arguments are the same as Oedipus's, and it will be interesting to compare their speeches.

Gender is also a topic often pursued when discussing this play. Both Ismene and Antigone have differing views: Ismene doesn't want to contravene the orders of men, but Antigone, on the other hand, is only carrying out a task assigned to women out of tradition. Government and tradition, then, seem to oppress women. For this reason, Antigone is not, as some have characterized her, the model feminist hero. Furthermore, she doesn't actually cause Creon's downfall. He does that all by himself. Her rigidity and equally temperamental behavior cause her own destruction. But it seems like the audience is meant to pity her, just as the choir and everyone else does eventually. Even if she is not a modern feminist (in the way that Medea is), her behavior and relations with men, especially on the backdrop of the limiting society from which she comes, is particularly interesting.

Students should be encouraged to find ways of expressing the conflicts in this tragedy in more contemporary terms. In a very frightening way, this play is more relevant than many Greek dramas to our own world. Modernity is often about the struggle between rule of law and tradition. In Creon, we see a bit of the Mao Zedong who prohibited certain traditional practices in order to modernize his country. In many cases, these traditional practices came from the era in which those who were in power were those against whom Mao Zedong and other republican-minded individuals fought. While the cultural revolution was a disaster for China and everyone suffered, it also set about the chain of events that led to the modernization of the state and its eventual incorporation into the world today. Students should debate openly whether or not that sacrifice is worthwhile. Questions of state security and what comprises treason are also very relevant to the play. If Creon were alive today, would he be a leader we would want to get rid of, like a Mugabe or Saddam Hussein, or are we all, as Aristotle supposes, a little like Creon ourselves?

Discussion

1. Is this play about Antigone or Creon? *Oedipus Rex* seems clearly about Oedipus and his fate, but what about *Antigone*? Creon faces a situation quite similar to Oedipus at the end of the play, something of which we are meant to be aware. Discuss whether tragedy should just be about the fate of the individual in society or whether it can be about groups of people.

2. Gender and age are both creators of hierarchy in this play. Haemon is younger, and Antigone is a woman, thus they are meant to obey the king. In what way does Sophocles undermine this traditional way of thinking? What role does the chorus, which is comprised of old men, serve in mediating this hierarchy?

3. Who has done the greater wrong, Antigone for acting against the law or Ismene for not obeying tradition? What about Creon and Antigone? Who is more clearly wrong? Why? What values did the Greeks prize so much that they made Antigone, despite her character flaws, such a heroine?

Connections

1. Despite Creon's rough personality, he does try to act in the interest of the city. He buries Polynices *before* rescuing Antigone, which is what needs to be done to make right his offense of the gods. When he shuts Antigone in the cave, he doesn't kill her. Why is this? [Hint: Consider the aspect of pollution in *Oedipus Rex* (p. 899) and the two plays of *The Oresteia* (pp. 806 and 858).]

2. In Tiresias's speech, he describes a sacrifice that has gone horribly wrong. Some scholars have noted that sacrifices often go astray in tragedy. In *Agamemnon*, another sacrifice is described (that of Iphegenia). What is similar or different between these two descriptions?

Groups

1. Have students relate the conflict of this drama, man-made legal codes versus religious traditions, to contemporary events. Ask them to produce a short documentary through annotated photographs and illustrations of similar crises and problems in the world.

2. Assign a character to each group. Let students comb through the text, looking for three or four lines or couplets that might serve as the motto of that character. How do these statements embody the character who speaks them? What is the significance of the connection between language and personality?

Writing

Ask students to write a short paper in response to one or more of the following:

1. Sophocles' plays often seem to support the idea of democracy. What specific statements and events in the text make this true? If you disagree, then show through citations how Sophocles' plays are actually undemocratic.

2. The choral odes in this play are extremely relevant to the circumstances in which they are sung. Choose one, and show how it develops its meaning from the conversation preceding or following it.

BEYOND THE CLASSROOM

RESEARCH & WRITING

1. Creon rebukes his son for putting "some woman" before the laws of the state and before his own father. Furthermore, Ismene says that women should be obedient to men. Clearly, there is some kind of problem of gender equality being exposed here. Describe the gender conflict in greater detail, quoting from the text.

2. Some scholars have seen Creon as being a kind of fascist. After researching fascism and its features, describe the tendencies and language used by Creon or those around him that encourage this idea. It may be helpful to note that some productions of the play show the city in complete disarray and full of people at the beginning of the drama, then spotless and well built by the end of the drama, with nobody but Creon and the bodies of his son and wife.

Projects

1. Jean Anouilh wrote his own version of *Antigone* for the times in which he lived (it was published in 1942). In this version, some have seen a sympathetic reading of Creon. After reading Anouilh's short play (or viewing the movie based on it), comment on the similarities and differences between the two works.

2. Many movie and opera versions of *Antigone* have been created. Choose one of them, and compare the director's version and choices with the text. How well does the director make the play relevant to the audience? Do the conflicts that are present in the text of Sophocles remain strong in the movie or opera?

WWW   For additional information on Sophocles and annotated Web links, see *World Literature Online* at bedfordstmartins.com/worldlit.

FURTHER READING

Anouilh, Jean. *Antigone.* 1942.
Bowra, C. M. *Sophoclean Tragedy.* 1944.
Goheen, R. F. *The Imagery of Sophocles'* Antigone. 1951.
Jones, J. *On Aristotle and Greek Tragedy.* 1962.
Knox, B. M. W. *Oedipus at Thebes.* 1957.
———. *The Heroic Temper.* 1964.
Reinhardt, K. *Sophocles.* 1979.
Segal, C. *Tragedy and Civilization.* 1982.
Winnington-Ingram, R. P. *Sophocles: An Interpretation.* 1980.

WWW   See *World Literature in the 21st Century* at bedfordstmartins.com/worldlit for information on the relevance of Sophocles in today's world.

MEDIA RESOURCES

VIDEO

Antigone
111 min., 1984 (Films for the Humanities & Sciences)
Antigone is perhaps the most easily accessible of all the great classical tragedies, its theme clear and up-to-date: the conflict between moral and political law. With Juliet Stevenson, John Shrapnel, and John Gielgud.

Antigone: Sophocles
50 min., 1985 (Insight Media)
Presented by Bruce Williams, this video provides a thought-provoking interpretation of Sophocles' classic play. It rejects a narrow focus on the character of Antigone and explores the rhythm of the numerous conflicting views within the text.

Antigone
95 min., 1991 (Insight Media)
This production of Sophocles' play was produced and directed by Arlena Nys and stars Carrie O'Brien and Chris Bearne.

Antigone
90 min., 1972 (IMDB)

Based on a script by Jean Anouilh, Genevieve Bujold, Stacy Keach, and Fritz Weaver star in this adaptation of the Sophocles tragedy that presents a world of honor, treachery, and fateful consequences.

Antigone
86 min., 1962 (Library Video Company)
Director George Tzavella brings Sophocles' drama to the screen. Discover Sophocles' conclusion to the tragic story of Oedipus and the curse on the royal house of Thebes. (Greek with English subtitles.)

Antigone: Rites of Passion
85 min., 1991 (Library Video Company)
Amy Greenfield, Martha Graham, and Bertram Ross address Sophocles' tragedy of family honor, guilt, and revenge in this feminist interpretation. The program enhances the essentials of the plot through movement, sparse voice-over, and scene locations. Features the work of contemporary composers Glenn Branca, Diamanda Galas, Palu Lemos, Elliot Sharp, and David Can Tieghem.

Sophocles' Antigone: Revenge of the Gods
70 min., 1998 (Insight Media)
Antigone's desire to obey ancient customs governing the burial of the dead clashes with her Uncle Creon's ruling that the body of her traitorous brother Polynices receive no burial rites. This production examines how the tragic outcome of the conflict between divine and human law illustrates the folly of ignoring traditional culture and wisdom.

WEB SITES

The Internet Classics Archive — Sophocles
Classics.mit.edu/Browse/browse-Sophocles.html
Read the complete e-texts of Sophocles' plays at this site.

Poetry Archive — Poems by Sophocles
www.poetry-archive.com/s/sophocles.html
At this site, users will find several poems by Sophocles as well as links to other sites about the author and his works.

Sophocles
www.imagi-nation.com/moonstruck/clsc1.htm
Visit this site for background on the life of Sophocles as well as links to other useful pages.

Sophocles Links
www.vroma.org/~riley/sophocles/portrait_links.html
Providing users with numerous links, this site is a good place to begin research on Sophocles. Find links to images, biographies of the writer, pages about ancient Greek culture and art in general, secondary sources, and information about contemporary performances of plays by Sophocles and other ancient Greek dramatists.

EURIPIDES, *Medea* (p. 999)

WWW   For a quiz on *Medea*, see *World Literature Online*
at bedfordstmartins.com/worldlit.

Euripides was perhaps one of the most popular playwrights among the common Athenians. His dramas are highly realistic, lacking the deception of seers and prophets and instead relying on human ingenuity. In his plays, he toys with audience expectations and with the conventions of tragedy itself. For this reason, he is often seen as the most extreme Greek dramatist. Some plays end with a happy reunion between brother and sister or husband and wife, and others, like *Medea*, end with gory murder and dismemberment. Euripides can be incredibly comical and shockingly violent, even in the same play. His popularity after his death is evident on the basis of the survival of his plays. Of his ninety plays, nineteen of them were preserved, more than twice that of any other tragedian. He was probably born around 480 B.C.E. and, despite popularity among the Athenians, was not well liked by the judges at the dramatic festival: He won only four times. He left Athens some time around 408 B.C.E. for the court at Macedon, which was becoming a strong regional power. For a variety of reasons, we are able to date Euripides' plays with greater precision than those of Sophocles or Aeschylus. *Medea*, in 431 B.C.E., is one of the earlier plays.

In a play written by the comedian Aristophanes called the *Frogs*, Euripides is portrayed as a man who tried to go against the grain and break with tradition. It also critiques Euripides' desire to confront the harsh, violent, and brutal plots available to the tragic poet. Aristotle writes that Sophocles makes men "as they ought to be," while Euripides portrays men "as they are." The ancient literary critic Longinus believed that Euripides was particularly adept at displaying the psychological condition of his characters, women in particular.

Typical characters of Euripidean drama display many layers of personality. Some of them appear to "act" for the other characters on the stage. For example, when we hear Medea off-stage, she seems to rage incoherently, but when she is on stage and before the audience, she transforms into a capable speaker and an actress who manipulates those around her to achieve her goals. At the same time, Euripides employs the tactic of "*deus ex machina*," or "god from the machine," in order to rescue his characters. The effect in *Medea* is meant to terrify, but sometimes it draws the play to an unexpected positive conclusion. Rather than make the play less tragic (as it may seem to us), it helps to create a greater release of emotion for the Greek audience. Sometimes, such as at the end of his play the *Bacchae*, about Agave's tearing her son Pentheus to pieces, the "*deus ex machina*" never comes, and we are left in still greater despair, having no sense of closure whatsoever.

Euripides' talent lies in small picaresque scenes of everyday life on the backdrop of tragedy. The chatter of the nurse and the tutor at the beginning of *Medea* is not there for a kind of comic relief, like the sentry in Sophocles' *Oedipus Rex*. Rather, it closes the distance between the audience and the disaster about to unfold. Euripidean realism is not like a journalistic Emile Zola or a fact-by-fact account but rather is a transformation of characters and scene from the formal and "out-of-the-distant-path" type that Aeschylus and Sophocles used in less heroic and more ordinary people. This makes the truly villainous characters or those with heightened degrees of passion, like Medea, all the more frightening.

As with the other tragedies, students should set about trying to find the conflicts that are present in this tragedy. This will be difficult since whereas Sophocles was interested in the situation that produced tragedy, Euripides was more fascinated with the psychology of the characters involved in tragedy. On one hand, it is easy to be sympathetic with Medea: She has been abandoned by her husband who has dragged her from her far-off home. But her response seems hardly defensible. The power of life and death has been given to a single figure who is meant to appear as motherly as possible. Jason, on the other hand, is a weak character. He wants to legitimize the citizenship rights of his children by marrying a Greek. While his half-Asian children might never be princes of the realm, their future will be secure if they are related to legitimate brothers. It is a situation that would have been common in Athens. Full Athenian citizenship was granted only to those whose father and maternal grandfather had full citizenship. There were constant legal battles trying to disinherit individuals of their rights based on their mother's origins.

Euripides explores a number of issues, then, which would have pressed upon the minds of *Medea*'s Greek audience. The concept of citizenship and its rigid requirements produced an unhealthy rivalry between mistresses and wives. In the case of Jason, it permits him to have a second wife. Since this *creates* the witch-like figure of Medea, it can be seen as a conflict: the desire to produce legitimate children endowed with citizenship against the treatment of wives who have produced healthy sons. But this was not the only conflict. In an era when the Athenian self-image was so great as to lead to their downfall, it is interesting to watch a play about Greek encounters with foreigners. Indeed, many of Euripides' plays deal with Greek and non-Greek relations. At the time of *Medea*, Athens believed that its naval might would protect it from rival Sparta. However, it could not protect them from a land siege in 432 and 431 B.C.E. Growing Athenian imperialism under Pericles led to a dangerous self-confidence in the face of a growing threat from other lands. When Jason argues that she should be thankful for his having taken her to Greece, some of this Athenian superiority comes out in his language. Students should have no trouble finding contemporary issues related to those in *Medea*. Cases where mothers kill their own children have a profound psychological component and have been prominent in the media. Furthermore, questions of citizenship, deportation, and exile are all relevant to our present society. Euripides remains the most modern of all the Greek playwrights, haunting us with his in-depth knowledge of the human psyche.

TEXT & CONTEXT

The story of *Medea* follows that of *Jason and the Argonauts*, an epic cycle that does not survive, although it became a popular subject for poetry during Hellenistic times (the later fourth and third centuries B.C.E.). It was already known at the time of the making of Homer's *The Odyssey*, since Odysseus hears about the story. It describes the adventures of its hero Jason, who went to Colchas — on the far end of the Black Sea in Asia Minor — in order to get the Golden Fleece. He succeeds with the help of the king's daughter Medea, who has supernatural powers. She helps him because she has been struck with love for Jason. A later poet, Apollonius of Rhodes, wrote an *Argonautica* in the fourth century B.C.E. that describes the sorceress-like qualities of Medea. This characterization of Medea may well have been influenced by Euripides' *Medea* and was certainly a model for the figure of Dido in Virgil's *Aeneid*. Jason, who has been exiled from his native land for failing to resurrect his father with Medea's help, finds himself and Medea in Corinth.

The play by Euripides takes place many years after the adventure in Colchas. Medea has given birth to two children whom Jason evidently cares for very much. But he has left her, as we find out from the nurse and the tutor in the opening scene, for Glauce [GLAU-kay], the daughter of Creon — who is the king of Corinth — where they also live. It might be useful to tell students that this is by no means the same Creon as the tyrant of Thebes in *Oedipus Rex* or *Antigone*. *Creon* is close to the Greek word for power, *kratos*, and probably only means "a powerful ruler." Medea takes Jason's abandonment of her very hard. She wants to kill herself, her children, and nearly everyone around her. And yet, when confronted in a public place, she becomes calm and composed. The chorus, which is made up of local Corinthian (hence, Greek) women, tries to be loyal to Jason and wants from the outset to reason with Medea. It is they, however, who are convinced by the clever Medea to take revenge on Jason.

But this conversation is interrupted by Creon, who wants to preemptively deport Medea lest she pose a risk to his own daughter (who is, remember, betrothed to Jason). Creon believes that he is protecting his house and people from her imminent revenge and tries to stand firm but is finally convinced by Medea to be given twenty-four hours to "get her stuff together." In the end, he says, "I'm no tyrant by nature. My soft heart has often / Betrayed me;

and I know it's foolish of me now" (ll. 315–16). It is almost as if she has cast a spell over him at this point. Medea begins to plot as soon as Creon leaves, and she tries to find sympathy from the women: "We were born women — useless for honest purposes, / But in all kinds of evil skilled practitioners" (ll. 369–70). The chorus does not exactly cooperate, but they do sympathize.

Again, just as Medea is about to tell her plan, she is interrupted by another male authority — this time Jason. He tries to tell her that she could have stayed in Corinth, but she speaks in such a way that poses a risk to his children and the royal family. He offers friendship and tries to help financially. It is hardly the image of the enemy that Medea has painted thus far. But she rages violently against him, launching into a long speech about how she has always helped him and how ungrateful he is. The chorus is alarmed at the height of her anger, and Jason responds that he has tried to help her and has taken on this marriage so that his sons by Medea could be well off. He asks her to be thankful, then, for his own sacrifice in marrying Glauce in order to benefit his family with Medea. But he finishes his speech with taunting misogyny, saying it would be better if one could have children without women. The chorus responds that it is wrong for a man to abandon a wife. These constant interruptions by the chorus prove that Jason and Medea are not speaking directly to one another but rather are pleading as though in a court before a jury.

Only at this point, in fact, do Jason and Medea begin to truly argue. Jason insists that he is doing everything for his children's sake, but Medea is convinced that Jason is interested in a younger woman's bed. Only after the arguing couple has split up can the chorus finally give their traditional opening ode. They lament on the dangers of love and the horrors of exile. Opportunely, King Aegeus of Athens arrives to ask advice from Medea. He has been given an oracle, "not to unstop the wineskin's neck," which he needs to have interpreted. There may be a subtle joke here: Either the whole audience understands what the oracle means, or there is a delicate sexual overtone here. Medea doesn't interpret it but waits for Aegeus to ask her how she is doing. Again, Euripides appears to have made Aegeus a very weak character, something emphasized by his lack of children. Nevertheless, Aegeus, hardly as firm as Creon, is willing to accept Medea and her children in Athens as exiles. She binds him with an oath, which seems to confirm for the audience that she truly intends to take Aegeus's offer. But Medea's real reason is that she wants Aegeus to accept her even if she is polluted by the murder of Glauce and her own children. She tells her plan to the chorus, who tries to talk her out of it.

The chorus addresses the audience indirectly, praising Athens, and then Jason arrives. Medea now enacts her plan, behaving sweetly to Jason and asking for his forgiveness. She encourages her children (who, out of convention, must remain silent) to greet their father and to pass on a gift of a dress and golden crown to their new stepmother, Glauce. The chorus, perfectly aware of the trick that has been committed, prophecy the future. Usually choruses are as unaware of the coming events as the other characters, but these women of Corinth are like the audience, knowing how things will turn out but not sure when or how. In fact, both the audience and the chorus are surprised when the tutor, who we are sure will announce Glauce's death, instead comes in to tell Medea how delighted was Jason's mistress with the gifts. Since Glauce has permitted the boys to stay in Corinth, it seems all will be well, but Medea is in despair, nearly giving up the plan to kill the children, but in the end resolving to do the horrible deed.

After this, the chorus speaks on the difficulty of having children and how sweet it is to have children but also the heaviness of the responsibility. The argument seems to fall on Jason's side, since he has been saying that he has made his decision out of responsibility for his children. A messenger finally arrives with the news that the princess has died. He describes in gory detail how the garment consumed her. Again, the conventions of tragedy dictate that a messenger must deliver a speech speaking of the death of someone. But, at this point, there are children's voices heard offstage as well. This is highly unusual and would have alarmed the audience. The next victims, while not killed on stage, are killed within earshot of the audience. Jason appears, trying to storm the house to save the children. But Medea reappears in a chariot driven by snakes (or dragons, since the word is the same). We know that Euripides must have used the *skene*, since even in this early a play, Medea appears *above* the door; otherwise Jason would have run right into her. They fight again, and she curses Jason. She announces her plan to go to Athens (which is ambiguously good or bad for Athens).

IN THE CLASSROOM

I. Making the Monster of Medea

As with most works from the ancient world, students will lack the requisite foreknowledge to understand the play at the outset. Whereas the Athenian audience knew perfectly well what Medea was going to do and why, we moderns will not have heard these legends before. *Medea* is interesting because we gradually gather a picture of what Medea and Jason have done in the past from various speeches they make. However, it will be clearer for students if they understand the plot of *Jason and the Argonauts* as well as Euripides' *Medea* before they read the play.

Students may want to debate whether or not the values of an ancient society can be converted to a modern society. Perhaps, as relevant as the play seems on the backdrop of current events in the media, the conclusions it reaches are difficult for us to understand. A critic once said that Euripides was either a misogamist, a feminist, or both. If Euripides created the figure of Medea, a horrible witch who murders her own children, was this how he viewed women? Did he believe that they were all susceptible to psychological depravity? Or is he simply emphasizing how badly men treat women and how unequal was the society in which his heroines lived?

The comparative approach should also be employed here. Students may have read Sophocles' *Antigone*, which is also seen by some to contain feminist sentiment. Aristophanes' *Lysistrata* also deals with many of the problems of inequality and unfaithfulness that are described in *Medea*, except in a more contemporary and comical fashion. Students should compare these gender and power conflicts and how the author deals with each one.

Discussion

1. Unlike the other plays where the gods make themselves present by either being on stage or by bringing on plagues or other disasters, in *Medea*, the gods are curiously absent. In the final scene, Medea appears from the top of the *skene*, where gods should traditionally appear. What is the meaning or significance of this? What does this imply about the condition in which Medea finds herself? What gods, if any, are appealed to and why?

2. With which character is Euripides the most sympathetic? While he makes Medea the most affected of the two main figures, he also turns her into a sorceress and murderer. On the other hand, Jason, who has acted wrongly, tries to defend himself. Does Euripides try to portray Jason as fairly as possible?

3. Much of *Medea* is concerned with oratory and being clever at speaking. During the same period of time, a group of philosophers known as the Sophists (who were not from Athens) offered lessons in how to speak cleverly. In the Athenian legal system,

where one could be constantly sued by any Athenian citizen, it was useful to know how to speak cleverly. What tricks of speech are used by Medea and Jason? How can we tell that they are involved in an oratorical contest?

4. The nurse shows some understanding of the character of Medea before we even meet her. While speaking to the children, she warns them of Medea's nature. How does this affect our initial impression of Medea? Is she pitiable when we first meet her? How about at the end of the play? What makes her pitiable?

5. In one of the odes (p. 1015), the chorus describes how power was taken from women and now returns to women. They also see the princess of Corinth as someone who possesses power over Jason. Elsewhere, the nurse also claims that Jason is a "prisoner" of the princess's bed (l. 128). How is the princess granted power throughout the play? In what ways is she seen to be someone who is powerful? Over whom does she hold this power?

Connections

1. In Aeschylus's *Agamemnon* (p. 806), Clytemnestra kills Agamemnon by means of a woven cloak, just as Medea kills Glauce with a dress she has woven herself. Throughout both plays, there is much use of the metaphor of netting and weaving. We know that the creation of nets and woven materials was traditionally assigned to women. How do these metaphors work similarly in *Agamemnon* and *Medea*? Are there differences as well? How does this similarity help to characterize the personalities of Clytemnestra and Medea? What do they have in common?

2. The idea of "pollution" (in Greek, *miasma*) has been a common theme in all the plays. This was a cultural value that we do not have in our own society. In each of the plays we have read, discuss how concern about pollution has changed or affected the outcome of the plays. For example, Clytemnestra is polluted with Agamemnon's murder, Orestes with Clytemnestra's, Oedipus with the murder of his father Laius, and Creon tries to avoid polluting himself with the murder of Antigone. One might also want to consider whether or not pollution is a value in the societies reflected in Homer's world.

3. In Henrik Ibsen's play *Hedda Gabler* (Book 5), the heroine, Hedda, comes from an aristocratic family and has married into a bourgeois family. Likewise, Medea is the daughter of an Asian king and believed that in marrying Jason she would marry a prince. How have her expectations been changed? In what ways do the two women behave similarly toward their husbands and their fate? What are the differences in their behavior?

Groups

1. Assign a choral ode to each group, asking students to relate the choral ode to events preceding or following the ode. Have students describe how the odes link together different parts of the play. Does the choir react to recent events, or do they predict future events? What are their concerns? How do they change throughout the play?

2. Divide the class into two groups: those writing a defense speech for Medea and those writing a defense speech for Jason. Have each group compose their speech based on actual lines from the text for use as evidence and testimony.

Writing

Ask students to write a short paper in response to one or more of the following:

1. Aristotle once said that while Sophocles showed men "how they *should* be," Euripides portrayed them "how they *actually are*." Is this statement true? Using *Medea* and any play of Sophocles, compare the characterization of these plays.

2. Although Medea is neither a male nor a Greek, she appropriates much of the language of the Greek hero. What does she say in the attempt to make herself seem like a Greek hero?

3. How would you stage the last scene of the play? Describe where Jason would stand, where the chorus would stand, and where Medea and her chariot would be. What would the chariot look like, and how would the bodies of the children be displayed? How would Medea sound, and what other effects, if you were staging a modern version of the play, might you use?

4. Another Asian woman who is captured by a Greek male is Cassandra in Aeschylus's *Agamemnon* (p. 806). However, Cassandra acts somewhat differently from Medea. What are the similarities and differences between these two women?

BEYOND THE CLASSROOM

RESEARCH & WRITING

1. Medea often appeals to the chorus because its members are women just like she is. What does she say to them? How does she try to show that the women of Corinth have had a common experience with her?

2. How would you describe the character of the nurse? What role does she play in introducing the drama? How does she treat Jason, Media, and the children?

Project

1. Do research on postpartum disorder and infanticide. Some studies show that infanticide is much higher among women who have been abandoned by the babies' fathers. Based on what you have learned about the syndrome, could you say that Medea might suffer from such a disorder? Do you suppose that conditions in the ancient world might have caused many instances of infanticide?

WWW   For additional information on Euripides and annotated Web links, see *World Literature Online* at bedfordstmartins.com/worldlit.

FURTHER READING

Burnett, A. P. *Catastrophe Survived.* 1971.
Lloyd, M. *The Agon in Euripides.* 1992.
Loraux, B. *Tragic Ways of Killing a Woman.* 1987.
Murray, G. *Euripides and His Age.* 1946.
Pucci, Pietro. *Medea, The Violence and Pity in Euripides' Medea.* 1980.
Webster, T. B. L. *The Tragedies of Euripides.* 1967.
Zuntz, G. *The Political Plays of Euripides.* 1963.

MEDIA RESOURCES

VIDEO

Euripides' Life and Times: The Trojan Women
38 min., 1986 (Insight Media)
Including professionally acted scenes from *The Trojan Women*, this program illuminates themes of Euripides' tragedies, providing insights into daily life in ancient Athens, the status of women in Greek society, and the effects of war on the populace.

Medea
107 min., 1959 (Insight Media)
Euripides' classic is brought to life in this 1959 production. Judith Anderson plays the title role of the young princess, who has betrayed her family and homeland to steal the Golden Fleece for Jason.

Medea
87 min., 1982 (Films for the Humanities & Sciences)
This stunning Kennedy Center production of *Medea* stars Zoe Caldwell as Medea and Judith Anderson as the nurse. The English text is by Robinson Jeffers.

WEB SITES

Euripides
www.emory.edu/ENGLISH/DRAMA/Euripides.html
This page from Emory University offers an interesting excerpt on Euripides from Edith Hamilton's *The Greek Way.*

Euripides' *Medea* Study Topics
Iws.cccd.edu/kennedy/studyguides/EuripidesMedeaStudyTopics.htm
Find here a list of helpful study topics on Euripides.

AUDIO

Seven Classic Plays
8 tapes or 10 CDs, 11:25 hrs. (Blackstone Audiobooks)
Now, for the first time on audiocassette, Blackstone presents seven great plays in one volume, illustrating the development of European drama from ancient times to the threshold of the modern theater. Not mere readings, these are full performances that use the resources of audio to full advantage. All seven plays were taped with a repertory company in New York during the spring of 1985 and were finished in Chicago. The plays are *Medea, The Tempest, The Imaginary Invalid, Camille, An Enemy of the People, Arms and the Man,* and *Uncle Vanya.*

ARISTOPHANES, *Lysistrata* (p. 1044)

WWW   For a quiz on *Lysistrata*, see *World Literature Online*
at bedfordstmartins.com/worldlit.

Everyone knows that there are three famous ancient Greek tragedians: austere Aeschylus, philosophical Sophocles, and avant-garde Euripides. But among comedians of the classical period in Greece, there was only one that stood out far above the rest — Aristophanes. Although Eupolis and Cratinus were popular, the fact that no complete play of either of these comedians survive is very good evidence that Aristophanes was the best and, by any record, the most prolific of the ancient comedic playwrights. Born between 460 and 450 B.C.E., Aristophanes witnessed the height and fall of the Athenian empire by the time of his death around 386 B.C.E. We know next to nothing about the man, despite having eleven of his plays survive intact. Because nobody escaped his political satire, we do not even truly know what views he espoused. In Plato's dialogue, *Symposium*, Aristophanes is a dinner guest at Agathon's house (a famous tragedian of the time), and he tells an intriguing myth about love. Whether or not this was a caricature of the true Aristophanes is hard to say. In Plato's

Apology, Socrates claims that it is Aristophanes' play, the *Clouds* (produced in 423 B.C.E.), that leads to the bad opinion people had of Socrates and his school.

Lysistrata was produced in 411 B.C.E., paid for by the wealthy Callistratus and performed at the Dionsysia, a dramatic and musical festival in honor of the god Dionysus. Comedy had been a regular part of this festival for sixty years before Aristophanes ever brought a play to the stage. Like tragedy, it has certain conventions that must be followed. However, unlike tragedy, comedy is usually about contemporaneous or hypothetical events. In *Lysistrata*, the action of which occurs during the years of the Peloponnesian War, women take over the assembly and impose a sex ban until the men negotiate a peace.

Athenian audiences watched comedy after a day of terrifying tragedies and an orgiastic satyr play. Unlike tragedy, the number of actors was probably four (or five, in some cases), although there was need for many extras. Stagehands as well as the audience played an important role in the comedy, since the characters frequently made fun of the audience. Main characters on the stage wore pants with padding to make them appear to be big in the bottom and had a comically large, leather dildo. It is possible that there were female nonspeaking actors (such as Reconciliation at the end of the *Lysistrata*), who would have either worn nothing at all or translucent clothing. The chorus was made up of men dressed as animals, clouds, fairies, or, in this case, girls. The plays are all meta-theatrical, that is to say, they all make reference to acting, directing, and producing. Their format is conducive to this. The plays begin usually with the main character telling one-liners and making fun of the audience (this part of the plays doesn't survive, since it was extemporaneous). After the farce gets under way, the chorus comes onto the stage, which is usually spectacular and mixes choral songs with solos. At some point, the actors have reason to leave the stage, and the chorus addresses the audience directly (this is called the *parabasis*). This is usually done in the voice of the author and is an opportunity for making fun of other playwrights. Then, the chorus reverts back to its dramatic role, and the play continues. However, in comedy, unlike tragedy, and indeed, much modern drama, there is little need to define a break between the fictional stage and reality. Aristophanic comedy has no limits in this respect; it would be as if Jerry or Elaine of the television comedy *Seinfeld* addressed the cameraman or studio audience in the course of their routine.

The play begins in the Cave of Pan (not far from where the play was performed, actually), on the hill of the Acropolis. Lysistrata, an Athenian woman, awaits a meeting with other women for some unknown plan. The other women are equally unaware of what Lysistrata is planning but show a strong desire to have sex, and repeated jokes are made to this effect. When Lampito arrives, a Spartan with a difficult accent (this is a feature of the Greek, but the translator has done a fine job of showing the different women's accents), the other girls make erotic jokes about her appearance — "My word! How neatly her garden's weeded!" It must be remembered that the audience (at least those nearest to the stage) and the author were male and that certain stereotypes did exist about women. Although Sappho never refers to her girlfriends in crude terms, on the comic stage, groups of women make erotic comments to one another to show the male perception of female society being focused largely on sex and shallow conversation. The comedy of this situation is precisely in that Lysistrata announces a rather serious plan about dealing with the war, hitherto the province of officious males. Aristophanes has no intention of elevating the status of women or starting a feminist movement of any kind. His choice of women is intended to mean something like "even *women* have the sense not to continue to fight." A modern play might use rats or cockroaches instead.

After Lysistrata announces the plan, the women all swear an elaborate oath and involve some foreign, non-Greek ritual elements borrowed from the nomadic Scythian female representative. Parodying religious ceremony and language is very common in Aristophanes' plays. Apparently, the Greeks did not have scruples about inventing new gods or rituals on the stage, making fun of the sacrifice, or the swearing of oaths. A group of old men enter, whose leader mentions the first literary joke of the play, about Euripides, who is always referred to as being a misogynist (in one play, Euripides disguises himself as woman but is found out). The men try to set fire to the assembly building recently overtaken by a group of old women. The chorus is overpowered by a group of old women, who put the fire out. A civil servant shows up, assuming that the women must be involved in a bacchic revelry of some kind. This is actually what men usually thought groups of women were up to. At least once a year, women went to a festival for women alone and performed secret rites they could not reveal. For women, this was an important rite of passage. However, some groups of women went into the wilderness and participated in cult rituals for women that were supposedly of a violent nature (a play by Euripides, *Bacchae*, describes their activities). It is said that Alexander the Great's mother participated in such rituals. As the police prepare to scuffle with the women, Lysistrata intervenes.

An interesting claim is made when the magistrate reacts with disbelief that the women will control the treasury. Lysistrata explains that women already fulfill this task domestically, so why not on a national scale? It is true that Athenian women were actually responsible for keeping track of household expenditures, but again, Aristophanes is not making a claim for female equality or superiority but is rather making fun of the incompetence of Athenian men. Aristophanes makes reference to many of the tasks that women perform (such as carding wool and spinning), which could have a political application and is more of a slight against politics than a praise of women's virtues. In answer to the men's objections, the chorus of women sings a list of rites they have passed on behalf of the state and argue for equality with men.

However, just as we begin to make note of the women's accomplishments, Lysistrata sees that things haven't been going according to plan, since some of the women are abandoning their oath. As in the opening scene, the women desire sex and are looking for excuses to return home. The audience will have been disappointed if they didn't get to peek at a domestic scene, however. The audience's anticipation will be rewarded. Before all collapses, Lysistrata's faithful disciple, Myrrhine, meets up with her unfortunate husband, Cinesias. Cinesias hasn't been with his wife for awhile and is *burning* for her, especially after all the compliments Myrrhine has ostensibly been handing him. However, she hides from him, and he must pinch the baby to get her to appear. But by grabbing the baby, Myrrhine avoids her husband's embrace. She is barely dressed and is ravishing, so he is persuaded to vote for peace if he can have one night. Myrrhine doesn't give in it to him right away, though. She delays, fetching a bed, then a mattress, then a pillow, then a coverlet, only then to disappear when he wants her the most.

Apparently, this scene has played itself out in many households. When the Spartan herald shows up at the Athenian magistrate's residence, there is nothing he can do to conceal the painfully large erection he has. After denying that he's hiding a sword, the magistrate asks "Well, what's that I see?" "A Spartan message-staff," the herald answers. Needless to say, the Athenians and Spartans make peace. A statue (or it just as well could have been a live female slave) is used as a "map" of Greece, and they divvy up her various "parts." The men cannot stand it any longer and begin to take their clothes off. Afterwards, at a banquet, the Athenians and Spartans discover that they like each other and have some things in common. Athenian women and Spartan women lead dances praising their nations' women, and the play ends on this joyous note of reconciliation.

The idea of a sex strike is not unique to *Lysistrata*, although it is arguably the oldest record of such a strike (even if fictitious). In July and August of 2001, women in the Turkish village of Sirt used a sex strike to convince their husbands to update the water system of their community (apparently the plumbing, not fixed since the 1970s, was repaired within a month!). These women were inspired by a 1983 Turkish film in which women held a sex strike against men who did no work and didn't contribute domestically. On March 3, 2003, while the United States was preparing to go to war with Iraq, performances and readings of the *Lysistrata* were produced all over the world in a massive antiwar rally called the "Lysistrata Project." Some protesters in front of the Australian parliament declared a sex strike during the same period. In the last fifty years, there has been a resurgent interest in producing ancient Greek drama. Picasso drew illustrations for a 1934 performance by Gilbert Seldes. Aristophanes also wrote *Thesmophriazusae*, a play in which women at one of their special rites try to get rid of Euripides, who has been writing misogynist tragedies. In *Ecclesiazusae*, produced in 392 B.C.E., women take over the senate and introduce communist-like legislation.

TEXT & CONTEXT

The play's backdrop of the Peloponnesian War (the war between Athens and her allies against Sparta and her allies) is critical for understanding its importance, its humor, and also its initial reception in Athens. Like the reproductions done in the early twenty-first century C.E., Aristophanes' plays were antiwar plays. The war was only popular with the politicians who waged it; the generals were reluctant to fight, and the population, simultaneously afflicted by plague and famine, blamed the politicians for their demise. It is admirable that, in the face of such political turmoil, Athens retained the freedom of speech to produce a comedy of such biting satire only a few meters from the ruling class of his time. Few modern societies would allow such public criticism in the midst of war.

Within a decade of Cleisthenes' political reforms in 508 to 507 B.C.E., hostilities began on the Eastern front of the Ionian states. In 490 B.C.E., the Persians began a plan to take over all of Greece, and a war of huge proportions was fought. They were defeated in battles at Marathon (490 B.C.E.), Salamine (480 B.C.E.), and Platea (479 B.C.E.). However, in order to defeat the Persians, the Athenians constructed a navy that they allowed other states to use in exchange for mutual defense treaties and an annual sum to be deposited in a treasury on the island of Delos. The league of Greek states under the Athenian auspices, called the Delian League, was created in 476 B.C.E. In 449 to 448 B.C.E., the Persians were thoroughly and finally defeated. Herodotus notes that, by this time, there was a rivalry developing already between Sparta and Athens. Under the direction of General Pericles, Athens became an imperial power with colonies throughout the Aegean, using membership in the Delian League as a weapon against other states (since nonparticipation implied loyalty to the Persian king). Naturally, the Athenian treasuries were overflowing from contributions in years of peace when no triremes (Athenian war ships) were built or manned.

When the smaller rival states of Corcyra and Corinth were at war, the Athenians became involved in 432 B.C.E. The Spartans and the Athenians lined up on opposite sides of what should have been a small conflict. Alliances began to form on both sides of the battle line. When Thebes, a Spartan ally, unexpectedly attacked Plataea, north of Athens, the war began. Athens proved an easy adversary on land and had to retreat within city walls, seriously damaging its economy and making it susceptible to a plague, which struck in the summer of 430 B.C.E., killing Pericles and much of the rest of the population as well. In 420 B.C.E., a peace treaty was signed but with little effect. A new arena opened up in Sicily in which the mighty Athenian navy was soundly defeated. Political crises ensued as generals and politicians traded blame and recalled one another from command. In 412 B.C.E., the council voted to establish an oligarchy. Unable to put up with delays, a round of assassinations intimidated the council to let the Four Hundred rule by force in 411 B.C.E. The democracy was briefly restored at the end of the year, forcing the oligarchy to flee in order to avoid persecution. It was in this year that *Lysistrata* was produced (whether the women represented the democrats or the oligarchs is unclear). The new democracy recalled the generals who were in charge of the Sicilian disaster. In 406 B.C.E., the Spartans offered peace, but the Athenians refused. Instead, in 404 B.C.E., the Spartans enforced their own rule over Athens with the Rule of Thirty, Spartan loyalists who formed the new Athenian government. There were several attempts to restore the democracy. In 399 B.C.E., the philosopher Socrates was tried, convicted, and executed. Within seventy years, all of Greece would be subsumed as part of Macedonia and the empire of Alexander of Great.

IN THE CLASSROOM

I. MAKE LOVE NOT WAR

Students invariably find *Lysistrata* to be a fascinating play because it reveals the uninhibited nature of the Greeks in their comedy. Aristophanes is as modern as any satire of our own time, and, in this sense, is much easier to understand and read than the tragedians. The culture of the Athenians is also somewhat more recognizable to us than the artificially resurrected archaic cultures of tragedy. You may want to begin a study of the work by showing pictures or videos of creative antiwar works. Since *Lysistrata* is a drama, it is a visual experience and should be compared to contemporary visual experiences that are protests against conflicts. Ask students to state their reaction to these images and to discuss whether or not these works have any lasting effect, and, if they do, the nature of that effect. Secondly, you might consider delving into the middling society portrayed by Aristophanes. This would be a typical group of Athenian characters with their typical prejudices and thoughts. Even as exaggerated as they are, it gives a window into ordinary Greek life. Ask students to try and reconstruct the society from the picture Aristophanes has provided for us. In particular, what are their attitudes toward women? How do Athenians view other cultures and people?

Discussion

1. How effective is *Lysistrata* as an antiwar work? In what ways does it make its argument clear? How might people react to it? In which ways does it fail as an antiwar work?

2. How might the visual experience of *Lysistrata* affect its reception as being political satire? If you were producing the play, what would you do to help enhance the visual aspect of some of the scenes?

3. In tragedy, there is a built-in sense of suspense and anticipation, causing tension and release in the reader or audience. Is this also achieved in comedy? Are there scenes in *Lysistrata* that cause some tension or anticipation? How does the author carry out heightened suspense?

4. What do the characters say about Athenian society? How does this society view women? How do they view the old versus the young? How do they view non-Athenians and non-Greeks?

Connections

1. Compare the different views of women offered in Hesiod's view of Pandora (p. 263) and Sappho's writings about women (p. 791) with the views offered by the characters in Aristophanes' *Lysistrata*. From what point of view is each portrayal of women? How do they differ? Can you tell that they come from the same culture? How?

2. Compare and contrast the antiwar views of Aristophanes in this play with the poetry of Wilfred Owen and to Takenishi Hiroko (both in Book 6). In many ways, these are the tragic corollary to this comedy. How do Takenishi's characters react differently to the affects of the atom bomb as compared to Lysistrata? What are the common themes? Does the gender of these characters make a difference?

Groups

1. Break the class into four groups portraying old women, young women, old men, and young men. Hold a mock debate over going to war. Each group must first agree on an opinion about the war and then produce an argument for or against it. How does gender or age affect someone's opinion about war and conflict, or does it have no affect?

2. Although we have the lines that the actors of the comedy spoke, we do not have either the stage directions or the extemporaneous jokes that would have naturally been part of the play. Dividing the students into several groups, have them act out part of the play without using a script, concentrating on following the gist of the lines from memory, extemporizing freely and using stage directions creatively.

Writing

Ask students to write a short paper in response to one or more of the following:

1. What are the arguments the women make for granting them authority instead of men? Are they persuasive arguments? Why? What effect might that have on the audience?

2. Aristophanes frequently makes fun of religion and ritual practice. What are some of the ceremonial situations he makes fun of in *Lysistrata*? How might you interpret this irreverence in light of the wider themes of the book?

3. How does Aristophanes make each character individualized? Give a description of each character, and describe how different they are and what they do that demonstrates their individual personalities.

BEYOND THE CLASSROOM

RESEARCH & WRITING

1. In Bharati Mukherjee's "A Wife's Story" (Book 6), an Indian immigrant discusses women's relationships with their husbands. Compare and contrast her views with the women of *Lysistrata* and the relationship they have with their husbands. Which is more realistic?

2. Are there any weaknesses or faults of which the women accuse the men? Are the women themselves guilty of these weaknesses?

3. What contributes to making this comedy funny? How is the humor achieved? What scenes in particular are very funny? Why?

Project

1. Read Aristophanes' *Ecclusiazusae*, a play about women who take over the senate written in 392 B.C.E. after the Peloponnesian War has already been fought. Compare the motives and characteristics of the women involved. What has changed now that the war is over? Are the characterizations of the women and men the same?

WWW   For additional information on Aristophanes and annotated Web links, see *World Literature Online* at bedfordstmartins.com/worldlit.

FURTHER READING

Barreca, Regina. *Last Laughs: Perspectives on Women and Comedy.* 1988.
Csapo, Eric, ed. *Crossing the Stages: The Production, Performance and Reception of Ancient Theater.* 1999.
Euben, J. Peter. *Corrupting Youth: Political Education, Democratic Culture, and Political Theory.* 1997.
Henderson, J. *Aristophanes Lysistrata/Edited with Introduction and Commentary by Jeffrey Henderson.* 1987.
Lord, Louis E. *Aristophanes: His Plays and His Influence.* 1963.
Pelling, C. B. R. *Literary Texts and the Greek Historian.* 2000.
Silk, M. S. *Aristophanes and the Definition of Comedy.* 2000.
Strauss, Leo. *Socrates and Aristophanes.* 1966.
Sutton, Dana Ferrin. *Ancient Comedy: The War of the Generations.* 1993.
Whitman, Cedric Hubbell. *Aristophanes and the Comic Hero.* 1964.

MEDIA RESOURCES

VIDEO

The Gods Are Laughing: Aristophanes, His Life and Theatre
52 min., 1995 (Films for the Humanities & Sciences)
Designed as a pseudo-biography, this video explains how Aristophanes became the father of political satire. It juxtaposes elements of Aristophanic plays with the activities of contemporaneous people.

Lysistrata
97 min., 1987 (Insight Media)
Shot at the Acropolis, this adaptation of the ancient Greek comedy by Aristophanes is a timeless injunction against the senselessness of war. For mature students. (In Greek with subtitles.)

Lysistrata
65 min., 1968 (IMDB)
Directed by Jon Matt, this is a U.S.-film version of Aristophanes' classic.

WEB SITES

Aristophanes
www.imagi-nation.com/moonstruck/clsc13.htm
Users will find a brief biography of Aristophanes at this site as well as summaries of several of his works.

Aristophanes — The Classic Text: Traditions and Interpretations
www.uwm.edu/Library/special/exhibits/clastext/clspg033.htm
From the library of the University of Wisconsin–Milwaukee, this site is a great place to learn more about translations and editions of the works of Aristophanes. It includes biographical information about the author and facsimile pages from translated volumes of his work in many languages and from many centuries, including etchings by Picasso and Beardsley of passages from *Lysistrata*.

The Internet Classics Archive — Works by Aristophanes
Classics.mit.edu/Browse/browse-Aristophanes.html

Read the complete e-texts of Aristophanes' works as well as students' discussions of his works.

Theatre Database — Aristophanes
www.theatredatabase.com/ancient/aristophanes_001.html
This site provides biographical background on Aristophanes' life as well as links to a number of relevant pages.

Theatre History.com — Aristophanes and His Comedies
www.theatrehistory.com/ancient/aristophanes001.html
Read a biography of Aristophanes here, and find a number of helpful links to research sites.

PLATO, *Apology, Phaedo,* and *The Republic* (p. 1083)

WWW   For a quiz on *Apology*, see *World Literature Online*
       at bedfordstmartins.com/worldlit.

These works may be read either in the order they are presented, or with the "Allegory of the Cave" in *The Republic* before *Apology* and *Phaedo*. *Phaedo* will provide relatively little for discussion (unless the whole dialogue is read), but it serves as an epilogue to *Apology*. This may be a good time to discuss how the Athenians ruled themselves. They possessed a democracy quite unlike our own. In many ways, it was more direct, but in others, susceptible to sycophants and corrupt officials. It was certainly a society of many socioeconomic classes, having emerged only recently from aristocracy. It may help, before reading *Apology* to do two things: (1) to discuss briefly the philosophy of Socrates' philosophy and (2) the charges against him. Many philosophers have viewed Socrates (c. 470–399 B.C.E.) as the breaking point between the earliest Western philosophies and the modern development of philosophy. For some philosophers, like the early modernist Nietzsche, this break was an artificial divide that prevented the true development of philosophy. For others, like Kant, the philosophy of Socrates was an important step toward man realizing his place in the world. Rather than finding out scientific scraps of information or examining myths to develop answers about his world, Socrates began with the foundation of approaching philosophy negatively. That is to say, he began with the assumption that he knew nothing and that everything he saw or heard was a mere appearance or phenomenon but not a true absolute. Thus when he asks his pupils "What is a table?," he rebukes them for offering examples of tables but not speaking as to the actual *form* of a table, or that which makes a table. The dialogue format adopted by Plato, which presumably derives from the Socratic Method (the method whereby the teacher asks questions that guides the student to discover knowledge for her- or himself), accomplishes this negative format of philosophy.

Forms, according to Socrates, are eternal and unchangeable; the divine properties of a thing. However, form also causes the existence of a thing (like the form of "surface" for a table). This separates them from "universals" like "wooden" or "blue," which could be used to create things other than a table (and, indeed, could be used to create almost anything). But Socrates, unlike the later Aristotle, was not interested in the biological categorization of items and events in his world. Rather, he became interested in the development of the soul through this search for the forms. He envisioned philosophy as a kind of pilgrimage, where the practitioner would constantly question things around him to find out the truth. The problem is that the perceptual world only approximates the ideal form. We must understand abstractly what "justice" is in the ideal sense, even though our own institutions demonstrate only a rough estimation of the ideal. Likewise, the guitar player tries to tune his instrument based on the abstract ideal of "being in tune," without ever really reaching it. In particular, the philosopher must eventually know the form behind goodness. The knowledge of forms is actually innate within us, according to Socrates. Our souls, once free of our bodies, could conceive the true forms directly, but our bodies, which are reliant on imperfect senses, imprison our souls and cause them to be unable to perceive true forms.

Socrates left behind no writings, so we cannot tell what were his particular beliefs and what were the beliefs of his student Plato, on whom we rely for most of our information about the philosophy of Socrates. Independent of Plato, there are other sources that confirm that he was very well known in Athenian society. Because he taught in the public square (the *agora*), he was often confused with the Sophists — a group of professors with whom Socrates often debated — who offered courses on how to speak well. In a play by Aristophanes, *The Clouds*, Socrates is ridiculed for being like the Sophists and for examining the unpractical. In addition, it seems that Socrates did not believe in the traditional Athenian pantheon but rather in different gods and in a different concept of the divine. In Plato's *Apology*, we hear Socrates argue that most people have formed an opinion about him based on *The Clouds* and not necessarily on direct experience. But the play was produced in 423 B.C.E., twenty-four years before Socrates would be sentenced to death.

TEXT & CONTEXT

CONTEXT AND SYNOPSIS OF *APOLOGY*

It is certainly true that, by itself, having different religious beliefs from other Athenians would not have gotten one in much trouble at all. In fact, we are not sure if educated Athenians really believed in the gods. In 399 B.C.E., the charges against Socrates were that he refused to acknowledge the gods that the *polis* (city-state) of Athens acknowledged, that he introduced new divinities, and that he corrupted the youth. Again, it is difficult to see why Socrates, based on other legal precedents, would have been put to death for these crimes. It is quite possible that Socrates was a scapegoat for a larger problem at hand. Athens was defeated in the war, and a postwar government known as the "Thirty Tyrants" greatly limited the freedoms and indeed murdered many of the city's citizens. Socrates was the teacher of some of these tyrants, Critias and Charmides. Later writers have speculated that it was because of this that Socrates had charges leveled against him. Another possibility was that he was the teacher of Alcibiades, who had, on the night before the Sicilian expedition in 415 B.C.E., chopped the penises off statues of Hermes that Athenians used to guard their homes. It was considered greatly inauspicious, and, as it turned out, the Athenians were soundly defeated at Syracuse. Alcibiades was to return to Athens on murder charges and be put to death, but he defected to Sparta instead.

Again, it seems unreasonable to think that twenty-three years after Aristophanes' play, or sixteen years after the Sicilian expedition, or indeed five years after the end of the rule of the Thirty Tyrants, that 280 citizens would condemn to death a man they had known so long for charges that seem difficult to equate with the man we read about in Plato. In all the dialogues, he certainly talks to young men, usually the sons of politically prominent people. He never dismisses the traditional gods of Athens out of hand. He dismisses what the poets say about them (Homer and Hesiod, especially), as do many of his contemporaries. In his discourses, he doesn't introduce new or strange divinities, although he begins to speak about a certain divine spirit that is central to his philosophical journey. But ancient Greek religion was not like Christianity: It was not a heresy to speak about the gods or to add or subtract gods. What *was* considered impious were certain modes of behavior or actions, such as Alcibiades' mutilation of the Hermae. Moreover, even if his teachings were considered dangerous to the state, the Athenians believed strongly in freedom of speech, and Socrates would have been exiled at most for expressing any views against democracy or the polis in general.

Tradition has it that Socrates remained completely silent during the whole trial, offering no defense. There are two versions of *Apology* made by Plato and Xenophon. The *Apology* of Plato has withstood the test of time and has served as a model defense speech over the ages; it also serves as a summary of the way in which this philosopher lived his life and wished to see others who wanted enlightenment to live theirs. He begins by saying that he doesn't know how to deliver a defense in court and that he is unfamiliar with legal language. The speech he gives, however, is very close in line with all the other defense speeches that have survived to the present day, and is, in fact, superior in many ways to them. Most speeches begin by saying that the accusers speak better than the defendant can, they mention how outlandish the claims are, and then proceed to speak about what an upstanding citizen the defendant is and begs the audience to imagine they are just a member of the family. Most defendants claim they have little money (so that the fine will be small) and that they have lived modestly. Socrates' speech includes all of these details. Plato even includes the vivid detail of a crowd reacting to certain items in the speech and Socrates attempting to silence them.

Socrates makes note of a few important facts that help to provide context to the trial. First, he tells his audience that they were children when they first heard the accusations against him, and he provides the detail that it was in a play of Aristophanes that they first saw someone by his name acting impiously. He tells them that they, like all children, were probably very impressionable and were not difficult to persuade. This is strangely the same claim the prosecution makes about his teachings, though. But in response to this, he tries to distance himself from the Sophists (with whom the Athenians identified him), saying that he is unable to offer the kind of services that they offer. He does not teach rhetoric, in other words. Mind you, he says this as he is producing a tour-de-force defense speech. When he claims to know nothing of which the Sophists profess, he has to quiet the outrage of the crowd.

He produces a story about an oracle given to him when he was young. His friend Chaerephon, whom apparently all of Athens knows, asked the oracle if there is anyone wiser than Socrates. The crowd again protests and Socrates must tell them to be quiet. The oracle answers, of course, that nobody is wiser than Socrates. He offers Chaerephon's brother as a witness. Socrates says that he thinks to himself "Why does the god say I am wise when I know I am not?" So, as he says, he goes to a very wise man (who is also politically powerful) and tries to find out what makes this wise man wise. It turns out that although the wise man *says* he is wise, he doesn't know anything. The conclusion we are supposed to reach is that *knowing* one does not know anything is far superior to *not knowing* one does not know anything. At any rate, Socrates, in his questioning of all these wise men, becomes a hated man.

Socrates goes on to say that, by chance, some wealthy men's sons congregated around him while he was asking these wise and prominent men whether or not they were wise. When these young people saw that these powerful people were not wise, and began themselves to question others, these "wise men" became irate at Socrates and invented slander against him — a slander identical to the charges to which he is answering in court. Socrates then says that the real reason they were upset is that they were unable to face their *not knowing* something. He names his accusers — Meletus, Anytus, and Lycon, all powerful liberally minded democrats of the time, representing different walks of life. Socrates cross-examines Meletus, a gesture that must have seemed quite threatening. The Athenian legal system is different from the British or American system in that all cases are civil cases. That is to say, the state does not prosecute anyone; an individual takes a person to court and sues for a fine or other punishment, whether his chicken has been stolen or his slave has been killed. Meletus is the individual who takes Socrates to court (for certain reasons, we believe it to be at the prompting of Anytus). When he has questioned Meletus, however, he states that he is not afraid of these individuals but rather of his reputation — the slander of the multitude — that will convict him. This is interesting because, for the first time, he acknowledges that he is unpopular and that he has to defend his reputation much more than the individual charges launched against him.

At this point, he seems more or less resigned, and what he defends are his choices for having become the person he has become in Athens. He compares himself with the ideal Greek hero, to Achilles, who killed Hektor even though he knew it would mean his own death. He also mentions his military service and how he faced death in battle. This is meant, one imagines, to stir up some patriotic feeling among the gathered citizens. He compares the fear of death to the belief that one knows when in fact one does not know. If one does not know death, he says, how can one fear it? He continues along this patriotic trend, however: Would he accept exile if he were offered it? No. His duty and responsibility, he says, are to the polis that raised him, and so he would continue questioning everyone, particularly citizens, since (so he says) the god orders him. He tells them that no matter their verdict, he cannot change and would not mind dying for the polis in this capacity (as questioner of its citizens). The audience is outraged again.

He begins to speak in a more threatening tone. The city will suffer more by killing him than letting him live. To kill a man unjustly invites evil, he says, since he is as though a gift from a god to the polis. He is a kind of "gadfly," something to prod and annoy the beast of the city. If the sleeping beast, annoyed by the gadfly, chooses to swat him out, then it will continue to sleep. Having established himself as a citizen of value, he becomes yet more personal, calling himself the father and older brother of each citizen. He claims to be absent from political affairs and to be directed by a small voice, a *daemon* (Greek for "spirit" or "minor divinity"). This is the first mention of a new god by him.

He then begins to outline his solitary political involvement on the Council. Like the jury system in modern courts, Athenian legislators were also rotated in from the populace, not elected as we elect our congressmen or members of Parliament. He was asked to judge a group of generals who had abandoned the dead and dying following victory at the battle of Arginusae in 406 B.C.E. Unwilling to give them the death penalty for this crime, Socrates alone did not vote for it. The crowd, superstitious about leaving the dead unburied (recall the plot of Sophocles' *Antigone*), urged the politicians to arrest and impeach Socrates. After reminding the citizens of this event, he then, not wanting to totally alienate his crowd, talks about his actions under the Thirty Tyrants. He confesses that he was summoned to be part of the council but only, he excuses himself, in order to implicate others in their reign of terror. He tells the crowd that, on a controversial decision, he left the room and went home. Again, it was not death he feared so much as doing the unjust thing.

Finally, he turns and lists his students who are in the audience. Why, he asks them, if their sons and brothers have been corrupted by him, have not their fathers, brothers, and uncles brought forth charges against him? If he has corrupted any of the youths, then why is it that neither they nor their guardians, as in Aristophanes' *The Clouds*, bring him to court? In his conclusion, he notes that he did not give a tearful address to the jury but rather that he spoke plainly. He says that he has not begged, but offered, a logical defense of himself.

At this point, the votes are counted, and the fate of Socrates has been decided: 280 against and 220 for him. He is surprised that so many voted for him and counts himself a victor since his principle accuser, Meletus, could not have obtained the necessary votes without accusations launched by Anytus and Lycon as well. His defense is genuine at this point because he has already been convicted. He did not try to enrich himself, become powerful, or join social clubs. He urged each citizen to care not about what he owned but about himself, and he told them to care not about what belonged to the polis but about the actual polis itself. Then, he considers various punishments: a large fine or exile. He proposes a fine of thirty minas (about $250,000 in today's U.S. dollars, but remember that Socrates had very little money for himself or his family). Again, the jury takes some time to vote between the fine (the penalty offered by Socrates) and the penalty of death (the penalty that was offered by Meletus). The latter is the decision. Socrates' response is interesting since, for a second time, he refers to the efficacy of his speech. He is not convicted because he could not produce a good defense speech but rather because he didn't say what they wanted him to say. Already an old man and near death, he begins to prophecy that Athens will not be relieved of the need of self-examination that he imposes. He then contemplates on what death will profit him, and here *Apology* ends.

In *Phaedo* and *Crito*, dialogues that occur during the imprisonment, a number of interesting arguments are made. In *Crito*, the polis is personified, and Socrates conducts a dialogue with it. Despite the huge *Republic* and *Laws*, the short dialogue in *Crito* is the most memorable for Socrates' conception of justice and the absoluteness of his convictions. In the *Phaedo* selection, we read the end of his discussion on the soul. Most of *Phaedo* has been concerned with the soul. It reminds us of the last lessons of Christ before his crucifixion: The most faithful disciples are gathered around, and the basic tenets of his beliefs are laid out. Socrates dies willingly and bravely, not delaying the taking of the poison (hemlock) and not allowing his family to see him or others who might become emotional.

THE "ALLEGORY OF THE CAVE"

It is difficult to see the difference between a "Platonic" and a "Socratic" view of the world. Plato certainly derived much from his teacher, although he also quickly learned that his dialogues need not serve as transcripts of lessons learned but rather could be employed as tools for disseminating Socrates' philosophy. The notion of the forms and ideals is clearer in the so-called middle dialogues, such as the *Phaedo* and *The Republic*. *The Republic* is a misleading name in many ways, since, in Greek, the title is more like "Governance: On the Soul." The word *republic* implies a country with an elected leadership. In Plato's *The Republic*, Socrates begins with the question "What is justice?" and, from there, builds a state he believes to be just. This state would seem contrary to all the democratic ideals we believe to exist in Athens. Socrates calls for a philosophical expert to be at the head of state and for various experts to be engaged in different fields. He also designs a rigorous education system (one that was perhaps used at the Academy, the school Plato later founded). However, he also censures much of traditional Greek literature, music, art and dance. In his effort to build the ideal state, he also tries to create the ideal citizen by a controversial molding process. The state Socrates designs, needless to say, is impractical and probably an unwanted utopia.

Within the seventh book of *The Republic*, Socrates discusses how a philosopher is fit for rule only in his kingdom, since the philosopher seeks out "the good," which is the highest goal of knowledge. If this sounds extremely abstract and without definition, then welcome to the world of Socrates. "The good" is a form only present in various kinds of moral virtues. Knowledge of the good, in earlier works of Plato, leads to happiness. The problem of knowledge is that there are various stages one must go through before knowledge, none of which, apparently, is any good: Imagining is useless but for seeing images, belief is misleading except for visible things, thinking helps only with science, knowledge is good for the forms, but intelligence (*noesis*) is what is needed to perceive the good.

The "Allegory of the Cave" comes after this description of the modes of thinking and before a discourse on the ten-year diet of mathematics Socrates intends to give his citizen-students. The cave as a traditional place of initiation (there are several caves along the face of the Acropolis) is replete throughout Greek literature. Later authors treated caves as places of mystery and surprise. Novices were led through the dark cave and then suddenly brought out into the bright light and revealed something that must have seemed, after sufficient amounts of smoke and wine, to be supernatural.

In Socrates' cave, the prisoners are held to be facing a wall on which they can see the shadows of items outside the cave. It may help to draw a picture of this. In modern parlance, it is as if we are watching someone pass a hand or other objects over a flashlight and make shadows. We are chained in such a way that we perceive only the shadows and believe those shadows to be the true nature of the objects we see. The lessons from this parable are many. When the released prisoner stands up and turns around, the light is too much for him, and he will believe the real objects to be an illusion, since he is accustomed to the shadow. Thereby, he will return to the recesses of the cave. Remember, Socrates believed that our souls were prisoners in our bodies much as these men are prisoners in the cave. But if a man is somehow forced to endure the bright light, and he becomes accustomed to it, he will realize that he now sees the reality of things. Once he sees the true forms in all their color, he will not want to return to the cave.

Consider now what happens in *Apology*. Socrates is being accused of corrupting the youth, essentially of leading them out of the cave. What Plato writes in *The Republic* must have been influenced by this greatly: "Men would say of [the one who went into the light and back down into the cave] that up he went and down he came without his eyes; and that it was better not even to think of ascending; and if any one tried to loose another and lead him up to the light, let them only catch the offender, and they would put him to death." Plato continues along this strain, saying it would be ridiculous for a man who was nearly blinded by a new light to have to stand and defend himself in court. There is some anger on Plato's part, coming out of the voice of Socrates, for having put his teacher to death.

The second lesson to be learned from the allegory is the nature of learning itself. Socrates says that it is not like making a blind man able to see or putting sight into sightless eyes. Rather, "the power and capacity of learning exists in the soul already." We need only to adjust to the light in order to be able to learn. The ability is with us all along. Gradually, we can be accustomed to the truth and life outside the cave without any need for new eyes or of someone adding something to our eyes to make us see. This is an important tenet of Socrates' philosophy: The soul is immortal and thus already possesses all knowledge. The only problem that remains is for us, with our souls imprisoned in our bodies, to remember that knowledge. The body, with its sensual needs, weighs down the progress of the soul on its journey to the highest good. Socrates rounds out the allegory by supposing that the body would be relieved of these desires of food and drink upon leaving the cave. In this way, those who have left the cave will make excellent ministers of state, unable to be bribed or corrupted. But in order for them to rule, they will be made to descend back into the cave. Socrates' students protest by saying that this is unjust. But the happiness of the state, the philosopher responds, depends on it.

This reveals another aspect of Socrates' political philosophy, something some scholars find to be akin to communism. He uses the metaphor of a hive of bees, with worker bees and a queen bee, all working in cooperation with one another. No one particular class (philosophers included) should be happier than the other classes in the state. If all classes perceive themselves as being benefactors of one another and conversely beneficiates of other members of the community, then they will all be bound together. Thus the philosophers who have emerged from the cave will have to descend into the cave, not willing to govern, out of knowledge that this is just. The philosophers will be rewarded not in gold and silver but in virtue and wisdom.

IN THE CLASSROOM

I. PUNISHMENT AND SELF-KNOWLEDGE IN PLATO

There is a lot to discuss in these selections of Plato. Each question that Socrates asks is a question worthy of asking anybody and each response Socrates gives deserves questioning. To begin with, the major issue of *Apology* is whether or not the polis is just in putting Socrates to death. One comparison that immediately springs to mind, although it is a young man rather than an old one, is the case of John Walker, who was captured in Afghanistan in 2002. He was an American citizen who went to help fight for the cause of an Islamic state. Although he was not directly responsible (or even really aware) of the terrorist attacks in New York, Pennsylvania, and at the Pentagon, and although it is not clear that he ever took up arms directly against Americans, his association with Al Qaeda and even his choice of faith made him a controversial figure in many Americans' eyes. His parents pleaded that he was a patriot in the end and that he believed in American ideals. Originally, the government even sought the death penalty, but his case was handled differently from most criminal investigations, and he may not have had access to legal help in Afghanistan. He went to the Middle East for ideals he was free to express in the United States, but, when he returned, the public had a different image of him.

How fair is the jury system? How impartial can we be? Questions of legality are very important in *Apology*. It is difficult to presume innocence if someone is standing in a courtroom. If someone has taken the trouble to arrest someone, then that person *must* have done something to lead others to believe he has done wrong. Furthermore, a trial is based on the question "Did he or she do *x*?" The answer determines whether or not the defendant will be punished. However, the *x* component is flexible. Did Socrates deny the gods as Homer and Hesiod wrote about them? Yes, sort of. Did he introduce new gods? It seems he may have. Did he corrupt the youth? Well, he did influence them. The laws are not made to fit the crime, but rather a law is found that has something in common with the crime. If Socrates was irreverent of the *polis* gods, a simple unqualified "yes" or "no" is the only thing a jury needs to answer.

The Greek word *apologia* means "a reasoning from after the fact," or a defense. It is not, as the English word *apology* might imply, a series of excuses or a statement of regret. Socrates is not regretful whatsoever. How does he characterize himself? Does he see himself as the philosopher who has gone out of the cave and sees the real situation, or is he, as Plato makes him out to be in *The Republic*, still squinting and defending himself at the same time? Does the Socrates of *Apology* ever answer to the charges leveled against him?

The consequences of the "Allegory of the Cave" will also provide much discussion on what is to be learned from it. Many of Socrates' arguments seem to be problematic. If some people leave the cave and discover it is better outside of the cave, how can you convince them to come back? The counterargument that they can only be bribed to return seems very plausible. Who would prefer their reward in wisdom and truth instead of money? After all, why are we really sitting in a university classroom? Will we be willing to return to the cave we came from without reward in silver? Socrates' society requires a kind of indoctrination of reliance, whereby the philosophers feel obliged to return, however unwillingly, to the cave. How effective is his plan? Will he produce a viable State in this manner?

Students may wish to view the movie *Matrix* (1999), which is based on this allegory. In the movie, machines are using human bodies for energy and feeding these humans dreams from which they never wake. All sensations of reality are created by "the Matrix," in which humans live and interact. Meanwhile, the machines take advantage of the human bodies. Some humans can be revived, however, and free themselves from the Matrix (with difficulty). These humans then must try to recruit other humans inside the Matrix and convince them to free themselves from the illusions provided by the machines. The movie offers a number of additional philosophical tenets of Judaism, Buddhism, and Christianity as well but may provide some room for interesting debate. How can we tell what is real and what is not? Is it viable to decide to stay in the imaginary world if that world is more pleasant, or are we obliged to go to the real world?

Discussion

1. Which philosophical ideas presented in *Apology* and the "Allegory of the Cave" are the same? How does Plato use those ideas to create the personality of Socrates?

2. What ideas in the "Allegory of the Cave" would Socrates have to defend in the courtroom? Are there any controversial subjects that may have been offensive to the mainstream Athenian public?

3. When is it acceptable to charge people for their beliefs? When does it happen that people's actions become dangerous enough that they must be arrested? How is it possible that Socrates may have become a danger to Athens?

4. What are the rhetorical features of Socrates' defense? How might this be similar to a modern-day defense speech? What are the weaknesses of his defense? What were the motives of those who voted against him?

Connections

1. In *Apology*, Socrates compares himself to Greek heroes. To which heroes does he compare himself, and how, in *Phaedo*, does he die?

2. The building of a utopia is a common theme in literature and philosophy. Name another work that tries to build a utopian state (for example, in some of Shakespeare's plays or in the works of Thoreau or Machiavelli). What are the arguments against such a utopia? What do most of these utopias have in common with one another?

Groups

1. Ask groups to create an outline of *Apology* and its arguments. Assign them different parts of the speech to outline, and have them write the outline on the blackboard and then reconstruct the speech. How effective is the structure of the argument? Does Socrates answer to the charges?

2. Hand out slips of paper, some of which have truths and some of which have lies. One suggestion may be to write genuine quotes from the Plato reading versus made-up ones. Each student should get at least five slips of paper. Give two or three students slips of paper that are truths. These students are "out of the cave." All students may trade these slips of paper freely, even trying to get more than one slip of lies for one slip of truths. Students who have truths will know because they recognize the text. Students with lies will not recognize their text. The goal of the game is to get as many slips of paper as possible with at least one of them being a truth. Some of the students outside the cave may elect not to trade their cards or to "go back into the cave," while others will try to go back into the cave to trade their truths. But beware: Students must have already read the text to know what will be true and false and those outside the cave will be indistinguishable from those inside the cave.

Writing

Ask students to write a short paper in response to one or more of the following:

1. What is the moral of the "Allegory of the Cave"? Like a parable from religious traditions, it is clear that this metaphor is meant to teach us. What is the most important thing Socrates wants us to learn?

BEYOND THE CLASSROOM

RESEARCH & WRITING

1. In what way is philosophy concerned with the opposition between truth and appearances? How does this apply to Socrates' defense of himself in *Apology* and the preconception the crowd evidently has about him?

2. Are there any modern situations that are similar to the "allegory of the cave"? Are we also deceived by the appearances of things, or has the scientific revolution of the Renaissance made us immune to the troubles of the cave? Can we acknowledge that progress has been made since Socrates spoke these words? Cite your examples by using other primary and secondary resources.

3. The descent back into the cave mirrors other characters' descents into the underworld, such as those of Dante in *The Divine Comedy*, Aeneas in Vergil's *Aeneid*, and Odysseus in Homer's *Odyssey*. However, instead of teaching in the underworld, these characters learn from the underworld. How, then, are the return to the cave and the trip to the underworld related? What key thing do philosopher and hero alike learn from their downward visit?

Projects

1. After watching the movie *Matrix* (1999) or any other film that mirrors the situation described in the "Allegory of the Cave," cite similarities and differences between the two. What are the major conflicts that the philosopher faces once he is outside the cave? Which is preferable, the reality outside the cave or the shadows within?

2. Read the speech by Lysias, "On the murder of Eratosthenes" (no. 1). This short speech is another example of a courtroom speech, written for the defendant, a man who killed Eratosthenes for sleeping with his wife. The speech gives much insight into Greek family life and husband-wife relations, but it is also a short and well-written defense speech (the defendant was acquitted in the end). Compare this speech to *Apology*. What features are similar? Which are different?

WWW   For additional information on Plato and annotated Web links, see *World Literature Online* at bedfordstmartins.com/worldlit.

FURTHER READING

Allen, R. E. *Socrates and Legal Obligation.* 1980.
Annas, Julia. *An Introduction to Plato's* Republic. 1981.
Burnet, J. *Plato's* Euthyphro, Apology, *and* Crito. 1924.
Cornford, F. M. *Plato:* Republic. 1941.
Guthrie, G. W. C. *Socrates* in *A History of Greek Philosophy*, vol. III, part 2. 1971.
Hackforth, R. *The Composition of Plato's* Apology. 1933.
Kraut, Richard. *Socrates and the State.* 1981.
Shorey, P. *What Plato Said.* 1933.
White, Nicholas. *Plato on Knowledge and Reality.* 1976.

MEDIA RESOURCES

VIDEO

Ancient Greece
48 min., 2000 (Insight Media)
This video explores the ideas of the great philosophers Pythagoras, Socrates, Plato, Aristotle, and Alexander the Great, considering how each was a pupil of his predecessors and how together they formed a golden age of thought and intellect. It includes footage of the ruins of ancient Greece as well as dramatic readings from the philosophers' works.

Greek Thought
30 min., 1989 (Annenberg/CPB Video)
Socrates, Plato, and Aristotle laid the foundation of Western intellectual thought.

The Greeks: In Search of Meaning
25 min., 1970 (Insight Media)
An introduction to Greece's golden age, this video features dramatizations of philosophical and moral debates. Socrates and his disciples argue about the value of friends and wealth, liberty and law, and the meaning of the good life. The program also presents scenes from *Antigone* and *Lysistrata* and re-enacts events leading to the death of Socrates.

Plato
46 min., 1987 (Insight Media)
Hosted by Bryan Magee, this video shows how Plato's ideas began as extensions of those of his teacher Socrates and then developed into original doctrines. It examines his ideas of knowledge as virtue, the immortality and tripartite division of the soul, and the theory of forms. It also considers his political philosophy.

Plato's Apology: The Life and Teachings of Socrates
30 min., 1962 (Insight Media)
Plato's *Apology* reveals how Socrates both inspired and outraged his fellow citizens. Using dramatizations of excerpts of *Theætetus* and the *Meno*, this video investigates the Socratic method of teaching and explains key aspects of Plato's philosophy.

Plato's "The Cave"
10 min., 1973 (Insight Media)
This animated video is based on the seventh book of Plato's *The Republic*. It presents the hypothetical situation in which four men chained in a cave mistake shadows for reality. One man who is released sees the real nature of things and shares his enlightenment.

Plato's Republic
23 min., 1996 (Insight Media)
Plato's *The Republic* has intrigued, provoked, appalled, and inspired readers since it was written over 2,500 years ago. Plato's concepts come to life through dramatizations of scenes from his writings and interviews with experts.

WEB SITES

Exploring Plato's Dialogues
Plato.evansville.edu
This user-friendly site provides an archive of Plato's dialogues, secondary materials, background on the philosopher's life, and a topical search engine that allows a search for relevant articles, images, lecture notes, maps, and bibliographies.

The Internet Classics Archive — Plato
Classics.mit.edu/Browse/browse-Plato.html
This site provides links to the complete e-texts of many of Plato's works.

Plato's *The Republic*
www.friesian.com/plato.htm
Users will find a couple of interesting articles about *The Republic* at this site, including one piece comparing Plato's work with Machiavelli's *The Prince*.

AUDIO

The Dialogues of Plato
5:25 hrs. (Blackstone Audiobooks)
The Dialogues of Plato rank with the writings of Aristotle as the most important and influential philosophical works in Western thought. None is more exciting and revelatory than the four dialogues — *Euthyphro, Apology, Crito*, and *Phaedo* — on themes evoked by the trial and death of Socrates.

The Mind of Plato
3:75 hrs. (Blackstone Audiobooks)
In this concise analysis, eminent Plato scholar A. E. Taylor examines the philosopher's theory of knowledge and doctrine of ideas; the ideal of the philosopher-king; social system advocated in the Republic; judgments on democracy; and belief in the immortality of the soul. Also considered are Plato's relationship with his master, Socrates; contribution to the idea of university education; attack on art; abstention from public life; and anticipation of Copernicus. Taylor also mentions historical misunderstandings of the one he deems the most original and influential of all philosophers.

Plato in 90 Minutes
90 min. (Blackstone Audiobooks)
In *Plato in 90 Minutes*, Paul Strathern offers a concise, expert account of Plato's life and ideas and explains their influence on man's struggle to understand his existence in the world. The book also includes selections from Plato's work, a brief list of suggested reading for those who wish to delve deeper, and chronologies that place Plato within his own age and in the broader scheme of philosophy.

In the World: Heroes and Citizens (p. 1117)

Begin this section with a conversation comparing heroes and citizens. When students try to describe their idea of a hero, they often use words like "provide a benefit to mankind" or "do some good." A citizen, on the other hand, is also supposed to contribute to society and to guard it from danger. And yet, the typical hero often goes against society or works against the established order, while the citizen feels part of the fabric of society and attempts to maintain it. We think of the hero as outstanding and somehow "above the rest," but the citizen is morally and ethically part of a community and thus more likely to simply be "at the right place at the right time."

These are all broad generalizations, but it is interesting to note that early heroes, like Achilles in Homer's *The Iliad* (p. 288), did not make good citizens. Achilles disobeyed his king and abandoned the Greeks in their time of greatest need for purely selfish reasons. But the citizens who are honored by Pericles' "Funeral Oration" (p. 1136) are nameless and buried *en masse*. The Greeks, too, saw this difference. The hero achieved the status of a god, as we see in Aeschylus's *The Libation Bearers* (p. 1134), in which the hero receives the same level of prayer and sacrifice as a deity. Already in Homer's *The Odyssey* (p. 421), it is noted that the gods are above morals and ethics and can behave with absolute self-determination. In some ways, a hero is like this, but a citizen must first belong to a community. At the death of Alexander the Great in 412 B.C.E., he was worshipped as a hero and god in Egypt and elsewhere. When Julius Caesar was murdered, Augustus and the veterans of Rome's civil war deified him. We read of his presence at the pantheon of the Roman gods in the first book of Ovid's *Metamorphoses* (p. 1270). Augustus, who took the name "princeps," or "first citizen," was deified upon his death.

Even in the twentieth century, this practice continues. After the death of Mao Zedong (Mao Tse-Tung) in 1976, despite his unpopularity during the cultural revolution, there was a tremendous outpouring of grief. This is the case in many totalitarian states. In China, however, Mao took on the status of a god. It is quite common today in China to find a bronze or even plastic statue of Mao with three sticks of incense burning before it. Sometimes this is done right alongside traditional ancestral worship or next to statues of Buddha or Guan Yin. Very few taxi drivers dare to drive a taxi that does not have a talisman of Mao hanging from the rearview mirror. As a brilliant military strategist, poet, calligrapher, and founder of the modern Chinese state, Mao held a natural hero status. It helped that stories circulated about his connections to the common people and to his love of the peasant. The Mao cult was outlawed in China from 1976 onwards, and he was posthumously criticized in 1981. After the tumult of 1989, however, the government removed Marx, Lenin, and Stalin from classrooms and the main square in Beijing (Tiananmen Square), replacing it with a a statue of Mao Zedong. It was not by government decree that Mao's popularity resurged. In fact, the government has recently taken advantage of his popularity among the masses to promote patriotism. Ironically, it was Mao who wrote:

> This land so rich in beauty
> Has made countless heroes bow in homage.
> But alas! Qin Shihuang and Han Wudi
> Were lacking in literary grace,
> And Tang Taizong and Song Taizu
> Had little poetry in their souls;
> And Genghis Khan,
> Proud Son of Heaven only for a day,
> Knew only shooting eagles, bow outstretched.
> All are past and gone!
> For truly great men
> Look to this age alone.   (Mao Zedong, "Snow," 1945)

In this poem, Mao lists a catalog of great heroes and famous poets from China's past but believes them all to have been outdone by the twentieth-century heroes who built the modern Chinese state. In the *Shu Jing*, the hero sets out the role that the leading citizens are obliged to play. A set of examinations, or trials, are set out to test whether or not Shun Yü will make a good leader. Similarly, this battery of tests is transformed into the imperial examination system, which was part of the Chinese system of bureaucracy sporadically for four thousand years, until C.E. 1911, when the last dynasty ended. The culture we read about in the *Shu Jing* advocated seeking equally among all men, the noble and the base, for the good citizen.

This system of tests is used in Chinese culture to seek the ideal citizen. In Western culture, we see the individual's battle with these tests as the mark of a hero. In heroic films like *Star Wars* or *Erin Brockovich*, the hero must pass a test or the test of coming into being on his or her own against the odds. Also, Heracles — the famous Greek hero — begins by being someone rather ordinary (or at least a mortal rather than a god), and he becomes a great hero by accomplishing the labors set before him by the Delphic oracle. Some of the labors are described in this excerpt of Apollodorus's summary of the myth of Heracles: acquiring the skin of the Nemean lion, killing the Lernaean hydra (a horrible monster that lives in the swamp of Lerna and eats whole cattle), fetching the golden apples of the Hesperides (the garden of the gods), and to bring Cerberus (a wild, dangerous dog) back from the underworld by traveling there. Along the way, we are offered a clue as to what will happen when he dies. Heracles tells Molorchus, a worker who he meets on his way to Hades, to wait thirty days and to make a sacrifice to the hero if he has died.

Countless records, often written on metallic tablets, give precise account for how a sacrifice to heroes and ancestors should be made. Although such practice differs from sacrifice to gods, it was not uncommon for people to make sacrifices at tombs and other places that commemorated heroes. In Aeschylus's *The Libation Bearers*, Electra, the daughter of the great military general and king Agamemnon, who was murdered by his wife — as recounted in Homer's *The Odyssey* (p. 421) and in Aeschylus's *Agamemnon* (p. 806) — offers a prayer and drink offerings at the site of her father's tomb.

With the rise of democracy, however, came greater individual responsibility for the governance and survival of the state. The traditional Greek army was formed on a unit called the *phalanx*, which relied on a group of men forming a compact fighting unit. If a single man were to abandon this group in fear, the whole phalanx would be defeated. This had strong implications for the communal life of the soldier and citizen of the early polis, or Greek city-state. What was formerly a military bond became a strong, elite society of Athenian males. Gradually, this was transformed to extend to care of the city governance, once the job of the tyrant or king. When the Persians attacked in 499 B.C.E., the Greeks, who were used to close quarters and hand-to-hand combat, could not withstand the rain of arrows the Persians unleashed. To defeat the Persians, the Athenians devised the greatest naval fleet of the age. As the war raged on and as civic duties became more complicated at home, Pericles, the great Athenian general and statesmen, invented the civil servant, paying those who would work for the administration. This meant that government jobs were available to the poor Athenian class, making Athenian citizenship very prized. The definition of citizenship changed under Pericles' new legislation. It became more difficult to claim Athenian citizenship, but the benefits and responsibilities were also increased. In the speech by Thucydides (p. 1136), we hear a bit of the patriotic character of Pericles and his expectations for the citizens of Athens. One of the more interesting parts of this speech is in his conclusion, where he addresses the women of Athens, bestowing upon them a duty, as if they were citizens themselves, to create and nurture more citizens of the city.

The direct democracy practiced by Athens, however, could be dangerous to individual citizens. There were few protections for the unwanted citizen. Socrates was condemned to death by the citizens of Athens following their humiliating defeat in the Peloponnesian War. Socrates was particularly interested in the role that the citizen should play in government and protection of the city. In several of his debates, he characterized the city as a real person in a dialogue, who was capable of expressing needs and wants and was susceptible to betrayal by citizens. In the excerpt from the biography of Socrates by Diogenes Laertius (p. 1142), we have an opportunity to see Socrates through the eyes of someone besides Plato and Xenophon and to view him as a citizen and person.

In India, as in China, tests were developed to determine who would make loyal subjects and ministers. Kautilya wrote a treatise on political science called the *Arthashastra*, which reveals much about the government of the Mauryas, who ruled India during the fourth century B.C.E. Some of the important attributes that this government attached to its citizens are shown by the qualities tested for in various examinations. These are piety, material gain, lust, and fear. Which test an individual passed determined which role they were going to play in the administration. Similar to the Greek view, the Mauryas believed that the individual held a responsibility toward government of the nation. However, ministers were not elected to office, but, as in China, they were chosen by the king based on their virtues.

TEXT & CONTEXT

It is commonly believed that in times of great political change, there will be a flourishing of philosophical schools. Not all the texts that we read in this section, however, derive from philosophical works. It will be important to discuss with the students *what* the work is, *where* it comes from, *when* it was written, and *why* it was written. This will influence greatly the work's perception of heroes and citizens and will help to distinguish between the works more clearly. The *Shu Jing*, although not by Confucius, is regarded as a Confucian classic for its compatibility with many of his ideals. By adding it to the canon of Confucian works, it gives greater legitimacy to the work and makes it contemporary to the Warring States Period of Chinese history, which was long after the reign of Shun. Apollodorus is credited with having written a work about Gods, and so his name is attached to the long collection of myths from the same period, called *Bibliotheca*, or "The Library." Apollodorus did not live in an age of mythmaking as did Homer. Many of his contemporaries did not have the religious tie to mythology that even the Athenian tragedians display in their tragedies. Instead, his work is an academic study of myths and their patterns, emphasizing the variation among different stories from different regions of Greece.

Aeschylus, on the other hand, employed myth for the purpose of demonstrating Athenian ideals on the tragic stage. Electra and Orestes offer sacrifice to Agamemnon and kill their mother. It is important to know that new citizenship laws discouraged Athenian males from marrying foreigners. By reading this speech alongside Thucydides' account of Pericles' funeral oration, we can see various treatments and reactions to the importance of males (heroes and citizens) and the treatment of women (heroes but not citizens) in classical Athens. The speech of Pericles in Thucydides' *History of the Peloponnesian War* is considered to be one of the greatest speeches ever written. The famous Gettysburg Address by Abraham Lincoln, "Four score and seven years ago . . . ," is heavily influenced by this speech. Diogenes Laertius was a biographer who had a geographic as well as chronological view of the schools of philosophy (similar to modern linguistic theory about the development of languages). His biographies of the philosophers are often a haphazard collection of anecdotes and actual philosophy. He also wrote some poetry that hasn't survived except in fragments and which one modern scholar has described as "wretched." Kautilya is credited with having written *Arthashastra*, but it is clearly a later work on linguistic and stylistic grounds. The manuscript for this work was discovered only in 1905, hundreds of years after it disappeared mysteriously.

IN THE CLASSROOM

I. THE GOVERNED AND GOVERNING CLASS

It will be useful to begin discussion simply by listing examples of heroes and citizens and then trying to sort out precisely the differences between these two categories of people. In this way, a set of criteria can be derived for finding the ideal hero or citizen. Then, compare this set of criteria with those set out by the culture that produced each example in this section. Further discussion can hinge on issues of gender, inclusion of wealthy and non-wealthy citizens, the hero's story and background, and the modern hero-citizen.

Discussion

1. What are the ministers that Shun appoints? What does this say about the priorities of this state? What are the requisite virtues of each of those ministers?

2. How does Heracles face his labor? What keeps him from giving up? What are his heroic qualities? Does his background and appearance have any effect on how he is perceived as a hero?

3. What does Pericles value in his citizens? How does he see the relationship between the government and the governed? What responsibilities does he place on the individual?

Groups

1. Ask the students to chart Pericles' comparison of the Athenian state with foreign states. Make a list for "non-Athenian vices" and a list for "Athenian virtues." How does Pericles use the relative lack of success in other states to the advantage of describing his own Athens?

Writing

Ask students to write a short paper in response to one or more of the following:

1. What does Socrates' domestic disposition say about him as a person? How might this affect his philosophical perspectives?

2. By using a system of tests or examinations to choose a leader, Kautilya proposes that the ideal minister will be found. What are the relative advantages and disadvantages of such a system? How might they be perceived to support or hinder citizen involvement in government?

II. CONNECTIONS

The story of the citizen and the hero is a common one in literature and in films as well. Ask students to consider the epics that they have already read but also other literature and films with which they are familiar. What makes these stories appealing? What are the common plots and crises of these stories?

Discussion

1. Heracles and Gilgamesh both face similar battles of life and death, including a trip to the land of the dead. Show the similarities in the plots of the *The Epic of Gilgamesh* (p. 55) and the account of Heracles' life that is presented in the text.

2. How is the world of war presented by Pericles' speech different from that found in Homer's *The Iliad* (p. 288)? Compare and contrast this speech with the speeches given in Books Nine and Twenty-four of *The Iliad*.

3. Compare and contrast the excerpt from *The Libation Bearers* with a poem by Catullus (p. 1174), in which he is at the tomb of his brother. How are the language and the treatment of grief similar? What is the common relationship between actions and speech in these two works?

Groups

1. Ask each group of students to choose another work of literature, not necessarily belonging to the ancient world, and to make a brief comparison of one of the selections in this section with that work. Then, each group should make a presentation demonstrating their reasons for the comparisons, either contrasting the two works, or showing their similarities.

Writing

Ask students to write a short paper in response to one or more of the following:

1. Describe the similarities and differences between Heracles' descent into the land of the dead, and similar voyages described in *The Descent of Inanna* (p. 23), *The Odyssey* (p. 421), and *The Aeneid* (p. 1181).

2. Compare this selection of texts and their point of view with *The Prince* by Niccolò Machiavelli (Book 3). What has changed in terms of point of view? How has the addressee changed? What might influence something like *The Prince* to be written instead of something like Pericles' funeral oration?

BEYOND THE CLASSROOM

Research & Writing

1. Imagine that you are traveling to a foreign land in the distant past. Choose one of your texts to locate yourself in the world and in time, and show how that text might help you to understand and interpret the culture that wrote it.

2. What are the values that all of the societies represented here try to enforce in their heroes and citizens alike? Why do those particular values make heroes and citizens?

3. Based on the texts provided in this section, what is the major difference between a hero and a citizen? Does it change over time? Compare our modern notions of the combination hero-citizen with examples from these ancient texts.

Project

1. Many of these texts imply a duty or responsibility that is part of the citizen's mandate. Compare this sense of duty and the culture that demanded it with a modern culture and its demands on the individual. One example might be to compare it with the role of the individual in Australian aboriginal culture. Another example might be to compare it with the individual in Japanese corporate society.

FURTHER READING

Antonaccio, Carla Maria. *An Archaeology of Ancestors: Tomb Cult and Hero Cult in Early Greece.* 1995.
Calder, William M. III. *The Unknown Socrates: Translations, with Introductions and Notes of Four Important Documents in the Late Antique Reception of Socrates the Athenian.* 2002.
Gaiser, Konrad. *Das Staatsmodell des Thukydides.* 1975.
Hard, Robin. *The Library of Greek Mythology Apollodorus.* 1997.
Kohli, Ritu. *Kautilya's Political Theory: Yogakshema, the Concept of the Welfare State.* 1995
Price, Jonathan J. *Thucydides and Internal War.* 2001.
Wilson, Thomas A. *On Sacred Grounds: Culture, Society, Politics, and the Formation of the Cult of Confucius.* 2002.

MEDIA RESOURCES

WEB SITES

Chanakya
www.top-biography.com/9046-Chanakya/

This is an extremely thorough site, giving information on the life, times, and writing of Chanakya (Kautilya).

Chinese Literature Classics
www.chinapage.com/classic1.html
This page provides access in English to many of the classic Chinese texts, including *The Book of History*.

Internet Encyclopedia of Philosophy
www.utm.edu/research/iep/
This is a very useful online reference that provides in-depth information on philosophies and individual philosophers. Check here for more information on Diogenes Laertius.

Internet Indian Sourcebook: The Kautilya
www.fordham.edu/halsall/india/kautilya1.html
This site from Fordham University provides translations from additional parts of *The Kautilya*.

Sources for Thucydides
www.perseus.tufts.edu/Thucydides/
This is the Perseus Project's page on Thucydides.

Summary of Apollodorus's Library
www.perseus.tufts.edu/Texts/apollod.summ.html
This is the Perseus Project's page on Apollodorus's Library.

ARISTOTLE, *Metaphysics* (p. 1151) and *Poetics* (p. 1153)

WWW   For quizzes on *Metaphysics* and *Poetics*, see *World Literature Online* at bedfordstmartins.com/worldlit.

Socrates and Aristotle (384–322 B.C.E.) are the two most prominent philosophers from the Classical Period at Athens (fifth to early fourth centuries). However, they differed in many respects. Socrates wrote nothing, so his philosophy survives only in the written dialogues of Plato, which try to re-create the Socratic Method — that is, the method of asking the disciple questions until they arrive at the proper answer on their own. Aristotle, on the other hand, wrote a staggering number of treatises, many of which survive due to a first-century B.C.E. collector of his works. Even more so than Socrates, Aristotle became an important philosopher during the Middle Ages for the Scholastics, a group of philosophers from the eleventh to sixteenth century C.E. who believed it was possible to prove the existence of God and the divine world through Aristotelian methods. One such philosopher was the famous Thomas Aquinas. Aristotle was also extremely important to Arabic philosophy, and most of his works survive in the Arabic language. At a time when Europe's civilization had declined somewhat, it is a great irony that Islamic civilization, which greatly prized learning, knew more about Aristotle than did the Latin West.

After Socrates' death in 399 B.C.E., Plato went into exile for a number of years, returning to Athens late in his life. The middle dialogues may be from this period. He founded a school called the Academy, which Aristotle entered at the age of seventeen, where he remained until Plato's death in 347 B.C.E. The main interests of Aristotle were mathematics and scientific inquiry, which characterize the majority of his works. He classified zoological subjects through a process called taxonomy, which grouped different animals, organs, or other biological phenomena into different classes based on similar properties. Most of this research was conducted on the island of Lesbos around 345 B.C.E. At the invitation of King Philip of Macedon, Aristotle served as tutor to Alexander the Great between 343 and 340 B.C.E. In 335, he returned to Athens to begin his own school, called the Lyceum. In the school was a covered walkway, or *peripatos*, in which Aristotle used to walk with his students as he taught. Because of this, his followers are called the Peripatetics. Aristotle spent much of his time at the school conducting research and assembling the school library, one of the first of its kind in the ancient world.

Begin the introduction to Aristotle by comparing the central themes of his philosophy to those of Socrates. While Plato and Socrates show us that the world's variety is still based on one pure form and is thus less diverse than it appears, Aristotle is interested in all the varieties and species of natural phenomena, which, for him, included psychology, ethics, politics, and language. His scientific approach makes him neutral in debates between philosophical opinions, always trying his best to understand the motives and benefits of two different arguments.

In particular, his philosophy delineated several oppositions useful in determining categories. In some way, these derive from Platonic ideas about the forms but are a more sophisticated and biological (i.e., taxonomic) way of envisioning the natural world. For example, *accident* is a property of a thing that is not part of the *essence* of the thing (the *essence* being a little like the Platonic form). *Accidents* can be used to make categories and subcategories of things, since they are composed of the small differences between things. Other oppositions are between *potential* and *actual* as well as *matter* versus *form*. From this, we can see that Aristotle's thought process did not try to derive some unique oneness but rather tried to imagine the differences between phenomena. It is important for students to recognize, especially as they read the *Poetics*, that Aristotle considered scientific inquiry valid for all branches of learning, including literature. While modern universities usually separate the sciences from the humanities, Aristotle believed that all phenomena were worthy of his method of study.

TEXT & CONTEXT

Metaphysics is so named because it came "after the *Physics*" (*meta phusika*), a series of books on natural phenomena. The word *metaphysics* now usually means those subjects that cannot be approached using scientific methods. Of course, this is in direct opposition to Aristotle's system of inquiry and has come to take on a more negative connotation of being excessively abstract or theoretical. *Metaphysics* is probably a collection of his notes made posthumously by his students. They are not grouped in chronological order, which is why some parts of the book disagree with other parts. The selection the students will read is from the beginning (*Metaphysics 'Alpha'*). It begins with the challenging statement, "All men by nature desire to know." This is perhaps Aristotle's most famous quote. Man is an inquisitive creature whose natural tendencies cause him to learn and thus to evolve. Aristotle immediately sets off to determine the difference between man's quest for knowledge and an animal's experience. (Note the nearly evolutionist point of view that Aristotle takes when he speaks of "first man.") Aristotle then turns to the inquiry of philosophy and how man came to that study. He says that all men have "first thoughts," that is to say, they ask "why are things the way they are?" But "second thoughts" are philosophical ones that look into a matter more profoundly. Aristotle uses a number of metaphors, like a large door or the blinded eyes of the bat, both of which are reminiscent of Plato's "Allegory of the Cave."

Only one book of the *Poetics* survives — the treatise on tragedy. In Umberto Eco's *The Name of the Rose* (1980), the portion on comedy is found but then lost again in a fire. This book was subsequently made into a movie in 1987. The *Poetics* is not a recipe book for how to make a tragedy (although many later readers of it used it in this way). Many of the concepts within the book, such as the notion of the "tragic flaw" (*hamartia*), are difficult to reconcile with the surviving tragedies. However, it is our earliest description of the general features of tragedy. Its importance goes beyond tragedy. It attempts to show the goal (*telos*) of literature in general. All literature relies on imitation (*mimesis*) of the natural world. Unlike other types of imitation, literature imitates not mankind but rather emotions and situations, or "action." Aristotle dissects tragedy and tries to find its different parts and inherent structure and how that structure has an effect on the audience. Students will profit by trying to understand each small part of his argument and comparing it to the tragedies they have read and even to tragic movies and plays from other eras, many of which were influenced by an understanding of *Poetics*.

Aristotle's style is compact in comparison to the gradual dramatic climax of Plato's works. This is partially because of the way his notes were collected and published and partially because of his approach. However, one cannot argue with Aristotle over clarity. He presents each compact statement and follows it up with a proof by way of example. Occasionally, however, he uses a polished metaphor to conclude a section or highlight a point. As a result of his compactness, it is not possible to read Aristotle quickly. However, small sections can be read aloud in group sessions and discussed with other examples. One of the most controversial aspects of Aristotle's philosophy is his attempt to organize everything into categories. Some students may find it alarming that he employs such a scientific manner for researching human thoughts and emotions. It is worth questioning, though, whether or not this is a profitable exercise and perhaps even giving the students a chance to try and write in his style.

IN THE CLASSROOM

I. The Evolution of Philosophy and Thinkers

Discussion should begin with a short introduction into the tenets of Aristotle's philosophy and, most importantly, how his method differs from that of Socrates. Afterwards, it may be useful to have students summarize the individual paragraphs of the selections so that the whole class will understand the texts. The writing is quite logical, so it should be easy to see the connection between parts of his argument. Discussion can center on the validity of Aristotle's methods and arguments and on potential alternative explanations for the phenomena he explores.

Discussion

1. Aristotle states that "all men by nature desire to know." He then proceeds to investigate the difference between human acquisition of knowledge and animal acquisition of knowledge. Are his conclusions correct? Do animals think differently from humans? Is it possible for an animal to be philosophical?

2. What is meant by Aristotle's paradox of philosophy? How is it that the "second thoughts" move in the opposite direction of "first thoughts"?

3. Why does Aristotle say that tragedy is an imitation of "action"? What is crucial to action that makes it more liable to being tragic than the imitation of a person or anything else?

Connections

1. What does Aristotle say about spectacle? How does it relate to the quality and goals of a work of literature? Give some examples of spectacle from tragedy or from contempo-

rary drama and cinema. For example, the sound of Medea's children calling out to her in *Medea* (p. 1004) or the description of Oedipus putting his eyes out in *Oedipus Rex* (p. 899). Did it contribute to the overall quality and goal of that work? What in Aristotle's culture may have been different that led him to his conclusions about spectacle?

2. At the end of the selection from *Metaphysics*, Aristotle speaks of the bat that is blind because it is unaccustomed to light. How does this relate to the "Allegory of the Cave"? (p. 1111). How might Aristotle have interpreted the cave metaphor?

Groups

1. Have each student summarize the argument of a specific paragraph of *Poetics*. Then, students should group themselves based on how related their paragraphs are. Have them summarize the basic argument of that group of paragraphs.

Writing

Ask students to write a short paper in response to one or more of the following:

1. How relevant are Aristotle's notes on tragedy to tragedies you have already read and are familiar with? Be sure and cite examples from that tragedy.

2. What are the similarities and differences between Aristotle's motivations for philosophizing in *Metaphysics* and that of Socrates in the "Allegory of the Cave" or *Apology*?

BEYOND THE CLASSROOM

RESEARCH & WRITING

1. Aristotle's writing on literature is usually concerned with the idea of *genre*, or species of literature (tragedy versus comedy, epic versus novel, etc.). Choose a genre of literature from which you have at least two works and write, in Aristotelian style, about the nature and form of that genre.

2. What are the similarities and differences between Plato and Aristotle in their philosophies? While some have seen Plato as an idealist and Aristotle a materialist, Aristotle never states that the universe is strictly material (as do Lucretius and Epicurus, for example). Furthermore, both believe that philosophy is the highest goal of knowledge. Citing examples from the texts, compare their philosophies. You may wish to read more Aristotle (for example, the first book of the *Nicomachean Ethics*) or Plato (the *Symposium* or *Meno*) to learn more about them.

Project

1. Read the entire *Poetics* (not a very long work but one that is very dense). Aristotle says that *Oedipus Rex* is the best example of tragedy. Show how *Poetics* may have been written by examining the structure of *Oedipus Rex*. Be sure and cite *Poetics* in as much detail as you can in order to profit from this exercise.

WWW   For additional information on Aristotle and annotated Web links, see *World Literature Online* at bedfordstmartins.com/worldlit.

FURTHER READING

Allan, D. J. *The Philosophy of Aristotle*. 1952.
Bridges, Tom. "Student Resources: Aristotle" (Montclair State University), http://www.msu.org/intro/content_intro/texts/aristotle/aristotle.html

Barnes, Jonathan. *Aristotle*. 1983.
Bremer, J. M. *Hamartia. Tragic Error in the Poetics and in Greek Tragedy*. 1968.
Grene, Marjorie. *Portrait of Aristotle. 1963.*
Jones, John. *Aristotle on Tragedy.* 1962.

MEDIA RESOURCES

VIDEO

Ancient Greece
48 min., 2000 (Insight Media)
This video explores the ideas of the great philosophers Pythagoras, Socrates, Plato, Aristotle, and Alexander the Great, considering how each was a pupil of his predecessors and how together they formed a golden age of thought and intellect. Includes footage of the ruins of ancient Greece as well as dramatic readings from the philosophers' works.

Aristotle's Ethics: The Theory of Happiness
36 min., 1962 (Insight Media)
Aristotle used the story of Croesus and Solon to answer the questions of "what makes a human life good . . . what makes it worth living, and what we must do, not merely to live, but to live well." Hosted by Mortimer Adler, this video presents the story, examines Aristotle's responses, and discusses his resulting "theory of happiness."

Greek Thought
30 min. 1989 (Annenberg/CPB Video)
Socrates, Plato, and Aristotle laid the foundation of Western intellectual thought.

WEB SITES

Aristotle
www.ucmp.berkeley.edu/history/aristotle.html
This site provides both a biography of Aristotle and links to his scientific writings at MIT's Tech Classics Archive.

Internet Classics Archive — Aristotle
Classics.mit.edu/Browse/browse-Aristotle.html
This wonderful site includes links to the complete e-texts of many of Aristotle's works.

Internet Encyclopedia of Philosophy — Aristotle
www.utm.edu/research/iep/a/aristotl.htm
This site presents users with an article on the life and works of Aristotle. Included are discussions of his views on ethics, metaphysics, art, politics, and nature, among others.

AUDIO

Aristotle
3:75 hrs. (Blackstone Audiobooks)
Writing to inform the beginner and stimulate the expert, eminent scholar A. E. Taylor presents a searching analysis of Aristotle's thought, including classification of the sciences, formal logic, theory of knowledge, matter and form, the four causes, God, physics, biology, sensation, ethics, theory of the state, and the fine arts. He also considers Aristotle's provincialism, errors regarding the nervous system and astronomy, and defense of slavery.

The Nicomachean Ethics
8:30 hrs. (Blackstone Audiobooks)
An unabridged version of *Ethics* read by Nadia May.

Rhetoric, Poetics, and *Logic*
14:25 hrs. (Blackstone Audiobooks)
Read by Frederick Davidson, this program provides the unabridged versions of Aristotle's
Rhetoric, Poetics, and *Logic.*

GENERAL MEDIA RESOURCES

VIDEO

Aspects of Classic Greek Theater
13 min., 1960 (Insight Media)
This program features scenes from Sophocles' *Electra,* directed by Dimitrios Rondiris of
the National Theatre of Greece — acclaimed authority on classical Greek theater and on
the movement and vocal style of the Greek chorus. Insightful narrative and a visit to the
site of Agamemnon's palace in Mycenae provide historic context for the tragedy.

Greece and Rome (1200 B.C.E.–200 C.E.)
30 min., 1989 (Insight Media)
Examining the philosophy, architecture, and culture of Greece and Rome, this video traces
the political evolution of Greece. It considers its colonization of the Aegean and Asia
Minor and chronicles the victories of Alexander the Great. It then describes the spread of
Roman control into Europe, North Africa, and Asia Minor.

Greek Civilization
30 min., 1970 (Insight Media)
This video investigates elements of Greek culture that have made an indelible imprint on
Western culture and institutions. It explores the influence of Greek drama on the development of the theater, discusses the origins and rituals of the Olympic games, and examines
the connection between Greek mythology and art, drama, and literature.

The Greeks
4-part series, 53–58 min. each, 2000 (Films for the Humanities & Sciences)
A major series that provides a thought-provoking synthesis of the values and contributions
of ancient Greece, setting our sense of beauty, good and bad, and right and wrong against
the searching questions about the nature of humankind.

The Greeks: Crucible of Civilization
2-tape series, 2000 (PBS Home Video)
The empire built by the Greeks in the fourth and fifth centuries B.C.E. is perhaps one of the
most breathtaking ever built. Not just a work of art and genius, the empire laid the foundation for modern science, politics, warfare, and philosophy. Come along and recount the
rise and fall of the legacy of an empire that marked the dawning of the great Western civilization — the grandeur of the great philosophers, the magnificence of the architecture, the
appeal of the great heroes. "The Revolution" takes you to ancient Athens, where Athenians
struggle against tyrants. "Golden Age" replays the heroic victory over the Persian Empire
and tells of the startling Greek transformation, and "Empire of the Mind" reveals the
downfall of a glorious empire through the eyes of Socrates.

Greek Drama: From Ritual to Theater
57 min., 2001 (Films for the Humanities & Sciences)
Why do plays well over two millennia old still speak to audiences today? This program traces Greek theater from ancient harvest rites to the golden age of Aeschylus, Sophocles, Euripides, and Aristophanes. Key scenes from *Antigone, Oedipus Tyrranus, Medea,* and *Lysistrata* show how these works remain relevant by exploring the timeless themes of honor, class, gender, sexuality, and politics. Essential concepts like catharsis, hamartia, and the use of masks and a chorus are discussed. Scholarly commentary by Helene Foley of Barnard College, Jeffrey Henderson of Boston University, Princeton University's Robert Fagles, and Peter Meineck of New York University's Aquila Theatre Company emphasizes the vitality of classical drama and the essential role it played in the everyday lives of the ancient Greeks.

Greek Theater
19 min., 2001 (Insight Media)
This program explores the ancient Greek theater, examining its origins and its role as a religious experience. It presents biographies of several ancient Greek playwrights and describes the competitions held among them. It also considers the purpose of the Greek chorus and depicts the staging of Greek plays, examining the physical structure of Greek theaters and tracing the evolution of staging techniques.

Greek Thought
30 min., 1989 (Annenberg/CPB Video)
Socrates, Plato, and Aristotle laid the foundation of Western intellectual thought.

Greece: A Moment of Excellence
36 min., 1995 (Time-Life)
Time-Life journeys back to ancient Athens, the world's first democracy, as Pericles helps usher it into a golden age of unparalleled achievement in philosophy, science, and art. Learn how this mighty city-state became the ultimate expression of the Greek drive for perfection, with architectural triumphs such as the Parthenon and the intellectual brilliance of Socrates, Plato, Aristotle, and others.

Philosophy and Government: The World in Greek Times
23 min., 1998 (Zenger Media)
This educational program examines how the rise of civilizations in Greece, China, India, and other parts of the world developed great philosophers and writers, who explored themes such as the citizen's role and responsibility in society and the government's responsibility to the people. Featuring dramatic readings and commentary by former Poet Laureate Robert Pinsky, the program covers works by Homer, Herodotus, Socrates, Euripides, Plato, Aristotle, Confucius, Lao-Tzu, and Buddha.

The Powerful Gods of Mount Olympus
50 min., 1996 (A&E Video)
Part of an A&E Network investigation into real-life mysteries. Explore the power of the Greek gods, and witness their impact on ancient Greek civilization. Legend says they could boil the oceans, electrify the skies, and split the earth. The Greeks honored them in magnificent temples with rituals, sacrifices, and other ceremonies. Yet Homer dared to poke fun at the gods in his classic epics. Were these figures divine or merely political?

WEB SITES

History and Culture in Ancient Athens
www.watson.org/%7Eleigh/athens.html
This site provides users with background information on ancient Greek theater, culture, mythology, and philosophy.

Internet Ancient History Sourcebook — Greece
www.fordham.edu/halsall/ancient/asbook07.html
The goal of the Ancient History Sourcebook is to provide and organize texts for use in classroom situations. Links to the larger online collections are provided for those who want to explore further. It also includes links to visual and aural material, since art and archeology are far more important for the periods in question than for later history. The emphasis remains on access to primary source texts for educational purposes.

Internet Ancient History Sourcebook — Hellenistic World
www.fordham.edu/halsall/ancient/asbook08.html
The goal of the Ancient History Sourcebook is to provide and organize texts for use in classroom situations. Links to the larger online collections are provided for those who want to explore further. It also includes links to visual and aural material, since art and archeology are far more important for the periods in question than for later history. The emphasis remains on access to primary source texts for educational purposes.

Internet Resources — Ancient Greece
www.ancientgreece.com/html/other_frame.htm
This is a wonderful and easily navigable site on all aspects of ancient Greek civilization.

Perseus Digital Library — Greek and Roman Materials
www.perseus.tufts.edu/cache/perscoll_Greco-Roman.html
The Perseus Digital Library, a Web site created and maintained by the Classics classics department at Tufts University, offers users a vast archive of ancient Greek and Roman images and e-texts.

AUDIO

Classical Love Poetry
2 CDs, 2:53 hrs. (Naxos Audio)
This anthology, the only one of its kind on audiobook, gives an insight into a more lyrical and tender aspect of Greek and Roman literature. From Homer's lofty lines on the loves of the gods to the earthier verse of Catullus to his mistress Lesbia, this recording encompasses the major love poetry written between the eighth century B.C.E. and the second century C.E. Translations are by British poets, including Dryden, Pope, Johnson, Marlowe, and Byron.

A History of Greece — Vols. 1 and 2
12 tapes, 17:20 hrs. (AudioBooksToday.com)
Volume I is the thrilling story of the rise to power and influence of the greatest civilization the world has ever known. *Volume II* continues with the bitter struggle between Sparta and Athens for mastery of the Hellenic world.

ROME:
CREATING THE MYTH
OF EMPIRE IN THE LAND
OF THE CAESARS

CATULLUS, Selected Works (p. 1164)

WWW   For a quiz on the poetry of Catullus, see *World Literature Online* at
bedfordstmartins.com/worldlit.

Catullus, who lived in the first century B.C.E., owed much of his poetry's liveliness and modernity to his Hellenistic predecessors. When Alexander the Great died in 323 B.C.E., there was an immediate contest for his throne and his rule over a vast part of Asia, Egypt, and the eastern Mediterranean. His son, Alexander IV, was too young to rule, so the empire was divided into the Hellenistic Kingdoms, each ruled by one of his generals. This ushered in a period of relative military stability (although intrigues within the royal houses were common), during which urban elites commissioned poetry for parties, religious observance, and — in order to contribute to the increasing importance of culture — as a determining factor in wealth and status. The system of patronage that ensued from this arrangement is what fed poets like Callimachus, Lycophron, Theocritus, Philetas, and Apollonius of Rhodes, all of whom lived between the fourth and third centuries B.C.E. These poets wrote on traditional and contemporary matters in highly allusive ways. Every poem was simultaneously a critical statement about the history of literature and a nod to predecessors, often short and witty. One epigram is a puzzle in which puns are played on the meanings of words; another reads the same forward and backward; another makes fun of the reader as he reads, anticipating his questions.

Meanwhile, Greece was in decline. When Philip V of Macedon signed up with Hannibal against Rome during the Second Punic War, Rome — whose greatest cultural influence had been Greece — took over Greece in 201 B.C.E. The only kingdom to remain independent was Egypt, which became part of Rome at the death of Marc Antony in 30 B.C.E. Tutors from Greece, including the great historian Polybius, were taken to Rome to educate the upper classes. It is at this moment in history that we witness the birth of Roman literature. Although Rome had been a Mediterranean power for some time and had existed since 753 B.C.E. or so, it had no real literature of its own. The most popular comedies and tragedies of the time were translations of Greek works by Menander and others. Epics were largely founded on the Homeric model. However, the flexibility of Hellenistic poetry would inspire distinctly Roman genres of literature. The shorter poems, or epigrams, by Hellenistic poets were collected by Meleager in the second century and made their way to Rome, where the local intelligentsia began to imitate and experiment with them. So, Catullus writes at the beginning of his "little book":

> To whom shall I give this new light-hearted little book,
> Smoothed down and shaved with pumice stone?
> To you, Cornelius: for you have long been accustomed
> To think that my meaningless poetry were something,
> When you alone of all the Italians dared to set forth
> A world history in learned and labored-over books.
> Wherefore, have this book, whatever it's worth and,
> Oh virgin goddess and patron, may it last over a century. (Catullus 1)

The opening lines match the opening lines of Meleager's collection, and the notion of smoothing and shaving the book (which was done to make the papyrus shiny but also refers to the editorial process of making the poems short and witty) is extremely Hellenistic. Catullus goes out of his way to introduce his poetry as trifling and superficial, also a Hellenistic virtue. Finally, he dedicates the book to his patron in typical Hellenistic practice.

Gaius Valerius Catullus was from Verona, even if he lived in Rome most of his life and circulated among the upper class. At a young age, he had remarkable poetic talent, but he was not cut out for becoming an orator (the equivalent of our lawyer or legislator), as his parents wished. He was invited to be part of a small club of poets, artists, and philosophers who were interested in new forms of poetry and who evidently made a number of political enemies in the process, either out of their love of things that were Greek or because of the politicians in their own group (who included the orator Licinius Calvus and the minor politician Helvius Cinna). This group was called *hoi neoteroi,* "the neoterics," in Greek and *poetae novae,* "the new poets," in Latin. We know few other details about the life of Catullus. He accompanied the governor of Bithynia (in modern day Turkey, near Istanbul), Memmius, throughout his term in 57 and 56 B.C.E. Combining this historical detail with a few others, we can say with certainty that Catullus was writing from about 61 B.C.E. to 54 B.C.E. If we are to make any inferences about when he died or when he was born, we have only the fact that he was very young to go on. If he died at age twenty-nine or thirty, then a date of 84 B.C.E. for his birth at Verona is not unlikely.

The collection of Catullus's poetry is roughly divided into three parts: the first group, poems 1 through 60, is usually called the *polymetric poems,* and they are a mixture of archaic imitations of Sappho and Archilochus and Hellenistic-style poems; a second group, poems 61 through 68, is called the *carminae doctae,* or "extended poems," since they are longer in length, like mini-epics. They treat various situations from Greek myths in complicated, ring-like structures. One of them, poem 68, uses this treatment of myth and history as a mirror of personal experience. In comparing the events of the Trojan War to his own bad luck in love, he is making a first in the ancient world. This will be the model for later writers of Latin love elegy, a distinctly Roman genre, whose authors use mythical themes to describe their troubles in love affairs. The later authors include Cornelius Gallus, Virgil, Ovid, Tibullus, and Propertius. Although none credits Catullus (except perhaps Ovid-Gallus is usually credited) with the invention of this genre, it is clear that his poetry served as the model. There is a third group, poems 69 through 116, which are all written in *elegiac couplets* (a hexameter line followed by a pentameter line), usually employing irony to talk about ideas and feelings that challenge the traditional bounds of the epigram. Catullus's poems are largely centered around three conflicts in his life: the untimely death of his brother, the political intrigues of Rome, and his love affair with Lesbia.

Acknowledging the influence of Sappho on his poetics, Catullus called the girl he loved "Lesbia" (a *nom de plume* according to Ovid), and he wrote using the rhythm and meter of Sappho's poetry (stanzas that are usually called "sapphics"). *Lesbia* is a feminine version of the noun *Lesbos,* the island on which Sappho lived. As we shall see, he even translated one of Sappho's poems to his own benefit. It is hard to say with confidence who Lesbia was. Some scholars have gone as far as to reject the whole idea that there was a single genuine Lesbia. But there is a comment in a much later author, Apuleius (a near contemporary of Petronius), that Lesbia was Catullus's code word for "Clodia." It turns out that there was a genuine Clodia, the wife of Quintus Caecilius Metellus Celer. Cicero, the great Roman orator (famous for defending the Republic against the imperial ambitions of Caesar and Augustus/Octavian), defended Celer in some private dispute, and that speech was published in Cicero's collected works. In that speech is a stunning damnation of Clodia and her lifestyle. Even if this was not the Clodia in Catullus's heart, it offers a window into the social revolution afoot in Rome during this period. Clodia turns out to be an adulterous, conniving woman, insinuated in an incestuous relationship with her brother. Catullus's choice to give her a Greek-sounding name is also telling. Roman prostitutes took on Greek names to use in professional activities. Furthermore, at several points, Catullus's condemnation of Clodia's behavior matches that of Cicero: "Live well and sleep with adulterous lovers, / three hundred men between your thighs, embracing / all love turned false, again, again, and breaking / their strength, now sterile" (Catallus 11) and "You whore! Where's your man to cling to, who will praise your beauty, / where's the man that you love and who will call you his, / and when you fall to kissing, whose lips will you devour? / But always, your Catullus will be as firm as rock" (Catallus 8). Elsewhere, he envisions her on her knees performing oral sex in an open alleyway.

Catullus thus transforms a noble woman and senator's wife into a prostitute and lover. Roman virtues and values were not as open-minded as were the Greeks and would not have been pleased with his poetic license. To add insult to injury, Roman men were not supposed to write or express any suffering because of love. A man in love was a cursed man to the Romans. It was womanly and unlike the Roman ideal (a combination farmer and soldier, a little like the early American ideal) to write in this way. Most of all, Cicero was offended by this new brand of Roman. It is true that Cicero probably only represented a narrow band of Republican sentiment at the time, but his description of the neoterics speaks not only of his estimation of their poetic values but also of their moral values. Cicero, in a letter to Atticus, calls a party a "delight," one at which Clodia is present. Catullus uses the same word to describe the verses of himself and Licinus, a fellow neoteric. But whereas Catullus takes this word to mean something like "sophisticated," Cicero elsewhere uses it only in an ironical way as a term insinuating a youthful and immoderate sentiment. The word for *new* did not usually have positive connotations in Latin. We moderns, assailed by marketing on all sides, associate "new" with improvement and progress, but the Romans only saw revolution in that word.

With the extremes of Cicero and Catullus, we can understand how he would have been received by many in his time; Elvis Presley and the Beatles were also viewed as being contemporaneous with ethical revolutions as well as musical ones. Changes in musical style invariably evoke and are accompanied by ideas of revolution and changes in ethics and values (Mozart's *The Marriage of Figaro* was not very well received by the court). Until the 1960s, there was no complete English translation of Catullus because of his use of expletives and graphic language. Harold Norris, a beat generation poet and novelist who lived with Allen Ginsberg in the "Beat Hotel" in Paris in the early 1960s, was often called "The American Catullus" and was, in some ways, influenced by the Roman poet. Even before the beat generation, however, Catullus was a hero to earlier revolutions; he is quoted by Shakespeare and hailed in John Cotton's poem "Catullus at Sirmio" (1982) and Swinburne's "To Catullus" (1883).

Poem 2, to Lesbia's sparrow, is an imitation of Hellenistic mock hymns to insects with the added twist of personal jealousy. If poem 2 is a mock hymn, then poem 3 is a mock dirge and was parodied by Ovid and other later writers. The surprise lies at line 17, where there is a sudden outburst against the sparrow that has caused grief and then the unexpected shift of focus to Lesbia. In poem 5, kisses are turned into a lover's currency, and he demands more of them from Lesbia, despite "what sour old men say." It is tempting to interpret the "sour old men" as Cicero and like thinkers of the time who did not appreciate Rome's gradual slide into decadence. In poem 8, we already have a picture of the poet denied his lover. He struggles between the intellectual understanding that Lesbia has been faithless and is no longer his and the emotional inability to write off his losses. Just as poem 51 marks the beginning of

Catullus's affair with Lesbia, poem 11 marks its end. It begins with a travelogue, a perhaps purposeful distancing of himself from Lesbia's Rome, and it ends with invective, carried by Furius and Aurelius. The debate surrounding this poem is that of other poems; Furius and Aurelius are spreading rumors about Catullus and Lesbia, and he curses at them in the most immoderate manner possible. So what does it mean to Furius and Aurelius passing the message for Catullus to Lesbia? Does he assume that they are now in her circle?

Poem 51 is a free translation of Sappho's poem "He is like a god" (translated as "He is more than a hero," p. 796). Catullus stays very close to Sappho's poem but changes it in several ways. Sappho writes, literally, "He is a god in my eyes — / the man who is allowed / to sit beside you — he / who listens intimately / to the sweet murmur of / your voice, the enticing / laughter that makes my own / heart beat fast." But Catullus writes, "He is changed to a god he who looks on here, / Godlike he shines when he's seated beside her, / immortal joy to gaze and hear the fall of / her sweet laughter." After these opening lines, Catullus shows that he is perfectly capable of producing an exact translation of Sappho's Greek. So why does he change the opening lines so much? Some have suggested that Catullus is emphasizing the conviction of his feelings for Lesbia, but this somehow seems unsatisfactory. Many scholars believe that this poem was originally given to Lesbia as a gift. Poem 76 shows the result of the relationship in a more controlled and rational manner than poem 8 or poem 11. There are some echoes of the language of both poem 8 and poem 51, which would be worthwhile to explore. In poem 85, we see some of love's schizophrenic results. In the words of the Catullus scholar Kenneth Quinn, "How can one both love and loathe? It is not something you do; it something that happens to you. And it hurts." Poem 85 is the most famous poem and is quoted frequently; nearly all students who have learned their Latin remember "Odi et amo — I hate and I love." Poem 101 is a poignant elegy to the poet's brother. The beauty of the poem lies in Catullus's recognition of his duty to his brother and in the futility of the ceremony to bring him back.

TEXT & CONTEXT

Usually, if an author's works survived the travails of the Dark Ages and made it to the end of the Middle Ages, they survived into modern times. This is especially true for Latin literature, since there was much less Latin than Greek literature, and since it circulated less widely during the Christian period. During the ninth century, an anthology of Latin poetry was created that included one work of Catullus (Catullus 62). In 966 C.E., the bishop of Verona discovered a manuscript of Catullus's 114 poems in an earthenware jar. After reading its contents, he blushed and wrote out a confession. The manuscript promptly disappeared again until after 1300, when it was supposedly "rediscovered." Almost as soon as it was found again, it was mysteriously lost a third time. Fortunately, it was copied at least twice and became a hit within fifty years. Francesco Petrarch (Book 3) imitated his work in 1347. The American scholar W. G. Hale found a third copy of the Veronese manuscript in the Vatican Library in 1896. Despite the disappearing manuscripts in post-classical times, Catullus was one of the most read poets in Rome. He lived in Republican Rome, but his poetry became of great importance in the Imperial Age that he never lived to see. In 44 B.C.E., the great military strategist and powerful political leader Julius Caesar was killed by his own senators. Marc Antony used his influence through his affair with Cleopatra VII, queen of Egypt (and previously an ally of Caesar), as well as his knowledge of the East to gain control. But Octavian, who had the support of Caesar's soldiers and veterans from the wars against Germany and Gaul, was also powerful. Italy was plunged into the second civil war and third revolution of the century. Octavian, promising peace, chased Antony's fleet to Actium, in northwest Greece, where he was victorious in 31 B.C.E. Cleopatra and Antony fled to Egypt, where they committed suicide in 30 B.C.E. In 27 B.C.E., Octavian announced that he had restored the republic, but he promptly went about assassinating all opposition (including the statesmen, Cicero) and creating propaganda for himself. By default, he was an emperor, although he called himself *princeps,* "first man." In this period, Horace, Virgil, Propertius, Tibullus, and Gallus and the great Augustan poets all wrote, heavily influenced by Catullus — even his antisocial poems. Ovid later gave credit to Catullus for the invention of Latin love poetry.

IN THE CLASSROOM

The youthfulness and modern pop sensibilities of Catullus may be attractive to some students. Roman culture went beyond the senate and the legions. Catullus's lyrics would have been attractive to the youth of his time and to those affected by the changes in the political scene in the bustling, urban, cosmopolitan center that Rome was. Begin, perhaps, by asking what makes a good pop song. What are the characteristics of the lyrics? What kind of personality does the pop artist have to have? Bring in a list of top hits of the week, and compare the lyrics from that week to those of Catullus. How close a match are they? Some students may think that this approach is "trying to make Catullus hip." The appropriate response is "Catullus is hip without trying."

Discussion

1. What are the main themes of Catullus's poetry? How would you describe his emotions? Is he angry, sad, passionate, or a combination? What are the words that tell you this?

2. What are the different roles of the sparrow? How does Catullus really feel about the sparrow in the sparrow poems? How do his emotions turn on the sparrow?

3. The pain of being in love can be as sharp as the pain of being rejected in love. Compare poems 51, 76, and 85. How have the physical symptoms changed? Who does each of the poems address? Why? What might that say about the author?

Connections

1. Compare and contrast Catullus's love poetry and the poems lamenting Lesbia's faithlessness with T. S. Eliot's parody of a man who is a failure in love in "The Love Song of J. Alfred Prufrock" (Book 6).

2. What are the differences between Catullus's version (poem 51) of Sappho's poem "He is more than a hero" (p. 796) and the original?

3. At the end of poem 11, Catullus speaks of a plow that knocks over a flower. Who is the flower, and who is the plow? Compare this poem with Sappho's "Lament for a Maidenhead" (p. 795) and also with the following poem by Meng Haoran, a poet of the Tang dynasty in China. [For more information on the Tang dynasty, see Book 2]

> Asleep in spring time, I did not notice the dawn
> Everywhere the sound of chirping birds
> Last night in the rain and wind
> How many flowers fell?

Groups

1. Divide students into small groups and ask them to answer how they might set Catullus to music (as Carl Orff did in *Catulli Carmini*). What kind of music would it be? Loud and rhythmical or soft and sad? What are the verbal clues that tell you the kind of music appropriate to his lyrics?

Writing

Ask students to write a short paper in response to one or more of the following:

1. Compare poem 8 with poem 76. These are from different parts of the collection. How have his emotions changed from one to the other? Which one do you suppose was written first? Why?

2. In poem 11, Catallus asks Furius and Aurelius, who are not friendly to him, to pass a message to Lesbia. Why does he ask them to pass the message?

3. Are there any similarities in the emotions of poem 101 with poem 76? How might these poems explore similar emotions? What are the circumstances of the two poems? Are they in any way related?

BEYOND THE CLASSROOM

RESEARCH & WRITING

1. Compare and contrast the themes and emotions, in particular the physical manifestation of love, in Egyptian Love Poems (p. 121) with Catullus's love poetry.

2. In poem 76, Catullus begins by trying to logically trace the source and the remedy of his grief. How does this logic begin to collapse as the poem progresses? What does Catullus have difficulty doing on his own?

Project

1. Outline the travels of Catullus in poem 11, drawing them on a map. What is the meaning of the first three stanzas? Why include this in a poem about a breakup with Lesbia?

WWW   For additional information on Catullus and annotated Web links,
see *World Literature Online* at bedfordstmartins.com/worldlit.

FURTHER READING

Fitzgerald, William. *Catullan Provocations: Lyric Poetry and the Drama of Position.* 1995.
Holoka, J. P. *Gaius Valerius Catullus: A Systematic Bibliography.* 1985.
———. *Catullus: The Poems.* 1966.
———. *The Catullan Revolution.* 1969.
Lyne, R. O. A. M. *The Latin Love Poets.* 1980.
Newman, J. K. *Roman Catullus and the Modification of the Alexandrian Sensibility.* 1991.
Ross, David O., Jr. *Style and Tradition in Catullus.* 1969.
Quinn, Kenneth. *Approaches to Catullus.* 1972.
Wiseman, T. P. *Catullan Questions.* 1969.

MEDIA RESOURCES

WEB SITES

Catullus
Catullus.iscool.net
This site provides terrific information on Catullus's life as well as links to much of his poetry, including the famous Lesbia poems.

C. Valerius Catullus Society
www.informalmusic.com/Catullus
This site provides links to several pages about Catullus as well as an online discussion forum.

Gaius Valerius Catullus
www.vroma.org/~hwalker/VRomaCatullus/Catullus.html
A site brimming with hyperlinks, users will find biographical information about the poet as well as interesting information about his friends, lovers, and rivals. Also available here is a complete list of his poems, with a side-by-side presentation of each poem in English and Latin.

VIRGIL, *The Aeneid* (p. 1174)

WWW   For a quiz on *The Aeneid,* see *World Literature Online* at bedfordstmartins.com/worldlit.

Virgil is indisputably the most influential and important Roman poet, and his *The Aeneid* is similarly the central text of Latin literature. Immediately following its publication shortly after Virgil's death in 19 B.C.E., the work was recognized as a literary masterpiece; the reputation of both poem and poet has survived, without interruption, to our day. During most of this time, *The Aeneid* has been read as a strongly nationalistic poem, extolling the glory both of the Roman state and people and of the new regime and its guiding personality, Augustus. That this interpretation is at least partially correct is beyond serious dispute. Yet there is a striking undercurrent in the poem that emphasizes the sheer human cost of the Roman enterprise, the suffering of those whose lives and interests must give way to it, and the cruelty and inhumanity without which Rome could not have gained mastery over the known world by force of arms. Much of the greatness of the poem consists in the tension between Rome's real and formidable grandeur and its long, dreary tally of victims. This tension, which Virgil explicitly locates on the cosmic level as well (i.e., between the allegedly providential governance of the world and the omnipresence of suffering in it), is neither resolved nor amenable to summary characterization.

An obvious way to approach this large issue is through the related problem of the character of Aeneas. There is much in him that is laudable and heroic, of course, but in some ways it is a diffident, flawed, and deliberately undermined hero that Virgil presents to us. Some of this undermining is intrinsic to the plot. For instance, in Book 2 our hero has to flee his doomed city, even though the heroic code would have him go down fighting instead. He loses his wife in the process, which hardly seems gallant, but is dramatically necessary in order for Aeneas to be single on his arrival at Carthage. And, of course, there is his rather caddish behavior in the Dido incident — true, that ill-fated liaison *had* to end badly, and Aeneas *was* fated to leave for Italy — but it would be a cop-out and a whitewash thereby to absolve Aeneas of all blame for his shabby and dishonest treatment of his lover. Although not included in the anthology, it is worth mentioning that the final scene of the poem has Aeneas, whose hatred of and contempt for war is obvious, declining to spare a defeated and helpless enemy, instead running him through in a fit of uncontrolled rage. Explore the relationship between the ambiguity in Aeneas's character and the other ambiguities suggested by the poem: the glorious versus the cruel Rome, the providential versus the pitiless nature of Fate, the violence that is necessary to ensure the safety and prosperity of a people.

Precisely *how* does *The Aeneid* manage to comment so heavily on issues contemporary to Virgil, when its plot takes place some thousand years before the poet's time? Aeneas, the

Trojan warrior, escapes with his small band of refugees upon the sacking of their city. He wanders the Mediterranean before finally settling in Italy and founding a settlement whose inhabitants, hundreds of years later, will eventually found Rome. The story thus connects Rome's origins to the literary and cultural world of Greece and (since Aeneas is the son of Venus, from whom Julius Caesar claimed descent) provides a legitimizing myth for the new regime. Moreover, in various places in *The Aeneid*, Rome's future destiny is revealed to Aeneas, thus allowing Virgil to give us history lessons in the future tense. Furthermore, it is a mistake to see the characters of *The Aeneid* as mere allegorical stand-ins for historical figures, neither is it wise to ignore parallels between Aeneas and Augustus. In particular, Aeneas's signal virtue, *pietas* (devotion to one's obligations to family, country, and gods), clearly meant to court comparison with Augustus, who as Julius Caesar's adopted son justified his participation in the civil war against Caesar's assassins on grounds of family loyalty.

The connections thereby made between the mythical past and the Roman present are paralleled by connections between Greece and Greece's literary culture and Rome and Rome's literary culture. *The Aeneid* will be the national poem of Rome and the center of Roman literary education, just as Homer was the poet and teacher of Greece; but it is in the differences between the two contexts that much of the resonance of the work is to be found. For example, Homer can narrate Odysseus's sacking a town for plunder without shame or anxiety, while Virgil shows profound concern for Aeneas's victims as well as his victories. Moral attitudes that prevail and make sense in that earlier culture are thus thrown into serious doubt and submitted to scrutiny — a process, incidentally, that has interesting links to the way in which the Christian New Testament plays off of and modifies its root text, the Hebrew Bible.

TEXT AND CONTEXT

Virgil lived from 70 to 19 B.C.E.; he composed *The Aeneid* during the last ten years of his life, leaving it just short of completion at his death. All but the last years of his life were marked by severe political strife and instability, some knowledge of which is necessary for an informed reading of the poem. During the second century B.C.E., Rome grew from being a regional power in Italy and the western Mediterranean to the imperial master of nearly the whole of the ancient world. The growth of this empire brought Rome unprecedented wealth, prestige, and access to the older and more established culture of the Greek East; it also led to a fatal weakening in its republican city-state system of governance. This system, though it had certain quasi-democratic features, was on the whole an elite government by the leading aristocratic families of Rome. Power and offices alternated within the ruling class, which by and large enjoyed a consensus within itself in favor of the prevailing constitution. During the first century B.C.E., this consensus frayed and ultimately broke, and, in spite of doomed efforts by some parties — notably Cicero and the assassins of Julius Caesar — to restore it, eventually gave way to one-man rule. Virgil lived through the climax of this excruciating process: the civil war between the factions of Julius Caesar and Pompey; Caesar's eventual triumph and subsequent murder; the temporary restoration of republican government; another civil war that saw the defeat of Caesar's opponents by his former supporters, led by Augustus and Marc Antony; the uneasy peace between these latter two; and finally the civil war between them that left Augustus the sole master of the Roman state.

If Virgil's times were marked by great shifts in the political life of Rome, they were no less noteworthy for the changes they saw in literary artistry. Of course, Virgil's chief models for *The Aeneid* are the Homeric poems, *The Iliad* and *The Odyssey*. The literary context of these poems, however, is far removed from that of Virgil's poems; the former are oral poems, arising from an organic and far less self-conscious poetic tradition of professional singers entertaining banqueters with tales of mythical heroes, while the latter is the product of a far more sophisticated, urban culture, with a literary and written tradition that spanned over half a millennium. In particular, Roman poetry in the first century B.C.E. borrowed heavily from the literary legacy of Hellenistic (third to first centuries B.C.E.) Greek poetry, which pioneered a kind of learned, allusive scholar-poetry, often eschewing longer poems in favor of a remarkable density and complexity of expression. Key figures in this movement are Callimachus and Theocritus; the closest modern equivalents are perhaps T. S. Eliot and Ezra Pound. In first-century Rome, engagement with these models brought forth great poetic achievement at the hands of poets like Catullus and Lucretius, to both of whom Virgil owes an enormous debt. Of course, *The Aeneid,* at least on the most obvious level of choice of genre, follows Homer rather than the Hellenistic poets; but the latter's influence is still deeply felt, particularly in the variegated ways in which Virgil consciously plays off of previous material, manipulating both similarities and differences to create divergent avenues of meaning and sentiment.

IN THE CLASSROOM

I. POLITICS AND HUMANITY

As we have seen, the problem of *The Aeneid*'s "position" on Augustus and the Roman Empire is a major interpretive issue in the poem. But it would be a mistake to see the poem's politics solely in those terms. *The Aeneid*'s richness extends to a broader sense of politics in terms of the way human beings live and conduct their affairs together, considering such topics as the nature of man; the interaction between leader and led; between winner and loser; the nature of power, love, hate, pride, and anger and their role in our lives; and family and gender relations. Some scholars have argued that *The Aeneid,* like Dante's *Divine Comedy,* shows us not only *a* world but *the* world — that is, a comprehensive picture and interpretation of the cosmos and of the way things are. That this universal aspect of the work should coexist with the particular, national, and Roman character of the poem on one level befits Rome and Rome's pretensions to be a universal state; on another it counts as still one more tense and carefully balanced dichotomy.

Discussion

1. Have students identify passages bearing on Augustus and the Roman state. Ask them to interpret the passages with a view toward trying to extract a message regarding Virgil's (or the poem's) own views. Is praise what it seems? Or are perceived subversive notes in the text false clues?

2. Discuss Dido as a counterpart to Aeneas. What is the relevance of her personal biography before meeting Aeneas? How are their similarities important for understanding their subsequent love affair? What historical points might Virgil be making by linking the origin of Carthage with that of Rome?

Connections

1. Dante's *Divine Comedy* features the ghost of Virgil guiding Dante through hell but unable to take him through purgatory and paradise. Think about Virgil's world as a complete picture of reality, and contrast it with what Dante saw as the fuller, divinely revealed truth about the world.

Groups

1. Have students in groups think of a character from literature or contemporary popular culture who, while heroic in some ways, is undermined and imperfect in a way similar to Aeneas. Challenge them to find the closest fit they can, and defend their comparison against the counterarguments of the other groups.

2. A frequent issue in Virgil scholarship is his optimism or pessimism with regard to human nature. Divide the class into two groups, one of which is to find and explain passages that present an optimistic view of the world, the other a pessimistic view. Discuss jointly the advantages and limitations of approaching the text in this way.

Writing

Ask students to write a short paper in response to one or more of the following:

1. What does Aeneas really think about Dido? Does he love her? Why or why not? What implications does your answer have for the work as a whole?

2. What role(s) do the gods play in *The Aeneid*? How are they like or unlike the human characters? What explains the differences?

3. Think about the issue of gender in *The Aeneid*. What generalizations can be made about the female characters, both human and divine, in the poem? The charge of sexism is frequently made against Virgil. Is this justified? Why or why not?

II. INFLUENCE AND APPROPRIATION
    The Aeneid cannot be understood without reference to other works of ancient literature. Of course, Homer is the most important influence, but he is far from the only one. Apollonius of Rhodes' *Argonautica,* a Greek epic of the Hellenistic age, had already pioneered the learned, self-consciously "literary" style of epic Virgil practices. Attic tragedy is influential, particularly for Book 4, frequently dubbed "The Tragedy of Dido." Lucretius's *De Rerum Natura,* a poem expounding Epicurean philosophy, is also central. In fact, Virgil's vision of a providential divine apparatus, however problematic, seems like a riposte to the antisupernaturalism of Epicureanism. Many such connections will be difficult for students who are not steeped in ancient literature to see; nonetheless, *The Aeneid* provides ample opportunity to consider what it means for a great poet to confront the legacy of an eminent predecessor. An accessible way of approaching this issue is through Virgil's use and reworking of the warrior ethical code of Homeric epic. What changes, what remains the same, and why?

Discussion

1. Ancient critics explicitly likened Homer's *The Iliad* to tragedy and his *The Odyssey* to comedy. Where does *The Aeneid* fit in this scheme? Or does it at all?

Connections

1. Greek tragedy is famous for exploring complex ethical issues. *Antigone,* for instance, considers the tension between the prerogatives of collective authority and individual conscience. *The Aeneid* seems rather to focus on the tension between the collective and individual good. How do these issues parallel each other in the two works? How do they differ?

2. Have students compare Aeneas with Odysseus. What might Virgil be saying by means of their similarities and differences?

3. Another literary figure worth considering is Job (but also recall that it is highly unlikely Virgil knew this text). Both Job and the narrator of *The Aeneid* (on Aeneas's behalf) comment on the difficulty of coming to terms with the fact that bad things happen to good people. Both suffer greatly and receive rather questionable recompense for their troubles. Do the two works share a conclusion? Do they even have one on this issue?

Groups

1. Have students in groups come up with explanations concerning why the ethical code of Homer would be considered to be in need of updating. Warn them not simply to call it "progress" or "evolution" but rather to consider what specific changes in society and culture led to these changes.

2. There is evidence that Virgil was an Epicurean. Epicureans disbelieved in divine intervention in human affairs. Ask students in groups to consider whether, and why, Virgil would include the traditional gods acting at crucial moments in his poem if he sided with Lucretius on such things.

Writing

Ask students to write a short paper in response to one or more of the following:

1. Find a specific passage in one of the Homeric epics with a parallel to *The Aeneid*. Trace in detail the appropriation and modification of the original, and comment on what purpose these features serve.

2. Compare Virgil's use of Homer with a recent film's use of a cinematic classic. Can anyone make a film about, say, the mafia without a tip of the hat to *The Godfather*?

BEYOND THE CLASSROOM

RESEARCH & WRITING

1. Ask students to read a work of modern literature that is heavily indebted to *The Aeneid*. Obvious examples would be *Paradise Lost* and the *Divine Comedy*. Students should research and write on how and why their author appropriates Virgil and his message.

2. Research Ovid's *Metamorphoses*. What does this work owe to Virgil? How does Ovid use intertextuality with Virgil to generate meaning? Are these the same ways that Virgil plays off of Homer, or are they different?

Project

1. Research a particular historical period. How was *The Aeneid* interpreted, and what political and moral uses were made of the poem? Particularly interesting cases are Victorian England and Fascist Italy.

WWW   For additional information on Virgil and annotated Web links, see *World Literature Online* at bedfordstmartins.com.

FURTHER READING

Barnard, John D., ed. *Vergil at 2000: Commemorative Essays on the Poet and His Influence*. 1986.
Bloom, Harold, ed. *Vergil* (Modern Critical Views). 1986.
Boyle, A. J. "The Meaning of the *Aeneid*: A Critical Inquiry." *Ramus* 1:63–90 and 113–151. 1972.

Camps, W. A. *An Introduction to Vergil's Aeneid.* 1969.
Farron, Stephen. *Vergil's Aeneid: A Poem of Grief and Love.* 1993.
Grandsen, K. W. *Virgil's Iliad: An Essay on Epic Narrative.* 1984.
Harrison, S. J., ed. *Oxford Readings in Vergil's Aeneid.* 1990.
Lyne, R. O. A. M. *Further Voices in Vergil's Aeneid.* 1987.
Martindale, Charles, ed. *Virgil and His Influence.* 1984.
Otis, Brooks. *Vergil: A Study in Civilized Poetry.* 1963.
Ziolkowski, Theodore. *Virgil and the Moderns.* 1993.

WWW   See *World Literature in the 21st Century* at bedfordstmartins.com/worldlit
for information on Virgil's relevance to today's world.

MEDIA RESOURCES

VIDEO

Virgil's Life and Works
18 min., 1993 (Insight Media)
This program offers all the known facts about Virgil's life and presents them in the context of the events of his time. The first section of the program emphasizes the historical events of the era, while the second half surveys Virgil's major writings, including *The Ecologues, The Georgics,* and *The Aeneid.* The works of various Roman artists and sculptors illustrate the program as well as some illustrations and manuscripts from later centuries.

WEB SITES

The Aeneid of Virgil
www.uoregon.edu/~joelja/aeneid.html
Find here the complete e-text of Virgil's *The Aeneid.*

The Classics Page — Virgil
www.users.globalnet.co.uk/~loxias/latin.htm
This page provides an e-text of *The Aeneid,* along with summaries of each book.

Virgil — The Classic Texts: Traditions and Interpretations
www.uwm.edu/Library/special/exhibits/clastext/clspg041.htm
This site provides biographical information about Virgil and facsimiles of pages from translated volumes of his works in many languages from many centuries, including the "Vatican Virgil" and a sixteenth-century Scottish edition of *The Aeneid* that is thought to be the earliest translation of Virgil into any English dialect.

Virgil.org
A wonderful place to begin one's research, this site offers a wealth of information on the poet, including a bibliography of editions of Virgil's works through the centuries, a history of his life, e-texts of his works, links to other useful sites, and background on Virgil's contemporaries. It also provides secondary sources on Virgil and maps of the ancient world.

The Virgil Home Page
www.dc.peachnet.edu/~shale/humanities/literature/world_literature/virgil.html
This site includes complete e-text translations of Virgil's works, links to other relevant pages, and links to many summaries of his works with several secondary sources.

AUDIO

The Aeneid
4 CDs, 5 hrs. (Naxos Audio)
Virgil's *The Aeneid,* one of the greatest classical poems, is superbly read by the great classical actor Paul Scofield, with Jill Balcon.

The Aeneid
14:25 hrs. (Blackstone Audiobooks)
This unabridged version of *The Aeneid* is read by Frederick Davidson.

OVID, *Metamorphoses* (p. 1265)

WWW For a quiz on *Metamorphoses,* see *World Literature Online* at bedfordstmartins.com/worldlit.

Before there was Carrie Bradshaw and *Sex and the City,* there was Ovid. The rise of Augustus was accompanied by a litany of moral legislation meant to curb the excesses of the late Roman Republic and the new youth. The emperor (or *princeps,* "first man," as he preferred to be called) ran a powerful propaganda machine to make him appear to be the moral authority of the land. He dressed in white, his somber image was engraved on any available free space, he declared himself a "man of the people," and could be seen among crowds. He also became the chief priest of the city and was called "father of the country," *pater patriae.* Some of the moral legislation passed in his lifetime included the so-called *Lex Iulia,* which was supposed to encourage marriage and the having of children. Meanwhile, the average Roman enjoyed his noontime gladiatorial spectacles and his evening prostitutes. Ovid wrote *Ars Amors,* or "Art of Love," which was intended as a combination sex manual and guide for men and women to find their matches. For this and an alleged involvement with his daughter and granddaughter (both named Julia), he was exiled to the literary desert of Tomis on the Black Sea. It had simply become too difficult for Augustus to maintain moral authority with the two Julias seeking lovers right in the forum he built and continuing to tarnish the image at which he labored. Ovid, a prominent member of the same circle as those who courted Julia, was the scapegoat of Augustan countermeasures.

Publius Ovidius Naso was born on March 20 in the year 43 B.C.E. He was thirteen years old when he saw Augustus's rise to power. Like all good upper-class children from the provinces, he was sent to Rome and later to Greece for his education. However, he followed the path of Catullus, Propertius, and Tibullus, not using his education to become a lawyer or politician. Instead, he became a poet, not of the approved epic and lyric styles of Horace and Virgil, the two greatest poets of the Augustan era, but of love poetry. Considering that Livy wrote a controversial history of Rome that did not necessarily portray Augustus in the best light and that Virgil and Horace both wrote poetry that could be interpreted as against the regime of Augustus, it is something of a surprise that Ovid was banished in C.E. 17, at the age of sixty. We learn from Ovid that his books were removed from the library (and perhaps burned as later authors suffered during the reign of Nero and other emperors).

Ovid wrote far more poetry than Virgil or Horace. His first work was *Amores,* a collection in three books of Latin love elegies. These owe a large debt to Catullus. As Lesbia was Catullus's love interest, the hypothetical girl of Ovid's love misadventures is Corinna, a female Greek poet. Corinna mourns a pet parrot similar to the sparrow that Catullus mourns on Lesbia's behalf. Ovid also wrote *Heroides,* "Heroines," which is a collection of letters from historical and mythical women. In this collection, we can see how well Ovid knew and admired Euripides.

Euripides' influence and dramatization of the female psyche can be seen in Ovid's choice of plays, especially in *Medea* but also in *Hippolytus*, which is about a stepmother (Phaedra) who falls in love with her stepson (Hippolytus) and, when he refuses her, claims to her husband (Theseus) that he has raped her, prompting Theseus to send his son into exile and thereby killing him. The letters are often poignant but sometimes a parody: Ariadne, a woman abandoned on a desert island, asks herself where she will find a postman to send her letter.

Other works of Ovid include a poem on make-up artistry (the *Medicamina Faciei Femineae*); *Remedia Amoris*, or the "Remedies for Love"; and *Fasti*, or "Almanac," which is a verse calendar on gods and festivals. From exile, he wrote *Tristia*, "Sorrows," books sent from Tomis that often take on the character of a book and the experiences a book might have if it were a living thing arriving in Rome. The poetry tries to defend Ovid's career and asks for imperial forgiveness. It also gives us an impression of the barrenness of the landscape the poet inhabits and the comparative urbanity of Rome. The *Epistulae ex Ponto,* or "Letters from the Black Sea" are letters written from overseas. The *Ibis,* named after an Egyptian bird, is based on lost Hellenistic models and is a catalogue of the poet's suffering. Other works we cannot date are *Medea,* a tragedy written by Ovid based on Euripides' model, and a translation of the Hellenistic poet Aratus's *Phaenomena,* a book about weather and astronomical signs.

Metamorphoses, or "Transformations," was probably written directly before Ovid's exile. It is an epic, somewhat in the same line of epics as *The Aeneid* in terms of the length of the poem, its arrangement into books, and the way it praises the office of the *princeps* (particularly in the last book), however ambiguously. But it is different in the sense that it is not a continuous narrative (although it sets out to be an "everything since the big bang" kind of history). Ovid's stories revolve around transformations of one individual into another, one place into another, and one being into another, combined with emotional transformations. Using tricks of language and shifting points of view, Ovid is able to recreate the sense of being "half-ling," or mid-transformation. Like Apollodorus, the author credited with writing *Bibliotheca* (see p. 1128), he was a collector of stories, stringing them together in unexpected ways, not always chronological. There is a postmodern, stream-of-consciousness approach to organization. Characters frequently tell their own stories, and sometimes the characters in their stories tell their own stories. This nearly disrupts the narrative, but it also offers a plurality of genres and allows Ovid to make more connections between events.

At first, it seems that Ovid is trying to provoke: Just as Michel Foucault identified in the *History of Sexuality* (although he makes no mention of Ovid's doing this), women with physical troubles or transformations tend to have issues deriving from sexuality. Medusa's prudish ways cause her hair to be full of snakes and her gaze literally petrifies men. Fathers and daughters, bulls and mothers — all mix in an array of the unnatural and bizarre. But Ovid is not really trying to shock so much as to show that the boundaries between divine and human or human and animal are always in flux. He has few examples of moral virtue in his work and many examples of disaster. The work doesn't appear, however, to be didactic or preachy. Like tragedy, he engages in dramatizing human failure and weakness and the emotions that ensue, but there are the scattered examples of good and pure characters that are not from the tragic stage. Ovid seems to deliberately avoid associating his work with a genre. In the process, we see a combination of emotional depth and psychological understanding (one that would easily rival Freud or Jung) on the background of all of earth's variety and changes (enough to impress Darwin).

"The Creation" episode promises to write a mythology from the beginning of time until the Augustan Age. It implies linearity, but the book itself transforms and becomes a little like Aesop's book of fables and a little like scenes from *The Aeneid,* with prophetic visions and the dangerous mix of god and man. The poem at this point reads very much like Psalm 104

(p. 205), which is about the creation of the earth from a Judaic perspective. The major influence, however, was Lucretius's poem *On the Nature of Things* (*De Rerum Natura*) (p. 786), even if creation is not compatible with the atomist philosophy of the eternal universe. It will be worthwhile to compare Psalm 104 with Ovid's poem and Hesiod's poem *Theogony* (p. 263). The chronology fits Hesiod, but the sense of mystery and the nearly monotheistic view that Ovid takes in his creation more closely fits Psalm 104. For the Jewish people, Yahweh is the creator of their universe, but for Ovid, it is Augustus Caesar. Because of the similarity and because Ovid wrote this in the year Christ was born, later generations tried to Christianize Ovid's poetry. But looking at early Christian images of Jesus, particularly in areas influenced by the Roman Empire, there is a stark similarity between the young Augustus, dressed in white with a divine halo for a crown, and the image of Christ on the throne. It seems more likely that, as Christianity became the official religion of the empire, a new king was formed using old imagery to enforce his rule.

"The Four Ages" is an attempt to move from this monotheistic creation toward a more recognizably Roman polytheism. It emulates the rugged primitivism of Hesiod's description but glosses over the *coup d'état* that Saturn (Ouranos, in Hesiod) suffers. Compared to *Works and Days*, *Metamorphoses* is less centered on the agricultural advantages and disadvantages of a particular period (although they still play a role heavily influenced by Virgil's *Georgics*). Instead, being the product of an urban society that he is, Ovid concentrates first on the roles of justice and law in each society balanced with the level of intrigue and violence. In "Jove's Intervention," when Jupiter (Jove, the Roman Zeus) intervenes, Ovid makes the remark that the Great Wheels of Heaven (an allusion to the opening of Lucretius's more atheistic poem) houses a palace not unlike to Palatine Hill (he even compares the Forum of Augustus with the Milky Way). Either Ovid is audacious by comparing a living emperor and his abode to the King of Gods, or Augustus is being audacious by letting such comparisons go. Ovid softens the blow, apologizing somewhat for the comparison, but a few lines later, the comparisons return: "They shuddered / In horror, with a fear of sudden ruin, As the whole world did later, when assassins / Struck Julius Caesar down, and Prince Augustus / Found satisfaction in the great devotion / That cried for vengeance / even as Jove took pleasure . . . ." It cannot be that Ovid is directly complimenting his patron and emperor; the comparison is so direct and obvious that it must veil a criticism of Augustus's self-aggrandizement.

"The Story of Lycaon" is interesting because it tells the story of Prometheus in Hesiod from the point of view of Zeus. This helps to reduce the savagery of the previous ages by giving a more legalistic defense of the punishment of Prometheus. But the relief is short-lived. Zeus plans to destroy the human race. A puzzling prophecy lies therein about the earth being consumed by fire. This apocalyptic view of the world cannot have been influenced by the Book of Revelations, which was written at a later date and not in circles that Ovid would have known. "The Flood," however, and the concerns that the other gods have, mirrors those found in *The Epic of Gilgamesh* (p. 55), whose flood is similarly unleashed by the most authoritative god in order to cleanse the world of evil, but the destruction of the human race threatens the livelihood of the gods who depend on sacrifice. The same series of events can be found in the story of the flood in the Book of Genesis, the first book in the Hebrew Scriptures (p. 134).

"Apollo and Daphne" is one of the most famous scenes in *Metamorphoses* and is the first example of Ovid's frequent pathology of female psyche and sexuality. In some sense, there is a worldliness about the myth: The father wishes that the daughter will bear sons and grandsons, but the daughter is not very interested in being a mother. This routine seems awfully close to the situation in the royal family: Augustus could not produce or keep alive a male heir or even adopt a satisfactory one. The conversation placed in Apollo's mouth is a fantastic metamorphosis in itself. He begins by saying that it is natural for animals to flee predators, but he is not a predator, simply someone being predated on by Love. Then, he expresses concern that she might trip and scratch her lovely legs. He promises to run slower if she will be careful and run slower, and then he transforms his strategy. Let her stop, and maybe she will find out she likes him; after all, he is rather powerful. Finally, it sounds almost as if he is talking to himself — "You foolish girl, / You don't know who it is you run away from, / That must be why you run. I am lord of Delphi / And Tenedos and Claros and Patara. / Jove is my father . . . my arrow / Is sure in aim — there is only one arrow surer, / The one that wounds my heart . . . I am called the Healer . . . Alas for me, love is incurable. . . ." Apollo surely recognizes the irony of his situation, and the idea of a troubled, nearly mortal god, is unique in classical literature. The god continues his pursuit, and, at the moment he is about to capture her, she transforms into a laurel tree. The transformation is magical because, after the fast chase, time seems to freeze as the author laboriously mixes up the word order and turns Daphne into the tree. But the tree turns out to be Apollo's possession anyway, and the link between Apollo and Augustus is made by the presence of the laurel tree next to Augustus' house.

"The Story of Orpheus and Eurydice" has been recreated many times and in many formats ever since Virgil's use of the story in *Georgics*. Orpheus, as the inventor of music, is a natural subject for opera and poetry. In poetry, Rilke wrote *Sonnets to Orpheus* (Book 6), and Ashbery wrote *Syringa*. Claudio Monteverdi wrote the opera *Orfeo*, and Gluck produced his most famous opera *Orpheus and Eurydice*. Stravinsky wrote a ballet, and the multi-medium artist Jean Cocteau wrote a screenplay *Orphée*, which was later set to music in a chamber opera by Philip Glass. It is the narration in Ovid's *Metamorphoses* that is the greatest influence on all these subsequent works. Orpheus and Eurydice are married, but the day does not go well. The traditional marriage torches do not light, and, as the bride is walking in the grass, a poisonous snake bites her ankle, and she dies (a scene echoed in Thomas Hardy's *The Return of the Native*). Orpheus makes his way to the underworld, like Aeneas in *The Aeneid* and Odysseus in *The Odyssey*, and he prays for the return of his wife. He is very political: He says he doesn't believe any of the bad things he has heard about all the creatures below, and he promises that his wife will return to the underworld if only he can have her awhile longer. There is an echo of Lucretius here as well, who says it is pointless for men to worry about death, particularly since they will be dead much longer than they will be alive. Orpheus's speech and music move the most awful and gory of the gods: Sisyphus, the Furies, and the vultures who feed on Prometheus's (here Ixion's) liver. They return Eurydice to him, making him promise not to look back before exiting the underworld. Of course, Orpheus *does* look back at Eurydice out of love, and he loses her a second time. He mourns and sings to the nature around him. Women come to him, but he has lost interest in them; only young boys can occupy his attention. The description of the listening trees and the place where he has his abode is very nearly lifted from Virgil's *Eclogues* and the *Idylls* of Theocritus, both of them great examples of bucolic poetry, or generally homoerotic poetry about shepherds, goatherds, and oxherds. In particular, the details about the "shining silver-fir," "friendly sycamore," and "slim tamarisks" are all standard references to Theocritus's poetry (later employed by Virgil). The transformation we witness is not only from human to cypress tree but also from the epic genre of poetry to elegy to bucolic poetry.

In *My Fair Lady* (1965, starring Audrey Hepburn), Eliza Doolittle is a poor girl who sells flowers in early twentieth-century England. Henry Higgins, a linguist, believes that diction is what makes a lady, and he tries to transform this girl into a society lady. His attempt to transform her through his brutal methods, however, teaches him that she has her own feelings and opinions, even if they are expressed differently. In the end, it is Higgins who is transformed. The movie is based on Shaw's play *Pygmalion*, based on Ovid's somewhat different account in "The Story of Pygmalion," which is essentially the story of Pinocchio. Pygmalion does not like the modern woman with her vices, and so he tries to create the idealized version out of ivory. In a prayer to Venus, he asks for a wife like the one he made of ivory, but his heart actually asks for his statue to be animated. When he returns home, she is there and, at his kiss, she becomes flesh. This is a good example of how it is easier to understand a passage in light of its reception than by reading it in isolation. Shaw's *Pygmalion* reveals that the idealized woman Pygmalion desires denies the superiority of a living and breathing being, despite its faults. Only true love can make someone "perfect," not a chisel or lessons in phonetics.

Even Venus falls in love in "The Story of Adonis." This is yet another example of a story within a story, since the episode with Atalanta is arguably more well-known than Venus's own story. There is a curious overlap between hunted and hunter in this story. Venus and Atalanta both identify with Diana, the goddess of hunting, and yet Venus wants anything but to be a virgin — she's hunting out Adonis (who hunts) — while Atalanta (who hunts) wants to be just like Diana (a virgin). Venus tells the story as if Atalanta wants to be with Hippomenes (whereas in most versions of the story Atalanta is tricked by Hippomenes and doesn't want to be with him). Venus changes the story, but the result is no different: Adonis dies. There is a curious repetition of events in *Metamorphoses* once again emphasized here. In the episode known as the "Calydonian Boar Hunt," Atalanta is nearly successful in killing the boar, much to the surprise of the men who are in the hunt with her. There is a complication each time a man is more like a woman and a woman more like a man. As Atalanta remarks to Hippomenes, "I wish at least you could run a little faster! / He looks like a girl, almost."

TEXT & CONTEXT

Metamorphoses was written in the years immediately preceding Ovid's exile to Tomis in 8 C.E. Ovid credits his expulsion from Rome to two faults: a *carmina,* or poem and an *error,* or discretion. The poet refuses to say what it is he has done wrong, saying that Caesar Augustus has already been harmed once by having to mention it, and it would do no good to repeat the offense aloud. As for the song, we know that Augustus called Ovid a "teacher of the obscene," which insinuates that it is the *Ars Amoris,* or "Art of Love," that sent him into exile. Another passage in his poetry suggests that Ovid saw something that he shouldn't have seen. If it had to do with Julia, Augustus's daughter, seeking lovers in the forum, then it is probably something that was common knowledge, but Ovid chose to publicize it in some form. On the other hand, it may have been a specific encounter Augustus did not want publicized, so he banished Ovid as soon as he realized the poet knew.

Despite having his books banned and not being present in Rome, Ovid's prolific output survived the Augustan Age, since there were frequent quotations from his works, and his books seem to have circulated widely. Even his erotic works survived years in the libraries of the moralizing Catholic Church. He was the most imitated poet in the Middle Ages (mentioned by Chaucer), and he was highly influential in Renaissance arts and letters. One of the earliest authors to be printed, there are countless renderings of his poetry and allusions in Titian, Dryden, Pope, and Shakespeare. Modern novels such as Italo Calvino's *Metamorphoses* have attempted to recreate his disorganized epic. Others, fascinated with the poet's life, have tried to reconstruct his experiences: David Malouf's *An Imaginary Life* and Christoph Ransmayr's *The Last World,* among these. More information about the reception of Ovid, particularly in printing and art, can be found at: http://etext.lib.virginia.edu/latin/ovid/index.html.

IN THE CLASSROOM

Students can consider discussing episodes in isolation, first in small groups, and then as a class, or discussing the work as a whole and looking for patterns in all the stories. It will also be useful to compare the work with Virgil's *The Aeneid*, since these were produced by the same culture and within only a few decades from one another. Although *Metamorphoses* claims to be an epic, it differs significantly from other epics students will have read. It may be a good time to introduce the idea of "reception" and to talk about the reasons for allusions and the ideas behind making nods and references to previous works. Finally, Ovid's understanding of gender is unique (with the possible exception of Euripides) in the ancient world. A discussion of early perceptions of female sexuality and Foucault's work in the *The History of Sexuality*, particularly on psychology and pathology, will be helpful.

Discussion

1. Both Virgil's *The Aeneid* and Ovid's *Metamorphoses* are epics. What are the major differences in composition between these two works? What still identifies *Metamorphoses* as an epic?

2. How does Ovid (and the translator) depict the passage of time or the sense that time is at a standstill (or the opposite)? What are the verbal cues?

3. What is the psychology of those who are in love? What kinds of things do they always say? How is it that they seem, in some way, injured or incapacitated in some way?

4. What does Venus tell Adonis the story of Atalanta? What is her motive? How is her situation similar to that of Hippomenes or Atalanta?

Connections

1. Compare and contrast the method of telling stories and trying to maintain an overall order in Chaucer's *Canterbury Tales* and Boccaccio's *Decameron* (both found in Book 2) and Ovid's *Metamorphoses* (p. 1270). In what ways did Ovid influence late medieval and early Renaissance works?

2. In Kafka's *The Metamorphosis* (Book 6), a transformation from human to insect is described. Although more grotesque than Ovid, and with more obvious social and political overtones, what are the similarities between these two works? How does reading Kafka's *Metamorphosis* influence your understanding of Ovid?

3. Compare and contrast the approaches to creation taken in Psalm 104 (p. 205) and in Ovid's description of creation. How is the creator addressed? What kinds of things impress Ovid and the author of Psalm 104?

4. Discuss how Apollodorus's organization of *Biblioteca* (p. 1128) resembles that of Ovid's in the *Metamorphoses*.

Groups

1. Have students divide up into groups and analyze paintings that are about the myths described in these excerpts. [Artworks based on Ovid's work can be found at http://etext.lib.virginia.edu/latin/ovid/index.html or at http://www.artchive.com.] How are the paintings influenced by Ovid's work? What are the details that give away a particularly Ovidian reading?

2. Let each group of students summarize one episode in the book, and produce a cartoon of several frames describing what happens in that episode. Which scenes does each group choose to depict? Is there a pattern to which scenes get highlighted the most?

Writing

Ask students to write a short paper in response to one or more of the following:

1. What is the role that Augustus plays in the composition of *Metamorphoses?* Is Ovid always critical or always complimentary? For what might Ovid be trying to answer in his discourse?

2. What are the places described in these excerpts from *Metamorphoses?* How are they depicted? What is the relationship between what a place looks like and the action that goes on there? Are there discernible patterns?

3. Compare and contrast the attitude toward women that seems to emanate from *Metamorphoses* with that found in Aristophanes' *Lysistrata* (p. 1049) and Hesiod's description of Pandora in *Works and Days* (p. 272).

BEYOND THE CLASSROOM

RESEARCH & WRITING

1. Compare and contrast Apollo's pursuit of Daphne with Atalanta and Hippomenes' race. How are the male and female components of the pursuit portrayed? What do they say (or not say) that makes them different?

2. Discuss the general disposition of males and females in these excerpts. In what ways are they strong or weak? What kind of language do they use? Are there any gender reversals? Why might this be relevant for stories about transformation?

3. Compare and contrast *The Satyricon* by Petronius with Ovid's *Metamorphoses.* Both are concerned with storytelling, and *The Satyricon* has often been seen as a prose mock-epic. Petronius also suffers under the tyrannical rule of Nero and is forced to commit suicide. What kinds of criticisms of the imperial regime are latent in both works? What narrative techniques remain the same? What new developments have arisen since Ovid's work that are present in *The Satyricon?*

Project

1. View a video recording of one of the operas (Gluck, Glass, Monteverdi) based on "Orpheus and Eurydice." What has the composer changed in his opera? What has he kept the same? What musical techniques does he use (e.g., tone and character of music) to emphasize the emotions and settings of the story?

WWW   For additional information on Ovid and annotated Web links, see *World Literature Online* at bedfordstmartins.com/worldlit.

FURTHER READING

Barchiesi, Alessandro. *The Poet and the Prince: Ovid and Augustan Discourse.* 1997.
Barkan, Leonard. *The Gods Made Flesh: Metamorphosis and the Pursuit of Paganism.* 1986.
Due, O. S. *Changing Forms: Studies in the "Metamorphoses" of Ovid.* 1974.
Galinsky, G. *Ovid's Metamorphoses.* 1975.
Hardie, Philip et al., eds. *Ovidian Transformations: Essays in the "Metamorphoses" and Its Reception.* 1999.
Hinds, S. *Ramus.* 1987.
Martindale, C. *Ovid Renewed.* 1988.
Syme, R. *History in Ovid.* 1978.
Thibault, J. C. *The Mystery of Ovid's Exile.* 1964.

Tissol, Garth. *The Face of Nature: Wit, Narrative, and Cosmic Origins in Ovid's "Metamorphoses."* 1997.

MEDIA RESOURCES

WEB SITES

Information on Publius Ovidius
www.croky.net/ovidius/
Here, users will find an extensive list of links to useful sites on Ovid as well as several other ancient Latin sites.

The Internet Classics Archive — Metamorphoses by Ovid
classics.mit.edu/Ovid/metam.html
This is the site to visit for an e-text version of Ovid's famous work and comments about it posted by users.

Ovid FAQ
www.jiffycomp.com/smr/rob/faq/ovid_faq.php3
This site includes a brief biography of Ovid as well as links to books, relevant sites, and Ovid discussion groups.

The Ovid Collection at the University of Virginia Electronic Text Center
etext.lib.virginia.edu/latin/ovid/
At this site, users will find e-texts of *Metamorphoses* in Latin and in several translations. Also available are links to several other relevant sites, along with fascinating images of Renaissance artists' interpretations of Ovid's famous work.

The Ovid Project: Metamorphosing The Metamorphosis
www.uvm.edu/~hag/ovid/
This site from the University of Vermont includes wonderful images of illustrated editions of Ovid's works which come from the university's rare book collection.

PETRONIUS, *The Satyricon* (p. 1293)

WWW   For a quiz on *The Satyricon,* see *World Literature Online* at
bedfordstmartins.com/worldlit.

IDENTITY OF THE AUTHOR

Unlike most other classical Greek and Latin writers, Petronius and his work cannot be introduced by listing basic biographical data on the author but rather by addressing the issue of his obscure identity. What is known is that a man of the name Petronius was a senator in the time of the emperor Nero (r. 54–68 C.E.) — his full name, which would normally consist of Roman *praenomen, nomen,* and *cognomen* is not known. Historian Tacitus gives the *praenomen* Gaius to the person whom he describes as consul and influential courtier of Nero (Book Sixteen of *Annals*), but Younger Pliny (*Natural History* 37.20) calls him Titus. Inscriptions found in the city of Herculaneum attest a consul named Titus Petronius Niger, while another document from Ephesus, attests an ex-consul called Publius Petronius Niger in 62 C.E. Tacitus draws a remarkable portrait of an amoral and decadent man, yet sharp, witty, and influential, whom he nicknames Nero's "arbiter of elegance" (*arbiter elegantiae*). According to *Annals,* he was a consul around 62 C.E. and was forced by Nero to commit suicide in 66 C.E. as a member of famous conspiracy against the emperor (other victims included the philosopher Seneca and his nephew, epic poet Lucan). It is somewhat of a problem that neither Tacitus nor Pliny allude in any way to possible literary activity of this Petronius. The fact that the author of the text that is discussed is noted in the manuscripts as Titus Petronius Arbiter, and the fact that the general atmosphere of *The Satyricon* seems to fit the picture presented in Tacitus, gives rise to now generally accepted opinion that the two men are one and the same. Also, the text has been identified as fitting into the Neronian period on linguistic and stylistic grounds as well as containing factual material that points to dating no later than Nero's principate. However, the matter is not decisively settled, and there are no conclusive proofs for the identity of this shadowy author (the name "Arbiter" might have well been introduced into manuscript tradition on the basis of testimony from Tacitus). Something by which students might be intrigued, and what might be pointed out to them, is a question as to whether a general tone and atmosphere of a literary work needs to reflect a character of the author's private persona or if the two are to be separated — in the case of Petronius, similarity between the work and the person described in other ancient literary sources played a significant role in assessing the identity of the author.

TITLE AND GENRE OF THE WORK

The text that has been transmitted to us under the title *Satyricon* (Greek neuter genitive plural: [books] of *Satyrica*) or *Satyrica* (Greek neuter nominative plural, formed on the noun *satyr* with derivational suffix *-ikos:* "satyr-like stories") is hard to place within the confines of one genre, although it is for the sake of convenience usually classified as a novel by modern critics (ancients did not have a term for a fictional prose narrative that would correspond). We don't know how long it was, except that it must have been of considerable length. What we have preserved is fragments of books 14, 15 (coinciding largely, it is believed, with *The Feast of Trimalchio*), and 16. It is unique in both form and content: written in prose but interspersed with poems performed by various characters on various occasions and with different relation to the actual narrative.

The title points straightforwardly to connection with Greek satyrs, proverbially lustful mythical creatures that are often represented accompanying the wine-god Dionysus. It also very probably alludes to Roman satire (*satura*), one of the literary genres that influenced the creation of this work. *The Satyricon* contains some features of satire, represented in works of Lucilius, Horace, Persius, and Juvenal — notably, realism and parody. However, one of the most striking characteristics of this work, in contrast to satire, is its complete lack of moral criticism and the author's distance from the events narrated. It is remarkable and unparalleled: Petronius presents a colorful array of dissolute characters of dubious moral values and their adventures in a remarkably realistic way, without idealization, yet he never expresses any kind of unambiguous ethic judgment on their behavior.

It is hard to identify genres that served as models for Petronius's complicated work: Apart from the mentioned connection with satire, *The Satyricon* can be compared with Greek romances and novels, Milesian tales, and the so-called Menippean satire. The complexity of the plot puts it within tradition of Greek romance narratives written from the first to fourth century C.E. , all of which are stories about pairs of lovers, their separation, subsequent adventures, and final reunion, and they feature standard motives like faraway travels, shipwrecks, intrigues, seduction, and confusion of identity (a standard example is Chariton's *Chaereas and Callirhoe*). Petronius takes over the basic structure of these novels but turns it into an outright comic work: Each of these typical motives is subtly inverted and ridiculed.

Connection of Petronius's work with the so-called Menippean satire is provided by alternation of prose and verse: Menippean in itself is by no means a clearly defined genre but rather is a designation applied to three major works of antiquity: the satiric narrative about Emperor Claudius's death, called *The Apocolocyntosis* (rendered as "pumpkinification") by the philosopher Lucius Annaeus Seneca and satires of Marcus Terentius Varro (preserved only in fragments) that are modeled on those by Greek philosopher Menippus, the originator of the genre — all of these share the feature of mixing prose narrative with various kinds of verse and blending elevated literary style with colloquialisms and vulgarisms of everyday speech.

Milesian tales, on the other hand, were racy and somewhat scandalous short stories, like those written by Greek author Aristeides (second century B.C.E.) and translated into Latin by the historian Sisenna (first century B.C.E.) — some of the interpolated narratives in *The Satyricon* are taken to be influenced by and modeled on this popular literary tradition.

THE PLOT OF THE SATYRICON

Our story, narrated by the young man Encolpius, is a long and tangled tale of his sexual adventures and various mishaps he shares with his companions, Giton and Ascyltos (the latter disappears in the later part of the story and a third party, the poet Eumolpus, is introduced). Students will undoubtedly be interested and amused by Petronius's parody of typical novelistic love-story narratives and in the way he turns a conventional heterosexual love triangle into one that is homosexual: He makes Giton a heroine of the narrative, with Encolpius and Ascyltus being rivals for his attention. Pointing out comic differences of *The Satyricon* with standard novelistic narratives is a good way to introduce the work.

The episode called "Dinner with Trimalchio" tells about a banquet of a wealthy freedman that the three main characters stumbled upon in a southern Italian town (it is mostly agreed that the scene is set in Campania, very probably in or near modern Puteoli). It gives a colorful picture of Roman *nouveaux riches* and their world during the Neronian epoch and is particularly interesting for revealing details about everyday life, material culture, social situation, and, especially, spoken language of the time. The scene is dominated by the host Trimalchio and his friends who were ex-slaves, and their conversations on variety of topics. Apart from the mentioned poetic insertions, there are several interpolated narratives within the text, typically, short stories narrated by the guests, which give us a glimpse of rich, undocumented popular folklore of antiquity.

TEXT & CONTEXT

The author of *The Satyricon* should be situated and discussed within the reign of Emperor Nero and his cultural policy. Nero has customarily been called "the histrionic emperor" because of his reported obsession with theater and public spectacles like chariot racing and gladiatorial shows as well as because of his own vigorous but artistically mediocre poetic activity (of which we have only second-hand reports — it should not be forgotten that our major sources on Nero are historians Suetonius, Tacitus, and Cassius Dio, who are by no means completely objective and that the notorious portrait of the crazy young tyrant is based on depictions with which they provide us). We do know that Nero had great enthusiasm for art and culture: He strongly advocated connection between literary activity and public festivals — and precisely these motifs are very prominent in "Dinner with Trimalchio." Frequent mention is made of gladiators, theater, and mime as well as the general attempt at glamour and refinement by the host, who is a hopeless social upstart.

GLADIATORIAL SPECTACLES AS A PHENOMENON

Gladiatorial combats, which originated as spectacles at funeral games in Etruria and were introduced to Rome in the third century B.C.E., became increasingly popular during the Empire. Gladiators were, like other public entertainers (actors, athletes, charioteers), a socially marginalized group with peculiarly ambivalent status: On one hand, they were admired and celebrated in a way that can be compared with modern treatment of music and movie stars, but, paradoxically, they were also despised and stigmatized, in a very concrete way, by their legal status as *infames,* that is, they were practically socially dead and had no lawful citizen rights. For Roman citizens of all social classes, gladiators held a particular fascination as figures representing both courage akin to military prowess as well as physical strength and sexual appeal. Some of them acquired a status of real stars in the arena: They were known under flashy pseudonyms, mentioned in graffiti that was scribbled on walls, and represented on decorative household items such as lamps or cups.

As much as we know that Petronius's work is not to be regarded as an absolutely faithful representation of contemporary society because of its parodic nature, there is still a great amount of facts about social realities that can be learned from the text.

It is only natural that guests at Trimalchio's party refer often to such pop culture phenomena as the circus and the arena: One of the details that helped date *The Satyricon* and situate it firmly in period of Nero's principate is precisely the mention of the famous gladiator Petraites (chapters 52 and 71), otherwise known from a Pompeian inscription and identified as a popular star of the arena under Nero. Trimalchio boasts of owning cups with representations of fights between Petraites and Hermeros, and wishes to have Petraites's combats displayed on his tomb (71.6). He also has a wall painting of a gladiatorial show funded by a certain Laenas, which seems very unusual and is probably to be regarded as an unprecedented social faux pas (there is no parallel for house owners displaying representations of public shows funded by someone else!). Indeed, it has been suggested that the whole setting of the banquet intends to evoke public spectacles, with various acrobats, singers, and other performers streaming through, as if the entire evening is one continuous theater play. Even the host himself is putting on a show, and so are his slaves and guests.

SOCIAL STATUS OF THE FREEDMEN IN THE ROMAN EMPIRE

"Dinner with Trimalchio" gives a hilariously funny, yet often also grim, portrait of a peculiar group within Roman society: freed slaves who amassed a prodigious fortune mainly through commercial activities but were unable to climb on a social scale, despite their striving to move into more elevated circles. In our text, each freedman is given individual character and is treated and described separately with great vividness and in detail. Language and style are important features in characterization: Various registers of speech are used to show sociocultural differences between the narrator Encolpius and the freedmen as a group as well as those between individual freedmen.

Petronius's text seems to suggest a certain social immobility in the case of emancipated slaves in the first century C.E.; originally, freedmen had not been entitled to Roman citizenship at all, until Emperor Augustus introduced Latin rights with the possibility of promotion to full citizenship. During the Empire, wealthy ex-slaves could hold some civic magistracies — like the position of *seviri Augustales,* which Trimalchio mentions in the account of his career — and thus gain some prestige. Trimalchio and his friends are the only *Augustales* depicted in extant literature. Still, although the holding of certain public offices was available to ex-slaves, they were socially almost stigmatized, albeit mostly unofficially: Behavior of Trimalchio and his guests reflects a kind of frustration stemming from their inability to penetrate the iron wall of social differences despite their wealth and is reflected in frequent allusions to slavery and in their overall strong consciousness of slavery-related issues.

IN THE CLASSROOM

I. SOCIAL MOBILITY
Discussion

1. It has been mentioned that Petronius devotes considerable care to the depiction of social classes in contemporary society and specifically to the status of freed slaves. The issue of social mobility is by no means a problem restricted to the ancient world. Have students discuss the situation in *The Satyricon* as compared with other epochs and societies. Why are the freedmen unable to move upward despite having acquired legal citizenship and considerable wealth?

2. What are the details, discernible to a modern reader, in which Trimalchio reveals his sense of inferiority and clumsiness in an attempt at being more refined? Consider Trimalchio's treatment of his own slaves now that he is a slave *owner:* He pretends to be a harsh and strict master but often displays a peculiar lenience, no doubt because he still remembers his days as a slave all too well.

Writing

Ask students to write a short paper in response to one or more of the following:

1. Read carefully through Echion's speech, and consider in which details his social awareness is disclosed. Is Echion different from Trimalchio in his attitudes toward issues like literacy, art, public spectacles, and culture in general?

2. Consider the language used by Trimalchio's guests, and, having read through several freedmen speeches, compare their style and diction. How do these differ from the narrative parts as told by Encolpius? What does it tell us about their social standing?

3. What is the narrator's attitude toward guests *chez* Trimalchio? What does it tell us about Encolpius's social standing? What about the author? Does he express any overt judgment on these people?

II. THEME OF DEATH
Discussion

1. The element of theatricality in depiction of Trimalchio's dinner has been stressed in preceding text. Equally prominent are repeated allusions to the imminence of death amidst drunken debaucheries of Trimalchio's guests: a clock ticking off the hours of Trimalchio's life (26.9), epigrams such as the one recited by the host in 34.10, the silver skeleton (34.10), Seleucus' story about attending the funeral (42.30), profession of the stonecutter Habinnas, and, finally, Trimalchio's staging of his own funeral at the end of our episode. Discuss these incidents in class and their meaning to the story overall.

2. Special attention is to be paid to Trimalchio's story about the prophetess Sybil at the town of Cumae, which was traditionally considered an entrance to the Underworld, because it is a direct intertextual allusion to book 6 of Virgil's *Aeneid*. Discuss this connection in class. Students could be led to make connection between the hero Aeneas descending into the Underworld and an anti-hero, Encolpius, descending into the "social underworld" of freedmen.

Connections

1. Look at the text of Virgil's *The Aeneid* (p. 1181), especially the excerpt from Book Six about Aeneas's visit to the underworld (pp. 1240–1265), and consider how Petronius

reworked the motif of hero's descent into the land of the dead, with special attention to Sybil at Cumae.

2. Consider the quotation of Trimalchio's words at the beginning of T. S. Eliot's *The Waste Land* (Book 6). What is the connection between Petronius, Geoffrey Chaucer's *The Canterbury Tales* (Book 2) and T. S. Eliot's work?

Writing

Ask students to write a short paper in response to one or more of the following:

1. Read carefully through the text, and find specific motifs that function as reminders of mortality at the banquet, whether in architecture, decor, performances, or conversation. How are these funereal allusions to be reconciled with the riotous drunken atmosphere and surroundings that suggest prodigious wealth and luxury?

2. What about the characters themselves — are there any references to death in their speeches, and how are these to be explained? Pay special attention to poetry recited by Trimalchio.

3. Consider the connection between allusions to public spectacles, especially gladiatorial shows, and the theme of death in the text.

BEYOND THE CLASSROOM

RESEARCH & WRITING

1. Names of characters in *The Satyricon* are almost invariably "speaking names"; they either have a specific meaning that reflects some traits of person bearing the name or allude to his or her origin and/or social standing. Investigate in the proposed bibliography the origin of names appearing in the episode: Encolpius, Giton, Ascyltus, Trimalchio, Fortunata, and/or others. After having found which language these names come from, reflect on their meaning and why they were chosen.

2. The tradition of Greek novel has played a significant role as an (anti-)model for Petronius's work. Read a translation of one of the Greek novels that is considered to have influenced Petronius (*Ephesiaca* of Xenophon of Ephesus, *Leucippe and Clitophon* by Achilles Tatius, *Chaereas and Callirhoe* by Chariton, *Daphnis and Chloe* by Longus, *Ethiopica* of Heliodorus), and consider the similarities and differences between that work and *The Satyricon*.

Projects

1. When Federico Fellini released his film version of *The Satyricon* in 1970, reactions were varied — it caused indignation on the part of many classicists, while at the same time it popularized Petronius's work among a wider audience. Watch the movie carefully, writing down your thoughts and remarks, and consider the differences between the film and the text. Compare your impressions with that of other classmates. How are characters represented? What about the visual effects — decor, light, and color? Do you find them cinemagraphically appropriate? Do they add to or take away from the story's interest?

2. Investigate Web sites that contain information under the search entry "Satyricon." Do they include mostly home pages of college departments and academic publications related to actual work of Petronius or commercial sites advertising random products that appropriated the name? On the basis of your Internet research, try to draw conclu-

sions about the afterlife of Petronius's work in popular culture work and the employment of the title.

3.   There are several English translations of Petronius available besides the one by William Arrowsmith that is printed in the book. Using your library's online catalogue, find at least one other translation, and read through the text of "Dinner with Trimalchio." Note the differences, and consider how various translators rendered original Latin colloquial speech into English. Which one do you find to be more natural? Do you think the English text is being modernized? What are the possible problems a translator might encounter in dealing with a work like *The Saytricon?*

FURTHER READING

Bodel, J. "The Cena Trimalchionis" in H. Hofmann, ed. *Latin Fiction.* 1999.
Boyce, B. T. *The Language of the Freedmen in Petronius' Cena* Trimalchionis. 1991.
Courtney, Edward. *A Companion to Petronius.* 2002.
D'Arms, J. H. *Commerce and Social Standing in Ancient Rome.* 1981.
Griffin, M. T. *Nero, the End of a Dynasty.* 1984.
Wiedemann, T. E. J. *Emperors and Gladiators.* 1992.

GENERAL MEDIA RESOURCES

VIDEO

Ancient Rome
49 min., 1996 (Films for the Humanities & Sciences)
At its zenith, the Roman Empire included North Africa, Spain, France, and Britain. The wealth that these conquests generated allowed Roman citizens to live in a sumptuous world of beautifully decorated homes and opulent cities. In this program, scholars discuss Roman unification of Europe, Roman culture and institutions, and the family structure. The role of the army as a major force in Roman society and politics, as well as its military structure and tactics, are discussed. The Christianization of Rome and the enduring legacy of Roman Law and institutions in Western government today are also analyzed. 3-D re-creations of the Coliseum and Pompeii allow students to see Rome as it was before the empire collapsed.

Ancient Rome
30 min., 2001 (Insight Media)
The Roman Empire stretched far beyond the city of Rome. At its peak, in 117 C.E., it reached from Britain to the Persian Gulf to North Africa. This video chronicles the rise and fall of the Roman Empire and explores the influence Roman culture has continued to exert on Western civilization in language, law, and architecture.

Rome: Power & Glory
DVD and video, 312 min., 2003 (Library Video Company)
Premiered on TLC and narrated by Peter Coyote, this six-volume collection is the most complete and revealing video history of Rome ever produced. Detailed re-enactments of ancient customs and conflicts, period art, original writings, and insights from scholars all paint a compelling and brutal portrait of life under this mighty empire. DVD enhancements include biographies, facts, and virtual reconstructions of great architecture (e.g., the Colosseum) as it appeared in the first century.

Empires of Heaven and Earth: The World in Roman Times
23 min., 1998 (Insight Media)
Featuring dramatic readings and commentary by the former Poet Laureate Robert Pinsky, this educational program covers the expansion of the empires in Rome, India, and China as it relates to the sophisticated poetry, dramas, and histories of the time. Explores the works of Plautus, Horace, Julius Caesar, Tacitus, Polybius, Lucretius, and more, and examines common themes found within their work. The program reveals how religious literature (including the New Testament), interpretations of Taoism, and Ashoka's rock edicts influenced society.

Greece and Rome (1200 B.C.E.–200 C.E.)
30 min., 1989 (Insight Media)
Examining the philosophy, architecture, and culture of Greece and Rome, this video traces the political evolution of Greece. It considers its colonization of the Aegean and Asia Minor, and chronicles the victories of Alexander the Great. It then describes the spread of Roman control into Europe, North Africa, and Asia Minor.

I, Claudius
780 min., 1977 (Library Video Company)
Dramatization of the reigns of the first four Julio-Claudian emperors of Rome as seen through the eyes of the fourth, the emperor Claudius, who was considered a most unpromising youth, yet survived the political dangers of decades to become a wise and just ruler. Derek Jacobi, John Hurt, and Patrick Stewart star in this BBC Masterpiece Theatre presentation.

Intimate Details of Roman Life
26 min., 1991 (Films for the Humanities & Sciences)
Robert Erskine conducts viewers through rooms in the British Museum, explaining particular artifacts and discussing daily Roman life. Cicero's letters describe — and coins portray — Caesar, Pompey, Brutus, Marc Antony, Cleopatra, and Augustus; the appearance of art in the service of the state is defined by Virgil and illustrated by artifacts. The progression of emperors is recounted up to Vespasian. The next 150 years show the heyday of trade in the Roman Empire and reveal the variety and extent of the world of Roman objects.

The Roman Empire and Its Civilization
83 min., 1983 (Insight Media)
Introducing Roman institutions, culture, and thought, this video discusses the daily life of ancient Rome and examines the various components of the individual Roman experience. It traces Roman history from the 753 B.C.E. founding of Rome to the rise of the Republic through the formation, decline, and fall of the empire.

The Roman Empire in the First Century
219 min., 2001 (PBS Video)
Presents an in-depth chronicle of the emergence of the powerful Roman Empire from a chaotic period of violent coups, assassinations, overarching ambition, civil war, and clashes between the classes as well as the sexes. Through the experiences and writings of those who lived it, stories are told of the emperors, slaves, poets, and peasants who built the most cosmopolitan society the world has ever seen, as they shaped the Roman Empire in the first century.

Rome: The Ultimate Empire
36 min., 1996 (Time-Life)
Time-Life discovers the essence of what it meant to live as an ancient Roman. Join researchers as they uncover the harsh life at Hadrian's Wall, experience the everyday lives of citizens through their personal letters, and glimpse the pleasure dens of Pompeii's brothels. Then, witness the spectacle of gladiators battling for glory and survival in the Colosseum and more.

Rome: Village to Republic
28 min., 2001 (Insight Media)
Chronicling the birth of the Roman Empire, this video tells the story of Romulus and Remus and reveals how the Roman rebellion against Etruscan rule led to the creation of a new republic based on democratic principles. It also considers the American Founding Fathers' use of Rome as a model for their republic.

WEB SITES

Forum Romanum
www.forumromanum.org/index2.html
Forum Romanum is a collaborative project among scholars, teachers, and students, with the broad purpose of bringing classical scholarship out of college libraries and into a more accessible, online medium. Toward this end, Forum Romanum actively contributes to the body of information available online, publishing texts, translations, articles, and other pedagogical resources. We also make a point of highlighting important materials that are available elsewhere in order to present a real picture of the state of classical scholarship online.

Internet Ancient History Sourcebook—Rome
www.fordham.edu/halsall/ancient/asbook09.html
The goal of the Ancient History Sourcebook is to provide and organize texts for use in classroom situations. Links to the larger online collections are provided for those who want to explore further. It also includes links to visual and aural material, since art and archeology are far more important for the periods in question than for later history. The emphasis remains on access to primary source texts for educational purposes.

Perseus Project
www.perseus.tufts.edu/cache/perscoll_Greco-Roman.html
Perseus is an evolving digital library, the primary goal of which is to bring a wide range of source materials to as large an audience as possible. The site provides access to many of the authors and their texts found in Book 1 of the anthology.

Roman Sites
www.ukans.edu/history/index/europe/ancient_rome/E/Roman/RomanSites*/Topics/General.html
This is a megasite developed at the University of Kansas that contains twenty-seven nonoverlapping subject pages of Roman Web sites. It provides a gateway site to literally hundreds of pages on Roman history, culture, and literature.

The Rome Project
www.dalton.org/groups/rome/
The largest catalog of Web resources on Roman history and culture on the Internet; originally authored by David Miele, a Columbia University student, and now maintained by Dr. Neil Goldberg.

AUDIO

The History of Rome — Vols. 1 and 2
12 tapes, 18:75 hrs. (AudioBooksToday.com)
These volumes present the story of a tiny market town on the Tiber, its rise to world domination, and then its slow, terrible plunge to utter ruin.

I N D I A : T H E T I M E L E S S W O R L D S O F P R I E S T S , W A R R I O R S , A N D C A S T E

VEDIC LITERATURE, *the Rig Veda and the Upanishads* (p. 1332)

WWW   For quizzes on the Rig Veda and the Upanishads, see *World Literature Online* at bedfordstmartins.com/worldlit.

The Rig Veda is a founding document not only of a religion but also of a people and a culture, all three of which remain vital presences in the world today. It is partly a compendium that makes the connection between religion and myth much clearer than does the Greek tradition. Fundamentally, however, it is a liturgical text to inform the performance of ritual in the major sacramental rites of naming, initiation, marriage, and death and the major annual ceremonies for the king and his kingdom. Both the concerns of these poems and the imagery with which they express them indicate the life situation of their audience as primarily being cattle breeders, with agricultural habits still developing. Both rain and sun were of great concern to them. Rainfall is generally plentiful in India, but several times each century the monsoon clouds fail to develop, rain does not fall, and crops do not grow. India has been primarily agrarian for millennia and remains overwhelmingly a land of farming villages.

The Upanishads reflect the growth of Vedic society from primarily being cattle herders to village dwellers and planters. As towns and cities became centers of economic and political power, the organization of agriculture that resulted led to grain surpluses, allowing for the elaborate differentiation of social roles. The Brahmanic class may be said to have developed out of a surplus of leisure resulting from the grain surplus, and, out of this new concentration of social roles, a revolution in thought arose that reflected on the Vedic world vision and created a distinguished new chapter. The introduction to India (p. 1323) refers briefly to this time "when doctrines and practices during the Brahmanic period became too rigid," leading to the founding of Buddhism and Jainism. The Upanishads, originating as commentaries on the sacred Vedas, both uphold traditional Brahmanic practices and suggest ways to transform and sometimes even undermine them in favor of a sweeping new transcendent worldview.

These points in a standard historical narrative of early India are mostly inferred from the content of the Upanishads, which develop the beginning signs of an inquiring attitude into mystery in the late hymns of the Vedas and carry them forward into the creation of a magnificent series of sustained religious and philosophical inquiries. If the overriding purpose of the Vedas is justification and praise of the mythic world system whose outlines it traces, the Upanishads is dedicated to the quest of the individual mind to discover the transcendent origin of the world order, to articulate the nature of the individual soul, and to seek the ultimate origin of the soul.

The permanent value of these works has been attested by many Western writers for over two centuries. The Vedas provide a much more specific map of connection of myth to society and worldview than do the Greek myths. They remain fundamental to the study of myth-based societies everywhere. The Upanishads may be read not only as cultural material and literary achievements but also, and primarily, as active stimulus to the inquiring mind. Their inventive means of inquiry through reasoning, analogy, and anecdote provide one of the world's great demonstrations of the resources of the human mind.

TEXT & CONTEXT

RITA AND DHARMA

Sacrifice is understood as a vital part of *rita*, the cosmic principle of good order that pervades all aspects of life in the Vedic worldview. Because of *rita*, the cosmos undergoes change without degenerating into chaos and the sun and moon rise and set; it is a principle of balance, regularity, and expectedness. When human beings observe *rita*, order prevails and there is peace. In worship, *rita* is the pattern of correct ritual performance, which ensures harmony between people and their relations with nature and the gods.

THE HORSE SACRIFICE

The horse sacrifice, or *asvamedha*, is crucial in maintaining the active sense of an established king as warrior-conqueror. In it, the royal horse was set free to roam wherever it chose, and those lands into which it wandered were thereupon declared the property of the king. The horse's sacrifice on its return to the kingdom was considered to transfer its vital energy to the king.

BRAHMAN, BRAHMA, BRAHMIN

Brahman is given an initial capital and a pronoun "he" in Mascaro's translation; other scholars have noted however that it is better to conceive of *brahman* impersonally, noting that the Upanishads refer to it in their most resounding phrase as "that." Personhood is a facet of *atman*, and there is a Great Self associated with the totality of *brahman*. But in any case, do not confuse three related terms:

* * *Brahman*, the ground of being, the power behind the gods
* * *Brahma*, the eventual personification of this creative energy in classical Hinduism as the creator god
* * *Brahmin*, the class of human beings who knew and used this power.

REINCARNATION

Contemporary popular culture tends to represent reincarnation as an added bonus to life — for example, a fantasy of a series of "role-playing" adventures. The Indian conception of reincarnation — which through Buddhism became widespread throughout Asia — was rather of a prison of suffering and death in which all living beings were caught. In the Katha Upanishad "From death to death" and "the End of the journey, from which he never returns" are references respectively to *samsara* — reincarnation, or literally "re-death" — and *moksha*, or release from reincarnation.

IN THE CLASSROOM

I. THE VEDAS AND THE STRCTURE OF COSMOS AND SOCIETY

The Vedic system envisions the king as the axis of transmission of cosmic order to the earthly world. Kingship combines the two quite different functions of conqueror and administrator, which in some ways are incompatible but are harmonized through the chief rituals of kingship.

"The Song of Purusha" also encapsulates the essence of Vedic thinking about the essential functions in a society and about their organization. The human body becomes an image of unity and a justification of hierarchical relationship. The Vedic imagination was driven to think holistically and cosmologically, dividing up the entire cosmos into coherent parts. "The

Song of Purusha" relates with uncommon concision several of those schemes: the mortals and immortals, material and immaterial (beings who eat and those who do not); the four *varnas*, or castes, in society; the types of animals; the chief forces of the natural world; and the general three-level division of space.

The Vedic gods were conceived of as residing in the heavenly realm, but several of them are identified at the same time with some of the primary natural forces a farmer might experience. The gods are thought of as existing in nature, as part of the natural order.

The wheel image that closes "Indra Slays the Dragon Vritra" is notable as an image of order and efficacy, of movement and sameness at the same time — a fitting image for the conception of *rita* as orderly change. Use this image as a point of departure for discussing the functioning of *rita* and its psychological implications for the Vedic people.

Discussion

1. Strictly logical readers may have a hard time making sense of "The Song of Purusha": In saying the primal man contains the cosmos, for instance, it seems to be saying the smaller thing contains the larger. Does he have a thousand mouths or one mouth? (If he is the personal and life-giving principle in all animated beings, that he has a thousand hands, eyes, and feet, what might be meant is that he is one with all created life.) If he contains all the gods, how do the gods sacrifice him? If he is everything, can it be right to kill him, even in sacrifice?

2. In "The Song of Purusha," how does each body part designate the social class that is made from it? It might be good to discuss with the class whether this is a good way to divide up the functions of society. Along with it should be discussed whether the oppressiveness of the caste system that is still quite prevalent in India is due to these categories or to the rule that one's family line will always remain in that caste no matter what.

3. Notice the combining of hero and king in Indra, although in essence they are quite different functions (conqueror and administrator). Where in ancient Indian texts and culture do we see combining of and distinction between these functions (the horse sacrifice; Rama)? Is the Vedic conception of power characterized by this unitary link to force? Does this explain why the *Kshatriya varna* combines warriors and rulers? Or is this identity characteristic of early (usually epic-producing) nomadic warrior societies?

Connections

1. In "Indra Slays the Dragon Vritra," note the way in which the narrative imagines the everyday world as really a battle of opposing forces with their warring magical powers. This is not too different from West African myth and poetry or from the frequently commented on "war in heaven" in the *Ramayana* and Western epic, from *The Iliad* to *Paradise Lost* (Book 3). Consider also to what extent the relation of Vritra to his mother Dana recalls Grendel and his dam in *Beowulf* (Book 2).

Writing

Ask students to write a short paper in response to one or more of the following:

1. Discuss the way in which one or more of the Vedic hymns lends justification and support to the role of king in Vedic society. Sun and horse, for instance, in different ways may be read as a metaphor of the king.

2. Analyze "The Song of Purusha" as an attempt to ground specific social structure in the mysterious cosmos.

II. THE ROLE OF SACRIFICE IN THE EVOLUTION OF CONSCIOUSNESS

Sacrifice is a topic that must be covered in dealing with virtually all ancient peoples: Especially as cultures grew more urbanized, reaction against sacrifice-centered religion was an important contribution to the revolution in ancient worldview constituted by the formation of the great world religions. Eventually, most early civilizations came to a "sacrificial crisis" in which the self-contradictory aspects of the practice were confronted. Still, for all the rationality of this general account, there is something going on here that rather addresses an epistemological need than a practical one: It seems to be a way of reassuring that the whole of the cosmos maintains an efficacious relationship with people in the present. As social practice moves away from herding, the need for sacrifice becomes steadily more questionable. In one of the Upanishads, it is imagined that when the individual who has duly followed good Vedic practice dies and expects to be united with his ancestors in *Svarga*, the Vedic heaven, he will instead be confronted by the souls of all those animals he has sacrificed and assailed for the murders he has committed.

Discussion

1. It is probably best to get modern ambivalent feelings about sacrifice out in the open. On the one hand, it could be said that modern meat processing and marketing masks our generally carnivorous nature to ourselves, whereas sacrifice is a way of bringing to consciousness and honoring the renunciation of life made by animals in feeding our species. On the other hand, the manifest brutality of the act cannot entirely be dispelled by glorious words, images, and purposes, and in ancient times.

2. In "The Song of Purusha," the sacrifice makes sense in terms of its religious purpose, which is to consecrate: In sacrificing Purusha, the gods were consecrating all of creation (hence the repetition of "that sacrifice in which everything was offered"). The circular logic of this extended image becomes explicit with the final verse: "With the sacrifice the gods sacrificed to the sacrifice." Ask students to restate this sentence in their own words. Such a paradoxical structure can be said to indicate perfection, completion, and wholeness. Throughout the ancient world, sacrifice was practiced, and the most profound thoughts about the nature of things grew out of the wisdom surrounding its practice.

3. Note the similarity, but now in present time, to the sacrifice in "Hymn to the Horse" to the sacrifice of Purusha. The horse sacrifice essentially re-consecrates the entire cosmos. The horse's reins (verse 5), images of the rational control of nature, symbolize the law. The Aryas were a people who conquered by the horse, hence its associations with cosmic power. As Ralph T. H. Griffiths clarifies, "the object of the sacrifice is to send the horse to the gods that he may obtain wealth and other blessings for his sacrificers."

Writing

Ask students to write a short paper in response to the following:

1. Discuss the purpose of sacrifice as founding and continuing order in one or more of the Vedic hymns.

III. THE UPANISHADS AND THE QUEST FOR THE SOUL
THROUGH THE ACTIVE ROLE OF CONSCIOUSNESS

The book introduction to the Upanishads states that the single underlying message of all the Upanishads is *"atman equals brahman"* (p. 1337) and that the purpose of life is to realize this connection. The last Upanishad excerpted ends with the resounding declaration "Thou art that." Its most immediate meaning, when read correctly, is that "little old you" are one with the power that makes and sustains the whole universe. But, more profoundly, it enunciates the same principle given in *atman* equals *Brahman:* As Sarvepalli Radhakrishnan articulates it, it is the discovery of the oneness of the ultimate as discovered objectively (Brahman) and the ultimate as discovered introspectively (Atman). It is thus the coming together of the endpoint of *two* arduous spiritual quests. "The real which is at the heart of the universe is reflected in the infinite depths of the self," writes Radhakrishnan.

The Chandogya Upanishad portrays Brahman as clay, gold, or iron — the "material" or "stuff" that is *molded* to make the object, used as an analogy to gain insight into how Brahman can be in all things or, more accurately, *pervades* all things. Hence Brahman is sometimes called "soul-stuff."

The Maitri Upanishad focuses on Brahman, "the Spirit supreme," who is identified as the Purusha in the selection from the Katha Upanishad. In portraying these supreme entities, the Vedas attempt to concretize what cannot be concretized as a gesture of affirmation and familiarization; the Upanishads approach through the openness of negating limited sense conceptions, employing many negatives to aid in taking the listener/reader down this path.

Note the role of consciousness as uniting the knower with Brahman in the Maitri Upanishad. No other ancient culture paints so boldly immaterialistic a portrait of the universe as is presented in the Upanishads.

The succession or ascending chain of entities given in the Katha Upanishad beginning with "Beyond the senses are their objects" is a rhetorical recapitulation of the essential spiritual act that is called for throughout the Upanishads. See if students can interpret in each case the way that one link in the stated chain is "beyond" the previous one — for example, that beyond the objects is the mind or that beyond the mind is reason. Ask then what sort of anthropology — that is, what model of human nature — is implied for Indian culture in this scripture.

In the Chandogya Upanishad, Prajapati's meditation produces first the Vedas; then, from his meditation, the Vedas themselves produce the *sounds* "earth," "air," and "sky." The Upanishads consistently emphasize consciousness as an active, creative force in making the universe. Three famous stories from the Upanishads feature a boy as the main character (Nachiketas in the Katha; Satyakama Jabala, the housemaid's son, who seeks to be a Brahmin; and Svetaketu in the Chandogya) because of children's natural inquisitiveness and very likely also because children have not yet learned to screen out their natural acceptance of the creative power of consciousness. The Chandogya Upanishad offers the analogy of the man attempting to get back to his home, asking people for directions, to describe the quest that is the subject of all the Upanishads — the process of seeking the truth and awakening to consciousness. Rather than something mystical, this anecdote portrays it as being practical and self-evident.

Discussion

1. Modern perceptions of the type of inquiry undertaken in the Upanishads tends to devalue them as "Other-worldly," subjective, impractical, and the like. What practical advantage might it give to think of the universe as created, sustained, and regenerated by consciousness? Could this be an encouragement to the mind to be more active in practical situations rather than seeing consciousness as a tiny, embattled light in a dark world or a mere distraction from the serious material concerns always pressing on one?

2. Make sure the class knows and can distinguish the difference between "transcendent" and "immanent." Discuss the Vedic gods, the Purusha, and "the Spirit supreme" of the Maitri Upanishad in these terms, paying special terms to prepositions like "in" and "beyond" and constructions like "neither . . . nor."

3. Ask students to "shift gears" and change the speed of their reading, gearing down to a slow and thoughtful consideration of a few of the simplest phrases, like "It is the ear of the ear" in the Kena Upanishad, so that these phrasings do not simply seem like meaningless formulas. Obviously, one cannot remain at this "speed" for too long, but it reveals the most creative level of these poems.

4. Have the class pay close attention to what the footnote on page 1150 says about "Thou art That." Ask students to rephrase what this concise statement means. (It is sometimes misrepresented as meaning something like "thisness" or particularity, when its actual meaning is the opposite.)

Writing

Ask students to write a short paper in response to the following:

1. Radhakrishnan has said of the Upanishads, "They give us knowledge as a means to spiritual freedom." Discuss the idea of freedom as it emerges in the Upanishads. What are its characteristics? From what and for what is it?

IV. LITERARY FORM AND STYLE

Much of the experience of this work, and the problems for non-Hindu readers of it, has to do with identifying the type of utterance or discourse of each portion. "Indra Slays the Dragon Vritra" presents a mythic hero narrative, with Indra as the god of battle, shaped by the migrating Aryas' military experiences. Indra's killing of the dragon is referred to numerous times throughout the 1,028 hymns of the Rig Veda. Though associated with rain, clearly Indra is not some kind of personification of rain but rather of the ideal powers and virtues of the males of the Aryan warrior class. His domain is the hazardous area where his worshipers must cope with hostile outside forces. This goes hand in hand with the tales of his physical hungers and his prodigious satisfying of them. He is not a god of morality but of rescue. The "Hymn to the Sun God" is a performance of a different genre, a poem of praise to the natural sun that is at the same time the sun god, Surya, and the ordainer of order throughout the existing world. "The Song of Purusha" is a creation or origin myth and is one of the most formative mythic narratives not only for Hindu belief but for the structure of Indian society. It is also a sacrificial hymn that explains the foundational nature of sacrifice whenever it is offered. "Hymn to the Horse" combines the poem of praise and the sacrificial hymn.

The introduction to the Upanishads uses the term *spiritual treatises,* in contradistinction to a unified philosophical system, to describe the Upanishads. What sort of characteristics go with this mode of thought and utterance?

Discussion

1. In the last verses of the "Hymn to the Sun God," note how the speaker's relation to this divinity becomes explicit. If we are expecting mystical consciousness, the down-to-earth and specific and even competitive nature of the speaker's wishes may seem surprising, comical, or small-spirited. Remember, however, the very practical and everyday nature of ancient worship. Do we still see religion addressed toward some of the most basic practical needs today?

2. The footnotes in the book suggest a dual reading of "Indra Slays the Dragon Vritra," a mythic one related to the practical everyday life of the farmer and herdsman, for which drought has a vivid life-related meaning, and a more philosophical and mystical one, for which drought has a spiritual meaning. When did this second layer of meaning come into formation? In this hymn, Indra is envisioned as fighting against the land's most threatening enemy, Vritra, the evil demon that withholds the monsoon. How much can be read

into the opposition? Is it a declaration of the power of the will to overcome the domination of nature? Of the invading Aryas to master the land into which they have come?

3.   In verse 4, note how this narrative of Indra's heroic exploit functions both as a creation narrative and as an allegory of drought-ending rain, which can recur throughout time. In the creation context, the storm cloud may be taken as what? A force opposing the emergence of the created world? Wanting it to remain in obscurity?

4.   Note the image of the storm cloud as an image for drought. What is notable about this? Does it not potentiate the image of drought by making it an absent presence, a plenty that is withheld? As such, is it particularly suitable as an image of hope but also of despair? (Consider the oppressive effect of the continual presence of the storm cloud that never breaks over the parched land.)

5.   Ralph T. H. Griffith's gloss on verse 14 (in which fear enters Indra's heart *after* he has killed the dragon and he flees), crossing "the ninety-nine streams like the frightened eagle" is: "This flight of Indra is frequently alluded to. It is said that he fled thinking that he had committed a great sin in killing Vritra" (*Hinduism: The Rig Veda*, p. 21, n. 14). Is this an indication of some complicating cowardice in Indra? Is it a reflection that to end an order, even an evil order, is a fearful thing? Or is it just an admission by the sages that things never really add up totally the way we expect them to?

Writing

Ask students to write a short paper in response to one or more of the following:

1.   In "Hymn to the Sun God," what features of the sun are used as evidence or imagery of the sun's majesty? What functional value does praise have? What about its psychological value on the person doing the praise? How is it likely to be overlooked or denigrated in a modern culture of self-interest? Does asking the sun god for advantage over one's enemy, as the speaker does at the end of the hymn, seem inconsistent with a religious purpose, or does it make us aware of a broader functionality of religion?

2.   The introduction to the Upanishads mentions the relation of these poems to the Vedas as "interpreting and completing" them. It says the later poems supplant "ritual with knowledge" and are "more easily translatable to other cultures." What do you notice as contrasts and differences between the style and content of the two works?

BEYOND THE CLASSROOM

RESEARCH & WRITING

1.   Students could be directed to read further in the Rig Veda, in either the selected Flaherty translation or the complete Griffiths translation. Its seemingly daunting length can be navigated with relative ease, since there is no great need to read it sequentially, and since hymns are either grouped together by subject (Flaherty) or bear notes indicating to whom they are addressed (Griffiths). Students could locate several hymns to Indra, to Surya the sun god or to the dawn, or to the horse and organize their findings into a report on the chief characteristics and importance of that major figure as found in several hymns.

2.   Students could also research the details of Vedic sacrifice, consulting works on Hindu religion as well as on ancient India.

3.   So that the Upanishads may not seem all rather high-flown utterance, one special assignment could be for students to read the actual story of Nachiketas and Yama, the

lord of Death. As the introduction tells (p. 1346), Yama wants not to answer the boy, but at last he utters a great poem disclosing the truths of *brahman* equals *atman, samsara,* and *moksha,* and the need for spiritual discipline or yoga. So substantial is this answer that the whole Upanishad may be compared with the Bhagavad Gita in form and scope. Note the importance ascribed to learning this story at the end of the Katha Upanishad selection.

4. The image of the charioteer in the Katha Upanishad is famous partly because it is highly comparable to the same image as used by Plato in his dialogue *Phaedrus.* It may be an occasion for looking at the background and the implications of the image as a modeler of human nature: Why is it an image that might easily have come to mind? What is it implying about human nature? With what kinds of models might it be contrasted, and what advantage or disadvantage would it present in comparison to them?

Project

1. Some evidence for the wisdom of the choice of the four categories is found in current organization theory, according to which there are three ways of motivating people: through force or fear, through the promise of material benefit, and through inspiration to an ideal. To these three, a fourth has recently been added in the concept of "servant leadership." Report on contemporary organization theory and its views of how people may be motivated. A number of Web sites make contemporary business theory available in full text. Students should stay close to the concepts of motivation and leadership.

FURTHER READING

Hinduism: The Rig Veda. Trans. Ralph T. H. Griffith. *Sacred Writings,* vol. 5. Jaroslav Pelikan, ed. 1992.

Basham, A. L. *The Wonder That Was India.* 1954.

Coomaraswamy, Ananda K., and Sister Nivedita. *Myths of the Hindus and Buddhists.* 1967.

Cuthbertson, Gilbert Morris. "The Fight with the Monster." *Political Myth and Epic.* 1975.

Dimock, Edward C. et al., eds. *The Literatures of India: An Introduction.* 1974.

Ions, Veronica. *Indian Mythology.* 1967.

Mascaro, Juan. Introduction. *The Upanishads.* 1965.

Radhakrishnan, Sarvepalli, and George Moore, eds. *A Sourcebook in Indian Philosophy.* 1957.

MEDIA RESOURCES

WEB SITES

An Introduction to the Upanishads
www.google.com/search?q=the+upanishads&hl=en&lr=&ie=UTF-8&oe=UTF-8
This very helpful site contains clear and concise information on the background of the Upanishads as well as a set of helpful links.

The Rig Veda
campus.northpark.edu/history/WebChron/India/RigVeda.html
This site out of North Park University provides some good background information on the Rig Veda and the Upanishads as well as excellent historical background on ancient India.

The Upanishads
www.hindunet.org/upanishads/
This site provides brief background on the Upanishads.

The Ramayana (p. 1351)

WWW   For a quiz on the Ramayana, see *World Literature Online* at
bedfordstmartins.com/worldlit.

The *Ramayana* is an enduring work of the imagination, a beloved narrative in India as well as an important part of world literature. Along with the *Mahabharata* and especially the Bhagavad Gita, it was crucial to the transformation of the culture and religion of the Brahmanic period in placing the great spiritual discoveries of the Upanishads in a social context. It envisioned a world distinctly transformed from that of the Vedas, in which the interaction of gods and people is central, a higher conception of morality and obligation is born, and these new demands on the selflessness of the person are justified and made sustainable by the central notion of personal devotion to a savior god who is also hero and king. Its story has been retold many times over the centuries in fresh literary form, and its influence extends fully into popular culture. It recently proved the freshness of its power when it was adapted and serialized on national television in India.

To students of world culture, it offers the opportunity to explore the prime values of a religious civilization and especially how conflicts between duty and desire, family and state, and man and woman are envisioned and resolved. As a landmark of world literature, it integrates the epic pattern as seen in Western and worldwide epic, with its divine mission and heroic quest, into a cosmic vision that makes full use of the elements of the life world, from animals to human beings to their technology, transforming them all freely in a supernatural context uniting love and war, fantasy and realism, the familiar and the transcendent, in a canvas of vast purposes. Its particularly Indian shaping of the heroic character makes renunciation and nonattachment the central heroic character trait.

TEXT & CONTEXT

VISNU AND VAISNAVISM

The "Hindu Trinity" of Brahma, Visnu, and Siva became the focus of worship in the epic period in which the epics were composed. The *Ramayana* is clearly a work of Vaisnavism, or devotion to Visnu, known as Visnu the Preserver, who is conceived as the protector of dharma, the proper and just order of the world. He is the only Hindu god who incarnates himself in the world, doing so in a series of *avataras*, avatars or incarnations. He is said to have only ten avatars throughout history, and all but the last — Kalki, who will dissolve the world order — have already appeared. An earlier avatar, known as "Rama with an Axe," is said to have brought the technological order to the human race; Rama himself to have brought the social order; and Krishna (the central divine voice in the Bhagavad Gita) to have brought the moral order. The worship of Rama became widespread in the medieval period in northern India, where Ayodhya is located, and the Hindi name "Ram" became a synonym for "God."

WOMEN AND POWER

Women were said to be in possession of *shakti*, the fundamental force of power in the world. *Shakti* makes action possible; without it men cannot transform their ideas and purposes into reality. This trait of women renders them fundamentally ambivalent in Hindu culture, however, and it is related to the strict rule under which women were required to be kept at all times according to the *Laws of Manu*. In the Hindu pantheon, the Devi (her name means simply "Goddess") is depicted as a wild warrior, dangerous but also a rescuer of the gods themselves. Every male god is also conceived of as being married to a female goddess who makes his purposes realizable. Visnu's consort is Laksmi, who is Sita's incarnation. The *Ramayana* depicts a conventional social world in which women are under strict control, but its action tells a different story: The power of woman overthrows a king and installs the heir of its own preference.

GRAMA AND ARANYA

Much of the symbolism of the *Ramayana* can be understood through the twin concepts of *grama*, which is ordered social space, and *aranya*, literally the forest, which is wild natural space. In *grama*, presided over by the king, order rules — hierarchy, obedience, good social practice, hospitality, and rationality. It runs out of the energy to sustain itself and must be restored from time to time by visiting *aranya*, where dangerous, violent, unsocialized beings lie in wait — but also where the energy to restore the kingdom may be acquired. These concepts structure such rituals as the horse sacrifice, in which a horse symbolizing the king is let loose to roam through outlying territory, accompanied by the king's retinue. Whatever territory the horse enters is considered "conquered" by the king, and the storehouses of his kingdom are refreshed by that territory. Rama's path in the epic (*Ramayana* means "the way of Rama") is from *grama* to *aranya* and back again.

IN THE CLASSROOM

I. THE RAMAYANA AS EPIC

The *Ramayana* is an epic of civilization and of religion. Its hero, like Aeneas in Virgil's *The Aeneid* but even more so, is a model of the virtues and the kind of life required to uphold the goals envisioned by the poet for a large, unified civilization. Rama's story, moreover, can be compared to Aeneas's in four major respects. He is denied his destiny as envisioned by his father (royal courtier at Troy; hereditary king of Ayodhya) in order that a greater destiny (founder of Rome; conqueror of demons and king for 11,000 years) may be achieved by his heroic action. He is required to go against his own desire and his personal sense of the good in marriage and love (Creusa, Dido, Lavinia; Sita). He is revealed a vision of order and destiny of which he has been unaware and which is so great that he cannot comprehend it himself and can only conform to it by acting in faith (eternal supremacy of Rome; Rama's identity as the ultimate god). And his heroic quest at its climax takes the form of a battle against an opponent who in many ways exemplifies an older ideal of the heroic warrior (Turnus; Ravana) but whose choices transform the battle into one of good against evil.

The virtues that such an epic of civilization stresses, therefore, entail denial of one's immediate self-determined goals in order to act in faith for a distant and invisible vision of the good, a vision moreover whose totality one cannot see but must trust is good. An ethic of responsibility, of keeping one's word, following the gods, honoring one's parents, and the like emerges out of this imperative. In further comparison, both Virgil's and Valmiki's poems involve their heroes in choices — the rejection of Dido and of Sita — that have been controversial to readers across the centuries and that, whether right or wrong, explicitly enact the conflict of the personal and the social in an advanced civilization.

In many ways, of course, the two poems are extremely different. The *Ramayana* was more central than *The Aeneid* was to its culture, even though it shares this honor with the longer *Mahabharata*. Whereas now *The Aeneid* is studied only in a classical education, the *Ramayana* remains an actively loved story by all Hindus today. Many of the differences, in fact, have to do with the status of the *Ramayana* as a religious epic. Like the Hebrew Bible and the New Testament — although again different from them in crucial ways — it is a definitive narrative of the involvement of the divine in the human world and human history. The divine commitment to the good of human beings becomes the motive for a broader definition of religious belief. The tenets of this belief are spelled out in the Bhagavad Gita, and the central doctrine of both poems is devotion — complete devotion to a transcendent deity who is a manifestation of the Ultimate Spirit and the Primal Man, and an ethic of *dharma*, duty to the requirements of one's place in society and nonattachment to the personal rewards that this world may offer.

The *Ramayana* operates by a different principle from the familiar method of the Western mimetic tradition. Homer lards his epics with details that place the reader in a real world, in which characters' actions and attitudes generally have the kind of consequences that readers might expect — even readers thousands of years later. Famously, this is true even when Homer portrays the gods. Valmiki's *Ramayana* is not without these moments, moments that render the complexity of motives and actions quite familiarly; its most prominent actions, however, require much more of a "willing suspension of disbelief." Hanuman is a human-like monkey-god (or vanara), but his leap into Lanka cannot be measured by human standards. It can be appreciated only on the basis of its rendering the cosmology within which it acts. Its realism is often a realism of the cultural imagination: Its "facts" are "checked" as often by knowledge of the Hindu cosmos as by verisimilitude to the household or the battlefield.

Without knowledge of the classical Hindu cosmology, readers of this epic can be dogged by questions such as: Why does the poet not just have the characters do anything he wants? Why this particular magical object or action and not another? Why is an event such as Hanuman's leap given such importance in the poem, augmented as Valmiki makes it with in-flight interviews by several supernatural personages? All this may seem rather arbitrary and childlike to Western readers, but it is presided over by a poetics designed to bring to life the abstract ordering concepts of the Hindu cosmos.

An unusual feature of the *Ramayana* is its self-reference in the poem. Its author is a character in the poem; its recitation is said and at times even demonstrated to have benign powers (in Sundara 31-33, Hanuman gets Sita to recognize her by reciting the story of Rama). This seems a breaking of the fictional contract, even a gesture that could be called "high modernist" or "postmodern." In Yuddha 98–99, Brahma tells Rama to listen to Kusa and Lava's recitation of the epic because it will narrate what has not happened yet. Modern readers may recognize this gesture from *One Hundred Years of Solitude* or from the more ancient *Popol Vuh*. Yet the practice is not irresponsibly self-promoting or ironic; it is related to the status of the poem as a sacred text. As the poem itself declares, "the holy epic Ramayana . . . promotes dharma. . . . He who listens to or reads this Ramayana propitiates Rama by this" (Yuddha 131). Not simply a promotional piece for Rama, the epic is intensely about spiritual qualities that it both portrays and praises. Hence the performative dimension in the text is meant to ensure both the continued revering of the *Ramayana* and its reception in the right spirit.

Discussion

1. What is the difference between devotion and duty? Why are these two qualities less highly regarded in the modern world? Discuss the positive and disadvantageous aspects of both.

2. Kausalya's parting blessing on Rama invokes his power of killing demons and anticipates this major aspect of his action to come. It establishes a textual parallel between

Indra's victory over Vritra in the Vedas and Rama's heroism to come. What else could you say to compare and contrast Indra and Rama in these roles of dragon/demon killer?

Connections

Have students individually or in groups:

1. Compare Aeneas and Rama as exemplars of moral integrity and heroic self-control.

2. Compare Homer's Penelope with Valmiki's Sita as paragons of wifely devotion and chastity in the midst of the direst situations.

3. Compare Homer's Odysseus's exile and return, the journey of encounter of dangerous or helpful others, or the journey of formation of character to the same things found in the Ramayana.

Writing

Ask students to write a short paper in response to one or more of the following:

1. In Aranya 14–15 (apparently already Dasaratha has died by this time, to judge by Lakshmana's last comment?), Jatayu declares his fealty to Rama. This is the first experience (in the excerpt included in the anthology) of the many nonhuman characters of the *Ramayana,* one of the things that makes it truly distinctive. Discuss the meaning of this and other instances of the nonhuman characters you find in the *Ramayana.*

2. Rama's journey forms the backbone of the plot of the *Ramayana.* What symbolism structures his journey, and what, in your assessment, is the ultimate meaning of his journey?

II. THE *RAMAYANA* AS EXEMPLIFICATION OF CLASSICAL HINDU COSMOLOGY AND ETHICS

Rama is a hero of renunciation and not simply of pleasures, riches, and self-indulgence. He is asked to renounce those goals that a man in society *should* want: his father's inheritance, his wife's devotion. If the nonattachment of which the Bhagavad Gita speaks is the supreme ethical goal in life, Rama's life is constructed to make him face the most painful consequences of that virtue. The *Ramayana* itself is constructed to explore the painful contradictions of the moral order discovered by the very classical Hinduism it promotes. Rama, the linchpin of the social system, becomes increasingly detached from society; beginning happy and spontaneously good, he ends his life in resignation.

Kaikeyi's denial of the throne to Rama elicits a response from him that is a radiant example of the moral order envisioned by Hinduism: He is untroubled in agreeing to his banishment, showing the perfection of his devotion to dharma, the duty of his station. He is a good son in obeying his father's wife and in defending the sacredness of his father's word even against the wishes of his father. Again, the poem creates extreme conflicts to test the new values it proclaims, and even in Rama's filial piety a sharp irony sticks, for to obey Kaikeyi, he must disregard and go expressly against his own mother, Kausalya.

The Ayodhyakanda is structured around Rama's heroic acceptance of exile. The attitudes several characters take in opposition to him only throw the idealism of his decision into sharper relief (see Discussion questions). As the Bhagavad Gita will argue, holding onto the desire for a particular end is what brings delusion and suffering into the world. The conflict in Ayodhya, the social world, centers on competing claims of self-interest, each of them reasonable enough in itself but bringing chaos in their conflict. In contrast, the central action in the Aranyakanda, the book of the forest, has to do with the pull of irrational, unstructured desire; thus in the contrast of *grama,* social space, and *aranya,* wild nature, two contrasting sides of the disruptive force of desire are shown. In the Aranyakanda, first Surpanakha and then Ravana, whom Surpanakha herself calls "addicted to sense-pleasure" (Aranya 34–35), exemplify uncontrollable desire. The sage, Marica, warns Ravana that, because of his life of pursuing pleasure, he is unfit even to understand what Rama is truly like, and, typically, Ravana seems to be acting and thinking on a completely different plane from Rama and Sita. Ironically, Ravana appears as his opposite, a wandering ascetic, in order to deceive Sita into letting her guard down. The great irony of this third book, however, is that the roles of Ayodhya are reversed, so that Lakshmana sees through Marica's too unsubtle disguise as the unearthly iridescent deer, but Sita does not, led astray by beauty. Rama too is seduced by the idea of gaining a princely trophy. Predictably, disorder ensues among the virtuous. In pursuit of Marica, Rama is led far away from guarding Sita. Sita, thinking Rama is in danger, makes remarks designed to sting Lakshmana's pride, and his self-regard makes him go off after Rama, although he knows Sita will be unsafe. The good do wrong and end in mutual accusation.

At the center of the fourth book is Hanuman. His leap and his visit to Lanka take up the undivided attention of the narrative, and readers might find this distracting and even childish if they fail to approach this part of the story with the spiritual goals of Hinduism in mind. Foremost among the spiritual qualities whose efficacy the *Ramayana* celebrates is devotion. We are told in the Balakanda that Hanuman was engendered as a support deity to Vishnu's avatar. A passage in the *Ramayana* that is left out of our selection shows Hanuman opening his chest to reveal the name "Rama" written over and over on his very bones. Hanuman exemplifies devotion in its perfection. His prodigious leap is possible because his devotion to Rama is so intense as to remove all self-doubt and concentrate his energies perfectly in a single movement of the will. "His whole being swell[s] with enthusiasm, fervour and determination" (Sundara Prologue) as he prepares for the leap, and, as he plants his foot, he gains the attention of "pleasure-loving celestials and peace-loving ascetics." This consummate resoluteness is the already achieved version of what the Bhagavad Gita seeks: the doctrine of nonattachment. Hanuman is free from any attachment to his own desires, and this "lightness" is brilliantly literalized in his leap. Once he is on the island of Lanka and searching for Sita, his internal monologues make this clear. He restrains himself from killing Ravana and all the other demons, even though he is powerful enough to bring an end to them all, because he wants to leave the rescue of Sita to the proper performer of the deed, Rama. He even reflects that lustful thoughts do not come to him as he looks on Ravana's sleeping wives because he is wholly engrossed in his mission for Rama!

Yet Hanuman's mood is not the serenity of the mystic. He worries incessantly, twice (in our selection) going so far as to imagine that his rash actions, though discharged with the best of intentions, will lead to the self-destruction of Rama and all his followers. In part, this train of thought exemplifies the ancient Indian concern with *karma*, the inescapability of the consequences of one's actions. But partly Hanuman's preoccupations and unexpected actions simply reflect with wit on the life of the everyday Hindu believer and worshipper of Rama. His "four virtues" are listed at the end of Sundara 1 as "firmness, vision, wisdom and dexterity."

Sita also is drawn into a line of self-questioning involving karma, as she asks whether some action in a past life has caused the misfortune she must suffer. Her inner agony shows her near despair while bravely resisting Ravana and the demonesses. She laments her "state of dependence upon others," the state to which women are relegated at all times in the Hindu social vision. Is she saying that this dependence makes nonattachment impossible? Sita admires as if from afar the spiritual state of sages "to whom the pleasant and the unpleasant are non-different," those who are truly not attached to the things and goals of this world.

Sita's purity and heroism of character become a central focal point in both of the last two books of the *Ramayana* as they lead to the two most troubling moments in the epic. In rejecting Sita, Rama is caught between his personal faith in her pure devotion to him and his dharma as prince and king-to-be (and later as king).

Discussion

1. Discuss the ways in which Kaikeyi, Dasaratha, and Lakshmana challenge Rama's perfect adhesion to dharma in the Ayodhyakanda through their personal goals and interests.

2. Hanuman is the model of the devoted worshipper of Visnu in Rama. Discuss how his special powers relate to this central quality and what effects Valmiki achieves by having a monkey exemplify the perfectly devoted Hindu. How do Hanuman's exchanges with the beings who meet him on his leap exemplify his nonattachment and devotion?

Connections

1. In the Ayodhyakanda, the good do wrong and end in mutual accusation. Ask students individually or in groups to compare the action here with *Paradise Lost* (Book 3) or even their understanding of the cosmogony in their own particular religions.

2. Rama is told by the pantheon of gods (Yuddha 120–21) that he is the cosmic being, Purusa. Compare conceptions of Purusa in the selection from the Vedas, the Katha Upanishad, and the *Ramayana*. Is there a logical development in the way descriptions of him change?

Writing

Ask students to write a short paper in response to one or more of the following:

1. Write a character analysis of Hanuman, considering him either as the figure of perfect devotion or as embodying "firmness, vision, wisdom and dexterity."

2. Dasaratha may be considered a model of the good man and the good king who is caught in the web of his own karma. Analyze the character of Dasaratha, especially in terms of attachment and nonattachment, and how these qualities relate to his suffering and his fate. Recall the goal of "grasping only by not grasping" as stated in the Kena Upanishad: How does Dasaratha measure up to this spiritual yardstick?

3. How does the *Ramayana* envision and dramatize dharma?

III. SOCIAL DOCTRINE IN THE *RAMAYAMA*

The introduction recalls that Rama is said in the Ayodhya Kanda to be fit to rule "the three worlds." Whether one takes that to mean the earth, the underworld, and heaven or as earth, sky, and heaven, our editor's interpretation of the phrase as meaning "politically, morally, and spiritually" is certainly justified. Rama is conceived as a summation of the princely virtues. An earlier avatar of Vishnu, Parasurama, is said to have conferred the agricultural or technological order on the human race, while Rama conferred the social order and Krishna (the avatar who reveals the divine purpose in the Bhagavad Gita) brought the moral order. The *Ramayana* defends the comparatively rigid social structure of ancient India through Rama's righteousness. However, the interactions it portrays between major characters sometimes tell a much more mixed story and make the *Ramayana* into as profound an examination as a justification of the social order.

Traits of the ideal king, the linchpin of the social order, are spread throughout the poem. Rama is the *dharmaraja*, the model of the king (*raja*) who follows *dharma*. In Bala 13–14, the people are guests at the banquet of the king and depend on his wealth and munificence, just as all do to Brahma, the creator god, who is honored in the horse sacrifice. In a profound but easily overlooked metaphor, the king is called in Ayodhya excerpt 1 "the very life of the people, moving outside their bodies." Conversely, Ravana is portrayed as an antimodel: the negligent monarch, self-devoted and careless of the welfare of his people. In Aranya 32–33, Surpanakha objects that he "has no spies": Spies were thought necessary to collect intelligence of his people for the king rather than as a noxious invasion of (a mostly nonexistent) privacy. The good king knows his people, and spies are his agents in this process. This turns out to be how Rama learns of his people's disapproval of Sita in the final Kanda.

This brings up the area that the poem exposes most troublingly: the status of women in this supposedly perfect model of society. Rama enunciates the social doctrine on woman to his mother: The supreme duty of women is to serve their husbands (Ayodhya 24–25). However, much of the poem's action describes women surmounting this command. Kaikeyi is seen at first exemplifying noble graciousness and trust, but her devotion is gradually eroded by Manthara's skillful manipulation of her fears and motherly concern for the welfare of her child. Whereas Kaikeyi entirely disregards social doctrine, Sita interprets to her advantage the dictum that the wife must be one with the husband and insists on the modicum of equality that this affords her in this situation. Her interpretation of the code of conduct for women is active and spirited. Sita invokes the cosmology of woman: "I am your half"; "I cannot live without you"; "a righteous wife will not be able to live separated from her husband"; "a devoted wife remains united with her husband even after they leave this earth-plane." She displays an even greater strength of inner character, an *amor fati* in which Rama believes in principle but that his somber attitude once he is not in the presence of his elders shows he has not adopted thoroughly. As Gavin Flood says, Sita is the ideal Hindu woman, fulfilling her "womanly duty" (*strisvadharma*) to the letter, yet retaining self-possession and an element of autonomy and identity independent of her husband Rama (109).

However, Sita is treated so harshly by the one who should be her most powerful supporter that she has been a figure of devotion for centuries by Indian women for her strength amid suffering. [See Richman's book for details.] And Rama rejects her not once but twice, as if to underline that this human inequity defies harmonizing with the existing order. Rama rejects Sita, as he says, "for the sake of preserving my honour." He accepted exile in order to preserve his father's honor, so he is not being disingenuous but rather extremely adherent to a principle he judges all-important to his authority. It is an extreme conflict of loyalties. Sita's response is true to her character as well: Deeply wounded, she cannot see the logic in placing such a theoretical honor over genuine love, and at the end she chooses her own death, as she could not do before when Ravana held her captive.

Discussion

1. Discuss the idea of the spy's role as agent of the king in the *Ramayana*. Note especially, in Sundara 2, Hanuman's discussion of the rationale for this policy.

2. Discuss the role that Rama's concept of honor plays in the two main crises of the epic, his acceptance of exile and his exiling of Sita.

3. Is Sita's second rejection by Rama, in Uttara 43–45, a redundant repetition of her earlier one? (Note that many scholars say the original epic ends with the Yuddha Kanda.) What is added to the poem by this final rejection of Sita? What does her being carried away by her mother Earth (Uttara 96–97) say about the Indian conception of women?

4. At the end of the story, is Sita required to go through the same ordeal that Rama had to go through at the beginning: banishment from home and from one's rightful position? Why is the result not similar? What do you think is the poem's assessment of her heroism?

Connections/Group Work

1.   This might be a good point at which to introduce the terms *shame culture* and *guilt culture* as concepts that can help explicate the concept of honor that drives Rama's selfless severity and Sita's tragic suffering. Eastern civilizations are sometimes portrayed as being more shame-oriented than Western, but historically all warrior cultures developed their ethical systems around concepts of honor and shame. Furthermore, the ancient Indian world of ideas is not completely oriented toward honor and shame: The project to discover the soul and its origin in the Upanishads results in a sense of the equality of all people that is essentially in tension with the concept of honor. Explain, or ask the class to research, briefly, these two concepts, and discuss their application in the *Ramayana* (e.g., are Rama and Sita in some sense "nondifferent" from each other, as she claims?).

2.   The conception of the king in the *Ramayana* bears great similarities to medieval European theories of kingship. Both stand in much greater contrast to the modern instrumental theory of kingship as laid out by Machiavelli. A discussion of the two conceptions of kingly or princely power and authority would yield illuminating results.

3.   Can the scene of Manthara corrupting Kaikeyi be compared with a scene like Satan's corruption of Eve in *Paradise Lost* (Book 3)? What elements are similar? Manthara is forgiven by Rama later in the poem. How do you think she has been viewed by readers over the centuries? Why?

Writing

Ask students to write a short paper in response to one or more of the following:

1.   What view of gender emerges from your reading of the *Ramayana?* Concentrate on how gender is modeled in two or three episodes, for instance Manthara's persuasion of Kaikeyi or Sita's carrying off by her mother Earth.

2.   The *Ramayana* sets forth the model of sacred kingship — the idea that the king, as father-provider of his people, is heaven's representative to the people and the people's representative to the gods. At the same time, it shows the stresses and cracks in this model.

BEYOND THE CLASSROOM

RESEARCH & WRITING

1.   Look at *Many Ramayanas*, ed. Paula Richman (University of California Press), to catalogue several of the different versions of the *Ramayana* or, alternatively, several ways in which it has been influential in Indian public life in the past two centuries.

2.   In Aranya 42, it is said "for it was in fact a hovercraft." This translation chooses to render the many magical devices used by Rama, Ravana, and others in terms of modern technology — like flying chariots are cars or spacecraft and ultra-destructive arrows are missiles. What is the effect of this way of translating? Is more gained or lost? Compare with readily available translations by those like Buck or Narayan.

Project

1.   Compare the spirit of pragmatism in Lakshmana's attitude to the position of Thrasymachus in Plato's *Republic* and of modern pragmatism in general.

FURTHER READING

Alles, Gregory. *The* Iliad, *the* Ramayana, *and the Work of Religion.* 1994.
Blank, Jonah. *Arrow of the Blue-Skinned God, Retracing the Ramayana Through India.* 1992.
Jacobson, Doranne, and Susan S. Wadley. *Women in India — Two Perspectives.* 1995.
Narayan, R. K. *The Ramayana.* 1996.
Richman, Paula, ed. *Many Ramayanas.* 1991.

MEDIA RESOURCES

VIDEO

Hinduism: Faith, Festivals, and Rituals
51 min., 1995 (Insight Media)
The majority of the Indian population practices Hinduism, which emphasizes right living, or dharma. This video explores the devotional ceremonies and observances of Hinduism and examines such sacred Hindu literary works as the *Ramayana* and the *Mahabharata.*

Spotlight on Ramayana: An Enduring Tradition
57 min., 1995 (Social Studies School Service)
Edited by Hazel Sarah Greenberg. A window opens on the culture of India through this study of the 2500-year-old Sanskrit epic of Prince Rama. This fascinating approach to Indian civilization through the Ramayana's plot and characters (who are as appealing as cartoon superheroes but signify profound spiritual values) can be used as a comprehensive interdisciplinary curriculum or a source of individual lessons. The kit includes 25 lesson plans with reproducible worksheets, primary source materials and background information on 356 loose-leaf on 8-1/2" x 11", three-hole-punched pages in a binder. Main themes are oral tradition, Hindu values and rituals, and the Ramayana's role within India's multicultural history and society; color video on the history and sociological significance of the Ramayana; 8 brightly colored 18" x 12" posters depicting heroes of the epic.

WEB SITES

ORIAS Monomyth Site: The Hero's Journey
ias.berkeley.edu/orias/hero/
This site provides information based on Joseph Campbell's monomyth providing information on three key world myths — *Sunjata, the Ramayana,* and *Yamoto.* On the *Ramayana* portion of the site, users will find information on plot and historical background as well as links to other key sites devoted to the epic.

The *Ramayana:* An Enduring Tradition
http://www.maxwell.syr.edu/maxpages/special/ramayana/
Created and hosted at Syracuse University, this site offers a wealth of information and links to additional sites on the *Ramayana.*

Web Resources for the Ramayana
www-learning.berkeley.edu/wciv/ugis55a/readings/ramayana
This site consists of the University of California–Berkeley's world civilization course's suggested Web sites that provide background on and resources for the *Ramayana.*

The Mahabharata (p. 1434)

WWW For a quiz on the *Mahabharata,* see *World Literature Online* at
bedfordstmartins.com/worldlit.

The *Mahabharata* is an epic of conflict; its nearest counterpart in Western literature is *The Iliad.* In comparison, the *Ramayana* is more like *The Odyssey,* dominated by highly foregrounded mythic themes, whereas the *Mahabharata* is structured by the relentless time of the eighteen days of the war. Rama's centrality focuses the *Ramayana* on the perfectly integrated man of Hinduism; the *Mahabharata,* however, stresses the efforts required to approach this integration. Hindu scholars describe the poem as *itihasa,* a history or chronicle — literally, "thus it was." In general, the *Mahabharata* is more novelistic than the *Ramayana;* it is divided into "books" (*parvan*) rather than, like the *Ramayana,* "cantos" or songs (*kandan*), and its author's name, Vyasa, means "compiler" or "editor." As the poem says of itself, "many things to be seen elsewhere are in the *Mahabharata,* but whatever is not in this poem does not exist anywhere else." The world's longest poem when unabridged, it is encyclopedic, a long-accreted effort at raising the entirety of ancient Indian culture into epic memory. It has received several renditions through the ages and is revered today in culture high and low: Peter Brook's massive cinematic production, Indian national television, and countless local performances of traditional popular dramas are based on it.

The large cast of characters, all with names difficult to spell and pronounce, presents an obstacle for reading and classroom study. A diagram listing the chief characters on each side, with a few salient facts about each, is indispensable and could be either handed out or assigned to students to make for themselves.

TEXT & CONTEXT

TRANSITION FROM THE VEDIC TO THE BRAHMANIC PERIOD

The national self-understanding of Hindu India, told in part in the Bhagavad Gita, includes a crisis of the old Vedic order, as people grew more urbanized and began to question the morality of sacrifice. The inner quest for the meaning of the soul and the Ultimate Spirit was said to have led to a mass desertion of the cities — an exodus to the forest — where searchers could be alone to seek union with the Brahman. Buddhism was born during this time. Classical Hinduism, expressed supremely in the Bhagavad Gita and the two great Indian epics, was said to have been born out of a sense that the people must come back out of the forest — back into social life and the duties of their social roles. In this context, the *Mahabharata* is an intense examination and ultimate affirmation of the worth of the warrior's life. The warrior, in turn, is a symbol of the active life and the possibility of just action.

KRISHNA

His enigmatic quality stems in part from his possible origin as an actual hero-king who came to be identified as one of the *avataras* of Vishnu. Through the development of his cult, culminating in the authoritative sayings of the Bhagavad Gita, he came to be identified with the "Supreme Person" or Ultimate Spirit himself. B. K. Matilal examines his conduct and the conception of his character in the *Mahabharata;* David Williams writes that Krishna's "essential role has been to encourage each individual to pursue their own *dharma* to the very end" and that "as a man, he has only ever been able to urge others tacitly to a point of self-knowledge" (183). These goals, Williams contends, are more important than morality for him.

Draupadi

The scene of Draupadi being humiliated before the Kauravas, but miraculously protected from being disrobed, makes her the central focus at the very moment she is being stripped of all social standing and enslaved and humiliated. Like Penelope, her sexual humiliation is postponed by unexpected means; like Helen, she will be fought over. The miraculous appearance of clothing upon her appeal to Krishna, "even as she was being shamed by the Kauravas," seems to enact the difference between a shame culture's code of honor/dishonor and the interiorized conception of innocence and guilt brought in by the world religions: The "miracle of the saris" is that she does not lose her honor, even as actions are taken to shame her. This is often taken as a key scene demonstrating the efficacy of nonattachment and devotion to Krishna in the midst of peril. In a nonreligious context, the scene has tremendous appeal, both for her strength in resistance and as motivation for the revenge and recovery of her honor. Draupadi is understood to participate in the fierce warlike nature of the Goddess (Devi) herself in her form as the warrior (Durga) and the destroyer (Kali).

IN THE CLASSROOM

I. The Way of the Warrior

Kshatriyadharma, in its largest sense, means the proper duty of the ruler and warrior class, the ethic of laying down one's life on the battlefield for one's king or of placing the strength and prosperity of one's kingdom as the highest good. The *Mahabharata* examines its formation and discovery in a past imagined in the "absolute past" of national tradition. Writing of this past, critic Mikhail Bakhtin has observed that "the world of epic is the national heroic past: it is a world of 'beginnings' and 'peak times' in the national history, a world of fathers and founders of families, a world of 'firsts' and 'bests'" (13). Rather than a realistic representation of warrior behavior, the epic work presents "only that which is worthy of being remembered," a gallery of images "projected onto their sublime and distant horizon" (18–19). All manifestations, including even the infractions, of the warrior code, then, are idealized.

In the *Mahabharata*, this is carried out to perfection. Discussions of the code cast it in hyperbolic terms that are nonetheless full of meaning. In XLII, Duryodhana declares that he is perfectly faithful to the warrior's code of duty, ready to "lie down on a bed of arrows in the battlefield." The poem uses this idealization as a motif in two ways. Implicitly, it measures how Duryodhana's conduct falls short of his own conception of the code, for, in LXXI, once he sees his side is irreparably defeated, he flees and hides himself in a lake. Explicitly, the image he has used becomes literalized only in the death of another warrior on the Kaurava side, Bhishma, who is regarded as a spiritual as well as military leader. Out of the distance between the two characters' fates arises a sense of how the *kshatriyadharma* must transcend its older, simpler definition of battlefield conduct to become an exemplary way of the human spirit in heroic action.

Bhishma is recognized as a spiritual authority by both sides in the conflict. His transcendence of the opposition in the conflict is exemplary of Hindu nonattachment (more will be said about that in the next section of this entry). Seeing this as the meaning of Bhishma's portrayal can help to overcome the sense of unlikeliness the modern reader may encounter in the courteous exchanges between foes. In LV, on the evening after they have battled fiercely and his men have shot many arrows in Bhishma, Yudhishthira comes to pay a respectful visit to him and is welcomed magnanimously. Granted, this setting aside of conflict in hospitality, while marvelous in itself, is not unheard of even in modern wars. But when Yudhishthira goes on to ask not only how the Pandavas might win the battle but how they might successfully kill Bhishma, and Bhishma tells him, the true ideal of the warrior's *dharma* shines through unmistakably.

Discussion

1. What specifics constitute the Indian warrior code? Find examples, and discuss their implications.

2. Pay special attention to the conduct of Bhishma. How does his way of dealing with others represent a new departure, a different level on which he sees the code? Analyze his scene on the bed of arrows, marked by several important exchanges.

3. The death of Karna in LXIX deserves discussion. Why does the fallen body of this less-than-perfect hero emit a light so powerful as to illuminate the sky? Does it reflect his character, or the fortunes of the Kaurava side, or a transcendent affirmation of the warrior's way? Is it a sign of triumph or of defeat?

Connections

1. How does the Indian warrior code compare with Greek and Anglo-Saxon codes as shown in *The Iliad* (Book 3), *The Odyssey* (Book 3), and *Beowulf* (Book 2)?

Group

1. In groups, have students examine two or three ancient literatures of war (*The Iliad, The Odyssey, Beowulf* alongside the *Mahabharata*), and discuss the ways each are alike and different.

Writing

Ask students to write a short paper in response to the following:

1. "The *Mahabharata* weighs the relative merits of a culture founded on force versus a culture founded on rational discourse and diplomacy" (p. 1436). But force has to be used anyway to secure a more high-minded and rational regime. Discuss how the poem and its characters deal with this paradox.

II. THE HINDU RELIGIOUS SYNTHESIS

Surpassing the old Vedic vision of life for which prosperity in life (and hence in war) is the greatest goal, the *Mahabharata* must also confront and supersede the Brahmanic vision based on the Upanishads, in which all actions that entail bad consequences must be avoided. The Pandavas are depicted struggling to find a way to conduct themselves in justice in the midst of the real world in which dire situations must be faced. Arjuna's crisis with the warrior's karma forms the heart of XLIX, the Bhagavad Gita section; Yudhishthira as well is shown several times agonizing over the outcome of actions he has chosen. The goal of nonattachment, as set forth by Krishna, is exemplified best in the anthology selection by Bhishma, who must be both a teacher of the just warrior's life and a defender of the Kauravas against the Pandavas. In XLV, for example, he agrees to lead Duryodhana's army but refuses to kill any of the Pandava brothers. In LVIII, counseling Karna, Bhishma enunciates the axioms of the Krishnaic code: "Be actuated by a desire to attain heaven" and "Where justice is, there victory shall be!" [See topic 1 above for other examples of Bhishma's action in nonattachment.] Rather than counseling a retreat from practical social action, the Hindu synthesis requires focus on action according to the model of *dharma*, within which justice resides; through faith in Krishna, it allows the hope of victory, not as the self immersed in the cares of this world might desire it but as heaven wills it.

A key motif in this shift of focus is the notion of illusion, to which all earthly desires and fears are relegated. Thus, in the final book of the poem, as told in the summary of the selection, Yudhishthira discovers in heaven that his fears of hell as his eternal lot and of the ultimate triumph of Duryodhana are his greatest illusions. The selections included in the book, however, present the motif of illusion in subtle, insightful ways. Arguably, Karna's acceptance of his foster parents and rejection of his true mother can be read allegorically as his being bound to illusion until he is able to renounce enmity and to accept, to forgive, and be forgiven by his true parents.

A more complex motif accompanies the development of Duryodhana's character. His embarrassment at mistaking the polished flooring of the Pandavas's hall for water and vice versa in XXI initiates the mistaking of illusion for reality in a natural way. The water/solid contrast reappears in his denouement in a heightened image. In LXXI, his retreating to the lake and solidifying it over him testifies to supernatural powers, seeming to suggest that now he has gained power over what before had discomfited him — that what the Pandavas achieved by art he has mastered by wizardry. In the following chapter, though, Krishna's power of enlightenment makes the Pandavas realize they are not bound by this illusion. The episode now emerges as an allegory of illusion unsuccessfully attempting to blockade justice as Krishna declares that Yudhishthira should use his own power of wizardry to dispel Duryodhana's magic. Rather than relying on special effects, however, Yudhishthira thereupon engages Duryodhana in dialogue, in effect dismantling his protective shield over the water, and then goes on to break apart Duryodhana's shield of rhetorical self-justification and self-preservation. It is an impressive scene of overcoming mythic power with the moral word, the new carrier of the divine will.

Discussion

1. Are Yudhishthira's asking Bhishma's permission to fight him and Bhishma's declaration in Book 5 that he would not kill any of the Pandava brothers good examples of action in nonattachment?

2. Why does Duryodhana emerge from the lake covered with blood? If one continues to read this scene as an allegory of illusion, this is the moment he emerges from the illusion he has generated about his self-justification. When he emerges from a lake covered not with water but with blood, the meaning is unmistakable that the element in which he has immersed himself is now revealed.

3. In LXXII, Duryodhana mentions an iron statue of Bhima as a substitute that absorbs the blows in Bhima's place as the Kauravas train to destroy him. In LXXXI, another iron statue of Bhima is produced by Krishna to receive the full anger of Dhritarashtra, while Bhima himself remains intact. In both cases, the statue receives a discharge of destructive passion, leaving the reality untouched. What does this motif suggest about the Hindu teaching on the passions and their relation to reality?

Writing

Ask students to write a short paper in response to the following:

1. The formula "desire = illusion = hell" could be said to encompass one important side of the *Mahaharata*'s religious teaching. What do you think it means? Discuss the insights of the *Mahabharata* into morality through these three motifs and what their equation means.

III. MORAL COMPLEXITY

"There can be no more effective condemnation of Pandavas misconduct than that uttered by its Kaurava victims," writes Ruth Cecily Katz in a chapter titled "Victory by Trickery" in her study of the *Mahabharata* (165). All the careful moral distinctions, the courage of not answering wrong with wrong, the placing of justice over might, seem to disappear as the last moments of victory are at hand for the Pandavas. In LXXIII, Krishna says, "Let [Bhima], by deception, kill the Kuru king who is the master of deception!" He is anxious for Bhima to use every means available, since the outcome is so much in doubt. The ideal code of the warrior calls for strict peer-to-peer single combat; here, however, Arjuna gives a secret signal to Bhima, following which he strikes Duryodhana a crippling and dishonorable blow below the waist, breaking his thighs, and then rushes over to kick his head with his left foot (left being the side of disgrace for many societies based on honor around the world). The teacher of both contestants, Balarama, Krishna's brother, decries Bhima's actions and character strenuously. Krishna blames Yudhishthira for allowing this disgrace, whereupon Yudhishthira joins the mass desertion of higher morality, saying in effect that Bhima's conduct is justified by the Kauravas's offenses: "I looked on his actions with indifference." In LXXXII, Bhima freely confesses that he acted unfairly in order to protect himself. The subplot of Bhima persistently examines the perennial appeal of revenge in the human heart: In XXIII, the crowd acclaims Bhima's vow to drink Duhsasana's blood, and when he does so in LXVIII, the narrative compares him to the Vedic god-king Indra after his slaying of Vritra (an episode depicted in the selection from the Vedas). In fact, all the acts of revenge on the Kauravas continue to be viewed with unqualified approval in many popular Indian versions and enactments of the story.

All these moral taints set the stage for their partial redress in Yudhishthira's offering of atonement to Gandhari in LXXXIII, in which he takes all the blame and welcomes her curses. Instead of an elaborate curse, she focuses her supernatural power on one of Yudhishthira's toenails, a sign that she recognizes the ultimately insubstantial nature of revenge. Krishna, on the other hand, she judges by his own yardstick. "Because you were deliberately indifferent to their destruction, you shall obtain the fruit of this act," she declares, and then curses him to a future of killing his kinsmen and dying ignobly in the forest, setting the stage for the final book of the poem. This paradox is how the poem handles the difficult portrayal of a personage who is both the Ultimate Spirit and a fully embodied participant in the war. Krishna's curse is logically consistent with a careful reading of the teaching revealed to Arjuna in XLIX, since he has counseled the faithful Hindu to do his duty and give over the fruits of his actions to Krishna.

The moral complexity of this work is something readers may want to call modern, but it is part of its ancient and lasting appeal. Its implication and overall tone is that human life is never a perfect reflection of dharma; of human order even less so. The Kali Yuga, the fourth and most disordered age of the world, is said to have commenced with the Pandava-Kaurava war. Tragically and ironically, the victory of the better over the worse brings disorder into the world in the form of resentment and cursed futures — the fruits of action. The best recovery of the moral order is interior, as Yudhishthira attempts atonement, and then, more reflectively, condemns himself in LXXXIV.

Discussion

1. Outline the case for and against Bhima's actions.

2. Discuss Krishna's highly partisan conduct — for instance, his rushing at Bhishma in LI and his affecting the duel between Bhima and Duryodhana. Is it consistent with his teachings? What kind of spiritual leader does it make him?

Writing

Ask students to write a short paper in response to the following:

1. The German philosopher Hegel contended that ultimately what is real is rational and what is rational is real. A verse in the *Mahabharata* says, "The unreal has no being; / The

real never ceases to be." What does the *Mahabharata* imply about what is ultimately real and what is not?

IV. PSYCHOLOGICAL COMPLEXITY AND THE STYLE OF THE *MAHABHARATA*

In its focus on the often conflicting imperatives of morality and of victorious action, the *Mahabharata* again shows its perennial greatness in examining the psychological motives for wrong action and the difficult process of self-questioning often involved in right action. It portrays the poem's chief antagonist, Duryodhana, for instance, as a man who embodies the wrong because of choices he makes rather than, like Ravana, because of his demonic nature. The paradox is that, in some ways, Duryodhana emerges as a character much more given over to evil than Ravana because of his complexity. By comparison, Ravana seems almost an innocent bully and sensualist, where Duryodhana is restlessly jealous, conniving, and treacherous.

In XXI, for example, Duryodhana's jealousy of the Pandavas's hall is not merely envy, as he confesses to his uncle, but attests to an unwillingness on his part to allow his rival cousins any prominence whatsoever, or even comfort. [Students may need to be reminded that the Pandavas have built their hall in Indraprastha because earlier the Kauravas asked them to leave their common patrimonial city of Hastinapura.] Duryodhana's embarrassment at mistaking polished flooring for water, and vice versa, is an ingenious narrative device linking his jealousy to a sense of injured pride, one of several ways that he may represent their difference from him as a grievance. It is psychologically acute that he forecloses on Dhritarashtra's wish to consult the wisdom of Vidura by blackmailing him with the threat of suicide; implicitly, therefore, he admits that his plan to cheat Yudhishthira is unwise but that he dares not confront his passion with this wisdom.

Dhritarashtra's invocation of fate to mask his inability to refuse his son continues the *Mahabharata*'s exploration of the ways of self-justification, and it is juxtaposed to a prime example on the Pandavas side when Yudhishthira, up to now a moral paragon, repeats the same pattern, going against his own better wisdom in agreeing to play in a rigged dice game with the comment, "But we all have to submit to fate and the will of the Creator." As a metaphor, his gambling compulsion ingeniously exposes this disorder in human desire, and the progress of the dice game shows it spiraling out of control. Then, in XXIV, to emphasize its irrational hold on desire, it happens all over again.

The prominent scenes of dialogue, questioning, searching, and self-accusation, by contrast, portray the Hindu moral world as coming into being in human consciousness and action rather than as fully formed. The dialogue that forms the Bhagavad Gita and other dialogues constitute crucial stagings of the struggle to transcend the old morality. The *Mahabharata* also follows the Upanishads in the sense that these scenes exemplify the newly crucial role of the soul's interior journey. Placed in the context of the war of the Bharatas, however, and in the "agonistic" form of dialogue, this struggle acquires drama, depth, and complexity. They deserve the kind of attention that is owed to Homer's Achilles in Book IX of *The Iliad*, in which he questions all the assumptions of the Greek warrior code. These dark scenes of questioning continue to repay the careful attention of readers living two millennia later, for such basic questions as the necessity of war or the extent to which one should be ruled by the pursuit of wealth, and such inescapable factors as the finality of death, remain fundamental today.

Yudhishthira's lament to Krishna in XL looks back ruefully at the Vedic world of values in which *artha*, or prosperity, is the chief end for which sacrifices to the gods are offered. The prince observes darkly that even for the enlightened such as himself, who subordinates desire for wealth to a higher sense of duty, the older code may have the last word after all. He then turns in the opposite direction and questions the foundations of the *kshatriyadharma*, the warrior code which has remained a constant in the transition beyond the Vedic world of self-enriching values. In saying "A Kshatriya kills another Kshatriya; a fish lives on another fish; a dog kills another dog," he is implying that the warrior's supposedly proud code in reality makes him no better than animals.

These scenes explore and refine the conception of the nature of *dharma*. In the most important dialogues, Krishna serves as guide. The conversation between Vidura and Krishna in the following chapter also questions the pointlessness of war, with Vidura taking the Brahmanic position that the world's evil should be withdrawn from and Krishna stating — and embodying — the synthesizing Hindu ideal of mediation.

Narasimhan's summary of XLIX can help readers to see the way the dialogue of the Bhagavad Gita functions in continuing and amplifying ongoing themes and patterns in the *Mahabharata*. Besides developing the depth of Arjuna's character and the Pandava brothers' deep interior lives, the episode counterbalances the wrathful revelation of Krishna's divinity in Book 5 with a loving revelation of his power. It is the premier example out of several in the poem of a crisis dialogue over the meaning of life and the conflict between *kshatriyadharma* and *brahmadarma*, and here the conflict is definitively resolved in the religion of devotion propounded by Krishna.

Discussion

1. Discuss the self-condemnation of Yudhishthira in Book 12 and the response to him by Vyasa, the author of the poem. How does this exchange re-enact the history of the development of Hinduism?

2. Look at the coronation ceremony that closes the book's selection. What does it suggest is the relation of the Hindu worldview to the old Vedic one? What is implied about the adherence to *dharma* of the new Pandavas reign?

Connections

1. Compare Achilles' intense questioning of the meaning and purpose of his life in Books Nine and Eighteen of *The Iliad* (p. 288) with Yudhishthira's self-questioning dialogues. What are the respective heroes' greatest concerns? How, if at all, are their crises of belief resolved? What general remarks can be made about the different concerns of Homeric and ancient Indian societies as shown in the two classic works?

Writing

Ask students to write a short paper in response to one or more of the following:

1. "Every strength is also a weakness and every virtue, especially if pressed too far, a potential vice." This is easy to see in Duryodhana, Bhima, and Arjuna but less so in Yudhishthira and Krishna. Choose one from each group, and compare how their strengths are related to their weaknesses or errors.

2. Compare the styles of the *Ramayana* and the *Mahabharata*. Both portray events based on the realities of a Bronze Age warrior society but with details exaggerated for the sense of epic distinction. Yet one epic projects a grave and realistic effect overall, whereas the other is magical and fantastic. Show how each accomplishes its effect, and discuss the relative advantages of each.

BEYOND THE CLASSROOM

RESEARCH & WRITING

1. Alf Hiltebeitel's *The Cult of Draupadi* presents an exhaustive two-volume study of the traditional popular dramas performed annually throughout India. Students interested in anthropology, theater, or the figure of Draupadi and the rationale for her elevation to divine status should be encouraged to wade through this rewarding compendium.

Project

1. Peter Brook's *Mahabharata* presents a rare opportunity to pair a major literary work with an ambitious film adaptation of it. It is five hours long, however. Instructors who are familiar with it may want to show selected scenes to the whole class; as an extra-credit project, however, the film could be screened in its entirety, with students taking this option to write a commentary or review of the film.

FURTHER READING

Bakhtin, M. M. "Epic and Novel." *The Dialogic Imagination: Four Essays.* Ed. Michael Holquist. Trans. Caryl Emerson and Michael Holquist. 1981.

Hiltebeitel, Alf. *The Cult of Draupadi.* 2 vols. 1988.

Katz, Ruth Cecily. *Arjuna in the Mahabharata: Where Krishna Is, There Is Victory.* 1989.

Matilal, Bimal Krishna. "Krsna: In Defence of a Devious Divinity." *Essays on the Mahabharata.* Ed. Arvind Sharma. 1991.

Van Nooten, Barend. *The Mahabharata.* 1971.

Williams, David. "The Great Poem of the World: A Descriptive Analysis." *Peter Brook and the Mahabharata: Critical Perspectives.* 1991.

MEDIA RESOURCES

VIDEO

Hinduism: Faith, Festivals, and Rituals
51 min., 1995 (Insight Media)
The majority of the Indian population practices Hinduism, which emphasizes right living, or *dharma*. This video explores the devotional ceremonies and observances of Hinduism and examines such sacred Hindu literary works as the *Ramayana* and the *Mahabharata*.

The Mahabharata
166 min., 1990 (Insight Media)
Beautifully staged by director Peter Brook, this video presents the saga of the world-shattering war between two feuding clans in ancient India. "One of the finest cinematic adaptations of a stage play . . . a magnificent presentation of one of civilization's most revered texts."

Making The Mahabharata
55 min., 1989 (Films for the Humanities & Sciences)
In Hinduism, the *Mahabharata* is a central text, an epic poem that forms an exposition on *dharma* — a code of conduct for a king, a warrior, or anyone seeking emancipation from rebirth. In this program, director Peter Brook, playwright and screenwriter Jean-Claude Carrière, and the international cast comment on the making of the film adaptation of this Indian classic and discuss the cultural and historical contexts of the poem.

WEB SITES

Lopa's Mahabharata Page
home.earthlink.net/~shubhrasudha/lopa3.html
This well-illustrated and interesting page provides a synopses for each part of the *Mahabharata*.

The Mahabharata — The Great Epic of India
Created and maintained by James L. Fitzgerald at the University of Tennessee-Knoxville, this site provides background information on the epic and a bibliography of additional secondary sources.

The Mahbharata — A Synopsis of the Great Epic of India
larryavisbrown.homestead.com/files/xeno.mahabsynop.htm
Larry Brown put together this well-designed site that provides a synopsis of the epic as well as an examination of its themes.

Bhagavad Gita (p. 1488)

www   For a quiz on the Bhagavad Gita, see *World Literature Online* at
bedfordstmartins.com/worldlit.

The worldwide fame of the Bhagavad Gita is unsurpassed by any other Eastern text. Next to the Bible, it is the most translated religious writing in the world. It is often considered the most central scripture in Hindu belief. Outside of Hinduism, it has lived a second life, not unrelated to the first, inspiring countless readers on its key themes of devotion, duty, and the discovery of the true self through discipline. This poem was inserted into the immense epic, the *Mahabharata*, during its textual compilation in the first century C.E.; it is in eighteen chapters and seven hundred verses, both numbers signifying completeness. (The *Mahabharata* is divided into eighteen books, and the war that the Gita prefaces, the central event in the epic, takes eighteen days.) *Bhagavad* means "of the Lord"; Krishna is frequently referred to as Lord Krishna, preserving the noble title of his role in the *Mahabharata* but with an added meaning similar to its usage in Judaism and Christianity. *Gita* means "song"; hence the poem is often called familiarly the Gita.

As a bedrock text of world literature, the Gita may be read at several levels. It is a great work of poetry, and the Miller translation reflects modern English poetic values well, just as the version by Sir Edwin Arnold epitomized Victorian diction. It is a moving dramatic dialogue, involving mind and heart in a quest culminating in a theophany unequaled in religious writing. It is a classic argument over perennial issues and may be analyzed for its reasoning, logic, and rhetoric. More deeply, it is perhaps the central text for understanding ancient India and Hindu tradition, incorporating and reintegrating the earlier works excerpted in the anthology. It is also a great work of cross-cultural inspiration, striking unexpected sparks from anyone who reads it attentively. German and English Romantics and American Transcendentalists are distinguished forerunners of today's students in this experiment, as are Gandhi and several other figures of consequence in world affairs.

References to the poem's text indicate chapter and line (or stanzas in Miller's translation) numbers parenthetically.

TEXT & CONTEXT

William Q. Judge writes, "*Dharma* means law, and is generally turned into duty, or said to refer merely to some rule depending upon human convention, whereas it means an inherent property of the faculties or of the whole man, or even of anything in the cosmos. Thus it is said that it is the duty, or dharma, of fire to burn. It always will burn and thus do its whole duty, having no consciousness, while man alone has the power to retard his 'journey to the heart of the Sun,' by refusing to perform his properly appointed and plainly evident dharma."

Dharma is developed into a central concept for the Hindu vision in this poem. Through Krishna's teaching, duty is redefined not by tribal or social but by heavenly standards. In the tribal standard, there is no totality. There is only the family and its needs. The heavenly standard posits a total right order for the cosmos, in which the righteous soul is to play a part based on the two determinants of his or her spirit and nature. [See the next entry in this section.]

SAMKHYA PHILOSOPHY

Sarvepalli Radhakrishnan writes that the Bhagavad Gita "integrates into a comprehensive synthesis the different elements of the Vedic cult of sacrifice, the Upanishadic teaching of the Absolute *Brahman,* the Bhagavata theism, the Samkhya dualism, and the Yoga meditation" (101). The Bhagavatas were a group who worshipped Krishna as the Supreme Spirit and an incarnation of Vishnu, the savior-preserver god. *Yoga* means "discipline," literally "yoke," and is the general name for the meditative practices developed as the spiritual impulses of the Upanishads became widespread social movements.

Samkhya philosophy deserves further explanation. The text's footnotes to 2.55 on *purusha* and 3.5 on *prakriti* help in defining these chief categories in Samkhya thought. Not a dualism of good versus evil, it is instead a way of distinguishing the immortal, universal self that is present in everyone from the conditions in which it is embedded. Human beings consist of both principles:

Purusha	+	*Prakriti*
Conscious subject		Unconscious object
Inactive consciousness		Unconscious activity
Spirit		Nature
Being		Becoming
Male		Female
Spirit, mind, imagination		Animating principle
(German *Geist*)		

Everything human beings are aware of has to do with *prakriti,* the manifest world. But consciousness itself is supernatural. *Prakriti* reincarnates; *purusha* does not — it is permanent but takes on incarnation from age to age. The goal of this philosophy is to become increasingly aware of the source of consciousness itself, ultimately identifying completely with *purusha.* Krishna's teaching in the Gita develops this vision without seeking to separate the human spirit entirely from nature, and it promises the easing of the difficult path to *purusha* through dedication to him.

IN THE CLASSROOM

I. HISTORICAL TRANSFORMATION AND SOCIAL ETHICS

The conflict Arjuna faces is one that forces him to choose between an older, unquestioned traditional way and a higher, but as yet still unclear, vision. The standard that leads him to his terrible crisis is a tribal one (1.34–37, 40–41): Both honor and good and evil are defined in terms of the treatment of one's kin. Although he mentions hell (1.44), the young nobleman's greatest fear is not so much his personal destiny in the afterlife as it is sheer awe at the magnitude of the crime against the family order he is preparing to commit.

This conflict can be seen cross-culturally as the struggle to conceive of ideals capable of justifying large civilizations. Aeschylus's *The Oresteia*, for instance, involves a no less intense search for the "justice of Zeus" over family blood claims. The classic Indian interpretation of its own past, however, envisions an evolution of values in three stages. The Vedic order of large family kingdoms, unified by central sacrificial rites, came to be challenged by the impact of the Upanishads, which relegated the sacrificial relation with the gods to spiritual insignificance when compared to the need to discover the true nature and origin of the soul, a quest in which society played little part. From this standpoint, Arjuna's crisis of belief in the imperatives of the tribal order at the beginning of the poem encapsulate that moment of historical change.

In the face of this fear, Krishna redefines "sacred duty" (see the footnote to 2.31), honor, and glory in the context of the total vision of sacred order, *dharma*, envisioned and willed by heaven (2.31–37). Fame and honor or shame are now to be thought of as spread about in heaven, superseding one's reputation among kin. A polemic against the extremes of the Brahmanic revolt against the social order begins in 2.47 with the instruction to avoid both attachment and inaction; equally Arjuna's linked chain of disasters resulting from killing family members in 1 is answered structurally by Krishna's list of the linked misfortunes that come from "brooding about sensuous objects" (2.62–63). The spiritual discipline (*yoga*) that Krishna now sets forth (1.39) is designed to free the earthly soul to act without fear and thus to succeed in performing its duty.

3.1 specifically asks for a justification of action. Arjuna's questioning embodies the history of Indian thought, which, in the Vedic order, embraced piety toward kin and then, in the Upanishads, steadily moved away from the scene of tribal activity toward discovery of the oneness of the spirit. Arjuna's question, here, then, is the key question that Krishna's synthesis founding classical Hinduism must answer.

Krishna answers by first laying bare the self-evident: To live is to act. The human being is immersed in nature, as the Samkhya philosophy affirms, and cannot get out of it until death; moreover, people are in nature for a purpose. In 3.5, he previews the clinching point he will make to Arjuna: Your nature will compel you to act anyway (18.59). This seems like equivocation: Arjuna *could* act, and in a noble manner, by opposing the war. But this is why understanding (knowledge) is as important as action and is also more powerful. For Krishna, the war is necessary; it is a war of the greater good against the lesser. In the context of the *Mahabharata*, all negotiations have failed and this is the only path left.

In 3.8–15, Krishna transforms the meaning of sacrifice while affirming that it still follows the teachings of the Vedas. "Action imprisons the world unless it is done as sacrifice": this uncompromising axiom broadens the field of religious activity from the isolated context of the sacrificial altar in the Vedic order to all action. The notion of detachment can now make sense within the context of devotion to a god, as in the most primordial sacrificial rites. (But, Krishna might add, what was done in darkness and ignorance then in Vedic times can be done in light and understanding now). He implies an interpretation that sacrifice was, from the beginning, a way of teaching human beings not to be attached to the material goods they hoped to get. Hence the men who "cook for themselves" (3.13) are "evil." 3.14 invokes the cycle of *rita* imaged in the Vedas, according to which the smoke of the sacrifice ascended to heaven, pleasing the gods, who in turn sent rain down to earth. (The Sanskrit word *rita* is a root of both the English words "rite" and "right"; it implies both ritual correctness and right order.)

On the face of it, an argument justifying war by means of a recuperation of sacrifice constitutes a strong religious legitimation of the status quo. This ingenious configuration of elements fortified a view designed to preserve the Hindu social hierarchy, especially the Brahmanic class, who were the most threatened by the defection of worshippers to Buddhism, Jainism, and other sects stressing meditation over action.

On the other hand, the Bhagavad Gita also opened a way to salvation for the lower castes and women, those "born in the womb of evil" and excluded from being "twice-born" (educated in the sacred Scriptures). It reaffirmed what the Upanishads had declared in passing, namely that the four immutable social orders of Vedic society were not to be based on birth but on one's internal nature. With Krishna at the center of all validation of meaning, however, any incitement of social change could be understood as besides the point. Hence over the centuries, the Gita has been read both as a bulwark against change and as an imperative for courageous social action. Gandhi embraced the abolition of the segregation of social roles and went so far as to argue that absolute nonviolence is the only logical culmination of Krishna's doctrine of "desireless action."

Discussion

1. What is Arjuna's fear, exactly? Can it be reduced to a personal concern for imprisonment in *samsara?*

2. In The First Teaching, Arjuna is worried about dishonor. What does Krishna say about honor in the Second Teaching?

3. In the Second Teaching, how is it that Krishna warns against inaction but ends with the image of the tortoise and counsels withdrawal of one's senses like the tortoise's limbs? If he does not mean inaction by this image, what does he mean?

4. Can Arjuna's answer to Krishna be reduced simply to "Don't think, just do your job as a soldier" ("Ours is not to question why, ours is but to do or die")? If the greatest happiness is to be obtained from performing action without attachment to it, is the poem saying, "Don't worry, be happy"?

5. How is the concept of duty ("sacred duty," 1.1) to be understood? If understanding (*jnana*) of the divine plan is necessary, how does this alter the concept of duty? Is it simply duty as society hands it to the individual ready-made? (Recall that Gandhi saw the Gita as validation of his ethic of nonviolence. How can this be argued, since the entire poem seems to be a justification of the warrior's duty to kill?)

6. Current interpretations of the Gita in India and Hinduism worldwide diverge on the interpretation of the very question that is central to the social meaning of the Gita: It is taken alternatively to justify a life of altruistic social activism or of withdrawal and seeking of mystical understanding. What are the chief elements justifying activism or of subordinating any action to mystical understanding?

7. How is "detachment" to be understood? If any longing for results subverts the moral and spiritual order, how is Krishna able to say, "act so as to gain victory"?

Connections/Group Work

Have students either individually or in groups discuss the following:

1. Compare and contrast the conception of action (*karma*) in the *Ramayana* and in the Bhagavad Gita.

2. Compare Arjuna's fears about dishonoring his kin (1.34–45) with Confucius's sense of the duties the gentleman must place first.

Writing

Ask students to write a short paper in response to one or more of the following:

1. Explain the argument in 3.4–9 by reference to the cultural history of religion in India, and discuss its meaning for the ethics of classical Hinduism.

2. Discuss the Gita as a work that preserves the values of the Vedas and the Upanishads while synthesizing them in a new vision.

3. Discuss the complex meaning of action in the Bhagavad Gita.

II. THE WAY OF KNOWLEDGE: THE GITA ON GOD AND THE HUMAN PERSON

Reading the Bhagavad Gita chiefly as an argument about action in the world — the point at which Arjuna begins the dialogue, and the focus of Topic 1 here — misses or downplays the surrounding visionary framework that Krishna says repeatedly is the point of his response to Arjuna. This framework is certainly heightened by the long-traditional practice of reading the Gita as a great scripture in its own right. When the poem is studied on its own, the literal events of the *Mahabharata* war now suggest a more general allegory of human life. Arjuna is the embodied human self; in this lifelong conflict, one's enemies are strong, potentially stronger than oneself (1.10), and they passionately desire one's destruction. The battle he faces is with folly (1.23). Later, Krishna declares that the true battle is with one's own passion and desire (3.37): "Great Warrior, kill the enemy / menacing you in the form of desire!" (3.43). Passion is dangerous not simply because it can seduce one away from one's social role, but because it obscures the vision the true self: It is like smoke obscuring the flame, or dirt covering the mirror (3.38).

Arjuna's crisis of faith in his social role is thus already the beginning of an answer to his dire question. In his lament, he sees that kingship (power, *artha*) and delights and pleasures (*kama*) constitute worthless goals for this wasting of life and limb (1.32–33). Krishna's counsel is designed to lead Arjuna from the initial insight that has brought about his despondency to an integrated vision of genuine wisdom and understanding (2.11). His first great argument is drawn from the Upanishads, the classic poems of spiritual discovery that announce that the individual soul is an organic part of the Supreme soul and is eternal (2.12, 17–24). The strict discipline of the senses that Krishna begins almost immediately to inculcate (2.14) is designed, he says, to make one "see reality" (2.16), to attain the consciousness needed to be "fit for immortality" (2.15). 2.49–53 stress the understanding that must be reached before the "swamp of delusion" (a description at once of ignorance, ordinary earthly consciousness, and *samsara*) can be exited, and a "place beyond decay" can be reached (which is both true consciousness and release from the cycle of *samsara*, or *moksha*). Arjuna must attain a consciousness of the "self within himself" (*purusha*, 2.55 and note) and act as befits this true self.

Scholars viewing the whole of the work have supported this view. Radhakrishnan thus contends that the ethics of the Gita "are centered on the concept of *yoga*: the three ways to progress toward liberation of the self, a new understanding of the unity and meaning of mankind, and union with God — *jnana-yoga* [the way of knowledge], *bhakti-yoga* [the way of devotion], and *karma-yoga* [the way of action in detachment]." The ethical teaching of the Gita is thus focused internally, on the person, as opposed to the external ethics that a reading concentrating solely on the social meaning of the work appears to disclose. Sri Aurobindo insists on this point more emphatically:

> The Gita . . . does not ask the awakened moral consciousness to slay itself on the altar of duty as a sacrifice and victim to the law of the social status. It calls us higher and not lower . . . The subjection to external law gives place to a certain principle of inner self-determination of action proceeding by the soul's freedom from the tangled law of works. (31)

The emphasis of the body of the poem bears out this claim. The Fourth through Sixth Teaching develop the main points of the *jnana yoga* while insisting that *Samkhya* (understood as renunciation of works) and *Yoga* (performance of works in the right spirit) lead to the same goal (5.1–12). Understanding by following the way of knowledge cannot alone lead to right action, for what the perpetual crisis of action requires is not formulated knowledge but *seeing*, that is, an intuitive grasp of the true self (as 2.39 and 3.43 insist). Hence, in 6.20, Krishna indicates that it is "when his thought *ceases*" (emphasis added) that the man of discipline may "see the self through himself."

At this point, the truly visionary part of the poem begins to unfold, for it is here that Krishna begins to speak of all creatures being in the self, of all creatures being in him, of the oneness of life (6.29–32). This is a prelude to the climactic theophany of 11. It also renders meaningful the revelation as a vision; as Arjuna puts it, "I wish to *see* your form / in all its majesty" (11.3). Seeing has already been established as a form of knowing that goes beyond understanding, for what one sees one grasps immediately as real and, in a sense, participates in. In making this request, Arjuna is already being the heroic warrior of disciplined impulse, for he jumps to the end of the mystic's path with one leap.

The *bhakti yoga*, the way of devotion to Krishna expounded in the poem from the Seventh Teaching until its conclusion, is what unifies the way of action and the way of knowledge and ensures their arriving at the same goal. In the Gita, Krishna reveals that he is at once the universal supreme Self, the container of all gods and human reality, and the individual reality that is Krishna. He unfolds the teaching of the *avatara*, according to which he is one of the preserver god Vishnu's incarnations in the world who visits it for its redemption in a time in which the forces of evil threaten to destroy the good in the human world. At the personal level, this means that Krishna knows and will encourage each devotee to be the fully realized self that he or she is destined to be. Thus complete devotion to him will both reveal all knowledge of the spirit and allow one to act righteously at all times; and it will lead ultimately to the release from the evil consequences of deeds and their atonement in continual reincarnations. Krishna's final exhortation is simply:

> Keep your mind on me
> be my devotee, sacrificing, bow to me —
> you will come to me, I promise,
> for you are dear to me.
>
> Relinquishing all sacred duties to me,
> make me your only refuge,
> do not grieve,
> for I shall free you from all evils. (18.65–66)

Discussion

1. Where does the poem emphasize "seeing," and how is this kind of knowledge different from formulated knowledge?

2. How is the term *self* used differently in ancient Indian thought from the way we in modern times use it? Why is that word used rather than simply *soul*?

3. Discuss the implications of "detachment," "relinquishment," and "renunciation," using practical examples from real life. What possible meanings for action can these terms have? Of these, which seem to be the most descriptive of what Krishna teaches?

4. Why is hope considered a kind of bondage in 6.10?

Connections

1. Compare Krisha's teaching of the twofold basis of good in the world (Third Teaching) with Thomas Aquinas on the two goals of life.

2. Compare the Stoicism of Epictetus with the discipline outlined by Krishna in 2.55–64.

Groups

1. In small groups, discuss what principles of the Upanishads are reflected in 2.12 and 17–25. Each group should then report their findings to the entire class.

Writing

Ask students to write a short paper in response to one or more of the following:

1. Explain the scheme of the three ways, and show how it defines the historical development of Hindu thought and practice.

2. Discuss the observation of William Q. Judge: "The despondency of Arjuna depicts a typical crisis in the life of one who has chosen the spiritual path over the material."

III. LITERARY PERSPECTIVES

The poetic form of the Gita (the "Song") and the high lyric tone of its verses, ably represented by Miller's translation, certainly make up a great part of the appeal of the poem over the ages, but they also influence its message: Arjuna is made more poignant and Krishna more graceful, tender, and gently self-confident by the rhythmic verses than any prose treatise could ever accomplish. Both characters in this intellectually resourceful dialogue give the impression not only of being full of ideas but of being fascinating persons in their own right, each balancing grace and power in their own way. This is crucial to the effect of the poem, since the religion Krishna expounds in it constitutes a new personalism on both ends: devotion to the god Krishna as solution to all things and discovery of one's true self as the goal of both action and meditation.

The poem is structured as a dialogue within a report. The frame of the dialogue enters the narrative when needed: to present the panorama of warriors in 1, to describe Krishna's theophany from a distance in 11 (implying that a more immediate presentation of it would be dangerous), and to affirm the holiness of the poem in closing. The blind king Dhritarashtra, to whom Sanjaya reports the dialogue, is only a symbolic presence in the poem but seems to represent the existing state of power in the world before Krishna's revelation.

The dialogue itself adapts existing forms to a new purpose. The *Ramayana* and the *Mahabharata* contain several examples of dialogues between a warrior and his charioteer, in each case creating an interlude in the action to bring in a deeper consideration of duty, justice, or the cosmic context for an action. Rama's charioteer Sumantra engages in two such dialogues, once with Rama and once with Lakshmana, each time before a major turning point in Rama's life. These moments bear the traits of the "threshold dialogue" as Mikhail Bakhtin defines it, a convention found in many works in which a significant, often life-or-death moment in a character's life applies the extraordinary pressure necessary to lead to the putting aside of conventions and engaging in a passionate inquiry into the meaning of life. The dialogue form is also found in the Upanishads, where it serves as a thematization of the quest for a higher truth. Somewhat like Socrates' dialogues, these conversations do not meander but instead proceed from one insight to a larger consideration and problematic, which is in turn illumined by further discourse, and so on in a technique of progressive illumination. Placed in the middle of the *Mahabharata*, the Gita is also sometimes called the Bhagavad Gita Upanishad; it is both dramatic and philosophical, and its ideational content is singularly focused on life situations.

Three kinds of images in the poem can be found readily. The most prominent are didactic images: clothes (2.22), the tortoise (2.58), the lamp sheltered from the wind (6.19), each used to illustrate a theological point. Linked to the dramatic situation are also several symbolic images that suggest complex meanings without stating or pursuing them, enriching the field of meaning of the poem. The frame of the poem, as discussed earlier, acts in this way, as does the evocative image of Arjuna slumped in his chariot. Finally, negative imagery, as in 2.23–24, in which a series of examples from ordinary life are given as not applying, works to lead the reader to a higher plane of consideration and builds the impression of the sublimity of the soul.

The theophany in 11 partakes in a cross-cultural feature of epics, wherein the hero is shown a comprehensive vision of the totality in which he is involved, as in Achilles' shield, Aeneas's dialogue with his father in the underworld, and Dante the pilgrim's final vision of the mystic rose. Again, the Gita mixes generic conventions, exceeding the epic with a scriptural purpose of revelation, in which the meaning is intended to sum up even more than the ideal worldview of a civilization. Such moments are familiar in the Book of Job and the Book of Revelations.

Discussion

1. As an example of small but significant detail, how do the attributes of the war conches that the Pandava brothers and Krishna blow (1.14–16) all suggest attributes of the righteous soul? Taken together, what portrait of the devoted soul do they sketch?

2. In the last chapter of the poem, Arjuna declares, "Destroyed is my delusion." Has Krishna effectively answered the concerns Arjuna has voiced? Diagram the elements of Arjuna's objection to action and the answers Krishna gives to each.

3. Why does Krishna's full revelation of himself bring out fear in Arjuna (11.45)? What components of this vision can you identify that might be terrifying, and how and why can they be in Krishna?

Connections/Groups

Have students either individually or in groups discuss the following:

1. Compare an epic or scriptural scene of vision from the Western tradition with the theophany in 11. What does each tell about the values of its culture, as understood in such categories as the imperatives for personal life, the goals of action, and the relation of heaven to earth?

Writing

Ask students to write a short paper in response to one or more of the following:

1. Discuss the added significance lent to the poem by its frame.

2. Krishna is a difficult figure to grasp for those unfamiliar with Hindu tradition. He is both a human character and a god who goes far beyond any Greek or Roman deity — the Supreme Spirit, the *Purusha* or "cosmic man." How is his human side portrayed in the poem? Write a character study of Krishna based on his dialogue.

3. Romantics understood the power of poetry as divided between the "beautiful," which the human imagination comprehends in terms of grace and form, and the "sublime," which defies the imagination's power to grasp it while evoking an impression of awe. Show how the Gita possesses both beautiful and sublime moments, and discuss what effect they have on the reception of its teaching.

BEYOND THE CLASSROOM

RESEARCH & WRITING

1. Here are some topics from other teachings in the Gita that are worth looking into as a next step:

   4.5–12: Vishnu's avatars

   4.23–32: Old sacrificial ritual, meditation, and action in detachment all seen as equally acceptable forms of sacrifice (implicitly the Vedas, the Upanishads, and the epics)

   5.1–12: *Samkhya* (renunciation of works) and *Yoga* (performance of works in the right spirit) lead to the same goal

   9.26–34: All classes of society can devote themselves to and be saved by Krishna (even though the lowest class is not allowed to study the scriptures; the route of the Upanishads was considered barred to them)

   13: More on *purusha* and *prakriti*

   18.20–39: Three kinds (good, passionate, dull — the *gunas;* see footnote to 3.5) of knowledge, of work, of doer, of understanding, of steadiness, and of happiness: a very interesting typology of everyday life. Students could even be asked to take this passage as a personal "rate yourself" quiz or to write about a moment in which they recognized their approach was "dull" and needed to rise to something higher.

2. Another great man of our times who was inspired by the Gita was Martin Luther King Jr. Read his "Letter from Birmingham Jail," and compare his program for social activism with the notion of sacred duty propounded in the poem. Look especially at his notion of "self-purification" as preparation for action.

Project

1. Compare Sir Edwin Arnold's translation with the present translation in terms of clarity of meaning and lyric quality. Specifically, with what shadings of character does Krishna's voice emerge in each version?

FURTHER READING

Translations:
The Bhagavad-Gita: Krishna's Counsel in Time of War. Trans. Barbara Stoler Miller. 1986.
The Song Celestial. Trans. Sir Edwin Arnold. 1891.
Western scholarship has provided good overviews of the interpretation and importance of the Gita in both Western and Indian contexts. For intelligent readings of the poem, the best sources are the best modern commentaries produced by Hindu scholars. Sri Aurobindo's, first published in 1922, is exceptionally readable and written with a wide readership in mind.
Aurobindo, Sri. *Essays on the Gita.* 1922.
Judge, William Quan. *Essays on the Bhagavad-Gita.* 1890.

Radhakrishnan, Sarvepalli, and Charles A. Moore, eds. *A Sourcebook in Indian Philosophy.* 1957.

Sharpe, Eric J. *The Universal Gita: Western Images of the Bhagavad-Gita.* 1985.

MEDIA RESOURCES

VIDEO

Hinduism and the Song of God: A Modern Interpretation of the Bhagavad Gita
30 min., 1975 (Insight Media)
This video explores the Hindu concept of self-realization. It explains the four yogas, the law of karma, the four stages of life, and man's purpose in life.

WEB SITES

Bhagavad Gita
ggl.bhagavad-gita.us/
Though this site has commercial overtones, it includes the full text of the Bhagavad Gita and a very nice section on illustrations that have been done to accompany it.

Bhagavad Gita
www.bhagavad-gita.org/
This site provides the full text of the Bhagavad Gita in English as well as providing some other interesting background information on it.

The Historical Context of the Bhagavad Gita
eawc.evansville.edu/essays/de.htm
Written by Soumen De, as the title suggests, this essay provides the context of the Bhagavad Gita.

AUDIO

The Complete Bhagavad Gita
7 CDs (Bhaktivedanta Ashram)
Sung in classical melodies by noted devotional singer Sri Vidyabhushana, this audio programs offers all seven hundred verses of the Gita with a beautiful accompaniment of flute, veena, sitar, mridanga, tabla, and tala. Set includes ten audio CDs (seven CDs of sanskrit chants, two CDs containing English translations for the entire Bhagavad Gita, and one CD providing an introductory lecture on the Bhagavad Gita by His Divine Grace A. C. Bhaktivedanta Swami Prabhupada).

In the World: War, Rulers, and Empire (p. 1515)

The selections included in this section raise a number of questions. The inquiry they provoke revolves around two topics, one political and one religious and moral.

TEXT & CONTEXT

Differences concerning East and West, and early, middle, and late antiquity, play a role in linking and distinguishing between positions in the selections presented in the book. The following table provides a rough spatiotemporal map to these readings:

	Europe	Near East	India	China
800		Sargon II 721–705 C.E.		
700				
600			Jainism 6th c. B.C.E.–1st c. C.E. 500	
400	[Alexander]			Mencius 371–288 C.E.
300			Asoka 292–232 B.C.E.	
				Laozi 4th–3rd c. B.C.E.
200				
100	[Julius Caesar]			
0	Flavius Josephus 37–100 C.E.			
100	Plutarch 46–120 C.E.			
200	Suetonius 75–160 C.E.			

IN THE CLASSROOM

I. POLITICAL THEORY OF EMPIRE

Sargon's annals narrate crisply the subduing of a populace. The single great moral imperative for ancient kings, as many texts in this anthology attest, is to make their kingdom and those in it prosper. The motive for empire is similar, and since the conquered lands and peoples become a part of the empire, imperial policies typically include the improvement of life in the territory. The governing assumption of any imperial policy, in fact, is that the subjects have no compelling reason to reject an orderly and materially improved life in order to rebel for the sake of freedom (self-determination). Improvement, of course, entails the imposition of taxation (tribute) and often also government by viceroy, as seems to be Sargon's custom. Hence existence as a client state in a larger empire rarely frees itself of a prevailing tension between material advantage and a thousand constant aggravations against the inhabitant people's preferences. Whereas conquered peoples are treated with a careful mixture of benefice and force, rebellion like Ia'ubidi's is dealt with in the harshest possible terms. The fates of Iamani and Ia'ubidi here demonstrate the tendency of empire to seek to transform war into police action wherever possible and to pursue the rebellious faction as criminals rather than opponents in war.

One can see without any advanced analysis that Sargon's real enthusiasm is for conquering and receiving tribute, especially in luxury goods, rather than for bringing benefits to all. This is a constant temptation, especially of empires in their formative stages, when aggression and dynamism are required. One becomes what one does, and the turn from conqueror to administrator-developer involves a sharp discontinuity in roles. A conqueror wants to go on conquering, the counteradvice of a philosopher-poet like Laozi notwithstanding.

What concern the "quietist" Laozi evinces about political matters centers on the welfare of the people and the insistence that the ruler make that welfare his main concern. In this, Laozi differs not much from his rival Confucius, but, characteristically, he stresses "naturalness" in contrast to Confucius's great metaphor of cultivation. Laozi's ideal of "actionless action" leads him to warn against acting rashly and to advise that the successful ruler will let the situation come to him: "He has done it because it had to be done . . . Let life ripen and then fall."

Ashoka Maurya's enlightenment comes fortunately just at the moment that he must make the turn from conqueror to administrator. He knows force may still be necessary for a ruler to rule justly (see paragraph 2 of the *Uttaradhyayana Sutra*, p. 1530). But like Laozi, he rejects warfare as a means of conquest — a position that is easier for an emperor to take once he has consolidated his empire. He combines his moral standards with the typical desire of empires to improve the standard of living of all its inhabitants, and he speaks in terms of "progress" that should be familiar to dwellers in the modern world.

The problem of maintaining various conquered peoples in peaceful coexistence occupies the empires of later antiquity. Ashoka decrees a cosmopolitan religious tolerance as being crucial to keeping the regions of India at peace with one another (see Topic 2 in this entry). For his empire, the great differences were not ethnic or cultural but ideological, and his response came as an ideological breakthrough. Plutarch's Alexander, facing an empire ethnically and culturally very diverse, goes much further in envisioning a realm that is not merely tolerant but unified. Even the cultural habits of the peoples should be "blended into one," "unit[ed] and mix[ed] in one great loving-cup." Intermarriage becomes a key in this blending process. Alexander's marriage policy is an ancestor not only of the modern melting-pot idea but of the central role of intermarriage envisioned by Virgil between Trojans and Latins in *The Aeneid* and later lamented by James Fenimore Cooper, in his strongly Virgilian Leatherstocking novels, as the road not taken between English colonists and Native Americans.

The Jewish War rolls this progressive history sadly backward, as mass killings, the complete destruction of Jerusalem, deportation, and population exchange follow the violent rebellion of an intransigent segment of Judaea.

Discussion

1. How do Sargon's annals preview the concerns and events recorded in the later passages, notably those by Suetonius and Flavius Josephus?

2. What is the advantage of the practice of population exchange that Sargon practices on the Arabs and Samaritans? In what ways is it an especially harsh measure?

3. If a policy of intermarriage is successful, will it solve the problem of ethnic, cultural, and ideological oppositions? Why is it not always a workable solution?

4. The introduction to *The Jewish War* (p. 1539) points out that, in his time, Augustus Caesar had tolerated the Jews' religious defiance. What factors brought this crisis to a head, and what other factors exacerbated it as the military campaign against the Jews took place?

Connections

1. In the *Book of Songs*, the procedure of the Zhou dynasty is to try defeated war generals in a criminal court. What strategic situations are likely to lead to such a resolution of a war, and what situations lead rather to a noncriminalized outcome in which the opponents basically agree to leave each other without further punishment? (The end of the slaughter of the suitors in *The Odyssey* (Book Twenty-two) might also be consulted, where Odysseus stifles the victory shout because the killings were a criminal proceeding).

2. Books 7 through 12 of *The Aeneid* deal with all the obstacles to the unification of empire. This second half of the poem is seldom anthologized. However, Anchises' speech to Aeneas in the afterlife in Book 6 treats all the difficulties that must be overcome to attain a dominant and internally unified Roman republic. Read it carefully, and pay special attention to Anchises' famous injunction to the Romans that closes this panorama. What position on empire does it encapsulate?

Writing

Ask students to write a short paper in response to one or more of the following:

1. Sargon refers to the "terror-inspiring glamor" of his divinity and the "trust-inspiring oracle" that assured him of victory. How do these phrases typify two of the ways in which religion is conscripted as a support structure for imperial power?

2. What are the advantages of treating rebels as criminals rather than opponents in war? Give examples of this either in literature or in the contemporary world.

II. RELIGION AND MORALITY

Sargon's concerns remain very much with the world today. Seeing them faced thousands of years ago, often in much more direct ways, can help in thinking about contemporary world affairs with a fresh eye. Another way to look at these passages, however, is as a comparative historical narrative in which the history being told is not of one emperor or empire but of the human race (or at least Eurasian civilizations) and its developing conceptions of order and justice.

After Sargon, the remaining passages in this section all postdate the cross-cultural revolution in organization and thought that occurred around 600–500 B.C.E. One of the results of this revolution was to develop the ideology of civilizations to a level beyond "might makes right" and justification through divine appeal. Freestanding concepts of justice and the good emerged into clarity across Eurasian civilizations around this time. The role of seer or philosopher became well defined as those who would have remained royal counselors turned to writing down their thoughts and gained a potential new audience and a certain autonomy of inquiry. The Jains, Mencius, and Laozi dramatically exemplify this freedom of inquiry as they dare to think independently of royal approval. The great emperor Ashoka exemplifies a dramatic turn when, in stark contrast with Sargon, he discovers justice and the good and reorients himself accordingly.

Mencius is an example of the direction in ethics exhibited in the great ancient civilizations. Christianity and Buddhism as well surpass the simple notion of justice, perhaps the founding moral concept of highly organized civilizations, with the notion of compassion, the idea that (as Russian novelist Fyodor Dostoevsky put it) "each is responsible for all." The transcending of clan lines that makes cities and then empires possible allows a perspective to emerge according to which all people, not merely one's relatives, are to be cared for with equal dedication.

Like Confucius, Mencius traveled around offering advice to rulers of various states. He repeatedly tried to commit them to the view that the ruler who wins over the people through benevolent government would be the one to unify the realm. He remarked ruefully, "If there were a ruler who did not like to kill people, everyone in the world would crane their necks to catch sight of him. This is really true. The people would flow toward him the way water flows down. No one would be able to repress them." Government by compassion and an inner sense of right and wrong was apparently a hard sell; but through it all, Mencius retained the conviction that the power of inner goodness (*jen*) was natural and irresistible.

Ashoka sees that "when an independent country is conquered the slaughter, death, and deportation of the people is extremely grievous," and he speaks of the "participation of all men in suffering." His is an Eastern cosmopolitanism, focused mainly on tolerance of religions. His inscription mentions "the essential doctrine of all sects" as a hypothetical vital thread that all religions share (or should share). However, within this doctrine of tolerance, there is no room for sects that do not "teach that which is good"; animal sacrifice, for instance, is prohibited in his empire. Nonetheless, the new program of empire, stated in the last two sentences of the selection, is one that would please Confucius, based as it is on expansion by good example rather than force.

Plutarch's picture of Alexander defines Western cosmopolitanism, based on a humanism and stated in political terms: All men are "of one community and one polity," "subject to one law of reason and one form of government." This belief is philosophical, arrived at by the Stoics in the Hellenistic era in which Alexander lived. The law of reason might not always prevail, of course, and so force is not prohibited as a last resort to bring peoples under his sway if persuasion fails.

Suetonius's portrait of Julius Caesar: Note: the verb "rallied" in the second paragraph (p. 1538) means "made fun of." If it is known that Caesar took Alexander as his ideal, interesting contrasts could be explored, for in Suetonius's account, Caesar appears to have dropped many of the more idealistic aspirations of empire to concentrate on subjugation, the improvement of life in the empire, and leadership by personal charisma.

The vivid narrative of *The Jewish War* makes it unmistakably clear how many factors conspire to make justice next to impossible once the decision for all-out war has been made. The burning of the Temple stands as a terrible contrast to all that Ashoka says about religious tolerance; does it, however, very much contradict the policies of Julius Caesar as Suetonius has outlined them?

Discussion

1. Judging from poem 30 of the Dao De Jing (Tao Te Ching), is Laozi against all war? What kind or kinds of war might he consider justifiable?

2. What happens to politics and the notion of conquest in the Jain *Uttaradhyayana Sutra?*

Writing

Ask students to write a short paper in response to one or more of the following:

1. What are some tenets that might be found in Emperor Ashoka's "essential doctrine of all sects"? In what ways might a particular religion disagree with that essential doctrine?

2. Contrast the cosmopolitanism of Ashoka and Alexander. What several factors — ideological, geographical, and the like — led each to fashion his cosmopolitan ideal for pacifying a large empire in his own distinctive way?

MEDIA RESOURCES

WEB SITES

Chaironeia: Plutarch
www.utexas.edu/depts/classics/chaironeia/
This site contains an exhaustive list of links on Plutarch.

The Edicts of King Asoka
www.cs.colostate.edu/~malaiya/ashoka.html
This thorough page provides background to King Asoka and his edicts, as well as a slew of useful links.

Internet Ancient History Sourcebook — Mesopotamia
www.fordham.edu/halsall/ancient/asbook03.html
The goal of the Ancient History Sourcebook is to provide and organize texts for use in classroom situations. Links to the larger online collections are provided for those who want to explore further. It also includes links to visual and aural material, since art and archeology are far more important for the periods in question than for later history. The emphasis remains on access to primary source texts for educational purposes.

Jain Principles, Tradition, and Practices
www.cs.colostate.edu/~malaiya/jainhlinks.html

This is a thorough source on Jainism; there is a section of the site devoted to Jain texts.

Sacred Texts
www.sacred-texts.com/index.htm
This wonderful site provides complete versions of sacred texts from around the world.

Internet Classics Archive — Works by Lao Tzu
Classics.mit.edu/Browse/browse-Lao.html
Read the complete e-text translation of the Tao Te Ching at this wonderful site.

Malaspina Great Books — Lao Tzu
www.mala.bc.ca/~mcneil/Tzu.htm
A great place to go for a wide variety of resources, this site includes biographical informa-tion on the author, links to his texts, and links to many secondary sources about Lao Tzu's philosophy. It also provides links to pages on other philosophers and religious leaders for comparative research.

BUDDHIST TEXTS, *Ashvaghosha* (p. 1543)

WWW   For a quiz on the Buddhist texts, see *World Literature Online* at
bedfordstmartins.com/worldlit.

Ashvaghosha's *The Life of Buddha* popularized the figure of the Buddha and Buddhist thought through his use of Indian Sanskrit poetics and Hindu teachings. In other words, Ashvaghosha's work did much to integrate the Buddhist ideas with the traditions already in place. *The Life of Buddha* instituted conventions as well: Several of the images Ashvaghosha used became characteristic of Buddhist literature. Consider the forest (*aranya* or *vana*), for example, which is often the setting of crisis. It is in the forest that one realizes the futility of one's worldly pursuits and devotes oneself to the greater project of spiritual wisdom. Draw students' attention to the stratagems of the king, whose attempts to prevent his son's envi-ronment from disclosing universal truths fail, and Siddhartha discovers the aspects of the human condition civilization cannot hide. Encourage students to compare the palace with the forest. Doing so will inform their grasp of what it means to renounce the world, the first step in Siddhartha's path toward enlightenment. You might point out that in further devel-opments of Buddhist thought, the forest renunciation that Siddhartha experiences becomes institutionalized in the form of town-and-village renunciation. In fact, monasticism in India developed within the framework of town-and-village renunciation. As a result, the *vinaya*, or teachings of the Buddha regarding proper conduct, became a pattern for correct behavior within communal organizations.

Following his renunciation of the world, Siddhartha makes a series of vows. His success or failure to fulfill his vows determines his path. Have students discuss the significance of the vow in his life. How does the vow exemplify the self-culture and self-restraint characteristic of the Buddhist way of life? Related to the vow, of course, is the self-declaration of enlight-enment. [Not included in the selection are the two other ways in which the Buddha's enlight-enment is recognized: (1) the cosmos responds in the form of an earthquake, rain falling from a cloudless sky, and trees producing flowers and fruit out of season; (2) Divine ele-ments, including the goods, seers, and so on, celebrate his attainment with offerings and praise.] It is through self-declaration that Buddha's enlightened status becomes recognizable to humans. Hence the Buddha's sermons both validate and demonstrate his experience. Ask students to categorize his experience (does it primarily constitute a challenge to social authorities? An affirmation of divine providence?). Emphasize the fact that Buddhism rep-resents a perspective on life more than a system of rituals and ceremonies.

An important effect of his attainment is the Buddha's possession of supernatural powers, which, in Ashvaghosha's account, take the form of *abhijna* (superknowledges). Although these powers distinguish the Buddha from the rest of humankind, they do not make him something other than human. Rather, he is an ideal human being, in as much as his life exhibits the perfection of human capacities. One way in which the Buddha is presented as superior to but nevertheless exemplary of humankind is in his equal treatment of others, regardless of social status. Direct students to examine his instructions to the Order in the *Mahaparinibbana Sutta*. How is the Buddha portrayed as human? To what extent does he recognize hierarchy?

For Buddhism, Sarla Khosla explains, "to be a human being is to have the potential of enlightenment and of a divine and supradivine status. To be a Buddha is to be a human being perfected and to manifest that transcendent potential in realized form. In other words, it is because — not in spite — of his humanity that [Siddhartha] can become the god above gods, the Buddha."

TEXT & CONTEXT

MEDITATION
There are four stages of meditation through which Siddhartha passes, which are conventional in Buddhist thought:

1. In which one passes entirely beyond the perceptions of bodily shape, so that distinction and diversity disappear, so that one perceives the infinity of space.

2. In which one passes entirely beyond the perception of space, so that one perceives the infinity of consciousness.

3. In which one passes entirely beyond the perception of consciousness, so that one perceives that "there is nothing," and attains and abides in the stage of nothingness.

4. In which one passes entirely beyond the stage of nothingness, so that one attains and abides in the stage of neither consciousness nor nonconsciousness.

FURTHER ASPECTS OF BUDDHIST THOUGHT
According to Buddhism, ignorance is the fundamental source of all of the suffering in the universe — specifically, the ignorance of the Four Noble Truths (see p. 1546). These four truths constitute the foundation for the attainment of wisdom, for they direct one to first identify what the pessimism portrayed is not. This investigation leads one to the realization that true existence is the Nothing, where the Nothing alone is certain.

COMMANDMENTS
Five rules of conduct (*Pancha Sila*) that hold for all Buddhists:

1. Let not one kill any living being.

2. Let not one take what is not given to him.

3. Let not one speak falsely.

4. Let not one drink intoxicating drinks.

5. Let not one have unchaste sexual intercourse.

The austere and pious then observe three more (*Ashtanga Sila*):

1. Let him not at night eat untimely food.

2. Let him not wear wreaths or use perfumes.

3. Let him lie on a bed spread on the earth.

IN THE CLASSROOM

Discussion and Writing

1. An essential step in Siddhartha's development is his discovery of the human condition and his realization that this condition (including ageing, sickness, and death) is common to all. How does Siddhartha's experience further constitute the human (questions of what it means to be the Buddha aside)?

2. Ashvaghosha's *The Life of Buddha* constructs a connection between the physical and the mental (exemplified, for instance, in Siddhartha's vow not to move from beneath the Asvattha tree, and the state of firmness and calmness — unmoved — he achieves through meditation. What function does this connection serve?

3. Universal compassion is a central component of the Buddha's enlightened personality. How does the opposition between passion and compassion structure the path to enlightenment? Examine the final section from Ashvaghosha and the selection from the *Samyutta Nikaya* in particular.

4. Discuss the spiritual significance of the natural cycle of things for the Buddhist. In so doing, you might consider the relationship between enlightenment and natural order.

5. To what extent does Siddhartha achieve immortality?

Connections

1. Examine the significance of enlightenment as it is attained in Ashvaghosa's account and in the "Allegory of the Cave" found in Plato's *Republic.* How is enlightenment related to virtue? In answering this question, you might compare the Middle Way to the Aristotelian mean described in the *Nicomachean Ethics.*

2. Compare the notion of suffering portrayed in the Buddhist texts with that depicted in Sartre's *The Flies.*

3. Compare the function of divine intervention as it is presented in Ashvaghosha's *The Life of Buddha* and any of the following: the Old Testament, the New Testament, Homer's *The Iliad* or *The Odyssey,* and *The Epic of Gilgamesh.*

BEYOND THE CLASSROOM

RESEARCH & WRITING

1. Find out more about Buddhism. Focus in particular on the role of prophecy in Buddhist culture. Compare what you find to the function of prophecy in Ashvaghosha's biography.

2. There are many accounts of other saints/Buddhas in the history of Buddhist thought. Read a few, and compare them with Ashvaghosha's *The Life of Buddha.* How are the ideals represented different?

3. Find out more about Mara. Discuss the significance of evil in Buddhism. What forms does it take?

Projects

1. Look at other representations of the Buddha in ancient and modern Indian art (paintings, sculpture, and the like). Discuss the changing face of Buddha. You might even go so far as to consider what kind of figure the Dali Lama embodies in terms of the Buddhist tradition.

2. Watch Bernardo Bertolucci's *Little Buddha*. Compare his representation of Buddhism with the selection presented.

FURTHER READING

Dutt, Ramesh C. *Buddhism & Buddhist Civilisation in India.* 1983.
Ergardt, Jan. *Faith and Knowledge in Early Buddhism.* 1977.
Khosla, Sarla. *Asvaghosa and His Times.* 1986.
Santiago, J. R. *Sacred Symbols of Buddhism.* 1991.

MEDIA RESOURCES

VIDEO

Ancient India
48 min., 1997 (Films for the Humanities & Sciences)
The antecedents of modern Indian culture can be traced back to the Harappan civilization, which flourished between 2300 and 1500 B.C.E. in what are now Pakistan and Afghanistan. This era saw the birth of the Hindu religion. The Aryan tribes from the Russian steppes invaded the subcontinent in 1000 B.C.E., bringing their language and culture. The resulting synthesis between the Aryan and Indian civilizations brought forth a unique society that included a caste system, which soon became entrenched. This program examines the religious tension between Hinduism, Buddhism, and Islam and the historical events that shaped the great Indian civilizations, from the Maurya empire through the Mughal empire. Maps and scholars provide insight into a culture that remains vibrant and diverse today.

Buddha: The Path to Enlightenment
43 min., 1999 (Insight Media)
Siddhartha Gautama, better known as Buddha, "The Enlightened One," renounced luxury and radical asceticism alike to attain spiritual freedom by taking the middle path. This program examines the life and teachings of Buddha, exploring the Four Noble Truths, Buddhist rituals, holiday celebrations, and such holy sites as Buddh Gaya and Mt. Kailash. It also considers aspects of monastic life and the concepts of karma and nirvana.

Buddhism: The Great Wheel of Being
52 min., 1995 (Insight Media)
This program explores the practice of Buddhism in Sikkim, a state tucked between Nepal and Bhutan, and Darjeeling, an adjoining district of West Bengal. It discusses history of Buddhism, highlights the Four Noble Truths, and looks at ancient monuments that testify to the enduring nature of the religion.

The Eastern Philosophers
3 volumes, 50 min. each, 2001 (Insight Media)
Examining the central doctrines of Confucianism, Shinto, Hinduism, Judaism, and Islam, this set examines the genesis of spiritual thought. The first volume explores the dominant

philosophical and spiritual ideas of the Far East, focusing on Confucius and Shinto. The second discusses the Hinduism and Buddhism of South Asia, with their focus on cycles of death and rebirth. The final volume considers the roots, rituals, and sacred texts of Judaism and the tenets and lifestyle issues of Islam.

Hinduism: An Introduction
29 min., 1999 (Insight Media)
Tracing the history of Hinduism's development and reformation, this video explains such spiritual concepts as karma, *dharma,* and God as both one and many. It examines the numerous Hindu scriptures and Hindu worship practices.

Hinduism: Faith, Festivals, and Rituals
51 min., 1995 (Insight Media)
The majority of the Indian population practices Hinduism, which emphasizes right living, or *dharma.* This video explores the devotional ceremonies and observances of Hinduism and examines such sacred Hindu literary works as the *Ramayana* and the *Mahabharata.*

India: Absorption of Brahman
42 min., 1998 (Insight Media)
The basic concepts of Hinduism have influenced Indian life from ancient to modern times. This video examines the roles of karma, rebirth, and caste in Hinduism. It also considers the Three Paths of Liberation and the Hindu concept of the Four Stages of Life.

The Jains
25 min., 1985 (Insight Media)
Observing life in the Jain community of Jaipur, India, this program outlines the main tenets of Jainism, explains its connections with Hinduism and local cults, and examines the tradition of spirit possession. It also explores ancient and modern Jain temples.

On Hinduism and Buddhism
35 min., 1994 (Insight Media)
This video presents an overview of Hinduism and Buddhism. It looks at the Hindu belief in reincarnation, the different kinds of yoga (Hatha, Jnana, Karma, and Bhakti), and the stages of life. It then considers the life of Buddha and his enlightenment, the role of meditation, and the philosophy of work.

Origins of India's Hindu Civilization
22 min., 1991 (Educational Video Network)
Long-ago Indo-Aryan invaders of India brought with them the pantheon of deities that evolved through the centuries into the complex Hindu religion that dominates the country's culture.

Religious Experience: Buddhism
60 min., 1999 (Insight Media)
This video explores the relationship among the religious impulse, the need to define meaning, and the impact of experience on spiritual understanding. It presents such fundamental Buddhist concepts as the Four Noble Truths, the Eightfold Path, egolessness, karma, *dharma,* and reincarnation.

What Is Buddhism?
52 min., 2002 (Insight Media)
This video introduces the history and fundamentals of Buddhism. The first segment explores the life of Siddhartha Gautama, the sixth-century (B.C.E.) prince that became the Buddha. The second highlights the *dharma,* the teachings of Buddhism, explaining the significance of the three jewels. The third addresses the current practice of Buddhism.

GENERAL MEDIA RESOURCES

WEB SITES

Ancient India
www.wsu.edu/~dee/ANCINDIA/CONTENTS.HTM
Richard Hooker's page (of Washington State University) provides an excellent overview of ancient India, including information on its history and peoples and culture, and many links to additional resources.

Internet Indian History Sourcebook
www.fordham.edu/halsall/india/indiasbook.html
The goal of the Ancient History Sourcebook is to provide and organize texts for use in classroom situations. Links to the larger online collections are provided for those who want to explore further. It also includes links to visual and aural material, since art and archeology are far more important for the periods in question than for later history. The emphasis remains on access to primary source texts for educational purposes.

AUDIO

Living Biographies of Religious Leaders
8 tapes, 11:25 hrs. (Blackstone Audiobooks)
This programs presents the lives of twenty great founders and leading advocates of the world's foremost religions. Here are the historical facts and legends associated with these forceful personalities who have inspired and influenced humankind through the centuries. Presented here are Jesus Christ, Moses, Isaiah, Zoroaster, Buddha, Confucius, John the Baptist, Paul, Muhammad, Francis of Assisi, John Huss, Luther, Loyola, Calvin, George Fox, Swedenborg, Wesley, Brigham Young, Mary Baker Eddy, and Gandhi.

CHINA:
THE ANCIENT WAY:
ANCESTORS, EMPERORS,
AND SOCIETY

The Book of Songs (p. 1573)

WWW   For a quiz on the *Book of Songs,* see *World Literature Online* at bedfordstmartins.com/worldlit.

The *Book of Songs* is a classic compendium of common political themes and situations, all woven through form and musicality into an immemorial brocade. With justification, the book compares them to the Vedas for India, yet they make a strange master text of a people. Surprisingly, fresh moments are "frozen" in these poems; there is very little mythopoetic founding of the four corners of the universe until late in the collection. Three traits constitute its contribution to world literature: its vivid picture of human life almost three millennia ago, its articulation of the chief political myths defining the Chinese people, and its elaboration of the lyric voice with a range and power equal to the work of the psalmist and the troubadour.

Confucius, who according to tradition edited the collection, said of them, "There are three hundred Songs and one phrase covers them all: 'No straying from the path'" (*Analects* 2.2). The "path" is the *dao,* the way of harmony and virtue. They encompass no narrow notion of morality but a view of human life that embraces its joys, sufferings, and emotions and finds a deep music running through them.

TEXT & CONTEXT

LEGENDARY AND HISTORICAL FIGURES OF THE ZHOU

The Zhou interpretation of history, justifying the rise of the house of Zhou to be the ruling power of China, is established in the *Book of Songs.* The odes especially substantiate the Zhou claim — the first assertion of the "mandate of heaven" — as resting on a history of righteous heroes, founders, and administrators. The following are the most important figures mentioned:

From the pre-dynastic period of myth and legend:

Jiang Yuan, mother of Hou Ji, impregnated when she trod on god's footprint

Hou Ji (Lord Millet), mythical male ancestor of the Zhou people, inventor of agriculture

From the Zhou royal period:

Wen Wang (King Wen, the Civil), originally Earl of West (Xi bo) under the Shang, married Tai-si, Lady Xin, designated first king of Zhou (traditional date 1134 B.C.E.)

Wu Wang (King Wu, the Martial), son of King Wen, defeated the Shang, established the Zhou dynasty in his father's name, capital at Hao (r. 1122–1116 B.C.E.)

Duke of Zhou, younger brother of King Wu, regent for young King Cheng (taken from Arthur Waley, pp. x–xi)

IN THE CLASSROOM

I. THE FORM OF THE *BOOK OF SONGS*

The anthology is traditionally arranged according to the origin and form of the poems, by gradations leading from the simplest lyric utterances to the lengthiest and most formal celebrations of mythic belief. The major divisions are as follows.

The *Airs of the States* (poems 17 through 75 and 148) are the youngest and most celebrated part of the collection, many of them thought by their form and diction to have originated in popular songs. They are direct in emotion and simple in structure and language. In this section, they are further grouped by the state of their origin. Two of these subgroups have notable features of their own. The "Airs of Zheng" (poems 24, 25, and 30) have been the most controversial in the book's interpretive history due to the frank passion they express, especially as voiced by women. Confucius called these poems "licentious" and said he "detested" them (*Analects* 17.18). Somewhat like the Song of Songs in the Bible, they have been reinterpreted by Confucian scholars to legitimize and control the erotic sentiment, not as religious allegories but as referring to royal and noble couples. The "Airs of Qin" (poem 148), coming from the small state that was later to provide the all-conquering Emperor Qin Shi Huangdi, are notable in sometimes singing of the warrior life as freely and easily as of a love affair.

The *Minor Odes* (poems 131, 132, 162, and 195) pull away from the constant joys and laments of village life to overlook life at a more aristocratic and courtly level. The poems and stanzaic forms are longer, the content seems to progress with forethought from scene to scene, and the voice expresses the consciousness of the clan and its members rather than individual experience. Agricultural work and military action are purposive, and feasting and merriment supply clan solidarity and allegiance to the lord.

The *Major Odes* (poems 238 and 241) zoom further outward to enunciate the chief myths of the Zhou people. These, typically, are myths about political order triply validated through religious belief, historical reference, and popular legend. The poems inculcate the sacred sense of calling as a statement about the meaning of all history. Joseph R. Allen observes that in these narratives of struggle of the Zhou people and their heroes the *Major Odes* accomplish "the creative imagining of the Zhou people as a cultural force." (225) Long when compared to the earlier poems, they nonetheless actually function as economical versions of epic.

Finally, the *Hymns* are the oldest poems in the collection. In diction the most austere and liturgical poems, they are grouped in three parts according to the dynasty of their putative origin, Shang and Zhou (with a third group from the state of Lu accorded equal solemnity, Lu being Confucius's home province). The Zhou Hymns compose the oldest layer of the *Book of Songs*. Poem 157, included here, achieves its distant, concerted, purposeful effect in part through speaking in the third-person plural. It presents a broad panorama that nonetheless takes delight in pointing out all the social types involved and the bustle of their activity. At its beginning, this hymn is all agricultural vitality, following the steps in making wine out of millet for offering to the elders. By the end, its sense of time palpably slowing, it has proceeded to focus on the solemn offering, the immemorial participation in the changeless ritual, and the silent pleasure of the dead ancestors. It is an artful rendering of a traditionalist society.

Discussion

1. What is the effect of placing the simplest poems first and the most formal and mythopoetic poems last? What would be the effect of the opposite arrangement?

2.   If Confucius "detested" the Airs of Zheng, why did he include them?

Writing

Ask students to write a short paper in response to the following:

1.   Trace the changes from section to section of the *Book of Songs* in terms of at least two of the following: diction, point of view, immediacy versus distance in presentation, and pacing in time. Discuss how these changes and their sequence present a concerted view of ancient Chinese life and mentality.

II. LIFE AND LOVE IN THE EIGHTH CENTURY B.C.E.

The love poems are remarkable for the freshness and daring of the women's voices and the variety of their situations. Each speaks with an individuality that shines through their quite typical entanglements. Poem 17, the most innocent, may be a transcription of an actual counting-game song. The poems of love affairs (24, 30, and 26) express a gamut of emotions, from the tension of desire and apprehension (the fear of breaking trees in poem 24 symbolizing the ruin of the girl's reputation) to the playful blindness of infatuation (the speaker in poem 30 wittily contradicts herself, "Of course people *do* drink wine in our lane," and so on), to the tableau of the lovers at dawn, so similar to the medieval European *aubade* or *alba*.

Poems 63 and 75 sympathize with equal frankness about the sufferings of young women whose unequal status leaves them helpless whether outside or inside marriage. Poem 63 alternates between brusque realism ("not so hasty, not so rough") and decorous metaphor (the dead doe) and metonymy (the handkerchief). Poem 75 uses imagistic resources — the metaphor of the tossed boat, the striking simile of the unwashed dress, and the reiterated negative comparisons: my heart is not a mirror, not a mat — I am not simply a reflection or instrument of social interests — to appeal movingly to the speaker's violated humanity.

From love, the subject matter moves to war, retaining somewhat its feel of spontaneous honesty in spite of the swing to the male voice and the opposite pole of experience. Poems 131 and 132 deal with Zhou campaigns against fierce tribes, providing a ground-level view of military action that is not permitted in epic or historical accounts. "We pluck the bracken" refrains from criticizing war openly — the warlord is presented as splendid — but nonetheless registers a realistic lament for the hard times war causes. Poem 132 presents a broader panorama in a narrative whose time scheme resembles the progress of a ballad. It is an interesting exemplar of the Minor Ode that stresses the gravity of the campaign, touching on other war poem themes as it goes, like the soldier's complaint, the warlord's praise, the wives' worries, and the change of seasons. The closure is definitive at the end as the Xianyun are brought to trial, and suddenly the poem has shaped its material up into a tale of civilization conquering lawlessness.

Poems 162 and 195, about preparing sacrificial offerings, desert the individual's view to express the exuberance of concerted action. Poem 162 uses ritual names for agricultural sacrifice. It moves quickly, with a time-lapse effect, from plowing to sowing to weeding. Poem 195 begins with an experiential *tranche de vie* like many of the airs, but its strange second stanza shifts the tone and pace quickly, using causal and analogical reasoning to lay out a grounding rationale for clans, and then swings to a wider frame as the ancestors are portrayed as watching. The rapid shifts evoke a microcosmic effect. (Only in retrospect does it become clear that the woodsmen have been cutting wood for burning at the sacrifice.) The following stanzas combine festivity and righteousness. "Virtue" in stanza 5 means essential strength, not morality. The last stanza is sheer group exuberance. It deserves chanting by the whole class!

Discussion

1. What is the situation of the young woman in poem 75? Why is its appeal especially surprising in a patriarchal society?

2. Are the speakers in poem 25 secret nighttime lovers, as some commentators seem to think, or are they husband and wife? Is the husband denying it is dawn because he is smitten or because he wants to sleep longer?

3. The images that the woman dwells on can be taken as symbols of marriage, home, and union. Is a positive view of marriage comparatively rare in ancient Chinese expression, or is it simply a less exciting subject for lyric poetry?

4. Catalogue the different time schemes employed in these poems. What alternatives to focusing on a single scene are used? How quickly or slowly do they proceed?

Writing

Ask students to write a short paper in response to one or more of the following:

1. What are the characteristics of the group voice in poems 162 and 195? How do the actions described in the poems work to overcome individual differences and create a group identity? What is gained and what is lost in this shift from the individual voice of the earlier poems?

2. Using the poems as a primary basis, describe a warrior's life in eighth-century B.C.E. China as fully as possible.

3. Western lyric poems are often said to achieve their intensity by portraying a "full moment," when the ties of one's existence to past and future fade and an intense feeling lays absolute claim on the speaker's consciousness, yielding an insight into the nature of joy or suffering. Do some of the Airs in this collection carry out this idea? What about the Hymn? What might a theory of the lyric based on the *Book of Songs* be like?

III. THE ZHOU PEOPLE

The "Zhou interpretation of history," in brief, is that the Zhou people were selected by heaven for their virtue and capability to succeed the Shang dynasty in ruling China. They originated the concept of the "mandate" or "charge" of heaven (*tian ming*), and, as these poems emphasize, such a concept means that the divine legitimation of a dynasty may be withdrawn if the rulers become corrupt and neglect the prosperity of the people. Moreover, in this view, dynasties always tend to begin in virtue and end in corruption, with the last king epitomizing the desecration of the royal role through atrocities and excesses.

Poem 241 is the chief articulation of this view in the *Book of Songs*. This ode will remind readers of parts of the Old Testament, with its strong sense of a people chosen by God, their essential righteousness (but the constant danger of their falling away from the path), their prophetic and patriarchal early leaders, and the authoritative overview of the generations from past to future. The Zhou are enjoined not to shame their ancestors but to "tend their inward power" so that the Zhou mandate may last forever. However, the fallen fortunes of the Shang serve both as a legitimation of the Zhou and as a "mirror" to them that "Heaven's charge is not for ever" but depends on their continuing righteousness.

Discussion

1. Compare the concept of the mandate of heaven with other notions of the king's responsibility toward his people. Does the threat of divine disfavor add anything significant to the idea? Practically, what good is it likely to accomplish?

2. Poem 238 presents one of the few origin myths in the collection. What is the role of agriculture in the legitimation of the Zhou? How is it connected to history and to the relation between the gods and humanity? Is agriculture given a more prominent place in Chinese myth than in the myths of other peoples? Considering that the great ancient epics arose out of nomadic warrior peoples, does the importance of agriculture in Chinese myth explain to some extent their lack of an epic?

Writing

Ask students to write a short paper in response to the following:

1. Here is your chance to write the "missing Chinese epic." Well, maybe not quite, but it is a good opportunity to discuss the epic elements of the Zhou mythology. Go on to sketch out what a Zhou epic might contain that would make it typical of other epics. (Another imaginative alternative: You are an archaeologist who has just found what you think to be the lost epic of the ancient Zhou. State your case as to why.)

BEYOND THE CLASSROOM

RESEARCH & WRITING

1. The *Book of Songs* rewards further reading. A library project could involve writing on the common characteristics of one of the sections outlined in this entry: the Airs of Zheng, the Minor Odes, or the Major Odes. In the last category, especially, much more material fleshes out the myth of the Zhou people.

Projects

1. Waley's note to poem 238 (p. 1587) is an accomplished piece of comparative mythology *à la* Frazer (*The Golden Bough*) and should be consulted for more interesting material. In the magical impregnating contact between god and woman, for instance, he draws a parallel to Sarah in the Bible, "another 'mother of nations,'" whose barrenness was removed by a miracle. The repeated and failed attempts to kill the hero as an infant, the child's exposure by enemies, its protection and nurturing by animals, and the early manifestation of his preternatural powers all suggest other familiar myths. Assign teams of students to collect comparable stories in other traditions, and present them to each other to discuss important variations in the stories and the importance and meaning they seem to have.

FURTHER READING

The Book of Songs. Trans. Arthur Waley. Ed. Joseph R. Allen. Rev. ed. 1996.
Owen, Stephen. Foreword. *Book of Songs.* xii–xxv. 1996.

MEDIA RESOURCES

WEB SITES

Book of Songs
mockingbird.creighton.edu/english/worldlit/wldocs/churchill/bksongs.htm
This site developed by Robert Churchill of Creighton University gives excellent background and a synopses of a number of works from the *Book of Songs.*

Shijing
www.chinavista.com/experience/shijing/shijing.html
This site provides illustrated examples of several pieces from the *Book of Songs.*

The Thirteen Confucian Classics
www.chinaknowledge.de/Literature/Classics/classics.htm
Billing itself as "a universal guide for China studies from Chinaknowledge, this site provides overviews of Confucian writings and also provides additional information on Confucius himself.

CONFUCIUS (Kongfuzi), *The Analects* (p. 1591)

WWW   For a quiz on *The Analects,* see *World Literature Online*
at bedfordstmartins.com/worldlit.

Confucius occupies a central position in the history of Chinese thought comparable only to founders of religions in the rest of the world. He is a renowned thinker on morality and the philosophy of life, and he might well be called the first philosopher of culture. Just as the Upanishads discover the soul and Socrates the mind (the possibility of attaining the truth by independent inquiry), Confucius is the first great thinker to enunciate the role of culture in shaping human life. His influence extended long after him, inspiring great ages of high culture more than a thousand years later in the Song dynasty and again in the Ming, and even in the flowering of the arts and culture in Japan.

A profoundly traditional thinker, Confucius equates devoted study of the tradition with the shaping of the person, an equivalency preserved in the West in the German word *Bildung* (which means both education and culture but literally means "forming"). His way of life and the style of his sayings, as recorded by his disciples in *The Analects,* have been almost as important as the content of his teachings. The marks of his epigrammatic style include brevity, inconsistency, tartness, and a preference for drawing lessons from experience and anecdotes. The humble, rustic nature of his voice and his claim to be only an editor and commentator, not an originator, are matched by the unassailable authority of his utterances.

IN THE CLASSROOM

I. THE CENTRAL NOTION OF *LI*

Li may be translated as ritual, custom, propriety, or manners. Its oldest meaning refers to the sacred rites of hospitality, particularly the ancestral rituals; hence *li* is nearly synonymous with religion. *Li* is the means by which life should be ordered and harmony established. It is the perfect reflection of the cosmic order, dao, as applied to human society. A person of *li* is good and virtuous; a state ordered by *li* is harmonious and peaceful. A land that does not follow *li* is uncivilized and therefore not fully human. The all-importance of this concept for Confucius amounted to the ritualization and sacralization of all of life.

Conversely, in his teachings, the specifically religious rituals became less important. *Analects* 6.20 instructs: "Devote yourself earnestly to the duties due to men, and respect spiritual beings, but keep them at a distance." This attitude refocuses religious concern onto human affairs. Ancient rites should continue to be performed, but, as Confucius saw it, their goal was really to reinforce the sense of order appropriate to all the affairs of life. Unlike the de-emphasizing of sacrificial ritual in the Upanishads, Confucius is reinterpreting ritual tradition not in the direction of greater transcendence but toward greater concentration on earthly life.

Li should not be thought of so exclusively as "ritual" as to suggest Confucius's approach to life is stiff and unresponsive. In a sense, *li* is undefinable except by its fruits, which are grace, harmony, and self-respect (see *Analects* 8.2 in the section "On Ritual and Music"). Another translation (by William Edward Soothill) states it thus: "The Master said: 'Courtesy uncontrolled by the laws of good taste becomes labored effort, caution uncontrolled becomes timidity, boldness uncontrolled becomes recklessness, and frankness uncontrolled becomes effrontery." Each pair of terms records the transition from a good quality to its graceless twin. *Li* is what makes the difference between the two. Like music, it can be learned only through submitting to repeated routine, but it becomes poised, harmonious, a means of free expression, and a way of life.

Discussion

1. In *Analects* 2.5, 3.11, and 10.7–8, is Confucius stressing the importance of following the actual ritual or the inner attitude one attains through following it? [Note: This question is related to the first writing assignment topic in this section.]

2. *Analects* 8.2 is a good saying to look at carefully in discussing the meaning of *li*. What examples from life can you think of that could illustrate the shading of difference between caution and timidity, and so on?

3. How does the meaning of *li* encompass relations to one's family, especially one's parents? Discuss Confucius's emphasis on filial piety as illustrated in the section entitled "On Filial Piety."

Connections

1. Compare *li* to the central notion of *dharma* in the Indian epics or the Bhagavad Gita. Both are universal concepts of order. How do they differ?

Writing

Ask students to write a short paper in response to the following:

1. Judging from the selections in the book, is *li* better understood as ritual or as an internal quality? In what way are both of these meanings involved in the full understanding of Confucius's concept of *li*?

II. THE IDEAL OF THE GENTLEMAN

Ren (pronounced approximately *rzhun* or, alternatively, *lun* with the *l* sound formed at the back of the tongue) is most often translated as goodness, humaneness, or humanity. It is the standard of which to aspire in conduct and the measure of individual character. As a goal of self-cultivation, it is to be thought of as the human quality that results from acting habitually according to *li* (see *Analects* 3.3). *Analects* 12.1 relates the two terms: "He who can himself submit to ritual is Good" (Waley); this can also be rendered, "To master or control the self and return to *li*, that is *ren*." Note that this priority of *ren* implies that the laws function properly as emanating from an inner attitude. [Compare the interiorizing revolution of thought in India.]

Whereas the more bureaucratic Confucians emphasized the control of individual impulses under the additional pressure of society, Confucius's emphasis remained with establishing an inner harmony, a goal toward which one should devote a patient and unceasing effort. Such is the message of the saying about the decades of life quoted in the book's introduction to Confucius (*Analects* 2.4). As a philosophy of formation of the person, this is a profound departure from the group order formed by the warrior peoples in India and China, the order centering on sacrifice. Even when compared with the Bhagavad Gita, the other great Eastern text on the philosophy of the person, the Confucian stance suggests a greater freedom. But it is freedom as the traditional world understands it: the freedom to conform to the way of heaven, not the modern understanding of freedom as the power to do whatever one wishes — until one is seventy! By that time, in a life devoted to *ren*, the personal will and the will of heaven can become one.

The context invoked by *The Analects* is one of corrupt times, dominated by men grasping for power over others. As a salutary counterimage, Confucius offers the *zhunzi* (pronounced *zhun-tseh*), the superior man or gentleman. Originally, the term meant "a person born to a position of wealth and privilege." Very significantly, Confucius changes the meaning of this term to mean "one who has good character." As the outer order becomes disorder, the inner order takes primacy. The *zhunzi* is cultured and reserved, observes good manners, and cares more for his own integrity and inner development than for wealth. He is above egoism and narrow self-interest. If he seeks public office, it is for the common good. He is not argumentative or contentious. He simply states the truth and disregards the consequences for himself. He is, as Confucius insists repeatedly, cultivated and not narrow. In him the arts flourish.

The *zhunzi* is a male ideal. In conformity with the differentiation of *yin* and *yang*, the ideal for a woman was to be obedient, supporting and aiding the development of virtue in her husband and children. Her job was to maintain order and contentment in her husband's family.

Discussion

1. *Analects* 3.3 states, "A man who is not virtuous (humane, *ren*), what has he to do with ceremonies (*li*)?" Which should come first and why?

2. Are the qualities attributed to Confucius in *Analects* 7.4 essential traits of the *zhunzi*? Why would these be important in a philosophy centered on honoring parents, ancestors, tradition, and ritual?

3. How are the traits discussed in *An.* 7.15, 7.26, 7.37, and 10.12 signs of a gentleman?

Connections or Group Work Assignments

1. As *Analects* 5.12 reveals, Confucius does not claim to provide a cosmology or a "total knowledge" but is steadfastly focused on cultivating human life and leading it toward the good. (See also *Analects* 11.11.) Use this as a point of comparison with Socrates, and go on to compare their senses of the goals of life.

2. *Analects* 6.28 suggests that Confucius's guidelines for conduct could be compared with the Golden Rule of Christianity. How do the two notions resemble each other? How do they differ?

Writing

Ask students to write a short paper in response to the following:

1. Outline the world of the Confucian gentleman: What are the chief entities in his world with which it is important to have particular relations (family, superiors, and the like)? Indicate a multiplicity of relationships and some idea of hierarchy in their priorities.

III. VIRTUOUS EXAMPLE AS AUTHORITY IN GOVERNMENT

Confucius claimed and believed that he was only trying to return to the original and proper way of the ancient sages. He thought of these as perfect beings, whose very presence in the world was enough to bring about a golden age. He names four in *The Analects*: Yao and

Shun, ancient kings, models of the perfect ruler; Yu the Great, protector of agriculture and water engineer; and the Duke of Zhou, brother of the dynasty's founder, protector of the boy king Cheng and the ideal scholar-administrator. These sages embodied *dê*, a combination of virtue and power perhaps best rendered as "moral force." The *dê* of the sages had the power to change the course of history by bringing about a harmonious order. Their virtue was so great that they could rule by "inactivity." Study and imitation of the sages became part of the Confucian way and was the motive behind his editing of the Five Classics. Those not born with *dê* could acquire it through devoted study. Confucius did not consider himself a sage but wrote that he strove ceaselessly to become one and to teach how to be one.

Analects 2.3, in the section "On Morality in Government," is a brief position statement by Confucius. To govern by decreeing laws and enforcing them by punishments was the ideal of the Legalists, a school of thought that had its greatest influence in the ruthless policies of the Emperor Qin Shi Huangdi some three hundred years after Confucius. However, to have to resort to such measures was to Confucius a sign either that the regime had lost its authority or that the people had grown utterly feckless. To Legalist doctrines, Confucius opposed governing by "moral force" (*dê*; the word is often translated as "virtue") and "ritual" (*li*). Freely interpreted, Analects 2.3 means: Show by your conduct the compelling power that the good has (*dê*), and always show others respect (*li*).

The driving force of Confucian politics is the power of virtuous example. He exercises a total, almost mystical belief in the power of the good to inspire others to order their lives and their relations with others, in a chain reaction of good order. Analects 9.13, a remarkable brief dialogue, envisions just such a reaction: "The Master wanted to settle amongst the Nine Barbarian Tribes of the east. Someone said, 'But could you put up with their uncouth ways'? The Master said, 'Once a gentleman settles amongst them, what uncouthness will there be?'" Here, the reversal of expectations, a device used in several of *The Analects*, indicates the reorientation of thinking that can be accomplished by belief in the power of virtue. The core idea is stated in a memorable image in Analects 2.1: "He who exercises government by means of his virtue (*dê*) may be compared to the north pole star, which keeps its place and all the stars turn toward it."

Discussion

1. Note Confucius's disregard for a government of laws without a moral sense resident in the people. Is this like or unlike American political theory?

2. What is the role of self-respect as indicated in *Analects* 2.3? In this saying "keep their self-respect" can also be translated as "have a sense of shame." Do you think shame can play a role in leading the people toward good order? Should it?

3. How is the maxim "Do not do to others what you would not like yourself" in *Analects* 12.2 made to relate to the principle of ruling by good example? (See also *Analects* 15.23.)

4. Does government by virtuous example presume that one has already attained the power over others, and their implicit assent, that is necessary to govern them?

Connections or Group Work Assignments

1. In *Analects* 12.11, Confucius implies that if everyone will simply live their role honestly and attentively, the society will be good. Using this as a point of comparison to the Bhagavad Gita on acting to fulfill the *dharma* of one's station in life, compare the ethic for action in society in ancient India with that of China.

Writing

Ask students to write a short paper in response to the following:

1. Václav Havel, playwright and former president of the Czech Republic, has remarked that Confucius "described what it means to wield genuine authority. His standards have very little in common with those who rule today by the whip. For Confucius, authority — whether for the father of a family or the ruler of a state — is a metaphysically anchored gift whose strength derives from heightened responsibility, not from the might of the instruments of power that the ruler may wield." Think of the world politics of the past hundred years: Soviet totalitarianism, the Nazi *Blitzkrieg*, the many small dictatorships of terror (how many of them have survived?), the constant threat of military destruction. Can you think of any examples of any political leaders having wielded true authority as Havel describes it? What would Confucius's comment be on the world of today?

BEYOND THE CLASSROOM

RESEARCH & WRITING

1. What is the goal of life, and how is it to be attained? A philosophy of life based on tradition can be compared most strikingly with a philosophy of life based on independent inquiry by studying Confucius's *The Analects* in comparison with Aristotle's *Nicomachean Ethics.* Several abbreviated editions of the *Ethics* are available and can make this project more manageable.

WWW   For additional information on Confucius and annotated Web links, see *World Literature Online* at bedfordstmartins.com/worldlit.

FURTHER READING

Confucius. *The Analects of Confucius*, 2nd Edition. Trans. William Edward Soothill. 1968.
Havel, Václav. "A Sense of the Transcendent." *The Art of the Impossible: Politics as Morality in Practice.* 1997.

MEDIA RESOURCES

VIDEO

Confucianism and Taoism
50 min., 1999 (Insight Media)
This video looks at the philosophies and rituals of Taoism, and examines how the philoso-phies and social doctrines of Confucianism have impacted Chinese culture.

Confucius
50 min., 1998 (Insight Media)
Few philosophers are cited more than Confucius. This program tells the story of Confucius's life, from his impoverished childhood to his position as a renowned teacher. It also examines China's feudal era, during which he lived.

Confucius: Words of Wisdom
50 min., 1996 (A&E Video)

From A&E's Biography series, this video explores the life and legacy of Confucius, whose timeless message remains influential to this day.

The Confucian Tradition — Chinese Poetry: Origins of a Literary Tradition
46 min., 1997 (Annenberg/CPB Multimedia Collection)
Learn the key elements of Confucian thought in China, and trace its impact on China's most important literary form, lyric poetry. This in-depth series includes readings from the Confucian *Analects* and the *Book of Songs* and presents the lives and works of many renowned poets. Produced by Columbia University's Project on Asia in the Core Curriculum of Schools and Colleges.

WEB SITES

Confucius
www.friesian.com/confuci.htm
This very helpful site provides background on the life of Confucius as well as notes on some of the basic tenets of his philosophy and teachings.

Confucius and Socrates
www.san.beck.org/C&S-Contents.html
This is a fascinating site that offers a thorough comparative analysis of the works of Confucius and Socrates.

The Internet Classics Archive — Confucius
Classics.mit.edu/Browse/browse-Confucius.html
This site provides the complete e-text versions of Confucius's work.

The Philosopher Confucius
www.csun.edu/~hbchm009/Confucius.html
This site provides links to several sites relating to the life and works of Confucius as well as images of two Confucius temples.

Stanford Encyclopedia of Philosophy — Confucius
Plato.stanford.edu/entries/Confucius
Find a biography of Confucius as well as links to relevant sites and a bibliography of primary and secondary sources at this site.

LAOZI (Lao Tzu), Dao De Jing (Tao Te Ching) (p. 1601)

WWW   For a quiz on Laozi, see *World Literature Online*
       at bedfordstmartins.com/worldlit.

There is a tendency in the Western classroom to classify "Eastern Religions" in one group, without distinction. Certain hallmarks, like mysticism, a belief in certain forces, reciprocity, and reincarnation, are singled out as elements of "Eastern Religion." However, many of these religions have their roots in what began as philosophical schools. Daoism and Confucianism are the two most famous examples of this. Daoism, like Epicureanism or Stoicism in the West, began as an explanation of how the universe worked. Its founder, Laozi, wrote several treatises, including the prose-poem Dao De Jing in the sixth to fifth centuries B.C.E. For students, it will be important that they know how to distinguish Daoism and Confucianism and how to distinguish their philosophical forms from their later religious practice. Confucius was interested in the political construction of China, the observing of hierarchies and the delineation of power. In his *The Analects,* Confucius sets down a system for order and peace based on virtues of loyalty and humanity. Confucianism never became much of a real religion except in the sense that he was worshipped as a hero and sage. Modern Christians and Buddhists or even Daoists will still claim to be Confucian in many parts of the Chinese world. In Singapore, Hong Kong, and elsewhere, Neo-Confucianism is considered a political policy, not a state religion.

Daoism, on the other hand, has no transparent aspirations to be political, except perhaps to advise the emperor that even he must follow the law of dao. In fact, contrary to the prevailing cultural desire for community over individualism inherent in Confucius's philosophy, Daoism (Taoism) is interested in the individual and in achieving inner harmony and peace, even to the neglect of social and political needs. While Confucius was largely a pragmatist, Laozi regarded involvement in state matters with disdain and preached an ascetic life governed by inaction. Both of these philosophers wrote in a period of political chaos and intellectual revolutions. Confucius believed that his system could put order into the state, while Laozi believed that a withdrawal to a more natural state of being was the answer to China's mounting problems.

Daoism relies on dao (sometimes written *tao,* but pronounced "dow," which rhymes with "plow") as the central force of its philosophy. Dao is a mysterious flow of energy that can be achieved by doing nothing. The catch is that doing nothing is harder than it appears. In the eighty-one short cantos of the Dao De Jing, there are many contradictions as to what constitutes "doing nothing," "nothingness" and "dao." Part of the challenge for the novice is to achieve a higher state of being and, ultimately, immortality, by learning the dao through practice. Reading the Dao De Jing is part of this exercise. The language is simple, short, and terse. But behind the simplicity is constant contradiction between nature and expectation.

ren fa di; di fa tian; tian fa dao; dao fa zi ran.

Earth rules men; heaven rules earth; dao rules heaven; the nature of itself rules dao. (25)

Unlike Confucianism, heaven and earth have no orderly natural state to attain. Whereas *ren,* "humanity" was the goal for men who followed Confucianism, Laozi writes, *tian di bu ren,* "Heaven and Earth are not humane" (5). The word *dao,* which I have not translated, is the character for "path" or "way." However, even a term as fundamental as *dao* is impossible to consistently translate in this work. Often it is a "path or "way" to enlightenment, but sometimes it is a force or being, and other times it is nothing. Laozi writes, "the *dao* is an empty cup that can still be drawn from, and needs not be filled" (4). The most famous description of the dao is in the opening lines, which are a challenge to the reader to be careful when looking for the dao: "Whatever you say is the *dao,* it is anything but the *dao*; whatever you call the *dao,* it is anything but the *dao.* The *dao* has no name" (1). The book professes to be the "Classic of *Dao,*" or a resource about Daoism, but it begins by saying that the dao cannot be defined. Does this sentence challenge presuppositions about the dao that the reader might have, or does it force you to reread the sentence and find a hidden meaning? Many interpreters of this passage have said that this is Laozi's attempt to show that language constrains the possible meanings of dao, which can only be known mystically and in practice, not by reading a text. Trying to understand dao from a few passages can be difficult. The empty vessel mentioned above is an illustrative example. Laozi writes, "We make a vessel of clay, but it is where there is no clay that the vessel is useful. We poke out the doors and windows of a building to make a house. It is only where there is nothing can we enter and use the house. Just as we must know how to use what exists, we must learn to use what does not exist" (11).

The title contains three words: *dao*, which is explained in the first thirty-seven chapters of the book; *de*, or "virtue," which is explained in the last forty-four chapters of the book; and *jing*, or "classic," which indicates that this is a collection of canonical writing, not a commentary or history. Chapters one and fifteen both describe how knowledge through language is constraining, but true knowledge, possessed by the ancient sages, is bottomless. Whereas the first chapter has the language of initiation in "the gate to all mystery" and in its near-address of the reader, the fifteenth chapter assumes the traditional relationship of master and apprentice. Laozi characterizes the master's virtues for the apprentice, who is expected to live a simple life with no wants or needs. In chapter sixteen, Laozi addresses the problem of whether or not thinking about philosophy is useful. He tells the novice to accept the cyclical pattern of nature passively as the first step on a ladder to an open mind, an open heart, a royal disposition, a divine disposition, oneness with the dao and finally, eternity. Here, he leaves his mark for immortality: "And though the body dies, the Tao will never pass away" (16). However, just as early Christians noted, pride in being without sin is also a great sin. Desire to be pure and without desire is also a desire. This paradox is phrased succinctly by Laozi in chapter nineteen: He tells the adherent to give up virtues so as not to invite the problems of desiring those virtues. Simplicity is all that is required. In chapter twenty, he goes further, asking students to give up learning as well. Desire of knowledge is also limiting. The student who has read chapter nineteen will assume that Laozi is making a similar claim here: Only give up knowledge, and enlightenment is yours. But the argument shifts directly to the notion of desire to be located someplace in the world. Knowledge is what the person who wants roots and power seeks; Laozi says he is rootless, nourished only by dao.

In chapter twenty-eight, the requirements of the student of Daoism are more metaphysical. The idea of balance is described in this passage. Traditional Chinese medicine and science depended on the notion of the opposition of *yin* and *yang*. Whereas *yin* is usually associated with women, *yang* is usually associated with men. *Yang* is white, but *yin* is black, and so on. The symbol for Daoism, the *yin-yang*, derives from this attempt to achieve balance: a cyclical revolution of black and white that are also composed of one another. In chapter twenty-nine, this balance is put into practice. By making no efforts to change things and by avoiding extremes, it is possible to be one with the universe. Balance, as chapter thirty-six explains, is part of nature, but it is the dao that holds together and produces the forces of *yin* and *yang*, of which all things are made (compare modern physical notions of matter and antimatter). The essence of dao is reiterated in chapter forty-three: "Teaching without words and work without doing / Are understood by very few" (43). Chapters forty-seven and seventy-four both lend short pieces of advice to the adherent about knowledge and fear, both of which sound familiar to those who have read Lucretius in the West. The final chapter of the Dao De Jing, chapter eighty-one, is perhaps one of the most practical. It lends advice for the novice who is living in the present: Speak the truth, do not argue, admit ignorance, do not horde, do for others, give to others, work effortlessly.

TEXT & CONTEXT

Some scholars contend that the philosophical doctrines of Laozi and Zhuangzi, the other major Daoist patriarch, were exceptionally compatible with local Chinese religious practice and beliefs as well as early Chinese science and technology. This is one explanation for how philosophical Daoism combined with local beliefs may have resulted in religious Daoism. During the Wei and Jin dynasties (220–420 C.E.), philosophical Daoism was transformed into a more mystical form of Daoism, which is the foundation for the religion practiced today. Religious Daoism is the only major religion to have been born on Chinese soil and has been central throughout the history of China. The tenets of this religion have had an immeasurable and lasting effect on Chinese architecture, music, painting, and literature. During the Tang dynasty (618–906 C.E.), Daoism became an official state religion and was highly influential in the court of Genghis Khan (1162–1227 C.E.). However, a direct competition with Buddhism arose during the following centuries, and Daoism threatened its popularity among the Imperial classes while retaining its followers among the poor and ordinary Chinese. In the last two dynasties, the Qing and Ming (1368–1911 C.E.), Daoism surged greatly in popularity. Currently, Daoism is one of the most eminent religions in the Chinese world. It is difficult to take statistics on Daoism, since its adherents typically believe in other local religions or Buddhism simultaneously. However, there are approximately 25,000 Daoist priests in mainland China alone. One of the most vibrant and active Daoist communities in the world is located in Hong Kong. In the last decade, a new religion, Falung Gong, which bases some of its tenets on Daoism, has achieved international media attention as it attempts to gain followers and political recognition.

IN THE CLASSROOM

RELIGION AND PHILOSOPHY OF THE COMMONS AND EMPEROR

Different avenues of discussion exist for the Dao De Jing, despite the brevity of the work as a whole. Regardless of it having its origins as a philosophical work, it has a definite metaphysical bent to it, perhaps qualifying it as a religious work as well. This is in fact how history has received the work. Students might want to discuss what makes a work religious and what defines the tone and manner of a religious work. The Dao De Jing can be compared to parts of the Koran or the Psalms in order to see what makes it stand out as a religious work. At the same time, Daoism should be compared to other philosophies with which students may be familiar, especially the Epicurean philosophy of Epicurus (p. 1633) and Lucretius (p. 785) and the Stoic philosophy of Cleanthes (p. 1636) and Marcus Aurelius (p. 1639).

Discussion

1. How do the more mystical and less practical portions of the Dao De Jing contribute to the work? What role do they play, considering the origins of the book as a philosophical work? How might you imagine them to be interpreted by their first readers?

2. How does Laozi confirm his beliefs in the work? What does he say to be as persuasive as possible that he has uncovered the truth? What are the problems with this strategy?

Connections

1. Compare Laozi's conception of fear and desire with Lucretius's writing in *On the Nature of Things* (p. 786) and the philosophy of Epicurus (p. 1633). Do the two philosophies try to attain happiness in the same way? How do they rationalize the connection between desire and fear?

2. Based on your reading of the Dao De Jing, in particular Laozi's characterization of himself, how is this similar or different from Cao Xueqin's portrayal of the Daoist in the opening chapter of *The Story of the Stone* (Book 3)?

Groups

1. In groups, have students summarize the content of one or two of the chapters of the Dao De Jing. Then, have each group rephrase the chapter in the plainest language possible for the rest of the class and provide a list of Daoist virtues based on the chapters they have summarized. As a class, discuss how the virtues are distributed and presented.

Writing

Ask students to write a short paper in response to one or more of the following:

1. How does Laozi contend with the difficulties and limitations of language? What does he identify as the problems of language?

2. What are the different forms in which dao is presented? How is it personified?

3. The first line of chapter 20 is believed to originally be the last line of chapter 19. Many scholars print it in both places, since it is difficult to be sure where it belongs. Based on careful reading of chapters 19 and 20, and on the conclusions of these chapters, where do you believe this line, "Give up learning, and put an end to your troubles," belongs?

BEYOND THE CLASSROOM

RESEARCH & WRITING

1. Laozi creates a description and typical expression of the Daoist monk or philosopher. Based on your reading, describe what the ideal Daoist philosopher would be like, according to Laozi.

2. What is the meaning of Laozi's "quietism"? How does it work in the context of practical application of Daoist philosophy? Use quotes from the text to support your conclusions.

3. How does the Dao De Jing explain nature? Could it be interpreted as a work of early Chinese science as well as philosophy? How does it compare with works by other philosopher-scientists like Aristotle or Leibniz?

WWW   For more information on Laozi and annotated Web links,
        see *World Literature Online* at bedfordstmartins.com/worldlit.

FURTHER READING

Barrett, Timothy Hugh. *Taoism Under the T'ang: Religion & Empire During the Golden Age of Chinese History.* 1996.
Csikszentmihalyi, Mark, and Philip J. Ivanhoe. *Religious and Philosophical Aspects of the Laozi.* 1999.
Kohn, Livia. *Daoism and Chinese Culture.* 2001.
Pott, William Sumner. *Chinese Political Philosophy.* 1925.
Qing, Xitai. Trans. David C. Yu. *History of Chinese Daoism.* 2000.

MEDIA RESOURCES

WEB SITES

Internet Classics Archive — Works by Lao Tzu
Classics.mit.edu/Browse/browse-Lao.html
Read the complete e-text translation of the Tao Te Ching at this wonderful site.

Lao Tzu Page
www.taopage.org/laotzu
This site provides biographical information on Lao Tzu and provides an overview of Taoist (Daoist) principles and practices. It is a useful site to discover the meanings of several key

Taoist terms. Also available here are links to a number of other pages related to Lao Tzu, Taoism, and Chinese philosophy in general.

Lao Tzu: Father of Taoism
www.chebucto.ns.ca/Philosophy/Taichi/lao.html
Visit this site to find background information on the life of Lao Tzu and on his famous work, the Tao Te Ching.

The Lucid Café — Lao Tzu
www.lucidcafe.com/library/96jun/laotzu.html
This site provides a brief biography of Lao Tzu and links to several sites related to his life and writings.

Malaspina Great Books — Lao Tzu
www.mala.bc.ca/~mcneil/Tzu.htm
A great place to go for a wide variety of resources, this site includes biographical informa-tion on the author, links to his texts, and links to many secondary sources about Lao Tzu's philosophy. It also provides links to pages on other philosophers and religious leaders for comparative research.

ZHUANGZI (Chuang Tzu), Basic Writings (p. 1611)

WWW   For a quiz on Zhuangzi's basic writings, see *World Literature Online*
at bedfordstmartins.com/worldlit.

Compared with Laozi's (Lao Tzu) more metaphysical and mysterious conception of dao (tao) and the impenetrable Dao De Jing (Tao Te Ching), Zhuangzi (Chuang Tzu) seems more like an analytical Western philosopher. He attempts to classify and arrange types of things and uses logic and reason as weapons of persuasion over more traditional ethical arguments. Laozi is ambitious in that his text is really meant to be a transforming experience for any individual who can read it, but Zhuangzi concentrates more heavily on liberating the individual through a description of the real world and its many inconsistencies. The format of Zhuangzi's writing reveals the fact that he was impeccably trained in the Confucian *Analects*. Although he works against Confucian moralistic and humanistic philosophy, his method is the same: His expert use of the dialogue is a way of personifying competing philo-sophical themes and pursuing the more logical goal. We might well compare Zhuangzi with Epicurus, the Hellenistic Greek philosopher on happiness and Laozi to Lucretius, his Roman follower several centuries later. While Epicurus wrote in prose in a clear style meant to show his philosophy by arguments from the positive, Lucretius wrote a poem that often resorts to argumentation from the negative.

Zhuangzi's dialogue form is only one of the forms that are employed in the whole work. In addition, he uses fables, anecdotes, parables, aphorisms, and even short couplets to bring across his point. In these conversations, sometimes with himself, Zhuangzi's Western-style analytical philosophy begins to emerge. Zhuangzi concentrates on determining that X *is equal* (*shi*, pronounced *shir*) to Y or that X *is not equal* (*fei*, pronounced *fay*) to Y. This dis-tinction is already viewed in the opening of the Dao De Jing: *Dao ke Dao FEI chang Dao*, "The *Dao* you call *Dao* IS NOT the usual *Dao*." In Laozi, this distinction between *shi* and *fei* leads to a rejection of language. But Zhuangzi does not reject language or describe it as inad-equate; it is only limited in perspective. In the episode entitled "What Fish Enjoy," Hui Tzu — who stands for the rival Mohist and Legalist philosophical traditions — and Zhuangzi argue about who knows what fish enjoy. Since Zhuangzi is not a fish, Hui Tzu argues that he cannot know what fish enjoy. But Zhuangzi, imitating Hui Tzu's naive form of argument, declares that since Hui Tzu is not Zhuangzi, he cannot know what Zhuangzi knows or does not know. Zhuangzi in fact knows because of his perspective: He has been "standing here beside the Hao."

In Zhuangzi's "The Wasted Gourd," we see some of the philosopher's pragmatism. A man has planted seeds that produce a huge winter melon so big that he could fit inside of it. However, the man can only think of how to dip the melon into a well or use it as a water barrel, and nothing else. Zhuangzi chastises his short-sightedness and recites a further anecdote about a sericulturist in Song who had a potion to prevent chapped hands. The man needed this potion to keep his hands useful after washing so much silk. However, only the man who realized that such a potion could help win a war in the middle of winter was rewarded by it. Zhuangzi seems to give this anecdote as part of a diatribe against the man he accuses of being so stupid. But the format of a semimagical story (there is no such potion) within another semimagical story (there are no melons this large) serves as a framework for the discussion of practical Daoism, constructed purposefully along similar didactic lines as Confucianism.

In "The Ailanthus Tree," the question about how something is used comes up again. The seemingly useless ailanthus tree, gnarled and misshapen, is a metaphor for Zhuangzi's philosophical tone. More likely, however, the metaphor is meant to be applied to Laozi or the character of Laozi: It describes something that can be interesting at which to look but impossible to put to use. The Dao De Jing, while profound and beautiful, could be seen by some to be highly impractical. Zhuangzi's response, however, is that the tree that cannot be put to use will not be cut down by an axe. He recommends, instead, that the critic lay down under the shade of the tree and relax. It is a clever response to criticisms of the usefulness of many intellectual pursuits (the same could be said for reading a book), but it happens to also promote the Daoist idea of inner tranquility. In Daoism, the axe would have been an interference, but by accepting the tree and not trying to use it for something else, the value of "doing nothing" is pursued. The portrayal of a Daoist as being ugly and deformed may remind students of how Socrates was typically portrayed.

Students will find the first paragraph of "Walking Two Roads" as either lacking sense or a fantastic puzzle. Unfortunately, this is the best one can do with the extremely compact Chinese original of this statement. After sorting through what these sentences mean, it is possible, perhaps, to compare Zhuangzi's statements to Descartes' *"cogito, ergo sum,"* "I think, therefore I am." Existence derives from the mere thought or use of something. Or, in Zhuangzi's terminology, "A road is made by people walking on it." However, Zhuangzi goes further, linking the idea of existence to value judgement. In order for something to exist, it must be of some use. In order for something to be of some use, it must have some good. Therefore, everything that exists is of some good. As a consequence of this generalization, nothing is completely good or completely bad. What unites the good and bad features of something is the dao. Only by following and seeing the world with Daoist eyes can one understand that seemingly broken or ugly things are whole and perfect. So far, Zhuangzi sounds like Laozi, proclaiming that all we have to do is change our view of the world and all will be right. But Zhuangzi continues in his typical style, offering an anecdote about the monkey trainer whose monkeys complain about the allocation of food. This little story is intended to be applicable to consumerism, politics, and other human behaviors.

In the "Penumbra and Shadow" and "The Dream and the Butterfly," a question is asked about reality that will be familiar to many students who have probably wondered the same thing. In the movie *Matrix* (1999), Neo wakes up to realize that his reality was a dream and his dream a reality. By choosing the butterfly, Zhuangzi alludes to changes in nature and the evolution of the individual. Reality is but a cocoon state of tomorrow's happy butterfly.

The story about Cook Ting (pronounced *ding*), "Cutting Up the Ox," is one of the most famous episodes from Zhuangzi's works. Cook Ting is frequently referred to by ordinary Chinese in speech as a master of the knife and the master philosopher of life. In this story, we also see some of the analytical philosophy behind Zhuangzi's Daoism. The space between the joints of the ox is infinite because the edge of the knife does not take up any space. No matter how close the joints of the ox become, the knife can get in between like air through a crack. Laozi says, "We beat metal to form a knife, yet the knife is useful where there is the least metal. . . . Just as we must know how to use what exists, we must learn to use what does not exist" (11). Building on Laozi's observation that emptiness or lack of material is useful, Zhuangzi lends us this story about the master Daoist, who can see emptiness where we only imagine a tight joint or thick knife. His knife is never dulled because it never touches anything, and yet he cuts oxen all day.

In "The Death of Lao Tan," "Transformations," and "Death of Chang Tzu's Wife," the philosopher explores reactions that men have to death and transformations along the way to death. Death and all of the changes that a person might experience are seen as part of the divine will of the creator, expressing a purpose that is otherwise perhaps difficult to comprehend. Students might be reminded of Job in the Hebrew Scriptures, who undergoes trials willingly because he believes that such trials must be intended for him. Master Lai acknowledges that one cannot accept some things from the creator and refuse others, since "If I think well of my life, for the same reason I must think well of my death."

In "The Job Offer" and "Yuan-Chu Bird," we see a typical view of the Daoist recluse who prefers not to take part in government. The disdain that this philosophical system has for politics is also seen in the "Woodworker," where the artist who has starved himself for seven days no longer thinks of the court. The heavily bureaucratic imperial system would be difficult, in Zhuangzi's day (to say nothing of the present day), to forget about. Part of the complexity of that system derives from its Confucian system of orders and hierarchies. In "The Swimmer," Confucius meets a Daoist swimmer who is not fazed by a deadly waterfall that is in his path. When Confucius asks him how he can swim in such waters, the man answers that he can because of what he is accustomed to, his nature, and fate all make it possible to float. When Confucius asks him what these things are, the man answers that dry land is what he is used to, nature is what he likes, and fate is the result of him not knowing why he does what he does. Here Zhuangzi denies Confucius's view of an individually controlled fate, replacing it with the more uncertain and unknown fate presented by Daoist philosophy.

"Happiness" is largely about the difference between the requirements for happiness and the requirements for what the world generally believes to be signs of success and tokens of happiness: a BMW, being on the cover of *People*, living to age ninety, universal respect, Banana Republic, vacations in Tahiti, and a Beethoven string quartet. Because these signs and tokens exist, people worry when they fall short of them because they are afraid that they will be unhappy. And yet, if the tokens or signs did not exist, people would not have to worry about not obtaining them, and they would be happy. Therefore, the very things that are signs of poverty are demonstrated in people who cannot obtain symbols of success: no sleep, fast food, rumpled clothes, no time to look at the scenery, no time to listen to a lover's words. Even the exceptionally good, like Martin Luther King Jr. and Jesus Christ, suffer for all the notoriety that they get. Neither Dr. King or Jesus die saying how happy their life has been. Therefore, for Zhuangzi, inaction or doing nothing at all is what produces true happiness. By not trying to obtain a symbol of wealth, power, eminence, or longevity, and by not trying to be so good to others, happiness is achieved. Inaction has no tokens or signs to represent it, so there is nothing to obtain or attain, and thus it is possible to stay happy and not worry about what one does not have.

TEXT & CONTEXT

THE AUTHORSHIP OF THE ZHUANGZI

With this selection, students will see a more concrete form of philosophical Daoism that they can compare with what they may know of other ancient philosophies. It will be useful for instructors to focus on the differences in form between Laozi and Zhuangzi and to trace what derives from what. Until relatively recently, it was simply assumed that the teachings of Zhuangzi derived from, and were subsequent to, those of Laozi. But archaeological and philological evidence has confounded this millennia-old assumption of who came first. Some now theorize that Zhuangzi invented Laozi as the interlocutor in his dialogue and that the hitherto anonymous Dao De Jing was called "The Laozi" on analogy with Zhuangzi's collection of writings, which are simply called "The Zhuangzi." But even those scholars who believe this theory must sort out what in "The Zhuangzi" is written by the man whose name the title bears and what was added by students and editors over the many centuries.

ABOUT CHINESE ROMANIZATION

There are various ways to Romanize Chinese names. The most modern and internationally used of these systems is known as "pinyin," designed to be as consistent as possible in pronunciation: Laozi, Zhuangzi, Dao, and Dao De Jing. However, the older Wade-Giles system is still used by some scholars who have grown accustomed to it and by some Taiwanese: Lao Tzu, Chuang Tzu, Tao, and Tao Te Ching. According to the *Chicago Manual of Style*, fifteenth edition, scholars are urged to use the more widely employed pinyin standard, except with proper names that have a long history in the West, like "Sun Yat-sen" and "Chiang Kai-shek," or are not proper to mainland China, like "Hong Kong" and "Taipei."

IN THE CLASSROOM

When students encounter Zhuangzi, they are able to make better sense of the general pattern of thought in Daoism. Some of the important concepts to review include *wuwei*, or "inaction"; Daoist perceptions of fate; and the physical world according to the Daoist. Students should compare the points of view as they are presented in Zhuangzi's illustrative way of writing with Laozi's style of writing. Finally, students should combine their knowledge of the two authors to try to imagine how the Daoist believer is characterized by his contemporaries and critics.

Discussion

1. On what does the Daoist perception of reality rest? Are they empiricists, that is to say, do they depend upon experience? Do they require concrete perception (through the five senses) to sense reality, or is their conception of reality more metaphysical?

2. What are the various ways in which Zhuangzi expresses *wuwei*, or "doing nothing"? How can "doing nothing" lead to lasting peace?

Connections

1. In "Woodworker," a special diet helps focus the Daoist artist's attention on his goal, while not making him goal-oriented (which would be against Daoist philosophy). In the Svetasvatara Upanishad (p. 1628), a special diet is also required of the Yoga practitioner. What other examples can you think of in which a person's philosophical outlook is also dictated by the food that is eaten by the person?

2. In Book 6 of *The Bedford Anthology of World Literature*, the philosophy of existentialism is introduced. In some ways, this philosophy, like Daoism, may seem pessimistic from

the point of view that man's ambitions are self-destructive. However, the philosophies are similar and different in key points. How do these respective philosophies deal with issues like fate, free will, government, and ambition?

Groups

1. Divide the class into groups, and have each group introduce a pair of selections from Zhuangzi. Each group should be responsible for showing what aspect of Daoism is demonstrated and, if possible, what relationship the text has with the works of Laozi.

Writing

Ask students to write a short paper in response to one or more of the following:

1. What is the Daoist reaction to death and old age? How is this demonstrated in actions?

2. What are the major differences between the Zhuangzi's and Laozi's style? How does this affect their ability to express philosophical views?

BEYOND THE CLASSROOM

RESEARCH & WRITING

1. What is the role of nature in Zhuangzi's works? How does he view the human interaction with nature?

2. Zhuangzi frequently uses animals to make comparisons or tell anecdotes in his works. How does his choice of animals and the way they are made human affect his characterization of different types of people?

Project

1. Research the contemporary religious practice of Daoism. How is it practiced, by whom, and what are the main traditions and tenets of its practitioners?

FURTHER READING

Des Forges, Alexander. *Gathering the Feng and Fei Plants: Individuals and Sacred Texts in Early Religious Daoism.* 1992.
Höchsmann, Hyun. *On Zhuangzi.* 2001.
Kupperman, Joel. *Classic Asian Philosophy: A Guide to the Essential Texts.* 2001.
Liu, Xiaogan. *Classifying the Zhuangzi Chapters.* 1994.
Qing, Xitai. Trans. David C. Yu. *History of Chinese Daoism.* 2000.
Watson, Burton. *Zhuangzi: Basic Writings.* 2003.

In the World: The Good Life (p. 1622)

At this point, students should be fairly familiar with methods of comparison and with the many ways in which a culture is reflected by the literature it produces. Students will already have learned how to see the texts as being relevant to the world around them and to learn to ask their own questions of the text. In this final section of the book, it may be profitable for the students to review everything they have learned thus far in terms of what geographical regions' literatures they have read, the kinds of religions and philosophical systems to which they have been exposed, and the histories of those cultures. What do certain cultures consider to be "The Good Life"? What is the goal of those civilizations? To what should we aspire?

In *The Iliad*, there is a famous decision that Achilles must make ("The Choice of Achilles"). Although it is not narrated in the epic, it is implicit throughout. Achilles is raised on Phthia, a grassy region of Thessaly that is good for raising horses. His parents, knowing he will die in battle, try to hide him by dressing him up as a girl and raising him among girls. When Odysseus comes to Phthia to raise troops for the effort against Troy, Achilles sees his weapons and tries them on. During *The Iliad*, Achilles nearly goes back to Phthia. He has a choice: to return to safety and to live happily but anonymously, or to stay at Troy and die famous. This freedom to choose between fates places a terrible burden on the human race. Philosophy and religion are meant to teach us to make better choices so that we can choose what will make us happiest in the end.

But happiness is difficult to measure. We can measure things that can contribute to happiness, like wealth, fame, and power. Happiness, however, can exist in the absence of these things; many philosophies and religions are concerned with trying to find happiness without the accumulation of things. These systems of belief teach that this kind of happiness will be more lasting and pure. In the story of Herodotus's Croesus, the king of Lydia, we encounter a man who has wealth, power, and fame and thus considers himself to be happy. In the selection, Solon says that there are many days in a man's life and that no two are alike. Until Croesus dies, Solon cannot say whether or not he is the happiest man he has ever met. Indeed, Croesus turns out to be very unlucky. He has two sons — one deaf and mute, and the other healthy and sound, named Atys. Croesus receives a suppliant from Phrygia (in modern Turkey), who has accidentally killed his brother. This man, named Adrastus, and Croesus's son go off to kill a boar that has been ruining the crops. Adrastus throws a spear that misses the boar but kills Atys. So Croesus, who has purified this man who has killed his own son, is quite unlucky. Later, when Cyrus destroys his empire and takes control of all Persia, Croesus recalls the words of Solon and cries out his name while he is about to burn at the stake. When he recognizes the truth of Solon's words and that he, too, is susceptible to fate, he saves Croesus from the fire and treats him well for life.

TEXT & CONTEXT

Herodotus lived in Halicarnassus, on the edge of the Greek world, peering into the Persian Empire and, for a time, controlled by it. His *History* covers the events of the Persian Wars (499–479 B.C.E.), the war between the alliance of Greek states and the Persian Empire. There were two attempts by Persia to colonize Greece, and both nearly succeeded. The result of the Persian War was Athenian prominence, due in large part to its successful navy. Herodotus attempts to write a universal history, that is to say, a history of many lands at once, including Greek and non-Greek lands. His book describes what was known about the tribes and cultures of India, Scythia, Greece, Egypt, and Africa. He includes information about the far-off tribes of the Hyperboreans and others who are too distant to even imagine. Although much of his history includes the compilation of myths and stories from these realms, his notes on other cultures show what was so remarkable about his own culture. He notes the ethnomusicological and linguistic differences between tribes of a particular civilization, how women are treated, and the origins of the gods of each culture. Most surprisingly, he was quite open-minded about other practices and admired greatly some cultures that no longer existed, such as that of ancient Sudan. His history, which records the Persian defeat, is not only a record of events and people, however. It also can be seen as a kind of tragedy writ large. There are lessons to learn that are similar to those in Aeschylus's *Agamemnon*. Croesus, Cyrus, Xerxes, and Darius all believed that they were great and powerful rulers, but all were crushed by their arrogance and desire to gain more than the gods had ordained for them. Herodotus's book is thus meant, particularly by the lessons it teaches as it draws to a close, to be a warning to Greek ambitions. Somewhat like the Old Testament, although less obviously so, it is a history with a moral and ethical code embedded in its pages.

The Upanishads were written between the eighth and fourth centuries B.C.E. They begin with a discussion on creation and the inquisitive nature of man and proceed to explain certain doctrines that were meant to be taught and expounded by a spiritual teacher. As part of a larger group of religious texts, the *Vedas*, they form a more practice-oriented part of religious study. In "Part 2: The Yogic Path" of the Svetasvatara Upanishad, the god Savitri inspires the mind and body to achieve harmony and focus through meditative exercises that are explained in the text. The passage looks back on tradition, asking for the hymns "of olden times" and confirming these hymns as the rock on which the practice of faith is based. The devotee is instructed to use the syllable *om* as a vehicle to ascend into a peaceful meditation. Next, breathing is regulated and health is monitored closely. The relationship between good health and a peaceful soul is very clear in this text. The body is to demand little and to get rid of little in the same manner that the soul is to be absent of desires.

Confucius (*Kong-zi* or *Kong-fu-zi*), who is sometimes called "Master" in Confucian works, lived in an era when various Chinese states and tribes warred endlessly with each other and within themselves. Confucianism, rather than being a religion, is more of a philosophical system that pervades a way of being. It was the official state religion of many Chinese dynasties and remains a prominent cultural influence throughout East Asia. Some high school students in China and Hong Kong even make a pilgrimage to his tomb before taking their college entrance examinations. There are three major components to Confucianism: being, doing, and goals or ends. This philosophical system is based on rationality rather than mystical transcendence. The main way of being involves *ren* (pronounced "rhen"), or acting humanely. This is defined by Confucius as "loving others" (*ai ren*). One of Confucius's major tenets is that one should not do to others what one does not want done to himself. Since Confucius lived during a time of changing governments, many of his teachings involve the art of rulership. He believed that it is best to rule by virtue (*de*, pronounced "duh"), not by force. His set of morals, then, instruct the individual to limit him- or herself and to view the greater good of society: He also urges us to gain profit for ourselves, which will also profit others. In modern Japan, this notion of "jiri-rita," or reciprocal benefit, is extremely prominent even in the business and political culture. In the selected passages, Confucius instructs the disciple on the hierarchy of behavior toward others: first the parents, then other elders, and so on until the rulers. This ever-widening circle of behavior helps to create an ordered state without the apparatus of religion. Each family unit is responsible for order, and each town, and so on up to the ruler, who is reciprocally responsible for all people.

Like Confucius, Epicurus (341–270 B.C.E.) did not touch on issues of the divine world, but rather tried to cultivate actions that could lead to a happier existence. The ideal state of mind for the Epicurean is *ataraxia*, or literally, "not to be shakable." The goal of the individual should be the pursuit of pleasure. However, since the desire of money, power, and sex is not pleasurable, it is best to dismiss those desires. This extends to how one eats and drinks. The Epicurean (despite the modern connotation of this word), does not eat or drink anything elaborate because she or he simply does not care about food or drink at all. The most important fear to dismiss is that of death. Since fear of death drives many men to try to acquire all they can while they are alive or to try to achieve fame, simple alleviation of this fear will cure one of much unhappiness. According to Diogenes Laertius, a historian of philosophy from the third century B.C.E., Epicurus lived simply because of the poverty of his youth and sought to find answers for the political turmoil following Alexander the Great's death. It is said that Epicurus was quite liberal, allowing women and slaves to take part in his discussions. He taught in a place called the Garden, which was maintained by a library and publishing house. In "Letter to a Friend," which is part of the writings preserved in Diogenes Laertius's biography of him, Epicurus speaks on the issue of choices between good and bad. He encourages us to be independent of such choices and thus to be free of anxiety, "escaping the bondage of opinion." His recipe for happiness begins with prudence (in Greek, *sophrosunê*). It is interesting to note that in his letter he calls for devotees to his way of life to study the precepts with a companion.

Stoicism developed as a rival school of philosophy roughly contemporary to the development of Epicureanism. It is so named because Zeno, its founder, taught in a painted archway (*stoa poikilê*). Stoicism is essentially materialist, believing the world to be made up of a substance (usually, like Heraclitus, fire), which is obliged to follow certain rules and thus is already determined. These laws, as a whole, were deemed to be "fate." They believed that even in such a world humans had free will regarding their actions and that they were morally responsible. Virtue (*aretê*) was all that was necessary for happiness, and emotions blocked the way to happiness. For the Stoics, virtue is both a moral virtue and a skill at using the world around oneself in a wise way. Reason and nature are inseparable notions they follow closely. The Stoics believe that a community of rational thinkers can converge to reach the truth. The Vulcans of the *Star Trek* series are a famous characterization of a Stoic community, wherein members always appeal to reason above emotion and are closely networked by their thoughts.

When Zeno died, Cleanthes (331–232 B.C.E.) took over the Stoic school. Cleanthes was not as important as his student, Chrysippus, but his "Hymn to Zeus" reveals some of the early philosophical trends of Stoicism, a school that was famously fragmentary. He believed that there were not moral rules to follow but rather basic principles like virtue and freedom from anxiety about pleasure. The "Hymn to Zeus" makes an allegory of Stoic ideas and the material nature of the universe, based very much on themes from Heraclitus. Marcus Aurelius (161–180 C.E.), on the other hand, was less interested in the philosophical ideas of Stoicism but rather in Stoicism as a way of life and as a moralizing tool. His writings read like sayings that are profound and beautiful, often inquiring into human psychology and the nature of things. For example, he once said, "a ball is a beautiful thing to a child," "a star never wears a veil," and "guide your life towards a single course of action."

IN THE CLASSROOM

I. LIVING ACCORDING TO PHILOSOPHY AND RELIGION

Students may want to begin by discussing the merits of each of the philosophies or religious systems presented. One topic of discussion may be to analyze how such systems arise. In particular, students might try to debate what is unique about the human condition or experience that evolves into these theories on being and the proper mode of life. Since this discussion assumes that all cultures will react similarly to the human experience, a follow-up question might involve how each philosophical system or religious doctrine is specifically adapted to the culture that adopts it. How, for example, is Confucianism particularly fit for the Chinese of the Zhou dynasty?

Many of the selections are moralizing in their tone. However, they achieve this through different means. Some speak directly as to the action to be taken, others speak of ideals, and still others present allegories and parables. Students should discuss these various techniques of the philosophical voice and how effective they are and what result they produce. Try, for example, to imagine a religious work that takes on a tone different from that native to it. For example, what would be the effect of the Upanishads written in an historical mode, like Herodotus's *Histories*? Students should discuss, with citations and examples, how these passages relate to the philosophies and religions they have been reading about throughout the first book. For example, whose voice sounds most like that of Aristotle? And whose most like that of Mencius?

Discussion

1. Why does Herodotus include the parable of Croesus and Solon in his history? What role does it play in the larger history being described? Considering that Herodotus is publishing his work at the beginning of hostilities between Athens and Sparta, what might his other purpose be in including this mark of wisdom from the Athenian philosopher?

2. One possible observation from these texts is that the Upanishads and Confucius seem to be concerned with actions that the human being should take up, whereas Marcus Aurelius and Epicurus are concerned with how people should be, exist, or conceive of themselves in the world. Is this a valid observation? What are the subtle differences between being and action?

3. The French philosopher Descartes once said, "I think, therefore I am." Is this compatible with any of the philosophers we have read in this section? What is the role of rationality in Stoicism, Epicureanism, and Confucianism versus the Upanishads and Solon's wisdom?

Groups

1. Divide students into groups and have them each introduce and represent a philosophical school and religion. After introducing the major tenets of their beliefs, each group should answer the question "What will make an individual happy?"

Writing

Ask students to write a short paper in response to one or more of the following:

1. Marcus Aurelius uses a number of allusions or metaphors to theater. What are they, and what do they mean in the context of his larger philosophical point of view?

2. Many of these philosophies and religions presented came to fruition during times of political crisis. Pick two passages, and show how they deal with issues of free choice and government. You may need to extrapolate from the philosophical tenants to answer this question. In other words, what kind of state would that philosophy or religion create?

II. CONNECTIONS: DOING AND THINKING

Authors and artists often use religion or philosophy as the wellspring of ideas for their creative works. Sometimes, these works become complicated allegories, like the "Song of Solomon" or Sartre's *The Flies*. In some cases, however, a system of thinking simply helps to reveal one of the cultural layers that forms a work of fiction, a painting, or an opera. Encourage students to draw connections between works of the literature they have read (or works of art they have seen or heard) and the concepts presented in the book. In particular, students should investigate how the cultural and educational background of an artist affects the outcome of his or her work and whether or not these are consciously a product of a philosophical or religious system or whether this happens naturally.

Discussion

1. In Herodotus's story, Solon is something like the proverbial Master in *The Analects* of Confucius. The wise man with a tale is a feature of many works of fiction as well.

Examples are Nestor in *The Iliad*, Jupiter as storyteller of the Lycaon episode in Ovid's *Metamorphoses*, and the old men who tell tales in *The Thousand and One Nights*. What is the role of such figures, and who are the figures endowed with knowledge of the mysterious universe?

2. Although the *Book of Songs (Shi jing)* come from a period before the life of Confucius, they were collected and allegorized by Confucian scholars. Reread "Tossed is that cypress boat" (p. 1579). How might a Confucian understand this poem? What does the boat signify? What about "King Wên is on high" (p. 1589)? Is it possible to see how this poem may have been attractive to scholars who followed the philosophy of Confucius?

3. Both Cleanthes's "Hymn to Zeus" and the Svetasvatara Upanishad consider the hymn and song to be an important way to contact a deity and also to dispense advice. This is also a feature of the Psalms and other texts. Why do people use song to communicate with gods as well as to serve a didactic purpose at the same time?

Groups

1. Epicurus says "plain fare yields as much pleasure as a luxurious table, provided the pain of real want is removed." This is a typical Epicurean idea that applies to all desires, not just those of good food. Lucretius, who follows the ideas of Epicurus closely, believes that love is just as dangerous a desire. The idea of physical pain associated with love or other types of desire is common. Consider, for example, Sappho's poem "He is more than a hero" (p. 796) or any number of poems by Catullus. Have each group adopt a theme of desire in the texts in the anthology (for example, from the Egyptian love poems, the *Book of Songs*, Sappho, Sophocles, or Ovid). Discuss whether or not this pain of desire actually profits us. Have each group respond to Epicurus's ideas about the pain of want from the point of view of the piece of literature students are representing.

Writing

Ask students to write a short paper in response to one or more of the following:

1. Drawing from one or more authors in the anthology who may have been influenced by Confucius or may be similar in ideology, discuss the significance of "He whose heart is in the smallest degree set upon Goodness will dislike no one."

2. Compare and contrast the heroes in *The Iliad* and *The Odyssey* with the "blessed" people Solon describes to Croesus. What does it say about the values of the Greek culture? What do they consider to be a great accomplishment?

3. In Petronius's *The Satyricon* (p. 1297), Trimalchio tries to present himself as a devotee of one of the philosophical sects in this selection. Try to guess which of the philosophies he claims to follow and whether or not he truly understands that philosophy. In what way has he potentially misinterpreted the teachings of that philosophy?

BEYOND THE CLASSROOM

RESEARCH & WRITING

1. Taking the "Choice of Achilles" (see above), write about how each philosophy or religion would respond differently to this choice. What would be their argument? How would each conclude Achilles should act?

2. Compare and contrast Epicureanism and Confucianism. In respect to the individual, they sometimes seem similar; however, they treat relations between individuals differ-

ently. What is more explicit in Confucianism? What is more explicit in Epicureanism? [Note that this same exercise may be conducted between Stoicism and Confucianism as well.]

Projects

1. Compare Cleanthes's "Hymn to Zeus" with the opening forty lines of Lucretius's *On the Nature of Things*. Lucretius makes his hymn to Venus but writes in a tone very similar to Cleanthes. Although they were from different philosophical schools, what similarities are revealed by close analysis of these two passages?

2. Research the relationship between meditation and health. Many philosophical systems, like that which we have read in the Upanishads, believe that a soul kept in good order promotes good health. What is the opinion of the medical community? Why do you suppose there may be a relationship between mind and body, and how do various religious or philosophical systems account for that relationship?

FURTHER READING

Bailey, C. *The Greek Atomists and Epicurus*. 1928.
Hartog, F. *The Mirror of Herodotus*. 1988 (English trans.).
Inwood, B. *Ethics and Human Action in Early Stoicism*. 1985.
Long, A. A. *Hellenistic Philosophy: Stoics, Epicureans, Skeptics*. 1986.
Rutherford, R. B. *The Meditations of Marcus Aurelius: A Study*. 1989.
Schofield, Malcolm, Myles Burnyeat, and Jonathan Barnes. *Doubt and Dogmatism: Studies in Hellenistic Epistemology*. 1986.
Van Zoeren, Steven. *Poetry and Personality: Reading, Exegesis, and Hermeneutics in Traditional China*. 1991.
Waters, K. H. *Herodotus on Tyrants and Despots: A Study in Objectivity*. 1971.
Zufferey, Nicolas. *To the Origins of Confucianism: The 'ru' in Pre-Qin Times and During the Early Han Dynasty*, 2003.

MEDIA RESOURCES

WEB SITES

Herodotus on the Web
www.isidore-of-seville.com/herodotus/
On this site you will find over two hundred links to resources about Herodotus and his age.

Cleanthes of Axos
theosophy.org/tlodocs/teachers/CleanthesOfAssos.htm
This page provides a very good overview of Cleanthes and his philosophy.

Epicurus and Epicurean Philosophy
www.epicurus.net/
This site introduces Epicureanism to both the serious student of philosophy and to anyone seeking useful and inspiring ideas. Epicurus helped lay the intellectual foundations for modern science and for secular individualism, with many aspects of his system still highly relevant some twenty-three centuries after they were first taught to the students of Epicurus at his school in Athens, called "the Garden." Follow the links to learn more about Epicurus and his philosophy.

The Internet Classics Archive
classics.mit.edu/Browse/
This site provides the complete e-text versions of many of the works included in "The Good Life" and often provides background information on the author of the works.

Internet Encyclopedia of Philosophy
www.utm.edu/research/iep/
This is a very useful online reference that provides in-depth information on philosophies and individual philosophers. Check here for more information on Epicurus.

The Philosopher Confucius
www.csun.edu/~hbchm009/Confucius.html
This site provides links to several sites relating to the life and works of Confucius as well as images of two Confucius temples.

GENERAL MEDIA RESOURCES

VIDEOS

Ancient China
47 min., 1999 (Films for the Humanities & Sciences)
From the creation legend of Panku to the demise of the Han Dynasty, this program traces Chinese history and explores the roots of Chinese culture. It visits the Great Wall of China, the Imperial Palace, and the Beijing Opera, whose works are an elaborate retelling of traditional folktales. The influences of Buddhism, Taoism, and ancestor worship in China are also examined, along with footage of the Buddhist caves and the Terra Cotta army.

Buddhism in China
30 min., 1983 (Insight Media)
This video explores the basic ideas of Buddhism and its influence on the character and life of the Chinese people. It surveys Buddhism from its introduction in China in the first century through the twentieth century C.E. Art, maps, animation, and live footage show the religion's historical evolution and philosophical and cultural impact.

China: Dynasties of Power
36 min., 1996 (Time-Life)
Time-Life joins Western and Chinese archaeologists to rediscover the powerful dichotomy haunting China's past. Trace the rise of China's earliest dynasty, the Shang, and witness the dawn of the Golden Age of Philosophic Enlightenment during the dynasty of the Chou. Then, watch the rise of Ch'in Shihuang Di, China's first emperor, who would raise the Great Wall through the blood and sweat of his vast slave-labor armies.

China: Heritage of the Wild Dragon
59 min., 2000 (Films for the Humanities & Sciences)
The fine loess soil of the Yellow River basin quickly established that region as the home of China's earliest recorded dynasty. This program focuses primarily on Bronze Age China and the contributions of the Yin (or Shang) dynasty, with a tangential emphasis on the reign of the Qins. Commentary by Tang Jigen, of the Chinese Academy of Social Sciences, and other experts; archival film of the excavation of Yinxu; armor and artifacts from the tomb of Qin Shihuangdi; footage of loess being used to replicate intricate Yin-era bronzes; and incredible 3-D computer animation provide penetrating insights into the history of ancient China.

The Eastern Philosophers
3 tapes, 50 min. each, 2001 (Insight Media)
Examining the central doctrines of Confucianism, Shinto, Hinduism, Judaism, and Islam, this set examines the genesis of spiritual thought. The first volume explores the dominant philosophical and spiritual ideas of the Far East, focusing on Confucius and Shinto. The second discusses the Hinduism and Buddhism of South Asia, with their focus on cycles of death and rebirth. The final volume considers the roots, rituals, and sacred texts of Judaism and the tenets and lifestyle issues of Islam.

Far East Religions
60 min., 1999 (Insight Media)
Addressing ethical and social dimensions of such religions as Confucianism, Taoism, Buddhism, and Shintoism, this video traces Eastern religion back to ancient folk practices. It considers the ethics of Confucianism, the quest for balance and harmony in Taoism, and differences between Eastern and Western spiritual perspectives.

The First Emperor of China
40 min., 1989 (Library Video Company)
This program chronicles the period of Qin Shihuang's rule. Much of the story has never been told before, and few Westerners are aware of his incredible achievements. As the vast and secret land of China opens more of its doors to Western eyes, there is a growing curiosity about the history and traditions of this nation of 1.2 billion people. *The First Emperor of China* offers viewers a unique opportunity to increase their understanding of the nature of ancient Chinese civilization and its extraordinary achievements. Narrated by Christopher Plummer.

The Great Wall
50 min., 1997 (A&E Video)
A&E examines the rule of Shih Huang Ti and the reasons behind the construction of this archaeological wonder. Leading historians discuss the reign of the first ruler of the Chin dynasty while examining the fascinating discoveries unearthed in Ti's tomb, including a life-sized army of over seven thousand statues. A remarkable portrait of a man driven by his desire for immortality and the Great Wall, which helped cement his legacy. As seen on the History Channel.

Overview of Chinese History
29 min., 1991 (Insight Media)
This video explores the central role of imperial rule in Chinese history for over five thousand years. It probes the influence of Confucius, travels to the Great Wall of China, and profiles the accomplishments of the Chin and Tang dynasties.

Religious Experience: Buddhism
60 min., 1999 (Insight Media)
This video explores the relationship among the religious impulse, the need to define meaning, and the impact of experience on spiritual understanding. It presents such fundamental Buddhist concepts as the Four Noble Truths, the Eightfold Path, egolessness, karma, *dharma*, and reincarnation.

Taoism
25 min., 1981 (Insight Media)
Set against the backdrop of contemporary China, this video illuminates the central tenets of Taoism and examines its call for a return to primitive social forms and an abandonment of conventional values. John Blofeld explains how it has influenced other Eastern religions and practices.

Taoism: A Question of Balance
52 min., 1978 (Insight Media)
Documenting the rituals of Taoism, this program from the *Long Search* series shows how religious life weaves together a Confucian respect for ancestors, the cosmic pattern of the Tao and its oracles, and a belief both in local gods who dispense justice and favors and the hungry ghosts of the dead.

Three Pillars: Confucius, Jesus, and Mohammed
53 min., 1998 (Insight Media)
This video studies the identities of the founders of three major religions — Confucianism, Christianity, and Islam. It looks at how Confucianism blended into the Chinese social and political structure; the significance of Jesus as a prophet for Muslims and as God incarnate for Christians; and the teachings of Mohammed and the Koran.

WEB SITES

Chinese Internet Resources
www.wsu.edu:8080/~dee/
Richard Hooker's page (of Washington State University) provides an excellent overview of links on ancient China.

Internet East Asian History Sourcebook
www.fordham.edu/halsall/eastasia/eastasiasbook.html
The goal of the Ancient History Sourcebook is to provide and organize texts for use in classroom situations. Links to the larger online collections are provided for those who want to explore further. It also includes links to visual and aural material, since art and archeology are far more important for the periods in question than for later history. The emphasis remains on access to primary source texts for educational purposes.

Internet Guide for China Studies
sun.sino.uni-heidelberg.de/igcs/
Edited by Hanno Lecher at the University of Heidelberg, this site offers links to all aspects of historical and contemporary China.

Book 2
The Middle Period
100 C.E.–1450

THE NEAR EAST:
CHRISTIANITY AND ISLAM

The New Testament (p. 23)

WWW   For quizzes on the New Testament, see *World Literature Online*
       at bedfordstmartins.com/worldlit.

There is perhaps no single text more important to the understanding of the medieval period and its literature than the Bible, in particular the New Testament. This is not only because of the pervasive religious mindset of the time and the formation of the early church but also because the Bible as a work of literature had a profound influence on nearly all the medieval authors of Britain, Europe, and the Near and Middle East. Writers from the *Beowulf* poet to Dante to Ibn Ishaq alluded to, interacted with, and responded to the Bible.

While its influence on the Middle Period cannot be overstated, the New Testament is also a great work of literature in its own right. It not only incorporates many of the themes and narrative elements of the pagan literature that came before it but also deliberately communicates in language that renders its contents subject to discussion and interpretation. Like the great works of Greek philosophy, the New Testament serves as a catalyst for reflection and self-examination. The language of the New Testament is also very sophisticated, incorporating both poetry and prose and employing literary techniques like symbolism, metaphor, and synecdoche. The King James Version, which is included alongside its American Version counterpart in several places for the purposes of comparison, is often praised for its authentic rendering of the language of the New Testament, even if it is also criticized for sacrificing a literal translation in favor of an aesthetically pleasing one.

The New Testament can be divided roughly into five unequal but thematically coherent sections. The first part contains the four gospels of Matthew, Mark, Luke, and John. These gospels detail the life of Jesus from Mary's pregnancy to Jesus' death and resurrection. The second part is the Book of the Acts of the Apostles. Acts, as it is usually called, is a record of the early spread of Christianity and the formation of the church. Luke is typically credited as the author. The epistles of St. Paul make up the third section. The word "epistle" is Greek for "letter," and in fact these books are a record of the letters that St. Paul writes to various communities such as the Romans and the Corinthians. These letters, for the most part, detail Christian doctrine and explain how to lead a Christian life. The fourth part contains epistles on the subject of Christian doctrine written by authors other than Paul. Finally, the last section is the Revelation of St. John. This vision, given to him on the isle of Patmos, depicted the events that would occur at the end of the world.

TEXT & CONTEXT

FOURFOLD EXEGESIS

In his work, *De Utilitate Credendi* (On the Usefulness of Believing), St. Augustine differentiates four levels of meaning in scripture. These levels — the literal, allegorical (or typological), moral (or tropological), and anagogical — constitute a semiotic theory that is still used to understand sacred texts today. According to this theory, the literal sense of a New Testament passage speaks about its events as historical facts, and the allegorical sense understands those events as the fulfillment of prophecy or completion of events in the Hebrew

Scriptures. The moral sense of a passage relates to the ethical obligations of the believers, while the anagogical sense connects past biblical events to the future, especially to what will occur at the end of time or in eternity. Although not every scriptural passage can be interpreted by means of all four of these senses, medieval scholars considered the fourfold exegesis an important interpretive tool. In medieval schools, a Latin verse was often employed as a mnemonic device to help students remember these levels of meaning: "The literal teaches history, the allegorical what you should believe, the moral what you should do, the anagogical where you are going" (*lettera gesta docet, / quid credas allegoria, / moralia quid agas, / quo tendas, anagogia*).

BIBLICAL GREEK

Classical Greek included a variety of dialects such as Ionic (the language of Homer) and Attic (the language of Plato and most of the ancient Greek playwrights). The language of the New Testament, sometimes called "biblical" or "koine" (common) Greek, evolved as a grammatically and structurally simpler form of these classical forms. The conquests of Alexander the Great in the fourth century B.C.E. helped spread Greek throughout the Mediterranean region. While there is some scholarly debate over the language in which the New Testament might have originally been recorded, the oldest extant copies of the text are primarily written in Greek, and there is no good evidence for the existence of earlier versions in Hebrew or Aramaic. It is likely that the historical Jesus and his disciples spoke Greek as a second language. As it was the common language of commerce and communication between peoples of different countries in the Near East, it makes sense that Jewish New Testament authors chose it to communicate their message to the wider community in which they lived. The most ancient manuscripts of the Greek New Testament, like older works in Ionic and Attic Greek lack punctuation, spaces between words, and chapter divisions.

IN THE CLASSROOM

I. THE NEW TESTAMENT AS LITERATURE

The New Testament's thematic and stylistic resemblance to the literature that preceded it and its influence on the works that followed place it in the center of the Western cannon. Moreover, its language, while not as poetic as that of the Hebrew Scriptures, is considered to be some of the most compelling in all of literature.

Discussion

1. Like many great literary works, the New Testament was meant to be both interpreted and read. It makes use of literary forms like narrative and poetry that students will quickly recognize. However, remember to point out to them and discuss the more specific forms like gospel, parable, and epistle. What are the major differences between each form? Why are these devices used in the places they occur? Does the form of the New Testament suit its content?

2. Verses 3 to 10 of chapter 5 of the gospel of Matthew are known as the "beatitudes," or blessings. Note the parallelism of the language, the repetition of the phrase "blessed are," in both the American and King James versions. What purpose does this poetic device serve? Is the repetition employed for emphasis, or is it meant to serve a meditative purpose like a chant?

3. Discuss some of the reasons that the New Testament is studied as literature, particularly in the context of the Middle Ages. Other than spiritual enlightenment, why are people interested in the text?

Connections

1. One of the New Testament's most powerful rhetorical devices is its claim to an intimate connection with the Hebrew Scriptures. Jesus himself notes this relationship on several occasions. In the Sermon on the Mount, for instance, he speaks of himself as a "fulfillment" of Hebrew Scripture prophecy, and, after his resurrection, he tells his awed disciples, "This is what I told you when I was still with you — that everything that is written about me in the Law of Moses and the Prophets and the Psalms must come true." Ask students to find other evidence that the New Testament is a continuation of the Hebrew Scriptures. Students may also want to consider the form and style of the New Testament, which is very distinct from its predecessor. How do the gospels differ from the prophetic works of the Hebrew Scriptures? Does the writing style of the New Testament help effectively convey its message to the Jewish population? What about to other peoples?

2. The active role that Jesus plays in the New Testament seems to contrast with the characterization of God in the Hebrew Scriptures. Although God appears in many of the books as a voice and in guises, his dealings with the people of Israel is very impersonal and distant, while Jesus' connection to his followers and disciples seems more like the relationship of the Greek gods to the people. Compare descriptions of Jesus with those of God from the Hebrew Scriptures and the Greek gods from *The Odyssey* and *The Iliad* (all in Book 1). How are the deities characterized? Are some more or less human than others?

Groups

1. Ask students to closely examine both the American Version and the King James Version of 1 Corinthians 13. The two versions are quite different. For example, the word that the American Version translates as "love" is rendered as "charity" in the King James. Have students discuss these differences and whether they are central to developing an understanding of the text. Do we still think of "love" and "charity" as synonymous? If not, what does the word "love" evoke today that the word "charity" does not? Point out that the opening line of the American Version of this chapter is "I will show you a far better way," which is absent in the King James Version. An inquiry into the reasons for this disparity in the two translations would make for a very interesting class discussion.

Writing

Ask students to write a short paper in response to one or more of the following:

1. The word "gospel" is often traced to a pair of Old English words that mean "god story" and "good news," respectively. With these definitions in mind, write a short description of the nature of a gospel by drawing on your experience with the texts.

2. In the Gospels, Jesus often speaks in terms of overarching issues rather than details. Write a short paper discussing the language that Jesus uses to speak to his disciples and the people both in the Sermon on the Mount and in the parables. You may wish to compare these with the language of Paul's epistle to the Corinthians or with Exodus 19:1–20 and 21 and Deuteronomy 6 and 7 from the Hebrew Scriptures. How do the style, purpose, and audience of these pieces differ from Jesus' as related by Matthew?

3. Write a short paper discussing Jesus' use of metaphor in one or more of the parables. How does he make use of language and situations that his listeners will understand in order to illustrate concepts that are difficult to grasp?

II. HISTORY IN THE NEW TESTAMENT

Like the Hebrew Scriptures, the New Testament contains an historical narrative as well as teachings or guidelines for conduct. In the Hebrew Scriptures, the narrative details such events as the lives of prophets and the exodus of the Jewish people out of Egypt, while the teachings include the Jewish dietary laws and other commandments handed down directly from God to the people through the prophets. In contrast, the narrative portion of the New Testament deals almost exclusively with the birth, life, and death of Jesus, while its teachings are split between the sermons and parables of Jesus himself and the interpretations of Jesus' teachings by his apostles.

Discussion

1. The New Testament Gospels reveal relatively little about Jesus' childhood. However, the incident in Jerusalem when he is twelve is a telling one. What are the reasons that Jesus gives for departing from his parents' company without their knowledge? What does Jesus mean when he explains that Joseph and Mary should have known that they would find him at the house of his Father? Why do they fail to understand him?

2. In Matthew 13, Jesus divides the people who hear his message into two groups — those who "are permitted to know the secrets of the Kingdom of Heaven" and those who "are not." He then goes on to divide them further in the parable of the sower. As a class, identify these groups and the ramifications for each group. What might it mean to be "good ground" for the seed of Jesus' teaching to be sown in? Is this an innate quality, a marker of grace as Augustine understands the word, or something that can be learned? Is it possible to migrate from one group to another?

3. The parable of the talents and the parable of the prodigal son both seem problematic at first. Discuss why the man who does not risk his master's money or the child who never transgresses against his father isn't favored in these stories. However, it is important to realize that part of the point of both parables is to emphasize the active part that Christians are expected to play in their religion. In each case, the onus is on the believer (represented by the man who wisely invests his master's money and the son who realizes his error and returns to his father) to take control of his or her own actions. How does this compare with the role that is given to believers in the Hebrew Scriptures or in pagan texts like *The Odyssey*?

4. In 1 Corinthians, St. Paul says that he would prefer that every man remain unmarried, but that marriage serves its purpose as well, and there is no sin in it. What is the purpose of marriage as St. Paul sees it? Under what circumstances does he believe that men should marry or stay single? How do Paul's views of marriage compare with those that Jesus expresses in the Sermon on the Mount?

Connections

1. The early life of Jesus is treated in the gospel of Luke much as Ibn Ishaq treats the birth and adolescence of the prophet in *The Life of Muhammad* (p. 134). Specifically, neither of these texts tries to exhibit the characteristics of a bildungsroman — a novel dealing with the moral, psychological, and intellectual development of a character from youth to adulthood. Compare these two accounts of the youth of holy men. Is the lack of detail concerning their youth and upbringing a problematic omission? Or do Luke and Ibn Ishaq gloss over these portions of the lives of Jesus and Muhammad in order to place emphasis elsewhere?

2. Many of Jesus' teachings are embedded in parables, and, although he exhorts his followers to "listen closely" to them, their meanings are not always readily apparent to all. Compare the way that Jesus teaches, through parable, with the teaching styles in *The Apology* (Book 1) and the Qur'an (Koran) (p. 97). How do Socrates and Muhammad teach? Are their audiences similar to those of Jesus? Which of the three styles do students find most accessible or convincing? Think about each as a historical reaction to the one before it. Can students articulate why each man might have chosen to teach in the style he employs?

Groups

1. Ask groups of students to choose another medieval literary work that makes use of the New Testament in some way. You might provide them with a list of works that make for easy comparison, or allow them to choose at will. A choice of authors might include Margery Kempe, Dante, Augustine, Langland, or the Qur'an. Ask these groups to identify and critically examine references or allusions to the New Testament that are present in these works. How is the author using the New Testament? Is his use satirical or ironic? Groups should be prepared to present an in-class discussion or mini-lecture on their findings. Alternatively, students might conduct the same examination on a work that seems to have influenced the New Testament. If this option is given, presentations should include an argument for their assertions, as New Testament references are rarely obvious and uncontested.

Writing

Ask students to write a short paper in response to one or more of the following:

1. On many occasions, Jesus faces people who do not understand or believe him. At times, even his mother and disciples suffer from doubt and confusion. Write about disbelief and/or lack of understanding in the gospel of Luke. You may want to trace the types of disbelief in the gospel, explain Jesus' responses to those who doubt him, or focus on one particular scene, for instance when he meets his disciples after his resurrection.

2. In Matthew 13, Jesus' disciples ask him why he teaches the people in "figures" or parables. Explain Jesus' reply to this question, using examples from chapter 13 as well as specific illustrations from one or more of the parables excerpted from Matthew or Luke.

BEYOND THE CLASSROOM

RESEARCH & WRITING

1. As the books of Matthew, Mark, Luke, and John deal generally with the same events, and in many cases relate identical stories from different points of view, it is possible to undertake a more critical comparison between a few or all of the four gospels. Provide students with corresponding passages from two or more of the gospels (or ask them to seek out these parallel passages on their own), and ask them to contrast the passages. Students may want to address the language of each piece or evaluate the central point the authors are trying to get across. Are the disciples simply reporting historical facts as they understand them, or are there perceivable attempts to interpret the events as well?

2. Alternatively, you might ask students to choose a passage from one gospel and compare several disparate translations of the passage. Is it possible that different translations lead to radically different interpretations of the message that is being conveyed?

3. Although it seems to refer to the afterlife, Jesus does not provide a specific interpretation for his assertion in Matthew 25 that "the man who has will have more given him, and will be plentifully supplied, and from the man who has nothing even what he has will be taken away." A similar, but far more specific passage occurs in "Sura 56: That Which is Coming" of the Qur'an (p. 97). Ask students to make an argument for or against the idea that the passage in the Qur'an can be read as an explanation of or perhaps a reaction to Jesus' statement. In addition to consulting scholarly works and other passages from the New Testament and the Qur'an, students may want to consider whether the spirit of Sura 56 accords with the general feeling of the New Testament teachings.

Project

1. The New Testament, particularly the story of Christ's crucifixion and resurrection — known as the "passion" — has inspired many composers from the medieval age to the modern. The Internet is a great resource for the study of these works. Web sites like Princeton's Gregorian Chant Home Page (www.music.princeton.edu/chant_html/) contain sound samples and scholarly treatments of the medium. Ask students to listen to medieval chants and other music that deals either explicitly with the New Testament or with the themes presented in the text. Knowledge of traditional music theory is not necessary, and students might also find it helpful to reference translations of the lyrics of some of these pieces. What does the music add to these stories or themes? Are the composers trying to interpret the events of the New Testament through their music? Students might also be interested in more modern classical works like J. S. Bach's *St. Matthew's Passion*.

FURTHER READING

Conzelmann, H., and A. Lindemann. *Interpreting the New Testament: An Introduction to the Principles and Methods of N. T. Exegesis*. 1988.
Flynn, William T. *Medieval Music as Medieval Exegesis*. 1999.
Gameson, Richard, and Henrietta Leyser. *Belief and Culture in the Middle Ages: Studies Presented to Henry Mayr-Harting*. 2001.
Kendall, Calvin B. *The Allegory of the Church: Romanesque Portals and their Verse Inscriptions*. 1998.
McDonald, Lee. *The Formation of the Christian Biblical Canon*. 1988.
Morey, James H. *Book and Verse: A Guide to Middle English Biblical Literature*. 2002.
Vanderbilt Divinity Library. New Testament Bibliography. 2002. <http://divinity.library.vanderbilt.edu/lib/bibliographies/newtestamentfall2002.pdf>
Wailes, Stephen L. "Why Did Jesus Use Parables? The Medieval Discussion." *Medievalia et Humanistica: Studies in Medieval and Renaissance Culture* 13 (1985): 43–64.

MEDIA RESOURCES

VIDEO

The New Testament
25 min., 1993 (Insight Media)
This program explores the major stories of the New Testament. It discusses the role of the apostles, the similarities and differences among the various accounts of the life of Jesus, the importance of the Sermon on the Mount, the pivotal events of Jesus' life, and the significance of the Book of Revelations.

Pillars of Faith
3 video set, 48 min. each, 1998 (A&E Video)
Nothing could deflect them from their chosen faith — not the hangman's rope, the executioner's axe, or the flames of burning fire. For two thousand years, history has recorded dramatic and moving accounts of Christ's followers braving incredible dangers to spread the word. This chilling and emotional video collection tells the stories of those who have become martyrs as well as the tales of men who bore witness to Christ's life and brought His message to new lands. The three videos in this set are *Celtic Saints* — in the earliest days of Christianity in Britain, the Celtic way of life had a strong influence in shaping the newly arrived religion; *New Testament Witnesses* — those who witnessed the events of Christ's life are the principal source of our knowledge of the savior; *Martyrs to Christianity* — no price was too high for them to pay, and in doing so, they strengthened the faith.

The Andalusian Epic: Islamic Spain
27 min., 1999 (Films for the Humanities & Sciences)
This program addresses the expansion of the Arab empire into Spain, where Muslims ruled with tolerance for more than seven centuries. The introduction and consolidation of Islamic power in Spain, the creation of the Umayyad emirate by the sole survivor of the Umayyad dynasty, the rise of Cordoba as a cultural rival of Abbasid Baghdad, and the gradual ebb of Arab rule on the Iberian Peninsula are all discussed. Special attention is given to the prosperous reign of Abdel Rahman III and the flowering of a Muslim culture that respectfully welcomed the contributions of Christians and Jews alike. (Portions are in French with English subtitles.)

The Birth of the Middle Ages
43 min., 1989 (Films for the Humanities & Sciences)
This program provides an introduction to medieval Europe by showing surviving traces to provide a feel of medieval style and practice, and by tracing the roots of the fall of civilization and the onset of darkness. Much that is medieval survives, sometimes in unlikely places: in a feudal community in sub-Saharan Africa, where an absolute ruler holds court surrounded by ministers, courtiers, and hangers-on, with paladins in mail and mercenaries who, according to local tradition, are descendants of the crusaders; and in numerous folk festivals held in modern Italy, which reenact the futile battles against the invading nomadic hordes. The program traces the fall of Rome and the development of fortified monasteries and their gradual transformation into centers of prayer, work, and the study of ancient learning. With the acceptance of Eastern peoples into the church of Rome, Europe achieved its frontiers.

Byzantium: From Splendor to Ruin
43 min., 1989 (Films for the Humanities & Sciences)
This program covers the founding of Constantinople as a second Rome, its flowering when the Roman Empire in the West was shattered, its gradual decline under the impact of Normans, Turks, Venetians, and the Crusades, and, finally, its fall in 1453. The program describes the history, art, and religious significance of Byzantium, its attempts to restore the Roman Empire, its influence in the West, and its heritage.

Christianity: The First Thousand Years
200 min., 2000 (A&E Video)
This four-volume set traces the rise of one of the world's great religions. Scholars explore the intertwined fates of the Roman Empire and the faith it first persecuted, then adopted. Theologians reveal how the New Testament was shaped and how pagan festivals were transformed into Christian holidays. Examine modern discoveries that shed new light on the dawn of Christianity. Drawing on ancient texts, the Scriptures, and visits to sites like

Istanbul's magnificent Hagia Sophia, this is a spellbinding journey through the early years of the Christian faith.

Christianity: The Second Thousand Years
200 min., 2000 (Insight Media)
This four-volume set documents the second millennium of Christian history. It begins with Christianity in the Middle Ages, exploring the Crusades and the Inquisition. It then examines the turbulence of the Protestant Reformation and the long struggle for dominance between church and state that sparked centuries of religious wars. The program ends with a look at the challenges posed to contemporary Christianity by science and modernity.

Crescent and Cross: Rise of Islam and Age of Crusades
59 min., 1998 (Insight Media)
Considering the Crusades as a response to the rapid rise of Islam, this video looks at various orders of Christian monks and their role in the preservation of religious, artistic, and cultural aspects of civilization. It addresses the issue of religious intolerance, focusing on the Inquisition.

Crusades
200 min., 1995 (Insight Media)
Filmed on location in Europe and the Middle East, this series explores the history and legacy of the Crusades. It discusses the reasons for the Crusades, the creation of a mythology of knights and chivalry, and the legacy of distrust between East and West.

The Crusades
23 min., 1989 (Insight Media)
Looking closely at the three major Crusades, this program examines the political and military divisions, economic incentives, and military pressures that gave rise to them. The video traces the path of the Crusaders to the Holy Land and considers the effects of the holy wars and the influence of the returning Crusaders on the developing culture of Western Europe.

The Eastern Philosophers
50 min. each, 2001 (Insight Media)
Examining the central doctrines of Confucianism, Shinto, Hinduism, Judaism, and Islam, this set examines the genesis of spiritual thought. The first volume explores the dominant philosophical and spiritual ideas of the Far East, focusing on Confucius and Shinto. The second discusses the Hinduism and Buddhism of South Asia, with their focus on cycles of death and rebirth. The final volume considers the roots, rituals, and sacred texts of Judaism and the tenets and lifestyle issues of Islam.

Faith and Feudalism: The Early Middle Ages
23 min., 1999 (Insight Media)
Featuring art reproductions, maps, interviews, and historical reenactments, this program recounts the rise of feudalism in Europe during the decline of Rome. It shows how religions such as Christianity in Europe or Buddhism in China were able to maintain the thread of culture in feudal periods. It also illustrates how religious writings gave people hope. Explores the songs, poems, plays, histories, and inspirations of the time, including *Beowulf* and Gildas's history of the Celts.

Great Religions of the World
33 min., 1995 (Insight Media)
This video explores the major beliefs, origins, and histories of Buddhism, Christianity, Judaism, Hinduism, Islam, and Taoism. It differentiates between ethnic and universalizing

religions, discussing how each of the universalizing religions developed from an ethnic base and expanded past national boundaries.

The Inquisition
DVD, 100 min., 1994 (A&E)
Recently opened Vatican archives bring to light compelling new historical information about the Inquisition and its brutal tactics.

Medieval Christian Europe
25 min., 2002 (Insight Media)
This program traces medieval Christianity's evolution into the Renaissance. It examines the influence of the scholarly and monastic traditions of St. Patrick, St. Benedict, Charlemagne, Hildegard of Bingen, and St. Francis of Assisi.

The Middle Ages
25 min., 1996 (Films for the Humanities & Sciences)
This program traces the evolution of Europe during the Middle Ages from a group of loosely tied kingdoms to a prosperous community of nations. Topics include the role of the church, development of the feudal system, the rise of the nobility, the Crusades, formation of the German Hanseatic League, the effects of the Plague, the growth of trade guilds, the discovery of printing, the urbanization of the peasantry, and the rise of science.

The Middle Ages
30 min., 1997 (Annenberg/CPB Video)
Amid invasion and civil disorder, a military aristocracy dominated the kingdoms of Europe.

The Middle Ages
34 min., 1992 (Insight Media)
This program explores the important figures and events of the Middle Ages through artwork and dramatic narration. It considers the influence of classical civilization on early Christianity and art, explores the so-called Dark Ages, discusses the Crusades, and examines the Gothic style of architecture.

Three Pillars: Confucius, Jesus, and Mohammed
53 min., 1998 (Insight Media)
This video studies the identities of the founders of three major religions — Confucianism, Christianity, and Islam. It looks at how Confucianism blended into the Chinese social and political structure; the significance of Jesus as a prophet for Muslims and as God incarnate for Christians; and the teachings of Mohammed and the Qur'an.

The World's Philosophies
60 min., 1994 (Insight Media)
In this video, Huston Smith defines three basic types of human relationships — with nature, with other people, and with one's self — and explains how these relationships correspond to the philosophical traditions of the West, of China, and of India.

WEB SITES

Bible/New Testament/Early Christianity Resources
www.artsci.wustl.edu/~cwconrad/nt.html
Created at Washington University in St. Louis, this site provides dozens of links to scholarly sites on Old and New Testament sources.

The New Testament Gateway
www.ntgateway.com/
Dr. Mark Goodacre of the University of Birmingham's site on the New Testament. This award-winning site features annotated links on everything from the Greek New Testament to Jesus in Film. Very thorough and user-friendly.

New Testament Resources
faculty.smu.edu/dbinder/resources.html
Dr. Donald B. Binder's (Southern Methodist University) excellent site on the New Testament. This index is designed to allow fast and accurate navigation to authoritative and precise information on New Testament Web sites.

AUDIO

A Poet's Bible
tape or CD, 3 hrs., 1991 (Audio Literature)
Rediscover the voices of the original text of the Bible in this fresh retelling of its most powerful stories. The author introduces the listener to many new authors, reveals the imaginative power of the original verse, and heralds a new era in biblical scholarship. With vivid, accessible language and playful metaphor, *A Poet's Bible* revitalizes the living poetry at the core of biblical verse and allows the secular listener to grasp this great classic in modern terms.

The Essential King James Bible
4 tapes, 6 hrs. (AudioBooksToday.com)
Beginning with the story of creation, and culminating with an excerpt from Revelations, this anthology is a beautifully narrated treasure. Half of the stories are from the Old Testament, half from the New. The brilliant, sensitive readings are accessible to listeners of all ages. Each performer reads individual stories in their entirety.

Living Biographies of Religious Leaders
8 tapes, 11:25 hrs. (Blackstone Audiobooks)
This program presents the lives of twenty great founders and leading advocates of the world's foremost religions. Here are the historical facts and legends associated with these forceful personalities who have inspired and influenced humankind through the centuries. Presented are Jesus Christ, Moses, Isaiah, Zoroaster, Buddha, Confucius, John the Baptist, Paul, Muhammad, Francis of Assisi, John Huss, Luther, Loyola, Calvin, George Fox, Swedenborg, Wesley, Brigham Young, Mary Baker Eddy, and Gandhi.

The New Testament
tapes or CDs, 21:75 hrs., 2000 (Blackstone Audiobooks)
Read by George W. Sarris, this program provides a full reading of the King James version of the Bible.

The New Testament
6 tapes or 6 CDs, 7:39 hrs. (Naxos Audio)
The New Testament tells the extraordinary and moving story of the life of Christ and the founding of his church. This generous selection from the texts which lie at the root of two thousand years of European civilization ranges between the powerful sincerity of the Evangelists and the ecstatic vision of John's New Jerusalem.

ST. AUGUSTINE, *The Confessions* (p. 70)

www   For a quiz on *The Confessions,* see *World Literature Online*
at bedfordstmartins.com/worldlit.

Tagaste, Africa, had been part of the Roman Empire for nearly five hundred years by the time of Augustine of Hippo's birth. However, Roman Africa was not foremost in the minds of the empire's leaders. A small Roman military force was kept in this remote section of the empire, but only African-born emperors spent any significant time there.

In Augustine's time, Christianity was slowly becoming the dominant religion in Roman Africa, even though the religion opposed the pagan traditions practiced by its parent — Rome. St. Augustine played a central role in the developing church. As Bishop of Hippo, Augustine made it his mission to help Christians understand more fully what Christianity entailed, to affect the Christianization of Roman culture, and to debate the subtleties of faith, grace, and salvation. In his lifetime, Augustine was a prolific writer on theological issues, devoting many pages to putting down church heresies and assisting in the canonization of the books of the New Testament.

But St. Augustine was a great deal more than an influential father of the early church. His life, from a modern perspective, served as a bridge between the civilizations of pagan ancient Rome and the Christian Middle Ages. Prior to his conversion, Augustine was a student and teacher of classical rhetoric who harbored political ambitions. Although his mother was a Christian, Augustine was not a believer early in life, preferring the writings of Cicero to the Bible, and Manichaeanism to Christianity. Yet, as is apparent in *The Confessions,* Augustine became disillusioned with the failure of academics and Manichaeanism to provide answers to some of the greater spiritual questions that haunted him. *The Confessions,* written by Augustine late in his life, is not only as a chronicle of his life and conversion but also presents some of the more thoughtful moral and philosophical problems of Augustine's age and our own.

The Confessions is a deeply personal and psychological work. Augustine's discussion of childhood at the opening of the work is easily comparable with much later thinkers like Sigmund Freud. Augustine's analysis, however, is not a general or impersonal one. He delves deeply into his own psyche in order to wrestle with the most significant aspects of religion and human behavior. The famous episode of Augustine and the pear in Book II, Chapter 4, is an example. When Augustine steals the fruit from his neighbor's tree, he confesses that he did not want to eat the pears at all, admitting "I sought nothing from the shameful deed but the shame itself." He presents what seems to be a small transgression, the stealing of a few pears from a neighbor's tree, as one of the greatest infractions imaginable. His distress over having stolen the pears just to steal speaks not only to the question of the Christian notion of sin but also to a more psychological concern.

The source of Augustine's shame lies not in the stealing of the pears themselves, but in the intentions behind the theft. Clearly, Augustine believes that his fault would have been less if he had stolen the pear because he had been "driven to it by any need." Although eight hundred years earlier Socrates asserted that no man deliberately chooses the bad, Augustine is tormented by this particular act because he knew the difference between right and wrong, and deliberately chose the wrong precisely because it was wrong. It will be helpful to have students compare Augustine's self-examination with that of the Underground Man in Dostoevsky's *Notes from Underground* (Book 5). Like Augustine, the Underground Man chooses wrong actions on purpose, but his reasons for choosing and reaction to the choices he makes are quite different.

TEXT & CONTEXT

ROMAN NAMES

Aristocratic Roman citizens typically had three names, a *praenomen*, a *nomen*, and a *cognomen*. For instance, the full name of Cicero, who Augustine mentions in Book III, Chapter 4, is Marcus Tullius Cicero. The *praenomen*, or forename, was a personal name that would have been given to a child at a naming ceremony. It was common for a family to use the same *praenomina* over and over again, and a first-born son often had the same *praenomen* as his father. Typically, only family members and close friends would use this name, much in the same way that we might use a nickname today. Both the *nomen* and *cognomen* were hereditary and derived from the family into which the child was born. Men of lower classes, like Augustine (whose full name is Aurelius Augustinus), often had only the first two. An additional *cognomen* like Magnus (the great) or Felix (the lucky) could be officially awarded to a man as a sort of honorific but could not be handed down to the man's children. A woman's name, on the other hand, would consist of the feminine form of her father's *nomen*, the possessive of his *cognomen*. If a family had more than one daughter, a modifier like "minor" (the younger) or *prima, secunda, tertia* (the first, the second, the third) was added to distinguish them. So, the third daughter of Cicero might be known as Tullia Ciceronis Tertia.

DONATIST AND PELAGIAST CONTROVERSIES

In the fourth century, a group known as Donatists split from the Catholic Church of North Africa. The Donatists accused Felix, bishop of Aptunga, of handing over sacred scriptures to be burned during Diocletian's persecution of the Christians in the early third century. When Felix later consecrated Caecilian as bishop of Carthage, the Donatists objected. They believed that the validity of any sacrament is dependent on the moral standing and holiness of the priest who administers it, and therefore considered Caecilian's consecration invalid. Donatists held that they, rather than the Catholics, were the true church. By the time of Augustine's birth, Donatists outnumbered orthodox Christians in Africa. Although the state repeatedly condemned their claims to authority and practices, it was the writings and teachings of Augustine that ultimately helped cause the demise of Donatism. The ideas of Pelagias, on the other hand, were a direct reaction to St. Augustine's teachings about divine grace and salvation, which he saw as being cruel and overly deterministic. As Pelagias understood it, Augustine taught that people are basically sinful and that God only saves certain people. Pelagias rebelled against the implication that those who are not chosen have no hope of achieving salvation. Pelagians denied the Augustinian idea of original sin and believed in the fundamental goodness and free will of man. While Pelagianism and semi-Pelagianism disappeared by the end of the sixth century, theological debates over questions of grace, free will, and predestination remain to this day.

IN THE CLASSROOM

I. AUGUSTINE'S LIFE AS EXEMPLAR

Augustine uses his own life as an *exemplum*, or story told to illustrate moral points. He intersperses the biographical story of his own life with specific moments that relate to his conversion to and life as a Christian as well as including minitreatises on various topics in theology.

Discussion

1. In reference to his infancy and early childhood, Augustine asks, "What matters that now to me of which I recall no trace?" Yet it is evident that something here does matter to Augustine because he spends the opening chapters of The Confessions discussing this

very thing in detail. Ask students to consider Augustine's purposes. What does he want his readers to take away from his discourses on infancy and childhood? Keep in mind Augustine's notion of original sin. There is a clear division between those behaviors that Augustine attributes to nature and those he credits to the grace of God. Can your students elucidate this division?

2. It is tempting to believe that Augustine's conversion happens in Book VIII, Chapter 12, when a voice exhorts him to "take up and read." However, a closer look will reveal that Augustine's conversion is a process rather than a quick flash of inspiration. According to his account, Augustine goes through stages of disbelief, confusion, and outright defiance of Christian teachings as he searches for meaning in the universe. Trace this process with your students, and discuss how Augustine's state of mind changes and develops throughout *The Confessions*.

Connections

1. In Book VI, Chapter 7, Augustine asserts that the "authority" of the sacred texts of Christianity is a matter of belief rather than reason. Students may wish to compare this account of faith with that in the New Testament (p. 23), or to view Augustine's logic about the authority of scripture in light of beliefs about the Qur'an (p. 97). It is interesting to note that prior to the fifth century, there was some debate over which books rightly belonged in the New Testament. Augustine played a significant role in the canonization of the work as we know it today.

2. Augustine speaks to his God in a way that indicates an intimate and personal relationship between the two. Although God does not speak directly, Augustine clearly believes that God listens and is concerned with his life. How does this relationship differ from the one between Muhammad and his God in the Qur'an (p. 97) or the relationships between the gods and the mortals in *The Iliad* and *The Odyssey* (Book 1)? Are there any similar traits? What can we tell about these various gods from the authors who speak to and about them?

Writing

Ask students to write a short paper in response to one or more of the following:

1. The importance of Augustine's first Christian influence, his mother Monica, is apparent from early on in the narrative. He is always conscious of the effect that her constant and sustained prayers for him have had on his life. Read the excerpts pertaining to Augustine's mother, paying particular attention to Book VI, Chapters 1 and 2, and answer one of the following questions. What role does Augustine's mother play in his young life? What does Augustine admire about Monica's actions?

2. In the *Meno*, Plato argues that all men desire the good and that no men desire evil. He maintains that when it seems that some men desire evil, this is because that they have mistaken that evil for a good in its own right. Augustine discusses this same phenomenon in Book II, Chapters 4 to 6. Write a paper that argues whether Augustine's concepts of evil and sin accord with those of Plato.

II. Influences on Augustine's Spiritual Development

In part because his mother felt that it would help him become a better Christian, Augustine received a traditional classical education. At this time, classical education would have included courses in the Greek and Latin languages and especially in texts by the Latin authors that influenced Augustine later in his life, like Virgil and Cicero. Despite his rejection of pagan thought, these authors continue to shape his verbal style as well as his thinking.

Discussion

1. Augustine admits that when he first reads the Bible, he find it "unworthy of comparison with the nobility of Cicero's writings" (Book 1). The particular work Augustine mentions, the *Hortensus*, is not extant. However, it should be fairly easy to find a few passages of Cicero to share with students if you wish. Discuss the techniques of rhetoric and oratory. It will be useful to notice that Augustine employs a sort of classical rhetoric himself, particularly in the less autobiographical passages such as "Why Men Sin." How persuasive and convincing is he?

2. Unlike Margery Kempe, who talks to an audience of her peers, Augustine talks directly to God. Ask students to consider what literary role God plays in the narrative. Is he a "character" in Augustine's story? a dialectic interlocutor like the men with whom Socrates talks? a member of Augustine's audience?

Connections

1. In *The Confessions*, Augustine looks critically at the actions of his youth and young adulthood. He evaluates these actions in light of his newer Christian beliefs and confesses his misdeeds to God. In the same way, Plato evaluates the actions that lead to his incarceration in his *Apology* (Book 1). While Plato insists that he should bear the consequences of his actions, unlike Augustine, he is not repentant. Have students compare these two pieces with an eye both to the differing moralities involved and to the nature of the personal evaluation in which each man engages.

2. In Book III, Chapter 2, Augustine details both his early love of the theater and offers a sort of psychological critique of the part of human nature that enjoys watching tragedy. After reading Aristotle's treatment of tragic theatre in *On Tragedy* (Book 1), ask students to compare the reasons Augustine gives for his delight with what Aristotle believes are the characteristics of good tragedy. Students might also wish to read or reread tragedies like *Oedipus Rex* or *Medea* (Book 1) with Augustine and Aristotle's views of tragedy in mind.

Groups

1. Despite the exemplary nature of Augustine's education and the fact that he himself taught, he is deeply critical of traditional classical education. With specific examples from the text and from your discussion as evidence, ask student groups to attempt to detail the sort of educational system that Augustine might condone.

Writing

Ask students to write a short paper in response to one or more of the following:

1. Augustine rejects many of the consequences of his classical education and seems at times to regret having studied the pagan authors, yet he still makes liberal use of them in the course of his narrative. Explore how one or more of these pagan authors (e.g., Cicero, Virgil, Plato, Aristotle, or Homer) has influenced Augustine's writing and thought. Possible questions to address might include: How does Augustine use essentially pagan authors to illustrate his Christian purpose? Can this be seen as doing a disservice to the classical authors? Does Augustine's education serve to strengthen or weaken his arguments?

2. Among Augustine's early influences was Bishop Ambrose, whom Augustine heard speak on several occasions. With reference to Book VI, Chapter 3, describe the effect of Bishop Ambrose on Augustine. How does Ambrose's influence compare with that of Cicero and Augustine's other classical influences?

BEYOND THE CLASSROOM

RESEARCH & WRITING

1. In Book VI, Chapter 4, among other places, Augustine dismisses the Manicheans, a religious group to which he had subscribed prior to his conversion. Research this Gnostic religion in more detail. What does Manichaeanism teach? Evaluate Manichean beliefs in light of both what Augustine says about his earlier years and his beliefs after his conversion. You might want to address how the Manichean doctrine of the forces of darkness and light are comparable or opposed to the teachings of Christianity, what Christianity offered Augustine that Manichaeanism could not, or how the move from Manichaeanism to Christianity might be seen as a progression in Augustine's thought.

2. Debates over Augustine's ideas about predestination have raged amongst scholars and theologians alike for many years. The crux of the debate centers on whether predestination can coexist with free will. For example, John Calvin used the writings of St. Augustine to support a strict theory of predestination that left no room for human free will. Unsurprisingly, many works of literature have raised these issues. With reference to *The Confessions* and at least one other primary text such as the Qur'an (specifically, Sura 5), Milton's *Paradise Lost* (Book 3) or any other work you find appropriate, tackle this debate yourself. Is there room for free will in the philosophy of these texts? How do the authors prove, disprove, or leave ambiguous the notion of free will? If primarily religious texts are used, it will be easy to fall into the trap of making arguments about whether Islam or Christianity is the better or more preferable religion, but try to look at the works as literature and to examine the logic of what is actually written in each text. No matter which texts are used, read outside scholarly sources to get a sense of the debate and to be specific and logical in your examination.

Project

1. In the late 1400s, Italian painter Benozzo Gozzoli painted a series of frescoes known as the St. Augustine Cycle. The cycle, located in the Church of Sant'Agostine in San Gimignano, depicts seventeen scenes from the life of St. Augustine. Refer students to the Gozzoli section of the Web Gallery of Art, which includes these paintings and brief descriptions of each (http://gallery.euroweb.hu/tours/gozzoli/frame3.html). Ask students to look particularly closely at the images that depict scenes excerpted in the anthology. How does Gozzoli's image correspond with Augustine's description of the events in question? Do the paintings reveal an interpretation or point of view on this episode in Augustine's life?

WWW For additional information on Augustine and annotated Web links, see *World Literature Online* at bedfordstmartins.com/worldlit.

FURTHER READING

Babcock, William S. *The Ethics of St. Augustine.* 1991.

Cary, Phillip. Augustine's *Invention of the Inner Self: The Legacy of a Christian Platonist.* 2000.

Fitzgerald, Allan D., et al. *Augustine Through the Ages: An Encyclopedia.* 1999.

Frend, W. H. C. *The Donatist Church.* 1952.

Hunter, David G. "Augustine and the Making of Marriage in Roman North Africa." *Journal of Early Christian Studies* 11, no. 1 (2003): 63–85.

Rist, J. M. "Augustine on Free Will and Predestination," *Journal of Theological Studies* 20 (1969): 420–47.

WWW See *World Literature in the 21st Century* at bedfordstmartins.com/worldlit for information on the relevance of Augustine to today's world.

MEDIA RESOURCES

VIDEO

The City of God
39 min., 1986 (Films for the Humanities & Sciences)
Augustine of Hippo is a symbol of humankind in early medieval times, seeking to understand the terror and destruction resulting from the barbarian devastations of the Roman world, seeking to find the hand of God — and finding it in the counterpart to the destroyed city of man in the city of God. The program covers the church resurgence, filling the vacuum left by the collapse of civil government and changing to meet its new obligations and fill its new role in society; the creation of the Vulgate Bible; mass conversions; the rule of Pope Gregory the Great — the last of the Roman popes and the first of the European; monastic life; Romanesque architecture; and the role of the pilgrimage in medieval society.

Saint Augustine: Late I Have Loved Thee
35 min., 1992 (Insight Media)
A compelling introduction to the works of St. Augustine, this video, written by James O'Donnell of the University of Pennsylvania, presents passages from *The Confessions* and *City of God* to acquaint viewers with Augustine's philosophy.

WEB SITES

Augustine of Hippo
ccat.sas.upenn.edu/jod/augustine.html
This site includes electronic texts of many of Augustine's writings, an extensive database of critical works, biographical information about the man and his times, a gallery of images, and essays examining Augustine's influence today.

Christian Classics Ethereal Library — St. Augustine
www.ccel.org/a/augustine
Found on this site are links to many biographical and critical sources on Augustine and e-texts of several of his works, including *The Confessions, The City of God*, and *On Christian Doctrine*.

EpistemeLinks.com — St. Augustine
www.epistemelinks.com/Main/Philosophers.aspx?PhilCode=Augu
This is a useful index of links to many sites related to Augustine as well as links to search engines for further research.

AUDIO

Confessions of St. Augustine
tape or CD, 12:75 hrs. (Blackstone Audiobooks)
The Confessions, read by Bernard Mayes, describes St. Augustine's conversion, shedding light on the questions that had troubled him on his way to the Cross. Outside Scripture, it is the most famous — and perhaps the most important — of all spiritual books.

The Life of St. Augustine
tape or CD, 6:75 hrs. (Blackstone Audiobooks)
Read by Frederick Davidson, this audio provides the life of St. Augustine.

The Qur'an (p. 97)

WWW   For a quiz on the Qur'an, see *World Literature Online*
at bedfordstmartins.com/worldlit.

The word *Qur'an* is an Arabic form of the Aramaic *qeryan*, meaning "reading" or "recital," which reveals one of most important of its liturgical functions: the basis for ritual prayer. Thus the Qur'an as text serves the same function as the Torah and the New Testament in their respective liturgical traditions. All three are distinct from Greco-Roman and other so-called pagan traditions in which there is no sacred, revelatory text or collection of texts that serves as the major source of prayers, sermons, and other religious celebrations (for example, in most Roman ceremonies, prayers followed strict formulas, much like Roman legal formulas). As is the case with the Bible, the Qur'an includes a mixture of genres; however, they are not as organized as the Torah-Histories-Poetic Books-Prophets pattern in the Old Testament, since thematic, not generic, principles are the guiding factors; nor are there quite as many genres in the Qur'an as in the Bible (e.g., the acrostic, folk song, lamentation, to name a few). Also, the subjects covered do not follow any easily discernable pattern, despite the quasi-rubric function of the name of each sura. To read everything in the Qur'an on a particular subject matter requires a literal *lectio dificilior*: an arduous picking out of the information from throughout various suras. If you are interested in nonlinear texts, the Qur'an serves as an excellent accidental prototype of late-twentieth-century exploded narratives.

The narratives of the Qur'an are scattered over its 114 suras. Each sura, with the exception of Sura 9 (Repentance) begins with a basmala (*bi-smi llahi r-rahmani r-rahim* or, in our translation, "In the Name of God, the Compassionate, the Merciful"). After the basmala, the beginning of Sura 2 (The Cow) and Sura 12 (Joseph) each includes a mysterious combination of letters, *alif lam min* and *alif lam ra*, respectively, and similar combinations are found at the beginnings of twenty-seven other suras. Their meaning is unknown, though their relation to the Hebrew and Greek alphabets is clear. Each of the suras is written, to a greater or lesser degree, in metrical lines of fairly equal length called *ayat*. Much like the Bible, the Qur'an is numbered according to sura and verse, as is seen in the margins, though there are some variations among printed editions. And, with the Bible, the poetry of the Qur'an is lost in translation.

The Western reception of the Qur'an begins with Petrus Venerabilis's Latin translation in 1143 (printed in 1543), which was done with apologetic and missionary purposes in mind. The first English translation (from the French!) was printed in 1649 "for the satisfaction of all that desire to look into the Turkish vanities," as the title page declares. The first translation from the Arabic, by George Sale, was published in 1734. In the nineteenth century, Qur'an scholarship in Europe benefited from the same philological attention as biblical scholarship, Theodor Nöldeke's *Geschichte des Qorans* (1860) being a watershed in the field. In the twentieth century, scholars continued the path of historicism by moving away from viewing the Old and New Testaments, Apocrypha, and other Judeo-Christian writings as source-texts for the Qur'an. They began to point out how the material underwent reinterpretations during its appropriation into the culture and viewed the Qur'an as an historical text containing significant information about Mohammad's time and culture. Whatever

other benefits this historical method may have, it does diffuse potential dogmatic disagreements on politico-religious grounds that tend to stifle open-minded, scholarly discussion
and therefore could be of use in class.

The study of the Qur'an as literature is still in its early stages. Thus linguistic (or philological) questions are still being posed in such areas as diction, register, imagery, and rhetorical devices. Investigations of that nature are readily available in libraries and on the Internet,
making this approach an easy way to avoid many of the political and theological issues and
prejudices surrounding the text. Of the selections in the anthology, Sura 55 (The Merciful)
is perhaps the most ostensibly poetic. It also allows for a comparison of poetic devices with
Psalm 137.

TEXT & CONTEXT

Though held by believers as a whole, some scholars, following Muhammad's life, have
drawn a distinction between eighty-eight so-called "Meccan" suras and thirty-six "Medinese"
suras. The distinction rests primarily on stylistic grounds, though there are other aspects of
the text that support the stylistic evidence. The most marked distinction is seen in the types
of speech acts in the two groups. According to this viewpoint, the Meccan suras do not contain commandments in the legal sense of the term, rather exhortations, pleadings, and
attempts at persuasion. The Medinese suras, however, contain commandments, usually in an
awkward legalistic style, since Muhammad had taken on the role of leader, legislator, and
statesman after the *Hegira* in 622. Furthermore, there is no mention of hypocrites in the
Meccan suras, while the Medinese suras do mention certain rivals to power in Medina,
specifically Sura 63 (The Hypocrites). Finally, the Medinese suras are addressed "to those
who truly believe." This theory can also be seen as a way of applying Muhammad's life to the
Qur'an's structure, or lack thereof. If Muhammad Ibn Ishaq's *Life* is on your reading list, you
may want to mention this theory to your students as, at the very least, a good way to bring
the two texts together. According to the theory, the following of our selections are Meccan:
Suras 1, 12, 55, 56, 93, 96, and 109; the rest are Medinese.

As is also the case with Judaism and Christianity, the Qur'an does not contain all that is
in Islam. Other "sources" are the Hadith (collections of sayings and teachings of the
Prophets). The Shia community also includes the tradition of the Twelve Imams as sources.
You may want to refer questions about Muhammad to the selections from Muhammad Ibn
Ishaq's *Life of Muhammad*. On the other hand, there are statements in the Qur'an that are
not necessarily to be taken literally (it is, after all, a poetic text). To counter overly literal readings, you may want to mention that Romans accused early Christians of cannibalism.
Communion, the (metaphorical) drinking of Christ's blood and the eating of his body by the
communicants, is based on the Last Supper. While the early church considered the transubstantiation of the Eucharist to be (in some sense) real, most Protestant churches now follow
the metaphorical level.

IN THE CLASSROOM

Discussion

1. What virtues does Joseph embody? Are they specific to Islam, or can they be considered
    universal? What other texts on the reading list also depict the same or similar virtues?

2. A comparison of Islamic and Jewish laws may prove useful in contextualizing the severi-
    ty or strictness of certain precepts in the Qur'an. Ask your students to point out what they

consider to be the harshest of the tenets in Sura 4. Then, ask them to consider certain laws from Leviticus (e.g., 19:18 — against clothing of linen and wool, 19:27 — against haircuts and beard-trimming, 19:28 — against tattoos; see also Exodus 35:2 — against working on Sunday). Ask students if they are in violation of any of those laws. Also compare the stipulations regarding a slave adulteress in Sura 4:25 and Leviticus 19:20.

3. Ask students to carefully read Sura 56 and then discuss how their own conceptions of heaven and hell compare with the ones in the Qur'an. How is the conception here depicted? For whom is it intended? Are their (pre-)conceptions any different?

Connections

1. Explore the significance of submission in the Qur'an in comparison with the *In the World:* The Good Life (Book 1, p. 1622) selection. How is virtue related to happiness?

2. Identify characteristics of the divine in the Qur'an. How does this portrayal contrast with that found in the Black Elk selection "The Gift of the Sacred Pipe" (Book 6, p. 166)? Comment on human access to the divine in both (perhaps comparing the visual and the oral).

Writing

Ask students to write a short paper in response to one or more of the following:

1. Write an analysis of the story of Joseph in the Old Testament from the perspective of the Qur'an.

2. Analyze the rhetoric of Sura 55. What literary devices are used? What is the basis of its poetic quality?

BEYOND THE CLASSROOM

RESEARCH & WRITING

1. Karl Marx wrote that religion is the opiate of the people. How do the Bible and the Qur'an serve that function? To what degree is this effect inherent in the message of the text or revelations? To what degree can it be ascribed to the organizations arising in the religious communities?

2. Write a paper or prepare a presentation in which you describe the Islamic conceptions of heaven and hell in relation to their conception in Judaism, Christianity, and (as much as possible) Hinduism and Buddhism.

3. Prepare a short presentation on the textual histories of the Bible and the Qur'an (include Sura 5). What "errors" did the compilers of the Qur'an wish to avoid? What power issues do the respective philological questions open up?

Projects

1. Two significant aspects of Islam have had extensive cultural implications in the Muslim world: (1) the ban on physical representations (paintings and sculptures but not designs) in its holy places; and (2) the requirement that believers read the Qur'an in the original Arabic (even if they don't understand the language). Ask a student or group of students to use similar cultural moments from European history (specifically the Puritan's argument against idolatry and the effects of their resistance, and the reasoning behind, as well as the effect of Vatican II or either Wycliff's or Luther's translation of the Bible) to define the cultural implications of such "radical" aspects of Islam.

2. Compare the Islamic stance on idolatry (e.g., in Sura 2) with the Puritan stance on idolatry. Be sure to include the social ramifications of both stances. What future does art have in the face of such zeal?

FURTHER READING

Abdel Haleem, M. A. *Understanding the Qur'an: Themes and Style.* 1999.
Barlas, Asma. *"Believing Women" in Islam: Unreading Patriarchal Interpretations of the Qur'an.* 2002.
Cook, M. A. *The Koran: A Very Short Introduction.* 2000.
Engineer, Asgharali. *The Qur'an, Women and Modern Society.* 1999.
McAuliffe, Jane Dommen, ed. *Encyclopedia of the Qur'an.* 2001.
The Quran: A New Interpretation. Textual exegesis by Muhammad Baqir Behbudi. Trans. Colin Turner. 1997.
Rippin, Andrew. *The Qur'an and Its Interpretive Tradition.* 2001.
———. *The Qur'an: Formative Interpretation.* 1999.
Sherif, Faruq. *A Guide to the Contents of the Qur'an.* 1995.
Wadud, Amina. *Qur'an and Woman: Rereading the Sacred Text from a Woman's Perspective.* 1999.

MEDIA RESOURCES

VIDEO

Doctrinal Dimension: Islam
60 min., 1999 (Insight Media)
This video explores the Islamic doctrines and ethical practices that underlie Islamic society. It discusses the five pillars of Islam, explores the meaning behind the prayer ritual, explains the significance of the Qur'an, and considers such key Islamic concepts as *shirk, sharia,* and *jihad.*

The Faith of Islam
29 min., 1988 (Insight Media)
This program describes the five pillars of Islam, presents a brief history of the religion, and shows the rituals of the *hajj.* It features the commentary of a Muslim religious leader and people who have lived and worked among Muslims.

Inside Islam
100 min., 2002 (Insight Media)
Available on video and DVD, this program examines the main tenets of Islam, the fastest-growing religion the world. It discusses the five pillars and explores the Qur'an's teachings on war, violence, and suicide. It features interviews with Muslim scholars, theologians, writers, and members of Arabic royal families.

Islam: Empire of Faith
120 min., 2001 (Insight Media)
Academy Award–winning actor Ben Kingsley walks us through the incredible rise of Islam. Within a few centuries, the Islamic empires blossomed, projecting their power from Africa to the East Indies, and from Spain to India. Inspired by the words of the prophet Muhammad, and led by caliphs and sultans, this political and religious expansion remains unequaled in speed, geographic size, and endurance. Hear the spectacular story of the great sweep of Islamic power and faith during its first thousand years — from the birth of

Muhammad to the peak of the Ottoman empire under the reign of Suleyman the Magnificent. Historical re-enactments and a remarkable exposition of Islamic art, artifacts, and architecture are combined with interviews of scholars from around the world to recount the rise and importance of early Islamic civilization. Increasingly, scholars and historians are recognizing the profound impact that Islamic civilization has had on Western culture and the course of world history.

Islam: The Faith and the People
22 min., 1992 (Insight Media)
This video examines the beliefs of Islam and their influence on the West. Explaining how Muslims view Muhammad, it shows how the five pillars of Islam dictate aspects of daily life. It considers the role of the mosque, looks at how the Crusades affected Islam, discusses the artistic and scientific contributions of Islam, and details the effects of colonialism on Islamic countries.

Islam and Christianity
30 min., 1993 (Insight Media)
Islam and Christianity share a large number of similarities, from their views on creation, morality, and the power of a supreme being. At the same time, they share a long history of conflict. In this program, Mohammad Masjed Jame'i, Iran's ambassador to the Vatican, takes an in-depth look at both religions, examining the roles of Christ and Muhammad, the Bible and the Qur'an, and the main differences of approach. The video also examines the reasons for the continuing conflict between Islam and the West.

The Koran: The Holy Book of Islam
15 min., 1995 (Insight Media)
Around 654 C.E., the teachings of Muhammad were written down and assembled into a single collection called the Qur'an, or Koran. Showing scenes of Muslims at prayer and in daily activities, this video explores the significance of the Qur'an to the religious and social life of Muslims and examines some of its teachings.

Muhammad: The Voice of God
44 min., 1999 (Insight Media)
Featuring footage of holy sites and rituals as well as modern life in Saudi Arabia, this program examines the biography of Muhammad, a merchant from Mecca, reportedly called by Allah to be his prophet and spread the Muslim faith. It discusses Islam's international appeal and considers why many non-Muslims fear the religion's spread.

Religions of the World: Islam
28 min., 2001 (Insight Media)
The world's fastest-growing religion, Islam is based on the teachings of the prophet Muhammad. This video investigates why the youngest of the world's religions has attracted so many followers, examining the history of the faith; the practices of its followers; the art, architecture, and science of Islam; its contemporary role in the world; and the effect of the colonial era on the faith.

Story of Islam
120 min., 1991 (Educational Video Network)
Take a journey through Islam's history, from its humble beginnings 1,300 years ago to its place in the world today, with more than one billion devout believers. The culture and philosophy of this major religion are examined in depth.

Three Pillars: Confucius, Jesus, and Mohammed
53 min., 1998 (Insight Media)

This video studies the identities of the founders of three major religions — Confucianism, Christianity, and Islam. It looks at how Confucianism blended into the Chinese social and political structure; the significance of Jesus as a prophet for Muslims and as God incarnate for Christians; and the teachings of Muhammad and the Qur'an.

What Is Islam?
26 min., 2002 (Insight Media)
Defining basic concepts of Islam, this video provides an introduction to one of the world's major monotheistic religions. It discusses the history of Islam and considers its significance to global culture.

WEB SITES

Exploring Ancient World Cultures: Medieval Europe Homepage
eawc.evansville.edu/mepage.htm
This site covers ancient Near Eastern history to the Middle Ages. It includes a thorough chronology of major events of medieval times and allows users to look into what was happening across cultures during various points in history.

Internet Medieval Sourcebook
www.fordham.edu/halsall/sbook2.html
A premiere Internet source on medieval studies created at Fordham University, the Internet Medieval Sourcebook is organized as three main index pages, with a number of supplementary documents — Selected Sources, Full Text Sources, and Saints' Lives. This is an excellent index of selected and excerpted texts for teaching purposes.

The Labyrinth: Resources for Medieval Studies
www.georgetown.edu/labyrinth/labyrinth-home.html
Based at Georgetown University, this site provides links to many medieval resources available on the Internet.

Listen to and Read the Quran
www.balaams-ass.com/alhaj/listen.htm
This site, requiring RealAudio, provides readings of portions of the Qur'an in Arabic.

The Online Medieval & Classical Library
sunsite.berkeley.edu/OMACL/
The Douglas B. Killings collection of some of the most important literary works of classical and medieval civilization.

AUDIO

Complete Holy Quran
20 tapes (UltimateQuran.com)
High-fidelity digital recording of the audio recitation in Arabic by Saudi religious scholar and native of Makkah (Mecca).

Living Biographies of Religious Leaders
8 tapes, 11:25 hrs. (Blackstone Audiobooks)
This program presents the lives of twenty great founders and leading advocates of the world's foremost religions. Here are the historical facts and legends associated with these forceful personalities who have inspired and influenced humankind through the centuries. Presented are Jesus Christ, Moses, Isaiah, Zoroaster, Buddha, Confucius, John the Baptist,

Paul, Muhammad, Francis of Assisi, John Huss, Luther, Loyola, Calvin, George Fox, Swedenborg, Wesley, Brigham Young, Mary Baker Eddy, and Gandhi.

MUHAMMAD IBN ISHAQ, from *The Life of Muhammad* (p. 134)

WWW   For a quiz on *The Life of Muhammad,* see *World Literature Online* at bedfordstmartins.com/worldlit.

Although we know that many early histories of Islam existed at one time, few have survived. Even Ibn Ishaq's *The Life of Muhammad,* the earliest biography of the prophet we know of, is no longer extant. What we have are various selections preserved most extensively in the writings of Yunus b. Bukayr (d. 199/814–15) and of Ibn Hisham (d. 218/833), augmented by further citations from Muhammad b. Salaam al-Harrani (d. 191/807), among other historians and compilers. Indeed at least fifteen different versions provide material for the restoration of Ibn Ishaq's original. The first original biographical document we have is Waqidi's *Kitab al-maghazi,* or *Book of the Wars,* which only recounts the Prophet's military efforts. Ibn Hisham's Sirat un-Nabi and Ibn Sa'd's Kitab ul-Tabaqat ul-Kabir follow, the first of which is the source of the text in the anthology. Many subsequent histories comment on Ibn Ishaq's work, even when they do not report its contents. He seems to have had a mixed reception, some praising his endeavors, others criticizing his accuracy with respect to Hadith. It is important to note that Hisham's version of *The Life of Muhammad,* which retains several of the not-so-favorable renditions of certain events, is nevertheless edited; in his prefatory discussion, Hisham explains that anything damaging has been excised.

Beyond the Muslim literary tradition, references to and accounts of Muhammad were, until the nineteenth century, generally biased and disparaging. In contrast with the seventh-century "Chronicle of Sebeos," which provides the first mention of Muhammad in Christian literature in the form of a brief historical sketch, later ecclesiastical discussions present Muhammad as a heretic. Byzantine records and contact with Islam through the Crusades formed the basis of such appraisals. An attempt to work from original sources was only made after the Renaissance, and the first critically "objective" portrayals appeared in the nineteenth century. Nevertheless, the problem of establishing the "factual" Muhammad remains for historians today, since the material on him is self-contained — one can only accept or reject the "evidence." This characteristic constitutes a similar sense of historical authenticity to that found in *The Life of Muhammad,* which, despite its inclusion of multiple perspectives, does not question the events themselves that are described. To be sure, Ibn Ishaq is as unreflective a reporter as Muhammad: Both merely announce what they have heard. Or is the narrator so unconscious? Examine, for instance, the psychological aspects of the narrator's account (e.g., in "The Story of Bahira," [p. 137]). What effect does this "realism" have?

In approaching the text, you might focus on the figure of Muhammad himself. What does he do that no ordinary human being could not do? Related to this question is the following: What effect do the supernatural stories have? How do they represent Muhammad as "an evangelist to all men"?

Encourage students to also consider the significance of Ibn Ishaq's account as a whole. What does Muhammad teach his people?

TEXT & CONTEXT

KEY TERMS AND LITERARY FORMS

Early Islamic history basically falls into four roughly distinct categories: *Hadith*, or prophetic tradition, detailing what Muhammad said and did, including *sira*, or accounts of Muhammad's life; *maghazi*, or accounts of the military campaigns he directed; *futuh*, or conquests; and *waqa* and *maqtal*, or particular cases, represent the first category. *Tafsir*, or commentaries on the Qur'an connecting Muhammad's life with the revelation of the suras constitute the second category; *adab* literature, which presents the doctrines of Islam in entertaining ways the third. Included here are *qisas*, which are myths concerning the prophets of the Qur'an or of the Old Testament narrated by *qussas*, or storytellers. Historiography comprises the fourth category and is organized mainly by historical period. Texts that represent any or all of these categories can be found in tabaqat, or works of biography, and in collections of *Hadith*.

THE HADITH

The Hadith, or the books of tradition, contain accounts of Muhammad's life, what he witnessed, and what he taught. At times, they also include what his companions said and did. Eyewitness reports (*matn*) provide the basis for these histories, often transmitted through a series of narrators (*isnad*). The great Hadith include the compilations of al-Bukhari (d. 870), Muslim ib al-Hajjaj (d. 875), Ibn Maja (d. 887), Abu Dawud (d. 889), al-Tirmidhi (d. 892), al-Nisai (d. 915), and Ahmad ibn Hanbal (d. 855). This last, the *Musnad*, incorporates close to 29,000 traditions.

BRIEF TIMELINE OF MUHAMMAD'S LIFE

570 C.E. — Birth
576 C.E. — Death of mother
578 C.E. — Death of grandfather
585 C.E. — First military experience: Battle of Fujjar
586 C.E. — Halful Fazul (reformist movement)
595 C.E. — Marriage to Hazrat Khadija
610 C.E. — Prophethood
611 C.E. — First revelation of Qur'an
613 C.E. — Announcement of his prophethood
615 C.E. — Migration to Abyssinia
620 C.E. — Ascension (*Meraj*) and the beginning of Islam in Medina
622 C.E. — Migration (*Hijra*) to Medina, followed by the institution of the Islamic state
and the declaration of jihad and the prophet's marriage (over the next several years) to Hazrat Hafsa, Umm-ul-Masakin, Hazrat Jowairia, Zainab, Hazrat Safia, and Hazrat Maimuna
630 C.E. — Conquest of Mecca
632 C.E. — Death

IN THE CLASSROOM

Discussion and Writing

1. What traits does Muhammad exhibit that make him a practical model for followers of Islam? To what extent is Muhammad human?

2. Characterize the role of revelation in the text. How is it experienced?

3. How is God portrayed? In what ways is he the author of the text?

4. Locate and identify a few contradictions in the text. What effect do they have on the biography (for example, do they constitute Ibn Ishaq's objectivity, detract from the believability, augment the realism of the text, since there is always more than one side to the story)?

5. Examine the account of Muhammad's ascent to heaven. What is the function of this story with respect to the rest of *Life?*

Connections

1. Both Ashvaghosha's *Life of Buddha* and Ibn Ishaq's *The Life of Muhammad* depict periods of development in a prophet's life. Compare the spiritual progress of each. What does Muhammad learn?

2. Compare Ibn Ishaq's relation of Muhammad's military activities with the texts included in *In the World: Muslim and Christian at War* (Book 2, p. 578). What role does God play in each?

BEYOND THE CLASSROOM

RESEARCH AND WRITING

1. Read more of *The Life of Muhammad,* focusing on the role women play. What model of virtuous conduct do they present?

2. Find out more about miracles in the Islamic tradition. How does Ibn Ishaq's biography inform the Islamic understanding of miracles?

3. Read other sira. What aspects of Ibn Ishaq's style are characteristic of the genre?

Projects

1. Watch the film *The Message* and/or the PBS program "Muhammad: Legacy of a Prophet." To what extent are the perspectives they take on Muhammad different/similar to those of Ibn Ishaq? How do they assert the objectivity of their perspectives?

2. Find out more about modern Islamic culture. What role does Muhammad play in Islam today?

FURTHER READING

Khan, Rahmat Ali, et al. *Prophet Muhammad in the Indian Context.* 1997.
Margoliouth, D. S. *Mohammad.* 1939.
Schimmel, Annemarie. *And Muhammad Is His Messenger.* 1985.
Warraq, Ibn, ed. and trans. *The Quest for the Historical Muhammad.* 2000.

MEDIA RESOURCES

VIDEO

The Middle Ages
25 min., 1996 (Films for the Humanities & Sciences)
This program traces the evolution of Europe during the Middle Ages from a group of loosely tied kingdoms to a prosperous community of nations. Topics include the role of the church, development of the feudal system, the rise of the nobility, the Crusades, forma-

tion of the German Hanseatic League, the effects of the Plague, the growth of trade guilds, the discovery of printing, the urbanization of the peasantry, and the rise of science.

The Middle Ages
30 min., 1997 (Annenberg/CPB Video)
Amid invasion and civil disorder, a military aristocracy dominated the kingdoms of Europe.

WEB SITES

Islamic Philosophy Online
http://www.muslimphilosophy.com/ip/old.htm
A Web site that provides better philosophical understanding of the Muslim world. Includes essays, definitions, links to other Web sites, and announcements of Islamic-related events.

In the World: Kings, Conquerors, and Fighting Saints (p. 158)

This section collects works that are separated by geographical, religious, and cultural differences but that share a common literary heritage. Accounts of the great deeds of extraordinary leaders and heroes are found even among the earliest writings known to man. By and large, these works do not contain the sort of magical and fantastic elements that cause us to label a work "mythological" even if there are historical truths at its root. Because of this, it may be very easy to treat these works as we would modern biographies and assume that they are essentially factual reports of events surrounding the life of an exceptional historical figure. However, encourage students not to fall into this trap, for to do so risks missing much that is important and worthy of note in these narratives. Stress that with one exception, *Joan of Arc by Herself and Her Witnesses*, the authors of each of these "biographies" were men who felt extreme respect for the subject about whom they were writing. Moreover, at this time, embellishment of the life of a famous person in order to produce a sense of mystery, fear, reverence, or awe was both common and acceptable. While these accounts should in no way be discredited as complete fabrications, they should be read carefully with an eye toward the authors' biases and the audience for which the works were intended. Remember that part of the reason that these works are literarily, and not just historically, significant is that they represent the production of an image of their central figure. If taken in this way, the texts yield a much wider set of interpretations, and you will find that rich comparisons will be possible not only with more traditional biographical texts but with heroic narratives and fictions as well.

IN THE CLASSROOM

I. IDOLS AND IDEALS

The works selected in "Kings, Conquerors, and Fighting Saints" are much more than mere factual accounts of the life and deeds of a famous figure. They also serve as *exempla*, illustrations of the ideals prevalent in the age and culture they represent. The lives of Charlemagne, Alexius, Saladin, Chingis Khan, and Joan of Arc are set out by their biographers as examples of lives worthy not only of admiration but also of emulation. As such, we can read these biographies in order to examine the subjects in their role as cultural icons as well as to understand the values and mores of the societies from in which they lived.

Discussion

1. The selection of Einhard's biography shows a personal side of Charlemagne that is far removed from a deifying, epic-style account of his battle prowess. It seems to reveal him

foremost as a man. Nonetheless, Einhard's prose still reveals the great respect that he has for the king. Why does Einhard focus on qualities like Charlemagne's manner of dress, temperance, and learning? What do you make of Einhard's characterization of Charlemagne as protector of Christians in predominantly non-Christian lands?

2. *The Alexiad* has been labeled both a history and a biography. Into which of these categories is the work most easily classified? What does she have to say about her father? about the crusaders? Alternatively, it has been suggested that *The Alexiad* reveals more about Anna Comnena herself than about Alexius or the history of Byzantium. If this is true, what literary genre is this work? Who is Anna? Who or what does she admire? Of whom or what does she disapprove?

3. Most of the figures in this section are praised for qualities that are still admirable to us today — their intelligence, bravery, compassion, or ability to lead. However, Chingis Khan's anonymous biographer seems often to glorify him for his brute strength and the relative mercilessness he shows toward his enemies. For what other qualities is Khan praised? Which of Khan's qualities are most admirable to his biographer? How do these qualities seem to us today? What might we consider commendable in Khan's character? How does he compare with the other leaders in this section?

4. Many of the great leaders portrayed here are at war with other powerful leaders. How do the authors of these texts portray the enemies of their subject? Are the enemies set up as foils for the great leaders or treated as opponents who are equally valiant? What do these techniques do for the narratives?

Writing

Ask students to write a short paper in response to one or more of the following:

1. Einhard describes Charlemagne as a well-spoken man who was good with foreign languages, who studied the liberal arts, and who was interested in legal reform and the preservation of literary works of art. Write a paper in which you define the Carolingian Renaissance and make an argument about Charlemagne's role in the movement. Questions to consider: What were the ideals of the Carolingian Renaissance, and what debt did they owe to earlier civilizations like the Greeks? Was Charlemagne an example of an model man under the ideals of the movement, or did he merely serve as the movement's patron? Did it matter that Charlemagne could not write?

2. Read the selections from Baha ad-Din's *A Life of Saladin* carefully, and write a paper on the use of the Islamic religion and, in particular, Islamic texts in the work. How does ad-Din make use of the Qur'an to illustrate the exemplary qualities of Saladin? What sort of conclusions about the similarities between Saladin and Muhammad can you draw from the text? Can you find evidence that ad-Din constructs his biography on the model of Ibn Ishaq's *The Biography of the Prophet*?

II. CONNECTIONS
Discussion

1. Einhard describes the "age-old narrative poems" that Charlemagne helps preserve as "barbarous enough, it is true, in which were celebrated the warlike deeds of the kings of ancient times" (p. 173). With this quote in mind, compare the account of Charlemagne given in *The Song of Roland* (p. 546) as well as some of the accounts in "Kings, Conquerors, and Fighting Saints" with descriptions of some of these "warlike" kings in Book 1 in works like *The Odyssey* and *The Peloponnesian War*. Were the deeds of Einhard's own time any less barbarous?

2. How does Anna Comnena's characterization of the Muslims, whom she calls Ishmaelites, compare with other accounts of Muslims (by both Christians and Muslims themselves) in the works you have read this year? Is she any fairer to the Muslims than she is to the Christian Crusaders?

3. Both Charlemagne in this section and Kublai Khan in *The Travels of Marco Polo* (p. 933) are described as being extremely generous. Compare these two accounts. How is the generosity of each leader depicted? Is there a difference between Khan's generosity toward the people under his rule and Charlemagne's generosity toward Christians even in other countries?

Writing

Ask students to write a short paper in response to one or more of the following:

1. The Middle Period is often seen as a tempestuous time; wars and other military endeavors were frequent, and writers often composed poetry and prose dealing with battle. Have students write a paper on the role of war in the literary productions of different time periods. In addition to the narratives in this section, students may wish to look at *The Iliad, The Aeneid, In the World:* Rulers and Empire (Book 1) and *In the World:* Literature from Two World Wars, Yeats's poems "Easter 1916" and "The Second Coming," and T. S. Eliot's *The Waste Land* (Book 6), or any other works you have read this year that are set in or pertain to times of war. What is the role of war in these works? How do classical, medieval, and modern authors feel about the wars through which they lived, and how are those wars portrayed?

2. The pieces excerpted here share some of the same heroic sensibilities as the great epics of antiquity. Ask students to compare one or more of these works with classical tales of heroic deeds like *The Iliad, The Odyssey, The Aeneid, The Epic of Gilgamesh* (Book 1), or others in order to formulate a working definition of the heroic in the Middle Ages. Students should decide whether their definition is similar to or distinct from the classical definition of hero and account for this difference in their papers.

BEYOND THE CLASSROOM

RESEARCH & WRITING

1. Unlike the works in *In the World:* Pilgrimage and Travel" (p. 933) and *In the World:* Travel Narratives (Book 4) as well as the works of Black Elk, Olaudah Equiano, Benjamin Franklin, St. Augustine, and Margery Kempe, most of the excerpts in this section are not autobiographies or memoirs. The people who are the central subject of the narrative did not write the works themselves. Have students write a short paper contrasting the genres of biography and autobiography. Students may want to address issues like image versus self-image, credibility, or narrative style in these two types of text. To illustrate the points they want to make regarding the two literary forms, students should use specific examples from at least one biography, at least one autobiographical work, and appropriate secondary sources. At least one of the biographical texts should be chosen from among the selections in "Kings, Conquerors, and Fighting Saints."

2. Quite a few of the works in this anthology deal explicitly with, or are written in a time period during or leading up to the Crusades. Though originally sanctioned by the pope in order to take Jerusalem from the Muslims, the Crusades spread and their implications

and influence were far reaching. Ask students to use one of the narratives they have read this year that relates explicitly or implicitly to the Crusades (for example, *The Song of Roland, The Alexiad,* or *A Life of Saladin*) as a striking-off point for a research paper dealing with some aspect of the Crusades. Students should be expected to familiarize themselves with a range of secondary historical and literary sources. Possible topics include the causes and effects of the Crusades, the perception Muslims and Christians had of one another, the effect of patriotic literature on the Crusade movement, or the literary legacy of the Crusades.

Projects

1. Joan of Arc is one of those medieval individuals, like King Arthur, whose story continues to capture the imagination of people long after her death. For this reason, there is both a wealth of extant information about Joan of Arc as well as a number of creative works that derive inspiration from her life. Have student groups make use of these resources by preparing presentations on one of the following:

   a. Research the details of Joan's canonization as a saint and the qualifications for sainthood in general. Include information about her reinstatement by the church, the movement to beatify her, and the miracles she is said to have performed.

   b. Compare Joan of Arc's visions with those of other medieval visionaries like Margery Kempe, Julian of Norwich, and St. Catherine of Siena. How can these visionary experiences be compared? What did each of the women see? Joan's visions caused her to leave her home and lead the French army. Are any of the other women prompted to act by their visions? How?

   c. Many, many films have been made based on the life of Joan of Arc. Watch a few of these films, and provide critical analyses and comparisons. Possibilities include Dreyer's *The Passion of Joan of Arc* (1928), Fleming's *Joan of Arc* (1948), Preminger's *Saint Joan* (1957), Besson's *The Messenger: The Story of Joan of Arc* (1999), and Duguay's *Joan of Arc* (1999). How do these films represent Joan, her allies, and her accusers? What decisions do the directors make in respect to her story? When are they faithful and unfaithful to the medieval accounts you have read and why?

   d. After researching in more detail the heresy trial of Joan of Arc, prepare a dramatic re-enactment of the testimony of Joan and the witnesses both for and against her. If you like, designate the rest of the class as jury, and ask them to decide whether Joan has committed any crime based on the evidence you present.

FURTHER READING

Astell, Ann W. *Joan of Arc and Sacrificial Authorship.* 2003.
Blaetz, Robin. *Visions of the Maid: Joan of Arc in American Film and Culture.* 2001.
Gouma-Peterson, Thalia. *Anna Komnene and Her Times, Garland Medieval Case Books.* 2000.
Martin, Henry Desmond. *The Rise of Chingis Khan and His Conquest of North China.* 1971.
McKitterick, Rosamond. *The Carolingians and the Written Word.* 1994.
Yaacov, Lev. *Saladin in Egypt.* 1998.

MEDIA RESOURCES

VIDEO

Charlemagne and the Holy Roman Empire
31 min., 1989 (Films for the Humanities & Sciences)
Out of the ashes of the Roman Empire rose the Holy Roman Empire, born during Christmas of 800 in the Basilica of St. Peter's in Rome. This program covers the antecedents and the life of Charlemagne, shows life at the court, life of the courtiers and of the peasants, recounts the battle of Roncevaux — site of the epic *Chanson de Roland* — and counterpoints the glories of the Carolingian Renaissance with the everyday realities of hunger, plague, and constant violence. The program concludes with the first of Europe's major confrontations between empire and church, in this instance between Henry IV and Gregory VII.

Genghis Khan
50 min., 2000 (A&E Video)
At the height of his power, Genghis Khan's empire extended from the Pacific Ocean to the Persian Gulf. But while none question his military brilliance, his abilities as a statesman and ruler are often overlooked. Genghis was, quite simply, one of the most effective rulers in human history. He fashioned his nomadic armies into the greatest fighting force the world had ever seen and extended his empire to the furthest corners of Asia and into Europe in a series of brilliant and devastating campaigns. From the plains of Mongolia to the pages of history, this is the riveting story of Genghis Khan.

Jihad: The Rise of Saladin
50 min., 1995 (Films for the Humanities & Sciences)
This program crisscrosses Syria and Jordan to discover how the Arab world launched a countercrusade to win back Jerusalem from the Christians. Through the writings of the powerful Muslim leader Saladin, it traces the political intrigues behind Saladin's ascension to power and the ultimate victory of the Turks. Arab studies experts provide interesting background on the battles.

Joan of Arc
50 min., 1998 (A&E Video)
A&E examines the life of the peasant girl whose defense of the French crown brought her both glory and death. Discover how this humble peasant girl convinced the French Dauphin to give her command of troops, who she led into victorious battles against the British crown. Learn of the reasons for her downfall, detailing the lengthy process of her trial, interrogation, sentencing, and eventual death on a burning stake. A gripping portrait of the "Maid of Orleans."

WEB SITES

Exploring Ancient World Cultures: Medieval Europe Homepage
eawc.evansville.edu/mepage.htm
This site covers ancient Near Eastern history to the Middle Ages. It includes a thorough chronology of major events of medieval times and allows users to look into what was happening across cultures during various points in history.

Internet Medieval Sourcebook
www.fordham.edu/halsall/sbook2.html

A premiere Internet source on medieval studies created at Fordham University, the Internet Medieval Sourcebook is organized as three main index pages, with a number of supplementary documents — Selected Sources, Full Text Sources, and Saints' Lives. This is an excellent index of selected and excerpted texts for teaching purposes. Includes full versions of *The Alexiad* and *The Life of Charlemagne.*

Joan of Arc Archive
members.aol.com/hywwebsite/private/joanofarc.html
This is an archive of information designed to present Joan of Arc as she was described in the historical documents. The site includes an overview of her life and trial, excerpts from the trial documents, letters, and other such manuscripts (either in translation and/or in the original Latin and French). Nearly three hundred pages are currently on the Internet.

The Labyrinth: Resources for Medieval Studies
www.georgetown.edu/labyrinth/labyrinth-home.html
Based at Georgetown University, this site provides links to many medieval resources available on the Internet.

The Land of Genghis Khan
www.nationalgeographic.com/genghis/index.html
This is the National Geographic's fascinating site devoted to the life, times, and campaigns of Genghis Khan.

The Online Medieval & Classical Library
sunsite.berkeley.edu/OMACL/
The Douglas B. Killings collection of some of the most important literary works of classical and medieval civilization.

Saladin Homepage
www.acsamman.edu.jo/~ms/crusades/saladin/saladin.html
This is a very thorough site that provides information on the life, times, and campaigns of the great Saladin.

GENERAL MEDIA RESOURCES

VIDEO

The Birth of the Middle Ages
43 min., 1989 (Films for the Humanities & Sciences)
This program provides an introduction to medieval Europe by showing surviving traces to provide a feel of medieval style and practice and by tracing the roots of the fall of civilization and the onset of darkness. Much that is medieval survives, sometimes in unlikely places: in a feudal community in sub-Saharan Africa, where an absolute ruler holds court surrounded by ministers, courtiers, and hangers-on, with paladins in mail and mercenaries who, according to local tradition, are descendants of the crusaders; and in numerous folk festivals held in modern Italy, which re-enact the futile battles against the invading nomadic hordes. The program traces the fall of Rome and the development of fortified monasteries and their gradual transformation into centers of prayer, work, and the study of ancient learning. With the acceptance of Eastern peoples into the church of Rome, Europe achieved its frontiers.

Common Life in the Middle Ages
30 min., 1989 (Annenberg/CPB Video)
Famine, disease, and short life expectancies were the conditions that shaped medieval beliefs.

Crescent and Cross: Rise of Islam and Age of Crusades
59 min., 1998 (Insight Media)
Considering the Crusades as a response to the rapid rise of Islam, this video looks at various orders of Christian monks and their role in the preservation of religious, artistic, and cultural aspects of civilization. It addresses the issue of religious intolerance, focusing on the Inquisition.

Crusades
200 min., 1995 (Insight Media)
Filmed on location in Europe and the Middle East, this series explores the history and legacy of the Crusades. It discusses the reasons for the Crusades, the creation of a mythology of knights and chivalry, and the legacy of distrust between East and West.

The Crusades
23 min., 1989 (Insight Media)
Looking closely at the three major Crusades, this program examines the political and military divisions, economic incentives, and military pressures that gave rise to them. The video traces the path of the Crusaders to the Holy Land and considers the effects of the holy wars and the influence of the returning Crusaders on the developing culture of Western Europe.

The Eastern Philosophers
50 min. each, 2001 (Insight Media)
Examining the central doctrines of Confucianism, Shinto, Hinduism, Judaism, and Islam, this set examines the genesis of spiritual thought. The first volume explores the dominant philosophical and spiritual ideas of the Far East, focusing on Confucius and Shinto. The second discusses the Hinduism and Buddhism of South Asia, with their focus on cycles of death and rebirth. The final volume considers the roots, rituals, and sacred texts of Judaism and the tenets and lifestyle issues of Islam.

Faith and Feudalism: The Early Middle Ages
23 min., 1999 (Insight Media)
Featuring art reproductions, maps, interviews, and historical reenactments, this program recounts the rise of feudalism in Europe during the decline of Rome. It shows how religious organizations like the church in Europe or Buddhism in China were able to maintain the thread of culture in feudal periods. It also illustrates how religious writings gave people hope. Explores the songs, poems, plays, histories, and inspirations of the time, including *Beowulf* and Gildas's history of the Celts.

Great Religions of the World
33 min., 1995 (Insight Media)
This video explores the major beliefs, origins, and histories of Buddhism, Christianity, Judaism, Hinduism, Islam, and Taoism. It differentiates between ethnic and universalizing religions, discussing how each of the universalizing religions developed from an ethnic base and expanded past national boundaries.

The Late Middle Ages
30 min., 1989 (Annenberg/CPB Video)
Two hundred years of war and plague debilitated Europe.

The Middle Ages
34 min., 1992 (Insight Media)
This program explores the important figures and events of the Middle Ages through art-work and dramatic narration. It considers the influence of classical civilization on early Christianity and art, explores the so-called Dark Ages, discusses the Crusades, and examines the Gothic style of architecture.

Three Pillars: Confucius, Jesus, and Mohammed
53 min., 1998 (Insight Media)
This video studies the identities of the founders of three major religions — Confucianism, Christianity, and Islam. It looks at how Confucianism blended into the Chinese social and political structure; the significance of Jesus as a prophet for Muslims and as God incarnate for Christians; and the teachings of Muhammad and the Qur'an.

The World's Philosophies
60 min., 1994 (Insight Media)
In this video, Huston Smith defines three basic types of human relationships — with nature, with other people, and with one's self — and explains how these relationships correspond to the philosophical traditions of the West, of China, and of India.

WEB SITES

Exploring Ancient World Cultures: Medieval Europe Homepage
eawc.evansville.edu/mepage.htm
This site covers ancient Near Eastern history to the Middle Ages. It includes a thorough chronology of major events of medieval times and allows users to look into what was happening across cultures during various points in history.

Internet Medieval Sourcebook
www.fordham.edu/halsall/sbook2.html
A premiere Internet source on medieval studies created at Fordham University, the Internet Medieval Sourcebook is organized as three main index pages, with a number of supplementary documents — Selected Sources, Full Text Sources, and Saints' Lives. This is an excellent index of selected and excerpted texts for teaching purposes.

The Labyrinth: Resources for Medieval Studies
www.georgetown.edu/labyrinth/labyrinth-home.html
Based at Georgetown University, this site provides links to many medieval resources available on the Internet.

Middle Ages
www.learner.org/exhibits/middleages/
The Annenberg/CPB site on the Middle Ages provides excellent and accessible information and images on the medieval world.

NetSerf: The Internet Connection for Medieval Resources
www.netserf.org/
Sponsored by the history department of the Catholic University of America, this is a wonderful gateway site to all things medieval.

The Online Medieval & Classical Library
sunsite.berkeley.edu/OMACL/
The Douglas B. Killings collection of some of the most important literary works of classical and medieval civilization.

AUDIO

Living Biographies of Great Philosophers
7 tapes, 9:75 hrs. (Blackstone Audiobooks)
Included in this program are Plato and Socrates, Aristotle, Epicurus, Marcus Aurelius, Thomas Aquinas, Francis Bacon, Descartes, Spinoza, Locke, Hume, Voltaire, Kant, Hegel, Schopenhauer, Emerson, Spencer, Nietzsche, William James, Henri-Louis Bergson, and Santayana.

Living Biographies of Religious Leaders
8 tapes, 11:25 hrs. (Blackstone Audiobooks)
This program presents the lives of twenty great founders and leading advocates of the world's foremost religions. Here are the historical facts and legends associated with these forceful personalities who have inspired and influenced humankind through the centuries. Presented are Jesus Christ, Moses, Isaiah, Zoroaster, Buddha, Confucius, John the Baptist, Paul, Muhammad, Francis of Assisi, John Huss, Luther, Loyola, Calvin, George Fox, Swedenborg, Wesley, Brigham Young, Mary Baker Eddy, and Gandhi.

INDIA:
NORTH AND SOUTH

The Tamil Anthologies (p. 212)

WWW   For a quiz on the Tamil Anthologies, see *World Literature Online* at bedfordstmartins.com/worldlit.

The poetry of the Tamil people constitutes a tradition whose significance is not limited to the representation of Tamil language and society. No other culture in India has produced an indigenous literary theory (including a metrics, poetics, prosody, and rhetoric). Tamil poetry also differs from other Indian literary languages in that it does not refer to figures or texts in Sanskrit — Tamil literature composes its own interpretative context. Finally, the literature of the Tamil is the only Indian literature that is both classical and modern; A. K. Ramanujan observes that contemporary Tamil poetry is "recognizably continuous with a classical past" on par with ancient Sanskrit or Greek literature. Instrumental in the formation of this tradition is one of its earliest works, the *Tolkappiyam*, which established the conventions of grammar and poetry in Tamil. As such, "Tamil literary conventions are not rules unconsciously followed by poets and codified by critics of a later age, like Aristotle's canons of epic poetry and those described by Horace. Ancient Tamil literary conventions were petrifications of old customs developed by the action of the environment on human life" and "were based on the actual customs and manners of the people" (Srinivas Iyengar, P. T., *History of the Tamils: From the Earliest Times to 600 AD*, 63). Since the selection the students have is in translation and the grammar rules are complicated, it may be most useful to highlight the differences and similarities between the literary tradition of the Tamil and that of Western civilization and to only address formal concerns in order to examine and interpret the poems' content. The poems' apparent simplicity, after all, make them less intimidating, especially for students unpracticed in analyzing poetry.

You might begin, then, by looking at the poems according to the way in which the subject matter of Tamil poetry was traditionally conceived and classified (See p. 214 for the distinction between *akam* and *puram* poems). Ask students to identify the depictions of love and war in each. Students should consider the relationship between love and war in Tamil society as they are presented in the poems. One way to understand their relationship is by focusing on the role nature plays in both love and war. Their juxtaposition particularly in "A King's Double Nature" and "A Leaf in Love and War" should prompt students to discuss the tension between survival and transience, a central theme in Tamil literature. The roles people play in the poems — father, mother, king, son, and so on — provide another way in which to approach the aims of love and war in terms of the continuance and greatness of a society. How do the stereotypes of these roles (characteristically portrayed in *akam* poetry) compare with their historical counterparts (characteristically portrayed in *puram* poetry)? Call students' attention to the stereotype of the thief in "25: What She Said" and the historical thieves in "His Hill."

The intimate connection between *akam* and *puram* poetry is further demonstrated in the following table.

AKAM–PURAM CORRESPONDENCES

Akam	kuriñci	mullai	marutam	neytal	pâlai
name of flower and poetic theme	(first) union of lovers	separation, patient waiting	infidelity, conflict	separation, anxious waiting	elopement; search for wealth & fame
Place (nilam)	mountains	forest, pasture	cultivated countryside	seashore *(akam)* open battleground *(puram)*	wasteland *(akam)*
Time (kalam)	night	evening	dawn	sunrise	noon
Season	cold season, early frost	rainy season	all seasons	all seasons	hot season, late dew
Common aspect	clandestine affair	separation from loved ones	refusing entry	grief	praise
Puram	*vetci*	*vanci*	*ulinai*	*tumpai*	*vakai*
poetic situation	prelude to war: cattle raiding	preparation for war	siege of a settlement	pitched battle	victory, the ideals of achievement

The Tamil poets thus identified basic human situations appropriate for poetic treatment that were based on a unified conception of the universe. By using the principle of economy and the technique of concentration, they would produce poetry that reflected what they saw as the entire scale of human experience. How does this make such simple poems epic?

TEXT & CONTEXT

THE BARDIC TRADITION

The *Tolkappiyam* concretized the bardic art that had flourished in Tamil for several thousand years. Founded on a secular oral bardic tradition, Tamil poetry stands in contrast to Vedic poetry and is comparable with the Greek or Welsh bardic tradition. Early Tamil poets were a highly esteemed, professional group of people that represented all classes of society. After receiving bardic training, they wandered about in groups, often poor but nevertheless influential. Their art did not involve moralizing about the ethics of war or the sexual conduct of the heroes. Instead, they focused on the impermanence of life in the world, or *kanci* according to the *Tolkappiyam*. Hence the unity of mankind Tamil poetry presents is not based on religious or cultural identity but on the nature of man and the acceptance of the human condition.

Partly responsible for this mantra was the political climate in which Tamil poetry was codified. A new military caste had replaced the old tribal and communal societies with chieftaincies ruled by princes, thereby ending the republican way of life. This age of transition informed the development of Tamil heroic poetry. What was present and significant in the affairs of men became the focus of bardic art, rather than the gods, for example. The rites and ceremonies of daily life, not religion, were reflected in early Tamil poetry.

THEMES AND FORMULAS

Ancient Tamil poetry is full of techniques associated with oral poetry. Epithets and stock phrases enable the bard to extemporize in meter more easily, producing the poetry's formulaic quality. In order to defamiliarize the presentation of the subject matter, the Tamil poets utilize suggestion. The use of historical allusions grounds the poems in reality and constitutes another dimension to the tradition the poems represent. Since these techniques shape bardic art per se, identifying the work of an individual author is virtually impossible. A good poem, the Tolkappiyam declares, is unified by a theme that is in harmony with tradition, such that it is exhibited in every aspect of the poem. As a result, the greatest poets of the anthologies are also the greatest technicians.

IN THE CLASSROOM

THE HEROIC

The heroes of classical Tamil poetry are idealized types derived from the common people and can be anonymous, as is the case with *akam* poetry, or historical, as in *puram* poetry. What makes them great, regardless of their birth or station, is the fulfillment of the duties associated with their position. Therefore, the hero is a valiant and honorable warrior in battle, a devoted husband and responsible head of the household in times of peace. Moreover, women could be heroic as the mothers of great men or if they displayed a courageous and martial spirit. The king's heroism depended on his qualities as a man as well as his performance as the leader of his people. For the ancient Tamil, the survival and prosperity of the kingdom depended on their success in harvest and in war, for which the king was responsible.

Discussion

1. How are the qualities of a great warrior related to the qualities of a lover?

2. The poems show that heroism does not depend on success or victory alone. How is loss presented as being heroic? Refer, for instance, to "A King's Last Words" or to "278: Mothers."

3. How is the opposition between peace and war portrayed?

Connections

1. Direct students to read Homer's *The Odyssey* and Virgil's *The Aeneid* (both in Book 1). How do love and war interact in other epic traditions?

2. On several levels, the Tamil poems contrast the inner with the outer. Compare the way they do so with the way the inner and outer function in Thomas Mann's "Death in Venice" (Book 6).

Writing

Ask students to write a short paper in response to one or more of the following:

1. Little is said about "the enemy" in the poems. Drawing on what the poems do present, identify what are the Tamil and their culture up against.

2. Beginnings and endings come together in many forms in several of the poems. In what way can the poems be interpreted as being cyclical?

BEYOND THE CLASSROOM

RESEARCH & WRITING

1. Find out more about what the *Tolkappiyam* says about poetry. Compare what you find with what Aristotle and Horace say in the *Poetics* and the *Art of Poetry*, respectively.

2. Inasmuch as Tamil poetry exemplifies the grammar of the language, all Tamil poetry (ancient and modern) is "grammatically correct." Read Terry Eagleton's essay "What is literature?" (the Introduction to his book *Literary Theory*), and write a paper about the implications of this characteristic for the way we define poetry in contrast to prose and/or everyday speech.

3. Part of what differentiates Tamil poetry from other Indian literatures is its independence from the Sanskrit tradition. Investigate what is characteristic of Sanskrit literature in comparison with the selection of Tamil poems in the anthology.

Projects

1. Read some modern Tamil poetry, and write about the relationship between the modern and the ancient variants.

2. The production of the anthologies is allegedly the achievement of the three academies. Find out more about this "creation" story, and compare it with the mythic origins of other literatures.

FURTHER READING

Kailasapathy, K. *Tamil Heroic Poetry*. 1968.
Kazhagam, V. *The Tamil Concept of Love*. 1962.
Varadarajan, M. *The Treatment of Nature in Sangam Literature*. 1969.

MEDIA RESOURCES

WEB SITES

The Tamil Literature Page
www.cs.utk.edu/~siddhart/tamilnadu/literature.html#Literature
An excellent and complete collection of links to sites devoted to Tamil literature.

Tamil Electronic Library
www.geocities.com/Athens/5180/index.html
Created by Dr. K. Kalyanasundaram of Lausanne, Switzerland, this site provides links to many literary, cultural, and historical sites devoted to Tamil India.

Internet Indian History Sourcebook
www.fordham.edu/halsall/india/100bhartrihari.html
This site created at Fordham University provides an unparalleled collection of links on Indian history, literature, and history.

KALIDASA, *Śakuntalā and the Ring of Recollection* (p. 230)

WWW For a quiz on *Śakuntalā and the Ring of Recollection*, see
World Literature Online at bedfordstmartins.com/worldlit.

Students should have little trouble responding to those parts of the play that directly enact the love between the king and Śakuntalā. Their mutual longing and their fears, hesitations, and misunderstandings are all depicted with a delicate psychological realism, in a manner that will make the story seem quite familiar. What may be harder for students to grasp is how a story of this sort can be seen as having great religious or cosmic significance. There is some parallel in the literature of medieval Europe, where the imagery of sexual love can, as in Dante's poetry, be used to convey ideas of spirituality. But in the European Christian tradition, there is usually at least an implied contrast between bodily and spiritual love: Only a chaste love — or at least one that is more selfless than sensual — can be considered truly spiritual. In the Indian tradition, there is no such contrast. Chastity is considered appropriate for certain people at certain times — Śakuntalā herself belongs to a community of ascetics when the play begins — but at other times a frankly sexual love is not only not a sin, but the only possible way to fulfill one's dharma (duty or path).

This relativity of right and wrong — to time, place, and a person's position in the scheme of things — may seem strange to students raised in the Judaeo-Christian tradition, but it is highly characteristic of the Indian view of morality, as given classic expression in the Baghavad Gita (Book 1). You may wish to point out other instances of this view in the play. Hunting, for instance, is shown as being a proper activity for a king but out of place in the Hermitage, where the taking of life is prohibited. The king impregnates Shakuntala without formally marrying her, but this is permissible to people of their high status, who are regarded as being capable of true marriage without ceremony, and is accepted even by Shakuntala's stepfather, the sage Kanva.

Kalidasa's greatness as a poet is not fully evident in translation; students will have to take it to some extent on faith. Nevertheless, the central role of imagery and metaphor in the play is clear, and students will gain from having their attention drawn throughout to this aspect of its language. The king, for instance is compared with a bee and with a rain shower, and S Śakuntalā with a vine as well as being associated throughout with plant imagery. Point out that such imagery, besides reinforcing the theme of fertility, can take on a deeper significance in a Hindu context than it might have in poetry of other traditions, for Hinduism doesn't just preach the interconnectedness of all life; through reincarnation, the life of a bee, a flower, or a human can actually be one and the same. Remind students also that much of the verse in the play was sung, and that the characters frequently danced as well, and used an elaborate code of gestures to reinforce the meaning of the words. All this would have created a much more palpable mood (*rasa*) than can be appreciated from a bare written text.

Emphasize that the story itself, which is taken from the *Mahabharata*, is a myth about the origin of India (Bharata, the son of Dusyanta, is the great king after whom India itself — *bharatavarsa* in Sanskrit — is named) and would have been familiar to the audience in the same way that the audience at a Greek tragedy would have known the outcome of the myths and legends they saw being enacted onstage. In neither case would there be any question of a surprise ending, and the predetermined quality of the action in both cases reinforced the idea of fate. But the Hindu view of fate, unlike the Greek, does not dwell on death and the destruction of human hopes. Death, according to Hinduism, is merely a passage from one incarnation to another, until the soul is finally released from the cycle of births and deaths into nirvana, or union with the godhead. There is therefore not so much scope for a sense of the tragic. Classical Indian drama instead seeks to convey a sense of inevitability and fulfillment, giving its plays, including the present one, a contemplative quality.

TEXT & CONTEXT

THE *NATYASHASTRA*

At the beginning of the *Natyashastra* (*Treatise on Drama*), a story is told both about the treatise's origin and about the origin of drama itself. Indra and the other gods approached Brahma, the Creator, saying that though all sacred wisdom had been preserved in the four Vedas, the common people had no access to it, and begged him to create another Veda that people could see as well as hear. Brahma therefore took elements from all four Vedas to create a fifth, which told the sacred stories by acting them out, with gestures, dance, and music. But this Veda was too complicated to understand, so Brahma gave it to the sage Bharata (not to be confused with King Bharata, Dusyanta's son) to simplify and codify. The resulting treatise became the *Natyashastra*.

The *Natyashastra* is in fact one of the primary documents not only on Indian drama but also on Indian dance, music, poetry, and aesthetics in general. The principles expounded in it, which are elaborated in great detail and cover everything from the construction of theaters to the tuning of musical scales, have influenced all subsequent theater, dance, and music not only in India but in other Asian countries as well, particularly those, like Nepal and Bali, in which Indian traditions have been adopted or absorbed. One can see traces of this influence everywhere: in classical Indian music, in classical Indian dance forms like the Kathakali from the Kerala region, and in many of the traditional theatrical arts of Indonesia and Southeast Asia. Even the popular Indian films made in "Bollywood" (Bombay), while often dealing with modern themes, use music, dance, costuming, makeup, and gestures in ways that still conform, in many respects, to the precepts of the *Natyashastra*.

THE THEORY OF *RASA*

By far, the most influential idea of the *Natyashastra* was that of *rasa*, a concept that later came to be applied not just to the arts of performance but to all the arts, including painting and sculpture. Literally, *rasa* means "juice," and in a broader sense, "essence" or "flavor." It thus denotes a quality that it is taken to be objectively present, not just the individual's emotional response to it, though it also refers primarily to a spiritual quality rather than to anything material. The eight *rasas* listed in the *Natyashastra* are *shringara* (the erotic), *hasya* (the humorous), *karuna* (the pathetic), *raudra* (the violent), *vira* (the heroic), *bhayanaka* (the terrible), *bibhatsa* (the odious), and *adbhuta* (the marvelous). Later, writers added a ninth *rasa*, *shanta* (the peaceful), but this is not accepted by all, on the grounds that though it is certainly a highly desirable state — prefiguring the state of nirvana, or bliss — it has no positive "flavor" of its own. Indian tradition also came to associate each *rasa* with a particular deity and a particular color. Of the two most important *rasas* in *Śakuntalā*, *shringara* (the erotic) is associated with the god Vishnu and the color bluish-black, while *vira* (the heroic) is associated with Indra and the color yellow (note the king's connection to Indra in *Shakuntala*; note also the very different associations of colors in the Western tradition).

A well-made work of art, on this theory, is supposed to be dominated by one *rasa* or combination of *rasas*. Other *rasas* can play a minor role, but certain ones are held to be incompatible, and that is why *bibhatsa* (the odious), for instance, cannot appear in a work dominated, as this play is, by the heroic and the erotic. *Hasya* (the humorous), on the other hand, is considered to be compatible with both of these, especially the erotic; it is represented in this play mainly by the buffoon Madhavya. *Karuna* (the pathetic) is likewise compatible with both the heroic and the erotic but not with the humorous: It makes a pronounced appearance in act 4 of the play, where the humorous element is notably absent.

THE PROLOGUE

When Sanskrit drama was first translated into Western languages at the end of the eighteenth century, one convention that struck European readers as novel was the prologue in which actors and director introduced the play. Of course, the idea of a theatrical prologue was not new in Western drama: It appears in Greek theater as well as in Shakespeare. But the unfamiliarity of this particular form of prologue gave it a fresh charm. Goethe, borrowing the idea from *Śakuntalā*, begins his *Faust* with a "Prelude in the Theater" (not included in the excerpt in Book 5) in which poet, theater manager, and clown discuss what they are about to present.

IN THE CLASSROOM

Discussion

1. Have students think of plays, films, or television shows in which actors step out of their roles and either address the audience directly or discuss amongst themselves the fact that they are in a performance. Do such devices make the action seem more or less real? Do they more often than not have a comic effect? What other effects can they have? How would one describe the effect produced by the prologue in *Śakuntalā*?

2. Direct students' attention to the delicate portrayal of the king's behavior during the scenes in act 5 in which Śakuntalā confronts him with her claim of being his wife. How is his character made to seem noble and sympathetic even when he is denying having married her?

3. The king's son is shown in act 7 playing recklessly with a lion's cub. How does this help the king to recognize him? Compare the king's reaction with the boy's behavior to the reaction of the ascetics. What values are represented by these different reactions? Are these values given equal due in the play? Explain.

Connections

1. Compare *Śakuntalā* to Shakespeare's *The Tempest* (Book 3). What similar elements can you find in the plots of the two plays? Does Shakespeare use a variety of different kinds of language corresponding to the speech of high-born and lowly characters in *Śakuntalā*? How is the role of magic and the supernatural similar or different in the two plays? Does the fact that the stage-world Shakespeare creates in *The Tempest* is not one that is an overtly Christian one account for any of the similarities or differences between the two plays?

Writing

Ask students to write a short paper in response to one or more of the following:

1. Analyze the king's role in the society depicted in *Śakuntalā*. What are a king's — or at least this king's — special responsibilities? Is kingship seen throughout as an enviable position to hold? How does the play's view of the king's responsibilities, privileges, and burdens compare with traditional European views of kingship?

2. Describe the interaction of the natural and the supernatural worlds in *Śakuntalā*. What sorts of beings other than gods or humans are mentioned or depicted in the play? What role do they have in the action? How powerful are the gods?

BEYOND THE CLASSROOM

RESEARCH & WRITING

1. The theme of recognition is pervasive in *Śakuntalā*. Write an essay identifying some of the many instances in which recognition occurs or fails to occur in the play. Explain whether, and if so how, each instance advances the story. Research the Hindu notions of *maya* (illusion) and *moksha* (liberation), and discuss how these notions might relate to the different kinds of deception and recognition depicted in the play.

2. Compare the imagery of love in *Śakuntalā* with the images used in medieval European poetry like Dante's or the *Lay of Chevrefoil* by Marie de France (p. 674). Identify common elements. Which images seem most bound to their cultural context, and which seem more universal?

Projects

1. Have students watch examples of Indian film, either classics like the films of Satyajit Ray, or the popular products of "Bollywood." Ask them to note elements that seem similar to elements in *Śakuntalā*. See if they can identify definite moods in either parts or the entirety of these films that correspond to one or more of the rasas listed in the *Natyashastra*. The same exercise may be performed with recorded examples of Indian music or illustrations of classical Indian art. You may also wish to have them take a non-Indian work of art and see whether the theory of *rasa* can be applied to it as well.

FURTHER READING

Ingalls, Daniel H. *Sanskrit Poetry from Vidyakara's Treasury*. 1968.
Natyasastra. Trans. and ed. M. Ghosh. 1995.
Paz, Octavio. *The Double Flame: Love and Eroticism*. Trans. Helen Lane. 1996.
Rangacharya, Adya. *Introduction to Bharata's Natyasastra*. 1998.

MEDIA RESOURCES

VIDEO

India
50 min., 2002 (Ambrose Video)
For over four thousand years, the lands of India have been home to a remarkable human civilization. This fascinating program journeys through the centuries to reveal the continuing story of the Indian people. Beginning with a graphic reconstruction of an Indus Valley city of the Second Millennium B.C.E., the Indian experience includes fabulous dynasties of kings, timeless belief systems, and golden ages of culture. India's greatest buildings especially reflect the character of a unique people, culminating in the glory of the Taj Mahal, the greatest monument to human love ever constructed and one of the most spectacular constructions anywhere on earth.

WEB SITES

Kalidasa Akademi
http://www.ujjain.nic.in/kalidasa_academi/kalidasa_academi.htm
A Web site devoted to the life and work of Kalidasa. Includes poetry and artwork relating to the fourth-century poet.

Internet Indian History Sourcebook
www.fordham.edu/halsall/india/100bhartrihari.html
This site created at Fordham University provides an unparalleled collection of links on
Indian history, literature, and history.

GENERAL MEDIA RESOURCES

VIDEO

India: From Moghuls to Independence
42 min., 1992 (Library Video Company)
This program covers the history of India from the time of Genghis Khan's first extension
of his domain beyond China. It explains the roles of Tamerlane and his descendant Babur
and shows the crucial battle of Panipat between Babur and the forces of Ibrahim Lodi, the
Afghan Sultan of Delhi. There would be many more battles (including a second battle of
Panipat) before the Afghans were beaten, but Babur had established Mongol hegemony
over a vast territory. The program traces the subsequent history of India: the exploits of his
son Humayun and his grandson, Akbar; the arrival of Europeans; the flowering of Moghul
culture epitomized by the Taj Mahal, and the decline; its submission to the British Empire
and its reawakening at independence.

Indus to Independence: A Journey Through Indian History
34 min., 2000 (Films for the Humanities & Sciences)
India, a rich amalgam of cultures and religions, bears the imprint of many civilizations.
Beginning with the Stone Age, this comprehensive program unfolds India's past, era by era,
covering the Indus Valley civilization, the Vedic Age, the Mauryan empire, the Gupta Age,
the southern kingdoms, the Muslim invasion, the Mogul and Maratha empires, the British
Raj, and independence. The impact of India's diverse religions — Hinduism, Buddhism,
Jainism, Islam, and Christianity — is also explored.

WEB SITES

Exploring Ancient World Cultures: Medieval Europe Homepage
eawc.evansville.edu/mepage.htm
This site covers ancient Near Eastern history to the Middle Ages. It includes a thorough
chronology of major events of medieval times and allows users to look into what was happening across cultures during various points in history.

The Labyrinth: Resources for Medieval Studies
www.georgetown.edu/labyrinth/labyrinth-home.html
Based at Georgetown University, this site provides links to many medieval resources available on the Internet.

NetSerf: The Internet Connection for Medieval Resources
www.netserf.org/
Sponsored by the history department of the Catholic University of America, this is a wonderful gateway site to all things medieval.

The Online Medieval & Classical Library
sunsite.berkeley.edu/OMACL/
The Douglas B. Killings collection of some of the most important literary works of classical
and medieval civilization.

AUDIO

Living Biographies of Religious Leaders
8 tapes, 11:25 hrs. (Blackstone Audiobooks)
This program presents the lives of twenty great founders and leading advocates of the world's foremost religions. Here are the historical facts and legends associated with these forceful personalities who have inspired and influenced humankind through the centuries. Presented are Jesus Christ, Moses, Isaiah, Zoroaster, Buddha, Confucius, John the Baptist, Paul, Muhammad, Francis of Assisi, John Huss, Luther, Loyola, Calvin, George Fox, Swedenborg, Wesley, Brigham Young, Mary Baker Eddy, and Gandhi.

CHINA: FROM THE COLLAPSE OF THE HAN DYNASTY TO THE MONGOL INVASIONS

TAO QIAN, Selected Writings (p. 302)

WWW   For a quiz on the writings of Tao Qian, see *World Literature Online* at bedfordstmartins.com/worldlit.

Tao Qian's poetry represents a significant transition in the history of Chinese literature. Throughout the Han dynasty and afterward, prose was preferred to poetry. Folk songs and ballads that depicted dynastic history, court life, and traditional ceremonies, rather than the everyday life of a common man, accounted for most of the poetry at the time. Such poetry was extremely formal and ornate, whereas the composition of the *gushi* (See p. 305) only required rhyming couplets and did not prescribe the position of tones within the verse (the Chinese equivalent to meter, involving level and deflected tones). Tao Qian's contemporary, Hsieh Ling-yün (385–433 C.E.), wrote nature poetry as well, but the difficulty of his diction and his numerous references to classical texts made his poetry more traditional. Hsieh Ling-yün was renowned, above all, for his landscape ("mountainand-river") poems — impersonal descriptions of the wilderness. In contrast, farms and their rustic surroundings compose the vistas in Tao Qian's work, the simple and intimate style of which was unprecedented. Previous poets had established connections between the historical setting and the individual, but on a grand scale, Pauline Yu explains, addressing "specific concerns with government, war, mortality, or immortality — and generally on rather formal occasions" (143). Tao Qian restricted himself to the ordinary person — "his retirement, farm, and family — and in the most casual of circumstances." His focus on the individual, his portrayal of nature, and his artless style greatly influenced subsequent poets and brought many to consider Tao Qian China's first modern poet.

The self-reflexivity of his rhapsodies and such poems as "Home Again among Gardens and Fields" and "A Reply to Secretary Kuo" will prompt students to focus on Tao Qian's portrayal of his feelings and his values. Direct them to develop this approach into an analysis of the interaction between place and state of mind. In so doing, students should identify the different kinds of places that illicit Tao Qian's poetic response. How is nature opposed to the world? How do his works figure forth the "natural"? You might instruct your students to respond to these questions first in terms of the physical and then in terms of the spiritual or philosophical.

Another important theme in Tao Qian's poetry and prose is the juxtaposition between change and constancy. Given the political turmoil at the time (see pp. 302–3), the order and harmony of nature, rather than social convention, came to represent stability. Many sought identification with the cosmic principle, which meant, for Hsieh Ling-yün among others, losing oneself in the vast wilderness of nature. Point out that Tao Qian does not lose himself in this way. Rather, you might suggest, in returning to nature Tao Qian returns to himself — for instance, to his nature. How, then, do the order and harmony of nature determine constancy and/or change in Tao Qian's works? Students should examine "In the Sixth Month of 408, Fire" and "Substance, Shadow, and Spirit" in particular.

Finally, Tao Qian's life and work illustrate his rejection of the Confucian's social obligations and his preference for the Taoist's "carefree" life. Ask students to identify what makes his life carefree, perhaps in comparison with the way a carefree life is typically envisioned in the West. How does such a way of life enable Tao Qian to achieve *tzu-jan* (see p. 304)? Encourage students to locate moments in the texts that demonstrate *tzu-jan*. To what extent is *tzu-jan* connected to one of the central themes in Tao Qian's work — the impermanence of life and/or manmade institutions?

TEXT & CONTEXT

CONFUCIANISM

The most important social institution in Confucianism is the government, which regulates all social interaction beyond the family. And since Confucianism had become state doctrine with the Han dynasty, Confucianism lost favor with its fall. Without a strong, central government, there was no encouragement to study Confucianism, and the Han government had not fulfilled the Confucian ideal of a good, stable government. Like Taoism, Confucianism also emphasized the development of the individual but specifically in order to serve the state. Civil service was the highest calling, and the relationship between ruler and subject came before all others.

TAOISM

Many civil servants retired into the countryside in the period following the Han dynasty. Such a retreat was symptomatic of the Taoist endeavor to live in harmony with the way of nature, which did not entail a set of rules but rather involved accepting things as they are or occur. The Taoist's life is therefore one of *wei wuwei* (to do without doing), whereby the force of the individual and that of the universe are balanced. Balance, of body and spirit, constitutes the natural state. Hence in Taoism, as opposed to Confucianism for instance, there is no central figure or institution of authority.

BUDDHISM

Buddhism became popular among the intellectuals in the south, where the aristocratic families of the north fled. It offered a more organized regiment than Taoism and was not as ascetic in various respects. While Taoism promoted sufficiency, Buddhism permitted luxury. Aristocrats could thus embody the virtues of Buddhism (self-discipline, piety, strict morality, cool rationality) and at the same time lead worldly lives.

TECHNIQUES OF CHARACTERIZATION

The tradition of historiography, Dore Levy explains, is the basis for Chinese techniques of characterization. Whereas the Western tradition emphasizes heroic action, through which the character of the hero is revealed, "Following the Chinese propensity for emphasizing ritual rather than mythological patterns of culture, individual *quality* rather than action is the issue, and so quality reliably determines action" (18) [Dore Levy is not in bibliography]. Tao Qian's poetry and prose clearly demonstrate his debt to this aspect of Chinese historiography; action is significant to the extent to which it expresses his will. Indeed, Tao Qian is considered a master at portraying the poet's intent. [Keep in mind that the Chinese poetic tradition developed without anxieties concerning authorial intention, such that the notion of the intentional fallacy is not relevant. See, for instance, the definition of poetry in the Great Preface to the *Book of Songs*, in which poetry is identified as "that to which what is intently on the mind goes."]

LITERARY CONVENTIONS

Part of the impact Tao Qian's poetry had on the poetry of later poets can be seen in the images he made conventional. Among these, Pauline Yu notes, are white clouds, denoting distant purity, chrysanthemums symbolizing longevity, and a bird returning home after venturing out into the world.

IN THE CLASSROOM

Discussion

1. Have students identify the qualities that Tao Qian disparages. To what extent are these "unnatural"?

2. Tao Qian rejects the order and tedium of life in a bureaucracy. How is this order different from the order that governs the natural life?

3. Contrast through parallelism structures much of the imagery in Tao Qian's work — winter and summer, morning and night, life and death are just a few. Have students focus on specific examples and discuss or write about the effect such contrasts have.

Connections

1. Nature and the natural order of things have composed an ideal in many literary texts. Compare the role nature plays in Tao Qian's writings with nature's function in Voltaire's *Candide* (Book 4), Whitman's *Song of Myself* (Book 5), or even Rousseau's *Social Contract* (Book 4).

2. The representation of the self shapes all of Tao Qian's works. To what extent does Tao Qian distinguish an authentic from an inauthentic self? How does this opposition contrast, for instance, with that of Rousseau in his *Confessions* (p. 70) or with Franklin in his *Autobiography* (Book 4)?

Writing

Ask students to write a short paper in response to one or more of the following:

1. To be surrounded by nature and/or his family seems to be everything Tao Qian wants. Nevertheless, he often characterizes himself as alone/solitary. Explore this seeming contradiction.

2. Explore the relationship between "reading" nature, reading poetry, and "reading" oneself. Consider, for instance, Tao Qian's description of himself in "The Gentleman of the Five Willow Trees," in which reading books provides as much sustenance as eating a meal, or the correspondence between Tao Qian reading *The Classic of Mountains and Seas* and the landscape before him.

BEYOND THE CLASSROOM

RESEARCH & WRITING

1. How do particular aspects of the Chinese language (e.g., the lack of tense and connectives or its idiographic representation — see *In the Tradition*, pp. 325–26) augment what Tao Qian communicates in his poetry and prose?

2. Read the official biography of Tao Qian in the dynastic history. How does this account compare with Tao Qian's self-representation in "The Gentleman of the Five Willow Trees," "Back Home Again Chant," and "Elegy for Myself" in particular?

3. Read or find out more about *The Classic of Mountains and Seas*. What significance does it have for Tao Qian's poem, "Reading *The Classic of Mountains and Seas*"?

Projects

1. Tao Qian is celebrated as one of the founders of Chinese nature poetry. Look at contemporary examples of landscape painting, and compare the way nature is represented in each medium.

2. Look at modern examples of Chinese nature poetry. What aspects of Tao Qian's style continue to shape the poetic representation of nature?

3. An early poet in the Western tradition similar to Tao Qian is perhaps Virgil. Read his *Georgics*, and compare Virgil's bucolic vision with that of Tao Qian.

WWW For additional information on Tao Qian and annotated Web links,
    see *World Literature Online* at bedfordstmartins.com/worldlit.

FURTHER READING

Lévy, André. *Chinese Literature, Ancient and Classical.* Trans. William H. Nienhauser Jr. 2000.
Levy, Dore. *Chinese Narrative Poetry: The Late Han through T'ang Dynasties.* 1988.
Shuen-fu Lin and Stephen Owen, eds. *The Vitality of the Lyric Voice: Shih Poetry from the Late Han to T'ang.* 1986.
Yu, Pauline. *Reading of Imagery in the Chinese Poetic Tradition.* 1987.

MEDIA RESOURCES

WEB SITES

Poetry of Tao Qian
www.chinapage.org/taoy2n.html
This site offers a number of Tao Qian's poems both in Chinese and English.

Tao Qian
www.renditions.org/renditions/authors/taoqian.html
This page includes a brief biography of the poet as well as a bibliography of English translations of his work.

In the Tradition: Poets of the Tang Dynasty (p. 318)

Traditionally, Chinese literature produced during the Tang dynasty is divided into four periods: the Early Tang (618–c. 713), the High Tang (c. 713–c. 790), the Mid-Tang (c. 791–c. 825), and the Late Tang (c. 825–907), reflecting literary developments of the time rather than changes in the historical context. Early Tang poets were circumscribed by the decorum and ceremony of the aristocracy and the court. Poetry had become a mannered form of social discourse that adorned, rather than addressed, affairs of state. According to the Sui Confucian Li O, "Poem after poem . . . never got beyond images of the moon and dew; tables were heaped and chests filled with nothing more than the descriptions of the wind and clouds" (*The Poetry of the Early T'ang*, 5). A tension between the traditions of court poetry and the impetus for change emerged during the Early Tang, on the level of composition as well as aesthetic taste. The nature of this change was determined by the "return to antiquity" that would become characteristic of Tang poetry, and quite literally in the *fu-ku*. For Early Tang poets, this return was primarily based on ethical grounds: Poetry should exemplify and thereby teach moral rectitude.

High Tang literature developed in reaction to that of Early Tang, mainly in terms of artistic freedom. Lack of decorum characterized the stylistic conventions as well as the subject matter of High Tang poetry. High Tang poets experimented with irregular meter and verse forms, informal themes, and the establishment of a distinctive voice. Their poetry represented and addressed the common people in plain and straightforward language and displayed the virtues of the individual more than the polish of social exchange. The political turmoil of the time fostered a poetry of reclusion expressive of a private voice, often the perspective of the exile poet. Of the poets included in the selection, Wang Wei, Li Bai, and Du Fu belong to the period of the High Tang.

By the time of the Mid-Tang, much of the poetry being written was personal. Poetry constructed the poet's identity according to established patterns, which included the characters of the lover, the hermit, and the scholar. In Mid-Tang poetry, such typologies become inadequate for the constitution of a writer's identity. Authenticity requires individual differentiation — the assertion of singularity — perceptible in the particularity of experience. Only then would poetry escape the falseness of cliché and conformity. Likewise, nature is no longer intelligible as an ordering mechanism, for life or for poetry. Instead of the architectural, purposive system it was in earlier representations, nature becomes an "aggregation of details," Stephen Owen explains, without a unifying principle or revealing its unintelligibility. Bo Juyi is a Mid-Tang poet.

Late Tang poetry reflects what has become a crisis of language and representation. The decline of the Tang dynasty shaped the sense of loss and melancholy that pervades poetry at the time. Historical associations often render the poems ironic or self-mocking, and, in general, demonstrative of the poets' awareness of the transience of life. Disorientation and confusion are characteristic of the world depicted in Late Tang poetry.

Providing a bit more background on the developing concerns of the Tang poets will enable you to approach the poems, in class discussion, as representative of a particular literary moment within a tradition and draw attention to the differences between the poets. For instance, Wang Wei, although regarded as a meditative, private poet, was also one of the more social and urbane of the Tang poets. This disjunction is more pronounced with Li Bai, who assumed various roles within his poetry (the eccentric, the brave, the drunk) other than his own (scholar-official). Li Bai deliberately constructed an image of the self in his poetry. Stephen Owen observes that "Unlike Wang Wei, Li [Bai] was not greatly interested in how the world was perceived; His was a poetry of self-creation" (*The Great Age of Chinese Poetry*, 137). Have students examine such poems as "To Subprefect Chang" and "Ch'ang-Kan Village Song" in order to discuss the construction of identity in Tang poetry. Often the natural landscape reflects Wang Wei's state of mind. Other questions to consider are: In what way does Li Bai construct a poetic subject in his poetry? What role does the poet speaker come to play in Bo Juyi's poetry ("An Old Charcoal Seller" and "Madly Singing in the Mountains" in particular)?

Another way to group together poems in order to distinguish the poets is by examining common themes. For example, direct your students to the poems in the selection that have to do with parting or separation. Contrast Wang Wei's "Seeing Someone Off" and Li Bai's "Seeing Off a Friend" with Du Fu's "P'eng-Ya Song" and "Dreaming of Li Po." How does exile affect the way separation is represented? Alternatively, have students discuss the relationship between the poet and the moon in Li Bai's "Drinking Alone beneath the Moon" in comparison to Du Fu's "Moonlit Night" or "Thoughts, Traveling at Night." Or you might focus on the contrast between the natural landscape and the city and what each signifies, particularly in such poems as Du Fu's "Spring Night, Delighted by Rain" and Wang Wei's "Crossing the Yellow River." What effect does this contrast have?

Finally, you might consider Bo Juyi's work in comparison with that of the other poets, since he belongs to a later period. How is the poet speaker's relationship to society in Bo Juyi's poetry different from that depicted in Wang Wei's "Hermitage at Chung-nan Mountain"? How does Bo Juyi's declaration "not one man!" in "Passing T'ien-mên Street in Ch'ang-an and Seeing a Distant View of Chung-nan Mountains" contrast with Wang Wei's "No sign of men" in "Deer Park"? How does Bo Juyi's commitment to the common people inform his perspective? One of the ways in which Bo Juyi aligns himself with the rest of the poets is in his recognition of the poetic tradition. Students should look at Bo Juyi's "On the Boat, Reading Yüan Chen's Poems" and Du Fu's "Dreaming of Li Po" in order to discuss the function of this reflexivity. What kind of a society do the Tang poets constitute?

TEXT & CONTEXT

THE INFLUENCE OF THE PAST

One of the most influential poets of the past for Tang poetry was Tao Qian, whose plain and simple diction, natural vocabulary, and intimate style offered an ideal alternative to the conventions of the court poem. Wang Wei was particularly influenced by his work.

BUDDHISM UNDER TANG XUANZONG

With the exception of Chung-tsung, none of the Tang emperors had been especially supportive of Buddhism, although they all knew how politically advantageous it was to maintain good relations with the Buddhist population. Hence many of Xuanzong's predecessors had built great Buddhist monasteries, provided for Buddhist monks, and allowed Buddhists political clout. Xuanzong, however, was determined to carry out broad economic and administrative reforms, beginning with policies mediating between church and state. With a series of edicts, Xuanzong relegated Buddhism to official places of worship, banned the construction of new monasteries, curtailed church holdings, and reduced the number of monks. Doing so eased the burden of the church for the state and enabled Xuanzong to allocate resources to other areas.

TAOISM UNDER TANG XUANZONG

By the end of his rule, Xuanzong had become enthusiastic about the occult and supported forms of Taoism and Esoteric Buddhism. He oversaw the translation of many Buddhist scriptures, the Tao-te Ching, and the composition of Taoist ritual music. First and foremost a Taoist, Xuanzong brought the Taoist clergy under the jurisdiction of the Court of Imperial Clan Affairs, demonstrating the imperial family's connection with Taoism.

IN THE CLASSROOM

Discussion and Writing

1. Have students examine the ways in which a journey is represented. How does the journey function? Direct students, for instance, to Du Fu's "P'eng-Ya Song," or "Thoughts, Traveling at Night" and Li Bai's "Going to Visit Tai-T'ien Mountain's Master of the Way without Finding Him," "Searching for Master Yung," or "Sent to My Two Little Children in the East of Lu."

2. Solitude is a recurrent theme in Tang poetry. Have students select poems from more than one poet and discuss the effect being cut off from everything/everyone else has for different poets. Consider Wang Wei's "To Subprefect Chang" and Bo Juyi's "Winter Night" or "Autumn Pool," for example. How do the conversation poems between Li Bai and Du Fu complicate this perspective?

3. Direct students to focus on moments in which the poets look to the past. How is the past portrayed? How does it compare with the present?

4. In opposition to the polite, censured themes of court poetry, many Tang poets made the corruption and injustice of the court significant in their poetry. What form does political critique take in the poems in the selection?

5. Each of the poets in the selection depicts a "way of life" that aligns the perspective of his poetry. Focus on one or two poets/perspectives, and identify what they consider essential in life.

Connections

1. The literature of the Tang dynasty was shaped, to a great extent, by the literature of the classical past. Compare the relationship between Tang literature and the tradition it invokes with the relationship between Neoclassicism and the Western classical tradition, as in Molière's *Tartuffe* (Book 4), or modernism and the Western classical tradition, as in T. S. Eliot's *The Wasteland* (Book 6), for example.

2. Tang poets greatly admired Tao Qian's poetry. What specific elements in Tang poetry display Tao Qian's influence?

BEYOND THE CLASSROOM

RESEARCH & WRITING

1. Read selections of the Tang *Wen-ching mi-fu-lun* and/or a few of the chapters of *Wen-hsin tiao-lung* (exemplary treatises on Chinese poetics in the time of the Tang dynasty) as well as pertinent excerpts from the *Classic of Poetry*. How do Tang poetics develop classical principles?

2. Find out more about the kinds of occasions that were deemed appropriate for poetry before the Tang dynasty. How does occasion function differently for Tang poets?

Projects

1. Find out more about modern representations of the Tang dynasty (for example, the reproduction of a Tang city, much in the same vein as Williamsburg, Virginia). What is the legacy of Tang poetry in China today?

2. Read translations of Tang poetry done by the Beat poets, and write about how Tang poetry influenced Beat culture.

FURTHER READING

Owen, Stephen. *The End of the Chinese "Middle Ages," Essays in Mid-Tang Literary Culture.* 1996.

——. *The Great Age of Chinese Poetry: The High T'ang.* 1981.

——. *The Poetry of the Early T'ang.* 1977.

——. *Remembrances, The Experience of the Past in Classical Chinese Literature.* 1986.

Wu, Fusheng. *The Poetics of Decadence, Chinese Poetry of the Southern Dynasties and Late Tang Periods.* 1998.

Yu, Pauline. *The Reading of Imagery in the Chinese Poetic Tradition.* 1987.

MEDIA RESOURCES

VIDEO

China's Cosmopolitan Age: The Tang
60 min., 2000 (Annenberg/CPB Video)
Take students on a field trip to an ancient democracy at the heart of a great empire, where new ideas about government, art, religion, and philosophy flourished. This was the Tang civilization of China, which lasted from 618 to 907 c.e. This video explores the immense influence of the Tang on future generations of Chinese, Koreans, and Japanese.

WEB SITES

Chinese Poems
www.chinese-poems.com/
This fabulous site presents Chinese, pinyin, and English texts of poems by some of the greatest Chinese poets. Most of the featured authors are from the Tang dynasty, when culture in China was at its peak, but writers from other periods are also included. Poems are listed by author.

Tang Dynasty Poems: Visions of Paradise
www.pureinsight.org/pi/articles/2002/9/16/918.html
This site provides a good number of Tang poems by several different poets.

Tang Poetry
members.tripod.com/~Dioscuri/poetry/poetry.html
This site gives an overview of Tang poetry and several translated examples of it.

GENERAL MEDIA RESOURCES

VIDEO

China's Cosmopolitan Age: The Tang
60 min., 2000 (Annenberg/CPB Video)
Take students on a field trip to an ancient democracy at the heart of a great empire, where new ideas about government, art, religion, and philosophy flourished. This was the Tang civilization of China, which lasted from 618 to 907 c.e. This video explores the immense influence of the Tang on future generations of Chinese, Koreans, and Japanese.

The Eastern Philosophers
50 min. each, 2001 (Insight Media)
Examining the central doctrines of Confucianism, Shinto, Hinduism, Judaism, and Islam, this set examines the genesis of spiritual thought. The first volume explores the dominant philosophical and spiritual ideas of the Far East, focusing on Confucius and Shinto. The second discusses the Hinduism and Buddhism of South Asia, with their focus on cycles of death and rebirth. The final volume considers the roots, rituals, and sacred texts of Judaism and the tenets and lifestyle issues of Islam.

Great Religions of the World
33 min., 1995 (Insight Media)
This video explores the major beliefs, origins, and histories of Buddhism, Christianity, Judaism, Hinduism, Islam, and Taoism. It differentiates between ethnic and universalizing religions, discussing how each of the universalizing religions developed from an ethnic base and expanded past national boundaries.

Marco Polo: Journey to the East
50 min., 1995 (A&E Video)
A&E's account of one of the greatest adventures in human history and a revealing portrait of the man who went where others dared not dream.

Three Pillars: Confucius, Jesus, and Mohammed
53 min., 1998 (Insight Media)
This video studies the identities of the founders of three major religions — Confucianism, Christianity, and Islam. It looks at how Confucianism blended into the Chinese social and political structure; the significance of Jesus as a prophet for Muslims and as God incarnate for Christians; and the teachings of Muhammad and the Qur'an.

The World's Philosophies
60 min., 1994 (Insight Media)
In this video, Huston Smith defines three basic types of human relationships — with nature, with other people, and with one's self — and explains how these relationships correspond to the philosophical traditions of the West, of China, and of India.

WEB SITES

Ancient China Index
www.crystalinks.com/china.html
This is a good gateway site to links of all kinds on ancient China.

Internet East Asian History Sourcebook
www.fordham.edu/halsall/eastasia/eastasiasbook.html
A premiere Internet source on East Asian studies created at Fordham University, the Internet East Asian History Sourcebook is a premiere site for information on the history, culture, and literature of Asian culture, both ancient and modern. Excellent links.

AUDIO

Living Biographies of Religious Leaders
8 tapes, 11:25 hrs. (Blackstone Audiobooks)
This program presents the lives of twenty great founders and leading advocates of the world's foremost religions. Here are the historical facts and legends associated with these forceful personalities who have inspired and influenced humankind through the centuries. Presented are Jesus Christ, Moses, Isaiah, Zoroaster, Buddha, Confucius, John the Baptist, Paul, Muhammad, Francis of Assisi, John Huss, Luther, Loyola, Calvin, George Fox, Swedenborg, Wesley, Brigham Young, Mary Baker Eddy, and Gandhi.

ARABIA AND PERSIA:
THE WORLD OF ISLAM

IMRU' AL-QAYS, *The Mu'allaqah of Imru' al-Qays* (p. 368)

WWW   For a quiz on *The Mu'allaqah of Imru' al-Qays*, see *World Literature Online* at bedfordstmartins.com/worldlit.

The *Muallaqat* is a collection of seven odes, each by a different poet. According to tradition, the manuscript was compiled in the eighth century by Hammad ar-Rawiya. Just why these seven *qasidah* by these seven poets (the others are Tarafa, Zuhair, Labid, Antara, Amr b. Kultum, and al-Harit b. Hilliza) were collected is still unknown. The poems of the collection already had something of a romantic air and a certain sanctity in pre-Islamic times.

Perhaps the most common approach to these poems is via orality: descriptions of Bedouin life in the desert in a long poem with only one rhyme. By focusing on the (to Westerners) illogical structure of poems by poets who seem to be ignorant of the concept of hypotaxis, you can point out how the oral nature of the composition determined the structure of the poem. It may be helpful if you let students voice any comprehension issues, and use these comments to introduce literary terms like *hypotaxis* and *parataxis*, or repetition and grammatical terms like *dependency* and *coordination*. Or, you can have the students perform a close reading of pages 78 to 82, since these lines are some of the most intricate in the poem. After these difficulties of the ode are dealt with, students should be better able to move on to the more aesthetically interesting issues. After a few readings, students should start to recognize that certain repetitions help the ode to cohere (especially if they pay attention to the footnotes).

MORE ON THE *QASIDAH*

Imru' al-Qays's *Mu'allaqah* loosely conforms to the structure of the *qasidah*. Loosely is the operative term here. According to Stetkevych, the poet has broken more conventions than he has upheld in this poem. She sees these unconventional aspects as signs for a different reading of the text. The opening, or *istiqaf*, of the *nasib* already puts the form on ambiguous ground. Toponymy sets the opening key in Stetkevych's reading. In other works, place names are found at the beginnings of odes, but here the names are rather indeterminate geographically and ambiguous semantically. Siqt (from *saqata al-janinu* meaning the fetus miscarried, aborted) comes between al-Dakhul (*dakhl* means sexual penetration) and Hawmal (*haml* means pregnancy). Such words may be a little excessive in what is supposed to be the elegiac or love lyric section.

The second part, or *rahil*, usually contains a panegyric to a leader or other notable person. It may also contain an extended retelling of ones own exploits, as is the case with the *Mu'allaqah of Imru' al-Qays*. On the other hand, this section of the *qasidah* is where an antagonist's ignoble deeds or his questionable ancestry are catalogued. Despite the lively, masculine nature of the content in this section, there is always some suggestion of immanent death. The harsh realities of desert life are not easily evaded. Thus one can say that looking death in the face is one of the main duties of the speaker of the *qasidah*. This is, after all, heroic poetry or perhaps a poetry of heroics, if you choose to depict it as such. Many of his deeds can be seen as acts of relinquishment or loss (and thus metaphors for death), like frivolously slaughtering his camel (Stetkevych, p. 11) or his seeming surrender to Fatimah (20ff.). And yet the catalogue of the speaker's deeds may also be read as self-criticism. In this context, verse 42 can be seen as a moment of self-awareness. The openness of the form and Imru al-Qays's handling of it have produced here one of the finest examples of pre-Islamic poetry.

A further aspect of the poetic qualities of this text is the use of extended descriptions. In the *qasidah*, these are usually static, exhaustive, and predictable (see Hamori). The static quality of the passages often have the power to turn the audience into participants. The exhaustiveness of the passages lends that which is described, usually a lady and a camel or other mount, to function to reinforce the belief system of which they are a part. Finally, the predictability of the descriptions functions to idealize the lady or the camel. Thus through these passages, the object is made almost tangible and yet distanced.

TEXT & CONTEXT

The concept of ritual helps explain the repetitiveness inherent in the *qasidah qua* form, if not that of an individual work. H. A. R. Gibb remarked on the hieratic quality of the *qasidah* in the Islamic period, when the genre had become, among other things, an instrument for summing up the desert life of what was by then a time of origins, an *illud tempus* (see M. Eliade, *The Sacred and the Profane*). But already in the sixth century, before the coming of Islam, these poems, rather than myths or religious rituals, served as the vehicle for the conception that sorted out the emotionally incoherent facts of life and death, and by the sorting set them at the bearable remove of contemplation.

Much like the Anglo-Saxon scop, the Bedouin poet solidified the community in which he was active by remembering and reciting the deeds of its members or by satirizing an enemy. A good poet could start as well as stop a war between tribes. The conflicts that ended in bloodshed were arbitrated via a system similar to the Anglo-Saxon/Germanic system of *wergeld*, or the acceptance of monetary compensation for the death of a family member in lieu of vengeance. When this system broke down, as it often did on the dry sand dunes of the Arabian desert as well as in the foggy dales of old England, it meant serious trouble for two or more families/tribes with feuds going far beyond anything of which the Hatfields and McCoys could have dreamed.

IN THE CLASSROOM

Discussion

1. At the end of the *rahil*, the speaker of the poem addresses a wolf with a comment on property or possessions. Ask students to discuss the contradictory role of property in Bedouin society (including generosity and nomadic life). Then, ask them to include Matthew 6:19–21 in their discussion. What differences are there between the two societies (the one nomadic and pagan, the other sedentary and Judeo-Christian) and the function of property in them? Why does Jesus admonish his audience? What significance does the communicative situation have in relation to the purport of both messages? This discussion can also include Qur'anic pronouncements on property, if you wish.

2. Bravado and boasting are significant elements of the *qasidah*. Ask students to discuss the significance of boasting and bravado in their lives as compared with their significance in Bedouin culture. A viewing of Jerry Springer or some other sensationalist talk show will give them adequate evidence, if such is needed.

3. One way of seeing the poem is as an extended description of arrested development: The speaker refuses to "grow up." Ask students to form two groups. One group is to argue for this interpretation, the other against it.

Connections

1. Like Imru' al-Qays, Rainer Maria Rilke (Book 6) is also known for exquisite descriptive passages in his poetry. Ask students to look at either "The Panther" or "Archaic Torso of Apollo" and one of the descriptive passages of the *Mu'allaqah* (e.g., 30ff.) and note how the description is constructed: Which senses are invoked (beyond sight, of course)? Does the use of more than one sense make a line or passage more evocative or more powerful, more spiritual or sensual, and the like? How do descriptive passages affect the interpretation of the whole work? If you prefer, one of Keats's odes will also serve.

Writing

Ask students to write a short paper in response to one or more of the following:

1. The most prevalent poetic device in the work is simile. Write a paper in which you demonstrate what effect the plethora of comparisons has on their interpretation of the poem. To what extent do the similes add to or detract from the poetry (e.g., in 38)? To what things are the women, the horse, and the storm compared? What differences are there in these similes, and how can the differences inform the interpretation of the poem?

2. Equilibrium plays an important part in the structure of Imru' al-Qays's *Mu'allaqah*. Write a paper on equilibrium in the form and content of this work. What formal aspects create balance? To what degree does the content support or work against the formal equilibrium?

BEYOND THE CLASSROOM

Research & Writing

1. There are many similarities between the rebellious and extravagant life of Imru' al-Qays and that of Julius Caesar (see Suetonius, Book 1). Ask students to compare/contrast their *gesta* and works of both men (using such resources as Suetonius, perhaps even Caesar's *Commentary* on either the Gallic War or the Civil War). See Stetkevychs, *The Mute Immortals Speak* (chapter 7), for her interpretation of the *Mu'allaqah* and a summary of Imru' al-Qays' life. The *tertium comparationis* can be Marcus Aurelius (Book 1), Buddha (Book 1), Christ (Book 2), or, to make things really interesting, Black Elk (Book 6).

2. Compare the depiction of Imru' al-Qays's deeds with that of Mohammad's in Mohammad Ibn Ishaq's *The Biography of the Prophet*. To what extent does Imru' al-Qays's work function as an early form of the *sira*?

Projects

1. Read A. J. Arberry's translation of the poem (in *Seven Odes: The First Chapter in Arabic Literature*. London: Allen & Unwin, 1957), and examine the ways the translators' different choices influence the reader's perception of the text's style, message, and function.

2. Read the *Mu'allaqah* of Labid and one other *qasidah*. Using all three odes as your corpus, abstract and present to the class an "ideal" or "standard" structure for the *qasidah*. Determine to what extent the form is open or closed. Beyond the formal aspects, determine what poetic or thematic aspects are common to all the texts in your corpus.

WWW For additional information on Imru' al-Qays and annotated Web links, see *World Literature Online* at bedfordstmartins.com/worldlit.

FURTHER READING

Haydar, Adnan. "*The Muʿallaqa of Imru' al-Qays*: Its Structure and Meaning." Part I: *Edebiyât* 2 (1977): 227–61; Part II: *Edebiyât* 3 (1978): 51–82.

Jacobi, Renate. *Studien zur Poetik der altarabischen Qaside.* 1971.

Stetkevych, Jaroslav. "Al-Qasidah al-'Arabiyyah wa Tuqus al-'Ubur." *Majallat Majma' al-Lughah al-'Arabiyya bi-Dimashq* 60, no. 1 (1985): 31–43.

MEDIA RESOURCES

WEB SITES

Cornell Library Middle East and Islamic Studies Collection: Arabic Literature
www.library.cornell.edu/colldev/mideast/arablit.htm
The comprehensive source of materials on Arabic literature includes general overviews of classic (pre-Islamic and early Islamic) and modern Arabic poetry, fiction, and some nonfiction as well as generous selection of works in English and Arabic from both periods and by dozens of important writers. Links to recent criticism, periodical articles, and a thorough bibliography make this an essential site.

Discovering Traditional Arabic Poetry
poetry.allinfo-about.com/features/arabic-poetry.html
An overview of Arabic literature with a link to an Imru' al-Qays's poem.

Poetry Dueling in Arabic
www.unc.edu/~yaqub/pdfdiss/chapter1.pdf
Though part of a much larger work, the first pages of this site show a fascinating exchange between two poets through riddle and reply.

Medieval Sourcebook: Pre-Islamic Arabia: The Hanged Poems
www.fordham.edu/halsall/source/640hangedpoems.html
This page contains full-text English translations of three of the "hanged" or "suspended" poems from the holy shrine of the Kaaba in Mecca, along with a brief description of the poems' key formal qualities.

ABU AL-QASEM FERDOWSI, from *The Tragedy of Sohráb and Rostám* (p. 382)

WWW For a quiz on the work of Ferdowsi, see *World Literature Online* at bedfordstmartins.com/worldlit.

The entire work can be divided into three sections. The first, the *asatiri*, or mythological, period covers the span of time from the beginning of the world up to the first shah Faridun. The stories of man's discovery of fire and preparation of foods, the invention of clothing, the domestication of animals, the construction of the first dwellings, the cultivation of fields, and the like, all fall into this period, which ends with the tyranny of the Dahhaks. Many of those secrets had to be forced from demons. In this section, the kings are presented as not only rulers but also educators leading the people to culture.

The second section is taken up with the *pahlevani*, or legendary, period. It begins with the revolt of Kawe, a smith whose sons had been sacrificed, that placed Faridun on the throne. He divided the world into three parts and distributed them to his sons. Salm, the oldest, rules the Eastern portion, called Rum; Tur, the second son, receives Turán; and the third son, Iraj, becomes king of Iran and Arabia. The subsequent wars among those three regions is blamed on Faridun's division. While in the early part of this period the rulers led their armies into battle, later on they step back and let the heroes take command. Therewith the heroes become the means to the end of political stability and instability in the world. The greatest of the heroes is Rostám. His duels against Afrasiyab, his campaigns against the Divs in Mazandaran, and his seven adventures are among the most striking in the *Shahname*. The significance of the heroes is translated into physical size and prowess in their literary descriptions. Rostám is gigantic — for instance, his head reaches into the heavens. Fighting is not their sole activity, though. They also feast, drink, and occasionally love.

The final section is the *tarikhi*, or historical, period. It begins with Darius III who loses to Alexander the Great. Cultural deeds begin to take the place of battles now. Politics, intrigues at court, hunting and festivals, international relations, the lives of the generals, priests, scholars, and musicians become almost as significant as issues of political hegemony. The invention of chess and the translation of the Sanskrit *Pancatantra* into Persian are seen as important cultural achievements and through the campaigns against the Eastern Roman Empire (Byzantium), the nomadic tribes of Iran and the Arabs form the unifying basis of the section. On the whole, this final portion of the work becomes more realistic in characterization and sober in presentation.

TEXT & CONTEXT

SOHRÁB AND ROSTÁM

The selection chosen, though very popular, is by no means indicative of the work as a whole, since neither hero is a shah, and the shah in this episode is anything but worthy of praise. However, this story is the one that has impressed itself on the European consciousness, partly due to its similarity to the Old High German *Hildebrandslied*, the Middle Irish *Aiged Aenfhir Aife*, and the Old Norse *Saga of Thidrek of Bern*, none of which are in the anthology. Yet the story itself provides plenty of action and psychology to rival the story of Oedipus.

Some additional background on the episode may be helpful if you want to avoid an overly oedipal discussion. Rostám is outside of society hunting when the encounter with Tahmina occurs. The shah's initial order to defend Iran from the Turánian invaders is met with resistance. Rostám goes on a drinking binge for three days before mustering. Key Kavus, in his anger, humiliates Rostám in public, ordering a courtier to hang him. Rostám fends off the courtier and says to the shah: "Don't nurse so hot a fire within your breast. / Each thing you do shames that already done. / You are unworthy of both throne and rule. You go and hand the brave Sohráb alive! / Take arms, set forth and humble him yourself!" (Clinton, pp. 66–67). Rostám leaves court with the comment: "I am . . . the lion-heart who gave this crown" (67). The court agrees that the shah is "crazed and foolish" (69), and an embassy convinces Rostám to calm down, not turn his back on his shah, and not lose fame by running away from a fight. They convince him to return to court, where Key Kavus apologizes for his outburst with the excuse "I am by nature rash in speech and act, / But one must be as God created him" (Clinton, p. 75). Rostám accepts the apology and returns to the fold. This background should make the shah's refusal to send the *nushdarú* to Rostám as requested seem as tyrannical as it is cowardly. According to one interpretation, the story of this father and son is used to test the limits of the father's loyalty to his shah, Key Kavus. Furthermore, this information makes drawing parallels between this episode of the *Shahname* and *The Iliad* that much easier.

THE *SHAHNAME* TODAY

For most of its history, the *Shahname* had been used as an instrument of state propaganda. After the 1979 revolution in Iran, the work fell from favor in its native country. The *Book of Kings* was associated with the last shah, and thereby the corruption of the government and its American ties. With the shah's exile and death, the *Shahname*'s political function had come to an end. The aesthetic merits of the work, however, have not been able to overcome the political coloring. Outside of Iran, the text has begun to enjoy a certain amount of scholarly attention. Its further depoliticization at the hands of myth and folklore scholars, structuralists, deconstructionists, and others may help it regain its former place in the Iranian canon.

IN THE CLASSROOM

Discussion

1. What narrative strategies, literary devices, and scenes from the text can be used to show that Ferdowsi was a monarchist?

2. How do the other characters attempt to console Rostám? What do they say? What images, metaphors, or allegories do they bring into their speeches? How effective are they in consoling Rostám? How effective would they be in consoling someone today?

3. To what degree is it justified to say that both Sohráb and Rostám are the victims of hubris? Explain.

Connections

1. Compare the characters and roles of the father/king figures in *The Tragedy of Rostám and Sohráb* and Molière's *Tartuffe* (Book 4). Consider to what degree their actions are motivated by character or office.

Writing

Ask students to write a short paper in response to one or more of the following:

1. Read the prologue to the section of the *Shahname* (e.g., Clinton 3–4). Then, write a paper in which you demonstrate how and where the themes of the prologue are worked out in the story itself. Perhaps, the most difficult question you will have to answer is: How is it just that Rostám must kill Sohráb?

2. Describe the function(s) of hyperbole in the story of Rostám and Sohráb. Where does it occur? What purpose does it serve? Does it have a thematic function? If so, to which themes does it contribute?

BEYOND THE CLASSROOM

RESEARCH & WRITING

1. Despite the many taboos on killing one's children, it is a topic in many works of literature. There are almost as many instances of parents exposing their children and it is an increasingly common occurrence in modern society. Using the story of Rostám and Sohráb, either Euripides' *Medea* (Book 1), *Iphigenia in Aulis* (not in the anthology), or

the Gretchen episode from Goethe's *Faust I* (Book 5) and either Sophocles' *Oedipus* (Book 1) or George Eliot's *Silas Marner* (not in the anthology), write a paper in which you explore the motivations and consequences of parents either exposing their children as infants or killing them later on. If the act is done to avoid some disaster, is it effective? What happens to the exposed child? Does it return to the biological parents? What constraints must the parents overcome or consequences must they face as a result of their act?

2. Try to apply Aristotle's theory of tragedy (Book 1) to the story of Rostám and Sohráb. Are there any cultural differences that make an application difficult or impossible? Is the story a tragedy according to his definition? Why or why not?

Project

1. Using the story of Rostám and Sohráb as your foundations, collect other stories and works of art that make use of a similar archetype (for example, Goya's *Saturn Devouring His Children* or Toni Morrison's *Beloved*). Your presentation should deal with the following questions: What function does it serve in the respective cultures? What aesthetic purpose does it fulfill in the work? Does applying the concept of an archetype help you understand the work of art better?

WWW For additional information on Ferdowsi and annotated Web links, see *World Literature Online* at bedfordstmartins.com/worldlit.

FURTHER READING

Clinton, J. W. "The Tragedy of Suhrab." *Logos Islamikos: Studia Islamica in honorem Georgii Michaelis Wickens.* Eds. R. M. Savory and D. A. Agius. *Papers in Mediaeval Studies* 6 (1984).

Nöldke, Theodor. *The Iranian National Epic.* Trans. L. T. Bogdanov. 1979.

Southgate, M. S. "Fate in Ferdowsi's 'Rustam v. Sohrab.'" *Studies in Art and Literature of the Near East in Honour of R. Ettinghausen.* Ed. P. J. Chelkowski. 1974. 149–59.

MEDIA RESOURCES

WEB SITES

The Epic of *Shahnameh* Ferdowsi
www.enel.ucalgary.ca./People/far/hobbies/iran/shahnameh.html
Found on this site are the complete electronic texts of Ferdowsi's famous Persian epic. The site also includes links to other pages about Persian literature and Iranian culture.

The Ferdowsi Society
www.ferdowsi.org
The official Web page of the Ferdowsi Society, this site is dedicated to information about the poet and his famous work, *Book of Kings.* It provides background on his life and times, and his philosophy and worldview as well as a links to a variety of related Web sites and information about the Ferdowsi Society.

Ferdowsi and the Illustration of the Shahnameh
www.princeton.edu/~jwc/shahnameh/illustrationt.html

This site includes an academic paper by Jerome W. Clinton of Princeton University that explores the relationship between images and text in Persian illustrated manuscripts by examining specific passages in the *Book of Kings* along with a number of fascinating illustrations.

Ferdowsi's Page
www.geocities.com/shaahnameh/ferdowsi/ferdowsi.htm
This page includes background on the life of Ferdowsi as well as an examination and explanation of some of the key elements of the *Shahnameh*; it also includes a gallery of images from illustrated manuscripts of Ferdowsi's epic.

IranChamber.com — Persian Literature — Ferdowsi
Iranchamber.com/literature/ferdowsi/ferdowsi.php
This site offers a useful biography of Ferdowsi as well as images of Ferdowsi and a photo of his tomb in Tus.

FARID UD-DIN ATTAR, from *The Conference of the Birds* (p. 406)

WWW   For a quiz on *The Conference of the Birds*, see *World Literature Online*
at bedfordstmartins.com/worldlit.

Central to Attar's poem is the relationship between God and the human soul. The title in Arabic, also meaning "language of the birds," refers in the Qur'an (27:17) to the ability God gives Solomon that enables him to understand this relationship — the secret of divine Love — as it is revealed in all beings. As such, the birds come to represent the various spiritual states humans exhibit, and the pilgrimage composes the never-ending process of self-discovery that realizes the love of God. And since each bird is concerned with the conditions of material existence at first and comes to recognize what matters only later, Attar is able to join the real with the transcendent — constructing an allegory that literally embodies the Qur'an's paradoxical insistence on God's transcendence and immanence. Attar's poem, therefore, does not simply begin with birds and end with God. Encourage students to identify ways in which the two come together before the poem's final lines. You might direct them, for example, to lines 83–84: "Renounce your soul for love; He you pursue / Will sacrifice His inmost soul for you" as well as lines 526–27: "With all the dangers that the journey brought, / The journey was in Me, the deeds were Mine."

In leading the birds on their pilgrimage, the hoopoe mediates between the material and spiritual paths that structure the poem. Ask students to characterize him as a guide. Have them compare the significance of his credentials — his deeds — with the significance of the journey. What does it mean to know the way to Simorgh? What is the difference between "showing" the path and "following" it? There are several stages that mark the path (p. 403): repentance, avoiding doubt, abstinence, poverty, perseverance, trust in God, and contentment. Have students find moments in the poem that represent any of these stages. You might contrast this "progress" with the progress of the stories themselves, which are mainly connected through free association. How does the sequence of stories add to the "reality" and/or "spirituality" of the poem? In approaching this question, you might draw students' attention to the places in the poem where the story and the hoopoe's moral create a dialogue (ll. 163ff, for instance). Alternatively, you might ask your students to contrast the hoopoe perspective with the that of the fool. To what extent does the figure of the fool facilitate or impede the progress of the poem?

One of the ways in which Attar aligns spiritual concepts with the physical traits of the birds is via fantastical aetiology. For example, the soaring height characteristic of the hawk's flight becomes representative of ambition, and the small physical size of the sparrow corresponds to the bird's little faith. Even inanimate objects can speak for the spiritual, through an artistic device called the "language of states" (*zaban-i hal*). Although there are no examples of this technique in the selection, several "states," including dreaming and death, are given spiritual expression. Have students focus on these moments in the selection, and discuss their significance.

Finally, you might examine the contrasts that abound in Attar's poem. Perhaps the most mysterious of these is represented in the reunion of the birds with the Simorgh, when "silently their shining Lord replies" (l. 509). At this point, the various reflected and reflective images in *The Conference of the Birds* converge, thus enabling Attar to comment on the nature of his story itself: The birds finding their experience recorded in the document the chamberlain gives them serves as a model for the reader's own experience reading the poem. Likewise, the Simorgh's silence is reflected in the ultimate silence of the poet. Ask students to discuss this manner of framing the journey. To what extent is the reader implicated in the birds' question "how is it true / That 'we' is not distinguished here from 'you'" (ll. 507–8)?

TEXT & CONTEXT

GREEK INFLUENCES

Neo-Platonic philosophy was well known in the Islamic world of Attar. Plotinus and his teacher Apollonius of Tyana even visited Assyria and Persia. Oriental philosophy, R. P. Masani explains, was what enabled Plotinus to relate the One to the Manifold as an active but also transcendent force. Sufi philosophy then benefited from the union of Greek and Oriental ideas. Hence the Greek *Logos* or Sufi *Aql-I-kull* (the Universal Mind) emanates from the Deity who, as the One Primal Unity, is "the source of all Existence, the cause of all matter, animate and inanimate, the ground of all being, the Highest Thought, the Highest Good, the Highest Beauty" (Masani, 41). The Universal Soul emanates from the Deity as well, connecting the Universal Mind with the world of sense. And since the material world is then the outward form of the reason that constitutes the Universal Mind, the sensual is reabsorbed, as it were, into the Universal Mind.

A VERY BRIEF SUMMARY OF THE ENTIRE POEM

An extended introduction opens the poem, addressing God in praise of his disciples and his precepts. Then, the various kinds of birds are distinguished according to their individual traits, which are symbolically interpreted. The hoopoe tells the assembly of birds, who want to find a king, that his name is Simorgh, and he lives behind the mountain Qaf. A long time ago, he dropped a feather over China from which all creation originated. The journey to Simorgh, the hoopoe notes, is arduous, but he will accompany anyone who wants to go. The hoopoe's description of the perils in store prompts the birds to present a parade of excuses, most of which center on the worldly. The nightingale, for instance, explains that he loves the rose of his songs and does not want to leave her. The duck suggests that he cannot leave the water. Hellmut Ritter points out that he is the ascetic of the birds: "He performs a major ritual ablution every moment (by diving under the water) and prostrates himself. — The hoopoe replies that the water is only good for those with an unwashed countenance." One by one the birds excuse themselves in ways that the hoopoe explains are trivial, since the things of this world are transient. The birds then ask him what sort of relationship they have to the king. The hoopoe replies that the birds come from the shadow Simorgh cast over the world. The birds then decide to go on the journey. The first thing they notice is that the road is completely quiet and lifeless: This is because silence signifies Simorgh's greatness. At one point in the midst of a vast expanse, the birds waver in their faith and ask the hoopoe several questions regarding their place in the world, the significance of death, and so on. The hoopoe's answers attempt to show the birds how to transcend their misgivings and earthly desires. Then, they arrive at the seven valleys they must cross. These are the Valley of Seeking, the Valley of Love, the Valley of Detachment, the Valley of Oneness, the Valley of Bewilderment, and the Valley of Denudation and Extinction. Many of the birds lose heart and die in this stage. The thirty who finally remain after the long flight to Simorgh's court realize the triviality of their existence, which the palace guard confirms when he tells them that Simorgh is their king regardless of whether or not they are there. And when they read the document Simorgh's chamberlain gives them (in which their experience is recorded), they disappear in shame. But the light of majesty gives them new life, and they finally recognize the Simorgh. They see themselves reflected in him and him reflected in themselves. They then disappear in Him, and after a hundred thousand eons they return to themselves, after which silence reigns.

IN THE CLASSROOM

Discussion and Writing

1. Attar's poem focuses on the way to the divine. What, by the end of the poem, can one say about the divine itself? In other words, how can the divine be characterized?

2. The figure of the fool appears many times, often providing a different perspective. Discuss the significance of his input.

3. Unlike many of the spiritual pilgrimages in the Western tradition, the journey on which the birds embark is primarily composed of changes in situation, rather than changes in scenery (for instance, allegorical landscape). To what effect?

4. The ostentatious bird's main objection centers on the uncertainty of the journey. How does Attar represent uncertainty? Consider, for instance, lines 247–48, when the pilgrim says "I have no certain knowledge any more; / I doubt my doubt, doubt itself is unsure" and line 430, "And blasphemy is faith, faith blasphemy."

5. *The Conference of the Birds* contrasts the physical and the spiritual in several ways (for example, in terms of goods, love, death, and the like). Focus on one example, and discuss the extent to which they are compatible.

Connections

1. Compare the way in which Pope's *Essay on Man* and Attar's *The Conference of the Birds* portray the relationship between self-knowledge and the knowledge of God.

2. In *The Ascent of Mount Ventoux*, Petrarch embarks on his own spiritual journey. What kind of "progress" do Petrarch's and Attar's works present?

BEYOND THE CLASSROOM

RESEARCH & WRITING

1. Read more of Attar's poem. Focus on the representation of Christians and Christianity. What function do they serve?

2. Investigate *The Risala of the Birds (Risalat al-tayr)*, the original work on which Attar drew. How does Attar reconceive the pilgrimage?

3. Identify a few of the references in Attar's poem to the Qur'an. How do these references construct an aesthetics or a way of reading *The Conference of the Birds*?

Projects

1. Read Jean-Claude Carriere and Peter Brook's *The Conference of the Birds* and/or take a look at Shirin Neshat's *Logic of the Birds*, both modern productions based on Attar's poem. What effect does the change of context/culture have on the poem's allegory? What effect does the change in artistic medium have?

2. Find out more about any one of Attar's other celebrated epics: *The Book of Secrets (Asrarnama), The Book of God (Ilahinama)*, or *The Book of Misfortune (Musibatnama)*. How does Attar develop the relationship between the physical and the spiritual elsewhere?

FURTHER READING

Davis, Dick. "The Journey as Paradigm: Literature and Metaphorical Travel in 'Attar's Mantiq al-Tayr,' " in *Edebiyat: The Journal of Middle Eastern Literatures* 4, no. 2 (1993): 173–83.

Hoffman, Valerie J. "Annihilation in the Messenger of God: The Development of a Sufi Practice," in the *International Journal of Middle East Studies* 31, no. 3 (1999): 351–69.

Ritter, Hellmut. *The Ocean of the Soul. Men, the World, and God in the Stories of Farid al-Din Attar*. Trans. John O'Kane. 2003.

MEDIA RESOURCES

VIDEO

The Andalusian Epic: Islamic Spain
27 min., 1999 (Films for the Humanities & Sciences)
This program addresses the expansion of the Arab empire into Spain, where Muslims ruled with tolerance for more than seven centuries. The introduction and consolidation of Islamic power in Spain, the creation of the Umayyad emirate by the sole survivor of the Umayyad dynasty, the rise of Cordoba as a cultural rival of Abbasid Baghdad, and the gradual ebb of Arab rule on the Iberian Peninsula are all discussed. Special attention is given to the prosperous reign of Abdel Rahman III and the flowering of a Muslim culture that respectfully welcomed the contributions of Christians and Jews alike. (Portions are in French with English subtitles.)

Chivalry and Commerce: The Late Middle Ages
video and DVD, 23 min., 1998 (Insight Media)
Revealing the religious zeal that built lofty cathedrals, sent armies on crusades, and impelled common folk to embark on arduous pilgrimages, this program chronicles the years from 1000 to 1450. It shows how curiosity about religion opened the courts of China's Great Khan to such explorers and merchants as Marco Polo; how religion inspired a literary awakening that contributed to the opening of church-run universities; and how models of chivalrous knights arose in books such as *The Tale of Genji* and the legends from King Arthur's court. It also discusses the Muslim preservation of classical learning.

Crescent and Cross: Rise of Islam and Age of Crusades
59 min., 1998 (Insight Media)
Considering the Crusades as a response to the rapid rise of Islam, this video looks at various orders of Christian monks and their role in the preservation of religious, artistic, and cultural aspects of civilization. It addresses the issue of religious intolerance, focusing on the Inquisition.

Crusades
200 min., 1995 (Insight Media)
Filmed on location in Europe and the Middle East, this series explores the history and legacy of the Crusades. It discusses the reasons for the Crusades, the creation of a mythology of knights and chivalry, and the legacy of distrust between East and West.

WEB SITES

Cornell Library Middle East and Islamic Studies Collection: Arabic Literature
www.library.cornell.edu/colldev/mideast/arablit.htm
The comprehensive source of materials on Arabic literature includes general overviews of classic (pre-Islamic and early Islamic) and modern Arabic poetry, fiction, and some nonfiction as well as a generous selection of works in English and Arabic from both periods and by dozens of important writers. Links to recent criticism, periodical articles, and a thorough bibliography make this an essential site.

JALALODDIN RUMI, from *The Essential Rumi* (p. 427)

WWW   For a quiz on *The Essential Rumi*, see *World Literature Online*
        at bedfordstmartins.com/worldlit.

One of the most fundamental distinctions in Rumi's poetry is that between "form" (*surat*) and "meaning" (*ma'na*). Whereas form is limited to a thing's outward appearance, meaning has access to a thing's inner reality. For Rumi, this distinction is related to the experience of enlightenment: "Form is shadow, meaning the Sun," he says in his *Mathnavi* (VI 4747). Many of the contrasts that permeate Rumi's imagery follow from this essential juxtaposition. His work demonstrates the way in which things become clear through their opposites by showing that spirit and body, teacher and pupil, fullness and emptiness, inner and outer are interdependent. Such contrasts are most striking in "A Basket of Fresh Bread." Ask students to locate and identify a few examples. Then, point out the one exception: God. He alone is without an opposite, as "Only Breath" exemplifies. The knowledge of contrasts thus establishes that which is without contrast: God as well as the limit of our knowledge — that which has no opposite. How does this difference between the nature of the world and the nature of God shape the role of the prophet/spiritual teacher? What can the teacher teach? Examine "I Come Before Dawn" and "The Gift of Water" in approaching these questions.

The goal of spiritual enlightenment is then in part to transcend contradiction. Doing so, for Rumi, involves the experience of contradiction itself. In other words, instead of perceiving oneself as a thing that exists among several other things that exist (constituting the world as we know it), one should recognize that in contrast to God, one has no existence. Since our existence is derived from His, He is the only thing that really exists. The realization of one's nonexistence therefore enables one to exist. Consider "When You Are with Everything but Me" in this context. Direct students to compare this perspective (which appears to transcend appearance) with the appearance of the contradiction of existence, presented in "The Food Sack" especially.

The classical Sufi term *fana* (annihilation) is therefore central to Rumi's portrayal of enlightenment. Only through annihilation of the self can one achieve subsistence (*baqa'*) with God, at which point one will know, actually rather than theoretically, that everything derives from God. This experience informs the Sufi notion of love (*'ishq*), which cannot be explained or known through words. For the experience of love is more real than anything else in the universe. The Sufi Beloved, after all, transcends everything we can conceive or imagine. What forms does the experience of love take in Rumi's poetry (for instance in "Checkmate")?

Finally, you might have students focus on the juxtaposition between gift and reward in "The Gift of Water" and "I Come Before Dawn." What experience of spiritual enlightenment does each entail? Encourage students to relate these concepts to selflessness in order to develop their understanding of the enlightened practical life Rumi promotes. In so doing, they might consider line 14 of "The Food Sack": "They [lovers] collect the interest without the capital." What sort of "property" does the enlightened person have?

TEXT & CONTEXT

THE POETIC TRADITION

Among the texts that influenced Rumi most were Hakim Sana'i of Ghazna's *Hadiqat al-haqiqa (The Orchard of Truth)*, one of the first Sufi didactic manuals, and Farid ud-Din Attar's *Manteq ot-teyr (The Conference of the Birds)*. Indeed, the former served as a model for all subsequent *mathnavis*, including the latter. A *mathnavis* is a didactic work written in rhymed couplets, whereby two rhyming hemistiches, or half-lines, compose each line. They usually contain several interpolated stories arranged in no particular order, many of which exemplify particular aspects of mystical experience. Rumi's own *Mathnavi* displays several other characteristic features of Sana'i's and Attar's works. Sana'i often used catchwords for Arabic meters, Annemarie Schimmel notes, or musical meters like "*tan tanna tanin tan tan-nana tan tanin*," although with Rume, such forms represent musical intoxication. In its meter (*ramal mosaddas*), Rumi's *Mathnavi* resembles Attar's epic, which Rumi especially esteemed.

But Rumi was influenced by other works as well, first and foremost the *Kalila va Demna*, attributed to Bidpai. By the end of the eighth century, this collection of fables had been translated into Arabic and formed the basis, Schimmel observes, for much of Muslim as well as European literature, all the way up to Lafontaine.

MUSIC AND SUFISM

Music traditionally played an important role in the Sufi life. A melody could induce an ecstatic experience, regardless of its lyrics. As a result, a profane love poem might have the same effect as the Qur'an, a consequence that provoked much criticism. By the twelfth century, such ecstasies had become ritualized in the form of a dance, the Ceremony of the Mevlevi (Whirling Dervishes), in which the Sufis, overwhelmed by music and poetry, whirled around and around, at times tearing their clothes. A flute made out of a reed was the main instrument that supplied the music for such dances.

IN THE CLASSROOM

Discussion and Writing

1. Several of Rumi's poems deal with the products of education ("A Basket of Fresh Bread" and "I Come Before Dawn," in particular). Examine the status of knowledge in his poems. In so doing, distinguish various kinds of knowledge. What does each do?

2. Bread and water are not the only nutriments Rumi's poetry presents. Identify other forms of food that Rumi describes, and discuss the significance of nourishment.

3. Rumi's depiction of the way to God often takes the form of work. Consider "Checkmate" especially in order to establish the relationship between work and enlightenment.

4. In "A Basket of Fresh Bread," Rumi says "Never condescend" (l. 20) and then later "put on humble clothes" (l. 26). With reference to the other poems as well, explain the lesson to be learned from such seemingly contradictory instructions.

5. Rumi addresses the reader directly in many of his poems, both in excerpts from the Qur'an and in his own verse. What effect does this direct address have?

Connections

1. Rumi discusses the function of the spiritual teacher in many of his poems. Compare the prophet/sheikh/dervish in his description with the apostle in Ibn Ishaq's *The Life of Muhammad*.

2. For Rumi, love mediates between God and humankind. How does such love compare with that portrayed in the selection of European Love Lyrics (Book 3)?

BEYOND THE CLASSROOM

RESEARCH & WRITING

1. Read more of Rumi's poems, focusing on the way in which Rumi portrays other religions, like Christianity, Buddhism, and Hinduism. What position does he take?

2. A central theme in Rumi's work is love, a key emotion for Sufism. In the Western tradition, love is often opposed to reason. What role does reason play in Rumi's poetry? In Sufi thought?

3. Music is an important element in Rumi's work as well as in Sufi practices. Find out more about the kind of music that would have produced an ecstatic experience at the time. You might even compare such music to modern music written as accompaniment to Rumi's poetry.

Projects

1. Performance poetry is one of the forms of Rumi's work today. Find out more about how performance poets interpret his poems. What effect does the performance of his poetry have?

2. Rumi's poetry has become enormously popular in the Western world. What factors have led to this reception?

FURTHER READING

Araste, Riza. *Rumi, the Persian, the Sufi.* 1974.
Harvey, Andrew. *The Way of Passion. A Celebration of Rumi.* 1994.
Lewis, Franklin. *Rumi: Past and Present, East and West.* 2000.
Lewisohn, Leonard, ed. *The Heritage of Sufism. Volume 1: Classical Persian Sufism from its Origins to Rumi (700–1300).* 1999.
Nicholson, R. A. *Rumi, Poet and Mystic.* 1950.

MEDIA RESOURCES

WEB SITES

Dar Al Masnavi
http://www.dar-al-masnavi.org/index.html
A Web site devoted to Jalaloddin Rumi and other Muslim poets. The site includes biographies, works, a discussion board, and links to other sites.

Rumi On Fire
http://www.rumionfire.com/
An online tribute to Jalaoddin Rumi with translations, poetry, biographies, and picture galleries. The site is designed to give viewers a deeper understanding of Rumi and his work.

The Thousand and One Nights (p. 435)

WWW   For a quiz on *The Thousand and One Nights*, see *World Literature Online*
at bedfordstmartins.com/worldlit.

Not too long ago, *The Thousand and One Nights*, or *alf laila wa-laila*, was considered fairly standard reading even for Westerners — in expurgated versions, of course. This status makes the *Nights* a prime source of Western misconceptions and stereotypes about the Middle East, for instance, Orientalism. For obvious financial reasons, Disney and Hollywood have never let go of some of these tales — Sinbad, Aladdin, Ali Baba — and that could make it even more difficult for students to come to terms with the text itself. A short opening discussion on the disparities between the Disneyfied or Hollywood versions and the flavor of the selections in the anthology may help set aside certain preconceived notions of the text. Mention, for example, that the stories of Sinbad, Aladdin, and Ali Baba are not in the earliest manuscripts. You can conclude this discussion by pointing out that the framework or framing narrative draws on three different stories taken from India: (1) the story of the husband who is shaken by his wife's infidelity but regains his health after learning that the same has happened to a higher ranking person; (2) the story of a supernatural being whose wife or prisoner is able to deceive him despite innumerable hindrances; and (3) the story of a young woman who is able to save herself, her father, or both, from a life-threatening situation. Thus the collection, having appropriated stories and structures from other cultures, was in turn appropriated and transformed in the hands of writers from even more distant cultures. Furthermore, you can point out that the full text contains not only adventure/fairy tales of the popular Disney variety but also gnostic literature, pornography, scatological jokes, and stanza after stanza of verse.

The number in the title of the earliest manuscripts, in Persian *Hezar Afsane*, in Arabic *Alf Chorafa*, meaning "a thousand stories/legends," originally signified a large indeterminate number. Only with further expansions, mostly resulting from the financial success of Antoine Galland's *Les Mille et une Nuit* (1704–1717) in Europe, was the number taken seriously and the accretion of tales enlarged to correspond to the title. This grouping of stories leads to the bundle of contradictions we have today. Divergent genres mix with contradictory value systems in this work, as can be seen in the editors' selection: nothing in the stories Shahrazad tells during the first eight nights (part of the so-called "wiles of women" section) would make the king change his attitude toward women; indeed, his misogyny receives only support. Some juggling may be in order, should one of your students notice this. Point out that in some versions and common translations Shahrazad tells Sharayar his own story, which then forces him to change his mind about killing women. Or, you can take this point as the basis for a connection to the medieval European *fabliau*, as in Boccaccio's story of Alibech and Rustico (pp. 864ff.), or, not included in this anthology, Chaucer's "Miller's Tale."

As with *Beowulf*, which was claimed to have "Christian coloring" some nineteenth-century translators and editors, like the German translator Enno Littmann, claimed that the entire collection was covered in an "Islamic varnish." It can be seen in the religious formulas the characters use in dire situations and in the severity of the punishment inflicted on the wife in the story of "Hasan of Basra." That demons and Jinns can be followers of Allah is taken from the Koran, which explains why the demon accepts the merchant's promise to return (p. 454). The recurrent invocations and prayers to Allah at the end of sections as well as a belief in fate are seen as aspects of the religious influence. The varnish, however, fails to cover the numerous scenes in which alcohol is drunk. Obviously, some of the "varnish" is integral to certain stories, since they were written down, if not created, as late as the nineteenth century. The punishment of women, central to the selections in the anthology, may cause some students to ascribe the misogyny of the texts to Islam — a fully unwarranted assumption.

TEXT & CONTEXT

One of the social functions of these stories, if not the primary one, was simple entertainment. Instead of a regent spending a hot, dry evening watching the trivialities of broadcast and cable television or the inanities of Hollywood's newest batch of B-movies as is the case today, he had expert storytellers entertain him and his retinue with fantastic and/or edifying as well as bawdy stories. The character Shahrazad makes full use of that function of storytelling, entertaining Shahrayar and keeping him in suspense with the refrain: "To be continued. . . ." The *Nights* have not usually been considered serious literature in Arabic-speaking countries for two reasons: (1) their subjects are fantastic, bawdy, and/or light, and (2) the earliest manuscripts were written in a form of Middle Arabic, the mark of trivial literature.

A careful examination of the entire collection reveals several severe anachronisms: Shahrazad knows stories of not only the legendary king Salomo (965–925 B.C.E.), but also of Mamluke Baibar (1233–1277 C.E.); furthermore, in the story of Ali Baba, coffee is mentioned. From such anachronisms, one can see traces of the oral situation that was the basis of this narrative technique, which only later came to be written down and collected under the title. This situation was one of exclusively male storytellers narrating and simultaneously adjusting their stories to, it is assumed, a predominately male audience.

IN THE CLASSROOM

Discussion and Writing

1. Have students find passages in which the misogyny of the narrator comes into play or is especially evident and also passages in which a form of protofeminism. Ask them to weigh these aspects and their positions in the text.

2. Have students compare the narrative situation of each of the stories. Ask who is telling the story to whom; what is the message; what effect, if any, does it have. Finally, ask if is there any relationship between narrator and effect.

3. In order for Shahrazad to stay alive, she needs to tell a story that is "more amazing" than the previous. Have students write short essays defining "the strange" in the *Nights*, and come up with criteria for determining the level of "strangeness."

Connections

1. Compare the image of women in the *Nights* with that in Homer's *The Odyssey* and Pericles' funeral speech from Thucydides (both in Book 1). What conclusions can be drawn about these "primitive" images of woman?

2. Both Dante (see *Paradiso*, not included in this anthology) and Faust (Book 5) learn life-saving, or soul-saving, lessons from female characters. What significance is there in the role-reversal of teacher and student that is seen in the European example?

BEYOND THE CLASSROOM

RESEARCH & WRITING

1. In the *Nights*, merchants appear to be on the winning side fairly often. Compare the social status of merchants in the *Nights* with their social status in European society and literature from either antiquity (who, for example, were the merchants in Rome?) or the Middle Ages (for example, in Chaucer's "Miller's Tale").

2. Using Haddawy's translation of the Mahdi edition, Burton's translation, and film resources such as Internet Movie Database (www.imdb.com), write a short paper on the popularity of various sections of the *Nights*. Which are the most popular stories? Which are the most successful? Are there any changes to the plots or characterizations that make them "sell" better? If so, discuss how these changes affect the story's "saleability."

3. Examine the concept and function of "orality" in the *Nights* and in at least one other work from an "oral tradition" (e.g., *Beowulf*, p. 482, *Black Elk Speaks*, Book 6, or just about anything from Book 1, like *The Epic of Gilgamesh*, the Egyptian Hymns or, not included in this anthology, the Homeric Hymns). Do not compare or contrast. Define the terms *orality* and *oral tradition* using two (or more) texts.

Projects

1. Have students choose and examine one of the stories Disney has appropriated, and read its corresponding portion of the full *Nights* (one of the older movies might be an easier choice). Using Internet resources, determine what Disney conceives of as its social function. How does that self-ascribed function affect the retelling of the story? How does Disney's social function compare with Shahrazad's and what sort of spin does that put on the story?

2. Ask students to examine the stereotypes built upon the *Nights* in light of now having read a small portion of the stories. Let them explain what changes, if any, have occurred in their image of people from the Middle East.

FURTHER READING

Hamori, Andras. *On the Art of Medieval Arabic Literature.* 1974.
Marzolph, Ulrich, ed. *The Arabian Nights: An Encyclopedia.* 2004.
Naddaff, Sandra. *Arabesque: Narrative Structure and the Aesthetic of Repetition in the 1001 Nights.* 1991.

MEDIA RESOURCES

WEB SITES

Bartleby.com
Online translations of stories from *The Thousand and One Nights*. The stories are translated by Edward William Lane and revised by Stanley Lane-Poole.

VIDEO

A Thousand and One Nights
92 min., 1945 (Columbia Pictures)
In this film, an Arabian prince seeks help from a genie to reclaim his throne.

Ali Baba and the Forty Thieves
87 min., 1944 (Universal Pictures)
This film follows Ali Baba through his many adventures, including the rescue of the Sultan's kidnapped daughter, and the discovery of the thieves' cave.

GENERAL MEDIA RESOURCES

VIDEO

The Andalusian Epic: Islamic Spain
27 min., 1999 (Films for the Humanities & Sciences)
This program addresses the expansion of the Arab empire into Spain, where Muslims ruled with tolerance for more than seven centuries. The introduction and consolidation of Islamic power in Spain, the creation of the Umayyad emirate by the sole survivor of the Umayyad dynasty, the rise of Cordoba as a cultural rival of Abbasid Baghdad, and the gradual ebb of Arab rule on the Iberian Peninsula are all discussed. Special attention is given to the prosperous reign of Abdel Rahman III and the flowering of a Muslim culture that respectfully welcomed the contributions of Christians and Jews alike. (Portions are in French with English subtitles.)

Chivalry and Commerce: The Late Middle Ages
video and DVD, 23 min., 1998 (Insight Media)
Revealing the religious zeal that built lofty cathedrals, sent armies on crusades, and impelled common folk to embark on arduous pilgrimages, this program chronicles the years from 1000 to 1450. It shows how curiosity about religion opened the courts of China's Great Khan to such explorers and merchants as Marco Polo; how religion inspired a literary awakening that contributed to the opening of church-run universities; and how models of chivalrous knights arose in books like *The Tale of Genji* and the legends from King Arthur's court. It also discusses the Muslim preservation of classical learning.

Crescent and Cross: Rise of Islam and Age of Crusades
59 min., 1998 (Insight Media)
Considering the Crusades as a response to the rapid rise of Islam, this video looks at various orders of Christian monks and their role in the preservation of religious, artistic, and cultural aspects of civilization. It addresses the issue of religious intolerance, focusing on the Inquisition.

Crusades
200 min., 1995 (Insight Media)
Filmed on location in Europe and the Middle East, this series explores the history and legacy of the Crusades. It discusses the reasons for the Crusades, the creation of a mythology of
knights and chivalry, and the legacy of distrust between East and West.

The Eastern Philosophers
50 min. each, 2001 (Insight Media)
Examining the central doctrines of Confucianism, Shinto, Hinduism, Judaism, and Islam,
this set examines the genesis of spiritual thought. The first volume explores the dominant
philosophical and spiritual ideas of the Far East, focusing on Confucius and Shinto. The
second discusses the Hinduism and Buddhism of South Asia, with their focus on cycles of
death and rebirth. The final volume considers the roots, rituals, and sacred texts of Judaism
and the tenets and lifestyle issues of Islam.

Great Religions of the World
33 min., 1995 (Insight Media)
This video explores the major beliefs, origins, and histories of Buddhism, Christianity,
Judaism, Hinduism, Islam, and Taoism. It differentiates between ethnic and universalizing
religions, discussing how each of the universalizing religions developed from an ethnic base
and expanded past national boundaries.

Three Pillars: Confucius, Jesus, and Mohammed
53 min., 1998 (Insight Media)
This video studies the identities of the founders of three major religions — Confucianism,
Christianity, and Islam. It looks at how Confucianism blended into the Chinese social and
political structure; the significance of Jesus as a prophet for Muslims and as God incarnate
for Christians; and the teachings of Muhammad and the Koran.

The World's Philosophies
60 min., 1994 (Insight Media)
In this video, Huston Smith defines three basic types of human relationships — with
nature, with other people, and with one's self — and explains how these relationships correspond to the philosophical traditions of the West, of China, and of India.

WEB SITES

Cornell Library Middle East and Islamic Studies Collection: Arabic Literature
www.library.cornell.edu/colldev/mideast/arablit.htm
The comprehensive source of materials on Arabic literature includes general overviews of
classic (pre-Islamic and early Islamic) and modern Arabic poetry, fiction, and some nonfiction as well as generous selection of works in English and Arabic from both periods and by
dozens of important writers. Links to recent criticism, periodical articles, and a thorough
bibliography make this an essential site.

Exploring Ancient World Cultures: Medieval Europe Homepage
eawc.evansville.edu/mepage.htm
This site covers ancient Near Eastern history to the Middle Ages. It includes a thorough
chronology of major events of medieval times and allows users to look into what was happening across cultures during various points in history.

AUDIO

Living Biographies of Religious Leaders
8 tapes, 11:25 hrs. (Blackstone Audiobooks)
This program presents the lives of twenty great founders and leading advocates of the world's foremost religions. Here are the historical facts and legends associated with these forceful personalities who have inspired and influenced humankind through the centuries. Presented are Jesus Christ, Moses, Isaiah, Zoroaster, Buddha, Confucius, John the Baptist, Paul, Muhammad, Francis of Assisi, John Huss, Luther, Loyola, Calvin, George Fox, Swedenborg, Wesley, Brigham Young, Mary Baker Eddy, and Gandhi.

EUROPE:
FROM EPIC TO
ROMANCE AND BEYOND

Beowulf (p. 482)

WWW   For quizzes on *Beowulf*, see *World Literature Online*
at bedfordstmartins.com/worldlit.

Although we don't have any information about the author of *Beowulf*, the manuscript
has an extraordinary history. Sometime in the tenth century, two scribes committed the
poem to parchment. *Beowulf* was bound together with four other Old English works: the
poem *Judith* and the prose works *Alexander's Letter to Aristotle*, *The Wonders of the East*, and
The Passion of St. Christopher. The record of the manuscript is then lost for several hundred
years. There is some suspicion that it was housed for a time in an English monastery, but, if
this is true, no one knows how it might have survived the destruction of books and religious
artifacts that occurred during Henry VIII's dissolution of these monasteries. We do know
that the Dean of Litchfield, Lawrence Nowell, owned *Beowulf*'s manuscript, as he wrote his
name and the date on the first page in 1563. The manuscript, which had by then been combined with another text of four works, resurfaced in the collection of the physician and anti-
quarian Sir Robert Cotton (1571–1631).

Cotton's library, at less than a thousand volumes, was not large by the standards of
other private libraries of the time, but it was nonetheless one of the most important collections of manuscripts ever collected. It contained primarily original legal and political
documents but also religious pieces like *The Lindisfarne Gospels*, a set of fifth- and sixth-
century illustrations of *Genesis*, manuscripts of *Sir Gawain and the Green Knight*, and, of
course, *Beowulf*. Cotton allowed scholars and intellectuals free use of his library, and his
loan lists included such important figures as the king, the queen, and Sir Francis Bacon.
The library volumes were catalogued based on Cotton's own utilitarian scheme rather than
any current bibliographical system. Each of his fourteen bookshelves contained a bust; the
twelve Caesars, Cleopatra, and Faustina watched over his collection. Each manuscript is
designated by its original location in the library. *Beowulf*'s manuscript is known as Cotton
Vitellius A.xv. This means that it was the fifteenth volume on the first shelf under the bust
of Vitellius Caesar in the Cotton library. This name includes all nine works currently
included in the manuscript. In order to differentiate the original five works of which
Beowulf is a part from the other four, the further designation "Nowell Codex" is used, in
reference to Lawrence Nowell mentioned above.

In 1629, Cotton's library was closed and seized by the king for examination, amongst
fears that it was dangerous for one man to own so many official documents. The library was
never returned to Cotton during his lifetime, but, in 1700 (during the Restoration), it was
willed to the British nation. The library was stored for safekeeping; however, in 1731, a fire
broke out that destroyed thirteen volumes and severely damaged hundreds more. *Beowulf*
survived when library trustees threw it and other manuscripts out of a window, but the pages
were burned along the edges and the entire manuscript became brittle due to heat exposure.
About fifty years later, an Icelandic scholar named G. J. Thorkelin made several hand copies
of *Beowulf* that preserved evidence of now missing or faded words. But it was not until 1845

334

that anyone began to take steps to preserve the crumbling pages from which about two thousand letters had been lost. Each page of the manuscript was mounted on a paper frame that stopped the deterioration but covered up some of the letters at the edges. The manuscript now resides in the British Museum along with the remains of Cotton's entire library. Recently, the pages of *Beowulf* have been examined by means of ultraviolet light to reveal some of the obscured letters, and the entire manuscript has been digitized and made available on CD-ROM.

TEXT & CONTEXT

WERGILD

If a man was unlawfully killed, the dead man's family would exact revenge by taking the life of a member of the murderer's family. This type of retributive justice often caused the murderer's family to counterretaliate and kill yet another man. Ultimately, family blood feuds emerged that lasted for generations. To prevent these feuds, many Germanic tribes, including the Anglo-Saxons, used an official system of payments called *wergild* in order to legally settle matters of serious injury or death. If one man killed or wounded another, he or his family could pay *wergild*, which literally means "man gold," to the family of the other man as compensation. The price paid was usually set by the appropriate king or lord and depended on the social status of the injured party and the severity of his injuries. By the ninth century, the *wergild* system had become quite complex, with a graduated schedule of payments for various injures. A set of surviving eighth-century laws lists increasing payments for each tooth that had been knocked out in a fight. In the event a man could not or would not pay the *wergild*, the injured family reverted to the old system and was within its legal rights to kill a member of the culprit's family of similar rank and status.

THE SCOP

Beowulf has also been called *The Scop's (or Poet's) Tale.* The word "scop" is related to our modern verb "to shape," and was most likely pronounced "shoap." A scop was a professional Anglo-Saxon storyteller responsible for singing the praises of kings and warrior heroes. While many scops sang *a capella*, others emphasized parts of their stories by accompanying themselves on an instrument, usually a harp. Even though scops were normally members of royal households, they were often nomadic; traveling from village to village, they exchanged stories for food, lodging, and money. A good scop was a respected member of his community and served as both an entertainer and historian. Often, a scop would become a "court poet" like the one referred to in lines 37–46 of *Beowulf* and sing about the accomplishments of his lord and his lord's men. Although scops and court poets were held in high regard, storytelling was not restricted to professionals. Anglo-Saxons of all trades shared stories with one another just as Hrothgar and his men do in Heorot, and the ability to tell an exciting tale was considered a valuable skill.

IN THE CLASSROOM

I. THE VALUE SYSTEMS IN *BEOWULF*

Although it was most likely composed and recited orally well before Christianity came to England, the written version of *Beowulf* was created at a time when British society was in a phase of religious transition between paganism and Christianity. The tension between the two modes of belief can easily be seen in the poem, where Christian elements coexist with the earlier folkloric and heroic traditions of the Germanic tribes.

Discussion

1. At the end of the poem, Beowulf's people praise him for being both "the gentlest of men and the most courteous, the most kindly to his people" but also "the most eager for renown." Discuss this seeming contradiction in the value systems of the poem. Is it possible to be both caring and ambitious? Are these standards meant to apply simultaneously or in different situations? Ask students to find other examples where elements of paganism and Christianity exist together. Do they mesh well together?

Connections

1. The epic battle scenes of *The Iliad*, *The Odyssey*, and *The Aeneid* (all in Book 1) can easily be seen to share many heroic elements with *Beowulf*. In particular, note that what is most desired after death is immortality through song. Rather than a lasting afterlife, the characters desire that their great deeds will be remembered and sung by future generations.

2. While the Christian morality that influenced *Beowulf*'s author can be seen in obvious places like the New Testament (p. 23) and *The Book of Margery Kempe* (p. 993), St. Augustine offers a more explicit treatment of pagan and Christian morals in *The Confessions* (p. 70) and a similar melding of pagan forms like the epic poem with Christian values can be seen in *The Song of Roland* (p. 540).

Writing

Ask students to write a short paper in response to one or more of the following:

1. Despite the seeming schizophrenia between pagan and Christian values in the poem, Beowulf is still primarily presented as the embodiment of all that is good. Keeping in mind the competing pagan and Christian ideals in the poem, discuss sources of positive value in *Beowulf*. You might want to address the question of what makes Beowulf good or, conversely, what makes him and his companions less than purely good. As part of this assignment, it may be necessary to formulate your own notions of how "good" and "evil" are defined in *Beowulf*, either in relation to one another or in relation to codes of behavior or belief established in the work. This differentiation of good and evil may be offered alone if a shorter assignment is desired.

2. Paying close attention to physical descriptions as well as the events of the narrative, compare and contrast Grendel, Grendel's mother, and the Dragon. Possible points to focus on include whether any of these characters is portrayed as the antithesis of the values that Beowulf and the men of Heorot personify (for instance, is one character "the embodiment of evil"?), whether one of them is more dangerous to Beowulf than the others, whether any of the three might be sympathetic characters, and whether they are all actually monsters in the way that we define "monster" today.

Groups

1. Our translation of *Beowulf* is in prose, but many excellent verse translations of the poem are available. Provide students with several additional translations of the episode titled "Grendel's Attack" in the book (pp. 502–3, ll. 710–90. For the best effect, try to choose at least one modern verse translation, like that of Seamus Heaney, and an older, more antiquated rendering. After having students identify differences in word choice and form, ask them to evaluate and argue for and against the effectiveness of each translation. They might want to note whether the verse translations attempt to retain the alliteration or caesura of the original poem and whether the translation seems proper to the

epic good versus evil struggle of this passage. Also, use this opportunity to give them a copy of the original Old English for the same passage. Using the translations as a point of reference, see how many words in Old English the class is able to identify.

II. IDENTITY IN *BEOWULF*

Beowulf is more than just an exciting story. As a record of the heroic deeds of its characters, identity is an integral part of the work. The world of the epic is one in which a man defines himself not only by his own deeds but also by those of his ancestors. Ancestral lineage and personal reputation served as identity markers through which a warrior could introduce and prove himself to others. In addition, a strong reputation could ensure a measure of immortality for a warrior, as poets would continue to sing about him long after his death.

Discussion

1. In the opening lines of the work, Hrothgar's family history is described in great detail before he actually appears. Notice that Scyld Scefing, Hrothgar's great-grandfather, is described as having been "found destitute" (p. 489). He is an orphan or foundling. Even though his surname, Scefing, is usually understood to mean Sheaf's-son, he has no identifiable father and must be distinguished by his own heroic deeds. Discuss with students the different ways that characters' identities are established in the poem. Is the way that Scyld's identity is developed significant in comparison with Hrothgar or Beowulf who, in addition to their own great deeds, can cite valiant and famous ancestors? Even though Scyld is explicitly praised as a great king, we are only given a short summary of his story. Is it possible that his lack of heritage affects his prospect of future fame?

2. In part, the prominence of family history in *Beowulf* highlights an emphasis on social bonds in general. One such bond is an arrangement known as *comitatus*, in which warriors pledge absolute loyalty to their leader in return for his protection and gifts of gold. Have students discuss the ways that various societal connections are presented in the poem. What is the relationship between Beowulf and his men? between Beowulf and Hrothgar? between Grendel and his mother?

Connections

1. Identity markers like lineage and reputation can be seen in many of the other epic poems. Characters in *The Odyssey* (Book 1) often have epithets like "wily Odysseus" or "wise Telemachus" but are rarely described in relation to their ancestors, while in the Hebrew Scriptures (Book 1) a more than complete lineage is often given for important characters. What might a poet be trying to convey with a focus on lineage rather than reputation or vice versa?

Writing

Ask students to write a short paper in response to one or more of the following:

1. Compare the importance of ancestral fame and personal reputation in establishing and developing identity in *Beowulf*. Is one of these clearly more important, or do the two work together to create the overall character of a warrior?

2. Women in Anglo-Saxon culture were not typically warriors and were not as concerned with cultivating their immortal fame through poetry and song. Address the topic of how the identity of women is developed throughout the poem. Does ancestry or reputation seem important to their characters?

Groups

1. In small groups (although this can also be done on an individual basis), have students sketch out several generations of a family tree. Ideally, the tree should contain not only the names of their ancestors but also their profession or an important distinguishing characteristic. Then, ask students to think seriously about the things they have accomplished in their own lives and what makes them unique. With these tools in hand, have students write a short piece in verse or prose introducing themselves as the hero of an epic or mock epic. Encourage students to make purposeful decisions about what information they incorporate into their epic introduction. If students are hesitant to write about themselves, give them the option of using a well-known literary character as the subject of their epic introduction. Recruit more adventurous students to serve as scops and read either their own or other students' epics aloud to the class.

BEYOND THE CLASSROOM

RESEARCH & WRITING

1. One of the things that connects *Beowulf* to both earlier and later texts is its status as an epic. Yet although the voice in which the *Beowulf* poet writes is recognizably similar to the voice in Homer's epics, each work has elements that are distinct as well. For example, note that at the start of *The Odyssey* the poet asks the muse for assistance in telling his story, while the *Beowulf* poet reminds the reader that we have all heard the stories of the Spear-Danes. Using one or more of the following works — *Beowulf, The Song of Roland, The Odyssey, The Aeneid, Paradise Lost,* or other epic works as primary texts, have students write a paper on some aspect of epic voice. This assignment should require a significant amount of research into various epic conventions as well as the difference between a primary and secondary epic and could also include investigation into current scholarly views of the form and function of the epic poem.

2. In 1939, the archeological discovery of Sutton Hoo — the burial site of an Anglo-Saxon king—broadened our knowledge of the Anglo-Saxon world and helped scholars offer new readings of *Beowulf*. However, some scholars have also attempted to interpret findings from the excavation using the poem, and this technique has sparked a heated debate in academia. Ask students to research Anglo-Saxon archeological sites like Sutton Hoo or the Anglo-Saxon cathedral beneath Canterbury Cathedral. How do the findings at these sites help us understand *Beowulf*? Conversely, how can *Beowulf* help us interpret the archeological findings and is this even a valid line of inquiry? Particularly relevant to this inquiry are lines 26–52 of the poem (p. 491), which describe the burial of Scyld Scefing.

Project

1. Many of the deeds in *Beowulf*, even those of the heroes, might be considered crimes in our society. In order to involve your students more directly with the characters and events of the poem, and to encourage them to read thoroughly, stage a mock trial prosecuting one of the main characters in the poem for his "crimes." Ask students to think creatively about these crimes. For example, if your class is interested in reading Grendel as a beast rather than a man, they might want to try Beowulf for animal cruelty rather than indicting Grendel for murder. While the culmination of this exercise will be in class, it will require a great deal of outside work. After deciding on the defendant and the crime involved, each student or group of students should be assigned a role: like judge, attorneys for each side, the defendant, witnesses. Students will have to closely

read the text in order to collect evidence for the trial and prepare their character roles. They will also need to familiarize themselves somewhat with court or mock trial procedure. Alternatively, to enhance the cultural aspects of this assignment, have students research aspects of Anglo-Saxon law prior to this assignment and try the character for crimes he may have committed in his own legal system.

FURTHER READING

Desmond, Marilynn. *"Beowulf:* The Monsters and the Tradition." *Oral Tradition* 7 (1992): 258–83.

Fulk, R. D., ed. *Interpretations of* Beowulf: *A Critical Anthology.* 1991.

Garde, Judith N. "Christian and Folkloric Tradition in *Beowulf:* Death and the Dragon Episode." Literature and Theology (1997): 325–46.

Gardner, John Champlin. Grendel. 1989.

Kendall, Calvin B. *Voyage to the Other World: The Legacy of Sutton Hoo.* 1992.

Kiernan, Kevin. Beowulf *and the* Beowulf *Manuscript.* 1981.

Owen, Gale R. *Rites and Religions of the Anglo-Saxons.* 1981.

Yale Law School. *The Avalon Project: Anglo-Saxon Law.* 2003. http://www.yale.edu/lawweb/avalon/medieval/saxlaw.htm

MEDIA RESOURCES

VIDEO

Background to Beowulf
25 min., 1995 (Educational Video Network)
This program explains the historical and literary traditions of this classic Old English epic poem. Students will learn about the historical and literary foundations that produced the poem, and a simple explanation of the origins of the English language is also provided. Students will also become familiar with the motivations of the characters and with the movement of the plot, and they will learn about the differences between the culture that produced *Beowulf* and modern culture.

Beowulf
30 min., 1998 (Zenger Media)
Swords fly as Beowulf battles the evil Grendel in this exciting animated adaptation of the epic poem. Incorporating fascinating sketch art and featuring the voice of Joseph Fiennes as Beowulf.

The 13th Warrior
102 min., 1999 (IMDB)
Starring Antonio Banderas and based on a book by Michael Crichton, this is an updated version of *Beowulf,* loosely based on the original poem.

The Ceremony of Innocence
90 min., 1985 (IMDB)
James Broderick and Richard Kiley star in this adaptation of Ronald Ribman's play that tells of eleventh-century England — a land bloodied, embattled, and beset by hordes of invading pagan Danes and disputatious nobles. The vacillating King Ethelred is drained of the decisive initiative he needs to save his throne and reputation. The production conveys the fear and violence of a period when lives were short and brutish.

Beowulf *and the Roots of Anglo-Saxon Poetry*
31 min., 1998 (Films for the Humanities & Sciences)
Beowulf is the oldest written epic in English literature. In this program, Dr. Robert DiNapoli — teaching fellow in Old and Middle English at the University of Birmingham, England — and Professor John Burrow of Bristol University examine the symbolism and the influence of Christianity in *Beowulf* and other masterpieces of English and Germanic poetry. *The Wanderer, The Seafarer, The Dream of the Rood,* and *The Battle of Maldon* are also analyzed. The program is an indispensable aid in teaching this watershed period in Western literature.

WEB SITES

The Electronic Beowulf
www.uky.edu/~kiernan/eBeowulf/guide.htm
Images of the *Beowulf* manuscript.

The Historical Background of Beowulf
www.angelcynn.org.uk/poetry_beowulf.html
A brief but useful overview of the times of Beowulf, along with some helpful links.

The Labyrinth: Resources for Medieval Studies
www.georgetown.edu/labyrinth/labyrinth-home.html
Based at Georgetown University, this site provides links to many medieval resources available on the Internet.

Old English at the University of Virginia
www.engl.virginia.edu/OE/
Peter S. Baker's site that provides information on Old English poetry. Especially interesting on this site are sound files of readings from Beowulf.

ORB: The Online Reference Book for Medieval Studies: Anglo-Saxon England
orb.rhodes.edu/encyclop/early/pre1000/ASindex.html
This is a very helpful site providing background on many aspects of Anglo-Saxon England.

Resources for Studying Beowulf
www.georgetown.edu/faculty/irvinem/english016/beowulf/beowulf.html
Created at Georgetown University, this site provides a student bibliography for Beowulf, information on Old English, and the ability to do a keyword search of Beowulf.

AUDIO

Beowulf
2 tapes or 2 CDs, 2:30 hrs. (HighBridge Audiobooks)
Seamus Heaney reads his acclaimed translation of Beowulf.

The Song of Roland (p. 546)

WWW   For a quiz on *The Song of Roland*, see *World Literature Online* at bedfordstmartins.com.worldlit.

It is important to help students distinguish *The Song of Roland* from the other epics they have read. Although important similarities exist between *Roland* and works like Homer's *The Odyssey* and *The Epic of Gilgamesh, Roland* has important unique features that set it apart.

The presence of feudalism in the poem should not be ignored. In a feudalistic society, the emperor granted land and other benefits to the aristocracy, who were known as his vassals, in exchange for military service. However, the relationship between a lord and his vassals was a complex one that involved mutual respect. Charlemagne demonstrates this respect when, early in the poem, he not only calls his Twelve Peers to ask for their advice on what to do about Marsilion but also adheres to their decision. Marsilion's court works much the same way.

The Song of Roland is as much a story about power struggle and conflict between allies as it is about battle. At two points in the poem, when Roland nominates Ganelon to go as envoy to the Saracens and when Roland and Oliver argue over whether to sound the oliphant, men who are on the same side engage in serious disagreements that end in radically different ways. Ganelon believes Roland has betrayed him by suggesting that he go to the Saracens with Charlemagne's message because the last two men that Charlemagne sent to Marsilion were killed. In retribution, he plots to betray Roland to his enemies and, in so doing, betrays the entire French army. Conversely, although Oliver knows that Roland was foolish not to sound the oliphant, he continues to fight the losing battle, and the two men make amends to one another before they die.

TEXT & CONTEXT

THE CRUSADES

The Crusades were a series of eight Catholic military invasions that are usually described as taking place between the eleventh and thirteenth centuries. However, these distinctions are largely arbitrary, and, in fact, crusade-like actions continued to take place up until the end of the seventeenth century. Sanctioned by the pope, the primary purpose of the crusades was to take back the Holy Land from the Muslims. Although the Crusades were touted as the pinnacle of righteousness, they were merciless, bloody massacres. The soldiers, largely made up of untrained and undisciplined peasants, felt their true mission was to rid the world of all non-Christians as they slaughtered, raped, and pillaged their way to Jerusalem. The actions were also often complete failures. For example, neither the crusaders of the Fourth Crusade nor the Children's Crusade reached Jerusalem. The crusaders of the Fourth Crusade sacked Constantinople, where they fought with Eastern Orthodox Christians, while many of the child crusaders died on the journey or were sold as slaves. In March 2000, Pope John Paul II issued an official apology for the crusades on behalf of the Catholic Church.

IN THE CLASSROOM

Discussion

1. The character Roland does not appear until about one hundred and fifty lines into *The Song of Roland* and is dead well before its end. Nevertheless, the poem is named for Roland, rather than for Charlemagne or the battle with the Saracens. What is the importance of Roland to the poem? Is this really his story? How so?

2. Pay attention to the poetic devices that the poet of *The Song of Roland* uses throughout the text. In addition to the typical repetition of oral-formulaic poetry, the poem often contrasts opposites in the same line like "Pagans are wrong and Christians are right" (laisse 70, l. 526). In the same way, the poet makes deliberate character parallels. Charlemagne versus Marsilion, Roland versus Oliver, and the Twelve Peers of Charlemagne versus the ten greatest men of Marsilion's army are all fruitful comparisons. How do these constant contrasts influence the way that you read the poem?

3. Ganelon, Roland's stepfather, makes it possible for Marsilion to attack Roland and the Rear Guard. Think about why Roland suggests that Ganelon be sent to take Charlemagne's message to King Marsilion, and discuss the reasons why Ganelon hands the French over to the Saracens. Is Ganelon a traitor to France, or are his actions justifiable? What do students make of the fact that Ganelon's grudge against Roland causes the death of thousands of French soldiers who played no part in the dispute?

Connections

1. *The Song of Roland* is an epic poem similar in style and content to *The Odyssey* (Book 1), *Beowulf* (p. 489), *The Aeneid* (Book 1), and *The Epic of Gilgamesh* (Book 1). Describe the characteristics of an ideal hero in these works. How does Roland stack up as an epic hero in comparison with these other heroes? What values have changed between the ancient Greek and Roman notion of a hero and *The Song of Roland*? How does the poem's overtly Christian subject matter play a role in what makes a good hero?

2. Compare what is said about the Saracens, who the poet calls Pagan, with suras 1 (The Exordium) and 5 (The Table of the Qur'an). What misconceptions does the poet of *The Song of Roland* hold about the Saracens? What does the Qur'an have to say about Christians, whom it calls "people of the book"?

3. Roland fails to sound his oliphant for fear that he "would lose [his] good name all through sweet France" (laisse 83, l. 544). It might be argued that this is a manifestation of the hamartia (from the Greek "to err") identified as an integral component of tragedy by Aristotle in *Poetics* (Book 1). Hamartia, usually translated as "tragic flaw" or "tragic error," often refers to the tremendous pride or hubris of a tragedy's hero that ultimately leads to his destruction. With this in mind, compare *The Song of Roland* with some of the Greek tragedies like *Oedipus Rex* (Book 1) or *Agamemnon* (Book 1). What does Roland's character have in common with the protagonists of these plays? How do they differ? Might *The Song of Roland* qualify as a tragedy?

Writing

Ask students to write a short paper in response to one or more of the following:

1. As an epitome of the traditional struggle between good an evil, *The Song of Roland* demonizes the enemy that fights against Roland's men — the Muslims. Write a paper that compares Muslim and Christian societies in *The Song of Roland*. How are the Muslims portrayed? Can these characterizations tell us anything about how Muslims were seen by medieval Christians?

2. Against the advice of his friend Oliver, Roland refuses to sound the oliphant until it is too late. Write a paper tracing the argument between Roland and Oliver in laisses 83, 85, and 129–33 over whether to sound the oliphant. What reasons does each man give for his position? Why does Roland finally blow the horn? Evaluate this discussion and its overall importance to the poem, particularly to Roland and Oliver's reconciliation in laisses 147–49 and the death scenes of each man.

3. Some historians claim that early crusaders may have recited *The Song of Roland* before marching into battle. Write a paper arguing whether inciting fervor for war, and in particular, for religious war, was the primary purpose of the poem. If refuting this claim, students should provide an alternative.

BEYOND THE CLASSROOM

Research & Writing

1. As Roland dies, he offers his glove to god "for all his sins" (laisse 174, l. 1061). Gloves also play an important role in other parts of the poem not excerpted in the anthology. When Charlemagne is trying to decide who will go as envoy to Marsilion, old Duke Neimes says "I'll go there for your love; / Give me therefore the wand, also the glove," (laisse 17, ll. 24–47), and, after Ganelon is named as the envoy, he drops Charlemagne's glove (laisse 25, ll. 331–33). Ask students to write a paper that explains the symbolism of the glove in *The Song of Roland*. This assignment will require that students not only give careful attention to the contexts in which gloves are used in the poem but also that they have recourse to secondary sources in order to determine the significance of gloves in medieval society.

2. Charlemagne has two prophetic dreams that warn him or Ganelon's betrayal. With reference to *The Song of Roland*, at least one other medieval text, and several secondary sources, have students write a research paper on the role of dreams or visions in these works. Consider the importance of the dream or vision to the work as a whole and whether the dreamer changes his or her behavior because of the dream. Possibilities for other texts include Genesis in the Old Testament (Book 1), *Purgatorio* (p. 689), Augustine's *The Confessions* (p. 70), and *The Book of Margery Kemp* (p. 993).

Project

1. Unlike many epic poems and tales of heroes, *The Song of Roland* doesn't end with the death of the hero or the defeat of the enemy. Roland's death and the subsequent rout of the remaining Saracen army by Charlemagne's men come only about halfway through the poem. The remainder describes a further battle, the trial and punishment of Ganelon, and ends as a war-weary Charlemagne is called to fight again. Have students or student groups construct their own ending for the poem. This assignment may take the form of a creative work or a persuasive essay that makes a case for the proposed ending. Alternatively, students may want to write an essay defending the original ending or arguing that the poem should end where the excerpt in the anthology leaves off.

WWW   For more information on *The Song of Roland* and annotated Web links, see *World Literature Online* at bedfordstmartins.com.worldlit.

FURTHER READING

Ashby-Beach, Genette. The Song of Roland: *A Generative Study of the Formulaic Language in the Single Combat.* 1985.

Ashe, Laura. " 'A Prayer and a Warcry': The Creation of a Secular Religion in the *Song of Roland.*" *Cambridge Quarterly* 28, no. 4 (1999): 349–67.

Lyons, Faith. "More about Roland's Glove." *Société Rencesvals: Proceedings of the Fifth International Conference*, Oxford 1970 (1977): 156–66.

Madden, Thomas F., ed. *The Crusades: The Essential Readings.* 2002.

Menocal, Maria Rosa. *The Arabic Role in Medieval Literary History.* 1990.

Taylor, Andrew. "Was There a *Song of Roland?*" *Speculum: A Journal of Medieval Studies*, 76, no. 1 (2001): 28–65.

MEDIA RESOURCES

WEB SITES

Introduction to Medieval History: The Song of Roland
www.ku.edu/kansas/medieval/108/lectures/roland.html
Professor Lynn Nelson's brief but interesting overview of the context of *The Song of Roland*.

The Medieval Epic
newman.baruch.cuny.edu/digital/2000/c_n_c/c_04_medieval/medieval_epic.htm
An interesting site out of CUNY-Baruch that gives an overview of three key medieval narratives — *The Song of Roland*, the *Poem of the Cid*, and the *Book of Kings*.

The Song of Roland
ishi.lib.berkeley.edu/history155/manuscripts/roland.html
Out of the University of California-Berkeley, this site contains a sound file of Professor Joseph J. Duggan singing selections from *The Song of Roland*.

AUDIO

The Song of Roland
(Blackstone Audiobooks)
A three-hour audiobook dramatizing in English the famous twelfth-century French epic poem.

In the World: Muslim and Christian at War (p. 578)

At the time the First Crusade began, the Islamic world was fragmented and weak. The achievements of Arabic civilization were great, but the political climate was unstable. Conflict broke out toward the end of the eleventh century in Palestine and Syria between the Seljuq Turks and the Fatimids. The former, who ruled the eastern Islamic world, were Sunni Muslims, whereas the latter, with an empire extending from Egypt, were Isma'ili (Sevener) Shi'ites. Christian crusaders were so successful against the Muslims at first because another ideological war was already waging in the East. The Seljuq Turks and the Abbasid caliph formed an alliance against the Fatimids, and the fighting that ensued continued during the Crusades and composed, in a sense, an Eastern counterpart. Point out to students that from 1092 to 1094, every major political leader in the Islamic world east of Egypt changed. In many respects, Pope Urban II's recommendation to "Let hatred . . . depart from among you; let your quarrels end; let wars cease; and let all dissensions and controversies slumber" addressed conditions that existed in both Europe and the East. You might approach the texts in the selection by examining how this rhetoric of peace constructs the foundation for a rhetoric of war. How does the pope develop the contrast between Christian and Islamic societies?

Focusing on the pope's differentiation between Christian and Muslim should help students identify differences between Christian and Muslim perspectives. How do the anonymous author of the *History of the First Crusade* and Ibn al-Athir portray "the enemy"? Students should notice similarities in their depictions as well as differences. To what extent do either perspectives change in these or other texts included in the selection?

Certainly, one of the changes documented in the *History of the First Crusade* involves the crusaders' understanding of the Crusade. How do the knights and footmen perceive the Crusade by the end of the excerpt? What kind of loss do the crusaders experience? You might go on to consider Conon de Béthune's "Alas, Love, what hard leave" in this context. Then, turn to the Muslim experience of loss. This comparison might lead you to discuss how reference to God or Allah mediates either experience.

Finally, every one of the accounts is concerned with virtue, be it virtue in battle or the virtues of either culture. Focus on this aspect, particularly in the excerpt from Usamah ibn Munqidh's *The Book of Reflections*. How does familiarity with European civilization inform or change his impression of his own?

TEXT & CONTEXT

SHORT CHRONOLOGY OF THE CRUSADES FROM PRE-INVASION TO 1291

1055 — Baghdad is ruled by Seljuk Turks

1071 — Seljuks defeat Byzantines at Malazgerd, gaining control of Asia Minor and soon the entire Muslim East (not including Egypt)

1095 — Proclamation of First Crusade at the Council of Clermont

1096–1102 — First Crusade

1096 — Kilij Arslan (sultan of Nicaea) triumphs over invading Franks (led by Peter the Hermit)

1097 — First great Frankish expedition; Nicaea is taken; Kilij Arslan is defeated at Dorylaeum

1098 — The Franks take control of Edessa and then Antioch

1099 — Jerusalem falls and is plundered; Godfrey of Bouillon becomes Jerusalem's first Latin ruler

1101 — Armies of the First Crusade defeated in Asia Minor by the Turks

1107–1808 — Crusade of Bohemond of Taranto

1109 — Tripoli is captured after a two thousand–day siege

1110 — Fall of Beirut

1114 — Catalan crusade to the Baleraric Islands

1118 — Pope Gelasius II's crusade in Spain

1120–1125 — Pope Calixtus II's crusade in Spain and the East

1120 — Foundation of the Knights Templar

1123 — Crusade decree of Frist Lateran Council

1124 — Tyre falls to the Franks, who now occupy the entire coast (except for Ascalon)

1125–1126 — Alfonso I of Aragon raids Andalusia

1128–1119 — Hugh of Payns organizes a crusade to the East

1128 — Franks fail to take Damascus

1139–1140 — Crusade to the East

1144 — Muslims recover Edessa (the first of the four Frankish states of the Orient)

1145 — Pope Eugenius III proclaims the Second Crusade

1146 — Zengi, the Muslim ruler, is murdered; his son, Nur al-Din, succeeds him

1146–1147 — Second Crusade

1147 — Lisbon falls

1153 — Crusade in Spain (renewed in 1175, 1193, 1212, 1229-53)

1154 — Nur al-Din takes control of Damascus; Muslim Syria is unified under his rule

1163–1169 — Nur al-Din gains control of Egypt; Saladin becomes vizier there

1171 — Crusade in the Baltic

1174 — Nur al-Din dies, whereupon Saladin takes Damascus

1177 — Philip of Flanders organizes a crusade to the East

1183 — Aleppo falls to Saladin, who now rules Syria and Egypt

1187 — Saladin triumphs over Frankish armies and reconquers Jerusalem (not to mention most of the Frankish territories — Tyre, Tripoli, and Antioch are left); proclamation of Third Crusade by Pope Gregory VIII

1188 — Saladin imposes a tithe in England

1189–1192 — Third Crusade

1190–1192 — Richard the Lionheart (king of England) helps the Franks recover several cities from Saladin (not Jerusalem)

1193 — Saladin dies in Damascus; civil war ensues

1193–1230 — Livonian Crusade

1197–1108 — German Crusade to Palestine

1198 — Proclamation of Fourth Crusade by Pope Innocent III

1202–1204 — Fourth Crusade

1202 — Zara falls

1204 — Franks take Constantinople and sack it

1206 — Danish Crusade to Ösel (and then to Estonia in 1219)

1209–1229 — Albigensian Crusade

1213 — Proclamation of Fifth Crusade of Pope Innocent III

1217–1229 — Fifth Crusade

1218 — Franks invade Egypt and take Damietta

1228–1229 — Crusade of Emperor Frederick II

1229 — A treaty gives Emperor Frederick II Jerusalem

1229–1231 — James I of Aragon organizes a crusade to Mallorca and then to Valencia (1232–1253)

1239–1240 — Crusade to help Constantinople

1244 — Franks lose Jerusalem

1248–1250 — Louis IX (king of France) invades Egypt; he is defeated and captured; Ayyubid dynasty ends and Mamluk rule begins

1258 — Mongols sack Baghdad

1270 — Louis IX dies near Tunis

1283–1302 — Crusade against Sicilians and Aragonese

1289 — Tripoli falls to the Mamluks

1291 — Acre falls to the Mamluks; two centuries of Frankish presence in the Orient end

IN THE CLASSROOM

Discussion and Writing

1. Describe the texts' depiction of value. What determined worth during the Crusades?

2. In what ways is Abu l-Muzaffar al-Abiwardi's poem similar to Pope Urban II's *Call to the First Crusade*? to Conon de Béthune's poem?

3. Read the first paragraph of the selection from *The Book of Reflections*, and discuss how the rest of Usamah ibn Munqidh's narrative relates to his initial position.

4. Although it was composed much later, Conon de Béthune's poem reiterates much of what Pope Urban II said in his *Call*. To what extent does the poem reflect the experience the crusaders had in the first two Crusades?

5. How do the narrators construct the historical accuracy of their accounts? To what extent does this depend on the objectivity of their perspectives?

Connections

1. Compare the rhetoric of empire portrayed in this selection with that of the Europe meets America selection (Book 3, p. 767) or Joseph Conrad's *Heart of Darkness*.

2. The book remarks on the Crusaders' lack of interest in getting to know the "enemy." Other narratives of imperialism do portray the other. Examine Mary Rowlandson's depiction of the Wampanoags and/or that of Western culture in Junichiro's *Aguri*.

BEYOND THE CLASSROOM

RESEARCH & WRITING

1. The book points out the Qur'anic source for Islamic jihad. What biblical justification can you find for the Crusades (note that Pope Urban II's quotations from the Bible do not directly call anyone to arms)?

2. Find out more about the role women played in the Crusades. What accounts of their experiences do we have?

3. Read more accounts from Muslim historians (see Gabrieli's *Arab Historians of the Crusades*). How do they understand the motivation for the Christian invasion? To what extent were Nur al-Din and Saladin religious as well as military heroes (see Baha ad-Din's *A Life of Saladin*, p. 179)?

4. Read a Christian account of the Sacred Lance, and compare it with that of Ibn al-Athir. To what extent were the Crusades a battle of faiths?

Projects

1. Take a look at contemporary portrayals of the Crusades (for example, the 1935 black-and-white movie *The Crusades*, Ridley Scott's *Kingdom of Heaven*, scheduled for release in 2005, or perhaps even the video game *The History Channel: The Crusades*). What image of the Crusades prevails in the Western world today? What about in Muslim society?

2. What influence did European art and architecture have in the Middle East as a result of the Crusades? What other aspects of Muslim culture were affected? How?

FURTHER READING

Edgington, Susan B., and Sarah Lambert, eds. *Gendering the Crusades*. 2001.
Erdmann, C. *The Origin of the Idea of Crusade*. Trans. M. W. Baldwin and W. Goffart. 1977.
Hillenbrand, Carole. *The Crusades. Islamic Perspectives*. 1999.
Powell, J. M., ed. *Muslims under Latin Rule, 1100–1300*. 1991.
Siberry, E. *Criticism of Crusading, 1095–1274*. 1985.

MEDIA RESOURCES

VIDEO

The Crusades
23 min., 1989 (Insight Media)
Looking closely at the three major crusades, this program examines the political and military divisions, economic incentives, and military pressures that gave rise to the Crusades. The video traces the path of the crusaders to the Holy Land and considers the effects of the holy wars and the influence of the returning crusaders on the developing culture of Western Europe.

Faith and Feudalism: The Early Middle Ages
23 min., 1999 (Insight Media)
Featuring art reproductions, maps, interviews, and historical reenactments, this program recounts the rise of feudalism in Europe during the decline of Rome. It shows how religious organizations like the church in Europe or Buddhism in China were able to maintain the thread of culture in feudal periods. It also illustrates how religious writings gave people hope. Explores the songs, poems, plays, histories, and inspirations of the time, including *Beowulf* and Gildas's history of the Celts.

The Fires of Faith: Dissidents and the Church
50 min., 1995 (Films for the Humanities & Sciences)
This program discusses papal reactions to church dissidents. Thirteenth-century fragmentation of religious orders into various sects is examined. Discussions include St. Francis of Assisi, the French Albigenses sect and the Albigensean Crusade, the fall of Albi, the Cathars and their extermination by the Inquisition, Pope Innocent III, the founding of the Dominican order, and the Ecumenical Council of 1215.

The Inquisition
100 min., DVD (A&E)
Recently opened Vatican archives bring to light compelling new historical information about the Inquisition and its brutal tactics.

ANDREAS CAPELLANUS, *The Art of Courtly Love* (p. 617)

WWW   For a quiz on *The Art of Courtly Love*, see *World Literature Online* at bedfordstmartins.com/worldlit.

The monk Andreas Capellanus is believed to have been a chaplain in the court of Henry of Troy in the late twelfth century. Henry's wife, Marie de Champagne, was an influential patron of the arts, most notably of Chretien de Troyes's *Lancelot*, and surrounded herself with poets and troubadours. Though a monk, Capellanus would have had ample opportunity to observe the love games of the court, and precisely because he was a monk, he might have been privy to some of the deepest secrets of the lords and ladies therein.

The Art of Courtly Love is written in the form of a letter to a young man, Walter, on the subject of love. The primary goal of the first two books of the text is to help Walter learn to attract, win, and keep a woman that he desires, while the third book (not excerpted here) serves as a retraction of the prior two books and a warning against involvement with courtly love. Students may struggle with the obvious sexism inherent in the text; the work is written primarily from a male point of view, women's experiences are mentioned only in passing, and, at times, Capellanus seems to condone rape by suggesting that it is acceptable for men to take what they want by force if a lady hesitates. It is true that women were largely considered to be, at best, sub par and, at worst, simple property during this period. Make Capellanus's assumptions about women and men into an opportunity for discussion about these topics both in the Middle Ages and in our time, and compare his views with those of Chaucer in "The Wife of Bath's Tale" and Margery Kempe.

Although Capellanus excerpted much of his material from Ovid's *The Art of Love* and other early Romantic texts, *The Art of Courtly Love* was nonetheless somewhat controversial for its time. The church condemned any sort of carnal love during this period because it was associated with the sin of lust; even sex between married people was sanctioned only for the purpose of procreation. Capellanus's book, which even with the retraction of the third book was seen as dangerously in support of sexuality, became so popular that Bishop Stephen Tempier of Paris officially condemned it in 1277. Despite its popularity, there isn't a great deal of evidence that *The Art of Courtly Love* had an overarching influence on the conduct of people in the later Middle Ages. The work clearly had far reaching implications in the literary realm, but Capellanus's influence on the day-to-day life of even courtesans is likely a great deal more subtle.

TEXT & CONTEXT

ADULTERY

Many have labeled the institution of courtly love, as detailed in the works of Capellanus and the medieval troubadours, a form of sanctioned adultery. The most famous literary case of adultery, King Arthur's wife Guinevere's affair with the knight Lancelot, was romanticized by dozens of poets of the time. For example, although a law enacted in 1352 had stipulated that adultery with the king's companion was an act of treason, Sir Thomas Mallory still saw Guinevere as "a true lover" in his *Morte d'Arthur*. For its part, the medieval church considered adultery a more serious sin than simple fornication. Not only did adultery flout the marriage vows, but it also led to the possibility of producing illegitimate offspring. Despite this, adultery was so prevalent that courts in the late Middle Ages did not always consider adultery alone adequate grounds for divorce. However, adulterers, particularly if they were women, were often punished quite severely. In England, women could legally be expelled from their homes, sent to convents, publicly humiliated by their husbands, or stripped of their dowries. In some medieval Islamic societies, adulterous women could even be sentenced to death for their crime. Although an adulterous man's confessor might assign him a heavy penance and prescribe abstention from sex to cleanse him of his sin, a man's adultery often went undetected and unpunished by secular law except in the most flagrant of cases.

ELEANOR OF AQUITAINE

The commission of *The Art of Courtly Love* by Marie de Champagne continued a tradition of supporting the production of early courtly romance begun by her mother, Eleanor of Aquitaine. Eleanor was such an instrumental patron of these stories, particularly the early Arthurian romances, that Thomas of Britain wrote *Tristram* at her urging and Wace dedicated his *Brut* to her. Eleanor's own life reads much like a romance. It is rumored that before she divorced her first husband on the grounds that they were distantly related, Eleanor and her second husband-to-be, Henry II, met in secret much like Lancelot and Guinevere. When Henry tired of her, Eleanor returned to Aquitaine. There, she presided over a liberal and literary-minded court with her daughter Marie. The two women helped to set up a code of chivalry that became the standard for knightly behavior and even held contests at which they judged the behavior of lovers according to their standards.

IN THE CLASSROOM

Discussion

1. In Book I, Chapter 6, Capellanus writes "A married woman changes her status to match that of her husband, but a man can never change his nobility by marriage." This statement highlights Capellanus's tendency to differentiate starkly between men and women when it comes to love. Find other examples in the text where the author treats men and women differently. Are Capellanus's views on men and women typical of other authors in the medieval period? Is his audience for *The Art of Courtly Love* primarily male or female?

2. Capellanus stresses the necessity of secrecy in love if the relationship is to last. Is secrecy, like absence and difficulty, one of the things that makes love increase? What about the public sphere might be dangerous to love?

3. *The Art of Courtly Love* contains many seeming contradictions. For example, in "The Rules of Love," Capellanus writes "That which a lover takes against the will of his beloved has no relish." However, in Book I, Chapter 11, he encourages men who fall in love with a peasant woman "not [to] hesitate . . . to embrace her by force." Discuss these inconsistencies with your class. How might we explain this and other problematic sections? Are they a result of some bias on the part of the culture? of Capellanus? Are they even a problem at all?

4. In the third paragraph of Book II, Chapter 6, Capellanus breaks the flow of his somewhat impersonal narrative. He says, "I know that once when I sought advice" and then switches to the first person plural "we" in order to detail how a man falls in love with a woman he can never have. Notice how distinct and almost personal this language seems compared with his prior prose. You might have students underline personal pronouns in this chapter so that they can easily see the difference in this paragraph. Although Capellanus is a monk, does this section provide evidence that he has fallen in love? If Capellanus is not writing about himself, what else might explain his change in language?

Connections

1. Capellanus describes a courtly world much like the one in Lady Murasaki's *The Tale of Genji*. Using Book II as a guide, can you evaluate the relationships between Genji and the women in the novel? How do Capellanus's standards of love apply to Genji's world? Which author's conception of courtly love seems more complex?

2. In general, troubadours are described as poets who reject the Christian ideals of love and marriage in favor of practicing love as a religion. Yet Christianity does not discount love entirely. Compare *The Art of Courtly Love* with the Song of Songs in the Hebrew Scriptures (Book 1). Are the notions of love that are described in each piece radically different? On its surface, the Song of Songs is a traditional love poem, but it can also be read as an allegory for the love between man and God. Can Capellanus's work be interpreted this way?

Writing

Ask students to write a short paper in response to one or more of the following:

1. Capellanus describes love as "a certain inborn suffering derived from the sight of and excessive meditation upon the beauty of the opposite sex, which causes each one to wish

above all things the embraces of the other." Have students write a paper explaining this assertion using examples from one or more texts that you have read this year. What does Capellanus mean by "excessive"? Why does he think of love as a "suffering"?

2. Capellanus believes that love and marriage are separate phenomenon. With particular reference to Book II, Chapter 7, have students compare Capellanus's view of marriage with that of Paul in the New Testament. What are the views of marriage and love in each text? Under what circumstances does each man allow for or discount marriage?

BEYOND THE CLASSROOM

RESEARCH & WRITING

1. In Book II, Chapter 1, Capellanus warns "every man ought to be sparing of praise of his beloved when he is among other men . . ." Although he does not explain this assertion, it clearly refers to the famous classical story of the rape of Lucretia (Lucrece). Lucretia's story, originally told in Livy's *History of Rome*, has been retold many times, notably by Chaucer in *Legend of Good Women* and by Shakespeare. Have students research this classical story and evaluate the implications of Capellanus's opposition to bragging about one's love. Is Capellanus's concern derived directly from the Lucretia story, or does he have other concerns? How does his guideline to keep love from the public eye relate to this issue?

2. In the 1960s and 1970s, a scholarly debate emerged regarding whether Capellanus's *The Art of Courtly Love* was meant as a satirical piece or a serious one. Ask students to make an argument supporting one side of this debate. They should consult both recent scholarship and writings from the 1960s and 1970s, when the controversy began. You may also wish to ask them to read Capellanus's "retraction" of *The Art of Courtly Love*. In addition, students may want to think about whether courtly love existed at all in the Middle Ages or to evaluate Capellanus's description of it as accurate or flawed.

Project

1. Have students consult and study contemporary popular love songs, self-help manuals, advice columns, or advertisements to gain a sense of the guidelines that shape our current behavior when it comes to love. Then, ask them to construct a list of the rules of modern love. How have our conceptions changed from Capellanus's time? Does this exercise illuminate Andreas Capellanus's text?

WWW   For additional information on Capellanus and annotated Web links, see *World Literature Online* at bedfordstmartins.com/worldlit.

FURTHER READING

Allen, Peter L. "Ars Amandi, Ars Legendi: Love Poetry and Literary Theory in Ovid, Andreas Capellanus, and Jean de Meun," *Exemplaria* 1, no. 1 (1989): 181–205.

Burnley, David. *Courtliness and Literature in Medieval England.* 1988.

Hanawalt, Barbara A., and David Wallace, eds. *Medieval Crime and Social Control.* 1999.

Moi, Toril. "Desire in Language: Andreas Capellanus and the Controversy of Courtly Love." *Medieval Literature: Criticism, Ideology, and History.* Ed. David Aers. 1986.

Monson, Don A. "Andreas Capellanus and the Problem of Irony," *Speculum* 64 (1988): 539–72.

MEDIA RESOURCES

WEB SITES

Andreas Capellanus
cla.calpoly.edu/~dschwart/engl513/courtly/andreas.htm
Users will find a number of links to various Web sites devoted to Capellanus and his works, including biographical links, on this site.

The Medieval Sourcebook — Andreas Capellanus — *The Art of Courtly Love*
www.fordham.edu/halsall/source/capellanus.html
This page provides readers with an excerpt from *The Art of Courtly Love.*

In the Tradition: The Courtly Love Lyrics of Muslim Spain and the South of France (p. 628)

There are many ways in which antiquity influenced the development of the courtly love lyric, Plato's *Symposium* and Ovid's works perhaps most directly. The book states that *The Dove's Necklace* indicates their significance for Ibn Hazm, the former providing primarily a theory of love, the latter poetic conventions as well. For both, love has a transforming effect on humankind through the mediation of the divine. Have students identify examples in the texts of transformation. What form does the divine take? Sandra Alfonsi observes that the first secular portrayal of the ideal feminine as transforming, ennobling, and sweetening appears in troubadour love poetry, the Virgin Mary providing a parallel in religious works of the time.

The courtly love tradition emerged from the impact of Arabic literary modes on the Franco-Hispanic world as well. The rise of the Umayyads in the eighth and ninth centuries along with the relocation of the caliphate's political center to Syria instigated the decline of the Hidjaz aristocracy. Denied participation in politics, Hidjaz poets turned their attention to love. The description of amorous experience became the dominant literary theme by the eighth century. With its roots in the pre-Islamic *qasidah*, in which praise of the beloved only served to introduce a poem's main topic, Hispanic-Arabic poetry thus developed with love as its primary focus. That the feelings of the lover, rather than the depiction of the beloved through ornate simile and metaphor, composed love's formulation was the result of further Arabic influence. Arab poetry of the seventh and eighth centuries had centered on the lover's doubt and despair, exemplified in the *ghazal* (p. 631). These traditions came together in the production of poetry that portrayed the perspective of the unfortunate female, eventually displaying stylistic and psychological complexity. For by the tenth century, the Arab warrior ethic had become tied to the refined notion of love that had developed in the courts of Spain. Alfonsi explains that virile worth and love, love and heroic death, amatory mercy and social clemency were linked. Indeed the code of honor followed during the Almohad dynasty (1130–1212) demonstrated as much. Women were to be respected and virtue defended. The theory of love that had become conventional at court and in poetry by the twelfth century bore a remarkable resemblance to that which was developing in Southern France.

Like the Provençal love delineated in Capellanus's *The Art of Courtly Love*, Arabic love theory recognized several stages:

1. *istihsan*, or liking, which also counts as mutual friendship.
2. *i gáb*, or admiration.

3. *ulfa,* or companionship.
4. *kalaf,* or infatuation, which in the form of the obsession presented in love poetry is *'isq.*
5. *sagaf,* or amorous passion.

Have students locate these stages in the poems selected in order to distinguish the strands that collectively produce the experience of love. Students will be tempted to overlook the differences between the poems and reduce the poetry to the conventional. But such codes constituted an attempt to account, in part, for the transformation of love, for instance, that which is unruly, rather than a rulebook for love. Consider the confusion that reigns in Raimbaut's "Listen Lords . . . but I don't know what," the contradictions in Bernart de Ventadorn's "My heart is so full of joy," or the lack of restraint in "I am madly in love." You might also point out that the courtly love lyric, although originating in aristocratic circles, was not only an expression of high society, as Marcabru demonstrates. Expressions of love challenged gender conventions, too: How? Look at the Countess of Dia's and Castelloza's poems in particular. What these challenges to convention depend on is the personal experience of the individual. Although many courtly love lyrics take the conventional relationships between the speaker and his or her lover (unrequited love, abandonment, infidelity, and the like) as their subject, the personal "I" creates a singularity of perspective. Guillaume IX's "My companions, I am going to make a vers that is refined" and Marcabru's "By the fountain in the orchard" can be examined in this respect. In Donald Frank's words, "The troubadour lyric . . . reflects, in the literature of the twelfth century, a deepening awareness of the uniqueness and significance of the individual personality" (31).

The poets' own experiences are recounted in the *Lives of the Troubadours,* prose records from the thirteenth century written in Provençal that mix fact and fiction much like Guillaume IX's poem mentioned above. It is in these biographies that the term *troubadour,* which derives from the verb *trobar* (meaning "to find" or "to invent"), comes to denominate the poets collectively. Their work includes love songs as well as *cansos,* a form of long poem that developed during the twelfth century, and *sirventes,* a panegyric or satirical song, moralizing in nature. The impact of troubadour poetry can be seen in late twelfth century poetry in northern France as well as in *Minnesang,* the Germanic form of love poetry, the earliest extant specimens of which are from the twelfth century.

TEXT & CONTEXT

THE CATHARS AND THE TROUBADOURS

The Cathari (purist) doctrines developed a following at the same time the tenets of courtly love became conventional. For both, the desire for self-purification determined the relationship between men and women. The pursuit of a married woman, for instance, offered the poet-lover an unattainable ideal that provoked the emotional catharsis of platonic love, in keeping with the Cathari rejection of sexual relations. But the Cathari went further in shunning all emotional unions and held that women were responsible for the soul's imprisonment, not in terms of an ennobling and purifying conquest but as an instrument of the devil.

OTHER LITERARY FORMS

The *tenso* and *joc parti* (or *partimen*) were forms of poetic debate, the former usually on a topic of love casuistry. In the latter, a challenger is offered a choice of argument. The *planh* is a poem that laments the death of an important person. Both the *alba,* or dawn song, and the *pastorela* are characterized by narrative elements, including a climatic event. In the *alba*, the lady is already won, and at dawn the lovers must part to prevent discovery. In the *pastorela*, a knight attempts to seduce a shepherdess, who either succumbs (after displaying token resistance) or successfully resists in a witty manner. The *toza* of the *pastorela* and the troubadour's lady are similar in many ways that, Donald Frank notes, bring the superior status of the lady into question. Both heroines are playful at times, restrained at others. Neither tends to accept or reject her suitor's proposals more than the other, and both inspire idealistic as well as realistic poetry.

IN THE CLASSROOM

Discussion and Writing

1. Where do we see the theory of love Ibn Hazm puts forth played out in the poems themselves? How is the love that the poems portray different from Ibn Hazm's account?

2. What kind of concept of virtue do the poems depict? You might look at "Chastity," "By the fountain in the orchard," and "I've lately been in great distress," among others.

3. The poems often present love in terms of conquest. To what extent is liberation present?

4. War and conflict do not only occur between lovers in the selected poems. What effect does the political situation at the time have?

5. How is the authenticity of feeling constituted? That is to say, within the conventions of troubadour love poetry, what makes emotion real?

Connections

1. Compare the gender roles constructed in the poetry in the selection with that of Sappho and/or Ovid. How did the courtly love tradition depart from earlier models in this respect?

2. Explore the significance of the present moment in troubadour love poetry and in Marvell's "To His Coy Mistress." What do the similarities/differences reveal about what lasts in love?

3. The effect of love is not always idyllic. Examine this perspective in the selection and in Junichiro's *Aguri*. How do your findings compose a critique of the ideal that the troubadour poets maintained?

4. The power the poetic conventions of troubadour poetry accord women can be seen as an historical precedent for developments in the eighteenth century. According to Thomas Honegger, "this new, emotional tradition [of courtly love] became so influential that it established itself alongside, and often in conflict with, the older legalistic tradition, which viewed marriage as a business agreement between two families" ("De arte (dis-)honeste amandi," in *Authors, Heroes and Lovers. Essays on Medieval English Literature and Language*, p. 73). Refer to the selections in "Love, Marriage, and the Education of Women" (Book 4, p. 719), and discuss the relationship between law and convention.

BEYOND THE CLASSROOM

RESEARCH & WRITING

1. Read the troubadours' *vidas (The Lives of the Troubadours)*. How did their lives exemplify or betray the ideals they held forth in their works?

2. Read a few *Minnesang*, the Germanic form of love poetry that evolved out of the troubadour tradition. What aspects of troubadour love poetry were further developed?

3. Read more of the troubadour poetry by women. To what extent is their perspective different from that of the male poets?

4. Much religious writing was also produced at the time. Read a few texts, and discuss the difference between the way religious works and troubadour poetry portrayed love. Consider spiritual love, for example.

Projects

1. Examine the portrayal of women in other art forms of the time, particularly in paintings of the Virgin Mary, who had become a cult figure. To what extent do the conventions observed in the courtly love lyrics hold elsewhere? What other ideals other than Mary were upheld?

2. Read a modern version of a manual on love (e.g., Erich Fromm's *The Art of Loving,.* 2000). What aspects of courtly love remain current today?

FURTHER READING

Alfonsi, Sandra Resnick. *Masculine Submission in Troubadour Lyric.* 1986.

Denomy, Alexander. *The Heresy of Courtly Love.* 1947.

Frank, Donald K. *Naturalism and the Troubadour Ethic.* 1988.

Jaeger, C. Stephen. *The Origins of Courtliness.* 1985.

Nykl, Alois R. *Hispano-Arabic Poetry and its Relations with the Old Provençal Troubadours.* 1946.

Topsfield, L. T. *Troubadours and Love.* 1975.

MEDIA RESOURCES

WEB SITES

Muslim Spain and European Culture
http://www.xmission.com/~dderhak/index/moors.htm
A Web site that explores the history and culture of Muslim Spain and the effects of this culture on the rest of Europe.

Exploring Ancient World Cultures: Medieval Europe Homepage
eawc.evansville.edu/mepage.htm
This site covers ancient Near Eastern history to the Middle Ages. It includes a thorough chronology of major events of medieval times and allows users to look into what was happening across cultures during various points in history.

MARIE DE FRANCE, *The Lay of the Chevrefoil (The Honeysuckle)* (p. 674)

WWW For a quiz on *The Lay of the Chevrefoil*, see *World Literature Online* at
bedfordstmartins.com/worldlit.

We know virtually nothing about Marie de France save the small bits of information that she offers in her works. In addition to her fifteen *lais*, Marie translated a collection of 103 fables called "Ysopet" from English to French and wrote a longer poem called "The Purgatory of Saint Patrick." Her *lais*, like "Chevrefoil," belong to what is commonly known as the "love group" of the Breton Cycle, as they typically tell of the brave deeds that Breton knights performed for the sake of their ladyloves.

Since "Chevrefoil" is only a small portion of a longer tale about Tristan and Iseult, be sure to contextualize the poem for students either by summarizing the salient points of the Tristan and Iseult story or by having them read a version of the tale in tandem with the study of Marie de France's poem. You may wish to point out that the love triangle represented by King Mark, Iseult, and Tristan mirrors that of King Arthur, Guinevere, and Lancelot. In fact, the two stories share many events, like the accusation of infidelity levied by the king at his queen and the banishment of the queen's lover.

"Chevrefoil," like all Marie's *lais*, was written in the vernacular language of her time. Even though Marie's works were written, they would often be recited orally. This allowed even the illiterate commoner to have access to the *lais* and increased their potential to reach a broad audience. In contrast, much of the literature of the church was written in and translated to Latin as a means of control over what writings the lay people could gain access. It is no wonder, then, that the rise of vernacular writings like Marie's caused the church considerable alarm. They regarded vernacular literature, particularly romances, as being seductive and dangerous works with the power to lead readers astray.

TEXT & CONTEXT

PENTECOST

As in many Arthurian legends, the feast that takes place in "Chevrefoil" is on the day of Pentecost or Whitsunday. The word "Pentecost" is Greek for "fiftieth," as the holiday is celebrated on the fiftieth day after Easter. Celebrations on this particular day date back to pagan times when sacrifices would be made to the gods in celebration of the first part of the harvest. In the Christian tradition, the Holy Spirit is said to have visited the disciples of Jesus on Pentecost. Afterward, when the disciples began to speak about Jesus to the people from various nations who were still gathered after Passover, each man heard the message in his own language. In the Arthurian tradition, Pentecost was an occasion for a great feast. Arthur often requested that all of his knights return to Camelot on Pentecost, and this day is the setting for many of the adventures of the Knights of the Round Table. In many Arthurian tales, Arthur has a standing rule that he will not sit down to the feast until a worthy adventure has been found.

ARTHURIAN LEGEND

Tales of King Arthur, a semihistorical king of the Britons, and the events surrounding his court were largely developed in the Middle Ages but are presumed to date back to ancient Celtic oral tradition. The earliest reference to Arthur occurs in the Welsh poem "Y Gododdin," written around 600 c.e. By 1100 c.e., Queen Guinevere is introduced and familiar knights like Kay, Beldivere, and Gawain make appearances in *The Mabinogion*, circa 1100

C.E. Geoffrey of Monmouth is credited with writing the earliest continuous Arthurian narrative in about 1139 C.E. His *Historia Regum Britanniae* (History of the Kings of Briton) identifies Arthur as the son of Uther Pendragon, mentions Arthur's adviser Merlin, and presents the basic frame of all Arthurian legend. The story of Guinevere's infidelity, the subsequent revolt instigated by Arthur's nephew Mordred, Arthur's death, and his departure to Avalon are all a part of Geoffrey's prose narrative. Many Arthurian tales focus on particular knights, couples, or peripheral characters, and it is not unusual for Arthurian legends to make only a passing reference to Arthur himself or leave him out entirely. The rich history and epic themes of Arthurian legend provided a fertile starting ground for medieval writers, many of whom, including Chaucer in "The Knight's Tale," added to the Arthurian cannon. In many respects, our fascination with King Arthur has not waned, as is evidenced by the abundance of Arthurian material still being created today.

IN THE CLASSROOM

Discussion

1. At the start of the poem, Tristan is nearly out of his mind for love of the Queen Iseult. What brings him out of his desire to "expose himself / to death and destruction"? What does he hope to gain from meeting with the queen?

2. Ask students to identify and explain the metaphorical significance of the poem. Why does Marie de France title her work "Chevrefoil"? What is the significance of the honeysuckle plant to the overall theme of the poem? Can students think of other examples of extended metaphor in the texts they have read?

3. Scholarly explanations of Tristan's message on the piece of wood vary, but the significance of the wood itself cannot be denied. Discuss whether students think this message was written in code. Is it important that the message was written on a piece of wood rather than another material? How do the nature and execution of the message relate to the metaphor of the honeysuckle and the hazel tree?

4. Marie de France is one of the few women poets whose works survive. Because many women were illiterate, men contributed the bulk of the literature of the Middle Ages. Marie was aware that her place in posterity was not guaranteed precisely because she was a woman. At the end of her fable "Isopet," Marie writes, "It may be that many writers will claim my work as their own, but I want no one else to attribute it to himself. He who lets himself fall into oblivion does a poor job" (trans., Mary Lou Martin). Discuss with students Marie's status as a woman who participates freely in a male-dominated pursuit. How might her position as an author differ from someone like that of Margery Kempe?

Connections

1. Marie describes Tristan's love for Iseult as something that he cannot control, so much so that he is driven to "expose himself to death and destruction." Compare Tristan's passion with the love of Dante for Beatrice in *Inferno* (p. 689) or between Genji and his various mistresses in *The Tale of Genji* (p. 1094). Is passion as dominant in these other works as it seems to be in "Chevrefoil"? Does passion seem to affect men differently from women?

2. The dominant metaphor for love in "Chevrefoil" is a description of the symbiotic relationship between the hazel tree and the honeysuckle vine. Note the similarities between

this section and the description of the bed that Odysseus built for himself and Penelope in Homer's *The Odyssey* (Book 1). Is the message of the two metaphors the same? How do the metaphors apply to the types of love in question in each text?

Writing

Ask students to write a short paper in response to one or more of the following:

1. Write a persuasive paper on the following question: Is Marie de France sympathetic to the plight of Tristan and Iseult, or does she condemn their adultery? Support your argument with specific evidence from the poem. For a more involved discussion, you might also address whether Marie's view of the lovers' plight is a typical attitude either for other writers of the Tristan and Iseult legend or for medieval love poets in general.

2. The beginning and ending lines of *The Lay of the Chevrefoil* serve as a sort of frame for the Tristan and Iseult story. However, unlike in Chaucer and Boccacio, Marie's frame does not provide a fictional setting for the main story. Rather, she uses these lines to address her audience directly. She first tells us that she intends to relate the story of Tristan and "the queen" and closes by assuring us that her account is true. What purpose does this serve in the overall scheme of the poem? Are Marie's first-person asides comparable to those of other medieval authors?

BEYOND THE CLASSROOM

RESEARCH & WRITING

1. *The Lay of the Chevrefoil* is only a piece of the larger Tristan and Iseult story that was being constructed at approximately the time Marie was writing. Have students read and research other medieval versions of the Tristan legend, like those by Chaucer and Gottfried von Strassburg. Ask them to look for the incident related in "Chevrefoil" in these more complete tellings and to analyze the role of this event in the larger tale. Students may want to use this analysis to answer the larger question of why Marie might have chosen this particular detail as the subject of her poem or to argue about the nature of love in the Tristan and Iseult story.

2. Compared with many other medieval romances, the woman in "Chevrefoil," Iseult, seems to have an extraordinary amount of freedom and will. She commands the group of knights who accompany her with ease and is comfortable enough with Tristan that she can "[tell] him whatever she like[s]." Ask students to research the life of a typical medieval woman and evaluate Iseult's behavior in light of the social norm. Is Iseult radically different from her archetypal counterparts? Students should keep in mind that Iseult is a queen rather than a member of the lower classes. As part of this research project, it may be helpful for students to compare Iseult's character not only with a historical or scholarly "norm" but also with some of the other medieval literary women they have encountered, like the Wife of Bath, Shaharazad, or Margery Kempe.

Project

1. After students have read and researched the Arthurian genre, have them write their own Arthurian story. Depending on what you would like them to get out of the exercise, their tale may be a retelling of a familiar legend, like Tristan and Iseult, or one entirely of their own making. Students who wish to undertake a more difficult approach to this assignment may attempt to emulate Marie de France's brief style or her poetic form. Ask stu-

dents to think carefully about their purpose in writing their particular story. Is there some point that they intend to illustrate? If so, will they communicate their message directly, as in a first-person address to the reader, or more subtly through metaphor and the manipulation of their poetic subject?

WWW   For additional information on Marie de France and annotated Web links, see *World Literature Online* at bedfordstmartins.com/worldlit.

FURTHER READING

Block, Howard. *The Anonymous Marie de France.* 2003.
Grimbert, Joan Tasker, ed. *Tristan and Isolde: A Casebook.* 2002.
Hammond, P. W. *Food and Feast in Medieval England.* 1993.
Higham, N. J. *King Arthur: Myth-Making and History.* 2002.
Wynne-Davies, Marion. *Women and Arthurian Literature: Seizing the Sword.* 1996.

MEDIA RESOURCES

WEB SITES

International Marie de France Society
www.people.vcu.edu/~cmarecha/#Online
This page, created at Virginia Commonwealth University, includes bibliographical references, on-line translations, links to biographies on the author, and information about contemporary performances of her work.

The *Lais* of Marie de France
Web.english.ufl.edu/exemplaria/intro.html
This site offers a complete translation of the *lais* of Marie de France and includes brief commentary on the translations by the translator, Judith P. Shoaf.

The *Lais* of Marie de France — Study Guide
www.wsu.edu:8080/~brians/love-in-the-arts/marie.html
This site offers brief summaries of several of the *lais* and includes questions for further study.

Women's Comedy — Marie de France
Home.earthlink.net/~dianska/mariedefrance.html
This page helps students look at some of the humorous aspects of the fables and *lais* of Marie de France. It also offers a close reading of several passages, examining how the author uses comic elements like sarcasm and the grotesque.

DANTE ALIGHIERI, *Inferno* (p. 689)

WWW   For a quiz on *Inferno,* see *World Literature Online* at bedfordstmartins.com/worldlit.

Today, Dante is acknowledged with Homer, Aeschylus, Chaucer, and Shakespeare as one of the greatest poets in the world, and his poems have had a remarkable influence on English literature. It was not always so, however. Chaucer mentions Dante in "The Monk's Tale," but Dante's work was not truly recognized by English writers until the end of the eighteenth century, when the first English translation of his work was rendered. The nineteenth century saw a resurgence of interest in Dante, when poets Shelley, Byron, Browning, and Tennyson honored him in their poetry. Although exiled from his native Florence, Dante's influence is felt throughout the art world in Italy, and it is often said that he helped shape the spirit of his home country as well as exterior perceptions of it.

Dante wrote at a time when Latin was the language of literature, politics, and high culture. Evidently, Dante feared that composing his works in the vernacular would cause him to be censured by his peers. In 1306, he published *De Vulgari Eloquentia (Of Literature in the Vernacular)*, a treatise defending literature written in what he called the "mother tongue" of the poet. In *De Vulgari Eloquentia*, Dante argues that certain vernacular languages, like the French Provençal, are particularly suited to poetry. Dante successfully merges Italian and Roman traditions in *The Divine Comedy*, which, while written in the vernacular, constantly alludes to Latin literature like *The Aeneid* by taking the form of an epic journey and including one of the greatest Latin poets, Virgil, as a teacher and guide.

It may be difficult for students to gain a firm grasp of Dante's view of religion in *The Divine Comedy* and in *Inferno* in particular. Dante's scathing criticisms of church corruptions that do not spare even those in the highest positions should not be confused with heresy. On the contrary, one of the primary purposes of *The Divine Comedy* is to help reform a corrupt society and bring those who have strayed from God back to virtue. Dante's condemnation of several corrupt historical popes to hell merely serves to underscore the seriousness with which he views the office.

Dante's Christian beliefs are grounded in philosophy and natural reason as described by Aristotle and Boethius. He firmly believes that through the light of reason, represented by Virgil, combined with a spiritual revelation, represented by Beatrice, man can transcend earthly life and attain an eternal one.

Encourage students not to become discouraged by the sheer amount of religious, political, and personal allusions in *Inferno*. Although an understanding of these allusions is helpful, particularly for those with historical interests, it is in no way necessary to recognize every person Dante consigns to hell in order to understand *Inferno*.

TEXT & CONTEXT

COSMOLOGY

The architecture of hell, which Dante envisions as nine concentric circles, is based on medieval cosmological concepts developed by Plato, Aristotle, and Heraclides in the third and fourth centuries B.C.E. and eventually Ptolemy around 150 C.E. In the Ptolemaic system of the universe, the Moon, the Sun, and the five visible planets were perfect, unchanging spheres. These bodies were located within concentric spheres that fit one inside the other, much like Russian nesting dolls, with the earth at the center. The space in which the earth was situated, called the sublunary sphere, was made up of the four basic elements of earth, water, fire, and air, and contained all of the imperfect elements in the universe. Above the earth were located in order: the spheres of the Moon, Mercury, Venus, the Sun, Mars, Jupiter, Saturn, and, finally, the sphere on which the stars were supposed to be fixed. While the ancients conceived of an ultimate sphere inhabited by a rational mind they called the prime mover, the medieval church placed the heavens in an unbounded area outside of the sphere of the fixed stars. In *The Divine Comedy*, Dante locates the circles of the inferno inside of the earth, those of purgatory between the earth and the moon, and those of paradise above the sphere of the fixed stars.

THE GROTESQUE

Although the term *grotesque*, a French word derived from the Italian word for "grotto" or "crypt," did not come into use until the sixteenth century, medieval art, architecture, and literature had its share of grotesque imagery. Characterized by a distortion of human faces and bodies or bizarre depictions of imaginary beasts, grotesque figures could be disturbing or comical. Grotesque carvings on churches, like gargoyles and half-human animals, often represented moral tales or the anguish of hell and may have served as lessons to the illiterate masses. However, the meanings of grotesques are not always easily discerned, and some scholars argue that in many cases these monstrous figures may have been nothing more than fanciful decoration.

IN THE CLASSROOM

Discussion

1. Ask students to identify and describe the levels of hell. What sorts of people are being punished in each level, and what sins did they commit? How do the punishments received by the condemned fit the crimes they committed in life (this concept is called *contrapasso*)? For example, why is Dido relegated to hell? What do Dante and Virgil have to say about her plight?

2. Discuss Dante's conception of sin. What behavior does Dante identify as sinful that we would disagree with today? Note the differences between upper and lower hell and which types of sins are in the lowest levels of hell. Why are traitors considered the worst sinners? What does this say about the role that the will plays in sin?

3. Homer, Socrates, Plato, and other virtuous pagans are consigned to the first level of hell, sometimes called "Limbo." Why are these men here, and what is the nature of their punishment? Have students compare Limbo with the pagan idea of life after death in the Elysian Fields. Are they really being punished at all? Compare the characters in Limbo with the figures from Greek and Roman literature and mythology who reside in the other circles of hell.

4. Many of the figures with which Dante peopled hell, like the seven popes, Alexander the Great, and Vanni Fucci, are historical ones. Many of them were Dante's enemies during his lifetime, while others were church figures who Dante believed were steeped in corruption. It will be helpful to students if you look up a few of these key figures and gloss their lives and/or their connections to Dante for your students. However, this information is not necessary to engage students in discussions about Dante's methods and purpose. Why does Dante choose to punish these men for an eternity in literature? Is there a significant difference between his condemnation of his contemporaries and people long dead? between real and fictional people? between Christians and pagans?

5. Dante asks Virgil to explain the inscription over the archway into hell that reads, "Through me the way to the city of woe, / through me the way to eternal pain, / through me the way among the lost. / Justice moved my maker on high. / Divine power made me, / wisdom supreme, and primal love. / Before me nothing was but things eternal, / and I endure eternally. / Abandon all hope, you who enter here" (Canto III, ll. 1–9). What is Virgil's explanation? Does it seem adequate? Does Dante heed Virgil's advice? What does it mean that hell was built by justice, wisdom, and love?

Connections

1. Dante's journey through hell (and on through purgatory to paradise) is much like the voyage of Odysseus in *The Odyssey* and the flight of Aeneas in *The Aeneid* (both in Book 1). Each story is an epic journey: Odysseus struggles to get home to his land and family, Aeneas flees the ruins of Troy to fulfill his destiny as the founder of Rome, and Dante undertakes a metaphysical journey that leads him from a dark wood of spiritual confusion to salvation in paradise. While Dante's journey takes place entirely in the realm where people go after they die, both Aeneas and Odysseus also visit the underworld. Have students compare the depictions of Hades in *The Odyssey* and *The Aeneid* with Dante's descriptions of hell. Despite the thematic and structural similarities in the three works, note the significant stylistic differences.

2. In his "General Prologue" to *The Canterbury Tales* (p. 885), Chaucer uses comic description to make fun of many of the religious and political figures that he considers corrupt, like the Pardoner and the Summoner. Dante is just as incensed about the excesses of the church and governmental corruption as Chaucer, but his satirical depictions of contemporary holy men are scathing rather than humorous. Why might Dante and Chaucer have chosen the methods they did? Which set of portrayals do your students find more effective? Can they give evidence for why a medieval audience would have been more convinced by one of the two types of satire?

Writing

Ask students to write a short paper in response to one or more of the following:

1. It is curious that Dante chooses Virgil, a pagan poet unacquainted with Christianity, as his guide through hell. Write a paper that analyzes Virgil's appropriateness as a guide. Dante calls Virgil his master. Is the relationship between Virgil and Dante one of teacher to student? Does the relationship change from canto to canto? It may be helpful to know that while Virgil guides Dante all the way from hell through most of purgatory, he is replaced by Beatrice in canto 30 of *Purgatorio* because he is not permitted to enter paradise.

2. *The Inferno* contains a number of deliberately recurring images. Trace one of these images through the poem, and make a claim abut the meaning of the image. You may choose your own images after reading the text, or you may want to pursue one of the following suggestions: fire, water, the weather, metamorphoses, beasts, or poetry.

BEYOND THE CLASSROOM

RESEARCH & WRITING

1. More than once in *Inferno,* Dante seems to sympathize with the condemned. The most obvious case occurs in canto 5, when the poet meets the lovers Paulo and Francesca. Ask students to critically analyze this passage and make an argument about Dante's attitude toward the lovers. Students may want to consider the true nature of Paulo and Francesca's sin or to compare it with romances like Marie de France's "Chevrefoil" (p. 674) and the story of Ghrismonda and Tancred in Boccaccio's *Decameron* (p. 853). How does Dante react to and interact with the lovers? Does Dante somehow condone or even participate in their transgression? How is Dante's love for Beatrice free of the sin committed by Paulo and Francesca? The Keats sonnet "A Dream, After Reading Dante's Episode of Paulo and Francesca" may shed some additional light on this episode. Alternatively, you may allow students to address Dante's sympathies toward other inhabitants of hell like his former mentor, Ser Brunetto.

2. Dante's journey through *Inferno* is the first step toward alleviating the confusion with which he begins the poem. Have students write a paper that makes a case for what, if anything, Dante has learned in his travels through hell. Is Dante closer to salvation than he was at the beginning of the poem? Is he a better person? In the course of this assignment, students may find it helpful to approach this assignment by comparing Dante's behavior with that of his guide Virgil. Pay particular attention to the scenes in cantos 8 to 9 when Dante and Virgil face the wall of Dis and 21 to 22 when they encounter the Malebranche. What are Dante and Virgil's reactions in each situation? What accounts for the differences in their behavior?

Projects

1. Ask students to design their own inferno, modeling their design after that of Dante. This assignment may take one of several forms. The design may be a written one, where students describe their inferno and identify the people or literary characters that populate it. Students should spend significant time explaining the conditions under which someone is relegated to each level of their inferno and the punishments they would receive there. What moral system is used to designate someone as a "sinner" for the purposes of this assignment? Do the punishments fit the crimes committed? Another way to complete the assignment would be for students to construct a visual representation of either their own inferno or that of Dante. Students may choose to render a drawing or to construct a three-dimensional model. What does the physical space of the inferno look like? How might its design be suited to its purpose? If trying to depict Dante's inferno, can students defend their design in light of his descriptions of the place? This could also be a group assignment, where students design and visually depict their infernos collectively.

2. *Inferno* is one of the longer works in the anthology, and it may be helpful to students to discuss it either a canto at a time or a circle of hell at a time. As class time doesn't always permit this sort of leisurely pace, students can take some of the responsibility for sections of the text. Start by setting up an e-mail list or a listserv for your class so that you and your students may have an ongoing discussion outside of class time. Assign each student (or let them choose) one or more sections of the text for which they will write a set of two to five discussion questions or comments. Students will post the comments or questions for their section to the listserv on the appropriate day. Other students may respond directly to the list, or you may use these questions as a jumping-off place in class. If an electronic format is not desired, students may bring their questions and comments to class, and the class can spend a set amount of time discussing them during each meeting.

WWW   For additional information on Dante and annotated Web links, see *World Literature Online* at bedfordstmartins.com/worldlit.

FURTHER READING

Gallagher, Joseph. *A Modern Reader's Guide to Dante's the Divine Comedy.* 1999.

Levine, Peter. "Why Dante Damned Francesca da Rimini," Philosophy and Literature 23, no. 2 (1999): 334–50.

Maddox, Donald. "The Arthurian Intertexts of Inferno V," *Dante Studies* 114 (1996): 113–27.

Mandelbaum, Allen, Anthony Oldcorn and Charles Ross, eds. *Lectura Dantis: Inferno. A Canto-by-Canto Commentary.* 1998.

Princeton University. *The Princeton Dante Project.* http://etcweb.princeton.edu/dante/index.html

Reynolds, Suzanne. "Dante and the Medieval Theory of Satire: A Collection of Texts." *Libri poetarum.* 1995. 145-57.

WWW See *World Literature in the 21st Century* at bedfordstmartins.com/worldlit for information on the relevance of *Inferno* in today's world.

MEDIA RESOURCES

VIDEO

The Circles of Light: The Divine Comedy
50 min., 1995 (Films for the Humanities & Sciences)
The most celebrated work of Dante Alighieri is certainly the *Divina Commedia* — a vision of hell, purgatory, and heaven that provides a strangely surrealistic view of medieval attitudes on religious dogma and the price of disobedience. In this program, dramatizations of scenes depicting courtly love, sexual love, love of God, and love of the Virgin Mary are featured.

Dante: Divine Comedy
50 min., 1999 (videopreview.safeshopper.com)
This introduction to one of the greatest works of medieval literature draws on new dramatic filmed sequences, contemporary images, and the works of artists inspired by Dante's epic voyage. Features visual interpretations of *The Divine Comedy* by the Topiary Dance Group, the Dore Illustrations that were first published in 1861, and footage from Florence — Dante's birthplace. Also features interpretation and analysis of the themes, plot, and characters by Professor Zygmont Baranski of Reading University, Dr. Catherine Keen of St. John's College at Cambridge, Dr. Simon Gilson of Warwich University, Dr. Robin Kirkpatrick of Robinson College at Cambridge, plus author and leading Dante authority, Dr. Anna Lawrence.

Dante — The Divine Comedy
50 min., 2000 (Kultur International Films)
A powerful introduction to the greatest work of medieval literature. This unique program features visual interpretations of Dante's masterpiece and new location footage from Florence as well as an in-depth look at the themes, plot, and characters of the work. Also includes interpretation and analysis by leading Dante scholars.

Dante's Inferno
88 min., 1993 (Films for the Humanities & Sciences)
This ambitious program, produced by the award-winning film director Peter Greenaway and internationally-known artist Tom Phillips, brings to life the first eight cantos of Dante's *Inferno.* Featuring a cast that includes Sir John Gielgud as Virgil, the cantos are not conventionally dramatized. Instead, the feeling of Dante's poem is conveyed through juxtaposed imagery that conjures up a contemporary vision of hell, and its meaning is deciphered by eminent scholars in visual sidebars who interpret Dante's metaphors and symbolism. This program makes Dante accessible to the MTV generation. (Caution to viewers: program contains nudity.)

Dante's Inferno: An Analysis
116 min., 1994 (Insight Media)

Explaining the nature of allegory, this set focuses on the law of symbolic retribution and the structure of Dante's hell as it reflects the Thomistic soul. It considers how one should read *Inferno* for the first time, analyzes Dante as a new epic hero and his journey as a new epic "action," and discusses Dante's purpose in writing *Inferno*. The program also addresses the episode of Paolo and Francesca.

Dante's Ulysses and the Homeric Tradition
28 min., 1987 (Insight Media)
The differences between Dante's *Ulysses* and Homer's *The Odyssey* relate to their different symbolic functions for two different cultures. This video compares the linear trajectory of Dante's *Ulysses* with the circular pattern of the homeward-bound Homeric hero.

The Divine Comedy: Visions of Violence and Beauty
60 min., 2001 (Films for the Humanities & Sciences)
Two of Italy's greatest artists are eternally linked, one genius having paid homage to another. Two hundred years after Dante Alighieri wrote *The Divine Comedy,* Sandro Botticelli illustrated the classic with a series of exquisite drawings crafted at the height of his career. In this program, translator Mark Musa, art historians, clergy, and other experts guide viewers through Botticelli's exquisite portrayal of Dante's *Inferno, Purgatorio,* and *Paradiso,* images that have had a lasting impact on the collective imagination of Western civilization. This program surveys Dante's epic and the ninety-two surviving illustrations to provide an unparalleled tour of two masterpieces of literature and art.

Divine Poet and Wandering Exile
45 min., 1987 (Educational Video Network)
The literary masterpiece of the Middle Ages, Dante Alighieri's *The Divine Comedy* was an imaginary journey from hell, through purgatory, to paradise. The great poem is peppered with memories of his own exile.

Inferno
51 min., 2001 (Films for the Humanities & Sciences)
Through his *Inferno,* Dante fleshed out the spatial and moral geography of hell for the first time ever, bringing it to life in a way that both terrifies and edifies. This program tracks Dante's allegorical journey through the underworld while providing background on the visionary poet, life in the Middle Ages, and *Inferno*'s influence on the arts and pop culture. Interviews with *Inferno* translator Robert Pinsky, Dante scholars Ronald Herzman and William Cook, the Reverend Stephen Happel of The Catholic University of America, and others are featured as are readings by three-time Poet Laureate Robert Pinsky and dramatizations of scenes from *Inferno* and Dante's life.

WEB SITES

Dante Alighieri on the Web
www.greatdante.net/commedia.htm
A must-visit site, this page offers a wide variety of resources and research possibilities. Available here are e-text translations of several of his most famous works as well as links to related authors, including Bocaccio. Also offered is a biography of Dante and a background on his time and works.

Digital Dante
dante.ilt.columbia.edu
This site contains a wide variety of Dante resources, including e-texts of translations of his writings and links to scholars' critical works on Dante as well as more unusual offerings,

like an image gallery of considerable size devoted to displaying artists' interpretations of the *Comedy* and Dante over the centuries.

AUDIO

A Life of Dante
1 CD, 1:20 hrs. (Naxos Audio)
Dante's vision, *The Divine Comedy,* has profoundly affected every generation since it first appeared in the early fourteenth century. Here is a brief account of his life, compiled from various sources (including his first biographer, Boccaccio) by Benedict Flynn. It sets the known facts of Dante's life against the turmoil of the times and puts the very personal nature of his poetry into perspective.

The Divine Comedy
10 tapes, 14:25 hrs. (Blackstone Audiobooks)
The unabridged Carlyle-Wicksteed translation is offered on this set of tapes.

The Inferno
3 CDs, 3:57 hrs. (Naxos Audio)
Dante's hell is one of the most remarkable visions in Western literature. An allegory for his and future ages, it is, at the same time, an account of terrifying realism. Passing under a lintel emblazoned with these frightening words, the poet is lead down into the depths by Virgil and shown those doomed to suffer eternal torment for vices exhibited and sins committed on earth. The inferno is the first part of the long journey which continues through redemption to revelation — through purgatory and paradise — and, in this translation prepared especially for audiobook, his images are as vivid as when the poem was first written in the early years of the fourteenth century.

The Inferno of Dante
tape, 3 hrs. (Audio Literature)
"Midway on our life's journey, I found myself in dark woods, the right road lost. To tell about those woods is hard — so tangled and rough. . . ." So begins Dante Alighieri's epic poem of a journey through hell. With the poet Virgil as his guide, Dante travels through the nine circles of hell, listening to the voices of the condemned until at last, "we came forth, and once more saw the stars." Poet and essayist Robert Pinsky's translation captures the intensity and passion of the literary masterpiece, and world-renowned actor John Cleese contributes a profound and electrifying performance.

Paradise
3 CDs, 3:35 hrs. (Naxos Audio)
With the release of "Paradise: From The Divine Comedy," the seminal work of Western literature is now available for the first time on audiobook. "Paradise" is the final part of Dante's great epic trilogy *The Divine Comedy*. Having said farewell to his faithful guide Virgil, Dante is left to make the final journey to paradise.

Purgatory
3 CDs, 3:57 hrs. (Naxos Audio)
"Purgatory" is the second part of Dante's *The Divine Comedy*. We find the Poet, with his guide Virgil, ascending the terraces of the Mount of Purgatory inhabited by those doing penance to expiate their sins on earth. There are the proud — forced to circle their terrace for eons bent double in humility; the slothful — running around crying out examples of zeal and sloth; while the lustful are purged by fire. Though less well known than *Inferno*, "Purgatory" has inspired many writers, including, in our century, Samuel Beckett, and has played a key role in literature.

GIOVANNI BOCCACCIO, *The Decameron* (p. 853)

WWW   For a quiz on *The Decameron,* see *World Literature Online* at
bedfordstmartins.com/worldlit.

Although the son of a merchant, Giovanni Boccaccio turned his back on business and
the study of law in order to study and write literature. He became involved in court society
in Anjou, where it is supposed that he met Maria d'Acquino, who appears in more than one
of his works under the name Fiammetta.

In addition to being numbered with Francis Petrarch and Dante Alighieri as one of the
greatest Italian poets, Boccaccio was one of the earliest and most important Renaissance
humanists. Humanism was a movement begun in the Middle Ages that sought to revive the
language, art, science, poetry, and, in some cases, even the values of Greek and Latin antiquity. Boccaccio was a prominent classical scholar and was familiar with French fabliaux tales
as well as the works of Homer, Tacitus, and Livy in their original languages. Like other
medieval authors, many of Boccaccio's stories were retellings of older works, and classical
influences can clearly be seen in many of his works, including *The Decameron.*

As much as Boccaccio was influenced by his predecessors, he was just as much of an
influence on those who came after him. Boccaccio's *Teseide* is a telling of the romance of
Palamon and Arcite, which Chaucer retells in "The Knight's Tale," while *Il Filstrato* tells the
story of Troilus and Cressida, retold both by Chaucer and Shakespeare. It is clear that
Chaucer drew directly and heavily on many of Boccaccio's works, but whether the English
poet was intimately acquainted with *The Decameron* is unclear. The two works have a similar structure, in which a narrative frame is provided as a pretext for the telling of tales, and
many stories from *The Decameron* reappear in *The Canterbury Tales.* Some scholars argue
that Chaucer not only read *The Decameron* but that he may have met Boccaccio himself
while living in Italy in the 1370s.

Like those in *The Canterbury Tales,* the stories in *The Decameron* are episodes that are
told inside a frame structure. However, Boccaccio's organization is a bit more complex than
that of Chaucer. There are not one but two narrative frames. The first consists of a semi-
autobiographical prologue and epilogue, reflected in the anthology in the "Conclusion,"
where Boccaccio addresses his audience directly. The second details the specifics of the
plague and the flight of the seven women and three men from the city. *The Decameron*'s
structure, in which ten stories are told on each of ten days, prefigures the plan that Chaucer
intended — for his pilgrims to each tell a story both on the way to and from Canterbury. By
allowing each of his characters to tell ten stories, Boccaccio achieves an intricate characterization of each of the young women and men. This makes for an interesting comparison with
Chaucer's "General Prologue" as method of characterization.

Frequent critical comparisons between Boccaccio's work and that of classical authors,
medieval contemporaries, and Renaissance writers will yield interesting discussions about the
authors' views of their worlds and the place of Boccaccio's work in the cannon of literature.
Note Boccaccio's treatment of gender difference, sexuality, moral virtue, and his characters'
seeming lack of concern with the traditional medieval values of chivalry, piety, and humility.

TEXT & CONTEXT

THE PLAGUE

The Decameron is set within an event that changed the socioeconomic climate of Italy
and Europe forever. The black plague broke out in the mid fourteenth century in the East

and was carried to Italy by people attempting to escape the epidemic by boat. Caused by a bacillus carried in the digestive tracts of fleas, the plague manifested itself in four forms. The most common, bubonic plague, was transmitted only via a bite from an infected insect. Characterized by large buboes, or swellings in the glands (especially under the armpit), it was the least deadly of the four. Pneumonic plague occurred when the bacillus migrated into the lungs and could be transmitted from one person to another. The septicemic and enteric plagues, when the bacillus infected the bloodstream and digestive system respectively, were rare, but always fatal. There is no official account of how many died during the plague epidemic, but it seems that throughout Italy at least half of the population died. The world of medieval Italy was thrown into a sort of chaos. Some preached religion in the belief that the plague was a divine punishment for sin, while others adopted a "live for the moment" philosophy, participating in excesses of decadence and extravagance. People stopped working and performing religious or societal rights, abandoned their friends and family, and fled the city. Economically, the scarcity of workers caused extreme inflation and was actually of benefit to surviving serfs, as their work was now so in demand that they garnered a competitive wage.

FORTUNE

The theme of the third day of *The Decameron* is to tell stories of "the fortune of such as have painfully acquired some much-coveted thing, or, having lost, have recovered it." Like Boccaccio, much of medieval society was greatly interested in the workings of Fortune, which they viewed as a capricious element of their everyday lives. Fortune was often depicted as a wheel with four human figures representing the four stages of fortune. The ascending figure on the left of the wheel is often labeled with the Latin equivalent of "I will reign," the topmost figure "I reign," the figure sinking on the right side of the wheel "I have reigned," and the bottom figured "I have no kingdom." Another traditional representation of Fortune is as the goddess Fortuna, an enormous but unpredictable woman who must be tamed by the reason and will of a man. She is often depicted turning or cranking the Wheel of Fortune in accordance with her whim. This iconography accurately represents the medieval conception of Fortune, that a man might enjoy good Fortune at the top of the wheel one moment but in the next he might swing down to the bottom position of the wheel, losing everything.

IN THE CLASSROOM

Discussion

1. At the beginning of the first day, Boccaccio sets the stage for his tales. He describes the flight of the seven women and three men from the city into the country in the wake of the plague that has devastated Italy. Ask students to consider why Boccaccio spends so much time detailing the horrors of the plague. Is there a moral to this part of *The Decameron?*

2. As young women, it is likely that the women in Boccaccio's story are obliged to stay at home and care for the sick and dying. Why do the seven young women decide to abandon the city and their families? How does the plague make them see their obligations and actions in a different light?

3. The story of Ghrismonda and Tancred is a variation on a traditional theme known as the "eaten heart motif." Usually, the husband of an adulterous wife kills her lover and secretly serves the lover's heart to her as a meal. The husband then reveals his deed but not before the wife has feasted on her lover's organ. In Boccaccio's story, however, Ghrismonda drinks wine that she herself pours into a goblet containing her murdered lover's heart. Why does Ghrismonda do this? What message is she trying to send to her

father? How does this turn the "eaten heart motif" on its head? Are there larger implications to this scene?

4. Boccaccio's women and men discuss sex and desire explicitly in the tale of Alibech and Rustico. What is the effect of this candor on the narrative? How do Boccaccio and his characters treat the subject of male and female desire?

5. Many medieval authors end their works with a retraction — a short essay often completely renouncing the content of the work. Whether these retractions are genuine, are simply narrative devices, or are intended to protect the author of a controversial work from church and societal backlash is a matter of active debate. In contrast, Boccaccio's conclusion defends *The Decameron*. He says that he is going to reply in advance to any objections that people might levy against his work. What are the objections Boccaccio imagines might be raised? How does he respond to them? Is this conclusion a sort of retraction or something completely different?

Groups

1. For a great creative assignment, have the class spend a few days constructing stories as did Boccaccio's men and women. Divide the class into several groups. Each group will be responsible for choosing the theme of one day and then will work together to create one short tale that fits into the theme for each day. Groups will choose one member to tell their tale to the entire class on the appropriate day. At your discretion, if groups have particularly good storytellers in their ranks, the stories may be written down in note-card form to allow the storyteller a little free reign in recitation and to remove the awkwardness that often accompanies reading aloud from a written piece.

Connections

1. *The Decameron*'s narrative frame is easily comparable with Chaucer's *Canterbury Tales* (p. 885) and *The Thousand and One Nights* (p. 435). Discuss the connections between the frames and the stories within them. Do the stories in these texts all bear the same sort of relationships to the frames that contextualize them? Would all of these texts work just as well without the frame? Why or why not?

2. Ask students to consider whether Boccaccio is expressing a system of values in *The Decameron*, particularly in the introduction to the First Day and the Conclusion. What are these values? How does Boccaccio's value system come out in the stories themselves? How do the values expressed in *The Decameron* differ from those in other works with a very strong value system like the New Testament (p. 23) or *The Song of Roland* (p. 540)?

3. Scholars argue that Boccaccio was greatly influenced by Dante's *Inferno* (p. 689). Both men painted the organized church and their class-based society with a critical brush. Is it possible to see Dante's effect on Boccaccio in the tale of Alibech and Rustico or that of Tancred and Ghismonda? Are Boccaccio's criticisms exactly the same as those of Dante? How do the purposes of the two men differ?

Writing

Ask students to write a short paper in response to one or more of the following:

1. When the women are contemplating whether to leave the city, Filomena says "Remember we are all women; and any girl can tell you how women behave together and conduct themselves without the direction of some man. We are fickle, wayward, suspicious, faint-hearted & cowardly . . . Indeed men are a woman's head and we can rarely succeed in anything without their help." With evidence from the text, formulate

an argument about Boccaccio's representation of women in the selections we have read. Do his stories lead one to think of Boccaccio as a feminist or antifeminist writer? What is Boccaccio's attitude toward women? Pay particular attention to the introduction to the First day and the Conclusion and consider whether the young ladies actually believe Filomena's statement. If they do not, why do they want to include men on their journey? Alternatively, your may want to compare Boccaccio's treatment of women in *The Decameron* with Chaucer's in "The Wife of Bath's Tale."

2. Choose one of the two tales excerpted in the anthology and write a paper about the primary subject of satire in the tale. The paper may take the form of an argumentative essay that seeks to prove exactly what Boccaccio is satirizing in a particular story, it may compare Boccaccio's satire to that of another author you have read this semester, or it may be a critical examination of Boccaccio's satire and its implications.

BEYOND THE CLASSROOM

RESEARCH & WRITING

1. Bawdy stories like the tale of Alibech and Rustico are part of a primarily French tradition known as the *fabliaux* and were very popular in the Middle Ages. Ask students to research the *fabliaux* form as well as to read several of the more popular medieval fabliaux like Chaucer's "The Miller's Tale," Marie de France's "About a Woman and her Paramour," Eustache d'Amiens's *The Butcher of Abbeville*, John Bodel's *Gombert and the Two Clerks,* or Guerin's *Beringer of the Long Arse.* For their paper, students may want to compare Boccaccio's fabliaux with one or more of these stories or with the typical fabliaux. They may also wish to examine the fabliaux form in general, making reference to particular stories solely as examples to support their assertions. As they read and write, have them consider the following questions: Do the fabliaux have a purpose other than entertainment? Of what do the fabliaux make fun? What do Boccaccio's fabliaux reveal about the way Boccaccio perceives the world?

2. In some ways, Ghismonda is a revolutionary figure, breaking the social conventions of her time. Not only does she decide that she will take a lover when she realizes that her father does not intend to find her a second husband, but her lover is of a lower class. Ask students to write a paper that compares Ghismonda with other literary women who break the conventions of their time (or conversely, fail to do so). Good comparisons can be made with figures like *The Odyssey*'s Penelope (Book 1), Margery Kempe (p. 993), or many of the women in *The Tale of Genjii* (p. 1094). Students will want to think about the decisions the women make as simultaneously personal and affecting the world around them. What are the social implications of their actions? Are Ghismonda's father or Penelope's suitors, for example, right to be angry? What do these stories say, if anything, about love and social classes?

Projects

1. Brown University's Decameron Web at http://www.brown.edu/Departments/ Italian_Studies/dweb/dweb.shtml contains a great number of resources for teachers and students — from translations to a search engine for the text to maps of Boccaccio's world. A number of on-line activities are suggested there that make use of the material contained on Decameron Web. Use the "class activities" Web page on Decameron Web at http://www.brown.edu/Departments/Italian_Studies/dweb/pedagogy/activities-class .shtml, or develop your own assignments to make use of these excellent resources.

WWW   For additional information on Boccaccio and annotated Web links, see *World Literature Online* at bedfordstmartins.com/worldlit.

FURTHER READING

Bagliari, Agostino Aravicini, and Francesco Santini, eds. *The Regulation of Evil: Social and Cultural Attitudes to Epidemics in the Late Middle Ages.* 1998.

Brown University. *Decameron Web.* http://www.brown.edu/Departments/Italian_Studies/dweb/dweb.shtml

Cantor, Norman F. *In the Wake of the Plague: The Black Death and the World It Made.* 2001.

Hollander, Robert. *Boccaccio's Dane and the Shaping Force of Satire.* 1997.

Koff, Leonard Michael, and Brenda Deen Schildgen. *The Decameron and the Canterbury Tales: New Essays on an Old Question.* 2000.

Norris, J. Lacy. *Reading Fabliaux.* 1993.

Potter, Joy Hambuechen. "Boccaccio as Illusionist: The Plays of Frames in the *Decameron*," *The Humanities Association Review* 26 (1975): 327-45.

WWW   See *World Literature in the 21st Century* at bedfordstmartins.com/worldlit for information on the relevance of Boccaccio's *The Decameron* in today's world.

MEDIA RESOURCES

VIDEO

Boccaccio: Tales from the Decameron
71 min., 1996 (Films for the Humanities & Sciences)
This marvelous video demonstrates what fun late medieval to early Renaissance literature can be. Chaucer lifted the concept, tone, and even some of the stories from *The Decameron* for *The Canterbury Tales.* Here are six of Boccaccio's tales executed with style and wit with live-action animation of shadow puppets. Teachers who would not offer their classes "The Miller's Tale" unexpurgated should be forewarned that while the stories themselves and the visuals are the soul of propriety, the brilliant and witty translations can be racy.

WEB SITES

Boccaccio
www.humanistictexts.org/boccaccio.htm#9
This page offers a brief biography of Boccaccio as well as excerpts from several of the stories in *The Decameron.*

Decameron Web
www.brown.edu/Departments/Italian_Studies/dweb/boccaccio/index.shtml
This beautiful and essential site created at Brown University provides complete English and Italian editions of Boccaccio's *Decameron* and some of his minor works. Also available are a biography of the writer, critical essays on his work and their cultural and social background, maps of medieval Italy and Europe, a comprehensive bibliography, and gorgeous artwork and graphics.

The Geoffrey Chaucer Page — Boccaccio
icg.harvard.edu/~chaucer/special/authors/boccaccio/

Part of the much larger Chaucer site, this page includes a biography of the writer as well as links to his *Decameron*.

AUDIO

The Decameron
4 tapes or 4 CDs, 5:20 hrs. (Naxos Audio)
At the time of the plague that ravished Europe in the 1340s, a group of friends in Italy enclosed themselves in a castle in an attempt to survive the maelstrom outside. To pass the time, they told stories — ten stories over a period of ten days. This remarkable collection, with an equally well-known preface, has delighted readers ever since with its wit, bawdiness, and invention.

The Decameron
11 tapes, 30:75 hrs. (Blackstone Audiobooks)
Giovanni Boccaccio, Dante, and Petrarch were the leading lights in a century that is considered the beginning of the Italian Renaissance. *The Decameron*, or *Ten Days' Entertainment*, is his most famous work, a collection of stories considered representative of the Middle Ages as well as a product of the Renaissance. The work is both, as it not only encompasses literary legacies of the medieval world but also goes far beyond Boccaccio's own time, transcending in tone and style artistic works of previous as well as later periods.

GEOFFREY CHAUCER, from *The Canterbury Tales* (p. 885)

WWW For a quiz on Chaucer's work, see *World Literature Online* at
bedfordstmartins.com/worldlit.

Of all the authors in Book 2, students are most likely to have heard of Geoffrey Chaucer, and for good reason. Like all great poets, Chaucer's language is both aesthetically pleasing and complex. However, what sets Chaucer apart from his contemporaries, like Langland and the Gawain Poet, is his subject matter. Although he addresses spiritual and political issues in his works, they are not his primary concern. Rather, as the scholar Lee Patterson points out, he deals above all with questions concerning the individual. In *The Canterbury Tales*, each pilgrim can be classified by his or her station in life, and, indeed, the General Prologue lists them this way: a knight, a squire, a merchant, the Wife of Bath, and the like. However, the portraits of each pilgrim and the tales that they tell have less to do with their position than with issues that are of interest to all people. In this way, Chaucer is a very modern poet. The contemporary idea of writing for the sake of character owes a great deal to Chaucer, and it is no wonder that Chaucer's works have been so admired and influential throughout time that even the poet John Dryden considered Chaucer to be the father of English poetry.

Although *The Canterbury Tales* are often considered to be unfinished because the General Prologue indicates that each person catalogued should tell one tale on the outbound journey and one on the return trip, there is some scholarly debate about this. The existing tales, some argue, do fit together as a unit, and Chaucer may not have intended to write each story told on the journey. Although we have only an excerpt of the full *Canterbury Tales* here, the class will be able to see this connectedness on a smaller scale.

While the tales are perhaps themselves inseparable from one another, it is even more difficult to separate the tale from the pilgrim who tells it. For example, the Wife of Bath has survived several bad marriages in which she was mistreated or undervalued, but she eventually finds happiness with her fifth husband, Jankin. At the end of her Prologue, we learn that she at first willingly surrendered the governance of her land and her person to Jankin. However, this agreement did not work out in the Wife's favor. After a physical fight that the Wife wins, she asks for these powers back from her husband. Jankin agrees to bend his will to hers, and they both live happily thereafter. Her tale, of a knight who desires knowledge of "what women really want," reflects these events in her life. Ultimately, when the knight surrenders his will to that of the old woman he has married and allows her to choose whether to be old and faithful or beautiful and possibly adulterous, the tale ends happily. The woman gains control, and the knight gains a wife who is both beautiful and faithful.

The message of the tale is integrally connected with the personality of the Wife of Bath and could not have been told by the Prioress or the Miller. Bring students' attention to this correspondence between tale and teller, and solicit their opinions. The Wife of Bath has the longest Prologue of any of the pilgrims. Do her Prologue and Tale have *identical* messages? If so, why does Chaucer feel the need to repeat the message twice? If not, what are the subtle distinctions between them?

Do not let students forget that, while Chaucer does have messages and ideas to convey, the General Prologue as well as the Wife of Bath's Prologue and Tale are at times intended to be humorous. Nearly every character described in detail in the General Prologue appears to be at least a bit comedic. For example, the Knight appears, for the most part, as a knight should — in armor and on horseback. However, he is also quite bedraggled in a manner unbefitting his station. His armor is rusty in spots, and he is spotted with the gore of a recent battle. Have students search for these humorous moments, and discuss the reasons for the comedy and the methods of conveying it.

Chaucer is one of the easiest authors to place in a world literature context. He was an incredibly well-read poet. Some accounts claim that he, himself, owned sixty books, an enormous sum for the fourteenth century. Also, there is evidence to suggest that Chaucer could read in several different languages and even might have visited other countries. Naturally, his writings reflect the influence of numerous authors and texts, both European and non-European. Chaucer makes reference to Boccacio and Petrarch, just to name a few. More importantly, however, Chaucer's work can be seen as part of a worldwide storytelling tradition. During the pilgrimage he describes, Chaucer's characters share entertaining, amusing, and enlightening stories with one another orally, just as the peoples of all cultures have done since before the time of the written word. For this reason, students will be richly rewarded for comparing Chaucer with just about any other text in the anthology.

TEXT & CONTEXT

WOMEN AND MARRIAGE

Although the treatment of women varied in different parts of the world, in general, girls in medieval Europe were brought up to expect to marry. Wealthy families could afford to support their unmarriageable daughters in a convent, but lower-class girls who could not marry would have been forced to find their own means of support. However, married life was not an easy path. Married women were expected to subjugate themselves to the will of their husbands at all times. Legally, a married woman had no presence or rights in the public sphere. She could not own property, run a business, or enter into legal agreements in her name alone. On a personal level, married women faced additional hardships. Although midwives attended most births, childbirth was nonetheless extremely dangerous, and many women died while in labor. In addition, peasant women were expected to bear, rear, feed, and clothe their children as well as tend to their houses and sometimes participate in their husbands' labor or business. This brutal and laborious existence was also short. Few people, men included, in the Middle Ages could expect to live past the age of thirty, but the average life-span for a woman was twenty-four.

ESTATES SATIRE

In the later Middle Ages, literature concerned with social classes or "estates" was very popular. These works were often bitingly satirical, meant as a critical comment on society as a whole as well as an individual estate. Traditionally, there were three estates, and each estate had its particular failings. The clergy, meant to minister to the spiritual needs of their people, suffer from the very sins they are meant to absolve in others. The aristocracy, whose function is to uphold justice, to protect the weak, and to defend the church, are powerful and money hungry, and mistreat the working class. The workers, who through labor provide for themselves and the other two estates, are dishonest and litigious. As the pilgrims in the *Tales* span a wide range of estates, some Chaucerian scholars argue that *The Canterbury Tales,* especially the General Prologue, are a type of estates satire. The first evidence that Chaucer intends to criticize society lies in the opening of the General Prologue. The narrator explains

> Also, I prey yow to foryeve it me
> Al have I nat set folk in her degree
> Here in this tale, as they shold stonde.
> My wit is short, ye may wel understonde.

Shortness of wit seems a poor excuse for failing to place the pilgrims in proper rank order in the text. Although the varied nature of the pilgrims allows Chaucer to comment on the society and class structure of his time, one should not read the *Tales* expecting to find Chaucer's definitive position on the estates. His subtlety is purposeful, meant to illustrate the difficulty inherent in forming moral and social judgments.

IN THE CLASSROOM

I. CHAUCER'S MODE OF NARRATION

One of the more interesting aspects of Chaucer's style is his mode of narration. Although ultimately Chaucer himself writes *The Canterbury Tales* and is solely responsible for its content, the *Tales'* narrator is not identical with Chaucer the poet. The narrator comments on individual pilgrims and has thoughts and opinions that may not be identical with those of Chaucer. Furthermore, Chaucer makes use of a sort of nested narration. Each tale is first told by a pilgrim, like the Wife of Bath, and is then passed to the narrator who presumably tells the entire story to Chaucer.

Discussion

1. Many authors make explicit textual comments about the characters and events in their stories. Typically, this is referred to as the "authorial voice" of a work. In *The Canterbury Tales,* however, Chaucer seems to substitute a "narratorial voice" for an authorial one. Why? Point out some comments made explicitly by the narrator, and notice how he addresses the audience at the beginning of the General Prologue. Is it possible to identify comments that might have been made by Chaucer rather than the narrator?

Connections

Mode and method of narration is an important factor in any discussion. Interesting comparisons can be made between Chaucer's way of addressing his audience and that of nearly any author.

1. Have students look at excerpts of *The Odyssey* (Book 1) to see an older, more epic form of address. Note the formality and "timelessness" of the opening lines of the poem. The story of Odysseus seems simultaneously to have taken place long ago and in no particular time at all. In comparison, Chaucer seems casual, and he has located his story within a very particular framework. Is Chaucer's narrative voice more "modern" than that of Homer, or just different? Might each author have chosen a voice to fit thematic elements within his story?

2. Compare *The Canterbury Tales* with two approximately contemporary works: Boccaccio's *Decameron* (p. 853) and Dante's *Inferno* (p. 689). Note that while Boccaccio writes about events that took place in and before the time of Homer, his narration is remarkably similar to that of Chaucer, and he uses many of the same techniques. Dante, on the other hand, is both narrator as well as author of *The Inferno:* He places himself in the story. Also see *The Thousand and One Nights* (p. 435) for another example of stories told within a narrative frame.

Writing

Ask students to write a short paper in response to one or more of the following:

1. The technique of nested narration allows Chaucer to distance himself from the *Tales*, as he claims that he merely retells them rather creates them. Some argue that in this way he verbally shirks responsibility for his own work, as he claims merely to retell rather than create. Why might Chaucer not want people to equate him and the ideas in his texts? Might this technique in itself say something about Chaucer the poet? Is Chaucer practicing a sort of humility (false or in truth) about the greatness of his own works, or is he afraid that the content will offend?

2. Occasionally, Chaucer (or his narrator) refuses to describe or narrate an event. Often, this refusal, called "occupatio," is followed by a detailed description of the very thing that he had just declined to narrate. Address this narrative technique using examples from the General Prologue. Does this technique allow Chaucer to draw his readers' attention to something by the very act of pretending to pass over it? If so, why would Chaucer want to emphasize particular passages in this way instead of in a more direct fashion?

II. CHAUCER AND MIDDLE ENGLISH

Unlike the language of Old English texts like *Beowulf*, Chaucer's Middle English bares a close visual resemblance to the English written today, relying less on a strict case structure and more on word order and prepositions. However, the English speakers of Chaucer's day had not yet adopted the pronunciation that we associate with the sounds of English. In the period between the fifteenth and eighteenth centuries, vowels changed their sound in a move known as "The Great Vowel Shift." Vowels that in Chaucer's time had been pronounced near the back of the throat were pronounced higher up in the mouth after this shift. Despite this, Chaucer's language is easy for students to understand with a little practice, and it is worthwhile to attempt, as much of his verbal humor and poetic style is lost in the translation to modern English.

Discussion

1. Provide students with an untranslated passage from *The Canterbury Tales*. The entire General Prologue can be excerpted easily, and a good edition, like *The Riverside Chaucer*, will provide footnotes that translate difficult words into modern English. Discuss the two versions side-by-side, noting which Middle English words are easily identifiable and those that are more difficult to recognize.

2. Ask students to take turns reading sections of Chaucer's original language aloud to one another. If you like, provide a pronunciation guide (see *The Riverside Chaucer*) to help them with the sounds of Middle English. Even without a guide, the students should be able to get some sense of the language. Does reading the text aloud help with understanding? That is, did particular words or passages that were difficult to understand on the page become clearer when read out loud? Are there passages for which more than one interpretation seems possible?

Connections

In the medieval period, the English language was changing at an amazingly rapid pace. Between *Beowulf* in the eighth century and Chaucer in the fourteenth century, English changed much more than it did in the similar span between Shakespeare and today.

1. Compare some of the works from these periods. For instance, provide students with a short section from *Beowulf* in Old English so that they may compare it with the Middle English of Chaucer. [Note that they will not likely be able to read any of this passage, but it will serve as a useful illustration of the differences between the two languages.] Then compare these passages with an excerpt of Shakespeare (Book 3) and one from a contemporary author like James Joyce (Book 6). Although Shakespeare's syntax and style might sound strange to modern ears, it will seem just as readable and recognizable as Joyce's language, while Chaucer will be much further removed, and *Beowulf* will not seem to be written in English at all.

2. Have your students compare even the translated version of *Beowulf* (p. 482) with *The Canterbury Tales* selection to perform a simple comparison of style. In the section on *Beowulf*, we noted that, as a primarily oral text, *Beowulf* uses formulas and the repetition of key phrases in part to help the performer remember the poem. This has the effect of making the poem stylistically similar throughout. *The Canterbury Tales*, however, do not rely on such devices, perhaps because Chaucer knew that his work would be read from a printed source rather than performed from memory. Discuss the differences and similarities between oral and written literature.

Writing

Ask students to write a short paper in response to one or more of the following:

1. Take a fifteen- or twenty-line section from the Middle English, and render it into modern English. You may want to simply write a prose summary of the section or try to emulate some aspect of Chaucer's style (for example, rhyming couplets, ten syllables per line). Refer to a Middle English glossary to look up words you do not understand.

2. The Wife of Bath is perhaps one of the most remarkable figures in *The Canterbury Tales*. Particularly interesting is the difference between her Prologue, in which she brashly and lustily gives the details her five marriages, and her Tale, which is both moral and quite charming. Address the difference between the Wife's Prologue and her Tale. How do the two relate and lend meaning to one another? The Wife of Bath has the longest prologue in *The Canterbury Tales*. Why does she feel the need to share this personal information with the pilgrims before she begins her tale?

BEYOND THE CLASSROOM

RESEARCH & WRITING

1. Based on the character portraits in the General Prologue, have students address in what way Chaucer might be satirizing one or more of the pilgrims. Alternatively, they might

take the position that Chaucer does not intend to satirize a particular pilgrim. They might defend their claim on the basis of estates satire or on the grounds of physical or other descriptions of the characters.

2. Some critics say that the Wife of Bath is the first "psychologically viable" woman in all of literature. By this, they mean that she is a well-rounded, three-dimensional character, rather than one who exemplifies only one or two traditionally female traits. Ask students to defend whether the Wife of Bath is a well-rounded character or a flat one. Have them give specific evidence from the text for their position. Have students compare the Wife of Bath with women in other texts you have assigned for class (Penelope in *The Odyssey*, Genji's various women in *The Tale of Genji*, Eve in *Paradise Lost*, in *A Simple Heart*, in "The Dead"). Is she better rounded than the older and contemporary women characters? Does she compare favorably or unfavorably in this respect with more modern women in literature?

WWW   For additional information on Chaucer and annotated Web links, see *World Literature Online* at bedfordstmartins.com/worldlit.

FURTHER READING

Brooks, C. N. L. *The Medieval Idea of Marriage.* 1989.

Harvard University's Chaucer Reference Pages. http://icg.fas.harvard.edu/~chaucer/

Leicester, H. Marshall Jr. "Structure as Deconstruction: 'Chaucer and Estates Satire' in the General Prologue: Or, Reading Chaucer as a Prologue to the History of Disenchantment," *Exemplaria: A Journal of Theory in Medieval and Renaissance Studies* 2, no. 1 (1990): 241–61.

Lucas, Angela M. *Women in the Middle Ages: Religion, Marriage, and Letters.* 1983.

Mann, Jill. *Chaucer and Medieval Estates Satire.* 1973.

Patterson, Lee. "For the Wyves love of Bathe: Feminine Rhetoric and Poetic Resolution in the Roman de la Rose and the Canterbury Tales," *Speculum* 58, no. 3 (1983): 656–95.

WWW   See *World Literature in the 21st Century* at bedfordstmartins.com/worldlit for information on the relevance of Chaucer to today's world.

MEDIA RESOURCES

VIDEO

Chaucer Reads Chaucer: "The Miller's Tale"
80 min., 1998 (Films for the Humanities & Sciences)
In Queen Victoria's day, this is the one they expurgated from the complete *Canterbury Tales;* fortunately, the modern sensibility responds with the intended laughter at the most notoriously misdirected kiss in European literature. Here the tale is told as Chaucer might have told it — in Middle English (with modern English subtitles) and appropriate costume, to an audience of contemporaries who shared Chaucer's own astonishing combination of grossness and delicacy. An excellent lesson in both literature and language.

Chaucer: The General Prologue to The Canterbury Tales
20 min., 1999 (Films for the Humanities & Sciences)

"Whan that Aprille with his shoures soote / The droghte of Marche hath perced to the roote," we meet Chaucer and some of his fellow Canterbury pilgrims. Our attention is drawn to Chaucer's sharply drawn descriptions of these characters and to the language of fourteenth-century England in which Chaucer wrote his verse. There follows a dramatization of part of "The Pardoner's Tale" by a group of students who have been examining some of the tales, the characters, and the language of *The Canterbury Tales*.

The Canterbury Tales
33 min., 1992 (Films for the Humanities & Sciences)
Written in the fourteenth century, *The Canterbury Tales* has stood the test of time as a landmark in the development of English literature. This innovative "frame story" owes its classic standing and impact to the diversity both of the narrators and of the styles of tales they tell. In this program, expert commentators Dr. Christiania Whitehead and Dr. Peter Mack, both of the University of Warwick, discuss the tradition of fourteenth-century poetry, the General Prologue, Chaucer's social grouping of the pilgrims and the themes they explore, and the poem as a reflection of medieval English society. Dramatic re-enactments of the pilgrims on horseback and numerous period images help bring the tales to life.

Prologue to the Canterbury Tales
14 min., 1991 (Educational Video Network)
Chaucer's contentious pilgrims have been delighting readers for six hundred years. This basic exposition of the characters will help students to visualize the motley travelers.

Chaucer
28 min., 1988 (Films for the Humanities & Sciences)
Chaucer is the first great English poet whose name we know and also the first great English storyteller. The Prologue to *The Canterbury Tales* is presented here in Middle English (with modern subtitles on screen); the "Pardoner's Tale" is acted out in Nevill Coghill's modern rendering. The performers are John Gielgud, Nicholas Gecks, and Ian Richardson.

The Wife of Bath
28 min., 1993 (Films for the Humanities & Sciences)
This program examines the character of Dame Alisoun, the wife in Chaucer's renowned *Canterbury Tales*. As one of the earliest important female characters in English literature, Dame Alisoun is discussed within the context of male/female relationships. Also addressed are many questions regarding the nature of those relations.

The Canterbury Tales Series
3 tapes, 1999–2000 (Library Video Company)
Students will experience the action and adventure of Geoffrey Chaucer's *Canterbury Tales* through these creative adaptations that feature stunning animation that depicts medieval life in Europe. These programs remain true to the original symbolism and imagery, and will generate student interest in the original texts. The programs will also serve as visual aids that clarify difficult passages. The voices are provided by the Royal Shakespeare Company. True to the style of Chaucer's original work, these programs depict scenarios that some educators may find inappropriate for classroom use. Part I (30 min.): *Leaving London* includes "The Nun's Priest's Tale," "The Knight's Tale," and "The Wife of Bath's Tale." *Part II* (30 min.): *Arriving at Canterbury* includes presentations of "The Merchant's Tale," "The Pardoner's Tale," and "The Franklin's Tale." *Part III* (30 min.): *The Journey Back* includes the "The Squire's Tale," "The Canon's Servant's Tale," "The Miller's Tale," and "The Reeve's Tale."

WEB SITES

Chaucer Metapage
www.unc.edu/depts/chaucer/
This page offers a wide variety of resources, including e-texts and audio files of Chaucer's works, biographical information, and scholarly commentary. The site also includes links to a number of helpful sites devoted to Chaucer, his contemporaries, and medieval literature in general.

Geoffrey Chaucer
www.luminarium.org/medlit/chaucer.htm
Part of a much larger anthology devoted to Middle English literature, this site is full of links to a wide array of resources and research possibilities, including a number of editions of *The Canterbury Tales;* audio excerpts from the *Tales;* e-texts of Troilus and Criseyde, The Book of the Dutchess, and several shorter poems; many biographical sources on Chaucer; critical essays by both students and scholars; and additional sources on the author.

The Geoffrey Chaucer Website
icg.fas.harvard.edu/~chaucer/
This essential resource for Chaucer research includes typical links to a biography and time-line as well as unusual offerings like "Teach Yourself Chaucer," a learning guide to Middle English, and informative descriptions of aspects of medieval culture and science, including courtly love, manners, and pilgrimages. Also available are the full e-text of *The Canterbury Tales* and links to other medieval and ancient writers.

Chaucer Bibliography Online
uchaucer.utsa.edu/cgi-bin/Pwebrecon.cgi?DB=local&PAGE=First
Visit this page from the University of Texas at San Antonio Library and The New Chaucer Society to search for both primary and secondary materials on Chaucer.

AUDIO

The Canterbury Tales — 1
3 CDs, 3:21 hrs. (Naxos Audio)
Chaucer's greatest work, written toward the end of the fourteenth century, paints a brilliant picture of medieval life, society, and values. The stories range from the romantic, courtly idealism of The Knight's Tale to the joyous bawdy of the Miller's; all are told with a freshness and vigor in this modern verse translation that make them a delight to hear.

The Canterbury Tales — 2
3 CDs, 4 hrs. (Naxos Audio)
Four more delightful tales from one of the most entertaining storytellers of all time. Though writing in the thirteenth century, Chaucer's wit and observation comes down undiminished through the ages, especially in this accessible modern verse translation. The stories vary considerably from the uproarious Wife of Bath's Tale, promoting the power of women to the sober account of patient Griselda in the Clerk's Tale.

The Canterbury Tales
13 tapes, 18:75 hrs. (Blackstone Audiobooks)
Read by Fred Williams, this unabridged reading of *The Canterbury Tales* tells of meeting at the Tabard Inn with thirty others to make the usual April pilgrimage to Becket's shrine at Canterbury. He describes his companions, who are of widely varying classes and occupations.

In the World: **Pilgrimage and Travel** (p. 933)

In the Middle Ages, travel was a slow, laborious undertaking that could prove deadly for the traveler. The three main methods of travel were on foot, on horseback, or by boat. Although theoretically a man on a horse can travel more than twice as far per day as a man on foot, twenty or thirty miles per day would have been considered a hard day's journey for a rider. The average pace was likely much slower.

In essence, horsemen and pedestrians faced many of the same challenges. In addition to procuring food, water, and shelter, a traveler had to find a suitable route to his destination. Though the remains of paved Roman roads still existed in some places, these roads were in poor repair, and most other roads were little more than dirt paths that became largely impassible after a rainstorm. Sea travel, while faster in some cases, came with its own hardships. Sea travelers often became sick, and if inclement weather resulted in a shipwreck, stranded survivors were unlikely to be rescued. Robbers who killed their victims after looting them were a danger on both sea and land, and land travelers in particular had to avoid traveling by night.

Most people, particularly those of the peasant working class, stayed within a dozen miles of their home, had little experience with the surrounding country, and knew almost nothing about foreign lands. Nonetheless, a surprising number of people traveled significant distances in the Middle Ages. These travelers, with many exceptions, fell generally into four main groups. Members of the nobility and royalty often traveled with a sizeable entourage of troops and servants in order to maintain order within the extensive lands under their rule. They would also travel to other lands to make alliances with or conduct war on neighboring rulers. High-ranking bishops and priests traveled back and forth between churches and monasteries under their jurisdiction in order to strengthen their influence and reputation. Pilgrims, a mixed group consisting of people from all classes and occupations, traveled to visit sites sacred to their religions. And finally, merchants undertook lengthy journeys for the purpose of trade and to obtain goods not available in their own countries.

The narratives excerpted in the book encompass everything from religious travel to simple exploration and are written in a variety of styles that include elements of both the sober and the fantastic. Egeria provides an almost journalistic account of her fourth-century journey to Jerusalem. Though she does not provide a great deal of detail about most of the things that she sees and experiences, her account seems to gain the most power from her extended description of natural phenomenon like the illusory quality of the height of the mountains. In contrast, Ibn Jubayr's writings give such exacting detail of the inside of the mosque at Mecca that it is possible not only to visualize it but also to draw a blueprint.

Both Xuanzang's and Ibn Battuta's writings seem in a way to be the mean proportional between pilgrimage accounts and those of secular travelers and explorers. Each combines the particulars of the geographic and cultural aspects of the places they visit with descriptions of holy places. Historical tales associated with the places he visits and snippets of Buddhist teachings characterize Xuanzang's writing, while Battuta is marked by his concern with describing in detail things that he finds marvelous.

The travel writings of Giovanni da Pian di Carpine, Marco Polo, and John Mandeville all focus largely on the characterization of specific people or cultures. The descriptions of all three writers seem to be bizarre and extraordinary. Di Carpine and Polo, though both on emissarial missions for their countries, paint portraits of the wonder and opulence of the Mongul courts. Yet their writings do not delve as deeply into the preposterous as those of John Mandeville, whose accounts should perhaps be taken with more than a grain of salt.

He was famed even in the Middle Ages not only for his travels but for his skill as an accomplished prevaricator. It has been argued that Mandeville never traveled at all and made up his *Travels*. If this theory were true, then Mandeville would still be lauded for an impressive work of fiction. Accusations that he plagiarized the narrative from a number of sources also seem to be inconsequential. Writing technique in the Middle Ages often included the rewriting of material from other sources; Chaucer himself borrowed heavily from Ovid, Virgil, and Petrarch.

TEXT & CONTEXT

HOLY RELICS AND PILGRIM BADGES

Many Christian pilgrims traveled to popular pilgrimage sites in order to visit a location mentioned in the Bible, like Mount Sinai, or to see a holy relic, like the veil with which Jesus wiped his face on the way to his crucifixion or one of the bones of a saint. The most popular destinations — Rome, Canterbury, and Santiago de Compostela — had established, well-traveled routes that allowed pilgrims to visit minor shrines and churches along the way. Since these routes were commonly known, charlatans would often travel with pilgrims or set up small businesses along the roadside to sell fake holy relics. Much like Chaucer's Pardoner (ll. 676–88), they would hawk scraps of common cloth and bits of animal bone off as genuine relics to unsuspecting pilgrims. Less dubious but still more in the spirit of commerce than spirituality, churches would often manufacture souvenirs to sell to pilgrims. The souvenirs, in the form of pewter badges, served a dual purpose; they allowed the pilgrims to show proof they had been to a particular shrine and also kept pilgrims from removing bits of the shrine to take back with them. Badges were unique and creative in their designs. For example, the badge of Saint James of Compostela was a scallop shell, while the badge of Saint Herbert depicted a hunting horn. Pilgrim badge manufacture was not limited to churches, however. Local merchants often made badges, and travelers could obtain badges depicting everything from secular locations to royalty to religious propaganda. In fact, pilgrim badge manufacture was such a lucrative industry that when Henry VIII forbade pilgrimage in 1559, the merchants of Dartford protested due to the loss of income from sale of the souvenirs.

IN THE CLASSROOM

I. STRANGERS IN A STRANGE LAND?

Each of these travelers, regardless of their purpose for traveling, left their home and traveled to an unknown place. As students read, they should reflect on how each writer deals with the terrain, people, and culture of another country. It will also be fruitful to think about what caused these travelers to take to the road. Not only was the travel itself not an easy undertaking, but voyagers must have, at least at first, had the sense that the lands into which they were walking were complete mysteries. Today, various media allow us a form of access to foreign places. We can be fairly sure that France is not full of monstrous beasts and rivers of gold, for example, because we can have at least a virtual experience of it through television, books, movies, and the Internet. Ask students to imagine how they might feel about traveling to a country where not only are they unfamiliar with the geography and the language but of which they had no prior experience or contact.

Discussion

1. Ibn Jubyr intersperses his narrative with prayer. Though Jubyr is a Spanish Muslim, his beliefs, embodied in this system of prayer, are his connection with the Muslims in Mecca, a culture that would have been in other ways significantly different from his

own. Do we imagine that he is offering these prayers in the course of the events about which he writes? What is the effect of these prayers on the reader?

2. Xuanzang is the only one of these writers to report conversations and dialogue directly — in quotations — rather than in an indirect way. Why do you think this is? Does the direct speech give us a sense of Xuanzang as an involved participant rather than merely a passive observer? What do you make of his relation to the culture of India compared with the way that the other writers relate to the cultures they visit?

3. Egeria writes, "I want you to be quite clear about these mountains, reverent ladies my sisters . . . They had been almost too much to climb, and I really do not think I have ever seen any that were higher . . . even though they only looked like little hillocks to us as we stood on the central mountain" (p. 943). This is the second time she has described the mountains, and each time she emphasizes their height. Why does she find this information so important to convey? What do they represent symbolically for her? Does the fact that her narrative is addressed to a group of nuns shed any light on why she focuses on these mountains or how she describes them?

4. In Marco Polo's discussion of "The Generosity of the Great Khan," he admires that Khan provides food to the poor and exempts his subjects from paying tribute if they have experienced hardship like plague, crop failure, or natural disaster. Yet Polo tells us that Khan's people would not even give alms to the poor before they "became familiar with the doctrines of the idolaters" (that is, before their conversion to Buddhism). In the same sentence, Polo applauds Khan's generous actions and yet condemns him as an idolater. Can these competing attitudes be reconciled? What might Polo have been trying to communicate to his audience? Do his words mark him as tolerant or intolerant with respect to the religion of the Mongols?

Writing

Ask students to write a short paper in response to one or more of the following:

1. Giovanni da Pian di Carpine calls his writings, curiously, *The History of the Mongols.* Write a paper in which you critically evaluate this title in relation to the work. Reflect on our modern definition of history and whether it can be applied to di Carpine's work. How far back do events have to be to be considered history? Do di Carpine's travel writings deserve this title? In what way can this piece be considered a "history"?

2. Xuanzang's account is rich in symbolic images. Explain one of the symbols and its importance either in relation to the excerpt or to Buddhism. Possible images include the Patali tree, the Bodhisattva figure that is half-buried in the sand, or the Bodhi tree. You may also wish to compare one or more of these images.

3. Ibn Jubyr and Ibn Battuta each visit Mecca, while both Marco Polo and John Mandeville travel to the palace of the Great Khan. Choose one of these two pairs, and compare their accounts. How are the respective places described, and in what sort of style are they written? Is there any significance to the differences in what Jubyr and Battuta each notice in Mecca? Does Mandeville's account of Khan's palace seem credible in light of that of Polo?

II. CONNECTIONS

Many of the selections in the anthologies include some form of travel. From Odysseus's wanderings to Aeneas's flight from Troy to Jesus, who accompanies his parents to Jerusalem, to the distraught travels of Kings Shahrayar and Shahzaman in *The One Thousand and One Nights* to the campaigns of Charlemagne as depicted in *The Song of Roland* and *A Life of Charlemagne* to Chaucer's pilgrims in *The Canterbury Tales,* the anthology provides ample possibilities for comparison. Also consider relating the medieval journeys represented in "Pilgrimage and Travel" with accounts of world explorers like Vasco da Gama (Book 3) in the Early Modern Era, and more recent accounts of travel like those in the "Travel Narratives" and imaginary voyages like *Gulliver's Travels* (both in Book 4).

Discussion

1. Although other works you have read this year may depict travel or pilgrimage, these seven authors have been compiled because they are travel narratives rather than narratives that include travel. This raises an obvious question: What makes a travel narrative? Should pilgrimage accounts be considered a distinct category or merely a subgenre under the rubric of travel writing? How do the accounts excerpted in "Pilgrimage and Travel" differ from works like *The Canterbury Tales*, which have travel as their setting?

2. In Dante's *Inferno*, Virgil escorts Dante through the levels of purgatory, while Egeria has holy men as her guides. What are the roles of guides like these in travel narratives? What is the advantage of having a guide? Why might a pilgrim choose to go it alone? Can the writers of these travels be seen as guides for their readers?

3. The Muslim *hajj*, while dictated by the Qur'an, is also in some ways a reflection of Muhammad's own journeys. Discuss the personal pilgrimage accounts of Ibn Jubyr and Ibn Battuta with the account of Muhammad's pilgrimage given in Ibn Ishaq's *The Life of Muhammad* and the spiritual journey that Muslims take by following the teachings of the Qur'an. What similarities can you identify? Do later pilgrimages mimic those of Muhammad? Can the Muslim *hajj* be compared with Christian pilgrimage to the holy land? Why or why not?

Writing

Ask students to write a short paper in response to one or more of the following:

1. Like Egeria, Margery Kempe makes her pilgrimage to the holy land that she describes in *The Book of Margery Kempe*. Have students write a paper comparing the experiences of these two pilgrims. Students may wish to compare the way that Egeria and Kempe are treated by the holy men and the other members of their pilgrimage party, to look at the way each woman behaves on her pilgrimage, or evaluate their writing styles. Make sure to note Kempe's tearful response at every holy site versus Egeria's almost girlish excitement at having holy places pointed out to her and appropriate Bible passages read.

2. Sir John Mandeville's accounts of travel in India, Java, Ceylon, and Cathay purport to be true accounts of what he observed on his voyages. Yet his descriptions are so fantastic that they read much like Jonathan Swift's fictional *Gulliver's Travels* (Book 4, p. 147). Write a paper comparing the stylistic idiosyncrasies of these two works. Can you find evidence (either textual or in secondary sources) that Twain may have read and been influenced by Mandeville?

BEYOND THE CLASSROOM

RESEARCH & WRITING

1. Understanding the experiences of medieval travelers is a difficult endeavor. Like other travel narratives, those generated in the Middle Period combine accurate observation, imperfect recollections, and wanton exaggeration. Ask students to construct a well-argued paper addressing either the way in which medieval travelers interacted with other cultures or the way they transmitted their experiences of foreign societies to their readers. This paper should not be a mere historiography, listing the varied reactions of

each traveler, but rather should attempt to evaluate the encounters from a particular angle. Students may focus on one primary text or take into account the views of several medieval authors and should incorporate at least two secondary sources to support their argument.

2. Have students write a research paper on some aspect of medieval pilgrimage in one of the readings that they have read for this course. Questions to consider include: What were the practices of pilgrimage, and what purpose did they serve? Were religious pilgrimages always undertaken primarily for religious reasons? When pilgrimage is used in a penitential fashion, is the strenuous nature of travel part of the spiritual cleansing process? In order to complete this project satisfactorily, students may need to read a larger portion of the work in which they are interested than is excerpted in the anthology. Depending on the nature of their paper concept, a good number of secondary sources may also be required. Although it is possible to write about more than one pilgrimage narrative for this assignment, it will be helpful if students confine their examination to one region or culture, rather than attempting to reconcile, for example, pilgrimage practices in Muslim Spain with those in Christian England.

Projects

1. Have each student to choose a work (or, at your discretion, a unified section of a larger work) that is either a medieval travel narrative or a secondary reading that addresses some aspect of travel or pilgrimage in the Middle Ages. Students should read these books and write a book review as if for a scholarly journal. Before beginning, students should obtain example book reviews from journals to which your library subscribes and familiarize themselves with the typical style and form of a scholarly book review. Students may also wish to research the guidelines for submission to a specific scholarly journal, *Speculum,* for example, and make sure the final format of their book review meets the chosen journal's guidelines.

2. Ask students to complete one or both of the following projects in groups:

    a. Research common medieval pilgrimage routes, like the route to Santiago de Compostela, Canterbury, Rome, or Mecca. Plot these routes on a map, making sure to identify prominent places that pilgrims would have stopped off to visit on the way to their destination.

    b. When they reached their destinations or other churches, pilgrims were presented with the intense visual experience of the architecture, art, and decoration of the church or holy building. Research an aspect or aspects of what pilgrims would have seen in one or more of the famous pilgrimage sites, and present your findings, with pictures if possible, to your fellow students. Possibilities include building façades and features; stained glass and pictorial windows; rugs and tapestries; wall, ceiling, and framed art; and mazes. Consider the effect these visual characteristics would have had on a medieval pilgrim and their significance to the pilgrim's journey.

FURTHER READING

Friedman, John Bloch, and Kristen Mossler Figg, eds. *Trade, Travel and Exploration in the Middle Ages: An Encyclopedia.* 2000.

Mackintosh-Smith, Tim. *Travels with a Tangerine: A Journey in the Footnotes of Ibn Battutah.* 2001.

Morrison, Susan Signe. *Women Pilgrims in Late Medieval England: Private Piety as Public Performance.* 2000.

Newton, Arthur Paul. *Travel and Travelers of the Middle Ages*. 2003.
Said, Edward. *Orientalism*. 1979.
Spencer, Brian. *Pilgrim Souvenirs and Secular Badges (Medieval Finds from Excavations in London)*. 1998.
Sumption, Jonathan. *Pilgrimage: An Image of Mediaeval Religion*. 1975.
Tzanaki, Rosemary. *Mandeville's Medieval Audiences: A Study on the Perception of* The Book of Sir John Mandeville *(1371–1550)*. 2003.
Wriggins, Sally Hovey. *Xuanzang: A Buddhist Pilgrim on the Silk Road*. 1998.

MEDIA RESOURCES

WEB SITES

Internet Medieval Sourcebook
http://www.fordham.edu/halsall/sbook.html
A Web site from Fordham University that has a very good resource page, though no specific link for travel. Includes sections on the Crusade and Exploration and Expansion, and Maps listed by country (a fine site for medieval maps).

Historical Maps, Perry Casteneda Library at the University of Texas
http://www.lib.utexas.edu/Libs/PCL/Map_collection/historical/history_main.html
Maps worldwide, including Europe at the time of the Crusades (twelfth century).

The Labyrinth
http://www.georgetown.edu/labyrinth/labyrinth-home.html
Resources for medieval studies, some background information.

Voice of the Shuttle: Anglo-Saxon and Medieval
http://vos.ucsb.edu/
Links to many other Web resources and background articles.

MARGERY KEMPE, *The Book of Margery Kempe* (p. 993)

WWW   For a quiz on *The Book of Margery Kempe,* see *World Literature Online* at bedfordsmartins.com/worldlit.

Margery Kempe is often grouped together with other medieval women mystics like Julian of Norwich, Hildegarde von Bingen, and Theresa of Avila. However, her life and story are unique in many ways. Because of her unconventional religious practices, Margery was a much more controversial figure than her counterparts. Margery insisted on wearing white even though she was neither a nun nor a virgin, her speech often approached the level of a sermon, and her uncontrollable weeping caused many to think her a charlatan.

Unlike Julian, whom Margery met in the course of her travels, Margery was forced to dictate her story because she had not been taught to read or write. While women's illiteracy was still somewhat commonplace in England, Margery's illiteracy is unexpected, because, by the late fourteenth century, more and more women of Margery's station were being taught their letters. However, her lack of formal education did not seem to hinder her to any great extent. She successfully argued with the archbishop of York and defended herself against charges of heresy. Moreover, despite the difficulties she faced and the reservations of her second scribe, Margery was able to convince two men to help her write her story.

Like many medieval manuscripts, the story of the discovery of *The Book of Margery Kempe* is an interesting and surprising one. Prior to 1934, only an eight-page pamphlet of devotional selections from Margery's autobiography was known. Wynken de Worde had published this pamphlet, entitled *A Short Treatise of Contemplation Taught by our Lord Jesus Christ, Taken Out of the Book of Margery Kempe of Lynn,* in 1501, and, of the five hundred copies, only one survived. An independent American scholar named Hope Emily Allen discovered the full manuscript somewhat by accident when she was called to examine a volume brought to the Victoria and Albert Museum by Colonel William Butler-Bowden.

TEXT & CONTEXT

RELIGIOUS WOMEN

The medieval period was an age in which spectacular demonstrations of personal piety were relatively common. Many degrees of religious service were available to women of wealthy families and were often sought in order to avoid the hardships of marriage and childbirth. Medieval nuns took vows of poverty, chastity, and obedience, and spent the greater part of their time in prayer, at Mass, and performing works like the copying of books and illumination of manuscripts. Anchoresses like Margery's counselor, Julian of Norwich, lived in enclosed, one-room cells that usually only had one small window. As women attached (or anchored) to a church, they lived a strictly solitary and ascetic life of contemplation and were very highly regarded by their church and community. In Europe, women could also become part of a community of religious women called Canonesses, who lived together under the direction of an Abbess. Although they took vows of chastity and obedience, they had a great deal more leeway than did Nuns or Anchoresses. Canonesses were typically engaged in the recitation of the prayers of the Divine Office, the care of church vestments, and the education of the daughters of nobility. Married and single women who wanted to devote their lives to spiritual work in the secular world could become Beguines. Beguines usually worked as nurses and teachers, did not take religious vows, and except for a brief novitiate period were not required to cloister themselves with other Beguines.

LOLLARDS

Because her extreme religious practices were not always understood, Margery Kempe was often wrongly accused of being a Lollard. Although the medieval church often used the term *lollard* as a synonym for heretic, Lollards were more specifically members of a reformist religious sect considered to be heretical by the church. Lollardy was based on the late-fourteenth-century teachings of the theologian John Wycliffe, who agitated for reform in the church. His followers, who multiplied quickly after his death, rejected the church's strict hierarchical structure, held that pious laypeople (including women) should be allowed to preach, and questioned both transubstantiation and the sacrament of confession. Lollards also are credited with the first translations of the Bible into English. The church, which preferred laypeople to learn doctrine from priests, mystery plays, and saints' lives, considered Lollardy such a troublesome movement that Wycliffe's books were burned and Lollard beliefs were declared heresy. In 1401, Henry IV issued the first order for the burning of heretics, and forty-one years after Wycliffe's death, his body was exhumed and immolated. Nonetheless, the church could not keep these ideas down for long; Lollardy is often seen as a precursor to the Protestant Reformation.

IN THE CLASSROOM

I. THE FORM OF KEMPE'S AUTOBIOGRAPHY

The Book of Margery Kempe is often cited as the first autobiography in English or the first written by a woman. However, the work is not an autobiography in the modern sense of the term. Margery does not tell the complete story of her life or even the complete story of a period of time in her life. Rather, she writes the story of her religious awakening and subsequent devotional practices.

Discussion

1. Discuss the genres of biography and autobiography with students. Talk about what distinguishes *The Book of Margery Kempe* as a work of autobiography rather than a memoir or journal. The concept of truth is particularly relevant to this discussion, as autobiographies are considered to be true accounts of a person's life. Does the fantastic nature of some of Margery's narrative, which is sometimes hard for even those who know her to believe, negate her authority as an author? Is it valid to call spiritual visions and accounts "facts," or do they exist outside of the factual realm?

2. Because she was illiterate, Margery was forced to dictate her story to priests and scribes. Ask students to consider the consequences of relying on a third party to relate one's story. Is it possible that the priests had their own agendas either similar or opposed to those of Margery that might be evident in the work? Note that Margery is often referred to in her narrative as "the creature." Have students think about what this appellation might mean in light of the treatment Margery receives from fellow Christians. While it is possible that this name is Margery's way of humbling herself before God, is it equally possible that her scribes viewed her with contempt?

Connections

1. Careful attention to other autobiographies and first-person accounts will shed light on Margery Kempe's narrative. Have students look at *The Confessions* of St. Augustine (p. 70). Although *The Confessions* is an autobiographical piece like that of Kempe, it is written from a first- rather than a third-person point of view. How does this change in point of view change students' impressions of the author? of the narrative? Also, pay close attention to the conversions Margery and Augustine experience. Both desire to devote themselves to a Christian life but are lured away by worldly matters. How do they finally come to lead the life they profess to have wanted all along?

2. In the Middle Ages, authors often wrote themselves into their own fictional accounts. How is the presence of the poet in Chaucer's *Canterbury Tales* (p. 878), Dante's *Inferno* (p. 689), or Boccacio's *Decameron* (p. 853) similar to or different from autobiography? How might the lines between fiction and reality be blurred in these works and in *The Book of Margery Kemp*?

Writing

Ask students to write a short paper in response to one or more of the following:

1. Margery's book does not declare its purpose outright, neither is her purpose in sharing her story immediately obvious. Yet she went to a great amount of trouble to have it written down. Write a paper addressing Margery's intentions in writing her story. Is she trying to praise God and His works or to bring others to the divine path? Is it possible, considering Margery's negative experiences with her pilgrimage companions, that she wants to validate her own life? Alternatively, you may want to address what function *The Book of Margery Kempe* might serve to those who read it.

2. Based on the class discussion of the genres of autobiography and biography, or on your own thoughts and reading, evaluate *The Book of Margery Kempe* as an autobiography. Is it proper to consider Kempe's work autobiographical? If so, might it be filed in a sub-

category of the genre? If not, explain and suggest a better classification. You may choose to look at the work either on its own or in relation to more modern autobiographical works like Benjamin Franklin's *Autobiography* or *The Interesting Narrative of the Life of Olaudah Equiano* (Book 4). How does Kempe's book stack up against these or others with which you are familiar?

Groups

1. This exercise is intended to simulate the conditions under which Margery was trying to dictate her tale and may work a bit like a written game of telephone. Split students into groups of three. One of these students will be the storyteller, and the other two will serve as scribes. The storyteller should get together with his or her scribes privately and tell each of them half of the same story. The story should be short and does not have to be autobiographical. You may choose to let the scribes make a few short notes or to ask them simply to listen to the story. The scribes will then go home and write up their half of the story as they remember it. If a scribe does not remember certain details like the names or relationships of the people involved, he or she should feel free to make them up. Groups should get together and see whether the completed stories bear any resemblance to the storyteller's original tale. As an alternative to make the assignment more interesting, you might want to assign one of the students to be a "hostile" scribe, much like Margery's second priest is said to have been.

II. The Focus of *The Book of Margary Kempe*

The primary focus of Margery's narrative is her spiritual relationship with God. Although she shares many of her life experiences, her connection with the divine is always her central theme. Her spiritual story is unique not only because she is a woman but also because she does not enter a convent or anchorage. Instead, Margery chooses to lead a spiritual life while remaining in the secular world.

Discussion

1. After Margery's first vision, she does not immediately devote herself to a religious life, but rather tries her hand at the worldly professions of brewing and milling. It is only after she fails at these endeavors that Margery "began to enter the way of everlasting life." Talk about this period as a time of transition between the worldly Margery and the spiritual one. Why doesn't she come to her religious life immediately after her first vision? Why must she try two separate failed businesses before she amends her ways? Consider whether her attempts at becoming a businesswoman are a way of beginning to assert her independence from her husband.

2. We are not told the nature of the sin that Margery tries to confess on her sickbed in Chapter 1, but the sin is mentioned again in Chapter 3. Students might be interested in trying to guess what this sin was, but encourage them to think more deeply about it. Talk about why Margery wants to confess this particular sin and how her failed confession affects her. What does it mean to Margery that she concealed this sin for so long? Note that even after she has confessed it once, Margery does not feel absolved of it. She writes that, "she was shriven sometimes twice or thrice on a day, and specially of that sin she so long had (hid) concealed and covered."

Connections

1. In Chaucer's *Canterbury Tales* (p. 885), the irreligious Wife of Bath explicitly discusses her five marriages and abundant sex life. Yet curiously, she does not mention children, and it seems possible that she has none because she is barren. By contrast, Margery's

spiritual reawakening seems to come to her as a direct result of the birth of her first child, and she does not succeed in convincing her husband of the importance of chastity until she has borne a total of fourteen children. What might these women's attitudes toward sex and childbirth say about their capacity for religious devotion? Margery trades her abundant physical fertility for a full spiritual life. Is the Wife of Bath's spiritual sterility indicated by her inability to have children?

Writing

Ask students to write a short paper in response to one or more of the following:

1. Argue whether and how Margery's gender affects her religious practices. You might want to discuss Margery's relations with her husband prior to her complete religious devotion. Notice that she must use prayer to God and negotiation with her husband to achieve her desire for chastity — she is not permitted to simply refuse his advances. She acknowledges this herself when she tells him, "I may not deny you my body."

2. Address Margery's actions and reception during her travels. According to church doctrine, women were forbidden from preaching, yet much of Margery's speech during her pilgrimage seems akin to sermon. Would people have been as uncomfortable with her if she were a man?

3. Margery explains that she weeps at first because of her own sins against God (Chapter 3), but later because "she had such great compassion and such great pain, at seeing Our Lord's pain" (Chapter 28). Critique this phenomenon and its repercussions. Can her weeping be seen as a form of dialogue or a medium through which Margery speaks? What are the positive and negative effects of this type of overt religious demonstration? You might want to address the fact that the weeping is a great source of tension between Margery and everyone from her neighbors to her fellow pilgrims. Some of them even accuse her of crying for dramatic effect — of being able to turn her tears on and off at will. Why does it disturb her companions? Does Margery's weeping really ring false to them, or is she seen as a threat to their own religious airs and practices?

Groups

1. Since scholars connect Margery Kempe so strongly to other groups like mystics and preachers, it would be helpful to students to have the opportunity to discover how *The Book of Margery Kempe* relates to other similar works of the medieval period. Assign each group (or have them choose) either a medieval woman mystic, a female preacher, or if you want to appeal to a broader range of interests, a male religious figure. If you allow students to choose their own research topic, stress to them the importance of having a primary source with which to start. Depending on your personal vision of this assignment, it may not be appropriate for students to research a figure about whom only third-person accounts exist. Groups should research their figure by reading both primary and secondary sources. For example, to research Julian of Norwich, a group should be prepared to read some or all of her *Shewings* as well as some contemporary historical and critical works that deal with her. The object is to have a broad historical sense of the individual as well as for students to make some critical determinations on their own. Each group should collect their research into either a formal paper or an oral presentation for the class.

BEYOND THE CLASSROOM

RESEARCH & WRITING

1. At the opening of our selection of *The Book of Margery Kempe*, Margery describes the event that serves as a catalyst for her first religious vision: the birth of her first child and her subsequent illness. Have students research pregnancy and childbirth in the Middle Ages. Were Margery's experiences typical? They might either undertake an historical project, perhaps including common practices, superstitions, and the role of doctors and midwives in the birthing process, or make an argument about how childbirth and motherhood (or the inability to have children) shaped the lives of medieval women. In addition to historical materials, these explorations should include other literary accounts of childbirth, if possible.

2. Hagiography is a type of Christian literature that concerns itself primarily with saints. Miracle stories, bulls of canonization, and accounts of the discovery of relics, among others, are included in the genre. *The Book of Margery Kempe* bears a striking resemblance to the most common type of hagiography — saints' lives. Rather than being a full biography, a saint's life is a record of the events that helped establish and reveal the saint's holiness. Have students research one or more saints' lives, and compare them critically with Kempe's account. Students may also wish to consult Ibin. How does Kempe's *Book* resemble or deviate from the saint's life model? Do the resemblances lend any authority to Kemp's account? Students might want to look specifically at the lives of St. Bridget of Sweden, St. Catherine, St. Margaret, Mary Magdalene, or Mary of Oignies, all of whom Margery mentions in the course of her account.

Project

1. For historical background on the topic of women, saints, and women's religious practices, show one or more of the following films: Carl Dreyer's *The Passion of Joan of Arc*, Chris Newby's *The Anchoress*, Peter Glenville's *Becket*, Luc Besson's *The Messenger*, Monty Python's *The Holy Grail*, or another film dealing with saints or facets of medieval religion. Ask students to watch the film actively, jotting down notes about the film as they watch, and have them turn in a two- to three-page critique of the film. This critique should not summarize the film but should include an analysis of the film as well as the students' impressions and general thoughts. After you have collected these essays, have students engage in some independent historical research about one of the medieval aspects of the movie, preferably something relating to medieval religion. This research should lead to a second essay, focusing on the way that the medieval is represented in the film. Did the film portray this aspect of medieval life accurately? If not, what effect did the movie create by changing the historical fact? Were the facts altered simply to appeal to a modern audience, or is there evidence that another agenda is at work? It might be interesting to some students to discuss whether the film shows the medieval world in a positive or a negative light. Is there any evidence of bias on the part of the filmmakers?

WWW   For additional information on Kempe and annotated Web links, see *World Literature Online* at bedfordstmartins.com/worldlit.

FURTHER READING

Collis, Louise. *The Apprentice Saint*. 1964.
Coon, Lynda L. *Sacred Fictions: Holy Women and Hagiography in Late Antiquity*. 1997.
Head, Thomas. *Medieval Hagiography: An Anthology*. 2001.

Ladd, R. A. "Margery Kempe and Her Mercantile Mysticism," *Fifteenth Century Studies* 26 (2001): 121–41.

Somerset, Fiona. *The Lollards and Their Influence in Late Medieval England.* 2004.

Watkin, E. I. *On Julian of Norwich, and In Defense of Margery Kempe.* 1979.

Watson, Nicholas, and Anne Savage. *Anchoritic Spirituality: Ancrene Wisse and Associated Works.* 1991.

MEDIA RESOURCES

VIDEO

Becket
148 min., 1964 (Library Video Company)
Richard Burton and Peter O'Toole star in this fact based Academy Award–winning film adapted from the play by Jean Anouilh about the friendship between King Henry II and Thomas Becket. Their friendship takes an ironic turn when the king tries to secure his throne by appointing his friend to be the archbishop of Canterbury. Watch as Becket finds himself moved toward a devotion to God, a rival with whom Henry II cannot compete, and discover the inevitable conflict this causes.

Cathedral
60 min., 1983 (PBS Home Video)
Illustrator David Macaulay hosts this highly praised PBS special. Animation and live-action sequences illustrate the cultural importance of the gothic cathedral and celebrate France's famous churches. The animation is derived from Macaulay's unique drawing style and depicts the design and construction of an imaginary but historically accurate cathedral near Paris.

Charlemagne and the Holy Roman Empire
31 min., 1998 (Films for the Humanities & Sciences)
Out of the ashes of the Roman Empire rose the Holy Roman Empire, born during Christmas of 800 in the Basilica of St. Peter's in Rome. This program covers the antecedents and the life of Charlemagne, shows life at the court, life of the courtiers and of the peasants, recounts the battle of Roncevaux — site of the epic *Chanson de Roland* — and counterpoints the glories of the Carolingian Renaissance with the everyday realities of hunger, plague, and constant violence. The program concludes with the first of Europe's major confrontations between empire and church, in this instance between Henry IV and Gregory VII.

Christians, Jews, and Moslems in Medieval Spain
33 min., 1989 (Films for the Humanities & Sciences)
Due partly to the weakness of its Visigothic rulers, partly to its proximity to Africa, the Iberian Peninsula was conquered by Berbers and by Arabs belonging to the Ommayad dynasty of Damascus. This program describes the history of Spain from the time of the first landing in 711 through the nearly eight hundred-year-long war that ended in the expulsion of both Moors and Jews in 1492; the development of a culture whose people spoke various Spanish dialects while the official language was Arabic; the role of the School of Toledo in preserving, translating, and making known the ancient Greek scientific texts as well as Arabic treatises on philosophy and science; the rabbinic center in Toledo; and the history of the Jews in Spain.

Cities and Cathedrals of the Middle Ages
30 min., 1989 (Annenberg/CPB Video)
The great churches embodied the material and spiritual ambitions of the age.

Common Life in the Middle Ages
30 min., 1989 (Annenberg/CPB Video)
Famine, disease, and short life expectancies were the conditions that shaped medieval beliefs.

Crusader: By Horse to Jerusalem
54 min., 1997 (Films for the Humanities & Sciences)
The march to Jerusalem was the greatest land journey of the Middle Ages. Recreating the 2,500-mile trip from the green lands of northern Europe to the burning deserts of Sinai, this program leaves from the castle of Duke Godfrey de Bouillon, hero of the First Crusade, plodding along on a one-ton descendant of the medieval battle charger across the lands of medieval Christendom, climbing the Anatolian plateau, seeing the Crusader castles and ancient battlefields in Syria, and finally crossing the Jordan River and reaching the jewel in the Crusader's crown, Jerusalem.

Crusades
200 min., 1995 (Insight Media)
Filmed on location in Europe and the Middle East, this series explores the history and legacy of the Crusades. It discusses the reasons for the Crusades, the creation of a mythology of knights and chivalry, and the legacy of distrust between East and West.

Knights and Armor
97 min., 1994 (A&E Videos)
A&E explores the chivalry and romance of medieval Europe, from the incredible true story of Sir William Marshal and the knights of the Holy Grail to the heroism of Excalibur. Filmed on location in the United Kingdom, Turkey, and Austria, this program also features the greatest collection of arms in the world.

The Late Middle Ages
30 min., 1989 (Annenberg/CPB Video)
Two hundred years of war and plague debilitated Europe.

Margery Kempe
24 min., 1999 (Films for the Humanities & Sciences)
As women mystics became more common throughout Europe in the late fourteenth and fifteenth centuries, the manner in which they expressed and practiced their devotion became more diverse. In this program, Kathy Garay of McMaster University presents Margery Kempe's unconventional life in context. Topics like bridal mysticism are discussed, along with Kempe's pilgrimage to Jerusalem. The transcription of her life into the first autobiography in the English language presents a portrait of a woman who defied social norms by following her visions and risked the charge of heresy in doing so.

Medieval Christian Europe
25 min., 2002 (Insight Media)
This program traces medieval Christianity's evolution into the Renaissance. It examines the influence of the scholarly and monastic traditions of Saint Patrick, Saint Benedict, Charlemagne, Hildegard of Bingen, and Saint Francis of Assisi.

The Middle Ages
25 min., 1996 (Films for the Humanities & Sciences)
This program traces the evolution of Europe during the Middle Ages from a group of loosely tied kingdoms to a prosperous community of nations. Topics include the role of

the church, development of the feudal system, the rise of the nobility, the Crusades, formation of the German Hanseatic League, the effects of the Plague, the growth of trade guilds, the discovery of printing, the urbanization of the peasantry, and the rise of science.

The Middle Ages
30 min., 1997 (Annenberg/CPB Video)
Amid invasion and civil disorder, a military aristocracy dominated the kingdoms of Europe.

The Middle Ages
34 min., 1992 (Insight Media)
This program explores the important figures and events of the Middle Ages through artwork and dramatic narration. It considers the influence of classical civilization on early Christianity and art, explores the so-called Dark Ages, discusses the Crusades, and examines the Gothic style of architecture.

The World's Philosophies
60 min., 1994 (Insight Media)
In this video, Huston Smith defines three basic types of human relationships — with nature, with other people, and with one's self — and explains how these relationships correspond to the philosophical traditions of the West, of China, and of India.

WEB SITES

The Book of Margery Kempe: Introduction
www.lib.rochester.edu/camelot/teams/kempint.htm
Written by Lynn Stanley, this site offers a critical and historical introduction to *The Book of Margery Kempe.*

Luminarium — Margery Kempe
www.luminarium.org/medlit/margery.htm
Part of a much larger anthology devoted to Middle English, this site offers links to a wide array of resources and research possibilities, including excerpts from *The Book of Margery Kempe,* many biographical sources on the author, critical essays, and additional sources.

Mapping Margery Kempe
www.holycross.edu/departments/visarts/projects/kempe
This digital library from the College of the Holy Cross offers a wide range of resources for examining the cultural, social, political, and religious contexts of *The Book of Margery Kempe.* It includes an e-text of the book, complete texts of other devotional writings, maps of pilgrimage routes, documents about daily life in fifteenth-century Lynn, and an extensive bibliography.

Margery Kempe
Home.infi.net/~ddisse/kempe.html
This site provides a brief biography of Margery Kempe as well as links to several other helpful sources.

Medieval Women Writers — Margery Kempe
www.ce.mun.ca/dcs/courses/ms3351/margery.html
Created by a professor at Memorial University of Newfoundland, this site offers many interesting links to sites related to Margery Kempe.

GENERAL MEDIA RESOURCES

WEB SITES

The Book of Margery Kempe: Introduction
www.lib.rochester.edu/camelot/teams/kempint.htm
Written by Lynn Stanley, this site offers a critical and historical introduction to *The Book of Margery Kempe.*

Luminarium — Margery Kempe
www.luminarium.org/medlit/margery.htm
Part of a much larger anthology devoted to Middle English, this site offers links to a wide array of resources and research possibilities, including excerpts from *The Book of Margery Kempe,* many biographical sources on the author, critical essays, and additional sources.

Mapping Margery Kempe
www.holycross.edu/departments/visarts/projects/kempe
This digital library from the College of the Holy Cross offers a wide range of resources for examining the cultural, social, political, and religious contexts of *The Book of Margery Kempe.* It includes an e-text of the book, complete texts of other devotional writings, maps of pilgrimage routes, documents about daily life in fifteenth-century Lynn, and an extensive bibliography.

Margery Kempe
Home.infi.net/~ddisse/kempe.html
This site provides a brief biography of Margery Kempe as well as links to several other helpful sources.

Medieval Women Writers — Margery Kempe
www.ce.mun.ca/dcs/courses/ms3351/margery.html
Created by a professor at Memorial University of Newfoundland, this site offers many interesting links to sites related to Margery Kempe.

WEB SITES

Internet Medieval Sourcebook
www.fordham.edu/halsall/sbook2.html
A premiere Internet source on medieval studies created at Fordham University, the Internet Medieval Sourcebook is organized as three main index pages, with a number of supplementary documents — Selected Sources, Full Text Sources, and Saints' Lives. This is an excellent index of selected and excerpted texts for teaching purposes.

The Labyrinth: Resources for Medieval Studies
www.georgetown.edu/labyrinth/labyrinth-home.html
Based at Georgetown University, this site provides links to many medieval resources available on the Internet.

Middle Ages
www.learner.org/exhibits/middleages/
The Annenberg/CPB site on the Middle Ages provides excellent and accessible information and images on the medieval world.

NetSerf: The Internet Connection for Medieval Resources
www.netserf.org/

Sponsored by the history department of the Catholic University of America, this is a wonderful gateway site to all things medieval.

The Online Medieval & Classical Library
sunsite.berkeley.edu/OMACL/
The Douglas B. Killings collection of some of the most important literary works of classical and medieval civilization.

AUDIO

The History of English Literature
4 CDs, 5:15 hrs. (Naxos Audio)
Perry Keenlyside tells the remarkable story of the world's richest literary resource. The storytelling, the poetry, the growth of the novel, and the great histories and essays that have informed the language and the imagination wherever English is spoken.

Living Biographies of Religious Leaders
8 tapes, 11:25 hrs. (Blackstone Audiobooks)
This program presents the lives of twenty great founders and leading advocates of the world's foremost religions. Here are the historical facts and legends associated with these forceful personalities who have inspired and influenced humankind through the centuries. Presented are Jesus Christ, Moses, Isaiah, Zoroaster, Buddha, Confucius, John the Baptist, Paul, Muhammad, Francis of Assisi, John Huss, Luther, Loyola, Calvin, George Fox, Swedenborg, Wesley, Brigham Young, Mary Baker Eddy, and Gandhi.

JAPAN:
BIRTH OF A CULTURE

The *Man'yoshu* (p. 1018)

WWW   For quizzes on the *Man'yoshu*, see *World Literature Online* at
bedfordstmartins.com/worldlit.

The poems of the *Man'yoshu* fall under three types: *banka*, or elegies on the death of an emperor or a loved one; *somonka*, or expressions of love and longing; and *zoka*, or miscellaneous poems on nature, an event, and the like. Although *banka* portray political figures, Japanese poetry at the time was not political. Instead, poems often focus on the evocation of a mood or emotion. The poetic principle of *mono no aware*, a sense of the sadness of things, is integral to Japanese poetry, both in the *Man'yoshu* and today. Through *mono no aware*, Japanese poetry recognizes the universality of loss and sadness and witnesses the passing of things not with despair but with tranquility. Students will notice the elegiac tone that pervades the poetry. Encourage them to distinguish the different ways in which loss functions in the poems. Compare, for example, the loss that separates, as exemplified in "When He Parted from His Wife in the Land of Iwami: I" and "On the Death of His Wife: I and II," with the loss that unites, as in the "Lament Addressed to His Son-in-Law, Fujiwara Nakachiko." Loss is also a construct of time, as "A Lament on the Evanescence of Life" and "When He Passed the Ruined Capital at Omi" demonstrate.

Another principle that unites Japanese poetry is *aware*, a sensitivity to the things in the world, which is figured forth in the realization of an event or an object (many of the objects, particularly from nature, became conventional as a result of the *Man'yoshu*). Often *aware* takes the form of identification with nature. In the *Man'yoshu*, this process of identification involves the incorporation of the landscape into the poet's private reflections, whereby the landscape realizes the poet's own perspective. Such techniques render ornate language and elaborate metaphor unnecessary, so that even in the longer *choka* poems, the style is simple. Direct students to discuss the significance of place in the poems. You might point out that place names became conventional in Japanese poetry as a result of their romantic and poetic associations. This use of place names is called *uta-makura*.

One of the essential relationships that structure *Man'yoshu* poetry is that between macrocosm and microcosm. The two come together in single, inconsequential events or objects, and are at times formally represented in the relationship between a *choka* and its envoys. Have students examine the relationship between the *chokas* and their envoys. What function do the envoys serve? Often they signal a shift in perspective. What does this shift enable the poet to do? An investigation of perspective should lead students to consider "Upon Seeing a Dead Man Lying among the Rocks on the Island of Samine" and "Dialogue between Poverty and Destitution." What effect does identifying the reader with the dead man in the former have? What does the reader's perspective have in common with his perspective?

Finally, issues of time pervade *Man'yoshu* poetry. The clearest distinction that emerges, again and again, is between the past and the present. What distinguishes the one from the other? How does this division construct the authenticity of the moment presented in the poem? Point out to students that Japanese poetry is anything but abstract or metaphysical in its construction. Any universal significance emerges from the concrete.

TEXT & CONTEXT

THE IMPACT OF BUDDHISM

By the seventh and eighth centuries, Buddhism, having arrived in Japan from China during the sixth century, had become integrated into the state. As a result, great temples were constructed, including the *Horyuji* in 607 and the Great Buddha *(Daibutsu)* of the *Todaiji* in 752. During this time period, many Japanese art forms were influenced by Buddhist iconography. Nevertheless, Japanese literature remained unaffected, primarily because Buddhist models, representative of abstract thought, were imitated in Chinese, whereas literature, committed to the concrete in its portrayal of inner emotion, found expression in Japanese.

PROSODY

Japanese verse is structured according to number of syllables because of its phonetic language. Without any clear distinction between stress or syllable length, the number of syllables has become the determining factor in Japanese prosody. Since all syllables end in a vowel, Japanese poetry is harmonious even without rhyme, and some historians claim that the poems of the *Man'yoshu* were originally sung. Parallelism is the most prevalent rhetorical device and is characteristic of the *choka*. Other devices used include *kake kotoba* (pivot words), *makura kotoba* (pillow words), and *joshi* (introductory verses). Pivot words are words that have two meanings depending on the way in which a line is parsed. Shuichi Kato explains that the phrase "Osaka barrier," for example, is sometimes written with 'Au' (in *kana*, meaning "meet") instead of 'O', which rendered the expression either "Osaka barrier" or "to meet at the Osaka barrier." Pillow words are fixed epithets that modify a word either in terms of sound or sense association (comparable, to some extent, with such epithets as "wise" in "wise Odysseus" in Homer). Although they are often five syllables in length, pillow words are not limited to adjectives, and function, in Kato's example, like "where it always rains" in the expression "Manchester where it always rains." *Joshi* modify the verse that follows in a similar, if more substantial way, and are often connected to the poem with a pivot word. You might ask students to identify the pillow words in the poems and discuss their effect.

IN THE CLASSROOM

Discussion and Writing

1. Place and memory are connected in many of the poems, "At the Time of the Temporary Enshrinement of Prince Takechi at Kinoe" and "When He Parted from His Wife in the Land of Iwami: I," for example. To what extent is memory geographical? What effect does locating memory have on what is remembered?

2. How is greatness represented in the poems (for instance, via comparison, understatement, and the like)? Consider "When He Passed the Ruined Capital at Omi" or "At the Time of the Temporary Enshrinement of Prince Takechi at Kinoe" for the greatness of a ruler and "On the Death of His Wife: I and II" or "Longing for His Son Furuhi" for the greatness of love.

3. Discuss the significance of survival in such poems as "A Lament on the Evanescence of Life" and "Dialogue between Poverty and Destitution."

4. Several poems portray the contrast between not knowing and knowing something. What does enlightenment represent in these poems? Examine "Upon Seeing a Dead Man Lying among the Rocks on the Island of Samine" and "Lament Addressed to His Son-in-Law, Fujiwara Nakachiko," in particular.

5. Despite its position at the beginning of the Japanese literary tradition, the *Man'yoshu* nevertheless presents a sense of tradition not necessarily tied to prior texts. How does tradition emerge in the poems?

Connections

1. Ruins have connected the past and the present in many literary texts. Compare the significance of ruins in the *Man'yoshu* with the ruins in Neruda's "The Heights of Macchu Picchu" (Book 6).

2. Explore the significance of death in the *Man'yoshu* and in *Beowulf* (p. 482). How is death represented as a part of nature in these seminal texts?

BEYOND THE CLASSROOM

RESEARCH & WRITING

1. Find out about the function the gods serve in Japanese culture. How does this role inform the representation of the divine in the poems of the *Man'yoshu?*

2. The *Man'yoshu* also includes many poems by women about the men they love. Read a few of these, and compare them with the way the male poets represent love.

Projects

1. Examine the *tankas* in the *Man'yoshu* as part of the literary tradition of Japan. Read later *tankas* in the *Kokinshu* as well as some modern *tankas*. What aspects does this form of poetry make characteristically Japanese? To what extent does the *tanka* develop?

2. Compare the representation of nature in the *Man'yoshu* with contemporary representations of nature in painting and sculpture.

FURTHER READING

Ebersole, Gary L. *Ritual Poetry and the Politics of Death in Early Japan.* 1989.
Miner, Earl. "Waka: Features of its Constitution and Development," in *Harvard Journal of Asiatic Studies* 50, no. 2 (1990): 669–706.
Plutschow, H. E. *Chaos and Cosmos: Ritual in Early and Medieval Japanese Literature.* 1990.
Yiu, Angela. "The Category of Metaphorical Poems (*hiyuka*) in the *Man'yoshu*: Its Characteristics and Chinese Origins," in *Journal of the Association of Teachers of Japanese* 24, no. 1 (1990): 7–33.

MEDIA RESOURCES

WEB SITES

Asuka and the Man'yoshu
www.asukanet.gr.jp/asukahome/ASUKA2/MANYOU/asuka_manyou.html
This page provides background on the *Man'yoshu* and links to individual works.

The Man'yoshu
www.shef.ac.uk/japan2001/manyoshu.shtml
This terrific site gives an introduction to the forms of the poems, background on them, access to individual poems, and links to individual *Man'yoshu* poets.

Kokinshu (p. 1051)

WWW For a quiz on the *Kokinshu,* see *World Literature Online* at bedfordstmartins.com/worldlit.

With the compilation of the *Kokinshu,* poetry composed in Japanese became a legitimate component of "official" culture. Although the concept of an official literature had been imported from China, and the earliest imperial anthologies focused on poetry and prose in Chinese, the institution of *uta-awase* and the development of *karon* made the shift to Japanese "official." *Uta-awase* were poetry contests in which *waka* (see p. 1046) were written on one particular topic so that they could be compared and the best determined. Since the excellence of the *waka* had to be based on objective criteria, *karon,* or treatises on *waka,* were formulated and consulted. Many of the poems included in the *Kokinshu* were the product of *uta-awase* and were critiqued in *karon.*

Uta-awase made spontaneous composition a common condition for the production of official poetry. This approach upheld many Japanese poetic ideals, like the natural expression of genuine emotion. A poet could nevertheless show his skill in the ingenious metaphors he employed or in concluding a poem with a clever twist. Word play and indirection were often used but not to the extent that the significance of the poem becomes obscure. Most significant, therefore, is the imagery, which students will find more accessible than other poetic devices. Ask students to distinguish various kinds of imagery. Are the images dynamic? Static? To what effect?

Of course, many of the images are from nature, several of which had become conventional with the *Man'yoshu* (p. 1018). With the *Kokinshu,* nature acquired a different aspect. Instead of the poet's state of mind composing the landscape so that nature embodies the emotion evoked, nature became a poetic subject per se. Encourage students to examine the effect this way of representing nature has on the emotion presented in the poem. To what extent are nature and emotion contrasted rather than united? Also, what kind of nature is depicted (wild, civilized, harmless)? Students might discuss the "genuineness" of this nature.

In addition, the representation of sound is an important element in the poems that should be addressed. Direct students to focus on the source of sound and the way in which sounds express the interaction between the human and the natural. Consider poems 162, 412, and 804, in particular. An interesting approach for bringing students to appreciate the function of sound in the poems is to have them recite one (which they might even memorize!), an exercise that will also emphasize aspects of the poems' structure. After all, sound is one of the many ways in which contrast is developed in the poems. Encourage students to identify other forms of contrast, perhaps beginning with a discussion of parallels between sound and image in poems 635 and 804, and then move to the contrasts in poem 645, for instance.

Finally, the theme of loss permeates the poems in the *Kokinshu* and certainly ties the anthology to the Japanese poetic tradition. Have students describe the ways in which loss is portrayed in the *Kokinshu* (via indirection, imagery, and the like). Doing so should enable them to tackle questions like: How does the *Kokinshu* present the universal with reference to the transient? What does the here-and-now signify?

TEXT & CONTEXT

SOCIAL CLASS

Unlike the poets of the *Man'yoshu,* those of the *Kokinshu* belonged exclusively to the upper echelons of society. To be sure, anonymous authors contributed almost a third of the poems included, yet the vocabulary and subject matter of these poems rule out the possibility that provincial peasants produced them. Moreover, the closed society of the court, where "official" poetry flourished, was such that most of the poets came from the lower aristocracy, where one had access to the life of the court, but did not participate in the power struggles of the elite. The four editors were all low-ranking aristocrats.

POETICS

The *Standard Poetic Forms (kakyo hyoshiki)*, written in 772, represents the first attempt to analyze Japanese in terms of Chinese literary principles. Ki no Tsurayuki's preface is regarded as the first attempt to establish a Japanese poetics that benefited from but did not replicate Chinese models. The basic terms that then shaped analysis of Japanese poetry include "heart" *(kokoro)* and "words" *(kotoba)*. *Kokoro* denotes "the capacity of being affected, the conception resulting, and the informing cognitive element," whereas *kotoba* designates "that which has been expressed by an affected poet — language, materials, subjects; so also the literary expression" (*Princeton Companion to Classical Japanese Literature*, 284–85). A balance between the two is the Japanese poetic ideal. This achievement is the composition of a poem's *sama*, a term with multiple connotations that is perhaps best understood as the *Gestalt*, or the appearance of the interaction between form and content.

IN THE CLASSROOM

Discussion and Writing

1. How does nature function in the *Kokinshu?* Consider the significance of seasonal change.

2. Although most of the poems present a first-person perspective, a few, including poem 304, offer a more "objective" view. What effect does this distance have?

3. Several of the poems portray the contrast between dreams and reality. Explain what each represents. What does it mean to wake up?

4. How is time depicted in the *Kokinshu?* How does time create both order and disorder?

5. Like their Chinese counterparts, many of the poems in the *Kokinshu* were composed with specific occasions in mind. How does "occasion" shape emotion in the poems?

Connections

1. Discuss the way in which transience figures in the poems of the *Kokinshu* and in Marvell's "To His Coy Mistress."

2. Compare genuine or authentic feeling in the *Kokinshu* with Keats's "Ode to a Nightingale." Alternatively, discuss the representation of dreams in each.

BEYOND THE CLASSROOM

RESEARCH & WRITING

1. In *Japanese Court Poetry,* Robert H. Brower and Earl Miner suggest that "no small part of the history of Japanese court poetry can be summarized as 'Po-Chü-i half-understood' " (180). Read the selection of Bo-Chuyi's poetry included in the anthology and explain to what extent this claim is accurate. You might also refer to the play *Haku Rakuten,* by the Nō dramatist Zeami, in which Chinese cultural dominance ends when Bo-Chuyi's boat is blown back to China.

2. Investigate Japanese nature watercolors. Compare the way in which nature is portrayed in the watercolors and in the *Kokinshu.*

3. Read Ki no Tsurayuki's preface. To what extent do the poems in the *Kokinshu* reflect the principles he describes as being essential to Japanese poetry?

Projects

1. In the Western tradition, color is traditionally associated in terms of poetics with the "colors of rhetoric." Find out more about the "colors of rhetoric," and discuss their relationship to color in the *Kokinshu* (in poems 113, 381, and 792, for instance).

2. Research theories of photographic art. How are the poems photographic?

FURTHER READING

Brower, Robert H., and Earl Miner. *Japanese Court Poetry.* 1983.
Chamberlain, Basil Hall. *The Classical Poetry of the Japanese.* 2000.
Lacure, Jon W. *Rhetorical Devices of the Kokinshu: A Structural Analysis of Japanese Waka Poetry.* 1997.
Miner, Earl. "Waka: Features of its Constitution and Development," in *Harvard Journal of Asiatic Studies* 50, no. 2 (1990): 669–706.
Raud, Rein. *The Role of Poetry in Classical Japanese Literature.* 1994.

MEDIA RESOURCES

WEB SITES

The Kokinshu
www.shef.ac.uk/japan2001/kokinshu.shtml
This terrific site gives an introduction to the forms of the poems, background on them, access to individual poems, and links to individual *Kokinshu* poets.

The Poems of Kokinshu
etext.lib.virginia.edu/japanese/kokinshu/intro.html
This page from the University of Virginia's Japanese Text Initiative gives a brief yet helpful background on *Kokinshu* poetry.

SEI SHONAGON, from *The Pillow Book* (p. 1063)

WWW   For a quiz on *The Pillow Book,* see *World Literature Online* at
bedfordstmartins.com/worldlit.

Detailed records of women's lives were not often kept in Heian-era Japan, and therefore we know relatively little about the writer Sei Shonagon. Not even her full name survives — Sei is a part of her family name, while Shonagon is a title referring to her position as a minor counselor. She was a lady in waiting to the Empress Sadako from about 993–1000 B.C.E., occupying a position much like the one that Murasaki Shikibu held in the court of Empress Akiko from 1005–13 B.C.E. Shonagon left the court after the death of the empress, and although some sources report that she married and subsequently became a Buddhist nun after the death of her husband, the end of Shonagon's life is largely a mystery.

Sei Shonagon is often contrasted with her contemporary, Murasaki Shikibu. Shonagon is seen as outgoing and even flashy, while Lady Murasaki is characterized by a darker, more ironic, introverted style. Lady Murasaki knew of Shonagon, and, in her diary, she harshly criticized Shonagon as "dreadfully conceited," and "one who has managed to survive this far without having achieved anything of note." History, however, does not bear out Lady Murasaki's opinions; Sei Shonagon is not only considered one of the foremost writers of Japan's Heian period, but *The Pillow Book* is seen as largely representative of the court culture of the time, and her work also became the model for the literary genre "zuihitsu," or what we would call a miscellany today.

The short, thematic form and interesting content of the lists in *The Pillow Book* make them quite accessible to students, but neither the grace of Sei Shonagon's language or the value of *The Pillow Book* as a historical look at the Heian court are evident in these sections. Be sure to have students focus on the more lyrical chapters, like "In Spring it is the Dawn" or "Especially Delightful is the Day," and the sections that deal with court life, like "When His Excellency, The Chancellor, Had Departed" or "When I First Went Into Waiting" as well as the catalogues. Although these chapters may not hold student interest as naturally as do the catalogues, they allow for valuable stylistic, historical, and thematic comparisons with other works in the anthology. Have students pay particular attention to the visual images Shonagon presents in many of her passages. It may even be helpful for you to read aloud the descriptions of the seasons given in "In Spring it is the Dawn" and then ask students to draw or describe in their own words one of the seasons that Shonagon depicts.

TEXT & CONTEXT

Essentially, pillow books began as sex manuals. In geisha houses throughout Japan, geishas would write and illustrate the specific sexual techniques they had developed. The images in these books often portrayed exaggerated genitalia in order to emphasize the body part to which the technique was to be applied. Gradually, pillow books evolved into more general forums for ideas, feelings, and dreams. Many Heian aristocrats developed the habit of keeping notepaper near their pillows in order to record stray thoughts and impressions. Rather than encompassing a coherent theme, pillow books were characterized by an almost haphazard treatment of various subjects. The stream of consciousness or free association writing style known as "zuihitsu," or "following the brush" because the writing instrument was thought to move the mind rather than vice versa, was commonly employed in pillow books. Just as often, pillow books contained extensive lists, like Sei Shonagon's "Hateful Things" and "Things that Cannot be Compared."

JAPANESE WRITING

The Japanese had no system of written language until about 400 B.C.E., when the Chinese system of pictographic writing was introduced to Japan over a period of several centuries. From these initial pictograms, each of which stood for a complete concept, the Japanese developed three distinct systems of writing: kanji, a pictographic form of writing very similar to the original Chinese, and katakana and hiragana, both phonetic writing systems that employ characters which are simplified types of kanji. Today, Japanese writing, though dominated by kanji, uses a combination of these three writing systems with hiragana used for words native to the Japanese language or borrowed from Chinese particles or verb endings and katakana primarily reserved for onomatopoetic and foreign words. During the Heian period, kanji was the language of priests and scholars. All serious writing by men was done in kanji, and its role in Japanese culture is approximately analogous to that of Latin in the Western world. Women, however, were not generally permitted to use kanji. It was believed that women were incapable of learning the complex characters, and they were taught only the much simpler hiragana script. As a result, the great Japanese novels written by women of the Middle Period like *The Tale of Genji* and *The Pillow Book* were penned primarily or exclusively using hiragana.

IN THE CLASSROOM

Discussion

1. *The Pillow Book* may be written in a style that is unfamiliar to students. The disjointed nature of *The Pillow Book*, which is often cited as the first example of the Japanese poetic form zuihitsu, makes it possible to open any page at random and find a short section worth reading. What is the overall effect of this quality? Discuss the peculiarities of Shonagon's technique and the reasons she might have chosen to write this way.

2. *The Pillow Book* provides another opportunity to discuss the intersection of prose and poetry. Although Shonagon does not write in an easily recognizable poetic form, her writing style bridges the gap between narrative and verse. The poetic language of passages like "But as noon approaches and the cold wears off, no one bothers to keep the braziers alight, and soon nothing remains but piles of white ashes" (p. 1064) are retained even in translation. Discuss the effect that this poetic style of prose has on the reader. Does this technique make Shonagon's descriptions seem more realistic or more dreamlike?

3. What was the role of women in the Heian emperor's court? Based on Shonagon's observations, how were they expected to conduct themselves? Discuss the similarities and differences between the courtly women of Japan and other women in this era, either in Japan or in other countries. Describe the relations between men and women of the court. What does Shonagon criticize in the behavior of either sex?

4. In the final chapter of *The Pillow Book*, "It is Getting so Dark," Sei Shonagon explains how she came to write the work, and says "it [was] written entirely for my own amusement," and she "regret[s] that it ever came to light" (p. 1085). What do you make of the statements that Shonagon makes in this final chapter? Many medieval authors, including Chaucer, affect what is known as the "modesty topos," a rhetorical device in which an author uses her very best prose to belittle her own skill as an author. Is "It is Getting so Dark" an example of this false humility, or does it seem genuine? Was *The Pillow Book* meant to be read by people other than Shonagon herself? What evidence can you provide from the text that your answer is true?

Connections

1. Sei Shonagon is one of the few women writers in the cannon of medieval literature. Compare *The Pillow Book* to the other works by women you have read in class like *The Lay of the Chevrefoil* (p. 674), *The Book of Margery Kempe* (p. 993), and *The Tale of Genji* (p. 1094). Do the works have any perceivable or significant similarities? Do the authors appear to have common interests or values? Is there any perceivable difference between these women authors and the bulk of the male-dominated cannon?

2. Like many of the authors in the anthology, Sei Shonagon writes about the aristocracy. Consider the portrait that she draws of the courtly culture of her time. Since they both write about Heian court culture, an easy comparison may be made between *The Pillow Book* and *The Tale of Genji* (p. 1094). However, ask students to broaden their understanding by looking at *The Pillow Book* alongside texts from other parts of the world. How do the aristocrats of her world compare with those in other works you may have

read in this class like *The Epic of Gilgamesh* (Book 1), *The Iliad* (Book 1), *The Lay of the Chevrefoil* (p. 674), and *The Decameron?*

Writing

Ask students to write a short paper in response to one or more of the following:

1. Much of Sei Shonagon's writing centers on very basic things, yet *The Pillow Book* also deals with many profound concepts and offers a portrait of sophisticated court life. Write a paper that makes a case for what this contrast between simple and sophisticated might suggest. Cite specific examples from the text in order to set up the contrasts you wish to address.

2. In the chapter "Hateful Things," Shonagon lists things, events, and situations that are not considered proper or of which she does not approve. Write a paper that addresses her method of evaluation. Are Shonagon's assessments based on reason? Do morals or values play a role in her judgments? Can you articulate the nature of these values? Can you determine from this list what she might consider to be praiseworthy?

BEYOND THE CLASSROOM

RESEARCH & WRITING

1. Miyabi, or "rule of taste," roughly refers to a refined taste in beauty, art, and manners and is related to the concept of *mono no aware* (awareness of things) that is ever-present in *The Tale of Genji*. In these works, a theory of aesthetics emerges. With reference to *The Pillow Book* of Sei Shonagon, *The Tale of Genji, The Tale of the Heike,* and at least one secondary source, have students write a research paper on the topic of aesthetics in Japanese Heian literature. Possible topics might include, but are not limited to, a discussion of whether the aesthetic theories presented in the three works are the same, how aesthetic values permeate Japanese culture in the Middle Period, or the role of different types of artistic expression in the literature.

2. Although not a deliberate autobiography like Augustine's *Confessions* (p. 70) or *The Book of Margery Kempe* (p. 993), *The Pillow Book* nonetheless contains a representation of its author, Sei Shonagon. With reference to *The Pillow Book* and at least one other text in which some representation of the author can be found in the text, have students write a paper that evaluates this quasi-autobiographical technique. This assignment will require that students read and reread the texts they choose carefully in order to find as many examples as possible for ways in which the authors reference, describe, or otherwise involve themselves in their narratives. Students should consider how the authors place themselves as writers as well as within the context of their culture, time period, social sphere, and gender. What sort of portrait of themselves are the authors trying to paint? Is it fair to equate an author with his or her "character" in a literary work (that is to say can we consider the author Geoffrey Chaucer to be the same as the narrator of *The Canterbury Tales* or the author Sei Shonagon to be the same as the Shonagon who appears in the text of *The Pillow Book*)?

Projects

1. Director Peter Greenaway's 1996 film *The Pillow Book* was inspired by *The Pillow Book* of Sei Shonagon. Though the film may not be suitable for some students (it is rated NC-17), you may want to give students the option of screening the film on their own. Greenaway's film is only tangentially related to Sei Shonagon's work, but nonetheless it is possible to see Shonagon's influence. What use does Greenaway make of *The Pillow*

Book in the course of his film? How does he portray Japanese court culture? Are his interpretations of Heian culture consistent with those familiar to you from and *The Tale of Genji*?

2. Have students compose their own pillow books. The books will be more interesting if the written assignments are a combination of entries that the students write on their own and ones for which you choose the topic. Ask them to make lists like the ones Sei Shonagon includes in *The Pillow Book*. You may choose to make up your own list of topics or consider using one of Shonagon's themes that are not included in this anthology, such as "Depressing Things," "Elegant Things," "Annoying Things," "Things That Have Lost Their Power," "Surprising and Distressing Things," "Things Without Merit," "Things That Are Distant Though Near," and "Things That Are Near Though Distant." While completing this assignment, students should keep in mind the following questions: How does one go about writing a pillow book? What should be included? How is this form of journal writing distinct from a diary?

WWW For more information on Sei Shonagon and annotated Web links, see *World Literature Online* at bedfordstmartins.com/worldlit.

FURTHER READING

Gottlieb, Nanette. *Kanji Politics: Language Policy and Japanese Script*. 1995.
Kristeva, Tsvetana. "Murasaki Shikibu vs. Sei Shonagon: A Classical Case of Envy in Medi-Evil Japan," *Semiotica: Journal of the International Association for Semiotic Studies* 117, no. 2–4 (1997): 201–26.
Morris, Ivan. *The World of the Shining Prince: Court Life in Ancient Japan*. 1994.
Morris, Mark. "Sei Shonagon's Poetic Catalogues," *Harvard Journal of Asiatic Studies* 40, no. 1 (1980): 5–54.
Shikibu, Murasaki. *The Diary of Lady Murasaki*. Trans. Richard Bowring. 1996.
Willoquet-Maricondi, Paula. "Fleshing the Text: Greenaway's Pillow Book and the Erasure of the Body," *Postmodern Culture: An Electronic Journal of Interdisciplinary Criticism* 9, no. 2 (1999): 50.

MEDIA RESOURCES

WEB SITES

Sei Shonagon
www.tl.infi.net/~ddisse/shonagon.html
This page provides a biography of Sei Shonagon as well as a bibliography of both on-line and print sources, including links to translated passage from *The Pillow Book*.

Sei Shonagon
www.geocities.com/CollegePark/Bookstore/4817/
Users will find a helpful biography of Sei Shonagon at this site along with a works cited list.

Sei Shonagon
www.taleofmurasaki.com/shonagonpage.htm
Another biography, this one with links to further information about *The Pillow Book* and the empress Teishi.

MURASAKI SHIKIBU, LADY MURASAKI, *The Tale of Genji* (p. 1094)

WWW   For a quiz on *The Tale of the Genji,* see *World Literature Online* at bedfordst martins.com/worldlit.

Very little is known of the Japanese author known as Murasaki Shikibu, or Lady Murasaki. Her name, Murasaki, which she also gives to one of the characters in *The Tale of Genji,* is thought to be merely a nickname, so even the author's real name is likely lost to time. Although there are no answers about the circumstances of *The Tale of Genji's* composition, the book is considered to be not only the first Japanese novel but also the first novel *ever.* Evidence suggests that the book had been widely circulated by about 1025 and was immensely popular among Murasaki's contemporaries in Heian Japan.

It is very easy for modern audiences to think of the character Genji as a playboy or sexist character, hopping between one woman and the next with very little restraint. It is one of the challenges of teaching this work, however, to insure that students do not come away with this erroneous impression. The two obstacles that stand in the way of a clear and full understanding of the *The Tale of Genji* excerpts provided are an understandable lack of knowledge of ancient Japanese culture on the part of Westerners and the necessarily short length of the selections excerpted, which cannot supply the thematic picture of the work as a whole.

It is helpful to understand that Genji's lifestyle was in no way considered unusual in Heian Japan. In the period directly before the Heian, marriage was known as "*Tsuma* (wife) *Toi* (visiting) *Kon* (marriage)." A man would come in the evening to the house of a woman he was interested in and woo her with music and poetry. If she reciprocated, she would invite him in. It was acceptable for a man to have several visiting marriages at a time, and, if he chose to stop visiting one woman, she might choose to receive a new visitor. The woman and her family would raise any children born of these unions. However, during the Heian era, a system that resembles today's traditional marriage was introduced. Instead of simply visiting his lady, a man would take a formal wife, often for political reasons. Nonetheless, it was still not atypical for a man to have one formal wife and several visiting wives.

The short selections provided for *The Tale of Genji,* while integrally connected, tend to slightly obfuscate some of the issues relating to Prince Genji's various affairs, in that the long-term changes that take place throughout the novel in Genji can be easily overlooked just based on these. Although the younger Genji makes a number of regrettable mistakes, the Genji of Chapter 25 actively cares for and supports his loves, both past and present. He arranges a good marriage for Tamakazura (to whom he is himself attracted) and keeps company with the lady of the orange blossoms (in whom he has lost all romantic interest). Moreover, he remembers fondly the lady of the evening and admits to himself that he would accept the daughter that she bore him even if the girl were to turn up in "some outlandish guise." Genji may have been a thoughtless and idle lover in his youth, but the older Genji's thoughts and actions are of an entirely different nature.

Each time Genji communicates — whether in writing or in spoken words — with one of the objects of his affection, he and the lady offer one another short snippets of allusive poetry. Although it seems to interrupt the flow of the narrative at times, it is important not to devalue these poetic interludes, as they are an integral part of both the style and the content of the overall story. Do not give in to the temptation to merely skip over these two-line verses without reading them. Unlike some other authors, who include lines of poetry within the body of their narrative fiction and then explain those lines in prose directly after, Lady Murasaki allows her poetry to stand on its own. In Chapter 25, after the reader has been told that Genji spends the night with the orange blossom lady out of affection rather than sexual attraction, the lady says: "You honor the iris on the bank to which / No pony comes to taste of withered grasses?" That she is both honored and flattered by his willingness to spend time with her is expressed in her poem rather than stated explicitly in the prose text. To ignore the poetry as superfluous would be to lose out on the subtle interaction between Genji and this lady he cares for but for whom he has no attraction. This intricacy of detail in relations between men and women is one of the things for which *The Tale of Genji* is famous.

In some ways, *The Tale of Genji* does not fit very well into the broad context of world literature. Although its story is one about romance and court life, the subject of many works of prose and poetry before and since, the peculiarities of traditions in the Japanese Heian era and the relative isolation of the book's popularity to Japan alone set it apart from more directly influential works. However, *The Tale of Genji*'s themes, in-depth studies of character, and complex narrative style tie it indirectly to nineteenth-century and later Western literature, when the novel came into its own as an art form.

TEXT & CONTEXT

THE *WAKA*

Throughout *The Tale of Genji*, the characters communicate with one another not through traditional letters but through short, telling poems called *waka*, the most popular poetic form in the Heian period. The thirty-one syllable, five-line poems contain lines of either five or seven syllables in the sequence 5-7-5-7-7. The *waka* were used widely until the seventeenth century, when the shorter 5-7-5 haiku came into favor. In Heian culture, an educated person's sensibility was on display every time he or she composed a *waka*, as the poems were seen to convey a heightened emotional awareness. The indirect language of poetry was an excellent way to express feelings in the characteristically reserved Japanese society, and skill in writing and interpreting poetry were considered marks of intellectual and spiritual fortitude. Not only were the content and sensitive use of images noted and examined, but the handwriting was carefully scrutinized as well. Nearly eight hundred *waka* appear in *The Tale of Genji* and form a vital part of its structure and tone. The poems are intrinsically bound up with the novel's concept of *mono no aware*, or "sensitivity to things." Genji's skill with *waka* was exemplary, and both he and the women in the tale were constantly judged on their ability to write the poems.

HEIAN COURT CULTURE

The Heian time period spanned from 794 C.E., when the capital of Japan was moved to Kyoto, to 1185 C.E. Because the era was a peaceful one, the aristocrats of Kyoto, like those depicted in *The Tale of Genji*, had a great deal of leisure time. The high born were acutely sensitive to natural beauty and the pursuits of poetry, music, calligraphy, and elegant clothing. Other than a woman's hair, which should have been thick and longer than she was tall, Heian gentlemen were not chiefly interested in a woman's physical beauty. A gentleman was mostly interested in a woman of impeccable breeding and dress and one who was skilled at calligraphy and the crafting of sensitive and clever poems. As the first part of *The Tale of Genji* shows, male courtiers had plenty of time for pursuing women, as little work was involved in their main occupation of attending the emperor, and ladies-in-waiting were free to pursue amorous liaisons with the gentlemen at court as well.

IN THE CLASSROOM

I. WOMEN AND MEN IN *THE TALE OF GENJI*

Although *The Tale of Genji* deals with many subjects, one of its greatest themes is that of relations between men and women. Genji, unlike most of the literature in this time period, was both written by a woman and deals with a great number of women characters. To a modern audience, it might be peculiar that — rather than one of these extraordinarily characterized women — the main character is a man and that the author seems at times to appreciate women for the same qualities that her male characters value.

Discussion

1. In Chapter 2, "The Broom Tree," Genji and his companions discuss the merits and faults of various types of women and the benefits and dangers of becoming involved with them. None of the men seems to have quite the same standards for choosing an ideal mate. One man warns that a man should be wary of a woman with too much experience in the ways of the world, while another brings up the dangers of marrying a child-like wife who must constantly be trained. What is the point of this discussion?

Connections

1. Nowhere in literature are women characters present in such a great number and also in such depth as they are in *The Tale of Genji*. For this reason, it is both interesting and almost necessary to compare the piece with other works of literature on the basis of these women. Compare the characterizations of women in *The Tale of Genji* with any other work that explicitly characterizes women. A comparison of the women in *Genji* with the Wife of Bath in Chaucer's *Canterbury Tales* (p. 878), for example, could lead to a discussion of women's thoughts on marriage and obtaining an ideal man. The Wife of Bath discusses her five husbands in much the same merits-and-faults way that Genji and his friends discuss women. The talents of woman as storyteller and intellectual companion can be seen in a comparison between the women of *The Tale of Genji* and Shahrazad in *The Thousand and One Nights* (p. 435). A discussion of women's independence, capability of strategic and diplomatic thought, and, of course, thoughts on sex will emerge from a comparison of the women in *The Tale of the Genji* with the women of Aristophanes' *Lysistrata* (Book 1).

2. It will also be fruitful to compare *Genji* with other works written by women like *The Life of Margery Kempe* (p. 993), *The Lay of Chevrefoil* by Marie de France (p. 674), or Sappho's poetry (Book 1). The works of each of these women deal in some way with the relations of lovers. Margery Kempe marries, bears fourteen children, and then manages to convince her husband that they should no longer have sexual relations in the name of spirituality. *The Lay of Chevrefoil* epitomizes the courting machinations between men and women present in all Arthurian legends. Sappho's poems speak eloquently about love of men and women. How do their opinions differ? Do they have any commonalities? How might they differ from a male author's treatment of the same subject matter?

Writing

Ask students to write a short paper in response to one or more of the following:

1. During the discussion, one of the men speaks of the woman who is a sweet and accomplished maiden tucked away in an unexpected place. Although at one point Lady Murasaki characterizes the discussion as containing "a number of unconvincing points," at least half of the women Genji subsequently becomes involved with in the novel (including the heroine Murasaki) seem to be of this unexpectedly charming sort. Write

a paper about one or more of Genji's women in these selections. Do their personalities fit into the types of women discussed in Chapter 2? How or how not? What might the author be trying to get across by making the women conform to or deviate from the expectations of Genji and his companions? What about the male characters in *Genji*? Do they fit into any types? What about Genji makes him so attractive to all women and yet basically undesirable to them as a serious mate?

2. In Chapter 2 (The Broom Tree), Genji and his friend To no Chujo have a discussion about women and class. Drawing from that discussion, with reference to other sections of the text, analyze the importance of class in *The Tale of Genji*. Consider what makes class boundaries seem firm and what makes class somewhat flexible, and think about whether class roles for men are different than those for women.

3. A belief that disturbed spirits wandered forth to do great mischief was prevalent in the Heian period. After the Rokujo Lady — with whom Genji has had an affair — dies, her spirit is blamed for a great deal of Genji's misfortunes in love including the death of Yugao in Chapter 4. Based on your thinking about this "disturbed spirit motif," are we meant to see the Rokujo Lady's spirit as a literal presence? What does the recurrence of the spirit of this lady say about Genji's character?

Groups

1. Due to the sheer number of characters in *The Tale of Genji*, and the movement of Genji between social circles, it is often difficult for students to keep track of the relations between Genji, his friends, and his lovers. Separate students into groups, and assign each group a character (like Yugao, Tamakazura, To no Chujo). At the end of the time that you have given them, each group should be able to describe their character's relation to Genji and the other characters in the selection as well as summarize the plot elements in which their character was involved. Have each group give a five-minute presentation to the class about their character. The presentation doesn't have to be anything prepared or spectacular, as the idea is just to clarify the traits of each character in your students' minds.

II. ATTITUDES TOWARD FICTION IN *THE TALE OF GENJI*

At the end of Chapter 25, Genji and Tamakazura discuss books, particularly the illustrated romances loved by Tamakazura and Genji's wife, Murasaki. At first, Genji is of the opinion that the romances are both useless and even perhaps dangerous because of their lack of truth. However, he quickly reverses his argument, and, instead of deriding the romances, defends their value. Genji is aware here that his opinions stand in stark contrast with those he remembers expressing to Murasaki some years earlier. Then, he cautioned his wife against reading love stories to his daughter because "we could not want her to think them commonplace."

Discussion

1. Discuss with students the value and purpose of fiction. Encourage them to think about fiction as it is currently written as well as fiction as it "should be." Are novels merely a form of entertainment meant to amuse but of no greater importance? What do they make of the "dangerous" aspect of fiction that Genji describes? Some people today still view books as being dangerous, but they are more likely to point to the ideas contained within the books rather than the fact that the books describe events that are untrue as the source of the danger. Is there something drastically different between the fiction of today and the sort of books that Genji and Tamakazura are discussing, or is it our notions of danger that have changed?

Connections

1. Throughout fiction, poetry, essays, and the like, the value of the written word has been argued for many years. This argument is broader than just the confines of whether or what we should write. It also has bearing on what we should read, both academically and in our spare time. The implications of this line of thinking can be seen in almost any work you choose, be it in the medieval period or the modern. Though the characters or the narrator of a work may not explicitly state it, every written work contains an implicit argument for its own existence. See canto 2 of Dante's *Inferno* (p. 689) and the introduction to the First Day of Boccaccio's *Decameron* (p. 853) for examples of authors discussing writing and reading outright, but have students keep this idea in mind as they read any work, and return to it in your discussions.

2. Marlowe's *Doctor Faustus* (Book 3) presents a different view of the dangers of books than the ones Genji describes. At the opening of the play, Faustus laments that although he has studied nearly everything of academic interest, he still feels restless and, in a sense, empty. He decides that he will study the occult, and it eventually leads to his downfall and demise. How do these dangers compare? Is one of them more likely? How might they be prevented?

Writing

Ask students to write a short paper in response to one or more of the following:

1. Because *The Tale of Genji* is a work of fiction, it is not necessarily true that Lady Murasaki's opinions coincide with those of her characters in this matter. Using the passage at the end of Chapter 25 (Genji and Tamakazura discussing books) as well as other selections from the text where applicable, argue whether or not the book suggests any overarching theory of the intrinsic value of fiction. If so, what is this theory? Do you think Lady Murasaki held a different theory of fiction for men and women? Does she make any distinctions between types of fiction? between fiction and poetry? How does *The Tale of Genji* as a work of fiction fit into the theories proposed by Lady Murasaki, Tamakazura, or Genji?

2. Although *The Tale of Genji* is primarily written in prose, it is interspersed with the short *waka* poems that Genji and his lovers use to communicate with one another. Write a paper about the interplay between poetry and prose in the narrative. Do the poems add to the complexity to the overall story or the meanings of particular poems in relation to the prose plot that surrounds them?

Groups

1. Divide students into several groups, and have each group write a short prose message. Ideally, this message will contain complex or abstract concepts, much like those that Genji tries to convey to his lovers. Then, ask students to write a version of their message in the 5-7-5-7-7 format of the *waka* poem. The goal here is to satisfy the requirements of the poem while accurately conveying the message. Students should not worry if this seems like a difficult task. They should assume that the group that receives their message will have to do some interpreting in order to properly understand it. Next, have groups exchange their *waka* poem messages. The receiving groups should try to summarize, or reword, the *waka* in simple prose language that is as short and to the point as possible. Finally, have groups write their *waka* on the board along with both their own prose version of the message and the summary that the receiving group wrote. Compare the two prose versions. Did the receiving groups correctly interpret their mes-

sages? If not, where did the problems lie? Discuss the difficulties inherent in using such a relatively restrictive form of poetry as one's primary means of communication, particularly in matters of love. Ask students why they think Genji and his lovers use this method of correspondence if misunderstandings are likely to result? Is there any evidence in the text that any of the *waka* are misinterpreted?

BEYOND THE CLASSROOM

RESEARCH & WRITING

1. Using *The Tale of Genji* and *The Tale of the Heike* as primary texts, research an aspect of the attitudes toward love in Heian-era Japan. For example, you could address the implications of the formalities of conduct that were observed or trace the history of the *waka* poem as a form of communication in the matter of love. You might also want to compare the lives of women and men or discuss the distinction between married and single life in the Heian court. Do you think *The Tale of Genji* is at all times in agreement with the traditional notion of love in the Heian era, or did Lady Murasaki intend to make an ironic or critical comment on her time?

2. It is known that Lady Murasaki was a Buddhist. However, some critics have suggested that the notion of good and evil in *The Tale of Genji* sometimes seems to correspond more with a Confucian morality. Research either of these two prominent Japanese philosophies or a broader range of Asian philosophical systems, and make a case for whether the morality in *Genji* leans toward one of these systems more than another. Alternatively, you may research these philosophies for the purpose of contrasting the philosophy in *The Tale of Genji* with that in Sei Shonagon's *Pillow Book*. How do the ideas presented in *The Tale of Genji* or *The Pillow Book* agree or disagree with the philosophical systems that you have researched? What is similar (or different) in the ways that these two works represent ideas of morality?

Projects

1. Several versions of scrolls and paintings depicting the story of *The Tale of Genji* can be found on-line with a simple search on Google or another search engine. For example, images of the eighteenth-century Genji hand scroll can be found on Dartmouth's "Screens and Scrolls" Web page (www.dartmouth.edu/~arth17/Genji.index.html). Either together in class or as an outside assignment, have students view these scrolls or other artistic renderings of *The Tale of Genji* that you find on-line. Discuss or have students discuss the content and/or formal elements of the various pieces. Can they identify the scrolls that depict the events of the selections they read? What class(es) of people are being represented in the various images, and what clues are we given about the social status of the people? More artistically minded students might also want to comment on the artists' usage of lines, perspective, color, and other formal elements.

WWW   For additional information on Lady Murasaki and annotated Web links, see *World Literature Online* at bedfordstmartins.com/worldlit.

FURTHER READING

Bargen, Doris G. "Yugao: A Case of Spirit Possession in *The Tale of Genji*," *Mosaic: A Journal for the Interdisciplinary Study of Literature* 19, no. 3 (1986): 15–24.
Japan 2001 Waka Web site. http://www.shef.ac.uk/japan2001/
Kamens, Edward. *Approaches to Teaching Murasaki Shikibu's the Tale of Genji.* 1994.

McMullen, James. Genji gaiden: *The Origins of Kumazawa Banzan's Commentary on* The Tale of Genji. 1991.

Miner, Earl. "Japanese and Western Images of Courtly Love," *Yearbook of Comparative and General Literature* 15 (1966): 174–79.

Murasaki Shikibu. *The Diary of Lady Murasaki.* Trans. Richard Bowring. 1999.

Murasaki Shikibu: Genji Monogatari. Dir. Gisaburo Sugii. Asahi Shimbunsha Japan. 1987.

MEDIA RESOURCES

VIDEO

The Genji Scrolls Reborn
60 min., 2002 (Films for the Humanities & Sciences)
Designated national treasures, the picture scrolls of *The Tale of Genji* were made in the twelfth century, one hundred years after Murasaki Shikibu wrote her classic story of Buddhist sensibilities and courtly romance in Japan's Heian period. This program combines readings from chapters corresponding to the paintings with a look at their meticulous restoration in order to rediscover an enduring literary masterpiece. Digital technology and painstaking reproductions allow the ancient pictures to be enjoyed in their original splendor, vividly bringing the world's oldest novel to life.

The Tale of Genji
110 min., 1995 (Films for the Humanities & Sciences)
This animated adaptation of Murasaki Shikibu's epic work narrates the turbulent life of a nobleman who is made a commoner. (In Japanese with subtitles.)

The Tale of Genji
60 min., 1997 (Films for the Humanities & Sciences)
Elegant and lyrical, *The Tale of Genji* — written by Murasaki Shikibu, considered by many to be the world's first novelist — predates the seminal *Don Quixote* by an incredible six hundred years. This extraordinarily beautiful program traces the plot, which centers on the romantic relationships of the noble hero Genji, through the panels of a series of illustrated hand scrolls dating from the early twelfth century. The program explains both Genji's adventures and the visual effects created by the paintings, decorated paper, and calligraphy of the scrolls, making accessible to Western audiences a formative work of Japanese culture and one of the milestones of world literature.

WEB SITES

Art and Culture — Murasaki Shikibu
www.artandculture.com/cgi-bin/WebObjects/ACLive.woa/wa/artist?id+1355
This site offers a brief biographical introduction to the life and times of Murasaki Shikibu, background information on the early novelist, and lists a number of links to other useful sources.

Diaries of Court Ladies in Old Japan
digital.library.upenn.edu/women/omori/court/court.html
Read here the full e-texts of this classic 1920 volume of translations of the diaries of Sarashina, Murasaki Shikibu, and Izumi Shikubu, with an introduction by the celebrated American poet Amy Lowell.

The Heroic Quest: The Tale of Genji
www.faculty.de.gcsu.edu/~dvess/ids/2305/lover.htm
This wonderful site provides links to all aspects of *The Tale of Genji.*

Murasaki Shikibu
www.tl.infi.net/~ddisse/murasaki.html
This page offers a biography of Murasaki as well as a bibliography of on-line and print secondary sources.

Murasaki Shikibu
Womenshistory.about.com/cs/murasaki/
This page lists several useful links to sites devoted to Murasaki, including e-texts of her writings, a summary of *The Tale of Genji,* and several critical essays about her works.

The Tale of Genji
mcel.pacificu.edu/as/students/genji/homepage.html
This site provides a summary of Murasaki's famous novel, brief character descriptions, an overview of the culture of the period, and a biography of the author.

The Tale of the Heike (p. 1154)

WWW   For a quiz on *The Tale of the Heike,* see *World Literature Online* at
bedfordstmartins.com/worldlit.

No one author is credited with writing *The Tale of the Heike,* and tradition holds that it was probably compiled from a number of different oral sources. The accepted date of the authorized version of the tale is 1371, but it is theorized that it was first written down sometime between 1198–1221. *The Tale of the Heike* is an example of a genre known as *gunki monogatari,* or military tales, which were usually recited by traveling blind monks called *biwa-hoshi* who accompanied their recitation by playing the lute. The tale glorifies military valor, promoting the values of loyalty to one's lord above all else, self-sacrifice, asceticism, and self-control, which probably helped shape some of the military ethics of its time.

The Tale of the Heike was recorded in the late fourteenth century, but its story tells the tale of a great war between two clans at the end of the Heian era of Japanese history. As such, the story is set in the world of Murasaki Shikibu and Sei Shonagon but is told from a significantly later perspective. Don't hesitate to emphasize this perspective when teaching *The Tale of the Heike;* this work will not read like either *The Tale of Genji* or *The Pillow Book,* both of which were written nearly four hundred years before. This does not mean, of course, that comparisons should not be made between the three works, only that students should keep in mind that the author of *The Tale of the Heike* was the product of a later era in Japanese history who was looking back on the origins of their culture.

While reading *The Tale of the Heike* with students, be sure to point out the major motifs present in the tale: a sense of history and the conflict of the old values with the new, the rise of the warrior class, and the religious underpinnings of Buddhism.

TEXT & CONTEXT

SAMURAI
In the Heian period, samurai, then pronounced "saburai," were not part of the regular imperial army. Rather, they were hired soldiers employed by the emperor or the aristocratic

clans exclusively to suppress rebellions. In contrast to the regular army, who were largely con-scripted and had to provide their own supplies, weapons, and armor, the samurai were paid and their equipment was provided for them. Originally, these warriors were farmers — members of regional clans who initially armed themselves to defend against the magistrates sent by the emperor to govern and collect taxes on their lands. These regional clans eventu-ally gained political as well as military power. After the Heiji and Gempei wars, in which the samurai played parts, the samurai gained control of the government. Although Minamoto no Yoritomo was ostensibly the victor of the Gempei war over his rival Taira no Kiyomori, he was merely a figurehead as emperor. The samurai, under a form of martial law, ruled Japan. Samurai were known for their exceptional prowess and military skill. The unwritten samurai code, called *bushido* or "way of the warrior," dictated that a samurai must uphold the virtues of loyalty, courage, honesty, compassion, honor, and respect for life. However, the samurai became much more than warriors. By the late Middle Period, the influence of Zen Buddhism could be seen in the samurai class. In addition to military training, samurai cul-tivated the arts of writing, calligraphy, philosophy, and painting. Many of the arts still prac-ticed today in Japan, like the tea ceremony, originated with the samurai.

BLACKENED TEETH

Tooth blackening, or *ohagura*, was a Japanese coming-of-age custom that dated from about the tenth century. Although at first confined almost exclusively to women, in the thirteenth century, tooth blackening spread to aristocratic men, including those of the samurai class, like young Atsumori in *The Tale of the Heike*. In the Heian era, tooth black-ening was primarily cosmetic, although it would regain greater significance in later years. It was believed that blackened teeth increased one's appeal to the opposite sex and also that the practice promoted healthy teeth. In married women, blackened teeth were sometimes seen as a symbol of faithfulness and obedience to their husbands. The tooth-blackening mixture was more of a lacquer than a dye, made by soaking hot iron or iron filings in sake or tea. This produced a liquid paste that, when oxidized, turned black and could be paint-ed on the teeth with a brush. By the eighteenth century, men were banned from blacken-ing their teeth, but the custom persisted in married women until the end of the nineteenth century.

IN THE CLASSROOM

Discussion

1. *The Tale of the Heike* centers on the rise and fall of the Heike clan. It will be helpful to take note of the way that the narrator describes the events that unfold. What is the pre-dominant mood of the work? How does the narrator feel about each of the characters? Which characters are sympathetic? Can you account for the sense of futility that per-meates some of the scenes?

2. Call students' attention to the notions of impermanence that are present throughout the narrative. When is this idea expressed, and what form does that expression take? How does a sense of the transient nature of life affect the way that the characters live their lives?

3. In the section "The Death of Atsumori," Naozane captures Atsumori, "a boy just the age of [his] own son," and finding it "easy to imagine the sorrow of this young lord's father if he were to hear that the boy had been slain," Naozane wishes to spare him. Why does Naozane ultimately kill Atsumori, and how does he feel about it afterward? What value systems are coming into conflict for the warrior?

4. Discuss the character of the Imperial Lady as presented in the final chapters of our selection. How does she conduct herself? What is the source of her profound sorrow? Why is she embarrassed to have the Retired Emperor see her in peasant garb? What is the importance of their conversation in "The Matter of the Six Paths"?

Connections

1. Religion is a prominent feature of *The Tale of the Heike,* with the final words of the section "The Death of the Imperial Lady" referring directly to the beliefs of a sect of Buddhism known as "Pure Land Buddhism." Other Japanese works of the Middle Period that are widely considered Buddhist classics are *The Tale of Genji* (p. 1094), *The Pillow Book* (p. 1063), and the *Man'yoshu* poems. Compare the spirituality in these works with that in *The Tale of the Heike.* Do all of these works share the same religious sensibility? How do the belief systems seem to compare?

Writing

Ask students to write a short paper in response to one or more of the following:

1. Three of the passages excerpted in the anthology deal explicitly with death: "The Death of Kiyomori," "The Death of Atsumori," and "The Death of the Imperial Lady." Write a paper discussing the attitude toward death in *The Tale of the Heike,* using evidence from these three sections. You may wish to compare the way each of the characters dies, to discuss under what situations characters are not afraid of death, or whether there is any connection between the attitude characters in the narrative have about death and their attitude about becoming a monk or nun.

2. With reference to the selections from Chapters I and VI, analyze the character of Kiyomori. You may wish to argue whether his death is a fitting one, how his character traits affect his clan, or whether his character seems to have changed over the course of the sections you have read. You may also choose to contrast Kiyomori's life and death with what they have read of the life and death of Atsumori.

BEYOND THE CLASSROOM

RESEARCH & WRITING

1. Many of the works in the anthology portray warrior cultures. With reference to *The Tale of the Heike* and at least one other primary work, students should construct a paper detailing the nature of warrior ethics in the Middle Ages. Reading *The Tale of the Heike* alongside *Beowulf* (p. 482), *The Song of Roland* (p. 546), or *The Iliad* (Book 1) will yield fruitful discussions, though other combinations are possible. Do different warrior cultures share common or comparable ethics? If so, how do you account for the similarity? Students may also choose to address this topic by writing about specific warriors in terms of the ethics to which they subscribe. They should keep in mind the ultimate fate of these warriors. Does it matter whether a desire to stick to their ethics or a renunciation of their system of values is one of the causes of their downfall?

2. The section "The Sea Bass" begins with a mythological tale that explains the continual good fortune of the Heike clan. Ask students to write a paper addressing myth and/or superstition in *The Tale of the Heike.* As there exist many excellent critical treatments of mythology and superstition, students should reference at least two secondary sources in support of their argument. Have them consider the role that myth and superstition play in the tale, both in terms of the culture that is presented and the literary project that is undertaken. Must the myths be taken literally to retain their power? Alternatively, stu-

dents may wish to tackle the role of myth and superstition in Japanese literature of the Middle Period or to compare myth and superstition role in a number of works you have read like *The Tale of the Heike* and another work like *The Tale of Genji* (p. 1094) or *The Aeneid* (Book 1).

Project

1. *Bushido*, the samurai code, was a critical element in the workings of Japan in the Middle Period. Divide students into two groups, and ask them to undertake a significant amount of research on bushido in order to prepare a short, argumentative presentation. The first group should focus on explaining how bushido would be a valuable asset to the military. At your option, students need not confine their discussion to the medieval Japanese military but could instead show how a *bushido* sort of code might benefit any military. The second group, on the other hand, should argue that bushido might be detrimental to society. This group should keep in mind the broader implications of such a code on society as a whole, particularly if that society comes under martial law. Have both groups make sound arguments and be prepared to provide concrete examples to illustrate their points.

FURTHER READING

Blomberg, Catharina. *The Heart of the Warrior: Origins and Religious Background of the Samurai System in Feudal Japan.* 1994.

Cormier, Raymond. "Twelfth-Century Heroic and Courtly Narratives: Cross-Cultural Perspectives from Homer's Troy, Medieval Japan and France," *Intercultural Communication Studies* 5 no. 2 (2002): 99–105.

Shirane, Haruo, and Tomi Suzuki, eds. *Inventing the Classics: Modernity, National Identity, and Japanese Literature.* 2001.

MEDIA RESOURCES

WEB SITES

The Tale of the Heike
www.meijigakuin.ac.jp/~watson/heike/heike.html
Michael Watson's (faculty of international studies, Meiji Gakuin University) page on *The Tale of the Heike* that provides information on the narrative style of the *Heike* and its influence on later Japanese art and drama, a short explanation of the rivalry between the Taira and Minamoto clans, and information on translations of the work.

Warrior Aesthetics: The Tale of the Heike and its Period
www.suntory.co.jp/sma/english/exhibition/20020910_genpei/
An interesting page about an exhibit of art based on *The Tale of the Heike* that took place at the Suntory Museum of Art.

ZEAMI MOTOKIYO, *Atsumori* (p. 1180)

The extreme compression and understatement of the *Nō* text, the lack of anything that we would think of as dramatic development in the action, and the reliance on nonverbal means like dance, costume, and music all make this kind of drama rather difficult to appreciate from the printed page. Perhaps the best that can be done is to make students aware of the sorts of things that are happening on stage at different points and the kinds of effects they are meant to produce. Once they have a sense of this, they should begin to gain some hint of the deeper resonance of the ideas and images expressed in such condensed form in the text.

In the beginning section, the waki, or second actor, enters and delivers a brief monologue that states the theme and basic situation of the play. This section is mostly sung in a slow tempo. At one point, the actor has to represent traveling a great distance, and the fact that he is required to somehow suggest this while actually taking only a few small steps is typical of the whole aesthetic approach in Nō. In the next section, the reapers enter, among them one who turns out to be the ghost of Atsumori. The *shite*, or main actor, who wears no mask at this point, plays him. This section is chanted alternately by actor and chorus and is highly atmospheric, with a more regular beat than the opening song. Then comes a section of spoken dialogue between the two principal actors. You may want to note the extended discussion of flutes and their music: This will prove significant later for the story of Atsumori's death. There follows another sung section in which it becomes clear to the audience (though not yet to the priest) who the young reaper actually is. The priest prays for the young reaper as requested, and the chorus concludes the first act with a solemn, emotional chant.

Before the second act begins, the *Aikyogen* (*Kyogen* actor) appears and explains the story in plainer language. As noted by the translator, this interlude is not considered part of the play's permanent text, and its wording varies from performance to performance. There is normally no music in it, and the dialogue can have comic elements. One version for the present play has the *Aikyogen* in conversation with the *waki*, still playing the priest, who asks to be told the story of the place. The *Aikyogen* tells the story of Atsumori and Kumagai, and says that he has heard Kumagai is now a priest who prays for Atsumori, but he doesn't believe his prayers are sincere and boasts that he will kill him if he ever sees him. The priest then reveals his identity; the *Aikyogen* is flustered, but Kumagai reassures him that he has come only to pray for Atsumori's soul. In modern performances, the language of the interlude, though still archaic, is much closer to modern Japanese, and, unlike the text proper, is readily understood by the audience.

In the second act, the main actor reappears masked and costumed as a young warrior. He announces himself to the priest as Atsumori, and the priest tells him that he has already prayed for him ceaselessly. At this point, the two former enemies are essentially reconciled. But Atsumori's ghost, to clear its karma, must still relive the circumstances of its death. In doing so, it will experience a last twinge of desire for revenge. This comes at the very end of the play. The *shite* performs dances in conjunction with the narration leading up to the battle scene. Most strikingly, for a warrior play, he does an elegant dance to flute music, reflecting the young Atsumori's artistic nature and the flute he had carried into battle, which Kumagai had heard from his camp the night before. The chorus and Atsumori take turns narrating, but the chorus quickly takes over the narration of the final combat, as the *shite* plays it out with increasingly vigorous movements. Although on stage the impact of physical movement is definitely greatest here, students will hardly fail to note that the scenes evoked by the words alone in this entire final section are, in their understated way, quite vivid and moving in themselves. The *shite* then mimes, in rapid succession, the death of Atsumori, the rising of his ghost to strike his enemy, and the final reconciliation. There is no real denouement, reflecting Nō's preference for "ending quickly."

TEXT & CONTEXT

Zen Aesthetics

The peculiar values of the Nō, like much of what we think of as most typical of Japanese culture, owe a lot to the form of Buddhism called Zen, which was a dominant force in

Japanese life from the twelfth century on. Most forms of Buddhism emphasize various methods of detaching oneself from illusion and suffering to achieve a state of enlightenment; Zen in its pure form has a violent aversion to any set method, seeing routine itself as being the greatest enemy of enlightenment. Instead, it stresses spontaneous, irrational acts that break through ordinary perception to reveal the mystery of things. This aspect of Zen had a great appeal to writers and artists of the Beat generation in America; in traditional Japanese art and culture, however, the Zen sensibility is most often subtly woven into what seems almost its opposite: an extreme ceremoniousness in which everything is done according to prescribed forms. The example most often cited is the Japanese tea ceremony. Here, the elements and their arrangement are all specified in minute detail. Yet without the appearance of the unpredictable, the irrational, the asymmetrical, which cannot be specified by rule, the ceremony would be regarded as incomplete and lacking in true beauty.

So it is with the *Nō*. The stage, costumes, masks, and instruments, the functions of each of the performers: All are fixed down to the smallest detail, and yet the performance must convey a sense of freedom and surprise, by means the performers can only discover spontaneously, within the performance itself.

WORDS, MUSIC, AND DANCE IN *NŌ*

Modern commentators on the *Nō* often say that dance is its central element. Zeami himself says, in his writings on the theater, that word and voice are the driving force from which the music and the dance both emerge. This difference of perception probably reflects the fact that modern audiences — even in Japan — without special study cannot really understand the archaic language of the *Nō*. The music clearly serves the story, and since gestures and movements are what most immediately convey the action to the modern audience (who usually know the story already), they are easily seen as being central. The climax of the play, as we have seen, is indeed dominated by dance and mime, though the words in this part are not negligible and reach a poetic climax here as well. In any case, unspoken elements clearly have a far greater importance in *Nō* than in most forms of Western drama. But this fits in with the general values of Japanese poetry itself: What is left unsaid is regarded as being at least as important as what is said.

STRUCTURE AND RHYTHM

A typical dramatic structure in the West consists of exposition, complication, climax, and denouement. In *Nō* drama the structure is seen as tripartite: There is an *introduction (Jo)*, an *exposition (Ha)*, and a *climax (Kyu)*. These terms, however, refer more to the tempo of the action than to its content. They are in fact originally musical terms and are applied not only to the work as a whole, but to each part of it, down to the individual phrase or movement. Everything follows the same curve: first, slow and tentative *(Jo)*, then faster and more measured *(Ha)*, and finally very fast *(Kyu)*. Once a *Jo-Ha-Kyu* cycle is completed, it is followed by an interval of emptiness or silence *(Ma)*. This is considered to be very important. The value of empty space or silence, in Western art, comes mostly from its setting off important shapes, words, or sounds. In *Nō*, these values are nearly reversed: The movements, the masks and costumes, and the sounds of chanting and music make us more deeply aware of the spaces and silences they frame. These, in the Buddhist view, best represent the inexpressibly profound reality of things.

IN THE CLASSROOM

Discussion

1. In the first act, the young reaper, who is Atsumori's ghost in disguise, asks his enemy, now a priest, to pray for him. One could imagine that a similar situation in a Western

play might result in the priest praying for his former enemy without intending to, and then being bound by his action later. Ask students how the action in the present play differs from this. Is the sense of drama diminished by such a treatment? Are there qualities that compensate for the lack of "complication" or suspense?

2. Have students find passages in the play in which Atsumori and Kumagai speak briefly in turn, completing each other's thoughts. As a class, discuss the following question: What major theme of the play is conveyed or reinforced by having the two main characters do this?

3. What do students see as the significance of Atsumori's ghost's appearance at the beginning of the play as one of the reapers? What associations are the rustic setting and the flute-playing intended to convey?

Connections

1. Compare the account of Atsumori's death given in the play with its source in *The Tale of Heike* (p. 1165). How do the styles of the two accounts differ? Does Zeami omit any important details of the original story? Does he add any that are not in the original? Do the two accounts on the whole have a similar effect?

Writing

Ask students to write a short paper in response to one or more of the following:

1. In the second act, the ghost of Atsumori says "It is to clear the karma of my waking life that I am come here in visible form before you." Discuss the notion of karma as it seems to operate in this play. What is it that prevents Atsumori's spirit from attaining peace? Compare European notions of spirits who cannot rest, like the ghost in Shakespeare's *Hamlet*. Is the notion of karma basically identical to the notion of sin? If not, how do they differ?

2. Trace the different images in the play that evoke the transience or impermanence of life. Which of these images seem most familiar from other literature you have read? Which seem different? Relate these differences to aspects of the Buddhist conception of life. How does the Buddhist view of life's transience resemble or differ from the Christian, the pagan, or other views?

BEYOND THE CLASSROOM

RESEARCH & WRITING

1. *Nō* was by far the most admired and imitated form of non-Western drama in the West during the twentieth century. W. B. Yeats, Bertolt Brecht, Paul Claudel, and Thornton Wilder were only a few of the writers who either wrote whole plays based on the *Nō* or incorporated aspects of its dramaturgy into their works. Have students familiarize themselves with some of these works and with Western writings (like those of Ezra Pound) on the *Nō*. Then, have them write an essay speculating on why this kind of drama was so appealing in the West.

2. Have students study examples of traditional Japanese ink painting, Japanese gardening, pottery, or other arts associated with the Zen tradition. They should then write a paper discussing the use of empty space, asymmetry, and "incomplete" elements in any or all of these arts, comparing it to the use of similar elements in *Nō* drama.

Projects

1. Invite students to collaborate on writing or improvising a *Kyogen* interlude for the play in a style that would appeal to a contemporary American audience. Their interlude must explain the basic story behind the play's action and may have either one or several characters. They may freely use anachronisms, jokes, slang, and non-Japanese elements. They may also try this kind of exercise with some well-known dramatic story from the Western tradition, like the story of Macbeth from Shakespeare, the stories of Adam and Eve or Noah's Ark from the Bible, or a story from Greek or other mythology. The story should be familiar but remote from modern life so that it could benefit from such a lighter interlude.

FURTHER READING

Leiter, S., and Ortolani, B. *Zeami and the Nō Theatre in the World.* 1998.
O'Neill, P. G. *A Guide to Noh.* 1953.
Pound, Ezra, and Ernest Fenollosa. *The Classic Noh Theater of Japan.* 1959.

MEDIA RESOURCES

VIDEO

Japanese History and Literature (552–1868)
160 min., 1996 (Annenberg/CPB Multimedia Collection)
Developed to provide background on Japanese history and literature for instructors of world history courses, this new series is also a valuable teaching resource. Covering the years 552 to 1868, the programs and guide provide an excellent overview of a fascinating time for this culture and its notable works of literature. Produced by Columbia University's Project on Asia in the Core Curriculum of Schools and Colleges. Integrates key historical themes with the literature of the time. Features renowned specialists on Japan from Columbia University.

WEB SITES

Atsumori Learning Site
http://www.glopac.org/Jparc/Atsumori/atsumori.htm
This site includes translations of Japanese works and biographies of their authors. There is also an interactive text of Atsumori.

GENERAL MEDIA RESOURCES

VIDEO

Classical Japan and the Tale of Genji (552–1185)
45 min., 1996 (Annenberg/CPB Multimedia Collection)
This program focuses on the Japanese genius for deliberate cultural borrowing; elements borrowed from China at this time include the centralized political state, Buddhism, Confucianism, and a written script. The evolution of *waka* poetry and prose demonstrates how the Japanese adapted the written script to their own spoken language and cultural tastes. Also discussed are the literary contributions of women during the height of Japanese court culture.

Japanese Literature
2 tapes, 28 min. each, 1976 (Insight Media)
Featuring readings from major works, this set traces the development of Japanese poetry and prose. It takes viewers from the Tokugawa period to modern times, exploring the effect of seclusion on Japanese writers, the changes that took place when the country was once again opened to the world, and the changes in Japanese literature during the modernization period.

Medieval Japan and Buddhism in Literature (1185–1600)
45 min., 1996 (Annenberg/CPB Multimedia Collection)
The warfare and disruption that characterized the feudal era in Japanese history set the context for this program. Similarities and differences between medieval Japan and medieval Europe — in political structure, bonds between warriors, and the importance of religion — are discussed. Selections from Essays in Idleness, Account of My Hut, and Nō drama demonstrate the resonance of Buddhism in this period's literature.

Ran
160 min., 1985 (IMDB)
Akira Kurisawa's great film. Although it is an adaptation of *King Lear,* its setting is medieval Japan and is about an aging warlord named Hidetora and his samurai sons.

Samurai Japan
48 min., 1996 (Films for the Humanities & Sciences)
From their ascension to power in the thirteenth century to the unconditional surrender of Japan at the end of World War II, the samurai, with their code of virtue and discipline, created a society that prized one's honor over one's life. In this program, scholars discuss the unique influence that this created and the impact of the samurai on Japan's institutions and history, including the role of women in political alliances. Also discussed is Japan's shift from feudalism to a bureaucratic and cosmopolitan society, symbolically ruled by the emperor and administered by shoguns.

Samurai Warrior
50 min., 1999 (A&E Video)
From their ancient origins in feudal Japan to the terrifying fighters of Hollywood blockbusters, here is the story of the legendary warriors known as samurai.

Shogun: Supreme Samurai
50 min., 2001 (A&E Video)
Providing history and vital backgrounds on some of Japan's greatest shoguns, this video is a glimpse at Japan's medieval history.

WEB SITES

Internet East Asian History Sourcebook
www.fordham.edu/halsall/eastasia/eastasiasbook.html
A premiere Internet source on East Asian studies created at Fordham University, the Internet East Asian History Sourcebook is a premiere site for information on the history, culture, and literature of Asian culture, both ancient and modern. Excellent links.

Recommended Sources on Premodern Japan
www.amherst.edu/~pwcaddeau/pwc_bib_premod.html#THEATREandDRAMA
This site created at Amherst College is a great place to begin researching early Japanese religion, literature, culture, and history in general, and Nō theater in particular. It lists a wide variety of links to primary and secondary sources available both online and in print.

AUDIO

Living Biographies of Religious Leaders
8 tapes, 11:25 hrs. (Blackstone Audiobooks)
This program presents the lives of twenty great founders and leading advocates of the world's foremost religions. Here are the historical facts and legends associated with these forceful personalities who have inspired and influenced humankind through the centuries. Presented are Jesus Christ, Moses, Isaiah, Zoroaster, Buddha, Confucius, John the Baptist, Paul, Muhammad, Francis of Assisi, John Huss, Luther, Loyola, Calvin, George Fox, Swedenborg, Wesley, Brigham Young, Mary Baker Eddy, and Gandhi.

Book 3
The Early Modern World
1450–1650

AFRICA:
EPIC AND EMPIRE IN MALI

Sunjata (p. 21)

WWW   For a quiz on the *Sunjata*, see *World Literature Online* at
bedfordstmartins.com/worldlit.

Sunjata is believed to be the founder of the Mali empire. His story, one of the great
myths of West Africa, is of both literary and historic importance and continues to be told
today. The epic of Sunjata has figured in the repertoire of Mande bards since at least the fourteenth century and now appears in written form as well. Although there is little physical evidence to corroborate his existence because of the many versions of his life, historians generally believe in his existence. However, the legend is interesting mainly because of its literary
aspects, not as historical relic.

Because it is an oral epic, it is important to pay attention to the ways the teller — in this
case Bamba Suso — situates himself historically and culturally. The central story of *Sunjata*
is the same in different versions, but each storyteller manipulates and creatively retells the
tale both to suit his audience and their needs and to better reflect his own situation. So,
embedded in the tale are important markers that reveal the teller and his specific location.
From the beginning of the tale in this version we learn: "It is I, Bamba Suso, who am talking." Similarly, we are introduced to the teller's location and the genealogy of the teller and
the tale. This type of situation helps gain the listener's — and the reader's — trust and sets
the stage for the cultural narrative that follows. Direct your students to look for the other
genealogical narratives that follow and to consider what these markers tell the audience.

In order to understand the narrative, it is important to look for the cultural directives
throughout and for the ways the narrator distinguishes this hero from the people around
him. Sunjata is not an ordinary man; although he is the founder of the Mali empire, he is not
typical of his people. Through investigating his individuality and his exceptionality, readers
and listeners can better understand their own cultural expectations. From his parental origin to his strength of character and eventual physical and mental prowess, Sunjata stands
out, and his energetic spirit as a leader is called forth in wonder and admiration. At the same
time, it is necessary to remind students that this is a living story — an oral epic — and so the
history it enfolds is not rigid but changing, and the notion and expectations of a hero reflect
the contemporary society as well as the original one.

The legend of *Sunjata* and the people associated with it are the originators of the land,
family, and political system still in place, and people look to the legend for reminders of their
own lineage and access to power. Because of this, it helps to encourage students to look for
layering of meaning and for its meaning as a conglomeration of cultural beliefs, desires, and
practices.

TEXT & CONTEXT

THE GRIOT

The French word *griot* is used to describe members of a hereditary caste of bards, workers in words and music. Griots are born into their caste and their place in that caste but can

rise within it based on individual merit. The most prestigious group, the *jalo*, is well-versed in political history, royal genealogy, and praise names. Its performances are accompanied on the *kora*, a 21-stringed harp; the lute; on the *bulo*, a xylophone with gourd resonators fixed underneath the keys; or on the *kontingo*, a small, 3-stringed plucked lute. Historically, the *jalo* (who attended on kings) and the *mansa griot* (who attended on kings and the court) were at the top of their profession. Below the jalo are the *danno*-jalo, or the hunters' griots, who attend on the caste of hunters. The *finolu* attend on a *sheriff*, or Moslem scholar descended from the Prophet or Companion of the Prophet, recite family history and religious history from the *Qur'an*, and are accompanied on a small drum. At the bottom of the hierarchy is the *mbo* jalo, a light entertainer unattached to a patron who sings, tells stories, dances, and amuses audiences. Originally, griots were attached to a particular family and were supported by that family. However, since colonial times, this relationship has changed and families are no longer able to support their griots. Although still linked to particular families, griots have been forced to fend for themselves, selling their entertainment at public functions like weddings and child namings. Griot performances have also changed: Formerly, performances followed a particular order, so the account of the host's family history began with an account of the ancestor who was connected to the *Sunjata* epic, then moved to more recent times. Now, the griot provides more entertainment than history, and the focus is on singing songs and reciting praises rather than historical narration. The audience has also changed, from elderly aristocrats to ordinary people.

HIERARCHY OF POWER IN MANDE SOCIETY

Mandean society is both patrilineal and age-based and follows the principle of *fa-siya*, which places into power the oldest son of the oldest son (who is not necessarily the oldest person). This system is represented from the family structure to the larger village and clan structures. The most immediate reproduction of the principle is the individual family, in which the *lu-tigi*'s ("household head") duties include the economic and social affairs of those committed to his charge, usually the family members in his compound but sometimes distant relatives also living there temporarily. Each compound is based on family structure and has a *lu-tigi*, whether or not he is involved in the political structure outside the compound. At the village level, authority is shared by two officeholders, one with political and one with religious credentials. The *dugi-tigi* (political chief or earth-village master) is originally associated with the power struggle in a legend relating to the mythical charter of the village. The *dugu-kolo-tigi* (ritual chief or earth-surface master) serves a ritualistic function and is the spiritual mediator between local earth spirits and the village; he maintains a balanced relationship through occult activities. The district, or *kafo/jamana*, is made up of several villages (often eight or more) and is presided over by the titular head of a lineage. The district chief, or *jamana-tigi*, is the senior man in the royal lineage of the district and rules by virtue of his place in the gerontocracy. There is also a three-part structure to Mande communities, with people divided up by lineage as descendants of slave or captives (*jon*); casted members of society (*nyamakala*) broken up into four groups: bards (*jeli*), blacksmiths (*numun*), cordwainers or leatherworkers (*garange*), and Islamic praise-poets (*fune*); and freeborn people (*haran*) made up of commoner and royalty (*masalen*) with clans dating back to Sunjata's era. The *jon* and *nyamakala* cannot hold office in the authority structure. Other members of Mande society include the stranger (*dunon*), who is welcomed because he may contribute to prosperity; the Muslim holy men (*mari*), who often combine the Qur'an (Koran) with occult medicine; and the hunter's societies (*donson-ton*), which are isolated because they are feared. The hunter's societies scorn set hierarchies, rejecting caste and lineage outright, and are believed to have powerful occult medicine since they spend so much time in the wilderness, the most dangerous place in Mande cosmology. Interestingly, the man of power (*faama* or *mogo-tigi*) can rise from outside the authority structure but only through the seemingly dangerous and antisocial behavior of a hero like Sunjata.

IN THE CLASSROOM

I. THE SUNJATA AS LITERATURE

Sunjata is a living story, changing with each telling and each teller; yet, as presented here, it is also a work of specific literary value. As such, have students consider the tale in multiple ways: as an avenue into understanding and exploring Mande culture, as revealing a long and changing society and that society's present values, and as evidence of a specific literary value. Students may also want to explore the connections the epic has to stories from other cultures — for example, the ways the idea of a hero both transcends cultures and is specific to one culture.

Discussion

1. Ask students to put themselves in the context of such a long, long history and tradition. Imagine participating in an oral tradition that has lasted for seven hundred years and that has served to direct and control a society. Ask if they can think up any stories that help to narrate their own lives or the culture in which they live.

2. Ask students to consider the benefits and the drawbacks of oral traditions versus written ones. What do we take for granted, for example, as readers of literary texts? How does knowing we have a specific, fixed printed text to come back to change the way we read and our expectations of the stories we engage?

Connections

1. Compare the hero in *Sunjata* to the hero in other early epics, such as *Gilgamesh* (Book 1). What makes this hero particularly Mandean? What makes him universal?

2. In another comparison, look for evidence of the layering of time periods in texts that were originally oral. In *Beowulf* (Book 2), for example, there is a hint of Christianity in an originally Pagan story. In *Sunjata*, the silk cotton tree the hero fells first came to the region with Portuguese traders in the fourteenth or fifteenth century.

3. Compare the story of Sunjata uniting the various Mande states with that of Moses and the Exodus (Book 1). Look at the differing senses of "nationhood" or group identity that emerges through the action of the heroes.

Groups

1. Have groups of students play a version of the game "Telephone." Give them a brief, specific story line and have them prepare an embellished version to present to the next class. After the presentations, discuss the ways the groups have changed the stories and what the new differences reveal about them and their creative impulse. Think about the ways in which oral tradition allows for fluidity of story and for adapting to changing circumstances.

2. In groups, ask students to prepare a reading of the epic out loud. What do they notice about the rhythm of the language? What seems specific to a text that was originally an oral narrative?

Writing

Ask students to write a short paper in response to one or more of the following:

1. How do Western notions of epic poetry, derived from experience with Homer and Virgil, apply to the Mande epic?

2. Investigate the use of proverbs in Sunjata. How do they work to draw in listeners and readers who are already familiar with them? How might they engage a more distant audience? What do they teach us?

3. Does the character of Sunjata develop over the course of the epic? Can we apply the category of round or flat character to an oral narrative?

4. Discuss the characteristics that make Sunjata a hero.

BEYOND THE CLASSROOM

RESEARCH & WRITING

1. Look into the development of the hero in a different cultural setting — Romulus and Remus, the rise of the comic book hero, the novelistic hero — and compare that hero to Sunjata. What do the shapes of our fictional heroes tell us about our aspirations? What do the changes in that hero reveal about specific times and places and changing desires?

2. Investigate the different versions of *Sunjata*. What do the differences reveal about the storytellers or their cultural or historic position?

Projects

1. Oral narratives are always changing, but who knows how until they have been recorded? The creative touch of the narrator or his or her take on their culture is often overlooked because an understanding of his adaptation is lost without an original fixed test. Compare the legend of *Sunjata* to one like *Little Red Riding Hood* and the film adaptation, *Freeway*.

2. Think about the role of the anthropologist in bringing a narrative like *Sunjata* into text. How might the presence of the anthropologist influence the telling of the tale?

3. Research the landscape of West Africa and suggest how that landscape plays a role in the narrative of *Sunjata*.

4. Research Mande cosmology, and investigate the ways it appears in the epic of *Sunjata*.

WWW   For additional information on *Sunjata* and annotated Web links, see *World Literature Online* at bedfordstmartins.com/worldlit.

FURTHER READING

Innes, Gordon. *Sunjata: Three Mankinka Versions*. 1974.
Obiechina, Emmanuel N. *Language and Theme*. 1990.
Okpewho, Isadore. *The Epic of Africa*. 1979.
———. *Myth in Africa*. 1983.
Ong, Walter. *Orality and Literacy: The Technologizing of the Word*. 1982.

MEDIA RESOURCES

VIDEO

Keita (The Heritage of the Griot)
94 min., 1995 (California Newsreel)
Keïta creates a unique world where the West Africa of the thirteenth-century *Sunjata* epic and the West Africa of today coexist and interpenetrate. Director Dani Kouyaté frames his

dramatization of the epic within the story of Mabo Keïta, a contemporary boy from Burkina Faso, learning the history of his family. During the film, Mabo and his distant ancestor, Sunjata, engage in parallel quests to understand their destinies, to "know the meaning of their names." (French with English subtitles.)

The Lion King
disney.go.com/disneypictures/lionking/index.html
This is the Disney site for the immensely popular animated feature based on *Sunjata*. On this site, there are images from and background information on the movie.

WEB SITES

African History on the Internet — Kingdoms and Ancient Civilizations
www-sul.stanford.edu/depts/ssrg/africa/history/hisking.html
Visit this page to find an extensive list of links to sites related to Ancient African civilizations. There are links to timelines, academic articles, maps, lesson plans, and libraries, to name just a few.

Background to the Epic of *Sundiata*
Courses.wcupa.edu/jones/his311/notes/sundiata.htm
Another good background site, this page includes information about the geography, politics, and religion of Malinke society.

The Kennedy Center African Odyssey Interactive
artsedge.kennedy-center.org/aoi/
This is a wonderful site that provides not only information on *Sunjata* but also very interesting background and exhibits on African arts and culture.

The Lion King on Broadway
www.lionking.net/
Audio and visual clips from the Broadway performance of *The Lion King*.

The Lion King (Hans Zimmer)
www.filmtracks.com/titles/lion_king.html#audio
Audio clips from the Disney movie of *The Lion King*.

ORIAS Monomyth Site: The Hero's Journey
ias.berkeley.edu/orias/hero/
This site provides information based on Joseph Campbell's monomyth providing information on three key world myths — *Sunjata*, *The Ramayana*, and *Yamoto*. On the *Sunjata* portion of the site, users will find information on plot and historical background of *Sunjata*, links to other key sites, and several useful video performances of the epic.

Sunjata the Lion King of Mali
www.jolofempire.com/SUNJATATHELIONKINGOFMALI.html
This site includes a brief biography of the historical figure Sunjata, the king who inspired the tale. It also provides users with an overview of the history of the Mali empire as well as information about present-day Mali.

GENERAL MEDIA RESOURCES

VIDEO
Africa: A History Denied
36 min., 1995 (Time-Life Video)
Time-Life treks inland to the remote site of great Zimbabwe, a fabulous "Lost City" that reached the height of its glory in the fourteenth century. Sift through the sands of time to

uncover the equally splendid culture of Africa's Swahili coast. The fabulously wealthy center of the thriving gold and ivory trades until the sixteenth century, its cities now lie all but forgotten, buried under centuries of indifference.

The Africans
9 1-hour videos, 1986 (Annenberg/CPB Video)
Explores history, culture, and politics of Africa. Includes discussions of the influences of Islam and the West. Tapes are: *The Nature of a Continent, A Legacy of Lifestyles, New Gods, Tools of Exploitation, New Conflicts, In Search of Stability, A Garden of Eden in Decay?, A Clash of Cultures,* and *Global Africa.*

The Ashanti Kingdom (Ghana)
15 min., 1992 (Films for the Humanities & Sciences)
The Ashanti are the best-known tribe of Ghana, comprising around two million of the country's twelve million inhabitants. All of the Ashanti kings belong to the Oyoko Dako clan, the clan of chieftains; they are the ones who have created and strengthened the Ashanti nation. This program shows the Ashanti kingdom: It explains the strict hierarchical organization of the village, the importance of the characteristic *kente* garment, the naming of children, the Ashanti religious beliefs, the importance of traditional values and traditional festivals, and the protocol surrounding the paramount chief of the Ashanti.

Caravans of Gold: Kings and Cities
114 min., 1984 (Video Library Company)
Produced in association with Nigerian television, Basil Davidson hosts this documentary that examines the medieval gold trade from Africa to India, China, and Italy. See how the coming of the Portuguese in 1498 signified the end of the great African trade. Also, learn about the African kingdoms and ancient rituals by traveling to Nigeria, where a king still holds court in his fifteenth-century palace.

The Glories of Ancient Benin
15 min., 1992 (Films for the Humanities & Sciences)
Long, long ago, three great hunters came upon a termitary from which emerged a nine-headed genie. A city was built on this spot, beside a pond named Abomiressa Adjaga after the god of the hunters. The Portuguese traders who arrived around 1600 called the city Porto-Novo (Newport). Teagmani, son of Pokbon, was king at that time, one of a long line of kings whose heritage is preserved in the Museum of Porto-Novo. Here, we can see the richly embroidered royal robes and some of the utensils used at court. The carved doors of the Royal Palace provide a window into the political, social, economic, and cultural life of the kingdom. Its symbols are as applicable today as in King Toffa's day: the snail, to show that the king must guide his people slowly and patiently; the tortoise, a symbol of invulnerability, means that while the king lives, no enemy can get on his back; the lizard symbolizes unity, for lizards hide in cracks, and if the country is unified, no enemy can hide; the duck symbolizes wisdom, for one who cannot swim should not go into the water, and one who is not sure of victory over the enemy should not attack. The museum and the palace contain a wealth of testimonials and memories of Benin's glorious past.

The Greatness of Africa
23 min., 1998 (Library Video Company)
Explore the civilizations that contributed to Africa's historical greatness. Intriguing facts combine with graphics to present an overview of ancient African civilization from the world's oldest monarchy to the incredible civilization of Egypt.

Wonders of the African World with Henry Louis Gates Jr.
3 tapes, 360 min. (Video Library Company)

Host Henry Louis Gates Jr. explores the origins of African cultures by touring the continent's ancient ruins and historical sites. *Volume 1* — Black Kingdoms of the Nile and the Swahili Coast — explores Swahili culture and looks at the Pyramids of Giza; *Volume 2* — The Slave Kingdoms and the Holy Land — looks at the truth about the slave trade and explores Ethiopia in search of the Ark of the Covenant; *Volume 3* — The Road to Timbuktu and the Lost Cities of the South — shows Gates traveling to Timbuktu in search of ancient books.

West Africa
47 min., 2001 (Video Library Company)
Elmer Hawkes explores Mali, Ghana, The Ivory Coast, Senegal, Timbuktu, and other African regions. The program looks at the people, cultures, geography, traditions, and history.

WEB SITES

Explore the Wonders
http://www.pbs.org/wonders/fr_wn.htm
This PBS site includes a few images, a short history of ancient Mali, and an on-line video interview on Timbuktu with Islamic scholar Ali Ould Sidi at Sankore Mosque, the heart of the extensive university system in sixteenth-century Timbuktu. Here, Sidi tells of more than 25,000 students under a rigorous ten-year program of astronomy, medicine, mathematics, and more.

The Kennedy Center African Odyssey Interactive
artsedge.kennedy-center.org/aoi/
This is a wonderful site that provides not only information on *Sunjata* but also very interesting background and exhibits on African arts and culture.

The Kingdoms of Classical Africa
www.geocities.com/ps5kingdoms/
An interesting general site about the five kingdoms of Classical Africa, developed by a non-specialist but still seemingly well done.

The Slave Kingdoms
www.pbs.org/wonders/fr_e3.htm
This is a fabulous site regarding the roots of slavery in Africa and how African slavery spread during the Age of Exploration.

EUROPE:
RENAISSANCE
AND REFORMATION

FRANCESCO PETRARCH, *The Ascent of Mount Ventoux* (p. 74) and *Canzoniere* (p. 80)

WWW   For a quiz on the *Canzoniere*, see *World Literature Online* at bedfordstmartins.com/worldlit.

It is tempting to say that Petrarch casts a long shadow over the history of European literature. But to picture Petrarch as a giant of the past would be to deny perhaps his most important insight — that, through writing, individuals can connect over vast differences in time and place. Petrarch's towering achievement is nonetheless intimate. He elevates personal, individual love and, in writings not included in the anthology, literary fame, to rivals for eternal salvation. Students can be expected to approach easily the bedrock emotions and experiences that Petrarch treats. Like Basho, his writing achieves a sense of casual familiarity even across centuries, continents, and languages.

If both you and your students are comfortable, relate experiences with unrequited crushes and disillusioned love. Ask them to compare the differing ways in which poets from different times and places present themselves as being jilted or disappointed lovers and the way this same theme appears in popular culture from songs to literature to film. Encourage students to think about popular music and the cult of love as it appears on FM radio. Is there a hint of spiritual longing, a remnant of Petrarch's concern with the dangerous distraction of his earthly infatuation, in "break-up songs" of today? Is there honor in being broken-hearted?

Most of all, encourage students to see the ways in which Petrarch felt intimately connected with others through writing. Petrarch, upon discovering the personal letters of Cicero in the Vatican library, was initially crushed to discover that his hero could be petty, mean, mundane, and vulgar. Ultimately, however, his disappointment turned to triumph as he realized the human connection between himself and the titans of the past; Petrarch's oeuvre includes familiar letters addressed to many of the ancients. As a humanist — that is, one who believes in the study of literature as an avenue to truth — Petrarch encouraged an elite group of scholars to see themselves as being members of a community with the Latin writers who, until his time, were untouchable, unquestionable giants. This connection allowed for scholarship as we know it: The delving into the contexts of texts is itself a result of humanist scholarship. Encourage students to recognize the continuing influence of Petrarch in our lives, as scholars and as people, as poets and as audience. How do (or can) students engage the world and create it through writing? Have e-mail and the Internet — the Information Age — changed their sense of connection to others, to their writing selves, and to writers of the past? What sorts of human relationships are possible in writing that are not possible in any other way?

TEXT & CONTEXT

POETIC FORM AND PERSONALITY
One cannot treat Petrarch without treating form. His mastery of the sonnet turned that particular form into the model of lyric poetry — of poetry that is concerned with the mind

and its transitory emotional states. Petrarch's use of oxymoron and paradox to describe the mind in conflict and his engaging use of metaphor and description influenced generations of poets. For some, the sonnet became a confining bondage, while others found the form flexible enough to reflect their inner experience even as it provided the structure that made it possible for them to connect with others through language. Moreover, the continuing popularity of the sonnet and its presence as a challenge for the aspiring poet suggest the ways in which an abstract notion like poetic form can occupy an intimate place in our lives.

PETRARCH AND ITALY

Italy in the time of Petrarch had not yet become a nation. Its political landscape consisted of a shifting series of alliances between and within its city-states or communes. Italy as a nation existed solely in the minds of a literary elite — for example, Petrarch's wistful appeals to Cicero and to Rome express his desire to unify a shattered country. Given the uncertain and contentious state of the Italian peninsula, this longing for the past makes perfect sense; the conflicting and fractious ideas that Petrarch portrays in his love poetry seem at least in part to reflect his political and social life. As in The Ascent of Mount Ventoux, Petrarch's remedy for his exile was to go into the natural world, where analogs to the experiences of his classical, pagan heroes could be found, and in that way he could travel to a kind of allegorical Rome. Petrarch, for all his devout Christian faith, insisted on and lived out the human scale of human inquiry. Petrarch's hike up the mountain lead, eventually, to great advances in philology — in the awareness of the situation of language in history. The introduction to this section shows how casually and familiarly we believe in a Renaissance kind of knowledge: The indispensable notion of "text and context" in many ways derives from that singular moment when Petrarch found Cicero in his personal letters and discovered that he was a small, petty human being as well as a great writer. Petrarch still seems familiar and intimate to us today because he thought of the "republic of letters" in such intimate and familiar terms — because he lived in a sense in ancient Rome even as he existed in Renaissance Italy. Literary form and literary experience thus become a way in which we connect over time and space with other human beings. If Petrarch is at home anywhere, it is in this republic of letters that he helps to found.

IN THE CLASSROOM

I. PETRARCH'S EXPERIENCE WITH FORM: THE SUBSTANCE OF LITERARY EXPERIENCE

Petrarch's experience in the world was shaped by his reading. It could profitably be wondered whether poets don't always live through words before — or as — they live through the world. Poets, in this view, are always of a double mind, delineating and anticipating their experience in their own words and the words of others. A. E. Housman's definition of poetry as a physical reaction to words applies to this phenomenon; it is experience that is useful to poetry, whether understanding or writing it. The experiences of writing and reading are themselves parts of living in the world, and for Petrarch, they are pre-eminent. Petrarch wrote beautiful calligraphy, and the manuscript copies of his books demonstrate his skill at writing in the most fundamental sense — as handwriting. Writing should therefore be a part of any study of Petrarch. Students can more easily understand Petrarch by trying to write sonnets and attempting to repeat experiences they have read about, or talking about the ways in which they involuntarily dramatize the experiences they see or hear or read. For contemporary students, thinking about situations like leaving a movie theater after seeing an action movie or the ways in which people choose music to suit their current activity can help them better relate to Petrarch's focus on written language.

As readers, students often approach the question of literary form as if the rules were prior to the performances, not ex post facto attempts to describe the features of a given literary form. Call students' attention to the ways in which musical styles like "gangsta rap" or country western set up expectations that its eager audiences embrace and even influences the ways in which its performers and listeners dress, speak, and act. Encourage students to see in Petrarch's sonnets an attempt not to establish a set of conventions but to describe his own mental struggles. This leads to the larger question of why so many poets across Europe would seize on the form he developed — whether to describe their own, similar mental states or to mimic the state so dramatically inscribed in Petrarch's poetry. Help students to think about the interplay between art and life and the ways in which lyric poetry, in particular, helps its readers to define for themselves inner experience — the subjective state through which one perceives the world.

The somewhat abstract question of poetic form becomes clearer when it is practiced; however, students can be both inspired and intimidated by the "rules" for a form. Reducing the number of rules can help students who say they cannot write poetry to give it a try. Students may be more likely to ease into poetry if you remind them that popular music, especially rap and hip-hop, are intimately concerned with language. Indeed, one good way to initiate the discussion of form might be to give students this assignment: Think of a song to which you know all the words. Without writing it down, write a poem in exactly that meter and rhyme scheme. This might also help them to feel how artistic, arranged language can be intimate. Similarly, the somewhat sheepish beginnings of the attempt to climb a hill because Petrarch did it can often give way to moments of what we might call authentic literary experiences, moments where the distinction between "book learning" and "real world" disappears and one understands both the world and the book anew.

Discussion

1. Ask students to think of a song that they listened to over and over in high school and of the situation in which that song seemed meaningful. Then, ask them how their personal context lends urgency to the words and music of that song? To what extent did their peer group embrace the same song? How did people define themselves according to the music they listened to?

2. Ask students to think about the way "oldies" music sounds to people for whom those songs were obsessive in high school. Have them think about their reaction to movie actors who were heartthrobs in their day — for example, James Dean or Marilyn Monroe. Can they feel the visceral reaction that their fans felt? Why or why not?

3. Divide the class into groups and have them write a sonnet. Have one group take the first quatrain of a Petrarchan sonnet, another the second, and so on. Come up with a subject for the sonnet — that is, a speaker and a situation in which she is speaking to her lover — and a general idea of the three statements she will be making about her relationship or about love. The group in charge of the couplet might have to write it on the spot, after hearing the three quatrains. How does converting the prosaic description of the sonnet into the sonnet itself bring — or fail to bring — the situation to life? How does poetry help the process? What role does versification (rhyme, meter) play in making the language more dramatic or less familiar, heightened in some way?

Connections

1. The physical feat of climbing Mt. Ventoux inspires in Petrarch both the admonition of his own pride and the essay itself, which is a commemoration of the physical feat and the blow to his ego. For Petrarch, the labor of climbing is a kind of literary homage, an attempt to reenact in the physical world his reading. His labor is thus never far from him — his exercise is not an escape but a kind of research. Have students contrast and com-

pare Petrarch's motives and the spiritual harvest he reaps from his climbing with the benefits, both literary and moral, that Bashō realizes from his walking trip into Japan in *Narrow Road Through the Backcountry* (Book 4). The psychological suggestion of Basho's title echoes the stated purposes for Petrarch's trip — an attempt to perform in space the historical sense that one accrues from voracious, committed reading. How well does Petrarch accomplish his goals? How does his admonition of his pride in reaching the top relate to Bashō's writing poems on signposts where his ancestors wrote on the rocks?

2. Petrarch's experience of love is painfully, obviously human. He views it as a distraction from his true calling as a human even as he feels its exquisite, agonizing pull. In some ways, Petrarch's attempts to define his love for Laura as a chain that binds him to earth are political in nature: He has to defend himself against charges that he valorizes temporal love, as his pagan heroes did, over eternal salvation. Compare these intrusions of the political with the political context through which Adrienne Rich (Book 6) understands her love. How close is the analogy between Petrarch's religion and Rich's politics? How do concerns about these larger group questions infiltrate their language about their innermost feelings?

Groups

1. Divide students into groups. Ask them to compare the position of the *volta*, or turn, in each of the Petrarchan sonnets in the anthology. How does that subtle shift in perspective, the victory of or introduction to some other side in his internal argument, appear? Does it fall in the middle? Does it coincide with the formal break after the eighth (or twelfth) line? Are there multiple turns? In the large group, ask whether the students' answers agree, and speculate on the ways in which the form allows the poet to represent the shifting, subtle nature of human thought, the ways in which we cannot always follow the form because our own slippery consciousness eludes it, and the ways in which the poet's use of form captures that slipperiness.

Writing

Ask students to write a short paper in response to one of the following:

1. We often counsel a jilted or hopeless lover to "get over it," to recognize that there are many other potential lovers who wouldn't spurn him or her. To what extent is this advice manageable? Use Petrarch's sonnets to discuss whether or not the lover can possibly take this advice, given the ways in which his or her perceptions are determined by his or her monomania.

2. Petrarch's sonnets are often seen as the beginnings of a new and different form of consciousness for Western Europeans. The struggle he delineates between desire and expectation, between religious and natural urges, begins to shape the outlines of human consciousness and to elevate this internal and individual drama to the level of nobility. The sovereign individual begins as the individual mind in dispute. To what extent does Petrarch's struggle reflect the internal conflict you feel and talk about? How is this internal conflict played out in popular song, television, or movies?

3. Try to write a sonnet. Write a paper detailing your attempt and its frustrations and triumphs.

II. PETRARCH AND ITALY

In *Power and Imagination*, historian Lauro Martines posits that humanism in Renaissance Italy is an elitist educational movement that serves the interests of an emerging administrative class. Petrarch and other humanists denigrated wealth and nobility as being impediments to true thought and learning, but even as they did so, they elevated the wealthy and the noble. How much more impressive is the learned king or nobleman, who can overcome these obstacles and be truly noble in morality, truly learned despite wealth? So, the revolutionary potential of Petrarch's insight into Cicero — that his personal letters show that he was ultimately "merely" human — is constrained by its confinement to an ambitious class of educated notaries and lawyers. The patronage system further consolidates power in the hands of the nobility. Ironically, even as humanists like Petrarch elevate themselves to the level of the ancients, they humble themselves before their contemporaries. Even as they defend the ancients from attacks based on their paganism, they show themselves to be true Christians. Thus what is sometimes seen as a transhistorical movement, the triumph of a superior idea, is ultimately the product of its time and place. Indeed, the very fragmentation of political power in Italy seems to encourage the eventual victory of the modern over the ancient.

Discussion

1. Encourage students to see how local politics take place on a more human scale than do national politics. For example, consider the kinds of criticism one indulges in of a mayor as opposed to the ways in which one criticizes the president. How does the sense of location empower one to assume a kind of authority over political affairs? Listen to talk radio, and consider the ways in which people feel compelled to present themselves as being authorities in local versus nationally syndicated shows.

2. Ask students to consider the ways in which one's sense of oneself depends on one's political situation. As college students, for instance, they might be unusually conscious of the effects of having had parental authority recently removed from their lives. In what ways do they have new responsibilities, and in what ways are they freer than before? How does this relate to issues raised by the question of free speech and the individual's right to say whatever he wishes?

Connections

1. Because humanism was an educational program focused on classical literature, which valued the moral and spiritual truths of the pagans even as it professed the superiority of Christianity, its proponents needed to defend themselves from charges that they were elevating pagan truth over Christian, revealed truth. This need emerges in Petrarch's sonnets and in his use of Augustine's *Confessions* (Book 2) atop Mount Ventoux. Compare *The Story of the Stone* (Book 4) and the ways in which Bao-yu has to negotiate his social and spiritual responsibilities. How do their solutions differ? In what way does the question of eternal reward and punishment shape the struggle of Petrarch differently from that of Bao-yu?

2. Contrast Petrarch's poetry to the Indian devotional poetry found later in this book (starting on page 921). Which seems more likely to you — erotic love as a competing influence to the divine or as a human metaphor for the divine? The selection from Song of Solomon (Book 2) is also intriguing in this context. For example, Calvinist theology felt compelled to read its eroticism in strictly allegorical terms in order to reduce the danger it saw in reading such a sensual text. What dangers might sensual and erotic metaphors for ecstatic religious experience pose for a culture in which sexuality is not connected with sin?

Groups

1. Divide the class into groups of four or more. Have students discuss the image of Laura that Petrarch develops in the context of popular culture. Does a movie like *There's*

Something About Mary have any common ground with Petrarch? Do the women or men represented in popular song bear any resemblance to the distant, cool beauty Petrarch attributes to Laura? Is there anything in popular culture akin to Petrarch's self-reproach?

2. In groups, discuss various curricular issues as they relate to the question of elitism. Is the study of literature an elitist one, the hobbyhorse of a privileged few? Does it bring about any change in the world, any difference in consciousness? Or does, say, the Internet do more to disseminate information and engage people in writing and reading than the confines of the classroom ever could? Would science or math classes benefit from an infusion of rhetoric, a renewed attention to the ways in which things are said?

Writing

Ask students to write a short paper in response to one of the following:

1. Discuss the role of human sexuality in your own spiritual tradition. Using Petrarch's and one other poet's attempts to negotiate the differences and similarities between sexual and religious ecstasy, advocate for one view of sexuality over the other — or take a reasoned stance between them, considering the pros and cons of each approach.

2. Write a letter to Petrarch. Introduce yourself to him, and react to his poetry as if you were an admirer in his own time, citing specifics and even quarrelling with some of his choices. Describe to him a hike or physical exertion of your own, and depict the spiritual insight — or lack thereof — you garnered as a result.

BEYOND THE CLASSROOM

RESEARCH & WRITING

1. The conscious influence of Petrarch over every poet since him — the primacy of the sonnet in discussions of poetic form — can be felt by browsing through any anthology. Read a number of sonnets from the widest possible range of cultures and ages or from the most diverse population of poets you can find. Using only twentieth-century English-language poets, one could range from E. E. Cummings to Countee Cullen to Elizabeth Bishop to Bernadette Mayer. Read the sonnets, read biographies of the poets, and speculate on the ways in which admission to the community of poets depended on writing sonnets, and on the extent to which the achievement itself allowed the poets to feel they existed in a meritocracy apart from their individual circumstances.

2. Research the role of the city-state in the founding of the Renaissance. How did the patronage system and the wealth of merchants make Renaissance humanism possible? How is Petrarch an example of this kind of humanism, and to what extent can we find his political life in his poetry?

3. Research the history of the depiction of love in popular songs. How does this depiction change over time? What continuities are there? To what extent can we see breaks in the depiction of love that are attributable to the political situations in which they occur?

Projects

1. Investigate the ways in which Renaissance architecture employed the Golden Mean, or the Divine Proportion, in its edifices. The Proportion was derived from Plato, yet it was modified by the Renaissance architectures. What comparisons and contrasts can you make between this classical borrowing and Petrarch's imitation of the poetry of Catullus, recently rediscovered?

2. Write a sonnet — or, better yet, a "crown," a sequence of seven sonnets in which the last line of one sonnet becomes the first line of the next, the last line of the seventh sonnet being the same as the first line of the first. Then, write a paper about the attempt, describing your plans, your triumphs, and your failures.

WWW   For additional information on Petrarch and annotated Web links, see *World Literature Online* at bedfordstmartins.com/worldlit.

FURTHER READING

Johnson, Paul. *The Renaissance: A Short History.* 2000.
Martines, Lauro. *Power and Imagination: City-States in Renaissance Italy.* 1988.

WWW   See *World Literature in the 21st Century* at bedfordstmartins.com/worldlit for a comparison of Petrarch's *Canzoniere* to modern popular songs.

GENERAL MEDIA RESOURCES

VIDEO
A World Reborn
57 min., 1997 (Library Video Company)
Featuring dramatic readings and re-enactments as well as on-location footage, this award-winning program explores the philosophical, political, artistic, scientific, and religious changes that occurred during the Renaissance. The program examines philosophical and scientific theories and artistic movements of the time, while identifying significant figures and their contributions, from Petrarch and Jan Hus to Brunelleschi and Machiavelli.

WEB SITES
The Petrarchan Grotto
Petrarch.freeservers.org
This site is a great first stop to make when researching Petrarch. It contains an extensive list of links to images, biographies, electronic texts (in Latin, Italian, and English translations), bibliographies, exhibitions, monuments, museums, and associations pertaining to Petrarch and his works. Be sure to check out the audio section as well.

Francesco Petrarch
Petrarch.petersadlon.com/index.html
View a wide variety of portraits of Petrarch on this site, which includes links to other pages devoted to the author, as well as biographical information and essays.

Hanover Historical Texts Project: Francis Petrarch — Selections from His Correspondences
History.hanover.edu/early/petrarch.htm
Read the full electronic texts of a large selection of Petrarch's letters here, including his famous "Letter to Posterity."

Petrarch: The Canzoniere
www.tonykline.free-online.co.uk/Petrarchhome.htm
Download any or all of the 366 poems of the *Canzoniere* from this page.

The Renaissance: Contexts and Comparisons
newman.baruch.cuny.edu/digital/2000/c_n_c/toc/toc_05.htm
This page was created by Paula S. Berggren and Marshall J. Schneider and contains not only very interesting background information on Renaissance literature, it also provides excellent comparative information on the Petrarchan and Shakespearian sonnets.

Dr. Vess's World Civilization Virtual Library
www.faculty.de.gcsu.edu/~dvess/pet.htm
Created by Dr. Deborah Vess of Georgia College & State University, this interesting site
includes an outline of a course on Petrarch and links to a number of pages devoted to the
author, including Petrarch's letters and writings on the plague.

In the Tradition: **European Love Lyrics** (p. 85)

In Renaissance Europe, the word was the beginning of all knowledge. Humanism was
not so much a philosophy as a course of study derived from *studia humanitatis*. Humanism
placed a renewed emphasis on the study of writing and rhetoric and on using the classics not
just as a source of knowledge — as, for example, medieval scholars had taken Aristotle's
works on natural science as a textbook and their original source of terminology and definitions — but also as a model for clear and elegant prose style. Unlike the scholastics, who
came from the ranks of the clergy, the humanists tended to be notaries and lawyers attached
to political rather than religious institutions. As laymen, the humanists were less interested
in conforming the texts to religious doctrine than the scholastics had been. Therefore, they
expanded the number and quality of Latin texts and extended their studies to include Greek
texts, many of which the humanists translated into Latin for the first time. These Greek texts,
lost to Europe but preserved in the Byzantine East and translated into Arabic, now suddenly opened up new fields of inquiry and new ways of thinking about the natural world to
Europe. Moreover, the humanists, as a result of this renewed attention to the study of language for its own sake, developed historical criticism and the study of grammar, particularly Greek grammar, to new heights. The practical uses of this new discipline were manifold.
For example, teaching the mercantile classes to read and write letters strengthened and
improved trade networks. Inevitably, perhaps, this attention to language and elegant expression led to a wider attention to ancient literature — to Homer, Sophocles, Isocrates, and so
on. This was how the written word achieved its prominence in Renaissance thought.

It seems only natural, then, that poetry should become an obsession in the Renaissance.
Lyric poetry, with its attention to the inner states of human beings and the emotional qualities of experience, combines musicality and emotional content with the seductive power of
words themselves. The word *lyric* is derived from the lyre, the stringed instrument that often
accompanied the recitation of poetry in Greek and Roman antiquity. In the Renaissance,
music was bent to the dictates of words. The tunes of madrigals sought to illustrate poems,
so that notes travel upward in pitch to reflect words about aspiring to heaven and downward
when grace descends from heaven. Along with this fascination with the word, written texts
became more and more accessible thanks to, first, an increasingly sophisticated network of
secular copyists taking advantage of cheaper and more plentiful paper and ink, and second,
the advent of the printing press and a flood of new books for an increasingly literate and
affluent reading public. That readership hungered to see itself represented in print, and the
subjective quality of lyric poetry brought new attention to the poet himself as an individual
like these new readers. Thus the possibility of achieving literary fame to rival the ancients
began to seem within the grasp of contemporary poets. With the growth of the publishing
industry, the law began to recognize poetry as a kind of property that belongs to the poet,
and the concept of copyright was introduced. The Renaissance, then, is an intellectual movement that had permanent, widespread effects in all areas of European culture.

Along with these material and educational changes, the notion of love underwent a revision. Castiglione's *The Courtier* (in portions of the work not included in this anthology), following the founder of the Platonic Academy of Florence, Marsilio Ficino, defines earthly love

as a means to salvation, a kind of golden ladder that leads the lover out of himself and toward the loved one. These exalted feelings can then point the lover ever closer to heaven and to love for God. The individual lover and the individual mystic share extreme emotional states, obsessive desires, an extravagance of expression and emotion that appeals to the Renaissance and its growing conviction that human beings are the center of the universe. This confidence in the power of human beings leads to new discoveries of every kind: By the time of John Donne (p. 107), the lover's internal state draws forth geographical metaphors ("O my America! my new-found-land") to express the capaciousness and extravagance of human feeling that seems to expand along with human knowledge.

Love fascinates painters as well as poets, and, like poets, painters tend to focus either on the person of the loved one or the meaning of love itself. Botticelli's *La Primavera* ambiguously illustrates the centrality of human love with a panoply of Greek gods surrounding Venus. The painting employs these gods to define the abstract concept of love. Compare this with, for example, Peter-Paul Rubens, who illustrates love by presenting specific, familiar scenes and intrudes a small figure of Cupid into his *Garden of Love* (p. 88). Where Botticelli treats the concept as a universal aspect of human life, Rubens treats its individual appearance among specific human beings in order to illustrate a universal. Poets and painters both have to deal with the specific and the universal at once; a universal is only universal when it is embodied in a familiar and approachable way.

TEXT & CONTEXT

EXPERIENCE AND THE WRITTEN WORD

These poems, while they express individual, intimate states of being also reflect an intellectual revolution that swept across the face of an entire culture. As you read through these lyrics, ask students to consider the ways in which these poets take in and extend the cultural currents of their times for individual readers. Bear in mind, too, the ways in which literary form both aids in this process, by outlining a practice that is almost meditative in nature, and transforms it, as each individual poet and reader performs the poem in his or her own way. Notice the differences between female and male lyric poets, and the ways in which female poets, as the expected objects of desire, manipulate the forms and perspectives of lyric poetry to make room for more authentic expressions from what seems, in most male poetry, to be the top of a pedestal.

Students can, obviously, be expected to relate to the concept of love and to its individual appearances. Encourage them to see both its universality and its malleability, the ways in which particular times and places configure human impulses in their own ways. In European love lyrics of the Early Modern Period, love was particularly ascendant. The selections in the anthology demonstrate the extent to which the concept served to exalt the individual human being and the capacities of all human beings.

IN THE CLASSROOM

I. A TRADITION OF IMAGERY

The love lyrics in this section employ increasingly exotic metaphors in increasing profusion as the Baroque taste for intricacy develops. The relatively simple red and white imagery of Garcilaso de la Vega's "While There Is Still the Color of a Rose" becomes, in Donne and Shakespeare, a compact web of conceits or, in Lope de Vega, a witty self-referential awareness of form. Direct students toward these subtle developments of form. Though this is a small sampling of poets, encourage students to consider the various national differences among French, English, and Spanish poets. Also, ask students to speculate on the ways in which familiarity with form leads to innovation, both in the poetry and in the states of mind that lyric poetry expresses.

Discussion

1. Ask students to trace the development of an image — maybe fire or flowers — in several of the poems. How do different poets refer to the same stock themes in different ways, taking differing attitudes and stances toward increasingly familiar conceits?

2. Ask students to notice the differences between male and female poets, and the different points of view they represent in their lyrics. How do female poets manage to overturn the conventions of the love lyric which, in the form of blazons of beauty, transform women into unreal, and therefore mute, objects of affection?

3. Direct students toward the impact of rhyme on the listener. Read poems aloud in class, and ask students to read them aloud, so that the sometimes delicate and subtle rhyme schemes of the sonnets can sound on their ears. In what ways do sound effects like these make poetry into a different kind of language, a language that means something by its surfaces even as it hints at deep moments of experience?

Writing

1. Write a short essay in which you trace the various permutations of the famous carpe diem theme — life is short, so seize the day — as they appear in this selection of poems. For example, you might compare and contrast Marvell's "To His Coy Mistress" with Ronsard's "To Cassandre." What metaphors do the poets use to embody this theme? How are they effective in portraying the brevity of life?

2. In a brief essay, consider the ways in which the act of writing is represented in these poems. How does the Renaissance infatuation with the written word shape the self-images of the speakers of these poems?

II. CONNECTIONS: WRITING AND THE WRITER

The most obvious connection is with Petrarch, the virtual inventor of the Renaissance lyric (p. 67). A bit less obvious, perhaps, is the way in which Petrarch's notion of literary fame as an enticement equal to immortal salvation might have driven these poets to see a grand love affair as being equal to a mystical union with God. Encourage students to speculate on the motives for the poets' hopeless aspirations for the objects of their affections. Direct students toward other texts in this book in which writers become self-consciously aware of the act of writing and its contradictory and dangerous power to bring into being what was not there before — *Doctor Faustus* (p. 389), in which the love of books and knowledge leads to a godlike prospect but at the expense of the eternal soul; *The Tempest* (p. 495), in which Prospero's magic, derived from his books, allows him to create illusory worlds; and the opening lines of *Paradise Lost* (p. 575), where Milton knows he addresses "the fit, though few" in order to "justify the ways of God to man." These connections can be expanded to include the *In the World* section, "Fashioning the Prince" (p. 140): How, for example, does the lover's individual sense of self and power compare with the arduous education through which one becomes a prince or a courtier?

Discussion

1. Ask students to think about their picture of the "Author." How do they imagine Petrarch or Donne or Bradstreet at their work? What do authors do when they write? What are authors thinking about when they write? You might start by asking students to give the

construction as it appears in their English classes. When English teachers talk about authors, how do those authors appear?

2. The identification of love with stars and astronomy seems natural, given the scientific discoveries that burst on European consciousness during the Renaissance. Ask students to notice the different attitudes toward these discoveries, and toward the stars themselves, that poets like Donne and Bradstreet evince in their lyrics. How might Bradstreet's physical position, as a colonist, lead to an altered view of her place with respect to the stars?

Writing

1. Write a brief essay in which you compare poets who focus on the body of a loved one to poets who focus on the abstract idea of love. How does the physical human being get represented differently in these different kinds of poems? How does the act of writing change as a result of these different stances toward the subject? Are these two approaches to the same idea, or do the two kinds of poets have absolute differences in their views of human love?

2. Compare the subjective self in love lyrics to the observed self that appears in the accounts of explorers. What allows Renaissance explorers to reserve for Europeans the soaring capacities they find in the abstract figure of Man?

BEYOND THE CLASSROOM

RESEARCH & WRITING

1. Research the early history of printed books and their influence on the self as it was fashioned through love lyrics in Europe during the Renaissance. Write an essay in which you speculate on the connections between copyright law and the vogue for sonnets, which reflect inner struggles and dramatize the interior lives of their poets. How does the attitude of readers toward the figure of the Author, as he begins to appear in printed texts, shape the ways in which poets wrote their lyrics?

2. Research a new development in science — particularly in medicine — that occurred during the Renaissance. How does this new notion shape the self-perceptions and cosmology of one or more of the poets represented in this selection?

Projects

1. Memorize and deliver for the class a couple of lyrics. In doing so, create a "backstory," a context within which a character delivers the lines of the poems. Before you recite the poems, set the stage for the class.

2. Research the ways in which the figure of love — or the feeling of love — is represented by Renaissance painters. Create a slide show or PowerPoint presentation that demonstrates the different approaches painters take to representing love visually. Do they rely on allusions to classical mythology? Do they paint the common people of their time? What different effects might these differing representations have on the ways in which people think about their own love relationships?

FURTHER READING

Levin, Phyllis. *The Penguin Book of the Sonnet: 500 Years of a Classic Tradition in English.* 2001.

Lewis, C. S. *The Allegory of Love: A Study in Medieval Tradition.* 1985.

MEDIA RESOURCES

WEB SITES

Golden Age of Spanish Sonnets
sonnets.spanish.sbc.edu/
On this growing site is a list of Spanish poets, each with their own home page providing biographical information on them. From there, you can link to individual sonnets of the poet, a bibliography page, and links to any external links currently available.

Literary Resources: Renaissance
andromeda.rutgers.edu/~jlynch/Lit/ren.html
Developed by Jack Lynch at Rutgers University, this site aimed at scholars and students attempts to cover all the significant and reliable Internet resources from Milton to Keats. The collection includes information on literature, history, art, music, religion, economics, philosophy, and so on from around the world.

Luminarium
www.luminarium.org
This wonderful site provides background and links on key authors of Medieval, Renaissance, and seventeenth-century Europe. It also includes links to high-quality general resources for the period.

The Renaissance: Contexts and Comparisons
newman.baruch.cuny.edu/digital/2000/c_n_c/toc/toc_05.htm
This page was created by Paula S. Berggren and Marshall J. Schneider and contains not only very interesting background information on Renaissance literature, it also provides excellent comparative information on the Petrarchan and Shakespearian sonnet.

Sonnet Central
members.aol.com/ericblomqu/sonnet.htm
This site contains information on the sonnet throughout Europe and throughout the ages.

Sonnet Poetry Forms
www.geocities.com/Bikies_poetry/sonnet1.html#ita
This helpful page provides a brief overview of the forms on the various types of sonnets.

The Sor Juana Inez de la Cruz Project
www.dartmouth.edu/~sorjuana/
Description, chronology, searching guide, recent bibliography, Cruz scholars, and exegeses.

Voice of the Shuttle: Renaissance & 17th Century
vos.ucsb.edu/browse.asp?id=2749
"The website for humanities research," the Voice of the Shuttle was developed by Alan Liu at the University of California, Santa Barbara, and provides extensive links to humanities and humanities-related resources on the Internet.

NICCOLÒ MACHIAVELLI, *The Prince* (p. 124)

WWW   For a quiz on *The Prince*, see *World Literature Online* at
         bedfordstmartins.com/worldlit.

     Machiavelli, it seems, has suffered the fate of all ironists: No one is exactly sure where he is serious and where he is slyly making some other point. *The Prince* is one of the most widely read books in the world, and it sparks furious debate among its readers, who tend to polarize into those who condemn Machiavelli's lack of idealism and those who laud his acute realism. What further complicates an attempt to read this work within its historical context is the fact that the book was circulated only in manuscript form during Machiavelli's time. Its first typeset version began to be sold five years after its author's death. It seems clear that Machiavelli thought the principate — ruled by a hereditary prince — an inferior form of government to the republic — ruled by a voting public, as were Florence and Livy's Rome — yet he was writing *The Prince* at least in part to regain the favor of the Medicis, who established principates, not republics. One way to read *The Prince*, then, is as an extended conditional: "If one must have a principate, then the way to act is as follows." Machiavelli did not merely employ irony, he was its victim: His desire for a political position, which impelled him to curry favor with the Medicis in the first place, ultimately left him out of favor when a republican government was restored in Florence toward the end of his life.

Still, the book is a handbook on how to gain and retain power that has been reviled and revered through the centuries since its composition, and the excerpt in this anthology perfectly demonstrates why it pulls no punches, and it makes no pretense that a ruler can be a good person and a good ruler at the same time. It is this assumption that so infuriates moralists and gives the book its peculiar clarity of vision. Machiavelli, of course, spoke from experience. In the fractious Italy of the fifteenth century, beset by the French, troubled by the aggressive Borgia popes, a ruthless, acquisitive prince was the best hope to protect Florence, reunify the Italian peninsula, and restore the glory of ancient Rome. Machiavelli, as much as Petrarch, seemed to live in the past even as he inhabited the present. Having read his father's dear-bought volumes of the Roman historian Livy, he wanted nothing more than a new republic that could restore a bygone era of peace and stability. Toward these ends, then, Machiavelli desired a powerful prince, not a compassionate and moral leader.

As dark and cynical as *The Prince* seems to be — and, for that matter, as truthful as it seems to be — there is a ray of hope in the book. Although an effective prince — in Machiavelli's view — cannot go to heaven because his position in life requires him to commit serious sins in order to remain in power and guarantee his subjects' safety and the stability of his principate, the prince nonetheless has important incentives to provide for his subjects. Happy, contented people also make for a stable government. The prince must be ruthless with his enemies, but he must be kind to his subjects, making sure he doesn't tax them too heavily, for example. If the successful ruler should aim to be feared rather than respected, he or she should also avoid being hated.

Even more telling, perhaps, is the story of Machiavelli's last words. Legend has it that Machiavelli had a dream just before he died. He met two groups of people. One, ragged and beggarly, was the company of saints on its way to heaven; the other, noble and grave, was the company of Roman philosophers and historians on its way to hell. When he told his friends about this, Machiavelli commented that he would be bored in the company of the saints and that he would rather go to hell to be with more interesting company. This outlook speaks volumes about the moral judgment that many of Machiavelli's readers wish to make on his book as well as about the moral judgment that Machiavelli himself made. Thus he could admire the ruthless Lorenzo de Medici even if he had higher aspirations for the Florentine government. Machiavelli was interested, above all, in the machinery of power as it really exists, not as it should be.

TEXT & CONTEXT

TURMOIL IN ITALY

During Machiavelli's life, the Italian peninsula was a scene of unending strife and shifting alliances. Though *The Prince* has sound, if morally questionable, advice for rulers and leaders of all kinds and in all places, it nonetheless arises from a specific context. Inform students about this context: France was making continual forays into Italy, conquering Milan and Pisa, among other city-states; the Borgia popes, especially Julius II, were acquisitive and greedy, political as much as religious leaders; the Holy Roman Emperor, Charles II, intended to assert his control over much of Italy; the various city-states were constantly acquiring and losing smaller cities and provinces, forming and breaking alliances. The rule of expediency certainly seems most applicable to such a situation, and given the fact that Machiavelli only circulated a manuscript copy of his book during his lifetime, it is intriguing to speculate on whom he intended to be its audience. Certainly, given his time and place, a measure of expediency was vital to maintaining power. Even the most idealistic and high-minded ruler could accomplish nothing until he or she had consolidated his or her hold on power.

Fortune and Gender in *The Prince*

The end of *The Prince* creates rather an interesting figure, a sort of bitch-goddess (like the Hindu goddess Kali in her most destructive phase) whose whims make rulers of various kinds, rash or careful, successful at various times. She is, in a sense, the wild card who evades Machiavelli's analysis, the unknown quantity that he cannot explain, merely account for. The fact that Machiavelli constructs the power of chance as a female divinity puts him squarely in the tradition of assigning to the female and to women the inexplicable and that which eludes reason. It also raises, however, the question of Machiavelli's own life and attitude toward women. It is a fuzzy area, to say the least. He was apparently a rather cold and distant husband, and he may or may not have frequented prostitutes. He described an encounter with one in lurid detail in a letter, but apologists have discounted this as a literary exercise. Moreover, Machiavelli knew personally — and admired — at least one female ruler, Catherine Sforza, who offered her children as collateral so that the occupiers of her city would let her return; once inside, she climbed the wall, exposed her genitals to the conquerors, and said she could always make more children.

IN THE CLASSROOM

I. Morality and Political Power: Is Expediency the Only Principle?

The question of morality and political leadership is always current, and current events will always pertain to such a discussion, for we are always discovering that political leaders are not necessarily moral leaders, however much we might like for that to be the case. Thus there will always be grist for an energetic discussion on these current events in class. The challenge, of course, is to keep bringing the discussion back to Machiavelli and to the precepts he derives from his experience of political leaders. Keep students focused on the seeming prescience of Machiavelli and on his accurate observations about the nature of people. At the same time, his utter disregard for moral questions remains troubling: Even if this is the case, is it always best to admit it? Perhaps, even if eternal damnation or the pangs of conscience are a kind of occupational hazard for politicians, we should allow them to seem moral in the interests of fostering a more moral society. Such an assertion is sure to spark more discussion because it is a troubling question in itself.

Discussion

1. Obviously, there are always current events to discuss in this context. Ask students to supply instances of the principle of expediency as it appears in contemporary politics. To what extent does terrorism combine expediency and idealism? For example, what expedients has terrorism forced from Israel and the United States? Are accusations of hypocrisy against rulers always pointless?

Connections

1. In *Tartuffe* (Book 4), Molière skewered the hypocrisy of rulers with the figure of a father, Orgon. To what extent are the hypocrisies of Orgon and Tartuffe excusable as expediency?

2. The African epic *Sunjata* (p. 21) is a meditation on the qualities of a ruler even as it is the narrative of a hero. Compare and contrast Machiavelli's picture of an effective ruler with the picture presented in *Sunjata*. Is weakness to be more despised in a ruler than hypocrisy?

Groups

1. Break students into two groups. Have one group list the characteristics of the best leaders they know, defining *best* as being the most effective for their followers, on one side of the blackboard. Have the other group list the characteristics of the ideal leader on the other side of the blackboard. Discuss the discrepancies and congruencies between the two lists.

Writing

Ask students to write a short paper in response to one or more of the following:

1. Trace the role of expediency in your life. To what extent do you need to be both a lion and a fox? Give specific examples, and don't forget to talk about your aspirations. Do you foresee yourself growing more hypocritical or more realistic as you progress in your life and career?

2. Argue for morality in leaders over expediency. Is there any way for a ruler to maintain power and be effective while also adhering to a moral code? Use examples from Machiavelli, from current events, and/or from your own experience as a leader and follower to support your claims for morality. Make sure to define *morality* carefully.

II. GENDER AND POLITICS: THE ROLE OF THE FEMALE RULER

It may be unfamiliar and even uncomfortable for students to discuss political power in terms of the family or to think of family arrangements in political terms; nonetheless, everyone has experience of a domestic arrangement, and every domestic arrangement includes authority and power. Indeed, the question of how to raise children can be seen entirely as an issue of when and how to most effectively apply power. Though women appear only as a metaphor for chance in the selection in the anthology, women are often rulers — particularly in monarchies — and the ways in which female monarchs have negotiated the competing demands of Machiavellian politics and cultural norms of femininity provide fascinating insights into the ways in which we arrange our hierarchies. A discussion and focus on these questions is also a way to alleviate the unremitting maleness of the topic of politics, especially historical politics.

Discussion

1. Ask students to think of the family as a political unit. To what extent is the role of the mother one of leader of the family? To what extent is the father only a figurehead? How do changing views of the ideal ruler change the views of the ideal parent?

2. Can a woman ever be elected as president of the United States? To what extent does Machiavelli's realism underlie our understanding of what a ruler should be, and to what extent is his prince necessarily a man?

Connections

1. Ramprasad Sen (Book 4), in his relationship to the bitch-goddess Kali, often pictures her as a cruel, diffident mother. Have students think about the ways in which capricious mothers can nonetheless be effective parents and the ways in which chance itself, as represented in Ramprasad and Machiavelli, is our true leader.

2. Look at the relationship between the narrator and Liza in Dostoevsky's *Notes from Underground* (Book 5). How are human relationships affected by the kind of politics Machiavelli outlines in *The Prince*? To what extent can private individuals benefit from the advice to be both lion and fox, and to what extent are morals more applicable to private than to public life?

Writing

Ask students to write a short paper in response to one or more of the following:

1. Discuss whether it is possible for the presence of women in large numbers in government to change the nature of politics — or whether the politics will inevitably change the women. Can any political movement, even one that seeks to bring the nurturing, cooperative ethos of home into public life, change the expediencies that dominate politics?

2. Discuss the politics of family life. Who are the natural leaders in your family? To what extent are they effective because they consider Machiavelli's observations about the effective ruler? To what extent are these questions improper when applied to personal, private relationships?

BEYOND THE CLASSROOM

RESEARCH & WRITING

1. Research the history of *realpolitik*, the attitude toward political science that makes Machiavelli "the Galileo" of political science. To what extent has he persuaded us that this is the way things must be and therefore made a self-fulfilling prophecy of his observations?

2. Look into the life of a successful leader — a rich and famous CEO, perhaps. Has this person taken Machiavelli's advice? Compare, if possible, an autobiography with a biography, paying special attention to the role of morality and accusations of hypocrisy in the different narratives.

3. Research the history of an extremist political group — like Earth First! or violent antiabortion activists. How has this group employed Machiavellian means toward idealistic ends? Is the use of violence and subterfuge in the service of a larger moral good sanctioned by Machiavelli?

Projects

1. In groups of three or four, design a Machiavellian utopia — that is, try to imagine a situation in which Machiavelli's observations about the nature of political power can be taken into account even as the ideals of good government are put into practice.

2. Using whatever research — from sociology, from political science, from history — make a presentation to the class on women as rulers. Compare, for example, a matriarchy with a patriarchy; does the nature of politics change when women are in charge, or are there political expediencies regardless of the gender of the rulers? Or consider

women like England's Queen Elizabeth I or Russia's Catherine the Great. How did accusations based on gender color their reigns? How did they manage expediency differently as women?

WWW   For additional information on Machiavelli and annotated Web links, see *World Literature Online* at bedfordstmartins.com/worldlit.

FURTHER READING

Curry, Patrick, and Oscar Zurate. *Introducing Machiavelli*. 1996.
Viroli, Maurizio. *Niccolò's Smile*. Trans. Anthony Shugaar. 2000.

WWW   See *World Literature in the 21st Century* at
bedfordstmartins.com/worldlit about the relevance of Machiavelli today.

MEDIA RESOURCES

VIDEO

Machiavelli on Political Power
28 min., 1982 (Zenger Media)
In this engaging, open-ended dramatization, Niccolò Machiavelli debates three humanistic scholars of Lorenzo de Medici. The debate contrasts Machiavelli's realistic approach to sixteenth-century leadership with his contemporaries' Christian-based conception of what a prince should be — virtuous, good, and just. Topics include innate goodness, absolute power, and means versus ends.

The Prince
52 min., 1996 (Films for the Humanities & Sciences)
Written to shock and reeducate its reader, *The Prince* still manages to cause a stir today. This program explores the moral ambiguities of power through Niccolò Machiavelli's treatise on political philosophy. Henry Kissinger; Yale University's Donald Kagan; Roger Masters, author of *Machiavelli, Leonardo, and the Science of Power*; Riccardo Bruscagli, of the University of Florence; former presidential hopeful Gary Hart; and others consider the ramifications of political realism and point out the influence of Machiavelli on American foreign and domestic policy. Reenactments from Machiavelli's life, period artwork, and location footage vividly evoke the man and his times.

The Prince
57 min., 1997 (Library Video Company)
Featuring dramatic readings, historical re-enactments, interviews with historians and politicians, and on-location footage, this award-winning program explores the inspiration for Machiavelli's book *The Prince*. Examines the policies of several European Renaissance rulers, including the Medici family in Italy, King Philip II in Spain, Queen Elizabeth I, and Oliver Cromwell, and highlights Machiavelli's observations of each incorporated into the text. The program explores how traditional ideas about power and politics were redefined during the Renaissance, while looking at Machiavelli's views on political structure and government.

WEB SITES

Hanover Historical Texts — Machiavelli
History.hanover.edu/early/mach.html
Visitors to this page will find a sizable archive of electronic text translations and original versions of Machiavelli's works. The site also includes links to e-texts of a number of secondary sources and Web sites devoted to Machiavelli.

Medieval Sourcebook: Niccolò Machiavelli — *The Prince*
www.fordham.edu/halsall/basis/machiavelli-prince.html
This site provides a relatively detailed biography of Machiavelli as well as e-texts of a few of his works, including *The Prince*. In addition, a bibliography of the author's works can be found here.

Niccolò Machiavelli
www.philosophypages.com/ph/macy.htm
This site provides a brief biography of Machiavelli and a description of his most famous works. It also includes a list of recommended secondary readings and several helpful links to Web sites on Machiavelli's life and writings.

Niccolò Machiavelli
www.orst.edu/instruct/ph1302/philosophers/machiavelli.html
Visitors will find a timeline of Machiavelli's life at this site as well as a brief biography and a link to a complete e-text of *The Prince*.

Niccolò Machiavelli — *The Prince*
www.the-prince-by-machiavelli.com/
This helpful site includes a biography of Machiavelli; a summary, outline, and complete e-text of *The Prince*; and links to sites where books by and about the author are available. Visitors may also view portraits of Machiavelli and read famous quotes from his writings.

Philosophy Research Base — Niccolò Machiavelli
www.erraticimpact.com/~modern/html/machiavelli_niccolo.htm
This page contains brief summaries of books by and about Machiavelli.

AUDIO
The Prince
4 CDs, 1997 (Tantor Media)
Narrated by Shelley Frasier, this reading of Machiavelli's classic gives a vivid portrayal of his world in the chaos and tumult of early-sixteenth-century Florence, Italy, and Europe. He uses both his contemporary political situation and that of the Classical Period to illustrate his precepts of statecraft.

The Prince
3 tapes, 3:75 hours (Blackstone Audiobooks)
Read by Glenn Mitchell, this is an unabridged version of *The Prince*.

In the World: Fashioning the Prince (p. 140)

Though we in the West think of democracy — rule by the people — as our form of government, we do not live in pure democracies; that is, the people do not choose without mediation. The majority does not decide in every case, nor does the majority decide on all of the functionaries who will make decisions for them. In the United States, for example, the president, senators, representatives, and state officials are all chosen in different ways, and elected leaders choose officials who make innumerable everyday decisions. The question of leadership, then, remains an issue in modern nations, and the debate over the ideal qualities of a leader is ongoing. Though this enduring question does not include concepts of nobility and royalty in the West today, we can still feel the pull of those notions as they appear in the texts in these sections. One wants one's leader to be better, or at least more effective, than oneself.

The Prince established Machiavelli as the "Galileo of political science," but the selections found in this section demonstrate differing opinions, less centered on observation, perhaps, but by writers who were no less involved than Machiavelli in the affairs of the world. That is to say, most of these writers were as familiar with the everyday compromises of statecraft as was Machiavelli, and Nizam al-Mulk, for example, insisted on a kind of idealism — conformity of civic laws to the Qur'an and *shari'a*, Islamic law — that has become the basis of government in countries like Iran to this day. Students accustomed to thinking of the separation of church and state as an absolute can be drawn into discussion about the merits of idealism and the insistence on a guide other than expediency to act as a check on the accretion of laws and policies devised to address the needs of the moment. When that guide is religious in nature, the question of the separation of church and state becomes more pressing.

Also, point out to students that the question of justice keeps arising in these selections. Though the assertion, during the Enlightenment, that the people have the right to disband the government when they find it oppressive is a revolutionary one, these selections' awareness of a prince's obligation to be just — for practical as well as idealistic reasons — may come as a surprise to students who are accustomed to thinking of monarchy as being unchecked, absolute despotism. Engage students on the question of how power also travels upward, even in a monarchy, even when the ruler rules by divine right. Though Machiavelli's assertion that it is better to be feared than to be loved encapsulates his supposed cynicism, he and the writers here were all aware that it is best to be both feared and loved, and consistent justice seems to be the best way to accomplish this.

IN THE CLASSROOM

I. LEADERSHIP AND EGALITARIANISM

The question of leadership — and of the qualities of ideal leaders — is one that occupies us in all times and places. In a democratic, egalitarian society that assumes people all begin on a "level playing field," the identification and selection of leaders — what Thomas Jefferson called "natural aristocrats" — is particularly problematic. If we are all equal, how do we decide who is qualified to guide us? Students can be expected to engage these writings on that level; how do the leaders in their lives — from bosses at work to teachers to university presidents to political figures — adhere to or ignore the guidelines presented in this section? Have they risen to the top by their merits? Who, among the various leaders they follow, should take what advice? Who abuses her power, and who understands his obligations to his followers?

Discussion

1. Have students imagine life in a caste system, in which leaders must be drawn from a given group of people. How would they find a way to be heard if they were not among the designated leaders? How could they influence policy?

2. The question of realism versus idealism permeates this entire section. To what extent does a leader need to disregard ideals in favor of staying in power, given that one must be in power in order to effect justice, compassion, and mercy in government? How does an adherence to a set of ideals help a leader, and how does it hurt her or him?

3. Discuss the benefits of homogeneity to a political unit. How does "group feeling," as Ibn Khaldun defines it, help people understand themselves? To what extent must a government regulate group feeling that doesn't focus on the government when it threatens to supercede devotion to country? How can a state religion help to foster the kind of group feeling that leads to stability and security, and is it worth giving up freedom of religion for that security?

4. List some of the leaders who are most influential in the students' lives. To what extent are these people influential as role models? Does an egalitarian society demand that each person be her own leader? Is this possible or desirable?

Connections

1. The most obvious connection, here, is with Machiavelli (p. 120); engage students, first and foremost, in the question of real versus ideal, reminding them that practicality need not always be limited to the cynical. The stories of most heroes — Quetzalcoatl (p. 721), Sunjata (p. 21), even Don Quixote (p. 262) — comment on the traits of good leaders. Help students to see how differing social circumstances value differing kinds of leaders, and also to see what traits of leaders seem suited to many circumstances. Ask them whether there are leaders who would be leaders regardless of situation and who would always find someone to follow them. Questions of honor and morality, of course, are also important, and the selection from Marguerite de Navarre's *The Heptameron* (p. 185) emphasizes the leader's moral obligation, or at least the potentialities of the moral leader.

2. Have students compare the feats of Quetzalcoatl (p. 721) with those of Sunjata (p. 21). Which text seems most interested in its hero as a leader? How might the interest in hero as a leader shape the narrative by directing the sorts of feats to be described? Which of them is more successful in Machiavelli's terms? Which would be a good courtier in Castiglione's view?

3. What benefits accrue to a moral leader? What stories have they read or heard or seen in which an upright and moral leader triumphs? Do any of the benefits of moral rule outweigh the benefits of being underhanded? To what extent must a ruler be suspicious? vain? cruel? egotistical? Who is the greatest leader who is also upright and upstanding that they know?

Groups

1. Assign groups of students to specific texts, and perhaps have them do a little research into the contexts of each of these texts. Ask them to delineate one ideal prince from another. What does their writer add that none of the others does? How does context shape the picture of the ideal prince? How does the specific situation of the writer change his emphases in terms of these ideal qualities? On which points would their writer disagree with the others?

2. Divide students into debate teams, with one side arguing for idealism in government and the other for realism. The goal might be to define a suitable balance between these competing demands.

3. Ask students to evaluate in groups one of the princes defined in this section. If they could live in a monarchy and be assured that the rulers would be compassionate, just, and strong, would that be preferable to a democracy in which the qualities of the ruler, for any given four years, are uncertain? Then, have each group report back to the larger group on why it chose a particular prince.

Writing

Ask students to write a short paper in response to one or more of the following:

1. Imagine yourself as a leader of some kind, whether in business, politics, or education. You are quite a success, due to your careful reading of the advice for leaders in this section, and are therefore in demand as a lunch speaker at places like the Rotary Club. What do you say as a motivational speaker? Do you extol the virtues of upright behav-

ior, or do you give them "the straight truth"? Write the ten- to fifteen-minute speech (because you have also learned the value of brevity) that you give to help others achieve the same success you have found.

2. Describe the ideal ruler. Place him or her in the most realistic setting you can imagine. Force that ideal ruler to confront the most difficult and contrary issues you can imagine. In a short story, play, or fable of no more than five pages, let your imagination both define and attempt to tear down the finest possible leader.

3. Women play a very small role in these pages, and they are mostly as a hindrance, if they are noticed at all. In a three- to five-page paper, discuss the following: To what extent does the presence of women in public life alter the political scene as these writers knew it? The few queens who ruled during the Early Modern Period knew they had to adjust themselves to the standards of male behavior in order to be convincing as sovereign rulers. What happens when that is no longer necessary, when women participate in the ruling class in large numbers? Is there any perceptible change in the public face of government? Does government approach its problems differently, notice different problems, ask different questions?

BEYOND THE CLASSROOM

Research & Writing

1. Read one or more business advice books or biographies of business leaders. In a five-page paper, answer some or all of the following: To what extent has the author or the subject of the biography learned or discovered the lessons of the authors in *In the World: Fashioning the Prince*, p. 140? Do any of them mention Machiavelli? What did they ostensibly learn from him? What could they learn that they should have learned? Your ultimate thesis, here, should be about the relevance of early modern ideas of the prince's duties to contemporary leaders.

2. Research two or three views of some recent event of horrific, state-sponsored violence: the Nazi Holocaust, the Killing Fields of Cambodia, the genocide of the 1990s in Rwanda, the atrocities against women by the Taliban in Afghanistan. Using Machiavelli and at least one of the other theorists in "Fashioning the Prince," debate the merits of this cruelty in "objective" terms; that is, morality aside, how did the atrocity in question undermine or support the regime that initiated it? What pragmatic conclusions might we draw from this particular event about the utility of morality, at least in terms of the ruler's own subjects?

3. Look into the history of terrorism. To what extent would Machiavelli find this mode of acquiring political power acceptable, especially given the rarity with which terrorist groups actually obtain their goal? Would Machiavelli be sympathetic to the logic that sacrifices innocent people for what, from the perspective of the terrorists, is a larger good?

Projects

1. Have students consider the TV series *The West Wing* to be a twenty-first-century version of the texts represented in this section. Can you distill, from specific moments in the series, a set of precepts for an ideal president of the United States? Which of the theorists represented would be most welcome among the writers of the show? Write and perform a scene for the show from the perspective of, say, Nizam al-Mulk. How might he account for and represent the charisma that has replaced the kind of luminescent royalty he describes?

2.   Have students undertake a team-building exercise called "The Electric Fence." A group of students is given a board and told that they must all pass over an imaginary electric fence that is six feet high. A rope is tied between two trees to represent the top of this fence. The group's task is to figure out how to get every member of the group from one side of the fence to the other without stranding or electrocuting anyone. Once students have done this, re-imagine it as a leader-training exercise as one of the theorists in this section, or Machiavelli, might design it. How could this same game be used to teach leaders to operate effectively (not necessarily morally) for the greatest good?

MEDIA RESOURCES

WEB SITES

Akbar
www.top-biography.com/9001-Akbar/spfeat1.htm
Though an online biography of Akbar, there is information contained on this page about Abu'l Fazl.

Internet Medieval Sourcebook: Renaissance
www.fordham.edu/halsall/sbook1x.html
This site out of Fordham University provides access to the full versions of *The Prince* and *The Book of the Courtier.*

Islamic Philosophy Online
www.muslimphilosophy.com/
This terrific site provides access to information on such Islamic political philosophers as Nizm al-Muk and Ibn Khaldun, among many others. It also contains a map of Islamic philosophy and where it fits in with other world philosophies.

The Islamic World to 1600
www.ucalgary.ca/applied_history/tutor/islam/learning/
This site provides the University of Calgary's excellent tutorial on the Islamic world, from its beginnings in the seventh century to the decline of its three great empires in the seventeenth century. Included is an overview of Islamic arts as well as the Islamic dedication to knowledge and learning, which resulted in significant advancements in medicine, astronomy, mathematics, and philosophy. Also included are brief biographies of eight Muslim scholars who contributed to knowledge in the Islamic world and who made certain scientific discoveries long before their counterparts in other regions of the world.

Japanese Neo-Confucianism
www.wsu.edu:8080/~dee/TOKJAPAN/NEO.HTM
This is Richard Hooker's (Washington State University) page on Neo-Confucianism, which contains a brief overview of Hayashi Razan.

The Italian Renaissance
history.hanover.edu/early/italren.htm
On this site from Hanover University can be found the complete e-text of *The Book of the Courtier* (along with many other key Renaissance documents), the complete e-text of *The Prince*, and Web links to information on Machiavelli.

The Renaissance: Contexts and Comparisons
newman.baruch.cuny.edu/digital/2000/c_n_c/toc/toc_05.htm
This page was created by Paula S. Berggren and Marshall J. Schneider and contains not only very interesting background information on Renaissance literature but also provides

excellent comparative background on Castiglione's *Book of the Courtier* and Machiavelli's *The Prince*.

Renaissance Documents
www.thecaveonline.com/APEH/renaissancedocument.html
This site contains an excerpt of Vespasiano da Bisticci on the prince and also includes excerpts from other documents on key themes of the Renaissance.

MARGUERITE DE NAVARRE, *The Heptameron* (p. 185)

WWW   For a quiz on *The Heptameron*, see *World Literature Online* at
bedfordstmartins.com/worldlit.

Princess and queen, diplomat and negotiator, religious reformer and writer, patron and practitioner of the arts, and considered to be one of the three major prose writers of sixteenth-century France, Marguerite de Navarre certainly epitomizes the ideals of the Renaissance. Her biography will likely fascinate students who are unaware of women like Navarre's influence on the politics and art of their day. Marguerite was a powerful woman, and an intelligent one, involved in the political intrigue and negotiations and the religious, intellectual, and artistic questioning of her time. She was involved in both the worldly and spiritual aspects of her society, and her struggle to negotiate the two is apparent in her writing. She was never willing to completely give up the gratification of the social world but was drawn to attempt to reconcile this part of herself with her understanding of spirituality. She was well aware of the corruptions in her society (and her religious institution) but believed in the possibility of reform.

Because of her close ties to the world, it is difficult not to read Marguerite's biography into her work. Indeed, the selection in the anthology from *The Heptameron* seems to come straight from her life. Like Florida, Marguerite was first married to a man she didn't love. Like Florida, she took her duties to her husband seriously. In Marguerite's case, she negotiated for the return of her husband and her brother from Spain, and when her husband became ill, she nursed him with constant dedication. Clearly, then, like Florida, Marguerite believed in her duties and the sanctity of her obligations. But also like Florida, and perhaps like Parlemente, Marguerite's second marriage followed her inclination and her belief in romantic love. Her difficulties in her marriage — her husband was not as faithful to this idea as was Marguerite — are perhaps also repeated here as we see the characters struggling with the idea of romantic love and the possibility of its realization in an idealized form.

While such dedication to duty might seem to us somewhat too self-effacing to be the sign of an independent, strong woman, Marguerite's life clearly evinces an inner strength and intelligence that must be admired. Just as clearly, as the selection shows, Marguerite was an untiring champion of women. She may not have been a feminist — such terms are anachronistic in the case of a Renaissance princess — but she provides a fascinating case of what a woman in power could accomplish, even if she is constrained by the definitions of her gender. Indeed, her apparent critique of contemporary social systems and beliefs are evocative of gendered critiques of society that are at the heart of feminism today. Encourage students to engage in a discussion of gender in Renaissance society as the selection presents it — how is marriage different for men and women? How does romantic love challenge the ideas of duty behind marriage? What do the various characters in the frame narrative provide as a contextual backdrop for this kind of critique? What do their "takes" on the story of Florida and Amador reveal to us about gender?

TEXT & CONTEXT

COURTLY LOVE: THE RISE OF THE IDEA OF ROMANTIC LOVE

Romantic love, in the West, begins with the troubadours, twelfth-century singers and poets in France who envision "courtly love" — an idealized love that includes complete devotion and self-sacrifice to the adored, usually the wife of a nobleman. The object of desire is always unobtainable, always above the lover in the strict class hierarchy of the time. The honor in courtly love comes from the self-sacrifice of a spiritual love, one which may never be consummated. This is a love based in the idea of adultery, and in the marriage-economy of the time. Love and marriage were not compatible, both because true love depended on giving oneself freely to the loved one and because marriages, at least among the upper classes, were social and political contracts. Several explanations for the rise of courtly love exist, but it seems clear that one reason for the popularity of this version of love for love's sake is that young knights — usually younger brothers left landless by the laws of primogeniture — could have their sexual desires channeled into socially productive actions. It also seems clear that courtly love literature arose in a different context from the Germanic sagas, and therefore these French stories of knights of yore from King Arthur's court catered to a more female audience: Rather than focusing almost exclusively on the heroic deeds of warriors, the troubadours' courtly love literature described love relationships, thereby providing more female characters and important roles more central to the plot.

IN THE CLASSROOM

I. REVISING NOTIONS OF LOVE

Marguerite has often been seen as a standard Renaissance neo-Platonist, repeating uncritically the "golden ladder" idea of Castigilione and others: Earthly love is a road to divine love, and the love of an exalted woman leads the lover to the consideration of the even loftier and more beautiful God. However, as the selection in the anthology clearly demonstrates, Marguerite was far more ambiguous and conflicted about the nature and purpose of earthly love. Amador certainly seems to be the perfect Platonic lover at the beginning of the story, as he is willing to sacrifice himself merely to serve his loved one, merely to be near her. Students can surely be counted on to notice, however, that Amador changes abruptly, becoming impatient with his Platonic situation. This in itself seems a critique of the notion of Platonic love leading to a religious love for God. Similarly, Parlamente's story supposedly reveals the perfect love of a woman. What does this notion of love tell us about Parlamente's, and maybe Navarre's, vision of women's love being one of denial? Have students consider the ways Navarre critiques belief in courtly love and perhaps all romantic love as being impossible for women. Students may be disappointed or feel that Amador's sudden turnaround is a flaw in the story; help them to see how the progress of the story exemplifies this Renaissance debate over the nature of love and honor.

Discussion

1. Ask students to define ideal love as Amador initially describes it. How does this idea of love change? Does Amador really believe it? Does Florida? How does this idea compare to the ideas expressed by the characters in the frame narrative? Have students try to distinguish between different ideas of love.

2. Ask students to consider the role of sexuality in the story and in the frame narrative. Do they reveal different ideas? If so, what are they? What type of sexuality and sexual desire is assigned to men and women?

3. Much is made of the clash between romantic love following the chivalric code and the duty inherent in marriage, but what about the duty to one's friends? Ask students to dis-

cuss the implications of Florida and Amador's relationship in terms of Florida's friendship with Avanturada. Have them compare this with Amador's allegiance to his king. Is there a similar code of allegiance between women?

Connections

1. Compare the conflict between romantic love and marital duty to that pictured in Chikamatsu's *The Love Suicides at Amijima* (Book 4). Does Amador's initial devotion to Florida (or hers to him) include suicide? Why or why not? What differences in ideas of love can be drawn from the two texts?

2. Compare the ideas of romantic love in *The Heptameron* to the nineteenth-century revisions of the notion apparent in Dostoevsky's *Notes from Underground* (Book 5) or Chopin's "The Story of an Hour" (Book 5).

3. Examine the apparent romantic hypocrisy of Amador with the religious hypocrisy of Molière's *Tartuffe* (Book 4). How are these similar? Are they equally horrible?

4. Amador teaches Florida chivalry and honor and is angered when he cannot overcome them for sexual gratification. Don Quixote (p. 262) elevates a peasant girl to a princess and thereby renounces all sexual aims. Compare Don Quixote's view of Dulcinea to Amador's initial view of Florida. How do the narratives they have created escape their control? Who has the greater possibility for true communication?

Groups

1. Have the class choose sides — those who believe in the possibility of "love at first sight" and those who do not. Using as evidence *The Heptameron* as well as other texts about love, both popular and literary, have students argue for their side.

2. In small groups, have students discuss the idea of marriage. Begin by asking them to list what duties spouses (or life partners) have to one another. Next, have students discuss the idea of marriage as presented in the text, that is, one of duty only. How does this idea mesh with their ideas of marriage and romantic love? What has changed since the Renaissance?

Writing

Ask students to write a short paper in response to one or more of the following:

1. The idea of courtly love was considered impossible to achieve in an actual marriage. It was incongruous because it was based on the idea of freely giving one's love, and marriage vows erased that possibility. Love in marriage was a duty. Examine the way Amador's demand of Florida's love (and her sexual submission to him) denies the possibility of this ideal love as exactly as any marriage. How does he erase her free will and so frustrate his own desire?

2. According to Amador, desire trumps duty because passion overwhelms reason (and so is forgivable). Similarly, the male discussants believe that their sexual desire should always be gratified, especially since that is the reason women were created in the first place. How does the switch in focus from Amador to Florida critique this idea in the selection from *The Heptameron*?

3. Discuss your idea of "true love," and examine it against the ideas of love set forth in *The Heptameron*. To what extent does Florida demonstrate true love for Amador by denying him and keeping quiet about her feelings or by the consistency of her feelings in the wake of Amador's changed behavior?

4. Examine the distinction between duty and desire in the text. How does it jibe with your own understanding of the conflict between the two? How do we see this same conflict represented today?

II. DENIAL, REFUSAL, AND SILENCE: THE POWER OF WOMEN

One of the fascinating things about this selection, and about Navarre's writing in general, is the point she seems to be making about women's voices and the impact that forced silence has on their lives. This is, of course, directly related to ideas of duty as being meek obedience. Remind students that this section is written by a woman who was well aware of the force of her own voice (as the diplomat who negotiated a king's freedom) but also of its limitations (both she and her daughter were married to men they despised). Have students consider the ways the women's voices — the possibility of articulating their desires — are compromised or erased by their circumstance. Florida never speaks her own desires; her sense of duty instead silences her. Marguerite is quite clear about the source and nature of women's power: They can refuse, stay silent, deny. The woman does not get to articulate an ideal, here. Florida's entire notion of chivalric love and honor come from Amador's tutelage, and she ultimately outdoes him in devotion to the ideal he has taught her. Her only power lies in staying silent; that is a woman's virtue. Indeed, Marguerite's honor is such that she keeps her very real desires for Amador hidden even after he has attacked her honor.

Discussion

1. Have students locate moments when Florida could speak her mind but instead remains silent. How do these moments of self-repression affect the outcome of the story? To what extent can you trace Florida's self-censorship to Amador's tutelage?

2. Have students consider how femininity and masculinity are defined in relation to voice — to speaking or keeping quiet? Consider, especially, times when characters act outside of their traditional roles, such as Amador's inability to speak when he first sees Florida or hears Florida's scream.

3. Give students five or ten minutes to freewrite on the question of which of their parents silenced him- or herself more often. After discussing what they have written, ask them to recollect their own self-censorship in relationships. Does this change from courtship to commitment?

4. Ask students to discuss the frame narrative and, specifically, the characters' reactions to Florida at the end of the story. Does anyone, besides Parlamente, laud Florida? Or are they more interested in Amador? What does this suggest?

Connections

1. Compare Chaucer's Wife of Bath's (Book 2) outspokenness with Florida's silences. Does being a widow allow the Wife of Bath more freedom?

2. Compare Florida's self-censorship to the narrator's attempt to reconcile herself to the "rest cure" in Gilman's "The Yellow Wallpaper" (Book 5).

3. Compare the storytellers of Navarre's text to Boccaccio's (Book 2): The former are constrained to telling true stories by the rules of their conversation. Thus the ideal is relegated to the discussions that come after the true stories, and a kind of empiricism comes into play. Can we see this as a sign of the times, the coming of science to literature?

Writing

Ask students to write a short paper in response to one or more of the following:

1. How can you reconcile the silences of the women in the story to the outspokenness of the women in the frame narrative? to the fact that a woman is telling the story in the first place? and a woman is writing it?

2. Does Florida, by her silence about her love and her adherence to the ideals of courtly love that Amador has taught her, become the ideal lover at the end of the story? How does the inability of the frame characters, particularly of the men, to see her as anything other than an object (or obstacle) make them unable to see this? How does the fact that Parlemente tells the story help us to see the ironies inherent in the conventions of courtly love, especially that the selfless devotion to the beloved is so often an erasure of the real woman, or of any woman's agency?

3. Are there any situations today where men or women are rightly silenced? Define the concept of acceptable and unacceptable censorship using *The Heptameron* and then try to find modern examples of both sorts of censorship.

4. Describe a time when you kept your silence. Discuss the reasons for this silence, and consider how speaking your mind might have changed the outcome of the situation.

BEYOND THE CLASSROOM

RESEARCH & WRITING

1. Read Boccaccio's *Decameron* (Book 2) and more of Navarre's *The Heptameron*. In a seven- to ten-page paper, comment on the nature of influence and criticism in the relationship between the two texts. Where does Navarre imitate, and where does she critique? Is this fundamentally related to gender or only marginally?

2. Research the use of frame narratives to collect a number of stories in one literary work. Does this device still exist? Do characters still comment on stories in the same ways?

3. Research the idea of romantic love. Is this a specifically Western idea, or does it appear in other cultures? Does the conflict between duty and desire take the same form in the art of other cultures?

Projects

1. A question that continues to provoke heated debate is whether art imitates life or vice versa. Consider this question in terms of the idea of romantic love, which seemingly got its start in the West with the medieval troubadours. Create a multimedia presentation on the rise of romantic love.

2. Present a reader's theater production of *The Heptameron*.

3. Write and perform a screenplay in which you insert an additional character into the frame narrator based on one of the other authors that you have read this semester, using his or her story as another in *The Heptameron*. How would the other characters comment on the new story? How would she or he comment on one of theirs?

WWW   For additional information on Marguerite de Navarre and annotated Web links, see *World Literature Online* at bedfordstmartins.com/worldlit.

FURTHER READING

Lewis, C. S. *The Allegory of Love: A Study in Medieval Tradition.* 1958.
Strage, Mark. *Women of Power: The Life and Times of Catherine de' Medici.* 1976.

MEDIA RESOURCES

WEB SITES

Blackmask Online — The Memoirs of Marguerite de Valois, Queen of Navarre
www.blackmask.com/books34c/cm04bdex.htm
Read the complete e-text of Navarre's memoirs at this site.

Marguerite de Navarre
Lib.virginia.edu/speccol/exhibits/Gordon/lit/marguerite.html
This page is part of a much larger site produced by the University of Virginia Library Special Collections Department that provides researchers with digital facsimiles of sixteenth-century printed books. It includes a facsimile of a 1560 edition of Navarre's *The Heptameron* and a transcription of the text. The site also provides a brief biography.

Other Women's Voices: Translations of Women's Writing Before 1700 — Marguerite de Navarre
www.tl.infi.net/~ddisse/navarre.html
A wonderful resource, this site gives a brief account of Navarre's life and publications. It also offers links to e-texts of several of her works, including *The Heptameron*. Many of these texts are translated, but some are in the original French. In addition, the site provides researchers with bibliographic information for a number of Navarre's works available only in print as well as for secondary sources.

MICHEL EYQUEM DE MONTAIGNE, *Essays* (p. 214)

WWW   For a quiz on *Essays*, see *World Literature Online* at
        bedfordstmartins.com/worldlit.

Montaigne, though sometimes frustratingly digressive, exudes geniality and tolerance, so students should warm to him. Be certain to help them catch Montaigne's tone of humility and open-mindedness, as that will help to offset his style — a style for which Montaigne himself did not apologize. He said that if you get lost reading his essays, it's because you are an inattentive reader. He also understood himself to be writing to a small and select audience. Neither of these facts will probably be very useful in getting students into reading Montaigne. His love for humanity and his respect for the variousness of human beings, on the other hand, will appeal to them. Montaigne invented, or at least named, the essay, and his method — described by Donald Frame as letting his mind wander as far afield as possible before pulling it back to the original topic and then filling in the space between — sets the standard for the leisurely, loose form that the essay has become. His famous medallion bearing the motto "What Can I Know?" may have been a starting point for modern skepticism. However, his answer to that question was not "nothing," or even "nothing for sure," but "myself, first and foremost." Once he felt he knew himself, he claimed an authority to know other things.

His *Essays* were sallies against the fortress of himself — attempts at his own personality — and he took them seriously as such. He called his book consubstantial with himself. When it was first published in 1580, *Essays* comprised only two books. By 1588, he had written a third book, and so a revised edition appeared. Montaigne revised this version for the next four years before his death in an unbound copy; these emendations consisted of about a thousand added passages. Montaigne believed in the inevitability of flux, and he embraced it; thus his book changed as he changed. *Essays*, according to Montaigne, had as much influence on him as he had on it, apparently a greater influence than his term as mayor of

Bordeaux — a public post that convinced him of Machiavelli's truth that one cannot be a politician and remain morally unstained. He preferred the self that he devised through his book to the professional, public self that the circumstances of his life offered him.

TEXT & CONTEXT

THE ESSAY AS KNOWLEDGE AND THE ESSAY AND KNOWLEDGE

Montaigne, in a late revision of *Essays*, inserted a passage in which he claimed that "I have no more made my book than my book has made me." Montaigne did not understand himself to be inventing a literary genre but discovering a self. He denominated the segments of the book *Essays* as "chapters." He used the term *essays* to describe the lifelong process of writing the chapter, which he thought of as an experiment on or test of himself, not the writing that his experiments produced. He was thus creating a kind of knowledge that was subjective. Though his method involved cultivating a sense of detachment from himself and his world, he nonetheless understood the world by first understanding himself.

It is important to note that Montaigne understood moral philosophy — the search for the proper way to live — to be the highest inquiry, and that it was, to him, as objective as the kinds of inquiry we denominate "scientific" or "empirical." Pointing out to students that Montaigne understood morality to be something that exists outside of human beings clarifies his tolerance of difference in the indigenous Brazilians he describes in "Of Cannibals": Montaigne does not declare all morality equal, but considers the Brazilians admirable because they have derived proper moral attributes from nature. They have found moral truth through God's creation, and Montaigne believes that God made all things good because God himself is good. Montaigne's criticism of civilization depends on his sense that civilized society betrays the direct revelation of morality in the Bible as well as the indirect revelation of morality through nature. Montaigne also believed, according to Frame, that God is a distant figure who has placed humans in a context so that they might fulfill their ultimate purpose of learning to conduct themselves in a manner worthy of the gifts of reason and soul that God gave them. He learned this through his attempt to understand himself. Another late passage inserted toward the end of the *Essays* states that although death is the end of life, it is not life's goal. Philosophy's ultimate purpose, for Montaigne, is to teach us how to enjoy our lives, not to accept our deaths; philosophy is not a set of precepts but an ongoing process that arises from enjoying, or at least living, our lives.

THE *STUDIOLO*, THE CABINET OF CURIOSITIES, AND MONTAIGNE'S STYLE

In the fifteenth and sixteenth centuries in Italy, the *studiolo*, a small room reserved for books and art, was an important status symbol and, according to Dora Thornton, an important way for the professional classes, who were some of the most active and ambitious of the humanists, to attain civic and political prominence. Over the course of the Renaissance, this sort of room — which the Medicis, in particular, commissioned art for, thus fulfilling the ideal of the prince as both man of action and well-read scholar — became the *wunderkammer* or *kunstkammer*, a "cabinet of curiosities," which is an ancestor of the modern museum. Montaigne's own study was more like a library than a museum, as its chief inventory consisted of one thousand books and only a few artifacts and artworks, but Montaigne seems nonetheless to have taken a view of knowledge and books analogous to the view of artifacts that a studiolo represents. Montaigne refers to several of the artifacts he did own in "Of Cannibals," but that's not the most important reference to the studiolo. More often, throughout his *Essays*, Montaigne presents us a collection of quotations from the authors of the past as artifacts in a verbal studiolo so that we almost seem to be browsing with him. While, certainly, he appeals to the authority of the ancients as any good humanist would, Montaigne also provides his readers with an idiosyncratic knowledge in the form of a collection assembled according to his interests.

The museum is intimately connected with the history of exploration and discovery; indeed, Western civilization has been described as a steamroller that smashes other civilizations to bits, then collects the bits and preserves them under glass. The age of exploration was also the beginning of the empirical age, and the wonders of nature were soon to become the objects of scientific study, but, in Montaigne's time, the wonders of the world still served as proof of the marvel of God's creation. Along with the knowledge of himself that Montaigne gained over the course of his book, he imparts such knowledge of the world as he has at his fingertips and draws from it lessons not about the functioning of the laws that regulate the world but moral lessons for the proper conduct of our lives.

IN THE CLASSROOM

I. MONTAIGNE'S EXPERIMENT ON HIMSELF

Help students connect with Montaigne's project to test himself through writing. The notion that writing is a discovery of ourselves continues to shape the teaching of writing, and many exercises from the composition classroom can be used to help students see this fact, and thus to realize the enormity of Montaigne's achievement as the first to set sail on the ship of reason for the dark and turbulent seas of the inner self. Ask students to think about how their own attitudes toward the world have been shaped, and encourage them to see how the process of education, particularly in terms of writing, eventually aims at providing them with the tools to fashion themselves, as Montaigne's book does for him. It is his lifelong testing of his own nature that Montaigne claims for his authority to generalize. Even as you introduce the concept of writing as exploration, engage students in the process of testing that claim. Can assuming an attitude bring that attitude about? Can we change the inner self by altering the outward appearance — or the attitudes we take toward things outside of us? When we discover what we think through writing, are we uncovering opinions, or are we making something entirely new which we then come to accept as our opinions?

Discussion

1. Does cultural relativism have its limits? Despite Montaigne's assertion that we cannot judge other cultures except against our own, he nonetheless takes the measure of both his own culture and the exotic other culture by comparing them to a set of standards he considers absolute. Is there an advantage to Montaigne's method? What are the pitfalls of accepting other cultures as they are and refusing to make moral judgments? Does that leave us anywhere to stand if we want to criticize, say, the Nazi Holocaust, the genocide in Rwanda, or female "circumcision" among certain African people?

2. Ask students to think about the ways in which schools do and do not foster the kind of thinking Montaigne values in "Of Cannibals." When Montaigne describes his witness of Brazil, he lauds him as "a simple, crude fellow" whose veracity he therefore trusts. What is he saying about relative levels of expertise? Is he ironically referring to his own limitations as an interpreter? Does he wish that everyone except himself were this sort of fellow? Do schools help to "weed out" such people? Should they?

3. Give students a chance to experience Montaigne's method for themselves, briefly, and discuss the results. Have students write a sentence of description about some other country whose social norms they admire — the Spanish and their siestas, for example, or Italians and their meals — and from that sentence develop a paragraph of moral lessons. In what sense is this an objective distillation of knowledge from fact, and in what

sense is it the addition of something on top of the facts? How does taking a genial, admiring attitude alter their feelings about the country they describe?

Connections

1. Perhaps the most obvious connections with Montaigne's "Of Cannibals" are other selections from the anthology that deal with travel and the meeting of different cultures; several *In the World* sections, especially "Imagining Africa" (Book 6), "Travel Narratives" (Book 4), "Pilgrimage and Travel" (Book 2), "East and West" (Book 5), and "Colonialism: Europe and Africa" (Book 6), treat this theme. In a large class, students could be grouped and given one of these sections; using Montaigne's moral questioning as a model, ask them to judge the reactions of the various writers to the exotic others they meet. In particular, Montaigne defines the "character fit to bear witness," which is either simple and crude or strictly honest; the awareness that we only have the standards of our own culture with which to judge; and the proximity of more "primitive" civilizations to nature as a recommendation for their greater purity. To what extent do the writers in each section agree with these precepts for the traveler, and to what extent do they disagree? How might these attitudes help or hurt us in the process of understanding others?

Writing

Ask students to respond to one or more of the following in a short paper. For the first topic, you might give them a list of nouns about which to write their essays:

1. Use Montaigne's method on yourself. With minimal library research, choose a topic that strikes your fancy, and follow your whims. Limit your Montaigne-like essay to two pages. On the third (and fourth, at most) page, discuss the kind of knowledge you derived from this experiment and/or whether it was indeed knowledge at all.

2. Describe a group of people you consider attractive and exotic, whose way of life, as you have heard it described or perhaps even experienced it, appeals to you. In as much detail as possible, within five pages, discuss this group. Don't worry about sticking to a thesis; let your mind wander, and worry later about making connections or cutting irrelevancies. So, research if you wish, or simply daydream from an advertisement in a magazine. Most of all, cultivate an attitude of respect for the group you describe, but do not succumb to the temptation to make them perfect. Consider, too, the ways in which, according to your own sense of proper conduct, their society falls short.

3. Write an essay about an incident from your life — the smaller the better — and then make that incident as significant as possible. Pile up as many interpretations of the event as you think it can bear. Look at Montaigne's "Of Training" for a model of this kind of writing and thinking about your own experience.

II. MONTAIGNE AND THE STUDIOLO

The studiolo, while it may have been a distant ancestor of the museum, was not a museum. It was not public but private; it did not seek to be comprehensive but to reflect a single person's enthusiasms. For his studiolo, Federico da Montefeltro commissioned a *trompe l'oeil* masterpiece of inlaid wood in which each illusionary shelf was stocked with objects that related to his enthusiasms. By his munificence and taste, he thus demonstrated his well-roundedness, being both a man of action and a scholar. The studiolo was important as a way not just for aristocrats to burnish their images but also for the professional classes to advance themselves in the civic life. Montaigne, even with all his humility, presents himself in his essays the way Montefeltro did in his studiolo: Each anecdote of his life, each quotation prized from ancient authors, serves to show how Montaigne is trustworthy, a man who is conducting his life in a proper manner and so can be a model for the rest of us. He is also a model of knowledge, or rather of knowing and of how to go about knowing things. Montaigne's way of knowing is not by the systematic construction of vast institutes of science but by the particular and individual interests of one human being, who then serves as a connection to others. Understanding the world begins with understanding yourself, and you can begin to understand yourself by understanding your enthusiasms and interests.

Discussion

1. Ask students about the notion of understanding themselves. What do we mean by it? How do we go about doing it? Begin the discussion by having students jot down, for five or ten minutes, all of their interests and activities. Ask them if their curricular and extracurricular interests help them to understand themselves, and discuss in what way for a few minutes, perhaps questioning specific students on how they arrived at their particular interests. Then, have all the students choose one of the interests they listed and freewrite, for five minutes, on the question of what this interest says about them. Point out to them that Montaigne's favorite pastime was roaming the countryside on horseback; what does this pastime say about Montaigne? Does it seem fitting? To what extent does Montaigne's personality direct what he can and cannot understand, what kind of knowledge he's bound to achieve and by what method he's bound to achieve it? Is his character — are all of our characters — destiny?

2. Ask students to write for a few minutes about collections they had when they were young. Do they still have those collections? What did they collect? If they have somehow lost that collection, voluntarily or involuntarily, does it feel like a loss? What part of themselves does this collection signify? If the class could have "show and tell" and share their collections, what would their collections say about them?

Connections

1. Although Montaigne's attitude toward others is in many ways exemplary, particularly given his time (see *In the World:* Discovery and Confrontation, p. 225, for a broader picture of Montaigne's milieu), he is nonetheless a member of the exploring class, the wealthy and acquisitive Renaissance Europe, and he nonetheless has a certain patrician attitude toward the peoples of the rest of the world. Contrast Montaigne's views with those of Okonkwo in Chinua Achebe's *Things Fall Apart* (Book 6). Does Okonkwo exhibit any of the moral characteristics Montaigne describes in his essay? Would these characteristics have helped Okonkwo adjust to the incursion of the missionaries into his world? Does the "subaltern" — the other who is by definition below the observer — have any reason to take the kind of tolerant, genial attitude that Montaigne can afford?

Groups

1. Bring a strange artifact into class. It might be an obscure part of a car, a kitchen gadget, an unfamiliar musical instrument. Name the place — it might be safest to choose an unpopulated place like Antarctica — and fictional group of people from which it comes. Break students into groups of no more than six. Have two students act the part of Montaigne, and describe the artifact to the rest of the group, deciding what function it serves in its society, including as much detail as they can invent about rituals, stories, and occasions for the use of the artifact. The remaining students, either singly or in pairs, should adopt an attitude toward the artifact: an intolerant judgment of the society and a tolerant but wary acceptance of the society's rituals. In the large group, have students discuss the ways in which these three roles made them feel about the nonex-

istent society. Did practicing intolerance make them, in fact, develop a dislike? Did tolerance do the opposite? Did the creation of supposedly objective knowledge about the culture make them more defensive of the culture? To what extent can knowledge determine attitudes, and to what extent can attitudes determine knowledge?

Writing

Ask students to respond to one or more of the following in a short paper:

1. Write an essay that includes some artifact from your home. Build that artifact into your essay as a piece of evidence that proves some point, perhaps about the wonder of the world, perhaps about its depravity. Provide, also, at least two quotations that support this same point; one of these quotations should be from Montaigne.

2. Read about skepticism in a general reference about philosophy. To what extent does Montaigne fit this definition? How does he figure in this particular reference book's history of skepticism? Do you think, based on "Of Cannibals," that Montaigne would enjoy being included in such company? If you like, write this paper as a dialog between Montaigne and the editors of the reference work, or write it as a dinner party attended by Montaigne and the other skeptics mentioned in the reference work's entry.

BEYOND THE CLASSROOM

RESEARCH & WRITING

1. Take a tour of the Museum of Jurassic Technology Web site (http://www.mjt.org). This mock-up of a museum points out the ways in which authority and structure, the trappings of science and institutional knowledge, nonetheless depend on individual interest and the passions of particular people. Having shown them the site, and the oddly plausible exhibits, engage them in the question of whether this is authentic. How does creating plausible but false knowledge about the world muddy the waters of knowledge? Is this a good thing or a bad thing? Should we lose faith in our capability of knowing? Should we approach learning and knowledge in a more personal way, allowing lab reports to be written in the first person, learning the history of science as a series of people rather than concepts? Or is there value in the sense that science, for example, proceeds of its own accord and can essentially plug faceless researchers into its method and continue to categorize and therefore know the entire world? Conversely, is every point of view valid? Are all of the truths that we create, even through misunderstanding and falsehood, somehow authentic views of the universe that deserve to be understood?

2. Look up the same word in two or three different collections of quotations, like *Bartlett's Familiar Quotations*. What quotations show up in all of them, and what quotations are unique to each? Do these similarities and differences say something about the concept you have looked up? Comment on the sort of knowledge that a collection of quotations produces. What is your experience of reading these collections of quotations?

3. Review a museum exhibit. Research the subject of the exhibit so that you can write knowledgeably about how the exhibit presents its subject. Be sure to describe the exhibit in plenty of detail. Does it serve as an introduction, or does it seek to be comprehensive? How does it go about trying to convince us of its authority? How convincing is it?

Projects

1. Collect artifacts and/or quotations that relate to your most cherished interest. Design (either in words or in drawings) or build a container that will display your collection.

Think about the ways in which the display can say something true about yourself and about your interest; display your finished product to the class in a ten-minute presentation.

2. Draw the floor plan for a museum you would like to see. Its topic can be real or imaginary; its approach to that topic should reflect your understanding of the ways in which a collection of artifacts or books can be an argument about that topic. Present your floor plan to the class in a ten-minute presentation. The best presentations will take special care to explain how the arrangement of the museum builds an argument both for its own authority and about the topic at hand.

WWW For additional information on Montaigne and annotated Web links, see *World Literature Online* at bedfordstmartins.com/worldlit.

FURTHER READING

Adorno, Theodor. "The Essay as Form." In *Notes to Literature*, Vol. 1. Rolf Tiedemann, ed. Trans. Shierry Weber Nicholsen. 1991.
Frame, Donald M. *Montaigne's Essais: A Study.* 1969.
Thornton, Dora. *The Scholar in His Study: Art and Ownership in Renaissance Italy.* 1998.

WWW See *World Literature in the 21st Century* at bedfordstmartins.com/worldlit for information about the twenty-first-century relevance of Montaigne.

MEDIA RESOURCES

VIDEO
Michel de Montaigne: "What Do I Know?"
32 min., 1996 (Films for the Humanities & Sciences)
This lyrical program examines the life and work of Michel de Montaigne. Excerpts from his writings are spoken by noted actor Francis Dumaurier, who aptly portrays him. Period and classical images, Renaissance music by the Baltimore Consort, and footage of France, including the tower hermitage at Montaigne's château in Dordogne, combine to paint a vivid portrait of the writer who firmly established the essay as a form of literary expression.

WEB SITES
Michel Eyquem de Montaigne
www.orst.edu/instruct/ph1302/philosophers/montaigne.html
This site contains a brief biography of Montaigne, along with a timeline of his life and links to e-texts of many of his essays.

Montaigne Studies
humanities.uchicago.edu/orgs/montaigne/
The Web site for the journal published annually by the University of Chicago, this is an indispensable resource. The site includes a large gallery of portraits of Montaigne, photographs of volumes from the university's Montaigne collection, and an extensive array of links to Renaissance Web sites. It also includes a listing of the journal's contents dating back to the first volume published in 1989.

Ralph Waldo Emerson on Montaigne
www.emersoncentral.com/montaigne.htm
This site contains the complete e-text of Emerson's essay on Montaigne from *Representative Men* (1850).

Renaissance Society of America
www.r-s-a.org/
This site provides a valuable database of Renaissance-related journals and books sponsored by the RSA as well as an index of links to sites concerning the Middle Ages and the Renaissance.

In the World: Discovery and Confrontation (p. 225)

This section provides students — and instructors — with a wider view of the potentialities of exploration. Voyagers can be pilgrims, conquerors, tourists, missionaries, explorers, discoverers, opportunists. The stance the voyager takes toward the world he investigates determines, obviously, what the voyager will find along the way. Help students to see how the perspective of the explorer shapes the journey. Vasco da Gama's first voyage, for example, clearly arrogated to itself the chore of sounding the Christianity of India. The crewman's journal tells a different story because of its writer's unusual situation. Da Gama comes across in the narrative as focused only on his mission, and one cannot escape the notion that the underlings were enjoying a joke on their superior, dancing while he wears himself out with his serious intentions. Similarly, the letter of Nzinga Mbemba to the king of Portugal holds the king's Christianity up as a mirror for him to follow, but here the subtext that the king's subjects do not act according to the dictates of his religion is not comic but tragic, the beginning of the decline of a civilization.

The voyager's purpose entirely shapes his narrative. For this reason, the journal of the Portuguese sailor from da Gama's first journey contrasts sharply with the history of China by Matteo Ricci. Although the civilizations of India and China are of comparable age, the former is given no credence, while the latter is discussed in detail and with respect. The explorer forces his way into the temple, assuming that a female deity must be the Virgin Mary and that paintings of gods must be saints, while the missionary gives rational arguments for the singularity and existence of God to his dinner hosts. Ricci takes a balanced and reasonable stance, seeing China with the strategic view of a lifelong missionary, one who seeks to persuade rather than confront, since he has a lifetime in which to accomplish his purpose. His respect for Chinese civilization leads him to a certain balance in his tone (and, incidentally, he published a book in Chinese about "the memory castle," a mnemonic device). Contrast this with the factual but more uncertain view of the Portuguese sailor, who does not trouble himself to explain why, for example, the landing party forces its way into an audience with the king and what happens to its hostile opponents once it has reached the king. At the other end of the spectrum, Evliya Çelebi nearly fawns on his subject, pushing his prose to portray the marvelous in what he has seen in his travels. According to Stephen Greenblatt, explorers writing about the New World employed the marvelous as a figure of speech that allowed them to take or deny possession of the unexplored in their writing. The ambiguity of the marvelous provided them an opportunity to indicate the strangeness of what they had seen. These writers are confronting civilizations that may include wonders but are undeniably civilized.

The purposes of the explorers, then — missionary work, establishing trade — may include less coercive means, and the viewpoint, as a result, may be more rational and objective. Help students to see the political purposes of these voyagers and how those purposes help to shape their narratives. Whereas da Gama was looking to establish a rather lopsided kind of trade (of which Mbemba's letter helps us to see the result), for example, Zheng-He (Cheng Ho) assumed a more directly acquisitive stance, demanding that the kingdoms he visited pay tribute to China merely on the strength of its reputation and Zheng-He's military might. The fact that his history is being written in retrospect, in order to glorify the Ming dynasty, also plays a key role in the matter-of-fact listing of his accomplishments. Ricci was more concerned with introducing Christianity into a civilized country, while Çelebi's sole purpose seems to be to see strange things. His writing seems to be the purpose of his voyage, and as a result, his narrative is the most embellished and ornamented, the most fun to read. All of these purposes help to explain the vastly differing narrative styles. Help students to see how writing — the most sophisticated "representational technology," in Greenblatt's terms, available to this era — helps these writers to achieve their various purposes.

IN THE CLASSROOM

I. Purpose and Truth, Expectations and Realizations

Students may come to the stories of Europeans among different cultures with a variety of strongly held viewpoints, from the notion that Europeans always act heinously in such a situation to the idea that Europeans always act magnanimously. These texts mostly present Europeans in the former stance, adopting a superior view and enforcing it despite moral strictures to the contrary. Ricci, through his respect for China, and Zheng-He, through his imperialism, help to counter a simplistic view of the relationships between cultures. Assist students in engaging in these texts on their own terms and to resist easy generalizations in favor of particular attention to the texts themselves. Most of all, we should bear in mind as we read these texts that the voyagers had to make momentous choices without any means of checking with their superiors. If they made egregious decisions as a result, we should recognize that they were individuals and not the entire culture.

Discussion

1. Have students speculate on the motives of each of the writers and the ways in which these motives shape what they see and how they respond. The first and most obvious difference in perspective is that between conqueror and conquered. How do the conquerors feel when the conquered refuse to act as if they are conquered? If da Gama is searching, as he tells the Indians, for "Christians and spices," what can students assume from this yoking about the Portuguese sailors' attitudes toward the two? How does the religious term square with the economic one? How does Mbemba negotiate with strange intruders?

2. Notice the differences in the nature of the contact between cultures. Vasco da Gama and Zheng-He assume a superior position to the cultures they encounter; Ricci a more objective one; Mbemba and Çelebi, in much different circumstances, a vaguely subservient position. To what extent are these rhetorical devices, and to what extent are they reflections of the true relationships between the cultures? Are the relative positions of the cultures inevitable, or do the voyagers' attitudes tend to become self-fulfilling prophecies?

Groups

1. Assign groups of students to each write a response to one of the texts in this section. For Mbemba, of course, this is easiest; they should assume the role of king of Portugal. In the other cases, the students will need to think about who they are and why they might be writing to the writer. Are they, for example, about to embark on a similar voyage and wish to have more information about what they are likely to encounter? In a large group, have a member of each group read the group's letter aloud, and discuss how they went about strategizing their letter.

2. Have students, in groups, consider how different one of these texts might be if the voyager had assumed a different attitude toward the culture he engaged. For example, they

might rewrite Mbemba's letters from the stance of an arrogant and inflexible ruler demanding that the Portuguese leave and never trade with them again. Discuss the likely consequences of various stances, making sure to return to the texts for particular evidence to support the assumptions they make.

Writing

Ask students to write a short paper, responding to one or more of the following:

1. To what extent might the purpose of the text — the market for the writing — shape the text? Çelebi is probably the only one who was writing for a literary market, and Zhang Ting-yu is the only historian. Contrast their differing methods of presenting information.

2. You are the leader of an expedition to a previously unknown culture, and you are in charge of making contact with this culture. You are trying to gain information about the culture, but your main purpose is to establish trade and see what advantages you can gain from this culture. You have several soldiers with you, carrying the most advanced weapons available to your culture. Write a journal or narrative history about what happens when you first meet this group about whom you have only heard that they are somewhat unreliable, sometimes reacting with hostility, and other times welcoming visitors with open arms.

3. Write an essay about a time when you were a tourist. As a thought experiment, speculate about what that experience would have been like had you been a conqueror or a missionary. Alternately, you might write about a time when a tourist or a group of tourists were particularly intrusive in your hometown, and speculate about what you would have done had you been a ruler and they, subjects far from home with no embassy in sight.

II. CONNECTIONS: EXPLORATION AND LITERARY IMAGINATION

One of the most obvious connections, here, is with Montaigne's "Of Cannibals" (p. 214), in which Montaigne, having heard of a culture in Brazil, proceeds to find them more moral and Christian, in some ways, than the Europeans. That accusation shows up, here, in Mbemba. How does it differ when it comes from an "outsider" — who may be a Christian but is nonetheless not one. Consider, too, the ways in which the tone of Çelebi's text — characteristic as it is of certain kinds of travel writing — might have influenced the metaphor John Donne employs in his "To His Mistress Going to Bed" (p. 111), namely, his lover as an undiscovered country. Also of interest is Machiavelli's *The Prince* (p. 124), particularly where he discusses the role of the prince in extending his empire. To what extent, for example, does the Ming dynasty follow his advice in sending out Zheng He to collect tributes? Finally, compare the pleasure gardens described in Coleridge's "Kubla Khan" (Book 5) to those described by Çelebi.

Discussion

1. Ask students to think about these primary sources and the ways in which Montaigne's philosophy, based on second-hand information, might have been different had he been one of the people on the voyage. Among the explorers presented here, whose attitude is most like Montaigne's? Whose is least like his? To what extent would Montaigne and Mbemba agree about the nature of the contact between European and African culture?

2. Have students trace the various strategies that the rulers in this section have for expanding empire and acquiring wealth through exploration. To what extent would Machiavelli have approved of this purpose and its strategies? Would he have been criti-

cal of overreaching, or would he have applauded the attempt to gain wealth for the prince's subjects?

Writing

Ask students to write a short paper, responding to one or more of the following:

1. You are the ruler of a small but militarily powerful country. You have just learned that a rich country has been discovered, well-populated, militarily weak, and incredibly prosperous. In a dialog between a prince and his advisers, or in a journal, or in a narrative history, relate the ruler's ideal response to this information. How can this ruler best increase her wealth without either embroiling herself unnecessarily or losing out to her greedy neighbors?

2. Analyze the rhetorical situation in which Nzinga Mbemba finds himself. How, from a position of weakness and need, can he convince the king of Portugal to reign in his subjects? How well has he done considering his circumstances? Can you think of any further arguments that Mbemba could use to influence the king? Does Machiavelli offer him any help?

3. Compare the marvels that Çelebi enumerates to those in Coleridge's famous poem, "Kubla Khan" (Book 5). Coleridge claimed to have written that poem in an opium-induced dream after reading an account in a different book of travels. How does the description of the sumptuous garden play out in the poem and in the prose narrative? Which seems more factual? Which takes more advantage of the exoticism of the locale?

BEYOND THE CLASSROOM

RESEARCH & WRITING

1. Read two or three biographies of one of the writers in this section, or of Vasco da Gama. How do different biographers portray their motives? Are they always heroic, or are they sometimes villainous? Do the biographers reveal different facts as they attribute to their subject differing motives?

2. Read *The Memory Palace of Matteo Ricci*. How do you judge Ricci's motives for writing the book in Chinese? Is his notion that he will attract Chinese to Christianity by showing them his culture's achievement arrogant or humble?

3. Research the role of written language in the advancement of civilization. Is writing a key invention that makes one civilization better than another, more capable of progress and technology? Or is it mere chance that the civilizations with writing prospered in the contact between cultures? Or is it perhaps a result of looser morals that come of having rules written down rather than memorized?

4. Choose a spice or a food — cinnamon or corn — and research the history of its introduction into Western European culture. How did people react to their first taste? What words did they use to describe it? Is there an element of the marvelous in their reaction? Do people worry that it will poison them? As the spice or food becomes more common, do the people remember where the food originally came from, or does it become a part of the native food?

5. Look into several science-fiction depictions of the encounter between two cultures, for example the books or movies *2001: A Space Odyssey, Contact,* or *Starship Troopers.* Other books include *The Left Hand of Darkness, Jem, Little Fuzzy,* and many others. This sort of book abounds, and there are many other choices. The important thing is to read

more than one, and trace the ways in which the real-life history of contact between cultures shows up. Do the books imagine a better outcome than the real-life one? A worse outcome? How do we judge the outcome?

FURTHER READING

Greenblatt, Stephen. *Marvelous Possessions: The Wonder of the New World.* 1992.
Levathes, Louise. *When China Ruled the Seas: The Treasure Fleet of the Dragon Throne, 1405–1433.* 1997.
Spence, Jonathan D. *The Memory Palace of Matteo Ricci.* 1984.

MEDIA RESOURCES

WEB SITES

Evliya Celebi: A Life of Travel
www.mfa.gov.tr/grupc/ca/caa/uu/marmara/muze/sadberk/ist/evliya.htm
Published by the Republic of Turkey Office of Foreign Affairs, this site provides a brief biography of Çelebi and the influence of his *Book of Travels.*

The Great Chinese Mariner Zheng He
www.chinapage.com/zhenghe.html
This is a well-illustrated page that provides brief information about Zheng He's voyages of discovery.

Matteo Ricci and the Jesuits
www.illuminatedlantern.com/christianity/page2.html
This site gives an excellent overview of Ricci's time in China.

The Ming Dynasty's Maritime History
www.ucalgary.ca/applied_history/tutor/eurvoya/ming.html
This site provides an overview and map of explorations that took place during the Ming dynasty and compares it with the European explorations of the era.

Rome Reborn: The Vatican Library & Renaissance Culture
www.loc.gov/exhibits/vatican/romechin.html
This page from the Library of Congress provides brief textual material about Roman influence on China accompanied by facsimile reproductions of original documents

The Story of Africa: Portuguese Intervention in the West
www.bbc.co.uk/worldservice/africa/features/storyofafrica/10chapter4.shtml
Created by the BBC, this site provides a wonderful overview of the effects of the Portuguese on West Africa and also contains audio files of Mbemba's letter to the king of Portugal.

MIGUEL DE CERVANTES SAAVEDRA, *Don Quixote* (p. 262)

WWW   For a quiz on *Don Quixote,* see *World Literature Online* at
bedfordstmartins.com/worldlit.

Don Quixote has been such a favorite with readers that it has been translated into almost as many languages as the Bible. Moreover, many of the readers of *Don Quixote* have been famous novelists whose work in some way reflects or comments on this great, rambling novel. From the spurious continuation written by "Avellaneda" to Henry Fielding to Jorge

Luis Borges, *Don Quixote* has served as inspiration and foil. The character whose delusions lead her into misadventures — whose skewed reality is more attractive and real than the degraded world around her — is nearly a stock figure in the tradition of the novel. The influence of this book is so wide and undeniable that it is sometimes hard to perceive the text through all of our associations with and expectations of it. Encourage students to first of all read the selections from the novel, trying to see the text as it is through the various interpretations and illustrations of the novel that have accumulated over the centuries. Once they have engaged it, then they can begin to see the myriad Don Quixotes in the world around us, from cartoons that portray various politicians tilting at windmills to the lunatic lovers in Adam Sandler or Jim Carrey movies. Students will no doubt wish to grant the "original" some priority over its progeny. Critical theory aside, they probably should be allowed to do so. The sense of accessing an influential original is one of the great pleasures of reading the literature of the past.

Vladimir Nabokov, one of the greatest twentieth-century novelists, called *Don Quixote* a "cruel and crude old book," and his lecture on "Cruelty and Mystification" elaborates this notion convincingly. Amid the slapstick fun and narrative geniality of the novel, and through the patina of years of "humanizing," we can forget the cruelty that lies at the heart of this great novel: People abuse Don Quixote in his madness; they mock him and beat him while playing to his *idée fixe*. Don Quixote's charming delusion, his insistence that peasant girls are really princesses, and that innkeepers are kings has been glossed by the intervening centuries of critics as idealism, a madness that is superior to much sanity. Though Don Quixote's madness does prove, in the end, a superior delusion to the one most of us operate under, he does not sail through life unscathed and oblivious. Rather, he suffers for his idealism, becoming, in Nabokov's reading, a kind of martyr for chivalry. The duke and duchess are particularly cruel, and Nabokov describes their setting up Sancho Panza with a government and putting Don Quixote through endless barbarous hoaxes as if they were big cats toying with their prey. It is well to remember that even though Don Quixote finally renounces his delusion, Sancho Panza seems to have taken the delusion up, like any good apostle, by the end of the novel.

Help students to keep in mind, then, that even if they don't know the name Don Quixote, or the song "The Impossible Dream," or the famous Picasso pen-and-ink drawing, or the phrase "tilting at windmills," they nonetheless have prior experience with Don Quixote. Consider as a class the ways in which our idea that the world is mediated by our perception of it has been anticipated and shaped by the novel.

TEXT & CONTEXT

DON QUIXOTE: ICON AND MYTH

It seems perfectly fitting that by the time Cervantes published the second part of *Don Quixote*, ten years after the first part, the Knight of the Mournful Countenance and his fat, worldly sidekick had already become famous figures. That the second part of the novel introduces Don Quixote's fame into the novel itself makes the book deeper and richer, a sophisticated meditation on the relationship between literary text and history. The duke and duchess recognize Don Quixote because of the book. In an episode not included in the anthology, another aristocrat fixes a sign to Don Quixote's back inviting people to mock and ridicule him by labeling him: "THIS IS DON QUIXOTE DE LA MANCHA," and, as a result, boys follow the Don all over town. In short, the deluded Don who tilts at windmills barely made it out of the ink bottle before he was reproduced and imitated endlessly. Encourage students to speculate on the reasons for Don Quixote's enduring attractiveness. Why do we continue to hold him up as a hero when he's clearly out of touch with reality? Why does the charge of "tilting at windmills" still carry a tinge of respectability — or does it?

SLAPSTICK, THE "REAL WORLD," AND DON QUIXOTE

Michel Foucault uses Cervantes' novel to illustrate a defining moment in the history of Western thought, the moment when text stops resembling reality and becomes a different thing from reality, a separate entity that comments on and points to but does not embody the world. One especially relevant characteristic of the novel is its use of slapstick comedy and low farce. These burlesque elements, bodily as they are, end up calling attention to one of the structural antitheses of the novel: Don Quixote's lean asceticism, the victory of spirit over flesh, opposes Sancho Panza's low, bodily thralldom to appetite and the flesh's incessant cry to the spirit. Slapstick comedy and laughing at another's pain helps the reader to avoid Don Quixote's fate by developing the critical distance this laughter entails. By calling attention to the divide between the written world and the real world, Cervantes offers us a defense against easy identification and leads us into more complicated forms of reading — the recognition of layers of fictionality and reality. Lead students gently into the twists and turns that following this line of thought entails. The connection between text and reality is one that is tenuous and complex. Be prepared for some rather contorted discussions, and keep the text handy as a sort of anchor (though it might seem to be made of papier-mâché).

READING AND DON QUIXOTE

Historically, the Renaissance was fueled by the appearance of the printing press (though before the printing press, the Renaissance was in full swing thanks to an increasingly sophisticated distribution network that used scribes) and a dramatic rise in literacy. Not surprisingly, then, the act of reading and the diluted and fragmentary responses that readers provide writers are characteristic concerns of *Don Quixote*. The self-conscious and palpable textuality of *Don Quixote* — its levels of narrators, its introduction of and commentary on stories such as Sancho Panza's abbreviated tale of the goats crossing the river — has evoked a great deal of commentary from all kinds of critics. Students need not be introduced to this tradition of criticism. Rather, instructors can point out the self-referentiality itself — the ways in which Cervantes anticipates the reader's reactions and comments on real reactions to the novel. This focus on the reader, and anticipation of the reader's response, evokes the oral tradition that Sancho Panza's proverbs illustrate and grant the reader a new power to choose within the text and to read with discrimination rather than to have his brains dry up and crack like poor Don Quixote's. Cervantes seems to invite us to read better, rather than to mock us for not reading well enough. Encourage students to talk about their experiences of reading, both of the selection from *Don Quixote* and of books in general. Help them to talk about how their reading has matured over time and how reading one novel shapes the way you read the next.

IN THE CLASSROOM

I. THE IMAGE OF DON QUIXOTE

The image of Don Quixote so persists in literature and art that it's difficult to think of a novel that hasn't in some way been shaped by Cervantes. Once students have engaged Don Quixote as he appears here and learned to admire his intransigence as everyone seems eventually to do, use the Don's ubiquity as a type to talk about the connections between fiction and history and the ways in which fiction can sometimes make history. It is the reverse of our usual way of thinking about the relationship, but it is just as valid; help students see how the membrane between reality and fiction is permeable in both directions.

Discussion

1. Encourage students to list as many quixotic figures as they can as well as from as many different artistic genres as they can. Students, with a little prompting, can list dozens of

melancholic idealists who, battered and bruised, make their skewed but admirable ways through the world to a final realization or denial of madness. Once a sizable list has been generated, engage students in thinking about the various ways in which these works comment on their quixotic figures. In the film *Don Juan de Marco*, for example, the man who thinks he is Don Juan is contrasted with a psychiatrist charged with "curing" him. The psychiatrist eventually indulges in the delusion himself, and that voluntary delusion recharges his relationship with his wife. The madman cures the doctor. Compare several of these artistic comments on the Quixote figure, and think about how characters represent *ideas* as much as they do *types*. *Forrest Gump*, particularly given the ubiquity of that quixotic figure in the wake of the movie's success, is another recent example that should provoke discussion and interesting comparison.

Connections

1. *Don Quixote* ties together a number of important themes from the Early Modern book of the anthology. The view of humanity promulgated in Castiglione's *The Book of the The Courtier* (p. 171) and Pico della Mirandola's "On the Dignity of Man" (p. 468) is simultaneously parodied and valued in the figure of Don Quixote. Show students how the interplay among these texts demonstrates that the Renaissance was constantly subject to revision and alteration.

2. Quixote figures abound in the anthology, including Okonkwo from *Things Fall Apart* (Book 6), Mister Kurtz from *Heart of Darkness* (Book 6), and the narrators of "The Yellow Wallpaper" (Book 5) and "Notes from Underground" (Book 5), to name just a few. Compare these various characters' connections with reality. To what extent are they saner than their surroundings? How do they speak the truth through their delusions? Do any or all of them seem to be speaking the truth when in reality they are merely deluded?

Groups

1. Divide students into two or three pairs of debate teams. Have them argue, using the text of *Don Quixote* as evidence, over which of the following pairs of terms is the more important concept to emphasize if one wishes to live a good and happy life: idealism versus realism, history versus fiction, writing versus speaking, wealth versus love.

Writing

Ask students to write a short paper, responding to one or more of the following:

1. Join in the fun: Create your own quixotic character, and set him or her to tilting at some of the windmills in your own landscape. In no more than five pages, give your character a conflict of some kind that arises from her skewed perception of some social reality — say, for example, the nature and efficacy of modern medicine — and decide whether he or she wins or loses and what that says about the reality beneath the social convention.

2. In a short, three- to five-page paper, compare the fate of Don Quixote with the end of one of the Quixote figures you have seen in books or film recently. Which is more believable? Which is funnier? Which is more thought provoking? What, ultimately, does the end of a quixotic figure say about reality and social convention?

II. Don Quixote and Physical Humor

Cream pie in the face. Slipping on a banana peel. Poke in the eye. Tweak of the nose. Moments of pain or embarrassment are often the source of low humor, the kind of humor that everyone can enjoy — except the immediate victim — because it is so direct. Sometimes called "physical comedy," slapstick was one of the earliest kinds of movie humor, and its broad appeal helped to make the movies into a moneymaking industry. But this kind of humor is much older than the movies, as a cursory glance at the selection from *Don Quixote* proves. Engage students in thinking about this kind of humor — which, because it is so immediate and bodily, sometimes evades description. Sancho Panza's attempt to defecate without alerting Don Quixote is another example of low, broad humor. Why is this kind of humor so enduring? Why does it appeal to the least common denominator? What does it say about the relationship between body and mind?

Discussion

1. Discuss with students the use of slapstick. One way to introduce the topic might be to show the skit from the movie *Monty Python: Live at the Hollywood Bowl*, in which a university don gives a dry lecture on the history of slapstick comedy, while assistants in plain jumpsuits illustrate his points. The humor lies in the demonstration: Even though someone stands there and explains the joke, the joke is still funny. What is the irreducible nugget of truth in slapstick comedy?

2. Why can Jackie Chan — born and raised in Hong Kong — emulate and elaborate the comedy of the sixty-year-old movies of Buster Keaton to such hilarious effect? Is it really true that the spectacle of a man suffering the most painful of blows will universally make us laugh as long as we are not the man who is doubled over grabbing his groin? Is slapstick a universal language? Think of specific gestures. How do they change over time? Is the pie fight dead?

Connections

1. Physical violence is, of course, a feature of much of literature, from war stories to slapstick comedy. Compare some of the violence in serious versus humorous works. Serious violence, that is, violence represented in order to horrify rather than amuse, occurs in such places as *The Iliad* (Book 1), *The Mahabarata* (Book 1), and the crucifixion of Jesus Christ in the New Testament (Book 2). How do these differ from the comedic violence of *Don Quixote* in their presentation? What might this difference indicate?

Writing

Ask students to write a short paper, responding to one or more of the following:

1. Think of a pratfall you have taken that happened long enough ago that you can now laugh at it. In an essay of no more than five pages, describe the pratfall, and comment on its humor. How long has it taken you to get over it? How would Don Quixote have reacted to it? Does he seem to appreciate his misadventures more as he ages? Why or why not?

2. In a paper of no more than five pages, consider the old question of whether cartoon or slapstick violence really leads to real-life violence. Exhibit A is *Don Quixote*: He reads ludicrous romances, and they lead him to attack defenseless monks in the road and to slaughter innocent sheep. On the other hand, no one has ever accused the novel of encouraging us to go around killing giants. Perhaps the humor *corrects* us rather than *incites* us. Use the story of the Knight of the Mournful Countenance as an argument for or against regulating violent images.

III. THE ROLE OF WRITING IN *DON QUIXOTE*

The role of writing — the difference between the written word and the oral one — structures the text of *Don Quixote* intimately. Indeed, the relationship between Sancho Panza and Don Quixote is in some ways completely shaped by the difference in literacy. Sancho cannot read, and he reasons by the use of preformed aphorisms he piles up as if they were proofs. Don Quixote has read too much, and the cracked brain that results from his attempting to read the convoluted sentences of chivalric romances is only corrected by his confrontation with the ultimate reality — death.

Discussion

1. Encourage students to think about their relationship to language, both written and spoken. You might have them freewrite on the topic of writing, then talk about what they wrote, and finally reflect on the difference between what they wrote and what they said. Who read parts of her freewriting aloud? Who summarized his freewriting? Why? Which feels most comfortable? What if the topic is more private? Which medium would he or she choose? Why?

2. Discuss with students the question of what Walter Ong calls "secondary orality" — the transformations of language and therefore of thought that come with new ways of transmitting language. The telephone and the radio have elements of writing — that is, the speaker can be absent from the listener. And the Internet and e-mail, especially with the growing popularity of instant messaging, have elements of spoken language. How might these technological advances be changing the ways in which we think about the world? How might they affect language?

Connections

1. Contrast Don Quixote to a "true hero" such as Achilles (Book 1), Sunjata (p. 21), Moses (Book 1), or Quetzalcoatl (p. 721). In what ways is Don Quixote more physically present, in our reading of his text, than these older presentations of heroes derived from oral tradition? To what extent can this physicality be attributed to the fact of writing and the absence of the storyteller from the audience?

2. Consider some earlier examples of writing that represents people telling stories for an audience: Boccaccio's *Decameron* (Book 2), Navarre's *The Heptameron* (p. 185), or Chaucer's *Canterbury Tales* (Book 2). Do the audiences in those cases serve the same function as does Don Quixote when Sancho Panza relates his story about the goats? Or when the duchess encourages Sancho Panza to tell her stories? To what extent — and to what purpose — does the audience comment on the way the story is told?

Groups

1. Divide students into groups of two or three. Each student is to tell his or her favorite story, in as much length as possible, to the rest of the group. Having told their stories, they should go home and write them down and bring them back to read the next day. Discuss how this odd method of generating text changed the way they wrote their stories. How did the voices of their auditors impinge on or improve their writing?

Writing

Ask students to write a short paper, responding to one or more of the following:

1. Write a short fictional dialog of no more than six pages between two characters who hold two radically different views of reality. By the end, there should be some kind of resolution between the two points of view — one persuades the other, one proves to be wrong but won't believe it, one changes her view as she talks about it, and so forth. What does the ending say about the differing points of view?

2. In a paper of no more than five pages, describe the difference between the passages that focus on Sancho Panza and the passages that focus on Don Quixote. How do the different characters' literacy and their different degrees of familiarity with the oral and written traditions inform these passages? Is Sancho Panza's illiteracy a handicap or an advantage?

3. In a three-page paper, comment on Cervantes' play with his authorship. Why does he create masks for himself, especially that of Cid Hamet Benengali? Why does he call our attention to his absence from the text and the fundamental anonymity of the author as opposed to the undeniable presence of the storyteller?

BEYOND THE CLASSROOM

RESEARCH & WRITING

1. Define physical comedy, and research its history. To what extent is Cervantes taking the easy road to laughs when he has Sancho Panza and Don Quixote suffer so many blows, and to what extent does he make us sensitive to the pain the blows must have caused? How much distance does he allow us from the pain, and why?

2. Read as much scholarly commentary on *The Three Stooges* as you can find. What is the effect of the content on the scholarly style? Are scholars of slapstick more or less formal than other kinds of scholars?

3. Read an English translation of *Amadis of Gaul*. Then, write a research paper in which you consider how Cervantes satirizes and at the same time valorizes the chivalric romance. The following questions are to guide your inquiry, though they are not all to be answered in your paper: What parts does he especially include, and what does he leave out of his novel? Is his criticism fair? Does it go too far? Not far enough? What role does translation play in your understanding of Cervantes' use of parody? To what extent has the narrator succeeded in reflecting the language of the chivalric romance?

4. Read the rest of *Don Quixote*. Comment on the editors' selections. What should have been included in the anthology but was left out? What was included that is not central to the novel? If you wish to include the entire novel in the anthology, what 600 pages of material can be removed, and how can it be accounted for? If you wish to cut the novel out entirely, what would you put in its place? How could the novel be better represented in the text, or is it important enough to be included at all? What could do *Don Quixote*'s job better than it does?

5. Read *The Female Quixote* by Charlotte Lennox, and write a paper about what happens to the quixotic figure when she changes genders. Imagine — or find — a female Quixote today. To what extent are female delusions part of the status quo? Can female quixotics ever question the authority of the official version of reality in the same way that can male quixotics?

Projects

1. Watch as much slapstick and physical comedy as you can find. Choose a specific gesture — the pie fight, looking at another person instead of a mirror, the pratfall, slipping on a banana peel — and try to come up with (and film or storyboard) a fresh context for that "sight gag." Can you do it? Why or why not? Present your conclusion to the class, and speculate with the class on the following question: Is it possible for a sight gag to become exhausted and unusable? Why or why not?

2. Make a PowerPoint presentation of several pictures of Don Quixote and Sancho Panza, making certain that you elaborate on the contexts for these illustrations/interpretations. How do the pictures reflect changing perceptions of, for example, the nature of knowledge?

3. Present a series of pieces of music inspired by *Don Quixote*. Over fifty composers of concert music, including Strauss and Tellemann, and many popular songwriters like Gordon Lightfoot, have written music about the novel. Describe the ways in which several of these musicians have interpreted *Don Quixote* through music.

4. Imagine a modern day Don Quixote, and write — or film — their reality. What would crack their brains? What would their reality be like? Perhaps consider the reaction to the Columbine killers and the role of video games in their tragedy.

WWW   For information on Cervantes and annotated Web links, see *World Literature Online* at bedfordstmartins.com/worldlit.

FURTHER READING

Alter, Robert A. *Partial Magic: The Novel as a Self-Conscious Genre.* 1978.
Birkerts, Sven. "Into the Electronic Millennium" in *The Gutenberg Elegies: The Fate of Reading in an Electronic Age.* 1994.
Bjornsen, Richard, ed. *Approaches to Teaching Cervantes'* Don Quixote. 1984.
Nabokov, Vladimir. *Lectures on Don Quixote.* Ed. Fredson Bowers. 1983.

WWW   See *World Literature in the 21st Century* at bedfordstmartins.com/worldlit for examples of the relevance of Don Quixote in today's world.

MEDIA RESOURCES

VIDEO

Miguel de Cervantes
43 min., 2002 (Films for the Humanities & Sciences)
Using drawings, paintings, letters, maps, and footage of notable landmarks, this program presents the adventures and tribulations of Miguel de Cervantes, arguably the best-known figure in Spanish literary history. In addition to *Don Quixote*, one of the most influential and widely read classics in Western literature, the program also introduces Cervantes' *Novelas Ejemplares*, a group of short stories that he claimed were the first to be written in Castilian. (Spanish with English subtitles.)

Don Quixote
30 min., 1999 (Library Video Company)
The Man of La Mancha rides again as Don Quixote battles windmills and evil with his faithful sidekick Sancho Panza — all in the name of his beloved Dulcinea. Features fascinating model animation and captivating music.

Don Quixote
120 min., 2000 (Zenger Media)
John Lithgow, Bob Hoskins, Isabella Rossellini, and Vanessa L. Williams star in this Hallmark adaptation of the novel by Miguel de Cervantes Saavedra. The story recounts the addled idealism of Don Quixote, a country gentleman who has read too many chivalric romances, and the earthly acquisitiveness of his squire, Sancho Panza. As Quixote sets out with a makeshift lance to set the world right, he is propelled into a series of adventures involving characters from every level of society.

Don Quixote (Ballet)
126 min., 1988 (Library Video Company)
The Kirov Ballet performs the ballet by Leon Minkus about the love of Kitri and Basilio and the chivalry of Don Quixote. This performance by the Kirov has been hailed as one of the greatest large cast ballet productions ever recorded on film.

Don Quixote: Legacy of a Classic
58 min., 1995 (Films for the Humanities & Sciences)
This program weaves art, music, and literature with Western culture to explore the enormous impact of Cervantes' classic on our world today. Artists, critics, and others, from novelist Carlos Fuentes to General Norman Schwarzkopf, reveal how the work — the most translated in history — has affected their lives. Mixing discussions of the text with music, poems, other writings influenced by *Don Quixote*, and clips from the many film versions of the work, the program explores the conflict between imagination and reality, masculine and feminine attitudes toward love, and other themes. This is a rich resource for the study of *Don Quixote* and of the influence of art on life.

Man of La Mancha
129 min., 1972 (Library Video Company)
Peter O'Toole and Sophia Loren star in this tale of Don Quixote de la Mancha, the knight errant who captured the world's imagination in Miguel de Cervantes' 1605 novel. O'Toole plays both Cervantes and Don Quixote in the film version of the Broadway play by Dale Wasserman. With loyal Sancho Panza, Quixote searches for causes to champion and damsels in distress to rescue.

Understanding Don Quixote
21 min., 1989 (Educational Video Network)
Learn about the eventful life of Miguel de Cervantes in this video, which also examines the major themes of his masterpiece, *Don Quixote*.

WEB SITES

Cervantes in CyberSpain
www.cyberspain.com/year/
Created in 1997 by the e-journal CyberSpain to celebrate the 450th anniversary of the birth of Cervantes, this page includes a short biography of the author as well as a link to a Spanish e-text of *Don Quijote de la Mancha*.

The Cervantes Project
www.csdl.tamu.edu/cervantes/
An essential research site, the Cervantes Project provides comprehensive information on the author's life and works, including an extensive bibliography and electronic versions of all of Cervantes' works. Students can also conduct searches for secondary sources on the site and can view numerous portraits of the author as well as artists' renderings of Don Quixote over the centuries. The entire site may be read in either English or Spanish.

Don Quixote Home Page
www.denison.edu/modlangs/dq/dqxhome.html
Written by a Cervantes scholar, this site offers a variety of approaches to the reading of *Don Quixote*, providing students of literature, history, philosophy, religion, law, and psychology questions, themes, and research topics to consider. Offered in both English and Spanish, the site also includes a reader's diary and links to other useful Cervantes sites.

H-Cervantes
www2.h-net.msu.edu/~cervantes/

This site is a member of H-Net Humanities and Social Sciences Online. A network for Cervantes scholars, it provides the user with a wide array of resources, including discussion logs, links, facsimiles of early editions of his work, and complete access to articles published in *Cervantes*, the journal of the Cervantes Society of America.

The Route of Don Quixote
www.mankato.msus.edu/dept/modernlang/webmaterial.html/lamancha.html
Take a tour of the route followed by Don Quixote. Created at Minnesota State University, this fascinating site leads users on a virtual video journey. It also includes music, photographs of the landmarks in Cervantes' novel, and a handy interactive map of La Mancha. A very useful and fun accompaniment to the novel.

A Tribute to Don Quixote de la Mancha
Homepages.together.net/~donutrun/quix.htm
Celebrating Dale Wasserman's musical *Man of La Mancha*, this fun and informative site provides lyrics to many of the play's songs as well as passages from the script. It also includes an audio excerpt and links to related sites.

AUDIO
Don Quixote
360 min., 1997 (Media Books Audio)
An abridged recording based on the book by Miguel de Cervantes and narrated by Christopher Cazenove. Tells the epic story about the life and adventures of the Man of La Mancha. After inheriting a large sum of money, the befuddled but well-meaning Spanish nobleman Quixote decides to become a knight-errant. Along with his faithful squire Sancho Panza, Don Quixote sets out on a comical quest to battle injustice in all forms.

Don Quixote
3 CDs, 3:17 hrs. (Naxos Audio)
The first European novel, and one of the greatest, is a marvelously comic study of delusion and its consequences: Don Quixote, the old gentleman of La Mancha, takes to the road in search of adventure and remains undaunted in the face of repeated disaster.

Don Quixote de la Mancha
13 tapes, 39:75 hrs. (Blackstone Audiobooks)
Don Quixote — the world's first novel and by far the best-known book in Spanish literature — was originally intended by Cervantes as a satire on traditional popular ballads, yet he also parodied the romances of chivalry. By happy coincidence he produced one of the most entertaining adventure stories of all time.

CHRISTOPHER MARLOWE, *Doctor Faustus* (p. 389)

www   For a quiz on *Doctor Faustus*, see *World Literature Online* at
       bedfordstmartins.com/worldlit.

Marlowe's *Doctor Faustus*, with its surprisingly contemporary characters and themes, is a delight to teach. Many students will be introduced for the first time to one of the sources of a familiar image: a devil on the left encouraging diabolic schemes and a good angel on the right influencing faithful actions. But what might seem a cartoon-like cliché in our day was certainly serious business during the Renaissance: The soul was a battleground on which different forces competed for dominance. While it is not clear whether a real Doctor Faustus ever lived, Marlowe's audience was familiar with the Faustian myth: Rumor, sermons, and numerous books about the magician Faust had created an influential, legendary figure by the time of Marlowe's adaptation. Marlowe modified these preceding medieval representations and crafted a decidedly early modern Doctor Faustus, who was obligated to grapple with contradictory Renaissance influences that escalated into a conflict of the soul.

The struggle that Faustus embodies reflects the intersection of medieval scholasticism and religious faith, Renaissance humanism, and modern scientific exploration. *Doctor Faustus* acknowledges medieval Christianity's moral and religious boundaries — it was a sin to sell one's soul to the devil. The Roman Catholic Church prosecuted the unfaithful with the Inquisition, promoting a forced orthodoxy by feeding fires of suspicion and fear. The Protestant Reformation, inspired by Luther and modified by Calvin, challenged this Roman Catholic orthodoxy (*In the World:* Challenging Orthodoxy, p. 661) but dictated its own orthodox adherence to new kinds of spiritual laws: Only the elect few were to be saved, but all people needed to adhere to revised, similarly strict doctrines. A competing school of thought was found in Renaissance humanism (*In the World:* Humanism, Learning, and Education, p. 661), which sought to restore stylistically pure Latin and ancient Greek influences in literature, rhetoric, poetry, and moral philosophy. The recovery of classical texts by humanist thinkers glorified man as God's special creation in the universe and acknowledged his powers of rational thinking. By careful study, man could arrive at rational conclusions — albeit reconciled with Christian principles — about how to better the world around him. Early modern thinkers, on the other hand, looked forward by embracing the revolutionary Copernican cosmology and promoting exploratory ventures into unknown lands and realms of knowledge. Like the humanists, early modern thinkers also looked back to the ancients; instead of retrieving classical sources, however, they excavated controversial mystical texts that challenged the boundaries of what Renaissance intellectuals considered to be scientific. By delving into these questionable (even occult) texts, early modern thinkers emphasized man's relationship to the natural macrocosm and attempted to uncover — without fear or prejudice — additional natural forces acting within the newly defined cosmology.

Begin your approach to this work by introducing students to these fundamental questions that define the modern period. Is Faustus the Christian overreacher who, through his own hubris, sows the seeds of his destruction? Does he, by his celebration of worldly power, pleasures, and beauty, exemplify the Renaissance man? Or is he the archetypal hero of the new age who risks everything to explore new frontiers of power and intellect? As students puzzle over this combination of disparate forces pulling for Faustus's allegiance, encourage them to trace specifically the influences of Christianity, humanism, and the spirit of exploration throughout Marlowe's work. Which of these influences is most pronounced, and which most determines Marlowe's fate? In this context, address the question of Doctor Faustus's ability to choose amidst these external pressures. As the Early Modern Period celebrates the defining of the individual, consider the options available to Doctor Faustus: To what extent does he have a choice? To what extent is he already condemned within disparate ideological systems?

The pronounced conflict in Marlowe's drama between the defining of the individual self in conjunction with or in contradistinction to external imposing ideologies quite literally sets the modern stage: Marlowe's daring — and perpetually ambivalent — illustration of Doctor Faustus's assertions of agency in the midst of conflict prefigures literary, political, and cultural identity politics of the next several centuries. Encourage students to examine how a theatrical production might further complicate Marlowe's already ambivalent text. Consider reading passages aloud in class, noting carefully how even voice inflection can modify an interpretation. How might directorial comments, stage directions, or set design today comparably influence how Doctor Faustus's choices are viewed and why he makes them? A presciently modern text, *Doctor Faustus* endures less because reductive answers can be found to answer the questions it poses and more because comparable questions about identity and ethics remain remarkably crucial in contemporary society. Ask students to identify modern equivalents to the issues that Marlowe illustrates. What modern collective ideological belief systems threaten individual identity? What traditional religious influences currently affect the public political, sociological, and cultural realms? What secularized moral, ethical, or rational systems of thought are at work in the public sphere? What kinds of modern technologies or knowledge seek to challenge those religious, moral, and ethical values? Discuss what Marlowe's work might prophesy for contemporary society: Do individuals today choose their fates? At what price? If this play is a cautionary tale, what exactly is its warning?

TEXT & CONTEXT

RELIGIOUS STRIFE IN EARLY MODERN ENGLAND

In 1517, Martin Luther's remarkable challenge to the Catholic doctrines of indulgences in the form of the Ninety-Five Theses pitted two poles of opposing beliefs against each other. On one hand, the Catholic Church adhered to a single, governing authority in the pontiff. In the Catholic orthodoxy, a deeply hierarchical institution, an individual's relationship to God was facilitated by the church's patriarchy — the priests, bishops, cardinals, and the pope as Christ's representatives on earth. Individuals witnessed miracles at Mass and participated in confession, pardons, absolution, sacraments, and even scripture through the mediating influence of the priest. On the other hand, Luther advocated a personal return to the living word of scripture. Luther maintained that both the conscience of an individual — and of the church — and the subsequent practice of religion should be dictated by a careful study of inspired texts, not by ritualized tradition. Unlike Catholics, Protestants believed that it was an individual's faith that determined salvation.

By the time Elizabeth took the throne in England, the Protestant/Catholic conflict had deeply divided the country. Complicating this tense religious conflict were the collective inherited decisions made by monarchs who preceded her. Despite Henry's VIII's title of "Defender of the Faith" for having written a tract against Luther, the king found his petition for a divorce from Anne Boleyn denied by the Holy Father. Undeterred, in 1531, the king declared himself "Supreme Head of the Church of England," established the Anglican Church, and granted himself the divorce. Subsequently, England saw Protestantism become more clearly defined during the reign of ten-year-old Edward and his Lord Protector, Edward Seymour (1547). Conversely, a resurgence of militant Roman Catholicism followed during "Bloody" Mary's reign immediately after Edward (1553). Elizabeth kept her own religious inclinations private, however. Not until she accepted the Crown (1558) did she reveal her acceptance of Protestant views. Nonetheless, Elizabeth carefully mediated between the disparate religious faiths by persecuting religious zealots of any kind, including Protestants. Despite persistent threats on her life from Catholic sympathizers, Elizabeth thwarted them all until she died in 1603 and maintained the Anglican Church as the Church of England throughout her reign. Elizabeth masterfully dictated an Aristotelean golden mean, accommodating most religious sects adequately but preserving her power absolutely.

IN THE CLASSROOM

I. INQUIRY: SCIENCE OR WITCHCRAFT?

Several times in his life, Marlowe was accused of religious heterodoxy, disloyalty to the Crown, and atheism. Although at one point Marlowe was surreptitiously employed in the Queen's service as a spy, it was his continued associations with freethinkers of the time that branded him a radical. His compatriots included Sir Walter Raleigh, Thomas Harriot, Nicholas Hill, and Walter Warner, each of whom proposed a rigorous pursuit of knowledge that would help man exert control over nature. This quest for "forbidden knowledge" extended far beyond accepted bounds of Renaissance scientific inquiry: These freethinkers resurrected neo-Platonist, Hermetic, and Cabalist texts that asserted man's power over nature to become godlike. Since one occult principle asserted that man could quite literally become one with God by experiencing universal knowledge as the mind expanded to comprehend the cosmos, too much knowledge was considered dangerous. Raleigh, Harriot, and Marlowe each ventured into the occult in this newly objectified search for truth and celebrated the concepts of human dignity, freedom, and power found in this tradition. But it was not only occult texts that interested these freethinkers. Traditional beliefs and institutions were also subjected to the intellectual rigor of logical analysis — even if that meant they would eventually be rejected. Raleigh advocated that new ideas should be explored, described, and conquered, just as unknown lands were; the pursuit of truth should neither be limited by idolatrous superstition nor by the strict confines of Roger Bacon's empirical science. Thus it was not only the occult that threatened orthodox institutions of church and state but freedom of inquiry. Definitions of what constituted science and what was deemed occultist remained vague during the Renaissance: It is important to remember that the scientifically observed and rational Copernican revolution inspired charges of heresy. Indeed, in England, the Anglican Church exercised its authority over any scientific advances or freethinking by making liberal accusations of witchcraft and necromancy. Freethinking of any kind could be mistakenly and fatally described as being occultist, just as the exposure of false witch trials in subsequent centuries and countries has shown. Rather than a conjuring black art, then, it is interesting to consider magic as a metaphor for human liberation from oppressive ideological forces, a striving toward independent knowledge, and an acknowledgment of distinctly human potential.

Discussion

1. Discuss students' preconceptions about the devil. Where do they come from? Ask them if the portrayal of Lucifer (or even Mephistophilis) in *Doctor Faustus* changes or conflicts with these preliminary ideas. Why or why not? What might the devil represent metaphorically?

2. What knowledge does Faustus shun at the beginning? What knowledge does he seek? Have students characterize the "forbidden knowledge" that Faustus lusts after, using specific passages in the text to support their observations. What might be called forbidden knowledge today? Like Lucifer and Mephistophilis, who might be said to be powerful enough to grant access to these guarded secrets?

3. Does morality conflict with the acquisition of knowledge? Ask students whether the struggle epitomized by the good angel and the bad angel still occurs in today's secularized world. Is Faustus's sacrifice of his own soul relevant today? What prices do students pay for knowledge?

4. Ask students to pinpoint specific passages in which Faustus exercises his magical powers. Have them identify the kinds of magic arts he uses and whether or not these powers are portrayed sympathetically. Is the attitude about magic that Marlowe seemingly hopes to evoke straightforward or ambivalent?

Connections

1. As a class, review basic principles of Aristotelean tragedy. Ask students to identify whether, according to classical principles, *The Tragical History of Doctor Faustus* is indeed a tragedy as its title suggests. Why or why not? If not, in what ways does Marlowe

modify Aristotle's definition as, perhaps, an early modern tragedy? Have students outline the principles that could define early modern tragedy as its own paradigm. What roles would seeking after knowledge and the transgressing of traditional boundaries play in this definition? Are these tragic flaws?

2. Have the students locate in the text the questions Doctor Faustus asks Mephistophilis about science and cosmology. Ask them to characterize Mephistophilis's answers, and compare them with the writing of Nicolas Copernicus (p. 684). Does Copernicus's Renaissance cosmological system support Mephistophilis's responses? What do Mephistophilis's explanations reveal about the type of knowledge (and by extension, power) that the devils possess? Discuss whether Mephistophilis and his obligations to Lucifer in hell form its own kind of ideological orthodoxy.

3. Ask students to compare Faustus's willful entrapment with Lucifer to Olaudah Equiano's unwilling enslavement by white captors (Book 4). What does this juxtaposition reveal about the privilege Faustus enjoys? What limitations are placed on Equiano's educational efforts that do not hamper the doctor's? Discuss who has access to the pursuit of knowledge during the European Renaissance.

Groups

1. One of the larger Renaissance projects involved discovering how man might exert control over nature beyond the bounds of religion and reason. Have students compare the magical powers of Marlowe's Doctor Faustus, Prospero in Shakespeare's The Tempest, and Wu Chengen's Monkey (perhaps in a chart or grid). Ask them to answer the following questions about each of these figures of Renaissance magic:

    a. How do these characters obtain their magical powers?

    b. For what goals are these powers used?

    c. In what ways are these powers limited? Do these figures succeed in exerting power over nature?

    d. What larger conclusions can be drawn from these examples about the validity of magical powers as an alternative to, say, scientific ones? Do you notice a difference across cultures?

    e. Are the magical powers portrayed in these works literal? Or do they have a deeper metaphorical significance? What might magical powers also represent?

    Then, as a group, consider addressing the following question: Is there a unified Renaissance view of magic and the occult as seen in these texts? Why or why not?

Writing

Ask students to write a short paper, responding to one or more of the following:

1. The suspicious circumstances surrounding Marlowe's death have convinced some that he died in part because of his unorthodox beliefs. How might Doctor Faustus similarly be considered a martyr for an unconventional, self-styled faith? What makes a modern martyr? Discuss whether unconventional beliefs based on transgressive knowledge are worth dying for.

2. Doctor Faustus and Milton's Satan both epitomize the unwillingness to repent or change, even though forgiveness is repeatedly offered. How do you explain this conscious choice *not* to repent? Would this pride be better characterized as a Renaissance position or an early modern stance? Justify your view with specific references from the text.

3. Once Faustus comes into power, are the decisions he makes ethical? Why or why not? If "knowledge is power" in a modern society, what responsibilities do individuals have to conduct themselves ethically when in possession of that knowledge? Consider contemporary dilemmas raised when science is at the frontier of knowledge — for example, in cloning, stem cell research, genetically modified food, or genetic engineering. Compare the doctor's principles with the different sides of these debates. How do Doctor Faustus's choices prefigure the problems inherent in modern scientific arguments? Consider especially, Faustus's successful wish to "possess" Helen of Troy: How might this scene prove to be a metaphor for unbridled scientific experimentation?

II. THE POLITICS OF NATION-BUILDING IN THE EARLY MODERN PERIOD

Although James would only coin the term *Great Britain* in 1707, Elizabeth was well on her way to establishing a mighty and modern nation-state. From authorizing the first forays into the New World abroad to creating a national, centralized government at the expense of the local and regional authorities, Elizabeth (following the Tudor Monarchs before her) bolstered the budding nation from without and within. To preserve unity, this seemingly innocuous virginal queen countered subversive voices during her reign with extreme and violent measures. During her reign, more than 6000 people were hanged and drawn and quartered. Ironically, the year 1571 saw the construction of the Triple Tree, a permanent structure dedicated to hanging as well as the first public theater. Indeed, hangings actually rivaled the theater as public spectacle. Spectators either stood close to the "stage," purchased actual seats in a gallery, or could rent neighboring rooms to watch the punishment. Vendors profited from the occasion by selling pies and fruits to onlookers. Printed accounts outlining the evil "plots" of the person being hanged were distributed. A sense of festive community was established, since both upper and lower classes mingled together. And yet, despite Elizabeth's efforts to demonstrate her monolithic power, occasionally those being hanged used their last breaths to speak out against the state, effectively subverting — however momentarily — her authority. Similarly, early modern theater became a site for continual play between affirming or denying the power of the state — and by extension, its religious, political, educational, and social appendages. The theaters themselves were purposefully built just outside the cities, on land outside the control of local municipalities, yet they were still under the watchful eye of national authorities. The Tudors encouraged the theater as the people's distraction from rebellion, yet the Privy Council regulated dramatic content through censorship. Especially in the subject matter of early modern drama, perceived threats to the state were contained and institutions legitimized on one hand; on the other, the omnipotent, squelching authority of the Crown was perpetually revealed, challenged, and even successfully — if momentarily — overthrown. Marlowe's play cleverly paints this paradox in the depictions of the Good Angel and the Bad Angel. While Faustus, the early modern (anti)hero, as well as early modern drama both swing to one side or the other of this dilemma, most often they are caught *between* these legitimizing and subverting forces and left to wrestle with the implications.

Discussion

1. Ask students who holds the most power in this text. God? Lucifer? Faustus? From what source is that power derived?

2. Have the class identify and list some of paired figures in the text who exist in relationships of domination and subordination (Lucifer/Mephistophilis; Mephistophilis/Faustus; Lucifer/Faustus; Faustus/Wagner; Wagner/Clown). Why does Marlowe employ this construction? Ask students what the pattern of repeated doubling reveals about power structures within the text. How might these constructions support Renaissance systems of authority?

3. Evaluate whether Faustus actually becomes powerful or not: If his power is dependent on another entity, what power is truly his? Encourage students to debate how Faustus makes use of the power he obtains. How does he take advantage of it? How does he squander it? Discuss what ultimate value this power actually has.

Connections

1. Call attention to the passage in the play when power first becomes a possibility for Faustus. What does Faustus first want to do when endowed with this power? Why do his aims involve voyages? Ask students to evaluate the institutions of power seated at his destinations. Whom does he propose to "conquer"? Compare his fantastic voyages with those of other travel writers such as Aphra Behn, Jonathan Swift, Denis Diderot (all Book 4) or the authors represented in *In the World: Europe Meets America* (p. 767). How do these accounts legitimize the power of the state? How do they reaffirm nationalistic designs and/or imperial expansion?

2. Ask students to compare the binary theological concepts presented in *Doctor Faustus* with those of the ancient Mexicans (p. 708). How do these binary constructions of heaven/earth, light/dark, creation/destruction, and spirit/matter play out between these radically different texts and cultures? In what ways might Faustus be seeking experiences outside Christianity but within the bounds of ancient belief?

3. Only a few decades after Faustus was performed under Elizabeth's all-seeing eye, the people of England challenged the sovereign authority of the king. The decapitation of the monarch in 1649 presciently foreshadowed the democratic revolutions of the next century in the American colonies, France, and Haiti. Review *In the World: Declarations of Rights and Independences* (Book 4). Does *Doctor Faustus* begin sowing the seeds of subverting monarchical power and promoting revolution? Why or why not?

Groups

1. Ask each group to write staging directions for the last scene of *Doctor Faustus*, complete with props, lighting, and visual effects. Encourage the students to reread the text carefully, describing (or even drawing) in detail what might be visible to the audience and what is visible only to Faustus. How might staging decisions affect the interpretation of this crucial scene? Encourage each group to identify how their representations demonstrate what Faustus actually chooses. Compare different groups' responses: Do they concur?

Writing

Ask students to write a short paper, responding to one or more of the following:

1. At the heart of the Elizabethan containment/subversion conflict is the problem of choice. Discuss the choices Doctor Faustus clearly makes and those that are made for him. To what extent is Faustus acted upon, and to what extent does Faustus fashion his own fate? At what point is Faustus damned? Consider analyzing when and why Faustus refers to himself in the third person.

2. Discuss theater as a means of sanctioned public subversion of governmental authority. Why might Marlowe have presented Faustus as a play instead of a narrative? In what ways might a live, theatrical performance that involves a large audience be more threatening to established authority than a written text?

3. Identify specific ways in which *Doctor Faustus* undermines the authority of the Catholic Church. Do your findings suggest that Marlowe affirms the power of the Elizabethan

monarchy? Why or why not? Discuss whether Marlowe's play ultimately affirms or denies specific embodiments of Renaissance institutional authority.

BEYOND THE CLASSROOM

RESEARCH & WRITING

1. Identify and research a specific medical ailment and its possible courses of treatment according to both Western medicine and a non-Western counterpart (perhaps in traditional Chinese medicine or another alternative treatment). Explain each in detail, and compare the focus of each approach: Which plan more closely achieves the Renaissance humanist aim (*In the World:* Humanism, Learning, and Education, p. 452) of finding dignity in humanity? Why?

2. Evaluate the use of capital punishment in other countries during the Early Modern Period by researching how other cultures viewed it. For what reasons did these cultures practice or not practice capital punishment, and how was it administered? Consider examining these same cultures in a contemporary context. Which countries today still legally practice capital punishment? Which do not? Compare the rationales each country argues, and discuss how capital punishment is currently viewed by the majority of the world's cultures. Should this Renaissance practice be continued? If so, under what circumstances? Identify the problems with this practice, and propose an alternative solution.

3. Research an influential occultist figure such as Alistair Crowley. Define this occultist figure's philosophies. Compare these philosophies with both religion and science, paying special attention to the commonalities that magic, religion, and science each share both in belief and practice. Identify why your chosen figure is classified as an occultist, and consider making an argument about whether he or she better might be better considered as a practitioner of religion or science. What continues to separate the forbidden knowledge of the occult from the accepted knowledge of religion and science? Hypothesize about the future: Do you envision a convergence of science, religion, and magic? Why or why not?

4. Why is God not more visible in *Doctor Faustus*? Compare Marlowe's play with Samuel Beckett's *Waiting For Godot* or another text that addresses God's physical or psychological absence among communities of believers (or agnostics). Describe in detail how the God of both texts might be characterized, and explain the purpose of God's absence. How do these two different versions of God reflect the respective anxieties of their times?

Projects

1. In a group, stage a scene from *Doctor Faustus*. Research theater architecture and conditions during Renaissance times, and present your scene accordingly. What production constraints would you have faced then? How would those constraints affect a Renaissance interpretation? Or, consider staging a modern interpretation of Marlowe's play. What more contemporary historical context might you use? How might a contemporary set and costumes change or illuminate different aspects of your scene? of different characters?

2. Find a recent science fiction or adventure film that involves seeking after forbidden knowledge. Compare this cinematic representation to *Doctor Faustus* by identifying the secularized powers that have replaced God and Lucifer. Why is this modern knowledge

hidden? Who authorized its hiding? Who seeks this knowledge? Discuss the motivations for possessing secret knowledge, the choices that are made to acquire this knowledge, and whether your chosen film depicts good winning over evil or vice versa. How would you evaluate the plight of the soul today?

3. Find the passages in which Mephistophilis tries to convince Faustus that hell might be a mistake. Based on those admissions, write a brief fictional account, *The Tragical History of Mephistophilis*. What choices did he make to arrive in hell? What did he sacrifice? Why might he regret his choices now?

WWW   For additional information on Marlowe and annotated Web links, see
      World Literature Online at bedfordstmartins.com/worldlit.

FURTHER READING

"Foucault, Michel. *Discipline and Punish*. 1977.
Greenblatt, Stephen. *Shakespearean Negotiations: The Circulation of Social Energy in Renaissance England*. 1988.
Laqueur, Thomas W. *The First Modern Society*. 1989.
Malleus Maleficarum (Hammer of Witches). 1486.
Mebane, John S. *Renaissance Magic and the Return of the Golden Age*. 1989.
Nicholl, Charles. *The Reckoning: The Murder of Christopher Marlowe*. 1992.

WWW   See *World Literature in the 21st Century* at
      bedfordstmartins.com/worldlit for how Faustus is relevant to today's world.

MEDIA RESOURCES

VIDEO

Doctor Faustus
93 min., 1968 (Library Video Company)
In this haunting drama, Richard Burton stars as Doctor Faustus, an aging scholar who makes a bargain with the devil for youth, knowledge and a woman, temptress Elizabeth Taylor. Mephistophilis, the devil's disciple, is sent to distract Faustus from questioning his decision. When Faustus encounters a bewitching seductress who transforms from one beauty to another, the fate of his soul is sealed. Enter a world of spectacular visions and erotic diversions.

Faust: The Man and the Legend
29 min., 1995 (Films for the Humanities & Sciences)
The historical Dr. Faust, and the legends that have arisen around him thanks to the writings of Marlowe, Lessing, and Goethe, are the subject of this fascinating program. The real Faust — excommunicated as a heretic — is presented as a victim of the political and religious tensions of his day. In a medieval world that believed in the corporeal presence of the devil, the accusation that Faust was in league with Mephistophilis seems strangely reasonable. Faust's mysterious death is seen as contributing to the subsequent legends that developed surrounding his character. Viewers gain a sense of Europe before the Enlightenment and of the legendary figure who continues to symbolize humankind's quest for scientific knowledge.

Marlowe's Faust
Two parts, 50 min. each, 1989 (Films for the Humanities & Sciences)
The potential of blank verse for drama was not truly recognized until Christopher

Marlowe's *Tamburlaine the Great*. Many believe his innovation greatly influenced Shakespeare's work. However, it is Marlowe's later work, *The Tragical History of Dr. Faustus*, that became his most celebrated. This play has mesmerized theatergoers for over 400 years and served as the inspiration for numerous books, films, television shows, and even a Broadway musical.

WEB SITES

Christopher Marlowe (1564-1593)
www.luminarium.org/renlit/marlowe.htm
From *Luminarium*, an online anthology of English literature from medieval times through the early seventeenth century, this site provides useful background information about Marlowe's life and works.

The Marlowe Society of America
http://icdweb.cc.purdue.edu/~pwhite/marlowe
The Marlowe Society of America is a nonprofit organization that serves as a forum for exchange of information between scholars, critics, and others who are studying Marlowe's writings, life, and times.

The Complete Works of Christopher Marlowe
http://www.perseus.tufts.edu/Texts/Marlowe.html
The Perseus Project is a digital library at Tufts University for the study of ancient Greece and Rome and Renaissance England. This page presents the Complete Works of Christopher Marlowe: An Electronic Edition.

The Marlowe Society
http://www.marlowe-society.org
This page presents news from the Marlowe Society, a biography of Marlowe, a description of his works, and information about tributes to him.

Selected Poetry of Christopher Marlowe
http://www.library.utoronto.ca/utel/rp/authors/marlowe.html
The Representative Poetry Online site at the University of Toronto Department of English presents the text of selected poetry by Marlowe.

In the World: **Humanism, Learning, and Education** (p. 452)

Renaissance intellectuals in Europe delighted in the recovery of the classical texts and artwork that would come to influence and redefine early modern moral, social, political, and economic institutions. During this flourishing of new thought, the medieval order of feudalism gave way to the development of the city-state; the self-discipline (and self-punishment) of intense religious practice dissipated as creative inquiry, the defining of the individual, and a renewed respect for humans' mental and moral capacities flourished. Renaissance attitudes shifted decidedly away from medieval repentance that anticipated a future heavenly life toward celebrating man's dignity during his earthly sojourn. Studies of classical sources also inspired in Renaissance thinkers an unconstrained curiosity that ambitiously attempted to uncover universal philosophical truths that united humanity — truths that could be discovered, defined, and understood through rational powers of inquiry. One Renaissance man — Shakespeare's Hamlet — praised reborn man effusively, calling him "noble in reason" and "infinite in faculties."

The power of reasoning did indeed make the Renaissance man "like an angel in apprehension . . . like a god!" (II.ii). Ironically, though, humanistic ideals in European, Islamic, and

Chinese thought maintained a symbiotic relationship with religious belief systems and did not completely follow their classical pagan counterparts: Reason was reconciled with Christian, Muslim, or Confucian principles. Humanists positioned man as a divine creation who had a special relationship to God. Like Hamlet, the authors in this section each esteem man as godlike. They also similarly express the love of learning, broad rational inquiry, and cultivation that will come to characterize Renaissance humanism.

That non-Western and Western thinkers alike address learning in similar ways across temporal and spatial boundaries underscores humanism's project of universalizing human experience. In this section, Zhu Xi defines study as the prolonged process of uncovering these all-encompassing principles. His approach advocates returning to the authentic discussions of the ancient sages, weeding out the textual commentaries that have overtaken them. Similarly, Ibn Sina's enthusiasm for truth drives him to examine new and varying textual sources in law, philosophy, and medicine, and yet he tempers his knowledge with an increasingly wise capacity of sound judgment. Abd al-Qadir Bada'uni's account of Akbar reveals an enlightened, open ruler interested in conversation, dialogue, and collaboration. Akbar revels in contact with disparate religious and scientific belief systems in his efforts to uncover truth. Niccolò Machiavelli, in the Western tradition, similarly advocates the all-importance of contact with the sages. By studying texts, he immerses himself in a different, liberating world governed only by the joy of learning. Francis Bacon imagines a perfect world of learning in which inquiry and the pursuit of universal principles are the economy that drives his utopia. But Giovanni Pico della Mirandola perhaps synthesizes these attitudes most comprehensively by echoing Hamlet's assessment: Man is the highest animal, created by a liberal God who endows man with "free judgment" to commence his own self-fashioning. In perhaps the most famous humanistic quote, Pico positions man as the "molder and maker" of himself. Perpetually aspiring, man enjoys a continual process of growth as a plastic creation, transformed by increasing knowledge and its moral applications. All men are permitted this metamorphosis, provided they have access to learning.

Yet even as Hamlet praises man as "the beauty of the world," he ironically deconstructs his own remarks: He confesses that "man delights not me" and, disappointed in man's foibles, esteems him as the "quintessence of dust." In true Renaissance fashion, ideals about man's potential were not always reflected in pedagogical — or lived — practice. Explain to students that the Renaissance commitment to education was not without its own set of contradictions. Conflicts abounded in Europe about corporal punishment inflicted on students that seemed to contradict any emphasis on students' dignity. Similarly, young men who did receive educations were those whose economic stations permit them to — most often the gentry and the highest of the commoners, if they were lucky — which negated the idea of a universal humanity. And, as the preferred pronoun was "man," women were not included in this educational reform: Although some were literate and studied some forms of literature and other arts, women were most often denied the rich classical education men were afforded. Perhaps most disturbingly, the enlightened humanist was defined in contradistinction to that which is beastly. While man is, as Hamlet stated, "the paragon of animals," he was also, as Pico observed, "made similar to brutes and mindless beasts of burden." Many were deemed by Renaissance intellectuals to be less than human and even bestial, including slaves, the dark-skinned other, the working classes, reprobate sinners (Jesus Christ came to save only the few elect), and women. The Renaissance veneration of learning and education thus remains a decidedly ambiguous influence because of its contradictory and exclusivist nature.

Consider beginning your approach to this section by asking some fundamental questions about education. How does learning take place? What responsibilities do both educators and students have in the learning process? On what premises do students base their beliefs about their own abilities to learn? Ask students to consider what their responses to these questions reveal about their own ontological presuppositions. How do they characterize — the quintessential Renaissance question — the nature of human beings? Introduce Renaissance humanism in this context to see how far-reaching the influence of the early modern humanist thinkers remains. Why is man worthy to be both the acting subject in as well as object of rigorous study? Describe the spirit of reborn confidence in human beings' abilities to discern for themselves — by the powers of reason and evaluation — the difference between truth and error. Invite students to analyze the systematic and dedicated approach to learning that the texts in this section illustrate, pointing out that this kind of careful textual examination is one of the surviving legacies of humanism — even studying "humanism" itself is a humanistic construction.

The ideas presented in this section stimulate fascinating discussions about education in general. What better place to discuss a love of learning and inquiry — including the power that knowledge engenders — than in a classroom dedicated to studying the humanities? These texts become contagious in their fervor for knowledge, and they invite instructors and students alike to reconsider the reasons for a university's existence. Students are fascinated to know how much of the current university system — as well as conflicts raised about general education — still reflect Renaissance ideals. Ask students, for example, why they decided to take a World Literature course. What are the values of studying the arts, literature, history, and philosophies of other cultures? What responsibilities does such an education imply? As students pursue the liberal arts, are they becoming more "free" (as the word "liberal" implies), more elitist, or both? Who might still be denied such an opportunity?

IN THE CLASSROOM

I. HUMANISTIC EDUCATION: NATURE VERSUS NURTURE

Although the word *humanist* first appeared in 1589, it is important to note that the word *humanism* was not coined until the nineteenth century. Indeed, attempts at a Renaissance definition only reveal how disparate the elements of emerging humanism were. The term *humanity* (from which the terms *humanist* and *humanities* are derived) had plural meanings: It signified peace and courtesy, but it also implied — hearkening back to Cicero — civility, doctrine, liberal knowledge, and gentility. Other Renaissance discussions of "humanity" distinguished philosophically between the divinity and brutality inherent in man's nature as well as defining an exclusivist "courtly humanism." Thus Renaissance humanism was more a discourse than an actual movement, more a sharing of ideals than a decided curriculum. Its inherent ontological uncertainties fostered the Renaissance nature versus nurture debate: Are virtue and character innate traits, or are they taught and modeled?

Renaissance educational reforms seemed to support both sides of this argument. On one hand, during the fifteenth and sixteenth centuries, the increasing number of grammar schools was largely reserved for aristocracy — except for a few wealthy common families. Heredity, in this context, determined intelligence and capability. On the other hand, blood alone did not determine brilliance: Students were also obligated to demonstrate intellectual and moral abilities to be considered as bright minds and potential future leaders, and certain poorer students who showed promise were permitted to attend. Thus a complicated relationship between instructor and student was born. Certain Renaissance writers compared the instructor/student relationship to a master gardener tending to his plant. The role of the teacher ranged from gentle, protective overseer to dominating disciplinarian; the student cultivated — "grew" — himself but also needed to be sometimes "pruned." Teachers were seen as supporting the patriarchal authority of monarchical rule by reinforcing its guiding precepts but also as those who presided over the independent and influential space of the classroom, thus simultaneously threatening that patriarchy. Similarly, students assimilated the ideals of the dominant culture, yet they also participated in the new Renaissance cult of independent critical thinking that encouraged them to evaluate questions of moral philosophy and existence rationally and to trust their reasoned conclusions.

The changing curriculum also supported both sides of the nature versus nurture dilemma. The new emphasis on the *studias humanitatas* (humanistic studies) during the European Renaissance modified the medieval curriculum of the trivium (grammar, logic, rhetoric) and the quadrivium (arithmetic, geometry, astronomy, and music) by emphasizing the more "humane" fields of grammar, rhetoric, history, poetry, and moral philosophy, especially as those fields involved reviving classical Greek and Latin works. While this definition of "liberal arts" varied among schools, regions, and theorists, transnational humanistic ideals placed the highest value in two distinct areas — tempering religion with philosophy and reading a large selection of the great works of literature. By reconciling these studies with Judeo-Christian principles, man would develop well-rounded artistic but moral, aesthetic yet reasoned abilities. He would also come to a better understanding of himself and of the larger project of a universal humanity. The responsibility, then, for bettering society fell squarely on the shoulders of these educated few, since they — echoing Cicero — were engaged in the public life and the pursuit of the common good, grounded in moral philosophy, and capable of persuading others to pursue the morally correct path. Such ideals reinforced the Renaissance paradox of promoting a burgeoning nationalistic power and, at the same time, sponsoring the development of a rational, liberal individual. The emphasis on the humanities in academe today still reflects the Renaissance liberal education that advocates a broad exposure to cultural ideas and artifacts tempered by a rational, critical analysis: One contemporary definition of humanism can still be defined as a devoted study of the humanities.

Discussion

1. Encourage students to discuss their goals in attending a school of higher education. What are they hoping to learn or gain? Zhu Xi states that "study is the only key to the comprehension of the principles of the world." Ask students to define what Zhu Xi means, and ask them to reflect about whether today's educational systems support Zhu's ideals. Do students attend school to learn the "principles of the world"?

2. Ask students to reflect on the importance of a liberal education in today's world. Are the fields of art, literary studies, and moral philosophy valued today? What kinds of bachelor's degrees do different contemporary cultures seem to reward? Why? Have students consider their ideas in light of Machiavelli's lament about poverty in his letter. What are his concerns? Discuss what makes Machiavelli's letter relevant today.

3. For each of the authors in this section, ask students to identify the specific realms in which learning is valued. Where does teaching and learning take place? Who is entitled to it? Ask students to discuss their findings and to compare their observations with an evaluation of their own cultures. Is learning for the few or the many today? Discuss how different levels of schooling may be more or less democratic or elitist, and identify what has or has not changed since the Renaissance in terms of education.

Connections

1. The Renaissance study of the liberal (from the Latin word for *freedom*) arts reflects Plato's discussion of the pursuit of truth in the Allegory of the Cave (Book 1). What

kind of freedom does the student find as he or she seeks to move outside the cave, away from the shadowed images? How does the study of the humanities in particular help to achieve Plato's ideal result?

2. Each of the thinkers in this section demonstrates a commitment to the pursuit of knowledge. Compare their quests to Monkey and Tripitaka's journey in *Monkey* (p. 837). What kinds of knowledge does each seek? How is that knowledge obtained? What is the ultimate goal for each thinker? Ask students to evaluate the criteria by which each thinker might consider himself successful in his journey.

3. Read the excerpt from Virginia Woolf's *A Room of One's Own*, "Shakespeare's Sister" (Book 6). What educational disadvantages does Shakespeare's fictional sister, Judith, face because she is female? What does Woolf's portrait of Judith reveal about the humanist curriculum of Elizabethan England?

Groups

1. In groups, ask students to design their own utopias, much like Francis Bacon does in *New Atlantis* (p. 481). Have them discuss what they would define as the best methods for understanding and bettering the human condition and creating an ideal society. What role would education play in the creation of their perfect worlds? What fields of study would be the highest priorities in their self-styled educational curricula? Have each group present their ideas to the class, comparing the various responses. Evaluate the values that each group's solutions reflect, and compare them to those represented in the texts of this section.

Writing

Ask students to write a short paper, responding to one or more of the following:

1. In *Areopagitica* (p. 680), Milton states that a "good book is the precious lifeblood of a master spirit, embalmed and treasured up on purpose to a life beyond life." Compare the attitudes that the authors in this section express about reading with Milton's assessment. How do modern-day readers compare with these Renaissance thinkers in their enthusiasm for a good book? Discuss whether or not reading for pleasure and in the pursuit of self-betterment is still a priority in today's world. Identify cultural emphases that may have supplanted reading, and explain why they have become more popular. What are the dangers for a culture that devalues reading?

2. Compare the forums in which the thinkers in this section learn. Identify the specific places in which these men study and whether it is in a group or in isolation. Compare the advantages and disadvantages of learning in communities and through individual study. Are both models necessary, or is one preferable over the other? Explain why you reach the conclusion you do, possibly using your own learning experiences as justification.

3. Ibn Sina's path to understanding begins at a very young age and in a dedicated way. He absorbs as much knowledge as is available to him in a perpetual effort to master it. How does today's educational system favor or hamper the kind of fervor that Ibn Sina demonstrates? Discuss specifically those aspects of modern education that both enhance and hinder learning, and propose solutions to the problems you identify.

II. HUMANISMS

The nebulous definition of humanism during the Renaissance prefigured the debates within humanism as a concept evolving over time: In subsequent eras, humanism has represented vastly different schools of thought. The debate about what humanism is continues to enjoy much attention among disparate humanistic circles. Today's humanism — an outgrowth of previous versions shaped by Ferdinand Schiller, John Dewey, and Jean-Paul Sartre, among others — poses special problems, since it is described as both "religious" and "secular." Each of these varieties can be individually defined as a philosophical system in which humans are free and natural beings who create their own values, morals, and world. Reason still drives these contemporary versions of humanism and especially emphasizes the necessity of evaluating available evidence through rational skepticism. The distinction between these views lies in a subtlety similar to distinguishing between scientific rationalism and empiricism. Some contemporary humanists have argued that Plato would be considered a religious humanist, Aristotle a secular humanist. Others chart the distinction between these two similar humanisms as an emphasis either on community or on the individual. For either system, all beliefs in the supernatural are dismissed, since they cannot be proven by the scientific method. Religious and secular humanists believe that humans will create ethical systems because they need them to survive; because humans exist in communities, a natural respect and tolerance for others' beliefs will naturally spring up. Despite their seeming differences, these two groups believe in the power of humanity to solve its own problems through the power of rational inquiry. Thus while certain tenets of Renaissance humanism remain — primarily the fundamental importance of reason and the belief in man's abilities — the roles of faith and God are removed completely from the equation.

Discussion

1. Ibn Sina studies texts voraciously, hungering after knowledge. After he listens carefully to a visiting Ismaeli, however, his "spirit [does] not assent"; when he does not understand something, he goes to the mosque to pray. Ask the students to consider Ibn Sina's methods of inquiry: Is his an appeal to powers of reason, to religious tenets, or both? Ask students to discuss how Ibn Sina reconciles faith and reason. Is his solution plausible? Generate a discussion about the benefits and disadvantages of combining rational inquiry with religious beliefs. How do students know when to believe or disbelieve something? What do their responses reveal about their own ontological presuppositions?

2. Ask students to identify specific parts of Francis Bacon's excerpt from *New Atlantis* in which both Christian humanism is celebrated at the same time contemporary rational skepticism and empirical science are embraced. In what ways does Bacon's bifurcated pursuit of knowledge illustrated in this excerpt prefigure contemporary debates about humanism?

3. Pico openly — and complexly — acknowledges divinity in his celebration of humanity. Ask students to identify specifically the ways in which Pico attributes or does not attribute the expansion of the mind to God. How does Pico's faith help or hinder his pursuit of knowledge? Ask students to discuss where God ends and man begins, according to Pico. How does acknowledging man as a divine creation encourage man's education? How do Pico's ideas compare with those presented by the other authors in this section?

4. Ask students to identify and discuss the ways the thinkers presented welcome new ideas, despite being devout believers in their respective faiths. Encourage students to evaluate their own open-mindedness as they encounter unfamiliar concepts. In what ways does modern religious faith encourage or discourage open dialogue?

Connections

1. Discuss the difference between rational scientific inquiry and direct revelation. Ask students to describe how God, Allah, or Buddha instructs different cultures. Have students

consider the nature of the revelation given in Exodus (Book 1) when God provides the Ten Commandments to the Israelites. How do the thinkers in this section comparably view revelation from God?

2. Li Zhi, in "On the Child-Mind" (p. 677), advocates maintaining an internal connection to the "genuine mind." Scholars lose touch with the child mind, Li Zhi argues, by "extensive reading and moral judgments" — and yet part of the humanist project involves reading extensively and judging morally. Compare Li Zhi's desire to maintain a Daoist state of being with the humanist ideals that are expressed. Are any versions of rational inquiry described by the authors compatible with a Daoist belief system? Why or why not?

3. Read an account of twentieth-century humanism by Jean-Paul Sartre from *In the World: Existentialism* (Book 6). Identify Sartre's argument for why existentialism might also be considered humanistic. In what ways does his version of humanism differ from Renaissance humanism?

Groups

1. Have groups of students choose one kind of humanism from any time period and research the tenets it espouses. Ask each group to present its findings to the class, outlining that humanism's specific beliefs and how they may have grown out of concepts found in Renaissance humanism. As a class, discuss specific differences between the types of humanism presented, paying special attention to the role faith plays or does not play within each version.

Writing

Ask students to write a short paper, responding to one or more of the following:

1. Zhu Xi reveals a basic tenet of humanism that "there is a principle for everything under the sun," and a "constant, eternal theory of the world." These principles are seemingly available to be discerned by any observant mind — and yet seem contradictory in the plural notions of humanism that abound today. Discuss the problems of universalizing the human experience: What are the dilemmas that arise when all-encompassing theories are said to undergird all cultures? If there are universal, underlying philosophical truths that govern human existence, how can the existence of multiple, contradictory religions be explained?

2. Compare Zhu Xi's and Li Zhi's (pp. 465, 675) assessment of scholars who live to create textual commentaries on the words of the great sages. Each of these authors advocates a return to some kind of essence inherent in previous utterances of the sages. Evaluate their views in contradistinction to the current humanist project of Western academe. In the practice of theorists within the humanities today, are intellectuals more like Zhu and Li or the scholars they criticize? Make an argument for whether textual commentary within academe has become a sort of religion in its own right. Can faithless endeavors also embody a form of faith?

3. Consider the accounts of two great leaders in this section: Akbar and the father of Salomon's House. Describe the influence each has over his respective kingdom, and compare how each of these leaders negotiates a balance between rational inquiry and faithful observance of religion. In what ways does science serve to inform their respective religious observances? How does religion underscore their scientific pursuits? Are faith and science mutually exclusive when governing a country?

BEYOND THE CLASSROOM

RESEARCH & WRITING

1. Research Renaissance painting, sculpture, or music. Find a work or a series of works that glorifies the human body, spirit, or mind. Perhaps by comparing a work of Renaissance art to a similar medieval counterpart, analyze specific ways in which the aesthetic representation celebrates the dignity of man and reinforces the principles of Renaissance humanism expressed in this section.

2. The study as an architectural space inside the home, complete with personal library, is a Renaissance creation. How does the study as a stand-alone room mirror the ideals of Renaissance humanism? Research the history of the study, and identify the Renaissance causes that made this architectural space possible, analyzing why these specific developments were necessary. What major political, sociological, and religious changes encourage private study?

3. Research current or past examples of Muslim education. How is religious faith combined with rational inquiry in these educational systems? Describe how the Muslim educational curriculum negotiates a productive marriage between faith and reason, and discuss the benefits and disadvantages of such a faith-based education. In what ways does such a religious education continue to either propagate or contradict Renaissance humanistic ideals?

Projects

1. Identify a debate about educational curriculum between what have been identified as "secular humanists" and their opponents (for example, whether the creation myth or evolution should be taught in schools). Research the conflicting stands the parties are taking and the possibilities for how the controversy might be handled in a practical sense. Imagine that you are a judge, given the power and discretion to resolve this conflict in an actual community. Write a verdict that summarizes the issue's different sides, gives your version of the issue's practical solution, and outlines the consequences you envision for the future.

2. What makes a great teacher? Watch a film that depicts the relationship between teachers and students (there are many examples; some include *The Blackboard Jungle; To Sir, With Love; Stand and Deliver; The Corn is Green; Goodbye, Mr. Chips; The Empire Strikes Back; The Miracle Worker; Finding Forrester; Shadowlands; The Paper Chase; Dead Poet's Society*). Evaluate the ideals of the teacher you have chosen to examine: Is this teacher worthy of emulation? Discuss the effectiveness of this teacher's methods and approach. How do this teacher's values compare with those expressed by the thinkers in this section? How does this teacher compare with other teachers you have had? Imagine that the teacher is a principal or department chair hiring a new instructor and write a detailed job description that reflects a superior teacher's required characteristics. Is this job description influenced by the humanistic ideals expressed in this section?

FURTHER READING

Bullock, Alan, *The Humanist Tradition in the West*. 1985.

Bushnell, Rebecca W. *A Culture of Teaching: Early Modern Humanism in Theory and Practice*. 1996.

Grendler, Paul F. *Schooling in Renaissance Italy: Literacy and Learning, 1300–1600*. 1989.

Pincombe, Mike. *Elizabethan Humanism: Literature and Learning in the Later Sixteenth Century.* 2001.

Remer, Gary. *Humanism and the Rhetoric of Toleration.* 1996.

MEDIA RESOURCES

WEB SITES

Humanistic Texts
www.humanistictexts.org/
This is an exceptional source of background information on humanist philosophers and writers. Found here are dozens of pages devoted to key humanist figures and texts, such as Chu Hsi, Francis Bacon, and Machiavelli.

The Islamic World to 1600
www.ucalgary.ca/applied_history/tutor/islam/learning/
This site provides the University of Calgary's excellent tutorial on the Islamic world, from its beginnings in the seventh century to the decline of its three great empires in the seventeenth century. Included is an overview of Islamic arts as well as the Islamic dedication to knowledge and learning, which resulted in significant advancements in medicine, astronomy, mathematics, and philosophy. Also included are brief biographies of eight Muslim scholars who contributed to knowledge in the Islamic world, and who made certain scientific discoveries long before their counterparts in other regions of the world.

Pico della Mirandola
www.wsu.edu:8080/~dee/REN/PICO.HTM
Richard Hooker's (Washington State University) site on Pico della Mirandola provides an overview of the Renaissance thinker as well as a translation of "Oration on the Dignity of Man."

Renaissance Humanism
www.historyguide.org/intellect/humanism.html
This page provides a brief overview of the intellectual currents of Renaissance humanism.

Rome Reborn: The Vatican Library & Renaissance Culture
lcweb.loc.gov/exhibits/vatican/humanism.html
This page from the Library of Congress provides a brief background information on humanism accompanied by facsimile reproductions of original documents from the Vatican Library.

WILLIAM SHAKESPEARE, *The Tempest* (p. 495)

WWW   For a quiz on *The Tempest*, see *World Literature Online* at bedfordstmartins.com/worldlit.

In the introduction to *The Tempest*, ways in which the play can be read as a study of the duties and responsibilities of the Renaissance prince in a colonial context are pointed out. Read from this perspective, *The Tempest* has profound connections to Machiavelli's *The Prince* and Montaigne's essays "Of Cannibals" and "Of Coaches." Shakespeare's play, of course, enriches the discourse of power and leads it into areas overlooked by Machiavelli and Montaigne, especially magic, art, and faith. Thus the play also has direct links to Marlowe's *Doctor Faustus* in that it goes beyond the rational dimension and questions the proper limits of human power. Teaching Shakespeare's works as literary texts without reference to the drama is always reductive, and ideally students should see a performance of the play to help them appreciate Shakespeare's dramatic magic and to hear for themselves the music of the play's language. Although many versions and adaptations of the play are available on film, it is always possible, and helpful, to have three or four students perform a scene or two for the class. It seems best to get the basic story straight before proceeding to more complex issues. Hence, one might begin by asking how Prospero has come to be on the island, why he has raised the storm to wreck the ship, what his relation is to Caliban and Ariel, and what he hopes to accomplish by scattering the various parties.

The Tempest raises questions about genre. Although it is often classified as a romance, the play presents a kind of hybrid genre that draws on various literary forms, including a masque that Prospero arranges for Miranda and Ferdinand. Of course, all of Prospero's manipulations — the raising of the storm, the separation of the various parties on the island, the meeting between Ferdinand and Miranda — are the result of Prospero's illusionist art. Like Machiavelli's prince, Prospero is a master of illusion, of creating spectacles to serve his interests. Thus in the play the boundaries between magic, art, and governance blur, and *The Tempest* — which some critics read as Shakespeare's farewell to the stage — focuses on some of the major issues about power and discovery that we have identified as major themes in the Renaissance. Overall, the play also embodies a sense of wonder that Renaissance exploration introduced to Europe, one that we see in Columbus's *Diario*.

Because Shakespeare has become a kind of cultural institution in his own right, it is often helpful to discuss just what we mean when we say that a work is "timeless." Does Shakespeare's work thrive because it contains immutable eternal truths and psychological insights into some unchanging human nature, or does it thrive because its artistry allows us to adapt his work and reconstruct its meanings to meet our own psychological, aesthetic, and cultural needs? A comparison of interpretations or performances of *The Tempest* over its history may be useful in attempting to answer this larger question, which is really a question about the function of literature and the nature of "great works."

TEXT AND CONTEXT

SEA ADVENTURE

There is some controversy regarding the inspiration for Shakespeare's choice of setting and description of the storm and shipwreck in *The Tempest*, but it is often argued that he drew from one or more accounts of the troubles encountered in 1609 by a ship called the *Sea Adventure*. One of nine vessels sponsored by the Virginia Company to carry cargo and 500 passengers to Jamestown, the *Sea Adventure* was separated from its group by a terrible storm and driven ashore at Bermuda, an island labeled by some sixteenth-century sailors as the "Isle of Devils." They found the island a much more hospitable place than expected and were eventually able to rebuild and finish their journey to Jamestown. Their miraculous arrival at Jamestown, almost a year late, was the subject of much celebration, speculation, and conversation in voice and print.

One reason for believing Shakespeare was familiar with this adventure is the fact that earls of Southampton and Pembroke, possibly close associates of Shakespeare, were connected with the Virginia Company. A more compelling connection is Shakespeare's association with William Strachey, a passenger on the *Sea Adventure* who had tried his hand as a playwright in London. Some scholars believe that Shakespeare must have read Strachey's letter, widely circulated to his friends in England but not published until 1625, describing the shipwreck and his experience on the island. There are similarities in Strachey's and Shakespeare's descriptions of the storm, the island, and the island's native inhabitants. One might note particularly Strachey's observation that the native inhabitants, like Caliban, were not especially receptive to the "civilizing" education of new arrivals. Further, the accounts of Strachey and others describe Bermuda — feared by many sailors as a dangerous and inhospitable place — as a fertile, welcoming environment with bountiful natural resources and natives who assisted the newcomers by showing them how to survive on the island. Readers of *The Tempest* might note that the play shares with records of the Bermuda shipwreck an attention to the themes of education, the power and influence of nature, and the tension between savagery and civilization.

IN THE CLASSROOM

I. DRAMATIC EFFECTS AND THEMES IN *THE TEMPEST*

While *The Tempest* may seem to some students a bit light on character development or plot complexity, drawing students' attention to the array of dramatic effects, themes and motifs, and symbols provides a field of investigation they will find wonderfully complex and challenging. Remind students that the play was performed at court, and highlight those elements that hold great potential for dramatic staging, such as storms, sprites, magic, monsters, music, and drunken humor. As you work through the text in class, ask students to imagine and describe how they would present particular passages, and have them discuss the intentions or reasoning behind their choices. In conjunction with this, spend time discussing ways the play comments on themes like the art of drama. Some scholars suggest, for example, that Shakespeare writes himself as Prospero and that Prospero's magic, especially his manipulation of events and beings, might represent a playwright's control of the stage. Some critics point to the tension between nature and nurture, or "civilization," in the play or to the importance of love as a potentially regenerative force.

Discussion

1. After familiarizing students with the conventions (and limitations) of Shakespearean drama, ask them to describe how they would stage a particularly dramatic moment of the play. Discuss how their choices are influenced by their interpretation of the text. How might they stage this scene differently on a modern stage? How might the changes communicate a different interpretation?

2. Discuss the major thematic conflicts or oppositions in the play — art versus nature, primitive versus civilized, and revenge versus forgiveness. Other themes to discuss include nature versus nurture, the responsibility of leaders, the nature of freedom, allegiance, the limits of vengeance, and the importance of forgiveness.

3. Keeping in mind Prospero's ability to manipulate it, ask students to define *nature* and explain its function in the play. How does Prospero's control over the environment of the island and its surrounding seas parallel a playwright's control over the setting of a play? What are the implications of this connection?

4. Address the function of the relationship between Miranda and Ferdinand. Concern for his daughter is clearly one of Prospero's motivations in the text. Why must Ferdinand undergo the trial he is put through in order to earn his bride? How does their example of virtuous love, or the promise of their union, speak to other themes in the text?

5. Discuss the importance of the epilogue insofar as it breaks the spell of the play.

Connections

1. Compare Prospero's use of magic to Faustus's (p. 389). What are the limits of their power? Do they use their power responsibly?

2. Prospero, Faustus (p. 389), and Monkey (p. 837) all use pranks, practical jokes, and games to achieve their ends. Compare Prospero's use of jokes and games with one or both of these other characters'. What is the effect of the comic subplot on our reading of the play?

Groups

1. Divide students into small groups, and assign to each of them one of the separated parties on Prospero's island: Prospero and Ariel; Ferdinand and Miranda; Caliban, Stephano, and Trinculo; or Gonzalo, Alonso, Sebastian, and Antonio. After some discussion, have them explain to the rest of the class what is happening within their particular party, the internal conflicts among the characters, their objectives, and their relation to Prospero's overall plan.

2. Divide students into groups, and have each perform a scene or two from the play for the rest of the class. Have each group bring in a few basic props. For example, a blanket, empty bottle, and a pair of swim fins are all that is needed to stage the Caliban/Trinculo/Stephano drunk scene (Act II, Scene 2). Consider asking two groups to enact the same scene so that, as a class, differences in interpretation communicated by the performances can be discussed.

Writing

Ask students to write a short paper, responding to one or more of the following:

1. Summarize and evaluate Prospero's motivation as it evolves through the course of the play. Why does he create the initial storm? At what point does his thirst for revenge begin to mellow, and what causes this change? What becomes his new motivation, and how is this change significant?

2. Discuss Prospero as an embodiment of Renaissance humanism.

3. Identify and analyze an important symbol in the play. For example, you might analyze the significance of Prospero's books. What function to they serve in Milan and on the island, and why does he not choose to take them with him when he leaves?

4. The scenes with Trinculo, Stephano, and Caliban are more than a comic subplot. Drawing from specific lines in the text, explore the ways they mirror, and comment on other hierarchical relationships in the play.

II. Shakespeare and His Attitude Toward Exploration and Colonialism

Miranda's famous line, "O brave new world/That has such people in't!" is the starting point for much scholarly speculation regarding Shakespeare's attitude toward exploration and the colonial enterprise. Though it is difficult to draw from the play a specific commentary on imperialism, *The Tempest* rewards readers with compelling explorations of issues of hierarchy, power, and cultural contact. Prospero's methods of control and attitudes toward authority — whether over Ariel, Caliban, his daughter, or the new arrivals — draw from his experiences in Milan and place that belief structure in a new environment. His own evolution of belief and the values he inherited are displayed and explored in the play. Does his inherited approach to the practice of power work in this new world? What has he learned from this experience about exercising authority, and what conclusions might readers draw from his education? The values, assumptions, and plots of the shipwrecked Europeans also introduce many layers to the exploration of issues of power and authority. Draw students' attention to shifting definitions of what it means to be a leader and to tensions based on the exercise of power or supposed superiority.

Discussion

1. Have students identify the grounds of Prospero's authority and the means by which he rules the island. Ask the class to draw from these observations a theory of the workings of governance. Discuss the implications of this theory as it comments on both European structures of power and the imposition of European power on the "new world."

2. Outline on the board the various hierarchical structures presented in the play (those from Milan and those on the island). Including rankings between humans and other-world creatures, discuss the ways these hierarchies, or the very concept of stratification, are challenged in the text. Then read aloud Gonzalo's proposal for a commonwealth. Ask students to examine the implications of Gonzalo's proposal. How does it comment on the process of ordering beings? (Looking at Montaigne's "Of Cannibals" is useful here.)

3. Discuss the relationship between Ariel, Caliban, and Prospero in terms of master, slave, and servant. For example, some critics argue that Caliban is "by nature" a savage, and this is why — though he claims a right to rule the island — he seeks a new master in Stephano rather than his own authority. In what ways does this play comment on the master/slave relationship? How does Shakespeare define the role of "civilization" or the concept of the "savage"?

4. What is the meaning of the word *brave* in the play? How does that term resonate throughout the play, especially in Miranda's "O brave new world"?

Connections

1. Compare Stephano and Trinculo's desire to rule the island to Sancho Panza's desire to rule in *Don Quixote* (p. 262). What do these texts tell us about the growing possibilities for social climbing introduced by the age of discovery, colonization, and exploration? Are these Faustian ambitions?

2. Apply Machiavelli's definition of the Renaissance prince (p. 124) to Prospero. Compare Prospero's performance of his princely duties to those of another Renaissance prince.

3. Compare Shakespeare's view of colonialism to those of Columbus, Montaigne, Sor Juana, and/or Machiavelli.

Writing

Ask students to write a short paper in response to one or more of the following:

1. Compare Gonzalo's response to the possibilities of the island to those of Sebastian, Antonio, Alonso, and Gonzalo. What implications do their responses have in terms of European colonialism and discovery of the New World? Compare these various responses to the New World with that found in Columbus's *Diario* (p. 773).

2. What conclusions might you draw regarding colonialism as portrayed in *The Tempest*?

3. Who is the "other" in this play, and how is that role portrayed?

BEYOND THE CLASSROOM

RESEARCH & WRITING

1. Focusing on the early seventeenth century, research narratives recording British explorations of new lands. Write a paper in which you use contemporary accounts of contact with an "other" to shed light on Shakespeare's exploration of the arrival of European peoples on an unknown island.

2. Research the reception history of *The Tempest*. Write a paper in which you present and analyze two to four differing reactions to the play. Paying particular attention to the perspective of each author and his or her cultural context, discuss the reasons for the divergence in opinions.

Projects

1. Write an act or scene in which the "foul witch" Sycorax would speak or take an active part. How might the play change if we could hear her version of the story?

2. Rewrite the story of *The Tempest* from Caliban's point of view. Compare his perspective to that of the Aztecs when Cortés arrives. Is Prospero at all like Cortés or Columbus? How does the Aztec situation differ from that of Caliban'?

WWW   For additional information on Shakespeare and annotated Web links, see *World Literature Online* at bedfordstmartins.com/worldlit.

FURTHER READING

Bradbrook, Muriel. *Themes and Conventions in Elizabethan Drama.* 1960.

Bush, Geoffrey. *Shakespeare and the Natural Condition.* 1956.

Murphy, Patrick M., ed. The Tempest: *Critical Essays.* 2000.

Richards, Jennifer, and James Knowles, eds. *Shakespeare's Late Plays: New Readings.* 1999.

Uphaus, Robert. *Beyond Tragedy: Structure and Experience in Shakespeare's Romances.* 1981.

Wells, Stanley, ed. *The Cambridge Companion to Shakespeare.* 1986.

WWW   See *World Literature in the 21st Century* at bedfordstmartins.com/worldlit for examples of the relevance of *The Tempest* in today's world.

MEDIA RESOURCES

VIDEO

Prospero's Books
124 min., 1991 (Library Video Company)
A uniquely structured retelling of *The Tempest*, starring John Gielgud as Prospero and directed by Peter Greenaway. Intricate staging, graphic nudity, and lavish art production are part of this nontraditional performance of the classic play.

Selected Sonnets
40 min., 2000 (Films for the Humanities & Sciences)
Four sonnets chosen to conform to a single classroom period: Sonnet 65 (read by Jane Lapotaire, commentary by Stephen Spender), Sonnet 66 (read by Michael Bryant, commentary by Arnold Wesker), Sonnet 94 (read by Michael Bryant, commentary by John Mortimer), Sonnet 127 (read by Ben Kingsley, commentary by A. L. Rowse).

Shakespeare's Sonnets
2 hrs., 30 min., 2000 (Films for the Humanities & Sciences)
Fifteen sonnets selected for what they tell us about Shakespeare — because of the individual addressed, or references to people or events, or because of their metaphors. The sonnets (numbers 8, 18, 25, 35, 53, 64, 65, 66, 87, 91, 94, 107, 127, 128, and 144) are read by Ben Kingsley, Roger Rees, Claire Bloom, and Jane Lapotaire, then analyzed by a noted critic

or writer (analysts include A. L. Rowse, Leslie Fiedler, Stephen Spender, and Arnold Wesker).

The Sonnet
30 min., 2001 (Films for the Humanities & Sciences)
Popular since the thirteenth century, the sonnet is one of the most well-known and powerful poetic forms. In this engaging program, three contemporary poets — Wendy Cope, Douglas Dunn, and Tony Harrison — discuss the sonnet's merits, its continuing relevance, and how its use has facilitated their poetry. The classic sonnets read and examined in detail are Sir Philip Sidney's "My true love hath my heart, and I have his"; Shakespeare's "When in disgrace with fortune and men's eyes"; and Charles Tennyson Turner's "Letty's Globe." Cope, Dunn, and Harrison also read and talk about their own sonnets, such as "The Sitter," "Sandra's Mobile," "Them and Uz," "Marked with D," and "Book Ends."

William Shakespeare
30 min., 1996 (Library Video Company)
Born in the country town of Stratford-on-Avon, William Shakespeare was educated at the local grammar school and in 1558 left for London to begin a career in the theater. He went on to become the world's most acclaimed poet and playwright, noted for his sonnets and for tragedies such as *Hamlet*, *Othello*, and *King Lear*. Discover the life and times of this literary giant.

William Shakespeare: A Life of Drama
30 min., 1996 (A&E Biography Video)
A&E Biography presents film excerpts, dramatic readings, and location footage that provide a glimpse into the little-known life and astonishing career of William Shakespeare. Discover the world's most influential writer, from his youth in Stratford-on-Avon and his marriage to an older woman at eighteen to the night of carousing that led to his death at age fifty-two.

William Shakespeare
46 min., 1995 (Films for the Humanities & Sciences)
He was simply the greatest poet and playwright of any age — a genius whose work still brings joy to millions throughout the world. This program tells the story of the man and his works. Featuring delightful dramatized extracts from some of Shakespeare's best-known plays, the program also includes memorable depictions of life in Elizabethan times. The program also features expert commentary and critical analysis by Stanley Wells, director of the Shakespeare Institute, and Robert Smallwood, deputy director of the Shakespeare Centre in Stratford-upon-Avon. The well-regarded Shakespearean actor Brian Blessed also makes a special appearance in this program, which provides a colorful and informative glimpse into the remarkable world of William Shakespeare.

William Shakespeare
50 min., 1997 (Video Library Company)
Through anecdotes, analysis and humor, author and storyteller Elliott Engel gives new insights to the life and accomplishments of William Shakespeare. Most people consider Shakespeare to be the greatest writer in the English language, but few know the real reasons why. Take an imaginative journey back through time, and attend a Shakespearean play with Professor Engel.

William Shakespeare: A Poet for All Time
30 min., 1997 (Video Universe)
Filmed on location in Stratford-on-Avon, celebrated Shakespearean actor Alan Howard presents some of the bard's best-known works. Includes performances from such classics as *Henry V*, *Romeo and Juliet*, *Julius Caesar*, *MacBeth*, and more.

Shakespeare in London
50 min., 1999 (Video Library Company)
Follow Shakespeare through sixteenth- and seventeenth-century London as he creates many of the most important works ever written. The story begins with the first written documentation of Shakespeare in London — his life on the banks of the Thames River, against the backdrop of the New Globe Playhouse. Queen Elizabeth I is on the throne, and Marlowe is at the height of his popularity, but there are rumblings in theatreland of a young upstart who has stolen ideas from the master. Illustrated by dramatic reconstruction of late Elizabethan life and scenes from the plays themselves, this program shows many sites known to Shakespeare — from the Tower of London to the taverns made famous by Falstaff and other characters. The program places the bard in the context of his time by using accounts of those who knew him and the major events of the time, including the Spanish Armada, political intrigue in the court, discovery of faraway lands, the plague, and the death of Christopher Marlowe.

Shakespeare Tragedies: Origins and Style
45 min., 2000 (Library Video Company)
This program helps students gain an appreciation and understanding of Shakespeare. After exploring Shakespeare's life and times, this program contains sections on understanding Shakespeare's poetry and the elements of Elizabethan drama. Also, by evaluating the tragic figure in Sophocles' *Oedipus Rex*, the Standard Deviants help viewers understand exactly what a tragedy is. Finally, the program offers a brief overview of Shakespeare's development as a writer of tragedy.

The Tempest
150 min., 1980 (Zenger Media)
Christopher Guard and Michael Hordern star in this BBC adaptation.

The Tempest
127 min., 1981 (Library Video Company)
This accent-free production, staged as it was seen in the sixteenth century, features award-winning performers Efrem Zimbalist Jr., William H. Bassett, Ted Sorel, and Ron Palillo, who act out the classic tale of spirits, sorcery, and shipwrecked scheming noblemen.

The Tempest
145 min., 1982 (Library Video Company)
John Cassavetes, Gena Rowlands, Molly Ringwald, and Susan Sarandon star in this loose, comedic adaptation of Shakespeare's tragedy. An architect, riddled with guilt for all the personal and professional compromises he has made, deserts his wife and flees with his daughter to a desolate Greek island. There, in the solitude of nature, he attempts to piece together his battered sense of morals and find his dignity.

The Tempest
28 min., 1993 (Films for the Humanities & Sciences)
In this program, viewers' willingness to suspend disbelief and imagine themselves into a drama of the literary magnitude of *The Tempest* is tested. Discussions focus on how Shakespeare draws attention to the power and implication of theatrical deception and illusion, and misrepresentation and manipulation.

WEB SITES
The Collected Works of William Shakespeare
the-tech.mit.edu/Shakespeare/
The complete texts of Shakespeare online with a search tool (giving you also the word or phrase's context) and a glossary to help you understand the meaning of unfamiliar terms.

Students interested in film interpretations of Shakespeare should also check out this site's related link.

Early Modern Literary Studies: A Journal of Sixteenth- and Seventeenth-Century Literature
purl.oclc.org/emls/emlshome.html
The best online journal on the topic, this site gives you full scholarly articles and their abstracts on topics potentially relevant to your own papers on Shakespeare.

Internet Shakespeare Editions
web.uvic.ca/shakespeare/index.html
ISE's growing site offers annotated, old-spelling transcriptions of the plays.

Mr. William Shakespeare and the Internet
daphne.palomar.edu/shakespeare/
Terry A. Gray at Palomar College created this annotated guide to Shakespeare resources available on the Internet. This enormous site — definitely one to look at before you begin researching and writing on Shakespeare — provides Shakespeare biographies, information about Elizabethan theaters, and excellent guides to finding secondary sources on Shakespeare on the Web. The scholarly articles (organized by individual play) also are available online for use in your papers.

Renaissance
shakespeare.palomar.edu/renaissance.htm
Developed by Terry A. Gray, this page is devoted to journals and text repositories related to Shakespeare, Elizabethan, and Renaissance studies. Web pages about Shakespeare's contemporaries (and near contemporaries) have also been placed here.

Shakespeare Illustrated
www.emory.edu/ENGLISH/classes/Shakespeare_Illustrated/Shakespeare.html
Offering a cross-disciplinary approach to Shakespeare, this site examines nineteenth-century paintings and performances of Shakespeare's plays and their influence on each other.

Shakespeare Internet Sites
web.uvic.ca/shakespeare/Annex/ShakSites1.html
Take some time to explore the many links (ranging from the academically rigorous to the quirky) at this site. Although there are many links to explore here, this site is most useful as a guide to stage and performance history in sixteenth-century England. Students interested in contemporary adaptations of Shakespearean drama (perhaps for a paper comparing or analyzing interpretations) can find good links here to information on a number of recent productions.

Shakespeare Resource Center
www.bardweb.net/
This site, designed by J. M. Pressley, provides a brief biography, a short essay on Shakespeare's works, synopses of the major plays, the text of Shakespeare's will, a summary of the Elizabethan era, a commentary on Shakespeare's language, and a reading list — plus links to related sites.

Shakespeare's Life and Times
web.uvic.ca/shakespeare/Library/SLT/intro/introsubj.html
Michael Best's extensive Web site is a valuable resource for information on the following topics: Shakespeare's life, the stage, society, history, politics, ideas, drama, literature, music, and art. There is interesting coverage of Elizabethan English, including brief sound recordings from *Henry IV, Part One* and *Julius Caesar* that illustrate Elizabethan pronunciation.

Such Stuff as Dreams Are Made On
members.aol.com/shakesp95/shakes.htm
This site has another interesting collection of Shakespeare links that are arranged by category.

Welcome to Shakey's Place
library.advanced.org/10502/
Developed by students, this site boasts a "3D Globe Theater Internet Experience."

AUDIO

Seven Classic Plays
8 tapes or 10 CDs, 11:25 hrs. (Blackstone Audiobooks)
A superb repertory company has been assembled for these recordings, joined by distinguished guest artists F. Murray Abraham, John Glover, Rosemary Harris, Lois Nettleton, Barry Morse, Fritz Weaver — all under the direction of veteran producer Yuri Rasovsky, who has won both the Audie Award for book production and the George Foster Peabody Award for broadcasting. These are not mere readings. Rather, they are full performances using all the resources of audio to full advantage. Just as stage plays are "opened up" when adapted to film, so these selections create greater intimacy. "Staginess" is avoided and lively theatrics are enhanced, while the substance of the works remains intact. The seven plays are *Medea, The Tempest, The Imaginary Invalid, Camille, An Enemy of the People, Arms and the Man*, and *Uncle Vanya*.

The Complete Sonnets of William Shakespeare
3 hrs. (Audio Literature)
Equal in epic proportion to his greatest plays, the vibrant sonnets of Shakespeare still bristle with all their original power since their first publication in 1609. These ever-quoted verses survive the scrutiny and interpretation of scholars through every generation and stand as testimony to the world's most notorious author. A host of celebrities, including Susan Anspach, Stephanie Beacham, Roscoe Lee Browne, Christopher Cazenove, Minnie Driver, Samantha Eggar, Robert Foxworth, Elliot Gould, Kelsey Grammer, Joel Grey, Edward Herrmann, Patrick Macnee, Juliet Mills, Vanessa Redgrave, Roger Rees, Julian Sands, Jean Smart, David Warner, Alfre Woodard, and Michael York, read these immortal rhymes that indisputably remain among the greatest poems ever written.

Great Speeches and Soliloquies
2 tapes or 2 CDs, 2:07 hrs. (Naxos Audio)
Many of Shakespeare's greatest and best-loved speeches are brought together in this superb collection, performed by outstanding artists who bring to vivid life words that are an integral part of our language, our culture, and our everyday lives.

A Life of William Shakespeare
2 tapes or 2 CDs, 2:30 hrs. (Naxos Audio)
A popular biography that looks at the life of the playwright in part through the plays themselves. The intricacies of Elizabethan drama set the background for the tale of the greatest dramatist.

The Life and Times of William Shakespeare
18 hrs. (Blackstone Audio Books)
This superb biography is both authoritative and extremely readable. It is the first modern biography of Shakespeare since the Victorian Age to pay full attention to his life and times, to his works, and to the numerous and subtle connections among them. Peter Levi emphasizes the background of Shakespeare's life — the local and national events that shape his experiences, his family and friends, and the Elizabethan people with whom he shared his

life and who populated his plays. Bringing together new work and new discoveries and reexamining the famous legends about Shakespeare, Levi uses the writings of modern historians to shed light on the poet's life. This valuable work will be the definitive life of Shakespeare for many years to come.

The Sonnets
2 hrs. (Caedmon Audio)
Shakespeare's timeless sonnets, which describe love in all its aspects, represent one of the finest bodies of poetry ever penned. They include the star-struck Sonnet 18 ("Shall I compare thee to a summer's day?"), the witty Sonnet 103 ("My mistress' eyes are nothing like the sun"), the despairing yet hopeful Sonnet 29 ("When, in disgrace with fortune and men's eyes, I all alone beweep my outcast state"), and more. As read by the legendary Sir John Gielgud, the sonnets in this selection come alive with all the passion and profound human insight of their brilliant creator.

The Sonnets
2 tapes, 2:25 hrs. (Blackstone Audiobooks)
Read by Fred Williams, this is the complete set of Shakespeare's sonnets.

The Sonnets
1:30 hrs. (Recorded Books)
The 154 sonnets of William Shakespeare contain some of the best-known, most-quoted lines in the English language. This collection brings dozens of those immortal poems to vivid life. Included here are Sonnet 18 ("Shall I compare thee to a summer's day?"), Sonnet 130 ("My mistress' eyes are nothing like the sun"), Sonnet 147 ("My love is as a fever"), Sonnet 151 ("Love is too young to know what conscience is"), and many more.

The Sonnets
3 tapes or 3 CDs, 3:09 hrs. (Naxos Audio)
For centuries, these wonderfully crafted, intense lyrics have stood for something valued about youth, love, and the emotional complexities belonging to that time of life. This new recording presents all 154 of Shakespeare's sonnets, using the New Cambridge Shakespeare texts.

JOHN MILTON, *Paradise Lost* (p. 575)

WWW   For a quiz on *Paradise Lost,* see *World Literature Online* at
bedfordstmartins.com/worldlit.

John Milton's epic *Paradise Lost* is dedicated to one of the most expansive themes of human history: man's first disobedience, the loss of paradise, and the subsequent consequences for the entire human race. It supports not only the sustaining myth of Christianity but is also an archetype of innocence and experience implanted deep in the Western psyche. The subject — or "argument," as Milton states — of *Paradise Lost* is rivaled only by its epic genre. Renaissance critics regarded epic as the queen of all literary expression, maintaining that Homer's classical epics contained all of the original liberal arts and sciences — history, rhetoric, philosophy, mathematics, geography, the art of war, and religion — within them. Milton's own epic echoes those of Homer and comprises multiple genres — narrative, drama, lyric (including sonnets, odes, hymns, love lyrics), and allegory — as well as pluralistic literary modes — heroic, elegiac, pastoral, tragic, satiric, and comedic. Because of its vast scope, its heavily Greco-Roman and Christian mythology, and its complex intermingling of genres, *Paradise Lost* can be imposing to teach and intimidating to students. Once students are oriented in Milton's universe and exposed to basic epic conventions, however, the text comes alive and absorbs them in fundamental questions of existence and humans' responsibilities in the face of free will.

Begin your approach to Milton's work with a textual analysis of the initial argument proposed by the bard (the narrator of the epic). As he invokes his "heavenly muse," Urania, he pleads for light and inspiration so that he can "assert eternal providence, /And justify the ways of God to men" (ll. 5–6). Discuss the significance of the bard's purpose: Why is it a poet and not a prophet who will reconcile mankind to God's ways? Why does the responsibility fall on a descendant of Adam and Eve — a fallen man — to assert eternal providence? Discuss the bard's desire to "justify": Is this an appeal to reason or to faith? Contextualize the bard's pronouncement within the larger project of European Renaissance humanism. Describe the humanistic celebration of man in his dignity as God's divine creation who, capable of rigorous studying, reconciles rational moral philosophy with Christian principles. Ask the class to consider the delicious paradox that allows the bard, as a fallen man, to invite readers — who are also fallen men and women — into the very councils of heaven and prelapsarian Eden. How does the bard manage to appeal to the very readers whose sin, folly, and fallen nature he exposes? Moreover, what redeeming qualities does Milton ascribe to the power of poetry?

Most students will already be familiar with God and Jesus Christ, Adam and Eve, and Satan but often only as one-dimensional entities who seem sometimes foreign in a modern world. Challenge students' preconceptions about these characters: Have students evaluate whether their initial views accord the first parents and their counterparts simplistic or complex natures and invite them to reconsider these originary actors through Milton's eyes. The characters of *Paradise Lost* appear more substantive as students identify each character's different struggles; students relate to characters choosing their way through perplexing situations using only their inexperienced powers of agency to guide them — and growing in the process. Consider reading passages of dialogue aloud in class, focusing on close readings to extrapolate the delicate nuances within each player's attitudes. Students come to view the cast of characters as complex beings reflective of complicated times, just as Milton himself was during the Renaissance. What Renaissance struggles do these characters — including the bard and Milton himself — embody? How are they both conservative and progressive, faithful and humanistic?

Another fascinating dilemma about teaching *Paradise Lost* is the notion of God's universe: Nothing and no one exists outside of it. Despite harboring drastically different views of the Father, the characters of Milton's epic all affirm that God exists. In the contemporary rational environment of academe, imagining God's universe as being real and absolute is both problematic and provocative. Encourage students to suspend disbelief about the existence of God enough to consider the reality of his heaven. In a postlapsarian world influenced by poststructuralist theory, a kingdom constructed without the ultimate goal of power seems hardly believable. And yet God's empire seems to be built on an immanent bliss that is as expansive as the cosmos it fills. Ask students to consider whether conceiving of such a state is even possible. Is a heavenly world such as this seemingly unreal because it cannot exist or, rather, because it is just too difficult to imagine?

Contrapuntally, challenge students to question the allocation of power within this state of bliss. Why must God have a Begotten Son? Why would hierarchies exist in this heavenly paradise? And the great irony: Why would God's chosen Son volunteer for his mission of self-sacrifice that would place him below all humans as seen through earthly eyes? But perhaps the greatest irony is in the testimonial text itself: It seems difficult to read *Paradise Lost* without at least reconsidering God's existence. Discuss the ways Milton's work skillfully positions the reader. How does the bard's — and Milton's — control of setting and view provoke a reaction within the reader? What effects do these clever maneuverings have on students? Discuss the implications. How is *Paradise Lost* a text that is defined by a reader's own religious or nonreligious attitudes and experiences?

TEXT & CONTEXT

FREE WILL, PREDESTINATION, AND FOREKNOWLEDGE

The relationship among predestination, foreknowledge, and human freedom is the key to Milton's moral and ethical system, which is grounded in his theology. By predestination, everything is determined by God before Time begins. By foreknowledge, God already knows what will happen. By human freedom, man has the capacity to choose good or evil. In strict Calvinist doctrine, predestination relates to human freedom much like fate determines Greek tragedy (even Oedipus's attempts at avoiding the oracle's prophecy only serve to fulfill it). But although he was a more orthodox Anglican (and therefore held more strict Calvinist beliefs) early in his life, by the time Milton wrote *Paradise Lost*, he — and the Church — had outgrown such exacting tenets. The doctrine of predestination had been modified to be a more general and conditional teaching. God predestines humanity to salvation if they are good, to damnation if they are bad. This modification suits Milton by its growing emphasis on free will, acknowledging in man a power of choice that entails greater consequences both in this life and the life hereafter. Since God is omniscient, existing in an eternal present, he knows and can see all — both what will happen and who will become saved. But although all the power stays with God, man is still responsible for his acts and can consciously choose them. Freedom is not extinguished by the existence of predestination and foreknowledge but rather is celebrated as man's primary responsibility and stewardship.

GOD AND EVIL

Milton's central argument is a theodicy: The bard desires to justify God's plan and justice to mankind. In that respect, *Paradise Lost* ingeniously portrays the problem of evil. To understand God's ways, basic assumptions are made about his nature: He is all powerful and perfectly good. If this is the case, how does evil exist in the universe? One explanation is that God can only will what is good, so evil — as a part of God's plan — must be a small player in a larger scheme of overall redemption. This glorification of the universal good, however, was parodied by Enlightenment thinkers who viewed it as being overly optimistic (as in *Candide*'s "best of all possible worlds"). Another explanation is that the introduction of evil in *Paradise Lost* is etiological, or a myth of origins. But to accept such a founding myth requires a discrimination between two different falls-the fall of Adam and Eve was predated by the heavenly fall of Lucifer from angel to monstrous devil. Distinguishing Lucifer as the source of evil certainly specifies him as the originator but does not answer the prior question: How was Lucifer tempted? Did he contain the seeds of evil as a creation of God? Another view of evil in *Paradise Lost* is influenced by Saint Augustine: Evil is the absence of good. Creations of God may thus choose, by their own free will, to abandon eternal pursuits in favor of earthly ones. Those who possess free will may then willingly move away from higher and more complete good toward lesser, fragmentary refractions of what once was goodness. Ironically, Satan demonstrates that he is still partly good: He seeks to love, to admire, to delight in beauty, and he is jealous of Adam and Eve's happiness. He weeps for his predicament but nonetheless consciously chooses not to repent and rejoin the heavenly hosts — and subsequently brings about the downfall of humanity. Such an interpretation would support the fact that God paradoxically placed a tree in paradise whose fruit represented the knowledge of good and evil and yet commanded Adam and Eve not to partake of it. By this doctrine of free will, God gave Adam and Eve commandments precisely so they could choose whether or not to follow them, thus deciding whether they are more good or more evil. In this context, God retains his perfectly good nature at the same time he allows men and women to exercise their agency.

IN THE CLASSROOM

I. EPIC

While Aristotle claimed that epic is second only to tragedy, Renaissance literary figures valued epic as the most advanced literary genre. Its grand scale, high drama, and mixing of literary genres and modes made it superior to tragedy in scope, substance, and form. Epic conventions were largely self-defined by the classical epics of Greece and Rome, and Milton logically turned toward the models with which he was familiar to produce his own masterpiece. In fine classical form, Milton begins his epic by invoking his muse, Urania, stating his argument, and raising the epic question. His drama, like epics before him, begins *in medias res*, with the fallen Satan building his own kingdom in hell.

Just as Milton both respects and yet revolutionizes the sonnet in his other poetic works, he obliges epic convention at the same time he modifies it. First, Milton respects classical epic convention by proposing a setting for the poem that is huge in scale. But where classical epics involve entire nations and civilizations, Milton's grand poem takes the origin, fall, and resurrection of mankind as his subject, reflecting not only the human civilization but the realm of the supreme God as well. Second, a classical epic's action involves a long journey interrupted by many battles in which superhuman deeds are performed. But as classical epic portrays a physical journey or nationalistic quest, Milton narrates a physical *and* spiritual journey: The fall is as much a change of space as it is a change of grace. Adam and Eve experience a physical death by becoming mortal but also experience a spiritual death by being banned from the proximal presence of God the Father. Third, gods or other supernatural beings participate willfully in the drama, intervening and interceding on the behalf of the hero and other humans. But the classical gods were fickle in their allegiances, sometimes backing one hero and sometimes another. Yet Milton's God is the God, the omnipotent, omniscient, mysterious prime mover of the universe. Unlike classical polytheistic belief systems, Milton's God is also a father, much like a human father, to all of humanity. First through Adam in humanity's creation, then through his other son, Jesus Christ, in humanity's redemption, Milton's God proposes that humanity can return to the "bliss" that characterizes being in his presence.

Also central to classical epic is the notion of an epic hero. Achilles in Homer's *Iliad*, Ulysses in *The Odyssey*, and Aeneas in Virgil's *Aeneid* each served as classical models for the epic hero that Milton would redefine. A figure of great national or even cosmic importance, the epic hero embodies the values of his culture. The driving force of the epic narrative is this hero's journey: He seeks out something of great value to the civilization he represents. As a larger-than-life character, he displays almost superhuman wit or abilities, accompanied by great courage and strength. But because of his mixed lineage or human weakness, the epic hero exhibits a complex character. Capable of great accomplishment, he struggles with the part of himself that is more human than hero. He encounters obstacles, often in the form of villains, monsters, or demons who are incredibly cunning and evil. Their maleficent talents far surpass any malicious inclinations everyday humans might possess. The hero's human weaknesses are painfully exposed during these confrontations, but his battles with evil forces are not in isolation. Gods intervene both directly in these challenges or indirectly away from them, fortifying the hero tactically or physically, thereby encouraging him to continue in his journey. In certain epics, heroes display growth through these adversarial experiences, another witness of their semihuman character.

Milton's approach to the idea of the epic hero is also revolutionary, since it is unclear exactly who he would nominate as his heroic candidate: The prospect of many ambiguous heroes remains provocative today. Adam would be a primary nominee because he certainly experiences challenges and rises above them in spite of his fallibility. But his heroism is questionable, since he does not proactively take the initiative to either fall or be saved. The hybrid demigod in this story is the Son of God or Jesus Christ, and yet his full redemptive powers are not called into question until *Paradise Regained*. The British Romantics nominated Satan as the epic hero, since he does choose to act proactively, defines his own quest, challenges adversarial powers, and crowns for himself a kingdom. Another interesting possibility is Eve. Condemned to be the initiator of original sin in Catholic doctrine, Milton's Protestant redefinition of the first woman paints her with many positive attributes. Eve sports a remarkable self-awareness and independence in her relationship with Adam and demonstrates an important aesthetic sensitivity. But it is she who, in her ignorance, first disobeys. And yet, if disobedience engenders a fortunate fall — the *felix culpa* — into a greater awareness of human freedom, is Eve not responsible for a her posterity's realization of free will? Whoever may be defined as the epic hero of this work, Milton supercedes the classical notion of a nationalistic warrior as the main character by placing a loving but quarreling domestic pair at the epic's heart.

Discussion

1. Milton aspired to write the greatest English epic of all time. Ask the students whether the creation of man and the problem of human freedom make the epic worthy — at least in subject matter — of that distinction. What other specific features of Milton's work might make this a sound categorization? What might not?

2. Ask students to detail the events of the war in heaven (Book V). Have them pinpoint how and why this epic struggle begins. What is Satan's character flaw? Discuss the consequences of his actions, and ask students if they think these consequences are justified.

3. Review the defining classical characteristics of an epic hero. Have students list the possible characters in *Paradise Lost* who fit these criteria. Who is the epic hero in this work? Adam? God? Jesus Christ? Satan? Eve? Sin? the bard? Ask the students to make arguments for the different possibilities and evaluate for which candidate the best argument might be made. Discuss the ways in which Milton's characters break the bounds of classical definitions of epic heroes. Ask students to note the instances of paralleled circumstances in the text (like councils in hell and in heaven, Christ and Satan both volunteering for a trying mission, the creations of Sin and Eve from their male counterparts, the couplings of Satan with Sin and Adam with Eve, Satan seducing angels as well as Eve). How do these doubled circumstances confuse or clarify who should be considered a hero?

4. Critics distinguish between two kinds of epics: primary (oral narratives spoken or sung repeatedly) and secondary (written texts that employ literary devices). Ask students to think about how the stylistic nature of language might differ between the two epic styles. How might rhythm and repetition of an oral text contrast with that of a written one? Discuss what kind of epic Milton's work is and the characteristics that would define it as such.

Connections

1. Ask students to hypothesize how Milton's epic compares with non-Western counterparts. Do both Western and non-Western epics follow the same conventions? Have students discuss the specific aspects of a non-Western epic through the eyes of Western lit-

erary convention — subject matter, length, book format, an epic hero, the intervention of divinity, and the idea of a journey — to determine where the similarities and differences lie. Consider using the *Creation Epic* of Mesopotamia (Book 1), *The Epic of Gilgamesh* (Book 1), the *Ramayana* (Book 1), Mahabarata (Book 1), or *Sunjata*, the Mande epic (p. 21), as possible works to discuss. What facets of non-Western epics exceed the bounds of Milton's grand poem?

2. Just as Milton's narrator — the bard — returns to his muse for guidance and inspiration, Indian devotional poetry (*In the Tradition*, p. 929) extols the relationship between a poet and his or her god. Ask the students to describe Urania, Milton's muse. Compare Milton's veneration to the adoration expressed in the Indian devotional verses. Generate a discussion about the importance of the connection between humanity and the divine in the moment of aesthetic creation. Compare the gods of each, the kinds of praises sung, and relationship the poets have with their muses. Does Milton approach Indian polytheism in his adoration of Urania? Why or why not? What position does Milton place himself in as poet when he takes it upon himself to "justify the ways of God to men"?

3. Machado de Assis, in "Adam and Eve" (Book 5), reverses the biblical account of Christianity's first couple. Ask students to compare Assis's retelling with Milton's by identifying the creator, the nature of paradise, and the consequences for Adam and Eve's fall in each story. Ask the students to consider which version of this tale is more convincing. What do their responses reveal about the differences between the Renaissance view of humanity and more modern views?

Groups

1. Do Milton's characters choose their epic fates? Assign groups of students to research one of the Renaissance concepts of predestination, foreordination, or human freedom. Ask each group to make an argument for how *Paradise Lost* reflects one of these concepts, perhaps using specific characters, their choices, and the consequences they suffer as justification. Once every group has presented its case, discuss how Milton's text might support all three arguments. Are these concepts mutually exclusive? To what degree does Milton allow for choice? What constraints are placed on those choices? What is already known about choices from the beginning? Determine whether Milton's portrayal of human agency reflects the dignity of mankind that Renaissance humanism espouses.

Writing

Ask students to write a short paper in response to one or more of the following:

1. Does Milton succeed in proposing a paradise of an epic scale in his portrayal of Eden? Outline the garden's defining characteristics, and discuss whether prelapsarian Eden would indeed be categorized as a Renaissance utopia, a place of perfection that is literally "no place." Compare Eden with another utopia, Francis Bacon's *New Atlantis* (p. 479). What values do each of these idealized states share? What does Eden lack? How does Eden compare with the values espoused by Renaissance humanism? Discuss what you might include in Eden that Milton neglects.

2. Satan's free will permits him to fabricate a new state of mind — of epic proportion. At the beginning of Book II, although he has been previously counted as one of the hosts of heaven, Satan states that it is "better to reign in hell, than serve in heaven" (l. 263). Similarly, in Book IV, Satan proclaims "Evil be thou my good" (l. 110). Why is it important for Satan to construct a new conception of his own existence? What about this

transformation makes it a decidedly modern notion and *Paradise Lost* a markedly progressive text?

3. Another convention of epic involves incorporating multiple genres. Discuss Milton's allegorical characters Sin and Death, the incestuous offspring of Satan (their creation takes place in Book II). Explain what the allegorical characters and their interactions signify. In what ways does this trio represent a perversion of the Holy Trinity? Why does Milton choose to employ extended allegory to characterize Sin and Death?

II. RENAISSANCE WOMEN

Complicated gender politics plagued Tudor-Stuart England. On one hand, the ideals of both the Renaissance and the Reformation encouraged more progressive attitudes about the nature of women. Courtly women were the objects of Renaissance love lyrics, glorified Petrarchan females who teased and delighted but remained forever ideal and unattainable. The Protestant Reformation fostered female literacy and even encouraged laywomen to participate in religious debate. Calvinist teachings permitted priests to marry, a practice that contrasted sharply with Catholic doctrines that celebrated celibacy as the highest form of reverence, thus placing a renewed value on married domestic life. Many Protestants believed that women had a naturally spiritual inclination that could be encouraged to be the influence of goodness in the home. The status of the home was thus more respected, and a woman's domestic role increasingly celebrated as a site for the affirmation of female agency. Continental advances in anatomical knowledge also began positively influencing medical attitudes toward women by discrediting the humoral system. Similarly, Christian humanism provided an impetus toward a more expansive education for women; certain humanist scholars argued in favor of exposing women to a male's education, if only so that her domestic sphere might be more enriched. Toward the later part of the seventeenth century, women themselves began publishing their own protofeminist arguments, asserting that women are not by nature inferior to men but rather that they should be provided the same opportunities of education that would challenge their equally rational minds.

On the other hand, much evidence contradicts such a progressive picture of women's experiences during the Renaissance. While certain Renaissance thinkers clearly expressed open-minded attitudes, these new perspectives were slow to be adopted. Almost all women were born into a state of subjection and submission by virtue of their sex. Renaissance positions on the nature of women were derived from and justified by the biblical narrative that God created Eve from Adam to be Adam's helpmeet as well as Aristotle's claim that women were physically inferior to men. These notions combined to perpetuate an active misogyny that named men to be of a superior nature, possessing greater intelligence, strength, skill, and bravery than women. The majority of men active in the realms of religion, medicine, law, and philosophy reinforced this patriarchal order in the public sphere. Similarly, in the private sphere, the man at home was the patriarchal head of his house.

Consequently, double standards pervaded the marriages of Renaissance couples. Husbands were granted the right to abuse their wives, yet a wife was punished if she defied her husband. Though rare, divorces were easier for men to obtain than women, and a man's transgressions were forgiven where a woman's were not. The instructional pamphlets and tracts that detailed women's duties and outlined domestic tasks (even those such as needlepoint) were ironically almost all written by men. And the few attempts to educate women in the humanist tradition have been seen by some critics as a further indoctrination in submissiveness and chastity. Moreover, women were considered to be chattel — property of their husbands. While men could come and go freely, women were told that they should leave their homes only to go to church, assist neighbors, or tend to household needs in the markets. Accordingly, most Renaissance women had few rights in marriage and in the domestic sphere that was to be their own.

A woman's treatment was also determined by her class: Not all women were equal. Within the aristocracy and gentry, women enjoyed an important influence politically by arranging marriages and being involved in patron-client relationships. Aristocratic women could propose potential spouses and begin initial marriage negotiations, often determining the fate of entire extended families and political alliances. Aristocratic women also enjoyed special privileges at court and could be asked to join the queen's privy chambers. Their duties included acting politically on behalf of the queen either covertly or overtly, even occasionally petitioning Parliament or helping coordinate parliamentary elections on behalf of family members. Nonetheless, the political efforts of aristocratic women were still seen through misogynist eyes and were considered to be trivial. Women of the elite were also actively involved in promoting the arts. They associated with authors, playwrights, artists, and clergymen, whose artistic works served to either glorify the Crown or their own family dynasties. Such sponsorships also enabled women to have a direct influence in shaping the nation's cultural heritage and — sometimes inadvertently — promoting protofeminist causes such as scientific research, Calvinist tolerance, and literary appreciation of women.

While a few aristocratic women enjoyed some social deference by Renaissance men because of heredity and station, most women survived deplorable conditions, drudging through the less than poetic practicalities of daily life. Women of the working classes spent their days providing basic needs for the children and men who depended on them. Their assignments revolved around domestic living, including cleaning, cooking, and washing laundry in what were almost primitive conditions. Women spent hours preparing a meal, including tediously making primary ingredients such as butter and cheese. Women were also expected to participate regularly in sexual activity with their husbands because it was believed to preserve their health. Absent effective contraception, women could be expected to bear children as often as physically possible, even at risk to themselves: One in two hundred women died in childbirth. Mothers took care of several children — both well and sick — only half of whom lived to adulthood. Without means for hiring physicians, women were also required to diagnose ailments and prepare medicines for household use. In addition, most common women would also increasingly seek employment in the burgeoning textile industry or urban centers.

Discussion

1. Ask students to discuss their preconceptions about Adam and Eve. Have them identify the sources from which they derived these notions. Are their sources textual or cultural? How does Milton's portrayal of this first couple contradict or reinforce these preconceptions?

2. After Eve is created, she sees herself in reflection and begins gazing in admiration (Book IV, ll. 449–491). Ask the students to discuss the significance of this moment. How does Eve resemble the mythological Narcissus? Discuss the interruption that leads Eve away from falling in love with her own image. What significance does this moment have in the context of future events in the garden?

3. Ask students to discuss the value that their cultures place on marriage. Discuss how and why the values they identify have evolved over the years, especially in regards to sexual intimacy. Have students compare their findings by characterizing the sexual intimacy between Adam and Eve. How is its moral value changed from prelapsarian to postlapsarian states? Discuss how Milton's view of sexual intimacy compares with Renaissance attitudes as well as the students' and society's changing perceptions.

4. As a class, create a list of ranks of characters presented in *Paradise Lost*, from highest to lowest. Identify the women in the text and where they would fit in terms of social rank by Renaissance standards. Have students consider Eve's position in the garden and the tasks she performs. Discuss whether the work she performs exalts or debases her. Does Eve reinforce or disturb Renaissance notions of women? In what ways does Eve's labor indicate the rise of a meritocracy in early capitalist England and Europe?

Connections

1. Renaissance love poetry (*In the Tradition:* European Love Lyrics, p. 85), especially the poetry coming from the Petrarchan tradition, glorifies the unattainable female. Compare Satan's flattery of Eve (Book IX, ll. 532–548, 568–612) with selections from Garcilaso de la Vega, Sir Thomas Wyatt, Maurice Scève, Pierre de Ronsard, Louise Labé, or Andrew Marvell. How does Satan's expression reflect or disagree with prevailing Petrarchan conventions? Ask students to compare Satan's assumptions about Eve with the other poets' assumptions about women. Whose portrait of womankind is more complex? Why? Have students compare Lope de Vega's assessment of woman in "Woman Is of Man the Best" with the bard's diatribe toward Eve (Book IX, ll. 404–411). Discuss what these latter texts reveal about attitudes regarding women and why these contradictory expressions about women are characteristic of Renaissance attitudes.

2. Ask students to compare Milton's portrayal of the first man and the first woman with the account of "The Creation of Man and Woman" in *Myths of Creation* (p. 715). Have students examine the means and purpose of the creation of man and woman in each of these texts. How do these creation stories shape their respective culture's beliefs about the relationships between men and women and the roles they should fulfill?

Groups

1. What roles do the sexes play in Milton's epic? Both Adam and Eve are given specific tasks to perform in the Garden of Eden. Ask students to identify these tasks as well as the passages in the text that discuss them. Have them outline the division of labor and answer the following questions:

    a. How do Adam and Eve each feel about their tasks? How well do they perform them?

    b. What do these tasks reveal about the character of each?

    c. How do these tasks compare with the division of labor during the European Renaissance? What commentary might Milton be making about the division of labor in his own time period?

    d. How does Milton's division of labor compare with modern-day standards? Is this division of labor an ideal one?

Writing

Ask students to write a short paper in response to one or more of the following:

1. Review Adam and Eve's argument in Book IX. Describe how and why Eve disagrees with Adam, identify the solutions Eve proposes, and describe Adam's reaction. Would you characterize her attitude and actions as retrograde or progressive? Does this portrayal support or subvert existing notions of Renaissance women?

2. Consider Milton's portrayal of the ideal marriage, including its noticeable lack of prelapsarian children. If Eden is a utopia, and Adam and Eve are the ideal couple, why do they not conceive immediately? Approach your discussion of this topic by considering the bard's celebration of sexual intimacy in marriage (Book IV). How does the bard consider extramarital sexual activity? Discuss the relationship between sexual intimacy for enjoyment and sexual union for procreation in an ideal marriage. Explain why Adam and Eve conceive only after being banished from Eden.

3. Compared to the biblical account, the bard considerably lengthens Satan's interaction with and temptation of Eve. Review the several passages in which these two interact. Describe Satan's strategies to approach Eve as well as his attempts at temptation. Why do his seemingly effective strategies take such a long time to become effective? Is Eve's fall a single event or a process? Make an argument for why Eve succumbs to Satan's plots.

BEYOND THE CLASSROOM

RESEARCH & WRITING

1. Research visual depictions of the fall of Adam and Eve of any time period, and compare them with Milton's version. How does your choice of artwork agree or disagree with Milton's representation? How is Eve characterized in particular? Describe the similarities and differences between the visual and textual representations and what your study reveals about Milton's opinions or Renaissance views of the first couple.

2. Research women's roles during the Renaissance. Look through diaries, journals, domestic instruction manuals, visual representations, or literary works to discover how you might characterize a Renaissance woman. Choose a female character from *Paradise Lost* and compare her to your findings. Does the female character you have chosen reflect typically Renaissance attitudes about the nature of women? How do these two women compare in station, respect, and beauty? Which woman might be said to be more specifically belonging to a Renaissance ideal?

3. There are many differing views about the fall of mankind. On one hand, Eve's choice and Adam's subsequent action mean that men and women must live in a mortal, earthly state, devoid of God's presence. On the other hand, some believe that the fall was a fortunate one, since men and women learned to distinguish between good and evil to become like God himself, rather than suffering in "ignorance" as Satan suggests. Research different positions about the fall of humankind, and compare them with Milton's text. Make an argument for which kind of fall you believe the text most strongly illustrates, using the text to justify your position.

Projects

1. Imagine you have been commissioned to write an epic that reflects your time and culture. Discuss whether writing an epic suits today's world or if the epic is a genre of the past. What modern topics might be worthy of this colossal genre? What kind of hero would this epic propose, if any? Would the gods play a significant role? Outline the plot that would drive your modern epic, and identify the specific aspects of language that would make it stylistically relevant to today's world.

2. Stage a scene from *Paradise Lost*. As you create blocking and rehearse lines, consider the gaps that Milton's text does not address. How do gestures change the meaning of conversation? What do facial expressions reveal about intentionality? What words are miss-

ing from the dialogue? Explain the conscious choices you must make as you fill in these gaps with interpretation.

WWW   For additional information on Milton and annotated Web links, see *World Literature Online* at bedfordstmartins.com/worldlit.

FURTHER READING

Frye, Northrup. *A Return to Eden.* 1965.
Giamatti, A. Bartlett. *The Earthly Paradise and the Renaissance Epic.* 1966.
Hunter, G. K. *Paradise Lost.* 1980.
Lewis, C. S. *A Preface to Paradise Lost.* 1960.
McColley, Diane Kelsey. *Milton's Eve.* 1983.
Walker, Julia M. *Milton and the Idea of Woman.* 1988.

MEDIA RESOURCES

VIDEO

Paradise Lost
160 min., 1971 (Library Video Company)
Bernadette Peters and Eli Wallach star in this adaptation of Clifford Odets's drama. Set during the depression in 1932. The story unfolds in a modest two-family home of Leo and Clara Gordon as misfortune strikes.

Paradise Lost
30 min., 1998 (Films for the Humanities & Sciences)
Patterned on Greek and Roman classics, yet achieving a voice of its own by defying the strict dictates of classical subject matter, Milton's epic poem is a masterpiece of monumental proportions. His diverse and often awesome use of language creates an effect as surreal and powerful as Dante's *Inferno.* This program features probing analysis by Thomas Winnifrith, University of Warwick, and Robert Wilcher, University of Birmingham. Topics include Milton's creation of hell as one of the great imaginative accomplishments of literature. Also examined are the poem's anti-Catholic tone; the use of the Narcissus myth; the weak, headmaster-like characterization of God; Eve as the strong, archetypal woman; Satan as hero; and criticism of Milton as a misogynist. A brief biography of Milton highlights philosophical debates of the period.

Paradise Lost
28 min., 1993 (Films for the Humanities & Sciences)
This program discusses the portrayal of women in this seventeenth-century epic poem and suggests that powerful negative myths concerning women are reinforced throughout the piece.

Milton by Himself
27 min., 1988 (Films for the Humanities & Sciences)
This program examines the life and times of John Milton through his major and autobiographical writings. The visuals — period art and location photography of the London and Cambridge sites associated with Milton — combined with the music of the time and Milton's own words, together trace the rise and fall of a tragic figure caught between the worlds of ancient glory and contemporary politics — a Renaissance man in the maelstrom of the Baroque.

WEB SITES

The Milton-L Home Page
www.urich.edu/~creamer/milton/index.html
This site, maintained by Milton scholars at the University of Richmond, is subscribed to by almost 500 scholars and students who want to learn more about the life and work of John Milton. This is by far the most exciting and comprehensive Milton site on the Web, offering news on Internet and audio-visual Milton projects, an opportunity to join an online discussion group, a detailed chronology of the author's life, the texts of his major and minor poems and prose, a list of scholarly articles about Milton's life and work, book reviews, announcements of events and symposia, and links to other Milton sites of interest on the Web.

John Milton
www.luminarium.org/sevenlit/milton/
Check this site for famous quotes by John Milton; a biographical sketch; text from his poems, prose, and essays; images from the rare book and manuscript library of Columbia University; and links to biographical information, online books about Milton's work, book reviews, and other Milton sites. This page is part of the *Luminarium* English Literature of the Seventeenth Century site, which includes similar information on Richard Lovelace, Andrew Marvell, John Donne, and Henry Vaughan.

The Milton Reading Room
www.dartmouth.edu/~milton/
This site, maintained by a professor of English and students at Dartmouth College, includes the text of Milton's *Poems, Carmina Elegiaca, Paradise Lost, Paradise Regain'd, Samson Agonistes*, and several pieces of prose. It also includes selected criticism from scholarly publications. This is a well-designed site and is excellent to use as a research tool.

Information about Paradise Lost from the University of Wisconsin, Milwaukee
www.uwm.edu/Library/special/exhibits/clastext/clspg117.htm
This page is part of a major exhibition, "The Classic Text: Traditions and Interpretations," at the University of Wisconsin, Milwaukee, and features extensive information on *Paradise Lost*

John Milton: Poet, Priest, and Prophet
www.shu.ac.uk/emls/iemls/postprint/jhill-milt/milton.htm
This site provides the full text of John Spencer Hill's *John Milton: Poet, Priest, and Prophet? A Study of Divine Vocation in Milton's Poetry and Prose.*

AUDIO

A Study Guide to John Milton's Paradise Lost
1:30 hrs. (Time Warner AudioBooks)
Paradise Lost is an epic poem that presents the Fall of Man and the Rise of Satan in exquisite verse. This study aid includes dramatic readings, a detailed narrative guide, critical analysis, and an introduction to Milton's England. Author Jayne Lewis is a professor of English literature at the University of California, Los Angeles, specializing in the eighteenth-century novel. The narrator is famed British actor Michael York.

Paradise Lost
3 tapes or 3 CDs, 3:55 hrs. (Naxos Audio)
Paradise Lost is considered to be the greatest epic poem in the English language. In words remarkable for their richness of rhythm and imagery, Milton produced characters who have become embedded in the consciousness of English literature — the frail, human pair, Adam and Eve; the terrible cohort of fallen angels; and Satan, tragic and heroic in his unremitting quest for revenge.

Paradise Lost
7 tapes, 9:75 hrs. (Blackstone Audiobooks)
Often considered the greatest epic in any modern language, *Paradise Lost* tells the story of the revolt of Satan and his banishment from heaven, and the Fall of man and his expulsion from Eden. Writing in blank verse of unsurpassed majesty, Milton demonstrates his genius for imagery and cadence. His style is rich and sonorous, his characterizations are heroic, and his action is cosmic in scale. *Paradise Lost* could only be the work of a mastermind involved in a profound search for truth.

In the World: Challenging Orthodoxy (p. 661)

One of the legacies of the Early Modern Period still apparent today is the idea that orthodoxy does not always uphold "truth." Modern conceptions of the ability to challenge orthodoxy owe a special debt to international thinkers during the that period, who based their findings on rational inquiry rather than faith or submission to traditional belief systems. The authors in this section each developed a reasoned method of examining orthodox principles and tenets and continued to seek after truth when the bounds of those orthodox systems no longer seemed rational. These thinkers not only promoted change by the conclusions they proposed — which were revolutionary — but also by the processes with which they experimented. An increasing emphasis on evidence derived from reasoned textual analysis, logical thinking, and scientific observation promoted an independence of mind that helped these authors unveil the "truths" that orthodoxy masked. Individual thinkers and researchers ironically began having more faith in their own perceptions and judgments than in those orthodoxy attempted to impose on them.

Luther's challenge to orthodoxy proposed a careful study of scriptural texts that emphasized the teachings of the "prophets and the evangelists." Deviations from these teachings were suspect; the accumulated traditions inherent in Catholic practice at that time were not mentioned by these scriptural authorities. Luther objected to what he considered to be false trappings of religion and challenged the Holy Roman Emperor — and indeed the entire Catholic Church — to disprove his textual analysis, a task they were unable to perform. Luther's ultimatum clearly illustrated the power of individual thought: He appealed to the power of scripture, reason, and his individual conscience as his guides, not prevailing Catholic doctrine.

Nanak's expressions in the Adi Granth also directly challenged what seemed to be overtly external religious practices of brahmins supported by and supporting the Hindu caste system. Instead, he advocated a direct, unmediated relationship with God. Like Luther, Nanak appealed to his own reason and conscience: He commands himself to abide by God's will as well as to "make [his] own" by writing it upon his "heart." Similarly, Li Zhi rejected the externalization of Confucian ideals expressed by textual commentators who had lost sight of the text in favor of their own words. Much like Nanak, Li Zhi promoted a return to the "core" of the "child-mind" — that which gave the texts life in the first place. The Way is lost to these commentators when the child mind is suppressed, rendering their analyses that intend to point out the Way ineffective. Li advocated dismissing commentaries about the writings of the Sages in favor of a rigorous but reasonable study of the original works.

The English orthodoxy that confronted Milton sported an interesting paradox: In order to prevent people from being exposed to — and thus choose — evil, the English Parliament voted to control the budding publishing industry. Milton's challenge to orthodoxy took an interesting form. He argued that a believer is a better Christian when he had knowledge of evil. Appealing to the classic biblical account of entering into the knowledge of good and evil,

Milton maintained that both agency and virtue required being tested: Man should be free to choose and, therefore, learn for himself. Milton's appeal to reason reconciled with Christian doctrine is a fascinating rhetorical strategy that appealed to the very audience he attempted to subvert.

Copernicus, Galileo, and Kepler each were members of a scientific community that were simultaneously dependent on and independent of Catholic orthodoxy. Copernicus's letter to Pope Paul III illustrates how much influence Catholic doctrine held over cultural communities — even if its area of expertise was not necessarily science. Copernicus appealed directly to an increasingly standardized science mediated by rational deductions about the movements of celestial bodies, describing for the first time a "method" of arriving at his conclusions. Similarly, Kepler appealed to both rational principles and scientific experiment in his desire to persuade Galileo to publicly support Copernicus's new theory: He reasons carefully through why a man of science should value more the opinion of "one intelligent man" than the masses but also encourages Galileo to test the theory scientifically. Galileo's reluctance to accept these new discoveries publicly in the face of this scientific proof illustrates the problem of cultural resistance to change and the power that orthodoxy possesses to perpetuate its erroneous tenets.

Begin your approach to this section by discussing the dilemma between traditional beliefs and a changing universe, established cultural norms and evolving cultural trends. Ask students to discuss the benefits and dangers of traditional belief as well as the risks and advantages to accepting change. Generate a discussion about how cultural institutions of any form — political, sociological, scientific, moral, religious — are created and how they become reified in collective consciousnesses. Who and what legitimizes these institutional bearers of orthodox beliefs in their own time periods and cultural contexts? Review the specific orthodoxies that prevailed during the Renaissance — the Catholic Church in Europe, the brahmins and caste systems in India, Confucian civil writings and authorities in China, European monarchies endowed by divine rights, and European scientific thought that was bound by church doctrine — under whose influence the thinkers in this section lived. Remind students how monolithic these orthodox institutions seemed to those who lived under their influences, some of whose authority had been in place for hundreds of years. Help students to contextualize their study of this section by considering how immense some of the changes were for their respective times and cultures — and how absolute orthodox authority seemed. Why might proponents of orthodoxy resist change?

Compare the reasons why each thinker seeks to challenge orthodox beliefs and/or practices. Discuss the special burden that being in such a pioneering position might bring. Outline the method that each of these thinkers employs: By what means does each investigate the problem that weighs on him? How does he reach a conclusion? Discuss the central role that reason plays during these processes of discovery and challenge to orthodoxy across cultures; help students to connect these rational inquiries to the goals of humanism and Renaissance education. Encourage students to characterize the thinker's reaction on arriving at what he defines as truth — is he enthusiastic or reluctant to deviate from orthodox institutions? Have students describe the appeals that these thinkers make directly to orthodoxy. By what means do they attempt to persuade their antagonistic audiences? The processes these thinkers employ and their courageous challenges to orthodox institutions lay the foundation for subsequent theorists. How do the methods used by these Renaissance thinkers anticipate philosophical systems to come?

Consider contextualizing these questions within a more contemporary time frame. Ask students to identify what current cultural institutions might be considered orthodox today. Are the strictures about challenging these institutions as severe as they were during the

Renaissance? Have students describe some of the major challenges to orthodoxy — in any field — within the past few decades. Ask them to define the orthodoxy challenged, who was pressing for change, whether the push for change was successful, and the methods of persuasion used by the challenging party. How were these changes received? Discuss what makes the Renaissance crisis between orthodoxy and its subversion a decidedly modern notion. In what ways are the struggles presented still relevant today?

IN THE CLASSROOM

I. THE RISE OF THE EARLY MODERN SUBJECT

Many objections arose against orthodoxy during the Renaissance, largely because the capacities of individuals were granted renewed respect. The Reformation encouragement of personal scripture study, an increased emphasis on rationality, the rise of scientific inquiry, expanding notions of individual rights, and the celebration of humanistic ideals — among other impetuses — encouraged individuals to trust their rational perceptions, even at the rejection of orthodox belief systems and practices. This newly interiorized subjectivity, however, resists quantifying even today, and critical debates about the Renaissance continue to thrive on defining specifically what constitutes an early modern subject. The Renaissance has long been heralded literally, politically, and historically as the championing birthplace of the liberal individual. And yet this traditional (perhaps orthodox) belief has been consistently challenged by critics. Those concerned with the growing protocapitalist agendas of protoimperial powers during the Renaissance, for example, identify an early modern subject who is increasingly exploited, alienated, and, ultimately, consuming. New historicist critics argue that collectively held values in orthodoxy can become synonymous with surveillance: A subject transforms collective shame into individual guilt. This version of the early modern subject polices himself on behalf of the state as a kind of psychic internalization of disciplining mechanisms. Other critics maintain that the early modern subject can best be understood by applying modern psychoanalytic theories to his conception of individualism. More recent criticism acknowledges the difficulty in describing subjectivity that remains both interiorized and heavily contextualized. Certain theorists advocate a shared subjectivity in which an individual simultaneously inhabits contrasting zones of externally imposed strictures and interior realms of agency. While many individuals will probably not effectuate such massive change as Luther or Copernicus, they can and do assert agency in "micro-subversions." Other critics have insisted that defining early modern subjectivity through contemporary theories risks denying the possibility of agency altogether: To understand early modern subjects, the standards by which these individuals themselves constructed their own identities must be engaged. Still other critics have downplayed this debate about subjectivity altogether by examining the objects and other paraphernalia that surrounded Renaissance subjects, recreating a link between early modern subjects and the world around them. Despite the differences between these varying definitions of subjectivity, the debate clearly illustrates that the rise of the early modern subject is distinctly marked by his or her individualism.

Discussion

1. Li Zhi describes the importance of maintaining the "child-mind." Ask the students to discuss how this concept defines and shapes an individual, according to Li. Who, does Li say, has lost the child mind specifically? Have students consider Li's discussion in light of Nanak's celebration of the divine. How is an individual most fulfilled, according to Nanak? Ask students to compare the ontological suppositions of each: How do these thinkers arrive at a different notion of what an "individual" is?

2. Ask students to define the concept of individual rights, and identify the source from which their perceptions about rights are derived. Discuss what life would be like without rights that were recognized in a formalized declaration. How does Milton define individual rights in *Areopagitica*? How does he justify their existence? Considering that the notion of natural human rights was not politically legitimized in Western culture until the eighteenth century, evaluate Milton's argument for its effectiveness.

3. Ask students to describe how Martin Luther relies on the importance of individual thought in his defense at the Diet of Worms. From what sources does he derive the authority to make his claims, and what does he argue are the only things that will convince him? How does Luther's response illustrate the early modern emphasis on the individual? Discuss the specific individual capacities that acknowledge man as an individual and why this acknowledgment rests at the heart of the Protestant Reformation. Why are these notions threatening to the Catholic Church?

Groups

1. Assign each group an author in this section, and have students research the specific orthodoxies that each of the thinkers challenges. Ask students to define how long the cultural institution in question had prevailed in the given culture and who had lived under its influence. Encourage students to discuss the culturally specific reasons why individuals may have preferred believing in orthodoxy rather than participating in change. As a class, compare notes: Is resistance to change universal or culturally specific? What similar obstacles to change do all of these cultures exhibit? Moreover, what are the consequences for individuals who challenge orthodoxy? Discuss the mechanisms that orthodox institutions use for suppressing change and whether or not they are effective.

Writing

Ask students to write a short paper in response to one or more of the following:

1. Nanak and Luther both advocated minimizing the external trappings of religion in favor of a direct, internal experience with the divine. What outward signs of worship does each of these reformers reject? How do the Nanak's and Luther's ideas come to influence millions of people? Compare Nanak's and Luther's ideas with those of the *bhakti* poets and the devotional Saints of India (p. 921). Describe how God's presence is found for each of these three approaches. How does an unmediated relationship with God specifically empower the individual in these traditions?

2. As reflected in the excerpts from Copernicus, Galileo, and Kepler, a scientist must carefully negotiate a tenuous balance between himself as a researcher and the scientific and cultural communities at large, among which are those who adhere to orthodox tenets. Discuss the importance of individual discovery in the context of this larger community. How do Kepler's concerns anticipate those that Copernicus reveals? Why do Kepler and Copernicus both reach out to orthodox believers? Explain what each of these theorists hopes to accomplish in communications with Galileo and the pope, respectively, and why these orthodox believers seem to be unreceptive.

II. CONNECTIONS

A significant number of early modern texts reflect the Renaissance struggle between establishing and challenging orthodoxy. Orthodox institutions, both those that were existing and those that were congealing into more formal collective powers, seemingly protected an individual at the same time they threatened his growing rights to choose. Renaissance fictional and nonfictional accounts alike record this crisis as it plays out across multiple contexts. Milton's Satan, for example, although living in the realm of God, directly challenges the Father by individually giving birth to Sin. Under Satan's influence, Adam and Eve likewise choose to disobey commandments from their all-powerful Creator, falling from grace into a postlapsarian world. Similarly, although an angel and even God appear to Doctor Faustus, Marlowe's main character deliberately rejects Christianity and medieval Scholasticism by signing a contract with the devil and making an individual choice not to repent. Wu Chengen's Monkey defies the Jade Emperor by stealing the fruit of the gods, ultimately acquiring spiritual power similar to that held by those in the pantheon. Just as Columbus and Cortés seek to impose collective authority over native people, Montaigne, Las Casas, and Cruz expose the inhumane treatment inflicted on those living in the New World by Europeans, demanding that natives be considered as individual human beings. Machiavelli justifies princely power only to have Shakespeare satirize the orthodox institution of the monarchy in *The Tempest* by revealing its abuses and colonial designs. Indian religion is heavily mediated by brahmins, yet devotional poets advocate a purer, more direct individual mystical experience with divinity. Even as Petrarch establishes poetic conventions for sonneteers, other European poets spurn these standards by transforming them into more ironic, satiric, and sophisticated expressions each in their own signature style. Thus even as collective Renaissance orthodox institutions become more established, so do individual challenges to them.

Discussion

1. Drawing on authors such as Columbus, Cortés, and Las Casas, compare the nonfictional accounts of New World conquest that detail the forced submission of the natives with Niccolò Machiavelli's, (p. 120) princely project in Europe. In what ways do princes and conquistadores both affirm their authority? Have students discuss the motivations and methods of each: Are these theories or attempts to enforce orthodoxy successful? Why or why not?

2. Ask students to consider fictional Renaissance accounts of the individual seeking to escape from imposed systems of authority (consider using *Sunjata* [p. 21], *Doctor Faustus* [p. 389], *The Tempest* [p. 495], Satan in *Paradise Lost* [p. 575], or *Monkey* [p. 837], among others). Have students describe the kind of orthodox belief system from which the character seeks relief and whether or not their challenge to it is efficacious. Is there a true escape from orthodoxy in the Early Modern Period?

Groups

1. Assign each group a specific arena of orthodox practice or belief — religious, political, sociological, economical, philosophical, scientific, or cultural. Ask each group to identify, research, outline, and present a modern orthodox belief within that specific category. Then, have each group characterize objections to this orthodox tenet: Who might challenge this belief and why? Are challenges to this belief carried out individually or collectively? In what manner? To whom are protests or challenges directed? As a class, discuss how principles of these modern controversies might find their roots in the Renaissance debate between orthodoxy and its subversion.

Writing

Ask students to write a short paper in response to one or more of the following:

1. Milton, in his tract *Areopagitica*, argues in part that allowing people to choose what they read will make them better Christians. Discuss how and why Milton appeals to ortho-

dox Christianity at the same time he challenges it, and evaluate his strategies for doing so. Choose another character from a work from this time period who effectuates a similar manipulation (such as Wu Chengen's Monkey or Satan in *Paradise Lost*). How does this character's strategy compare to Milton's? Argue whether this microsubversive tactic might effect greater or lesser change than a full-scale revolution.

2. The early modern struggle to challenge oppressive orthodox belief systems, practices, and institutions serves as a seminal notion that influences centuries of subsequent change. Briefly characterize this struggle as it is represented in this section, and analyze the relationship between it and the argument of at least one text of the following *In the World* sections: "Humanism, Learning, and Education" (p. 452), "The Spirit of Inquiry" (Book 4), "Declarations of Rights and Independence" (Book 4), "Love, Marriage, and the Education of Women" (Book 4), or "Science and Creation" (Book 5).

BEYOND THE CLASSROOM

RESEARCH & WRITING

1. Different cosmological systems are portrayed in Renaissance literature. Research the cosmology that Milton proposes in *Paradise Lost* (p. 575), and compare his representation of an ordered universe with the cosmology that is described in *Doctor Faustus* (p. 384). Define how each of these representations compares with Aristotelean, Ptolemaic, and/or Copernican cosmological systems. How do these literary accounts of the celestial orbs support orthodoxy or challenge it? Why might each character — or by extension, each author — take the position he does?

2. Renaissance lyrics were also a locus of establishing and upsetting orthodoxy. Research and outline the conventions that Petrarch establishes for Renaissance poets. Drawing on works by one or more of the authors from *In the Tradition:* European Love Lyrics (p. 85) — such as Wyatt, Shakespeare, or Donne — discuss how post-Petrarchan works often disrupt the conventions he established. In what ways does Petrarch's beloved Laura become transformed in later early modern poetry? How does the verse form change? What new kinds of conceits do these later poets employ? Discuss how and why the "challenge" proposed by early modern poets to Petrarch's "orthodox" conventions indicates a modern shift in aesthetics.

3. The rise of the individual subject in early modern Europe lays the framework for the Enlightenment debate about freedom and individual rights. Compare the assertions of reasoned individuals in this section with the American Declaration of Independence, the Bill of Rights, or the French Declaration of the Rights of Man (or with excerpts from *In the World:* Declarations of Rights and Independence [Book 4]). In what ways does the development of the early modern subject — including his challenges to hegemonic cultural institutions — anticipate the articulation of natural rights?

Projects

1. Practicing Sikhs often sing scriptures aloud with musical accompaniment rather than read them, just as many Protestants sing hymns to supplement their worship services. Research either or both of these traditions, attending live performances or finding recordings of these musical expressions. Carefully study the text of each musical work before listening to it. What faculties does music appeal to that a text does not? In what ways does musical accompaniment enhance a religious experience?

2. The censorship that Milton protested continues to prevent free speech in many countries — and some school districts — today. Research national censorship policies in a

given country (or banned books within a school district) to determine what kinds of texts are deemed dangerous. Using Milton's *Areopagitica* as a guide, write a letter to a chosen government or school district that argues for a change in censorship policy. How does the audience of your intended letter determine the argument's rhetorical strategy? Would Milton's arguments be considered effective today? Why or why not?

3. Not only was the Copernican cosmology a radical challenge to the orthodoxy of the Catholic Church, it also revolutionized science. Research more recent scientific discoveries: Is there a modern equivalent to the Copernican Revolution? Describe in detail the contemporary breakthrough you have chosen and how and why its unveiling directly challenged "orthodox" science. Discuss the reaction surrounding this discovery: Were modern scientists receptive? The public at large? Make a hypothesis about what the next major scientific breakthrough might be and whether or not contemporary society will reject or embrace this new knowledge.

FURTHER READING

Blasi, Vincent. *Milton's* Areopagitica *and the Modern First Amendment.* 1995.

Cassirer, Ernst. *The Individual and the Cosmos in Renaissance Philosophy.* 1972.

Ch'ien, Edward T. *Chiao Hung and the Restructuring of Neo-Confucianism in the Late Ming.* 1986.

Cohen, I. Bernard. *The Birth of a New Physics.* 1985.

Greenblatt, Stephen. *Renaissance Self-Fashioning. From More to Shakespeare.* 1980.

Hale, John Rigby. *Renaissance Europe: Individual and Society, 1480-1520.* 1972.

McLeod, W. H. *Guru Nanak and the Sikh Religion.* 1968.

MEDIA RESOURCES

WEB SITES

Eternal Glory of Sri Guru Nanak Dev Ji
www.srigurunanaksahib.org/
This fascinating site provides a great deal of information on Nanak and is even accompanied by an online video, unfortunately not in English.

The Galileo Project
es.rice.edu/ES/humsoc/Galileo/index.html
The Galileo Project is a hypertext source of information on the life and work of Galileo Galilei (1564–1642) and the science of his time.

Galileo's Battle for the Heavens
www.pbs.org/wgbh/nova/galileo/
PBS's wonderful site provides a biography of Galileo and links to portions of the site that go deeper into the works of Galileo. Well written and well illustrated.

Internet Modern History Sourcebook: The Reformation
www.fordham.edu/halsall/mod/modsbook02.html
A premiere Internet resource created at Fordham University, the Internet Modern History Sourcebook is a premiere site for information on the history, culture, and literature of the Reformation. Excellent links.

The Luther Project
www.augustana.edu/religion/lutherproject/
Gary Mann's (Augustana College) site that is devoted to interactive annotative study of the writing of Martin Luther.

The Milton-L Home Page
www.urich.edu/~creamer/milton/index.html
This site, maintained by Milton scholars at the University of Richmond, is subscribed to by almost 500 scholars and students who want to learn more about the life and work of John Milton. This is by far the most exciting and comprehensive Milton site on the Web, offering news on Internet and audio-visual Milton projects, an opportunity to join an online discussion group, a detailed chronology of the author's life, the texts of his major and minor poems and prose, a list of scholarly articles about Milton's life and work, book reviews, announcements of events and symposia, and links to other Milton sites of interest on the Web.

Nicolaus Copernicus
www.newadvent.org/cathen/04352b.htm
This is the Catholic Encyclopedia's entry on Copernicus. Embedded within the fairly detailed biography of the astronomer are hotlinks that provide even more information about his life, times, and works.

The Protestant Reformation
history.hanover.edu/early/prot.html
Developed by the history department at Hanover College, this site provides links to key documents and Web sites that provide background on the Protestant Reformation.

The Reformation Guide
www.educ.msu.edu/homepages/laurence/reformation/index.htm
Developed by Laurence Bates, this Reformation Guide is intended to provide easy access to the wealth of Internet information available on the Reformation period. The links to the original Web sites have been preserved so that users may access the most recent developments.

The Tomb of Li Zhi
www.china.org.cn/english/features/beijing/31030.htm
This site provides an overview of the life and teachings of Li Zhi.

GENERAL MEDIA RESOURCES

VIDEO

Elizabeth: The Virgin Queen
50 min., 1999 (A&E Video)
Trace the remarkable 45-year reign of the determined, vain, and brilliant woman who presided over one of the grandest periods in the history of her nation.

Florence: Cradle of the Renaissance
30 min., 1992 (Library Video Company)
This look at Florence begins at the time when this city's art, literature, and philosophy experienced rebirth in the fifteenth century. For 100 years after Brunellschi's dome went up on the Santa Maria del Fiore Cathedral in 1436, Florence was the cradle of Western civilization. Discover this home to Michelangelo, Botticelli, Da Vinci, Ghiberti, and others.

New Worlds and New Ideas
23 min., 1998 (Insight Media)
This educational program examines how the discovery of the Americas changed the world and how the quest for colonies, raw materials, silver, and gold brought about partnerships between monarchs and merchants. It explores how these alliances brought wealth and

power to and inspired ideas about liberty among the middle classes. Featuring dramatic readings and commentary by former Poet Laureate Robert Pinsky, the program covers works representative of the times, including Milton's *Paradise Lost* and Defoe's *Robinson Crusoe*. Examines how the scientific inquiries in the works of Sir Isaac Newton and John Locke helped to fuel social change.

Protestant Christianity
50 min., 1999 (Insight Media)
This video traces the rise of Protestantism in sixteenth-century Europe and chronicles its effects on the course of history. It explains the unifying tenets of Protestantism and discusses similarities and variations among such denominational groups as the Baptists, Calvinists, Presbyterians, Mennonites, Puritans, and Quakers.

The Reformation
14 min., 1979 (Insight Media)
The Protestant Reformation was catalyzed by discontent with the Catholic Church, the cultural reawakening of the Renaissance, the emergence of nation-states, and new interpretations of the Scriptures. This video examines the contributions of Calvin, Zwingli, Knox, and Luther.

The Reformation
30 min., 1989 (Annenberg/CPB Video)
Voiced by Martin Luther, Protestantism shattered the unity of the Catholic Church.

The Reformation: Age of Revolt
24 min., 1973 (Insight Media)
The sixteenth century represented an era of radical change in the areas of technology and ideology. This video focuses on Martin Luther, whose grievances against the Church produced a chain of events that profoundly affected the religious and political beliefs of the modern world.

Reformation Overview
180 min., 1995 (Insight Media)
This video explores the history of the Reformation, focusing on the key reformers and their belief that the Bible, not the Roman Catholic Church, should guide the people and that it thus needed to be translated from Latin to the vernacular. It profiles the lives and beliefs of Wycliffe, the Anabaptists, Hus, Luther, Zwingli, Calvin, and Tyndale.

Reformation: Luther and the Protestant Revolt
52 min., 1998 (Insight Media)
This video traces the history of the Protestant Reformation, the path of its founder, Martin Luther, and the subsequent rise of sects including Calvinism, Anglicanism, Presbyterianism, and Methodism.

Reformation to Modern Europe
25 min., 2002 (Insight Media)
Considering how the advent of science and printing pushed the medieval world toward modernism and individualism, this video highlights the influence of Martin Luther, who triggered the upheavals that led to Calvin, Loyola, Wesley, and later, Bonhoeffer and Vatican II.

The Renaissance
50 min., 2000 (Video Library Company)
This program looks at this historical period, which began with the invention of the Gutenberg printing press in the early fourteenth century and continued through the late

sixteenth century. Looks at the art of great Renaissance artists like da Vinci and Michelangelo, literary works by Shakespeare, and the voyages of Columbus, Vespucci, Ponce de León, Balboa, de Soto, and Marco Polo. The program features expert commentary from scholars at Yale University.

The Renaissance and the Age of Discovery
30 min., 1989 (Annenberg/CPB Video)
Renaissance humanists made man "the measure of all things." Europe was possessed by a new passion for knowledge.

The Renaissance and the New World
30 min., 1989 (Annenberg/CPB Video)
The video explores how the discovery of America challenged Europe.

Renaissance and Reformation
26 min., 1998 (Zenger Media)
This educational program examines how a return to classical thought engendered a rebirth in all the arts during the Renaissance. Looks at the emergence of powerful new empires — created by the new mercantile economy, world exploration, and trade — and examines how these new world powers influenced literature of the time, including Machiavelli's *The Prince*, Erasmus's *Education of a Christian Prince*, and the works of Molina, Cervantes, and Shakespeare. The program shows how the invention of the printing press, the rise of literacy, and worldwide communications influenced Martin Luther's Protestant reforms and religious skepticism.

Renaissance and Reformation
23 min., 1987 (Insight Media)
Focusing on the rebirth of humanistic philosophy and classical learning during the Renaissance, this program illustrates the symbiosis of the arts and the economic boom fueled by mercantilism. It considers the prevalence of court life as a subject in literature, showing how authors such as Cervantes and Molina poked fun at royalty, and discusses how religious questioning, fed by the rise of literacy, created the reform movement called Protestantism.

The Renaissance Explorers: A Voyage to the New World
CD-ROM, 1997 (Cambridge Educational Production)
This CD teaches about the equipment, navigation, and history of exploration from Marco Polo to Sir Walter Raleigh, using accounts of their discoveries and detailed maps. Focusing on the voyages of British explorer John Cabot, the program gives users a unique opportunity to learn about life on board a fifteenth-century ship.

The Renaissance, Reformation, and Beyond: Towards a Modern Europe
25 min., 1997 (Films for the Humanities & Sciences)
The Italian Renaissance's contributions to revolutions in architecture, art, religion, commerce, politics, and navigation are discussed in this program. The Signoria Tower, Ghiberti's Baptistry doors, and Giotto's Bell Tower exemplify innovative ideas in architecture and art; Martin Luther and John Calvin apply similar revolutionary thinking to religion; Portuguese seafarers boldly set out to discover a route to India, while Christopher Columbus, setting his sights westward, discovers the New World.

The World's Philosophies
60 min., 1994 (Insight Media)
In this video, Huston Smith defines three basic types of human relationships — with nature, with other people, and with one's self — and explains how these relationships correspond to the philosophical traditions of the West, of China, and of India.

A World Reborn
57 min., 1997 (Library Video Company)
Featuring dramatic readings and re-enactments as well as on-location footage, this award-winning program explores the philosophical, political, artistic, scientific, and religious changes that occurred during the Renaissance. It examines philosophical and scientific theories and artistic movements of the time, while identifying significant figures and their contributions, from Petrarch and Jan Hus to Brunelleschi and Machiavelli.

African Slave Trade and European Imperialism
www.cocc.edu/cagatucci/classes/hum211/timelines/htimeline3.htm
This site, developed by Professor Cora Agatucci of Central Oregon Community College, provides an excellent timeline of the spread of slavery from Africa; embedded are hotlinks to key events and documents.

The Catholic Reformation
history.hanover.edu/early/cath.html
Developed by the history department at Hanover College, this site provides links to key documents and Web sites providing background on the Catholic Reformation.

The European Voyages of Exploration
www.ucalgary.ca/applied_history/tutor/eurvoya/
During the fifteenth and sixteenth centuries, two nations — Portugal and Spain — pioneered the European discovery of sea routes that were the first channels of interaction between *all* of the world's continents, thus beginning the process of globalization in which we live today. This tutorial introduces the student to these two pioneering nations, their motivations, their actions, and the inevitable consequences of their colonization. It also examines the geographical, technological, economic, political, and cultural patterns of that era.

Internet Modern History Sourcebook: The Early Modern World
www.fordham.edu/halsall/mod/modsbook03.html
An Internet resource created at Fordham University, the Internet Modern History Sourcebook is a premiere site for information on the history, culture, and literature of the early modern world. Excellent links.

Internet Modern History Sourcebook: The Reformation
www.fordham.edu/halsall/mod/modsbook02.html
An Internet resource created at Fordham University, the Internet Modern History Sourcebook is a premiere site for information on the history, culture, and literature of the Reformation. Excellent links.

Literary Resources: Renaissance
andromeda.rutgers.edu/~jlynch/Lit/ren.html
Developed by Jack Lynch at Rutgers University, this site aimed at scholars and students attempts to cover all the significant and reliable Internet resources from Milton to Keats. The collection includes information on literature, history, art, music, religion, economics, philosophy, and so on from around the world.

Luminarium: 16th Century Renaissance English Literature
www.luminarium.org/renlit/
This wonderful site provides background and links on key authors and artists of the Renaissance. It also includes links to high-quality general resources for the period.

The Protestant Reformation
history.hanover.edu/early/prot.html

Developed by the history department at Hanover College, this site provides links to key documents and Web sites providing background on the Protestant Reformation.

The Reformation Guide
www.educ.msu.edu/homepages/laurence/reformation/index.htm
Developed by Laurence Bates, this Reformation Guide is intended to provide easy access to the wealth of Internet information available on the Reformation period. The links to the original Web sites have been preserved so that users may access the most recent developments.

Renaissance
shakespeare.palomar.edu/renaissance.htm
Developed by Terry A. Gray, this page is devoted to journals and text repositories related to Shakespeare, Elizabethan, and Renaissance studies. Web pages about Shakespeare's contemporaries (and near contemporaries) have also been placed here.

Renaissance: The Elizabethan World
renaissance.dm.net/index.html
This page contains a list of high-quality links on the Renaissance and the Elizabethan world.

Renaissance: What Inspired This Age of Balance and Order?
www.learner.org/exhibits/renaissance/
This Annenberg/CPB Web site provides a highly visual and entertaining overview of the Renaissance. Included here are pages on exploration and trade; printing and thinking; symmetry, shape, and size; focus on Florence; and related resources.

Virtual Renaissance: A Journey Through Time
www.twingroves.district96.k12.il.us/Renaissance/VirtualRen.html
Developed by C. S. Marszalek and B. Panagakis, this site is a collection of links on all aspects of the Renaissance world. It is a mixed bag of high and low culture, but it is worth a look for sites of interest.

Voice of the Shuttle: Renaissance and 17th Century
vos.ucsb.edu/browse.asp?id=2749
"The website for humanities research," the Voice of the Shuttle was developed by Alan Liu at the University of California, Santa Barbara, and provides extensive links to humanities and humanities-related resources on the Internet.

AUDIO

The History of English Literature
4 CDs, 5:15 hrs. (Naxos Audio)
Perry Keenlyside tells the remarkable story of the world's richest literary resource. The storytelling, the poetry, the growth of the novel, and the great histories and essays that have informed the language and the imagination wherever English is spoken are covered.

Living Biographies of Great Philosophers
7 tapes, 9:75 hrs. (Blackstone Audiobooks)
Included in this program are Plato and Socrates, Aristotle, Epicurus, Marcus Aurelius, Thomas Aquinas, Francis Bacon, Descartes, Spinoza, Locke, Hume, Voltaire, Kant, Hegel, Schopenhauer, Emerson, Spencer, Nietzsche, William James, Henri-Louis Bergson, and Santayana.

Living Biographies of Religious Leaders
8 tapes, 11:25 hrs. (Blackstone Audiobooks)
This program presents the lives of twenty great founders and leading advocates of the world's foremost religions. Here are the historical facts and legends associated with these forceful personalities who have inspired and influenced humankind through the centuries. Presented are Jesus Christ, Moses, Isaiah, Zoroaster, Buddha, Confucius, John the Baptist, Paul, Muhammad, Francis of Assisi, John Hus, Luther, Loyola, Calvin, George Fox, Swedenborg, Wesley, Brigham Young, Mary Baker Eddy, and Gandhi.

The Renaissance and the Discovery of the Modern World
50 min. (The Stanford Channel)
Gain new insight into the Renaissance and its effect on modern times with this fascinating lecture. Professor Ryan illustrates the three major themes of the period: the rediscovery of classical ideals in art, architecture, and literature; the rebirth of these ideals in new forms; and the discovery of the Americas. He also discusses how these three interconnected trends helped to shape our culture. Through it all runs the Renaissance notion of "humanism" — the study of how to make better human beings.

THE AMERICAS: AZTEC EMPIRE AND NEW SPAIN

The Ancient Mexicans (p. 708), *Myths of Creation* (p. 715), *The Myth of Quetzalcoatl* (p. 721), *The Poetry of Nezahualcoyotl* (p. 733), "The Conquest of Mexico" (p. 736), and *A Defense of Aztec Religion* (p. 765)

WWW   For quizzes on the ancient Mexicans, see *World Literature Online* at bedfordstmartins.com/worldlit.

By and large, education in the United States has neglected the Mesoamerican civilizations south of the border. For about a hundred years, racist assumptions prevented scholars from deciphering Mayan glyphs; it was assumed that the Maya were incapable of developing a written, phonetic language comparable to the hieroglyphic scripts of the Egyptians and Chinese. Students might remember something about human sacrifice among the Aztecs but know little about Mesoamerican art, schools, poetry, books, mythology, mathematics, and astronomy. Usually, an instructor must begin with the basics of history and the physical culture of indigenous peoples. The use of maps and photographs or slides of the major archeological sites, such as Chichén Itzá, Palenque, Tula, and Teotihuacán, will help students "chart" their understanding of the history and literature of this culture.

The literature of the ancient Mexicans provides an opportunity to make comparisons with the religious documents of Europe and the ancient Near East. Although it is difficult to make generalizations, there are clear differences between the worldviews of Renaissance writers like Marlowe or Machiavelli and the world view of Mesoamericans. One way to begin the discussion of these differences is to recognize that the creations stories of the Judeo-Christian tradition reveal that the identity and being of its deity were clearly separate from the world. This separation allowed for differentiation between what is sacred and what is secular, what is under God's dominion and what is under human dominion.

In the creation stories of the ancient Mexicans, several deities provide their bodies to create the world, the sun, and the moon. In this view, the world is a dismembered deity; "goodness" is not transcendent and separate but is immanent and integrated. The sacred is everywhere, residing in all things. Like many other native peoples, the Aztecs believed that all of nature was alive and vital. The word *pantheism* could be used if one is careful not to automatically dismiss native religion as pagan and to remind students about Christian angels, saints, and demons — the issue is not monotheism versus polytheism but the differences between immanence and transcendence. Christians tended to view the life on earth as a struggle between good and evil, Jesus and Satan, but Mesoamericans strove to balance the forces of light and dark, spirit and material.

The meeting of Old World and New World in the figures of Hernán Cortés and Moctezuma reveal other differences as well as similarities. Several spectacular omens led the Mexicans to expect the return of an important deity, Quetzalcoatl. European explorers often perceived their travels in terms of Christian beliefs: The discovery of Cape Verde in 1445, for example, called into question the mountain of Purgatory in the south. For a time, Christopher Columbus fantasized about the Orinoco River in Edenic terms. Both Spaniards and Aztecs could be warlike and aggressive as well as peaceful and compassionate.

TEXT & CONTEXT

TENOCHTITLÁN

Built on a low-lying island in the middle of the shallow Lake Texcoco, Tenochtitlán was founded by the Mexicas in the fourteenth century. Becoming one of the largest cities of the world at the time, some estimates suggest the population may have exceeded 200,000 by 1519, the year Cortés arrived. Because of the growing population, the inhabitants increased the size of the island by filling in parts of the lake. They created a series of canals, through which they traveled in canoes, which ran through floating gardens called *chinampas*. These gardens were created by putting dirt on top of a kind of raft built of branches or reeds. The city was divided into sections, a central plaza, in which religious and administrative buildings were concentrated, and three or four districts where the inhabitants lived and worked. It was connected to the mainland and other islands by causeways. The Spanish approached Tenochtitlán on the southern causeway, from Iztapalpa, and fled on the western causeway, to Tlacopan, on the famous "Night of Sorrows." Rituals and sacrifices like those described in "The Conquest of Mexico" (p. 736) were often performed at the top of the Great Temple, or *Templo Mayor*. This temple is also called the Pyramid of Huitzilopochtli, after the god that led the Mexica to this part of Mexico.

IN THE CLASSROOM

I. CREATION, DEVOTION, AND THE GODS

The first three selections in this section deal in some way with the spiritual beliefs and practices of the ancient Mexicans. Students will be familiar with a variety of creation myths and can draw on this knowledge as a point of departure for reading the Aztec "Myths of Creation" (p. 715). Encourage them to explore the ways these kinds of stories function in a society. What do they reveal about the lives and worldview of a particular people? Similarly, students will know the stories of several spiritual heroes, whether they be human or divine, and can draw from their experience with such figures in their approach to "The Myth of Quetzalcoatl" (p. 721). Call attention to the role of temptation in the story, the expectations surrounding Quetzalcoatl as spiritual model or leader, and the lasting impact of his actions on the physical environment. In what ways does this myth speak to the human endeavor to comprehend "the meaning of existence"? In "The Poetry of Nezahualcoyotl" (p. 733), human doubts and fears related to the transitory nature of earthly life are mitigated by faith in a place "where there is no death." Spend time in the classroom exploring the connection between the themes of these poems — nature and mortality — and the other writings of this section.

Discussion

1. Discuss student preconceptions about the Aztecs and Mesoamericans. What new discoveries about the life and thought of these indigenous peoples do the readings provide? For example, what do the creation stories reveal about the relationship between the gods and humanity? What cultural beliefs or values are revealed in the story of Quetzalcoatl?

2. The ancient Mexicans believed that they lived in a world balanced between sky and earth, light and dark, creation and destruction, spirit and matter. How do the creation stories express this view? Pointing to specific passages in the texts, ask students to articulate and explore these relationships.

3. As a class, generate a description of Nezahualcoyotl's vision of the divine. What role do nature and art play in this vision? What is the relationship between human beings and the "Giver of Life" in these poems?

Connections

1. Compare the Aztec creation stories with the stories with the story of Adam and Eve in Genesis (Book 1) and Milton's *Paradise Lost* (p. 575). How do pain and suffering play important roles in these stories?

2. The ancient creation story of Mesopotamia (Book 1) features a combat between a hero-god Marduk and a water goddess Tiamat; in the writings of the Greek poet Hesiod (Book 1), the first deities are involved in struggles between fathers and sons; rebellion and murder characterize the first stories in Genesis. Discuss the reasons why the creation of order from chaos might involve violence. What is the role of violence in the Aztec creation stories?

3. Indian devotional poetry (*In the Tradition:* p. 929) often celebrates a personal relationship between the poet and his or her god. Paying particular attention to the connection between humanity and the divine, the role of song and dance in spiritual expressions, and attitudes toward earthly existence, discuss the ways the religious beliefs and practices of the ancient Mexicans compare with those of the *bhakti* saints.

Writing

Ask students to respond to one or more of the following in a short paper:

1. How does "The Creation of the Earth" (p. 715) suggest that the ancient Mexicans lived in a volcanic region?

2. In the Aztec creation stories, Quetzalcoatl plays the role of a culture bringer, a primeval being who provides the basic necessities of a particular society. What necessities of Aztec culture does Quetzalcoatl provide? How do Aztec deities model important behavior for mortals?

3. The "Myth of Quetzalcoatl" (p. 721) combines the qualities of a deity with those of a cultural hero. What qualities of Quetzalcoatl make him the great, messianic hero of ancient Mexico even though he succumbs to temptation?

4. The Aztec creation stories portray an unstable world, subject to imbalance and even destruction. How are these concerns reflected in Nezahualcoyotl's poems?

II. CULTURAL CONFLICT

The last two selections in this section offer a poignant, disturbing record of the suffering and conflict attending the conquest of Mexico. "The Conquest of Mexico" (p. 736), an ideal text for discussing the colonial project and the concept of the "contact zone," provides a detailed picture of the differences in beliefs, motivations, and values of the Aztec and Spanish cultures. Students will be fascinated by descriptions of introductory contact moments like the report of the messengers on returning from the Spanish ships and the account of the Spanish army as it approaches the city. Encourage them to use these descriptions to gain insight into the worldview of both peoples. The religious beliefs of the Aztecs are nicely delineated in "A Defense of Aztec Religion" (p. 765). Call attention to both the language of the argument that is presented and the message it conveys regarding the inseparability of religious belief and cultural identity.

Discussion

1. Drawing from their experience with literature or knowledge of folklore, ask students to provide their own examples of omens and describe their literary or cultural function. Then look at the omens in "The Conquest of Mexico" (p. 736). What purpose do they serve in this text? What do they reveal about the values or beliefs of the Aztecs?

2. Ask the class to identify specific passages in the text that exemplify Moctezuma's reaction to the arrival of the Spaniards, and discuss his reasons for approaching the situation this way. Then, have students analyze his decisions and actions from both his perspective and the perspective of the Spaniards. Why were the people of the city critical of Moctezuma's decisions?

3. "The Conquest of Mexico" (p. 736) contains graphic descriptions of the violence and devastation resulting from the arrival of the Spanish. Ask students to analyze the motivation of each party involved in the conflict, and discuss how an understanding of these motives influences one's interpretation of violent actions.

4. Though they express admiration for the "book of heavenly words" and the "Lord of the World" introduced to them by the Spanish, the Aztec priests announce they will die before abandoning their own religious beliefs. Ask the class to describe the basic tenets of this belief system, and then discuss the reasons provided by the priests for their continued faith in it. In what ways are religious beliefs central to the identity of a people?

Connections

1. Does Christopher Columbus's *Diario* (p. 773) provide insights into Cortés's Renaissance personality and worldview?

2. Does Shakespeare's *The Tempest* (p. 495) raise issues about the relationship of Europeans with native peoples that might be relevant to the experiences of the Spanish in the Americas?

3. Denis Diderot's *Supplement to the Voyage of Bougainville* (Book 4) offers a critical comparison of European and Tahitian lifestyles. How does this text comment on European attitudes regarding the religious beliefs and life practices of the "other"? In what ways are these attitudes revealed in "The Conquest of Mexico" (p. 736) and "A Defense of Aztec Religion" (p. 765)?

Writing

Ask students to respond to one or more of the following in a short paper:

1. Analyze the similarities and differences between Cortés and Moctezuma. How is Cortés's view of the world different from Moctezuma's?

2. Drawing from specific passages in the text, define the Aztec view of "fate" and its role in human destiny. In what ways does this view of fate influence the events described in the text?

3. Summarize several passages that contain descriptions of "first encounters" between the Spanish and the Aztecs. For example, you might look at the report of the Aztec messengers after their initial visit to the arriving ships or the account of the Spanish army as it approaches the city. Then, discuss the significance of these first impressions. What do descriptions of the "other" reveal about the perspective and culture of the describer?

4. How are the qualities of courage and integrity revealed in "A Defense of Aztec Religion" (p. 765)?

5. Pointing to particular passages in the text, describe the tone and persuasive strategies of "A Defense of Aztec Religion." How does the tone shift as the argument progresses? In what ways are the persuasive strategies particularly appropriate for a European audience?

BEYOND THE CLASSROOM

RESEARCH & WRITING

1. One of the classics of American literature and history is William H. Prescott's *The Conquest of Mexico*, which provides an outsider's description of Cortés's personality and his military expedition. How is Prescott's perspective different from the Aztec account in this anthology? Does Prescott offer any insights into Moctezuma's reluctance to crush the Spaniards?

2. Examine other encounters between Europe and America. Did the worldviews differ? How might one explain the differences in values? Discuss the psychology of conquerors who presume that they have nothing to learn from the conquered.

FURTHER READING

Benson, Elizabeth, ed. *Mesoamerican Writing Systems.* 1971.
Burland, Cottie. *The Gods of Mexico.* 1967.
Caso, Alfonso. *The Aztecs: People of the Sun.* 1958.
Diaz del Castillo, Bernal. *The Conquest of New Spain.* 1963.
Flannery, Kent. *The Early Mesoamerican Village.* 1976.
Motolinia, Toribio de Benavente. *History of the Indians of New Spain.* 1950.
Nicholson, Irene. *Mexican and Central American Mythology.* 1967.
Soustelle, Jacques. *Daily Life of the Aztecs.* 1970.
Zorita, Alonso. *Life and Labour in Ancient Mexico.* 1971.

MEDIA RESOURCES

VIDEO

The Age of Gold
59 min., 1991 (Home Vision Entertainment)
Presented by best-selling Mexican author Carlos Fuentes and produced in association with the Smithsonian Institution. This program looks at the enormous wealth brought into Spain from the New World as well as the magnificent art and literature that was created during the life and rule of the mysterious King Philip II.

The Aztec Empire
50 min., 2000 (A&E Video)
Trace the astonishing story of the Aztecs who rose from a beleaguered band of barely over 1,000 to dominate nearly all of Mexico in just over 400 years.

The Aztecs
48 min., 1997 (Films for the Humanities & Sciences)
Aztec myth prophesied that a great city would one day stand on the site where an eagle, perched on a cactus with a serpent in its mouth, was found. Today, Mexico City stands on this mythical site. Although the Aztec empire fell on April 28, 1521, when Hernán Cortés and his army defeated Montezuma, traces of the thousand-year-old pre-Columbian empire still survive and influence world culture. This program explores Aztec culture and history, from the role of human sacrifice in the Aztec religion to their agricultural advances. Commentary by scholars, maps, and contemporary accounts provide an overview of the events that both shaped and destroyed an empire.

The Civilizations of Mexico
13 min., 1997 (Films for the Humanities & Sciences)

The archaeological sites at Monte Albán, Palenque, Uxmal, and Chichén Itzá speak of the great pre-Columbian civilizations: the Mayan solar calendar, mathematical system, and fabulous cities; and the Aztec Tenochtitlán, founded in 1325 and with almost a million inhabitants when Cortés "discovered" it.

Conflict of the Gods
59 min., 1991 (Home Vision Entertainment)
Presented by best-selling Mexican author Carlos Fuentes and produced in association with the Smithsonian Institution, this program retraces the Aztec world in Mexico and also depicts the gods of the New World, the introduction of the new European god, and the interplay between the two.

The Conquest of Mexico
35 min., 1997 (Films for the Humanities & Sciences)
This program provides a portrait of Cortés and his world — the real world and the imaginary one painted by theologians, mystics, imaginative travelers, poets, and liars; of the New World as seen by a small number of Spaniards; and of the civilizations of Mesoamerica before they were "discovered" — the world of the Maya and Aztecs, the nature of Aztec religion and politics. It describes the Battle of Mexico and explains how and why Montezuma lost — and why, today still, the descendants of the Aztecs speak Nahuatl.

Empire of the Sun
47 min., 2001 (Films for the Humanities & Sciences)
After Hernán Cortés destroyed the Aztec empire of Mexico, another conquistador, Francisco Pizarro, marched on the Incas of Peru with a mere 180 men — and won, filling the coffers of Spain with the treasures of the Andes. This program describes Pizarro's ruthless attack on the Inca empire amidst the aftermath of the civil war between the Inca ruler, Atahualpa, and his defeated brother, Huáscar. The rivalry between Pizarro and Diego de Almagro, the ransoming and subsequent execution of Atahualpa, and the Spanish occupation of the Inca capital, Cuzco, are discussed.

Hernan Cortes
30 min., 1995 (Zenger Media)
Fiercest of the Spanish conquistadors, Hernán Cortés (1485–1547) overtook Mexican cities and toppled the Aztec empire. Believing his actions were for the good of Spain and the glory of God, Cortés created an imposing army using the Indians who had survived his conquests. Though he eventually established himself as a colonial ruler and in many ways united the natives of Mexico, he left a controversial legacy and is remembered both as a brutal conqueror and as a courageous leader. (Available in both English and Spanish.)

Lost City of the Incas
50 min., 1997 (A&E Video)
A&E journeys high into the Andes Mountains to explore the spectacular remains of the Incan city of Machu Picchu. Long thought to be the result of legends, the city was discovered in 1911 by Hiriam Bingham and has been extensively studied ever since. Meet the men and women who have dedicated their lives to unlocking the many secrets hidden in the city just below the clouds.

Lost Kingdoms of the Maya
60 min., 1993 (National Geographic Video)
Long before Columbus, the Maya established one of the most highly developed civilizations of their time in the jungles of Mexico and Central America. Yet this advanced society of priests, astronomers, artisans, and farmers suddenly and mysteriously collapsed more than a thousand years ago. Accompany archeologists to Copan, Dos Pilas, and other spec-

tacular classic Mayan ruins as they unearth artifacts and huge temples of incredible beauty. Recently deciphered hieroglyphics and other new discoveries offer astounding clues to the lives of these ancient people. Hear the startling story of one kingdom's downfall and its final desperate hours of violent warfare. Through spine-tingling recreations, witness ancient rituals reenacted on sites where they originally occurred. And meet the enduring Maya, who still maintain many of their ancestor's traditions.

Machu Picchu Revealed
20 min., 1995 (Educational Video Network)
An overview of pre-Columbian civilizations in the Andes locates the Incas in time and place and investigates the ruins of Machu Picchu. Learn about the importance of this site and examine some of the theories about its creators.

The Maya
50 min., 1997 (A&E Video)
At one time, Mayan society dominated the area now known as Central America. A&E travels to the jungles of Mexico to answer the many questions surrounding this once great empire that all but vanished in 835 C.E. Climb Palenque's great palace and explore the Temple of Inscriptions, discovering why the Maya altered their historical records. Find out what is known of the Mayan ruler Pacal and the truths behind the persistent rumors of human sacrifice.

The Mayans
47 min., 1997 (Films for the Humanities & Sciences)
The most advanced of the pre-Hispanic peoples of Central America, the Maya rose to great prominence, only to suddenly decline around the year 900 C.E. In this program, cultural historian Iain Grain delves into Mayan history, investigating topics such as their mastery of mathematics, their extremely hierarchical society, their use of human sacrifice to induce rain, and their art. Many examples of Mayan architecture are provided as well, plus a computer re-creation of the temple at Chichén Itzá. Although there are still more than two million native Maya living in Central America, the exact origins of their ancestors and the fate of the ancient Mayan cities remain mysteries.

Mexican Pre-Hispanic Cultures
26 min., 1999 (Inside Mexico Video)
This video presents a panorama of the various pre-Columbian civilizations that existed in the Mexican territory: the mysteriously abandoned city of Teotihuacán, the impressive Aztec empire, the erudite Maya. Also shown are the fundamental traits of the indigenous civilizations that still exist in Mexico.

Mexico's Great Pyramids
50 min., 1997 (A&E Video)
At its zenith, the city of Teotihuacán covered eight square miles, making it the seventh-largest city in the ancient world. Not much is known about the people who made the city their home except for the physical remnants of a two-thousand-year-old urban wonder. A&E joins a team of archaeologists to unravel some of the mysteries surrounding the Teotihuacános, including who were their kings and priests, why they didn't develop a system of writing, and the purpose of the Great Pyramids.

Mayas, Aztecs, and Incas
25 min., 1996 (Educational Video Network)
The three leading American civilizations at the time of the Spanish conquest were the Maya and Aztecs of Mexico and the Incas of South America. Explore their cultures, and learn about their achievements.

The Mystery of the Maya
38 min., 1998 (IMAX)
Deep within the jungles of Mexico and Guatemala, and extending into the Yucatán Peninsula, lie the fabled pyramids, temples, and palaces of the Maya. While Europe still slumbered in the midst of the Dark Ages, these innovative people had charted the heavens, evolved the only true writing system native to the Americas, and had made tremendous strides in the area of mathematics and calendars. Without the advantage of metal tools, beasts of burden, or even the wheel, they were able to construct vast cities with an amazing degree of architectural perfection and variety. Filmed on location at numerous sacred sites throughout Central America, including the ruins at Palenque, Tikal, Tulum, Chichén Itzá, Copan, and Uxmal, *Mystery of the Maya* explores the culture, science, and history of these peoples. Narrated by Susan Glover. Originally presented in large-screen IMAX format.

Mythology of Ancient Mexico
19 min., 1990 (Educational Video Network)
Pre-Columbian Mexican culture involved the integration of the natural and supernatural worlds. Here are many insights into the great states that once ruled the land we now know as Mexico.

The Origins of Mexican Civilization
21 min., 1990 (Educational Video Network)
The Olmecs, the Zapotecs, and the residents of Teotihuacán established advanced cultures in Mexico long before the advent of the Aztecs. Learn about some of the amazing achievements of these ancient peoples.

Price of Freedom
59 min., 1991 (Home Vision Entertainment)
Presented by best-selling Mexican author Carlos Fuentes and produced in association with the Smithsonian Institution. This program explores the peoples and nations who fought for independence from Spain and examines the burdens accompanied by freedom.

Rise and Fall of the Aztec Empire
28 min., 1994 (Educational Video Network)
The Aztecs rose from obscurity to rule one of the great empires of preconquest Mexico. Eventually, their brutality fueled the resentment that helped to cause their defeat.

Teotihuacán: City of the Gods
18 min., 1987 (Educational Video Network)
When the Aztecs arrived in the Valley of Mexico 600 years ago, they found a mysterious city of great pyramids.

WEB SITES
The Age of Exploration
staff.esuhsd.org/~balochie/studentprojects/ageexploration/
Brandon Hall's site that contains information on the voyages of Columbus, Drake, Magellan, De Soto, Ponce de León, and Vasco da Gama.

Central and South American Chronology
campus.northpark.edu/history/WebChron/Americas/Americas.html
North Park University put together this site that provides a timeline of Central and South American history, complete with hotlinks to key events.

Civilizations in America
www.wsu.edu/~dee/CIVAMRCA/CIV.HTM
Richard Hooker's (Washington State University) phenomenally full and complete site on

the indigenous cultures of America. Be sure to check out the links under the drop-down menu to see more in-depth information on the Maya, the Aztecs, the Incas, and the Olmecs.

Conquistadors
www.pbs.org/opb/conquistadors/home.htm
This fascinating site from PBS gives background information on Cortés and Pizarro.

Creation Myths
www.magictails.com/creationlinks.html
Here are a large group of links to creation myths from a variety of world cultures.

The European Voyages of Exploration
www.ucalgary.ca/applied_history/tutor/eurvoya/
During the fifteenth and sixteenth centuries, two nations — Portugal and Spain — pioneered the European discovery of sea routes that were the first channels of interaction between *all* of the world's continents, thus beginning the process of globalization in which we live today. This tutorial introduces the student to these two pioneering nations, their motivations, their actions, and the inevitable consequences of their colonization. It also examines the geographical, technological, economic, political, and cultural patterns of that era.

The History of Mexico
historychannel.com/cgi-
bin/frameit.cgi?p=http%3A//www.historychannel.com/exhibits/mexico/
This is the History Channel's Web site that provides a comprehensive history of Mexico with specific sections of the site devoted to the Aztecs and the Maya. The links are excellent.

The History of Mexico: A Timeline Overview
www.mexconnect.com/mex_/history.html
This site, developed by Mexico Connect, contains an overview of the country's history that shows what the rest of the world was up to as Mexico evolved. Mexico's history is divided into several smaller categories in order to help you achieve a greater understanding of the evolutionary and revolutionary processes that have made Mexico what it is today.

Internet Modern History Sourcebook: The Early Modern World
www.fordham.edu/halsall/mod/modsbook03.html
A premiere Internet resource created at Fordham University, The Internet Modern History Sourcebook is a premiere site for information on the history, culture, and literature of the early modern world. Excellent links to sites on European exploration.

The Mariner's Museum: The Age of Exploration
www.mariner.org/age/index.html
This site provides a timeline, maps, and hotlinks to particulars of all of the major voyages of exploration of America by Europeans.

The Mexica/Aztecs
www.wsu.edu/~dee/CIVAMRCA/AZTECS.HTM
Richard Hooker's (Washington State University) phenomenal site on very full and complete background page on the Mexica and the Maya. Be sure to check out the links under the drop-down menu.

Quetzalcoatl: The Man, The Myth, The Legend
weber.ucsd.edu/~anthclub/quetzalcoatl/quetzal.htm
This is an in-depth site on the culture and beliefs of the ancient Mexicans.

The Sor Juana Inez de la Cruz Project
www.dartmouth.edu/~sorjuana/
Description, chronology, searching guide, recent bibliography, Cruz scholars, and exegeses.

AUDIO
History of the Conquest of Mexico
4 CDs, 5 hrs., 2003 (Naxos Audio Books)
In 1519, Hernán Cortés arrived in Mexico to investigate stories of a wealthy empire. What he encountered was beyond his wildest dreams — an advanced civilization with complex artistic, political, and religious systems (involving extensive human sacrifice) and replete with gold. This was the Aztec empire, headed by the aloof emperor, Montezuma. With just a handful of men, Cortés achieved the impossible, crushing the Aztecs and their allies, and effectively annexing the whole territory for Spain. One of the most extraordinary stories of conquest in mankind's history, it is told here in the classic account by the American historian W. H. Prescott.

In the World: Europe Meets America (p. 767)

Columbus's first contact with indigenous peoples in the New World has been much debated in recent years. Long celebrated as one of the great discoveries in Western history, Columbus's landing on the American continent introduced what Native American advocates have called a "holocaust" wreaked on indigenous people. To glorify this first contact is to celebrate the creation of a modern world with its navigational, military, scientific, social, and political achievements. And yet the development of this modern world also brought the destruction of entire peoples, the imposition of Eurocentric ideals on independent cultures, and the degradation of productive, agrarian systems of community development. The Doctrine of Discovery under which European explorers forayed into unknown territory revealed a decidedly Eurocentric value system. According to this Doctrine, militarized European states competed against each other to find uncharted lands; the nation who first discovered a virgin place was assured rights to its exploration and colonization — whether or not an indigenous population already inhabited the land. As such, indigenous peoples were legally rendered inconsequential within their own territories. Columbus's first contact in America, effectively between colonizer and colonized, prefigured centuries of a larger project of European imperial expansion that would spread to North and South America, the Caribbean, Africa, India, and elsewhere. Colonization — both in Columbus's time and throughout the twentieth century — was characterized by a calculated effort to identify and maintain difference: Race, ethnicity, culture, morality or religion, lack of (a recognizably European) government, and gender all became factors by which the project of colonial domination was legitimized.

As Columbus noted in his diary, the Spanish monarchy had barely retaken its own country from the invading Moors by the time he sailed for the New World. Spain, like many neighboring nation-states, found itself in a state of emergence. Renaissance exploration and conquest thrived at the same time a unified Roman Catholicism was becoming a fragmented Christendom. Emerging centralized governments began to shed a faith-based unity in favor of a more secular group of nations — what was to become known as Europe. Contact with the Other helped these nations — and Europe itself — construct individual and collective identities. Conquests and acquisitions in the New World aided many European countries to bolster their international political, economic, and military power. In many ways, the New World served as a mirrored stage in which European states could see themselves reflected in a position of superiority.

First contact with the New World and its native inhabitants also ignited another means of cultural domination: the Eurocentric textual representation of the Other. Private journal entries, diaries, logs, essays, and theatrical works attempted to reproduce "authentic" depictions that would be mimetic textual equals to the experiential knowledge of eyewitnesses. During this time, some Jesuits in the New World, such as Jacob de Acosta, began producing missionary protoethnographies, in which specific cultural practices of the indigenous population were recorded, so that missionaries would better understand how to convert the Other. While the texts in this section are not formal ethnographies and are not all missionary-based, the initial European contact with the New World nonetheless began to legitimize a certain generic protoethnography. The seeds of so-called objective observation — pseudo-scientific accounts of the Other and his culture, customs, habits, and points of difference — can be seen in these first textual records. The European — as observer and recorder — was perched in a position of superiority and civilization, a position from which he was able to make cultural observations that, in subsequent centuries, would come to serve as scientific fact.

For most of the literate European audiences during the Renaissance, texts were the only means possible to experience the New World, and textual accounts were often taken at face value. The indigenous people represented in these European texts generally fell under two categories. As Columbus and Cortés wrote in their diaries, native populations were ignorant, inferior to Europeans, suitable mainly for enslaving, and desperately in need of Christian saving. Conversely, other protoethnographers such as Las Casas and Montaigne depicted the Native Americans as innocent pre-Christians, humans, and much closer to being Europeans' equals. Each of these views proved to be problematic, however, since they both characterized the indigenous population as a sort of blank canvas onto which Europe and Christianity, as the bearers of native identity, could paint. Indeed, Cruz, in her loa, presciently depicts this struggle between indigenous populations — America and Occident — who contend desperately with European colonizers — Zeal and Religion — to preserve their respective identities, rejecting those that Europe wishes to impose.

Begin your approach to this section by discussing students' assumptions when faced with unknown cultures or peoples. Encourage them to be candid in the assessment of their own attitudes. Do they approach their first contact from a position of superiority or inferiority? On what do they base their preconceptions? How would students of different cultures approach an encounter of difference? Discuss how ethnographers similarly study unknown peoples. Starting with physical details, outline what observations might be readily made, then proceed to more abstract concepts regarding religion or general cultural values. Challenge students' preconceptions about the trustworthiness of assessing another person's or an entire people's identity through observation by asking them to consider the problem of objectivity: Can any observer ever be other than subjective? Can any observer escape his or her own culture? What kind of cultural biases are implicitly revealed in the categories students or ethnographers use to discuss different cultures? Compare the students' findings with the methods used by the authors in this section to represent their experiences with the indigenous American population to a European audience. Encourage students to pay special attention to the implied audiences in these texts, especially how each author speaks the "cultural language" of Europe. How does the author's audience affect the substance of what he or she writes? What specific markers of difference does the author identify, and how are they used to encourage or discourage colonial objectives?

Texts about conquest — even those that attempted to expose and oppose it — nonetheless represent the Other through the filter of European experience and cultural values. That none of the accounts in this section are written by native peoples suggests that each of them should be considered suspect to a degree, since even in defending the Other, Europeans (or those within the dominant culture) nonetheless speak for him. It is thus important to read these texts critically, with both author and audience in mind. In this context, it is also helpful to encourage students to avoid the Manichean extremes of seeing different positions or players within this debate as all good or all bad. It is as easy to praise Columbus as a pioneer just as it is tempting to glorify indigenous populations. But students should be informed that Columbus apparently believed that he had received revelation from God and perhaps (at least partially) believed that his discoveries of gold would help to build a futuristic Spanish Christian utopia that would help save the very people he colonized. Similarly, even though Cortés did conquer Moctezuma, the Aztec king was himself an unpopular leader of a fatigued and overextended empire who had so exploited neighboring countries that he had few allies. And, just as Las Casas eloquently pleaded to save the remaining native Taino Indians of Hispaniola (now Haiti) from extinction, he advocated importing African slaves in their place. It is important to consider all of the players as composite beings in ambivalent and shifting circumstances that were largely undefined in the Renaissance.

Remind students that indigenous peoples and their causes represented for a European audience often had less to do with America and more to do with Europe representing itself to itself (consider the Enlightenment example of Rousseau's glorification of the "noble savage" that was an implicit critique of European aristocracy and leadership). Encourage students to compare these accounts written by Europeans with primary sources written by indigenous peoples both during the Renaissance and after and to relate the dynamics of colonial projects with current world affairs. How are imperial forces still at work on a global scale? Where are current imperial practices observed, and what motivates them? Does a New World still exist in today's context? If so, where is it, and why is it considered as such? How do the texts presented here prefigure contemporary debates within global politics?

IN THE CLASSROOM

I. RELIGION: SPIRITUAL EMANCIPATION OR COLONIZATION?

Spaniards paired the territorial conquest of indigenous Americans with religious colonization, since Catholicism was utterly inseparable from Spain's cultural identity. More subtle than physical domination, religion wanted not native "immolation," as Cruz astutely noted, but "conversion." Missionary discourse ironically proved to be similar to the biblical double-edged sword. On one hand, faithful Christians believed that all mankind should hear the gospel of Jesus Christ and, by conversion, be saved from a damning afterlife. In this context, religion is seen as a positive force spreading light, peace, and salvation. On the other hand, the denial of indigenous religions and the imposition of Western belief systems communicated a different message: Religion was another means to maintain ideological control. By changing hearts and minds as well as physical circumstances, dominant cultures — in this case, Spain — could establish superiority of power both from external and internal pressures acting on a given colonized subject. In this context, religion is one of the most dangerous forms of colonization: It can actually usurp a colonized person's agency.

Discussion

1. Ask students to describe the savagery with which the native peoples of America are treated by pointing to specific passages from the accounts that are presented. Do any of these texts reflect the personified Zeal in Cruz's work? How does Las Casas expose the problems of violent behavior in the context of the Catholic faith? In what ways do his arguments reflect or not reflect Cruz's personified character Religion? Have students compare the different attitudes toward violence among the authors in this section. How do some justify violence? How do others argue forcefully against it?

2. Ask students to describe the complicated intersection of religious beliefs apparent when Cortés meets the Aztec ruler Moctezuma. Have students analyze Cortés's actions within the Aztec temple and evaluate the missionary discourse present in his account. How does Cortés use religion to accomplish his colonial objectives? In what ways is capturing a temple more influential than occupying a city? Discuss the possible reasons why the ancient Mexican belief system is so threatening to Spaniards, and, by extension, why indigenous religions make colonizers uneasy.

3. Discuss Montaigne's depiction of indigenous religion. Ask students to evaluate his tone. Does Montaigne approve or disapprove of these indigenous beliefs? Compare these observations with Montaigne's evaluation of the native state of nature. How does he characterize the innocent Native Americans, and what additional beliefs does he wish to impose on them? Have students discuss how Montaigne's approach differs from the necessity espoused by Columbus, Cortés, and Las Casas of imposing the Catholic religion on the indigenous population.

Connections

1. Columbus, Cortés, Montaigne, and Cruz each describe religious practices of the indigenous American peoples. Considering that each of these descriptions are representations of those practices filtered through European experience, have students compare these observatory accounts with primary sources written from another perspective. In what ways does "A Defense of Aztec Religion" (p. 765), for example, contradict or reinforce these European perspectives? Similarly, what do the omens in "The Conquest of Mexico" (p. 736) reflect about indigenous belief systems? How does the indigenous position on the inseparability of religion and cultural identity compare with European perspectives on the same issue?

2. Ask students to compare Bartolomé de Las Casas's attitudes toward the native peoples of the Americas with those held by Montaigne. According to these thinkers, what exactly is "barbarous" and what is worthy of emulation? Ask students to consider how these portrayals reflect the influence of Renaissance humanism (*In the World*: Humanism, Learning, and Education, p. 452). Similarly, how might these attitudes be said to prefigure the Enlightenment notion of the "noble savage" (Book 4)?

3. By the nineteenth and twentieth centuries, European colonialism was at its peak in Africa. Using texts from *In the World*: Colonialism: Europe and Africa (Book 6), ask students to compare colonizers' motivations. What exactly, for example, is the "White Man's Burden," according to Rudyard Kipling (Book 6)? Have students identify how modern thinkers like Fanon, Césaire, Ngugi Wa Thiong'o, and Chinweizu expose the multiple ideological forces of colonialism and how they propose becoming emancipated from these colonial influences. Discuss the ways in which these modern thinkers are responding to colonial forces similar to those found in Europe's first contact with America.

Groups

1. The unknown indigenous people in the New World discovered by Columbus became the object of an existing European rejection of the Other, in this case by the Spanish royal monarchy. Based on Columbus's diary and Las Casas's writings in this section, ask students to define who was already considered an Other in Spain. What religious or other ideological grounds separated "true" Spaniards from alterity? In what ways did the Spanish monarchy act to ensure that difference was maintained? Assign to groups of students another European country, and ask them to research the religions that specific

nation rejected. How do nationalistic governments act in relation to these groups deemed as outsiders? In class, ask the groups to compare their findings, noting especially any transnational patterns that become apparent and how those patterns reflect emerging Renaissance values. Why did differing religions seem so threatening to governmental authority during the Renaissance?

Writing

1. In her loa, Cruz chooses to personify the major players within this colonial relationship: America, Occident, Religion, and Zeal. Describe each of these characters in detail and evaluate her strategy of personification. How and why does this strategy make her argument more or less persuasive? Discuss other literary devices she might have used, and evaluate their effectiveness. Why might the strategy of personification especially influence a European audience sympathetically?

2. In "Are Not the Indians Men?" (p. 793) Father Fray Antonio de Montesinos challenges Spanish Catholics who, in turn, desire to "rebuke and frighten" the preacher. Why does de Montesinos call the Spanish consciences "lacking," and why does he state that the Spanish are ignorant and are in danger of "eternal damnation"? Describe the religious standards from which these claims are derived and how they support or derail colonial objectives. Discuss the problem of religious interpretation. How is Catholicism used to justify both violence against and pleas on behalf of indigenous peoples? What problems does this pose for religion's credibility in the New World?

3. The concept of race was only partially defined during the Renaissance and had not yet become fixed as a marker of difference attributed to skin pigmentation. Instead, European attitudes toward race still revolved around kinship structures, especially hereditary bloodlines and their associated rights of inheritance. Identify passages in which physical characteristics are specifically mentioned within the texts in this section. Compare the different versions of these descriptions, and evaluate what they reveal about the writers' attitudes. Why might race be used as a means to justify colonialism? How is race conflated with religion during the Renaissance? How do the attitudes presented prefigure racial strife that will characterize subsequent centuries?

II. CONNECTIONS: THE NEW WORLD AS UTOPIA

One way of representing Europe to itself was to project anxieties about European political, social, religious, or moral affairs onto a nonexistent textual stage. Sir Thomas More, a sixteenth-century Catholic humanist, revolutionized Renaissance thinking when he published *Utopia*, literally a "no place," in 1516. More's fictional account describes an ideal society that he maintained actually existed. More did indeed derive his portrayal of Utopia from a forged account attributed to Amerigo Vespucci, for whom America is named. A Florentine merchant who navigated voyages to the New World on behalf of Spain and Portugal, Vespucci documented his travels to the New World. Unfortunately, certain of his writings were freely changed in a volume entitled *The First Four Voyages of Amerigo Vespucci* (Vespucci made only two trips), which circulated in Europe in 1507. This volume contained a letter from Vespucci to Piero Soderini, the chief magistrate of Florence, in which Vespucci described the natives he encountered in the New World and glorified them in their Edenic state. The indigenous population Vespucci described enjoyed tremendous personal freedom, equality between the sexes, open sexual relations, a kingless government, a sense of honor, and the absence of slavery. Having borrowed material from this forged account, More fashioned his own fictional vision of Utopia, which in turn shaped European perceptions of America, since Europeans avidly read More's text and accepted it as an accurate description of the New World. More's Utopia is an island republic (note the similarity to England) whose liberal practices of universal education, communal property, devaluation of money, state-sponsored health care, and balance between hard work and intellectual pursuits sharply contrasted with the then-current social landscape of stratified Europe. Like subsequent depictions of Utopia, however, More's text is crowded with ambiguities: This ideal nation-state considers its neighbors inferior and depends on publicly humiliated slaves. The society operates by means of severe surveillance of its citizens who lack a sense of individuality and privacy. Thus while More's representation of the ideal society acts as the first literary representation that challenged European monarchies as a direct result of New World contact, it also simultaneously reflects some of the European states' imperfect practices. Even so, at a time when humanistic beliefs encouraged a return to an ideal, classical nation-state, More's text convinced many within the European audience that the New World indeed harbored such an Eden, setting the stage for Enlightenment thinkers to glorify the "noble savage." This utopian discourse also permanently imprinted the quest for the ideal in European cultural consciousness at the same time it justified an expanding colonial agenda.

Discussion

1. Both Cortés and Montaigne write of the industry and progress found in the New World. Ask students to describe the different innovative tools and ideas presented by the indigenous populations. How do Cortés and Montaigne view these technological developments? What do these accounts reveal about native technological capabilities? How do these accomplishments compare with European Renaissance utopian values? Ask students to compare their findings with similar innovative tools and ideas described in Francis Bacon's utopian community "New Atlantis" (p. 481). Why might Bacon's fictional representation be considered a utopia where the American reality is less appreciated?

2. Among explorers, the New World represented a utopia that was certain to contain vast treasures. Columbus searched in vain for gold, and Cortés embarked on a search for El Dorado. What utopian ideals does the acquisition of gold represent? Ask students to consider these two explorers' records in the context of Miguel de Cervantes's fictional account of Don Quixote (p. 262). Describe the fantastical utopia Quixote imagines in his mind, and compare it with the way both Columbus and Cortés define their quests. Have students then compare these accounts of Spanish explorers with Voltaire's fictional account of Candide (Book 4), who also searches for El Dorado. What utopian ideals does El Dorado represent across these disparate texts? For what reasons is it possible or impossible to find? Generate a discussion about the deeper significance of questing for utopia: Are utopia-seekers destined to Quixote's fate, or will they accomplish their missions? Why?

3. *Paradise Lost* (p. 575) is a fascinating example of a utopia gone wrong. Point out the irony to students that, in an age that so desperately seeks after the perfect society, Milton's monumental English epic depicts the fall from such perfection. Ask students to consider Milton's depiction of the fall in light of the etymological meaning of utopia — literally, a "no place" — and the emerging power of the Renaissance individual. How do Adam and Eve's choices preclude them from maintaining a position in Paradise? Using any utopian depiction for comparison, did Renaissance thinkers actually believe that humans could fashion such a utopia in reality? Why or why not?

4. Denis Diderot's *Supplement to the Voyage of Bougainville* (Book 4) offers a critical comparison of European and Tahitian lifestyles. Ask students to identify the specific Tahitian practices this text idealizes. Is Diderot more or less sympathetic to cultural ideals embodied in Tahiti? Ask students to compare Spanish accounts in this section with Diderot's appreciation of the Tahitian lifestyle. How sympathetic are the Spanish accounts to the cultural ideals of the indigenous populations?

Groups

1. Despite the pervasiveness of the utopian ideal during the Renaissance, authors differed on the elements that would characterize their perfect states. Have each group choose a different utopian literary representation and evaluate it according to specific criteria. Ask each group, for example, to consider its utopia's perspective on the ownership of property, social structure, valued objects, individual and collective work ethics, money, gender roles, the role of education, religious practices, courting and mating rituals, child care, slavery, association with neighboring countries, and other categories that students can define. Encourage students to evaluate the founding premises on which these utopias are constructed. Are Renaissance utopias political, moral, sociological, educational, or religious in nature?

Writing

1. Compare in detail the attitudes expressed by Columbus and Cortés about the indigenous populations they encounter. Synthesize the viewpoints of these two explorers by writing a composite textual description of their view of the indigenous American population. Compare these attitudes with Trinculo's assessment of Caliban's "worth" in *The Tempest* (p. 495). In what ways does Trinculo echo the Spanish explorer's observations? Describe Shakespeare's purpose in including both Trinculo and Caliban in his play. What is Shakespeare's own assessment of Caliban's worth? Is he condoning or satirizing colonizing attitudes?

2. At the end of his essay, Montaigne describes a Peruvian king who, being taken away as a prisoner, was still upheld by carriers who supported his coach. Even though these carriers were being slaughtered for metaphorically upholding their belief system, others continually came to take their places. Describe this passage as a metaphor. What right do people have to choose — to "carry" — their own ideologies, utopian or otherwise? Discuss the passage in conjunction with the struggle depicted by Cruz. Is it ever justifiable for one person or culture to impose a vision of utopia on another person or culture? What consequences can be expected? Are visions of utopia universal or culturally relative? Contextualize your discussion within a contemporary framework. Do nations still impose their visions of utopia on other nations with different belief systems? Is this practice justified?

3. Renaissance utopias grappled with the dichotomy of whether to be inclusivist — all people should be given equal status within a communal ideal — or to be exclusivist — privileges of rank, wealth, religion, and gender should be preserved. Jonathan Swift, in *Gulliver's Travels* (Book 4), presents a utopia in the land of the Houyhnhnms. Describe the inclusivist and exclusivist aims the Houyhnhnms propose and why they propose them. In what ways does the Catholic missionary project of conversion compare with a Houyhnhnm attitude? How does Las Casas portray Catholicism as inclusivist and exclusivist? What are the respective prices for entering into either a Houyhnhnm or Catholic utopia? Are these utopias ideal or flawed?

BEYOND THE CLASSROOM

RESEARCH & WRITING

1. Haiti — or the western half of Christopher Columbus's "Ysla Hispaniola" (Hispaniola) — was one of Columbus's first contacts in America and, under French rule, subsequently became the most profitable colony in the world. It was the first and only black republic to declare its independence during the existence of the slave trade. Research the

history of Haiti, and discuss the radical changes that have happened to it from the moment of first contact with Europeans. Describe what happened to the Taino Indians, the indigenous population at the time of Columbus's arrival, and compare that with the contemporary population's demographic makeup. Discuss Haiti's plight today as the poorest country in the Western Hemisphere. In what ways is Haiti still suffering from the first contact with Europe? Although declared an independent nation in 1804, what kinds of colonial forces are still present in Haiti?

2. Research extant accounts of first contact and subsequent colonization written by indigenous people. What accounts are available for study? Describe the indigenous interpretation of first contact. What assumptions did native people make about cultural foreigners? How do those assumptions compare with assumptions made by their European counterparts? Discuss whether native accounts reveal protoethnographic influences in the same way European accounts do. In what ways do native accounts differ in method and content? What are the undergirding belief systems and cultural values that make for a decidedly different native representation of this shared experience?

3. Read Sir Thomas More's *Utopia* and describe the specific kind of societal perfection he portrays. Is his utopia based primarily on political, cultural, psychological, moral, or class ideals? Discuss the practices found in More's "foreign land" that directly correlate to or contradict European societal standards. Identify what you consider to be less than ideal requirements within More's *Utopia*. How do certain of his prescriptions engender stratification within this society? As a textual representation of a new world, identify both the critique More makes of his own society and to whom that critique is addressed. What changes does More implicitly advocate within Europe?

Projects

1. Do an experiment in ethnographic observation. Watch a film in a foreign language and unfamiliar culture without reading the subtitles. As you are watching, jot down observations. After viewing the film, write a journal entry that describes the experience. What were your first impressions of the people? How did you create meaning out of this contact with a different culture? What specific cultural codes or behaviors seemed especially different? Describe the cultural instincts you may have discovered as you formed your perceptions and discuss the filters through which cultural experience becomes comprehensible. Consider watching the film again, this time reading the subtitles. How effective was your attempt at creating meaning? List the barriers that prevented understanding and describe what steps would need to be taken to remove them.

2. Part of the religious colonization undertaken by the Spanish in America included transforming physical space into protected mission communities. Research the rise of missions in the Americas, paying special attention to mission architecture. Using the medium of your choice, create a model of a mission community. Describe the function of each different space and relate it to Spain's colonizing mission. How does the mission's spatial demarcation reinforce or undercut colonial objectives?

3. Research the rights of indigenous peoples under international law today in the context of the early modern European Doctrine of Discovery. Are indigenous peoples protected against invasion and colonization today? As you discover policies that you consider to be unjust, outline why they seem inappropriate. If you had to write a loa-like play of personified players within the debate you discover, what would these major players be called? How do they compare with the entities Cruz identifies? Draft new legislation that would correct the problem you have uncovered. Consider writing to your con-

gressman or directly to the current UN ambassador to express your concerns and to share your proposal.

FURTHER READING

Alves, Abel A. *Brutality and Benevolence: Human Ethology, Culture, and the Birth of Mexico.* 1996.

Geertz, Clifford. *The Interpretation of Cultures.* 1977.

Hamlin, William. *The Image of America in Montaigne, Spenser, and Shakespeare: Renaissance Ethnography and Literary Reflection.* 1995.

Merrim, Stephanie, ed. *Feminist Perspectives on Sor Juana Inés de la Cruz.* 1991.

More, Sir Thomas. Trans. Robert Adams. *Utopia,* 2nd edition. 1992.

Padgen, Anthony. *Lords of All the World: Ideologies of Empire in Spain, Britain, and France, 1500-1800.* 1998.

Todorov, Tveztan. *The Conquest of America: The Question of the Other.* 1999.

MEDIA RESOURCES

WEB SITES

The Age of Exploration

staff.esuhsd.org/~balochie/studentprojects/ageexploration/

Brandon Hall's site that contains information on the voyages of Columbus, Drake, Magellan, De Soto, Ponce de León, and Vasco da Gama.

Central and South American Chronology

campus.northpark.edu/history/WebChron/Americas/Americas.html

North Park University put together this site that provides a timeline of Central and South American history, complete with hotlinks to key events.

Civilizations in America

www.wsu.edu/~dee/CIVAMRCA/CIV.HTM

Richard Hooker's (Washington State University) phenomenally full and complete site on the indigenous cultures of the America.. Be sure to check out the links under the drop-down menu to see more in-depth information on the Maya, the Aztecs, the Incas, and the Olmecs.

Conquistadors

www.pbs.org/opb/conquistadors/home.htm

This fascinating site from PBS gives background information on Cortés and Pizarro.

The European Voyages of Exploration

www.ucalgary.ca/applied_history/tutor/eurvoya/

During the fifteenth and sixteenth centuries, two nations — Portugal and Spain — pioneered the European discovery of sea routes that were the first channels of interaction between all of the world's continents, thus beginning the process of globalization in which we all live. This tutorial introduces the student to these two pioneering nations, their motivations, their actions, and the inevitable consequences of their colonization. It also examines the geographical, technological, economic, political, and cultural patterns of that era.

Internet Modern History Sourcebook: The Early Modern World

www.fordham.edu/halsall/mod/modsbook03.html

A premiere Internet resource created at Fordham University, The Internet Modern History Sourcebook is a premiere site for information on the history, culture, and literature of the early modern world. Excellent links to sites on European exploration.

The Mariner's Museum: The Age of Exploration
www.mariner.org/age/index.html
This site provides a timeline, maps, and hotlinks to particulars of all of the major voyages of exploration of America by Europeans.

The Mexica/Aztecs
www.wsu.edu/~dee/CIVAMRCA/AZTECS.HTM
Richard Hooker's (Washington State University) phenomenal site provides a full and complete background page on the Mexica and the Maya. Be sure to check out the links under the drop-down menu.

The Sor Juana Inez de la Cruz Project
www.dartmouth.edu/~sorjuana/
Description, chronology, searching guide, recent bibliography, Cruz scholars, and exegeses.

GENERAL MEDIA RESOURCES

VIDEO
The Age of Gold
59 min., 1991 (Home Vision Entertainment)
Presented by best-selling Mexican author Carlos Fuentes and produced in association with the Smithsonian Institution, this program looks at the enormous wealth brought into Spain from the New World as well as the magnificent art and literature that was created during the life and rule of the mysterious King Philip II.

The Aztec Empire
50 min., 2000 (A&E Video)
Trace the astonishing story of the Aztecs, who rose from a beleaguered band of barely over 1,000 to dominate nearly all of Mexico in just over 400 years.

The Aztecs
48 min., 1997 (Films for the Humanities & Sciences)
Aztec myth prophesied that a great city would one day stand on the site where an eagle, perched on a cactus with a serpent in its mouth, was found. Today, Mexico City stands on this mythical site. Although the Aztec empire fell on April 28, 1521, when Hernán Cortés and his army defeated Montezuma, traces of the thousand-year-old pre-Columbian empire still survive and influence world culture. This program explores Aztec culture and history, from the role of human sacrifice in the Aztec religion to their agricultural advances. Commentary by scholars, maps, and contemporary accounts provides an overview of the events that both shaped and destroyed an empire.

The Civilizations of Mexico
13 min., 1997 (Films for the Humanities & Sciences)
The archaeological sites at Monte Albán, Palenque, Uxmal, and Chichén Itzá speak of the great pre-Columbian civilizations: the Mayan solar calendar, mathematical system, and fabulous cities; and the Aztec Tenochtitlán, founded in 1325 and with almost a million inhabitants when Cortés "discovered" it.

Conflict of the Gods
59 min., 1991 (Home Vision Entertainment)
Presented by best-selling Mexican author Carlos Fuentes and produced in association with the Smithsonian Institution, this program retraces the Aztec world in Mexico and also depicts the gods of the New World, the introduction of the new European god, and the interplay between the two.

The Conquest of Mexico
35 min., 1997 (Films for the Humanities & Sciences)
This program provides a portrait of Cortés and his world — the real world and the imaginary one painted by theologians, mystics, imaginative travelers, poets, and liars; of the New World as seen by a small number of Spaniards; and of the civilizations of Mesoamerica before they were "discovered" — the world of the Maya and Aztecs, the nature of Aztec religion and politics. It describes the Battle of Mexico and explains how and why Montezuma lost — and why, today still, the descendants of the Aztecs speak Nahuatl.

Empire of the Sun
47 min., 2001 (Films for the Humanities & Sciences)
After Hernán Cortés destroyed the Aztec empire of Mexico, another conquistador, Francisco Pizarro, marched on the Incas of Peru with a mere 180 men — and won, filling the coffers of Spain with the treasures of the Andes. This program describes Pizarro's ruthless attack on the Inca empire amidst the aftermath of the civil war between the Inca ruler, Atahualpa, and his defeated brother, Huáscar. The rivalry between Pizarro and Diego de Almagro, the ransoming and subsequent execution of Atahualpa, and the Spanish occupation of the Inca capital, Cuzco, are discussed.

Hernán Cortés
30 min., 1995 (Zenger Media)
Fiercest of the Spanish conquistadors, Hernán Cortés overtook Mexican cities and toppled the Aztec empire. Believing his actions were for the good of Spain and the glory of God, Cortés created an imposing army using the Indians who had survived his conquests. Though he eventually established himself as a colonial ruler and in many ways united the natives of Mexico, he left a controversial legacy and is remembered both as a brutal conqueror and as a courageous leader. (Available in both English and Spanish.)

Lost City of the Incas
50 min., 1997 (A&E Video)
A&E journeys high into the Andes Mountains to explore the spectacular remains of the Incan city of Machu Picchu. Long thought to be the result of legends, the city was discovered in 1911 by Hiriam Bingham and has been extensively studied ever since. Meet the men and women who have dedicated their lives to unlocking the many secrets hidden in the city just below the clouds.

Lost Kingdoms of the Maya
60 min., 1993 (National Geographic Video)
Long before Columbus, the Maya established one of the most highly developed civilizations of their time in the jungles of Mexico and Central America. Yet this advanced society of priests, astronomers, artisans, and farmers suddenly and mysteriously collapsed more than a thousand years ago. Accompany archeologists to Copan, Dos Pilas, and other spectacular classic Mayan ruins as they unearth artifacts and huge temples of incredible beauty. Recently deciphered hieroglyphics and other new discoveries offer astounding clues to the lives of these ancient people. Hear the startling story of one kingdom's downfall and its final desperate hours of violent warfare. Through spine-tingling recreations, witness ancient rituals reenacted on sites where they originally occurred. And meet the enduring Maya, who still maintain many of their ancestor's traditions.

Machu Picchu Revealed
20 min., 1995 (Educational Video Network)
An overview of pre-Columbian civilizations in the Andes locates the Incas in time and place and investigates the ruins of Machu Picchu. Learn about the importance of this site, and examine some of the theories about its creators.

The Maya
50 min., 1997 (A&E Video)
At one time, Mayan society dominated the area now known as Central America. A&E travels to the jungles of Mexico to answer the many questions surrounding this once great empire that all but vanished in A.D. 835. Climb Palenque's great palace, and explore the Temple of Inscriptions, discovering why the Maya altered their historical records. Find out what is known of the Mayan ruler Pacal and the truths behind the persistent rumors of human sacrifice.

The Mayans
47 min., 1997 (Films for the Humanities & Sciences)
The most advanced of the pre-Hispanic peoples of Central America, the Maya rose to great prominence, only to suddenly decline around the year A.D. 900. In this program, cultural historian Iain Grain delves into Mayan history, investigating topics such as their mastery of mathematics, their extremely hierarchical society, their use of human sacrifice to induce rain, and Mayan art. Many examples of Mayan architecture are provided as well, plus a computer re-creation of the temple at Chichén Itzá. Although there are still more than two million native Maya living in Central America, the exact origins of their ancestors and the fate of the ancient Mayan cities remain mysteries.

Mayas, Aztecs, and Incas
25 min., 1996 (Educational Video Network)
The three leading American civilizations at the time of the Spanish conquest were the Maya and Aztecs of Mexico and the Incas of South America. Explore their cultures, and learn about their achievements.

Mexican Pre-Hispanic Cultures
26 min., 1999 (Inside Mexico Video)
This video presents a panorama of the various pre-Columbian civilizations that existed in the Mexican territory: the mysteriously abandoned city of Teotihuacán, the impressive Aztec empire, and the erudite Maya. Also shown are the fundamental traits of the indigenous civilizations that still exist in Mexico.

Mexico's Great Pyramids
50 min., 1997 (A&E Video)
At its zenith, the city of Teotihuacán covered eight square miles, making it the seventh largest city in the ancient world. Not much is known about the people who made the city their home except for the physical remnants of a two-thousand-year-old urban wonder. A&E joins a team of archaeologists to unravel some of the mysteries surrounding the Teotihuacános, including who were their kings and priests, why they didn't develop a system of writing, and the purpose of the Great Pyramids.

The Mystery of the Maya
38 min., 1998 (IMAX)
Deep within the jungles of Mexico and Guatemala, and extending into the Yucatán Peninsula, lie the fabled pyramids, temples, and palaces of the Maya. While Europe still slumbered in the midst of the Dark Ages, these innovative peoples had charted the heavens, evolved the only true writing system native to the Americas, and had made tremendous strides in the area of mathematics and calendars. Without the advantage of metal tools, beasts of burden, or even the wheel, they were able to construct vast cities with an amazing degree of architectural perfection and variety. Filmed on location at numerous sacred sites throughout Central America, including the ruins at Palenque, Tikal, Tulum, Chichén Itzá, Copan, and Uxmal, *Mystery of the Maya* explores the culture, science, and history of these peoples.

Mythology of Ancient Mexico
19 min., 1990 (Educational Video Network)
Pre-Columbian Mexican culture involved the integration of the natural and supernatural worlds. Here are many insights into the great states that once ruled the land we now know as Mexico.

The Origins of Mexican Civilization
21 min., 1990 (Educational Video Network)
The Olmecs, the Zapotecs, and the residents of Teotihuacán established advanced cultures in Mexico long before the advent of the Aztecs. Learn about some of the amazing achievements of these ancient peoples.

Price of Freedom
59 min., 1991 (Home Vision Entertainment)
Presented by best-selling Mexican author Carlos Fuentes and produced in association with the Smithsonian Institution, this program explores the peoples and nations who fought for independence from Spain and examines the burdens accompanied by freedom.

Rise and Fall of the Aztec Empire
28 min., 1994 (Educational Video Network)
The Aztecs rose from obscurity to rule one of the great empires of preconquest Mexico. Eventually, their brutality fueled the resentment that helped to cause their defeat.

Teotihuacán: City of the Gods
18 min., 1987 (Educational Video Network)
When the Aztecs arrived in the Valley of Mexico 600 years ago, they found a mysterious city of great pyramids.

WEB SITES
The Age of Exploration
staff.esuhsd.org/~balochie/studentprojects/ageexploration/
Brandon Hall's site contains information on the voyages of Columbus, Drake, Magellan, De Soto, Ponce de León, and Vasco da Gama.

Central and South American Chronology
campus.northpark.edu/history/WebChron/Americas/Americas.html
North Park University put together this site that provides a timeline of Central and South American history, complete with hotlinks to key events.

Civilizations in America
www.wsu.edu/~dee/CIVAMRCA/CIV.HTM
Richard Hooker's (Washington State University) phenomenally full and complete site on the indigenous cultures of America. Be sure to check out the links under the drop-down menu to see more in-depth information on the Maya, the Aztecs, the Incas, and the Olmecs.

Conquistadors
www.pbs.org/opb/conquistadors/home.htm
This fascinating site from PBS gives background information on Cortés and Pizarro.

The European Voyages of Exploration
www.ucalgary.ca/applied_history/tutor/eurvoya/
During the fifteenth and sixteenth centuries, two nations — Portugal and Spain — pioneered the European discovery of sea routes that were the first channels of interaction between *all* of the world's continents, thus beginning the process of globalization in which

we all live. This tutorial introduces the student to these two pioneering nations, their motivations, their actions, and the inevitable consequences of their colonization. It also examines the geographical, technological, economic, political, and cultural patterns of that era.

The History of Mexico
historychannel.com/cgi-in/frameit.cgi?p=http%3A//www.historychannel.com/exhibits/
mexico/
This is the History Channel's Web site, which provides a comprehensive history of Mexico with specific sections devoted to the Aztecs and the Maya. The links are excellent.

The History of Mexico: A Timeline Overview
www.mexconnect.com/mex_/history.html
This site, developed by Mexico Connect, contains an overview of the country's history that shows what the rest of the world was up to as Mexico evolved. Mexico's history is divided into several smaller categories to help achieve a greater understanding of the evolutionary and revolutionary processes that have made Mexico what it is today.

The Internet Modern History Sourcebook: The Early Modern World
www.fordham.edu/halsall/mod/modsbook03.html
An Internet resource created at Fordham University, the Internet Modern History Sourcebook is a premiere site for information on the history, culture, and literature of the early modern world. Excellent links to sites on European exploration.

The Mariner's Museum: The Age of Exploration
www.mariner.org/age/index.html
This site provides a timeline, maps, and hotlinks to particulars of all of the major voyages of exploration of America by Europeans.

The Mexica/Aztecs
www.wsu.edu/~dee/CIVAMRCA/AZTECS.HTM
Richard Hooker's (Washington State University) phenomenal site provides a full and complete background page on the Mexica and the Maya. Be sure to check out the links under the drop-down menu.

The Sor Juana Inez de la Cruz Project
www.dartmouth.edu/~sorjuana/
This site contains a chronology, searching guide, recent bibliography, Cruz scholars, and exegeses.

AUDIO
History of the Conquest of Mexico
4 CDs, 5 hrs.
In 1519, Hernán Cortés arrived in Mexico to investigate stories of a wealthy empire. What he encountered was beyond his wildest dreams — an advanced civilization with complex artistic, political, and religious systems (involving extensive human sacrifice) and replete with gold. This was the Aztec empire, headed by the aloof emperor, Montezuma. With just a handful of men, Cortés achieved the impossible, crushing the Aztecs and their allies, and effectively annexing the whole territory for Spain. One of the most extraordinary stories of conquest in mankind's history, it is told here in the classic account by the American historian W. H. Prescott.

CHINA:
THE GLORY OF THE MING

WU CHENGEN, *Monkey* (p. 832)

WWW   For a quiz on *Monkey*, see *World Literature Online* at
       bedfordstmartins.com/worldlit.

Although *Monkey* is easy and delightful reading, no familiar Western work is enough like it to show Western audiences how to read it. Like Mandeville's *Travels*, it is an account of an actual journey, the historical trek of Xuanzang (Hsüan Tsang) to bring the Buddhist scriptures from India back to China; and, like Mandeville's work, it contains a great deal of nonhistorical, legendary material. But *Monkey* is considerably more fabulous than Mandeville; its fantastic episodes are reminiscent of tall tales such as those recounting the exploits of Paul Bunyan or Odysseus's heroic deeds. The story of a religious pilgrimage, *Monkey* includes comic episodes that make it very different from Dante's deadly serious Easter pilgrimage and closer to the mixture of the comic and the serious in Chaucer's *Canterbury Tales*. The trickster Monkey, hero of Wu's tale, may be a little like such Renaissance tricksters as Don Juan and Doctor Faustus, and similar to figures such as Coyote in American Indian tales. Prospero's benevolent magic in *The Tempest* also may recall Monkey's magical services for Tripitaka. Among Western works, *Monkey* may be most like *Don Quixote*: Tripitaka's spiritual commitment resembles Quixote's idealism. Both narratives are constructed on a loosely connected series of adventures; and although Monkey and Sancho Panza contrast with their masters, both provide necessary common sense and practical support on the journey.

Students enjoy reading *Monkey* for its zany episodic adventures, but they should be encouraged to acknowledge contemporary Chinese religious and cultural practices for a more profound understanding of the text. Begin your discussion of *Monkey* by contextualizing it within the conflation of Confucian, Buddhist, and Daoist (Taoist) practices prevalent during the Ming dynasty. Point out to students that *Monkey* reflects this widespread syncretism without offering an explanation or demonstrating internal textual consistency. The cosmic hierarchy is incongruent with any single belief system; higher and lower order beings fluctuate in position and relevance. Consider, for example, the seeming discrepancy in Jade Emperor, a Daoist deity, controlling Monkey's destiny while the pilgrims seek out Buddhist scriptures from India with the help of a bodhisattva. Indeed, Kuan-yin and Buddha seem to possess powers superior to those of Jade Emperor and his court. In a similarly discordant way, members of the cosmic hierarchy such as Lao Tzu, the Jade Emperor, and Buddha each encourage Confucian moral values — including strict ethical standards — even as they transgress these norms themselves.

Most important, however, is the goal of the journey: The text suggests that the process of pilgrimage refers to the alchemical purification of religious Daoism as well as to the Buddhist aim of ego renunciation through self-enlightenment. The pilgrims thus enjoy processual Daoist self-cultivation — which one critic says serves as the defining trait by which a being's status can be evaluated — at the same time they extinguish the monsters of their own minds, a distinctively Buddhist proposition. Monkey's very name — Sun Wukong or "Aware of Vacuity" — suggests all three systems of Chinese thought concomitantly: It can mean a Confucian return to pure moral awareness, a Daoist refinement of the "holy embryo" that leads to immortality, and a Buddhist mastery of retreat from the problematic human tendency to create artificial dyads of form and formlessness, when neither exist in dharma — the Buddhist state of constant change.

These contradictions seem problematic when seen through Western eyes and become incredibly complex when the pilgrims' challenges and triumphs are metaphorically situated within the mind. Encourage students to step outside of Western "either-or" constructions or Aristotelean "A and not-A" logical reasoning to appreciate *Monkey* in its richness, as something other than an adventure story. Discuss the gaps in their own cultural knowledge that might prevent them from examining *Monkey* in this way and how they might begin closing those gaps. Consider reviewing basic tenets of Confucian, Daoist, and Buddhist thought and call attention to them as you encounter them in the text. While this syncretism might at first seem unfamiliar, ask your students how Western religions might also be considered syncretic as they have evolved over time. What examples of hybridization of church, state, secular, and even mystical beliefs might they find in Western religions during the Renaissance?

TEXT & CONTEXT

GODS AND MONSTERS: DEMONOLOGY IN *MONKEY*

Throughout *Monkey*, the eighty-one challenges the pilgrims face come in the form of demons. Rob Campany identifies a paradigm that describes these interactions between pilgrims and monsters. Almost every encounter, he argues, is characterized by a description of the demon's abode; a first meeting in which the demon is disguised; and an initial battle involving weapons and magic powers, during which either a stalemate or the pilgrims' defeat is imminent. On the brink of being vanquished, Monkey (on behalf of the pilgrims) discovers the demon's master to be a member of the Daoist-Buddhist pantheon (except for those episodes in which the bodhisattva intervenes). Some of these masters and lords of the cosmic hierarchy choose to show themselves directly to their errant servants. Others provide Monkey the knowledge or magic powers necessary to subdue the menacing demons. In either case, the demons inevitably surrender before their masters or are thwarted because of Monkey's newly acquired knowledge; their ability to disrupt is quieted, their true identities are revealed, and sometimes even restitution is made. Interestingly, the demons are not killed; rather, they are restored to their proper place within what Campany calls the "cosmic bureaucracy." (Consider how, in this excerpt, the wizard against whom Monkey struggles on the king of Crow-cock's behalf turns out to be Manjusri's lion in disguise, who is acting directly at Buddha's request.)

The reintegration of a monster into a cosmic hierarchy calls into question notions of good and evil, especially when read from a Western perspective. The demons described in *Monkey* are radically different from their Western counterparts (such as the Satan of Marlowe's *Doctor Faustus* or Milton's *Paradise Lost*) who embody pure evil. Instead of polarized, Manichean opposites of absolute good and absolute evil, *Monkey*'s demons reflect opposing forces that exist in harmony with and even encourage the pilgrims toward their collective processes of self-cultivation. Daoists believe, for example, that the energies called yin and yang complement each other, with each force containing the seed of its opposite. Where yin represents earth, winter, the female, darkness, negativity, and passivity, yang is associated with heaven, the male, light, positivity, and activity. Unlike Western conceptions of good and evil, however, neither yin nor yang seeks to win out over the other; rather, each is a necessary complement to the other. Since both are reflections of ch'i, or the energy of the universe, they are both influential forces but at different moments, often in relationship to seasonal or other specific circumstances. Similarly, in Buddhism, visible demons only assume an internal causation: The mind creates its own monsters. The creation of both bodhisattva and demon can be said to come from the same thought, since a primary Buddhist aim is to relinquish thought that imposes arbitrary permanence on a spontaneous universe. Gods and monsters are created in the mind itself; relinquishing them both is the only way to nirvana, or the ultimate emptiness.

IN THE CLASSROOM

I. MONKEY AND ALLEGORY

Since 1592 and throughout the Ch'ing dynasty, Chinese scholars and textual commentators have read *Monkey* as an allegory. Although sociopolitical interpretations became popular with the communist revolution, Western critics have recently returned to examining *Monkey* for its allegorical significance. Indeed, its primary, or literal, meaning only thinly disguises more profound secondary significations, which, in turn, can lead to proliferating additional interpretations. Read as such an indirect representation of ideas or truths, Tripitaka's and Monkey's pilgrimage reveals not just a journey to the West but a journey of the soul. The pilgrims' adventures, entertaining but sometimes repetitive when read merely for plot value, unveil clever subtleties when interpreted as the inner struggles humans face in the process of Buddhist and Daoist self-purification. As an allegory, *Monkey*'s message is clearly didactic: The pilgrims recognize — in the form of challenges — how their lives may be out of harmony with spiritual teachings and are given the opportunity to return to the path of Enlightenment or the Way. Through a process of self-cultivation, the pilgrims — and, by extension, the readers — become more aware of how to become saint-like within the Buddhist and Daoist traditions. Just as similar Renaissance allegories (*The Faerie Queene*, *Pilgrim's Progress*, and *Paradise Lost*, for example) treat the relationship of man to the gods as epic, *Monkey* grapples with the universal drama of human existence as well.

Also like many Western allegories of adversity, redemption, salvation, and self-purification, however, *Monkey* breeds opportunities for what one critic has called "fertile error." Allegorical characters seem to represent specific ideals within a given episode. Studied across multiple episodes, however, these same characters point to different allegorical significations: Their shifting identities destabilize the very allegory they are trying to construct. Similarly, the more readers of *Monkey* search for specific significance, the more they may be disoriented as meanings shift or even proliferate. The syncretic nature of Chinese religion further complicates this context, since allegorical markers may point to Confucian, Buddhist, and Daoist understandings simultaneously. Buddhism and Daoism both acknowledge the problems inherent in articulating that which cannot be articulated: Enlightenment is a relinquishing of form; the Way is only found when lost. Reading *Monkey* as an allegory can thus be a fascinating experiment in the ineffable world of Chinese syncretic religious existence. And since interpretation of allegory also depends on both the effort and enlightenment of the reader, *Monkey*'s insistence on the humorous takes on new meaning as readers experience the play — at multiple levels — in the text.

DISCUSSION

1. Begin your discussion by characterizing each of the pilgrims, including Tripitaka, Monkey, Pigsy, and Sandy. Ask the students to describe the allegorical significance of each. What sacrifices must each make to become a pilgrim? What changes does each make along the way?

2. Monkey is gifted at what he calls the "art of somersaulting through the clouds": He can travel extraordinary distances in almost no time. If this is the case, why is the pilgrim-

age necessary? Why can't Monkey bring Tripitaka with him? Ask the students to discuss the allegorical implications of the physical journey, especially within a Buddhist or Daoist context. What does the pilgrimage represent? How might Western readers naturalize this interpretation?

3. Explain to the students how *Monkey* might also be translated as *Journey to the West*. Ask the students why Arthur Waley preferred to retitle Wu Chengen's work as *Monkey*. Does this renaming affect the allegorical interpretation of the work, especially Monkey's role in it? How might this narrative be seen differently if it were entitled *Tripitaka*?

4. Ask the students to consider the references to Jade Emperor and the heaven he administers. Discuss the characterization of the realm of the gods in this story. Is Wu's depiction of heaven satiric? reverential? both?

Connections

1. Consider *Monkey* in the context of primary Buddhist teachings, such as The Sermon at Benares: The Four Noble Truths (Book 1). Identify how Monkey and Tripitaka live (or do not live) in accordance with these teachings. Who might be said to better represent these ideals — Monkey or Tripitaka?

2. Ask the students to compare the process of learning illustrated in Plato's Allegory of the Cave (Book 1) with the pilgrims' journey in *Monkey*. How might these two allegories be said to mirror each other? How is the ancient Greek definition of enlightenment different from a Buddhist or Daoist sense of illumination?

3. Compare an episode of *Monkey* with a parable taught by Jesus Christ such as those found in Matthew, chapters 13 and 25, or Luke, chapters 10 and 15 (Book 2). In what ways does fantasy enhance or hinder the didactic quality of an allegory? Are allegories or parables more effective as teaching tools? Why?

4. Voltaire's Candide (Book 4) makes a journey similar to Monkey's but for different reasons. Like *Candide*, might *Monkey* be read as a satiric allegory? Have students compare (a) the objectives for each journey, (b) the experiences Monkey and Candide each encounter, and (c) what or who is ultimately being satirized in each narrative.

Groups

1. Have students choose an episode from *Monkey*. As a class, sketch out the specific parts of the allegory's primary (literal) meaning for this episode. In groups, have the students discern the secondary (figurative) meanings for these same elements. Do all of the groups come up with similar secondary meanings? Why or why not? Call attention to the ontological premises from which the students in class might be operating. Are they imposing their own belief systems onto the text? Discuss whether myths such as *Monkey* are culturally specific or universal in nature.

Writing

Ask students to write a short paper in response to one or more of the following:

1. Discuss the nature of the monsters the pilgrims meet on their journey. If the pilgrims are experiencing an allegorical process of self-cultivation, are the monsters and demons they encounter real? Where do they reside? Explain what the allegorical equivalent might be of the physical struggle often necessary to combat these monsters. What internal weapons do humans inherently possess?

2. Consider the episode from *Monkey* in which Monkey encounters the six robber kings and kills them. What lesson does he learn? What powers does Tripitaka receive to control Monkey? Why is he given those powers? Discuss the allegorical significance of how these powers constrain Monkey.

3. The courts of the gods might be seen to parallel allegorically the courts of human rulers. If the Jade Emperor allegorically represents the emperor on earth, how would you categorize Monkey's attitude toward the imperial court? Using specific examples from the text, discuss whether the emperor is painted favorably or not as a character.

II. THE TRICKSTER

Monkey, Sun Wukong, is a stunning example of the mythological trickster. Principal characters in the oldest recorded tales, legends, and myths, tricksters embody imagination and play. From Hermes stealing Apollo's cattle in ancient Greece to Krishna eating all of his Hindu mother's butter, and then lying about it, tricksters appear across cultural boundaries. Tricksters are true to their names: These archetypes relish playing tricks on gods, humans, and animals. As Lewis Hyde suggests, tricksters are "boundary-crossers" who do not accept physical, social, or temporal constraints as real, and who seek deliberately to blur culturally fixed lines of distinction (male and female, sacred and profane, young and old, living and dead, and right and wrong). Tricksters avoid the traditional dichotomies of law-abiding and law-breaking, cultural code-sanctioning and taboo-transgressing: They seek to question and negate these binary constructions altogether and propose a new, different realm of existence.

As such, tricksters are innately contradictory characters, constructive and destructive at the same time. They are knowledgeable and cunning — often plotters, strategists, and master deceivers — and have special powers, including the ability to change form or shape. Despite obvious brilliance, however, tricksters are not without flaws: They can be painfully blind to their errors and are often tied to the physical world by biological cravings for food or sex. They occupy a liminal space, working for and against the gods, and have just enough power to threaten — and defeat — the reigning authority. Not surprisingly, tricksters often find themselves in trouble. And yet tricksters do not seek to flout authority just for defiance's sake but rather to question the very premises from which that authority is derived.

Hyde states that the trickster represents, in a larger sense, the human imagination itself, the kind that is "disruptive and playful," often difficult to keep bounded. Indeed, tricksters are at the heart of human societies, since they illustrate an imaginative response to the changing nature of life itself. At once jokers and heroes, thieves and saviors, tricksters seem to be free from values themselves and yet can ultimately shake up and redefine the mores of an entire culture. Hyde cautions societies who seek to purify themselves of tricksters, since suppression of the trickster's conspiring instinct might generate something entirely more severe than his typically playful response. Societies that thrive, Hyde insists, accommodate the trickster's paradox: They allow a space within culture to question culture. Ironically, tricksters can then preserve that culture because they can then provide comic relief, prevent stagnation, and contribute defining cultural innovations.

Discussion

1. Ask students to write down a list of the characteristics that would qualify Monkey as a trickster. Have them point to specific passages in the text to justify these claims. Compare Monkey to the bodhisattva. Might she also be considered a trickster? Why or why not?

2.   Have students point out passages from the novel in which Monkey deliberately deceives his companions. Ask them why he does this and whether or not his deception is justified.

3.   Ask students to identify specific cultural codes that Monkey attempts to destabilize throughout his adventures. Why does he do this? Is he effective? Why or why not?

4.   Have students discuss the challenges the pilgrims face. How might each struggle be considered as an internal battle? Ask them to relate the idea of the trickster to the activities of the mind. How might we each have tricksters metaphorically within us? What would they be called?

Connections

1.   Have students read Hesiod's accounts of Prometheus (Book 1). Ask them to compare Monkey with Prometheus, and discuss the trickster characteristics they might share. What taboos does each break? What are the punishments each receives?

2.   Ask students to analyze the relationship between Tripitaka and Monkey in comparison to the relationship of Don Quixote and Sancho Panza (p. 262). What binds each relationship together? Do tricksters need partners to be able to function? Why or why not?

3.   Ask the students to consider the generic conventions of *Monkey* and Gabriel Garcia Marquez's "A Very Old Man with Enormous Wings" (Book 6). Discuss the similarities and differences between the literary fantasy or the supernatural in Monkey and the magical realism in Marquez's tale. Do each of these literary styles help tricksters accomplish their goals? If so, why? If not, why not?

Groups

1.   Using the outline of Monkey's trickster characteristics (see above), have students think of contemporary figures from film, television, politics, or popular music that might exhibit similar characteristics. Would these modern-day characters also be considered trickster figures? Why or why not? How are these modern examples different from Monkey? Who are modern-day tricksters attempting to counter through their mischief? What power structures have replaced the gods?

Writing

    Ask students to write a short paper in response to one or more of the following:

1.   Using specific passages from the text, illustrate and discuss the different ways Monkey mediates between the gods and humans. How is he successful? What are his weaknesses, and how does he deal with them? Discuss Monkey's allegiances: With whom does he most ally himself?

2.   Explore the use of disguise in this narrative. Consider (a) who is able to disguise himself or herself; (b) who is able to recognize others in disguise; and (c) the purposes for which disguises may be used. Why would the arts of disguising and discernment be essential for a trickster figure to have? Explore and explain the metaphorical significance inherent in the power of discernment.

3.   Throughout the pilgrimage, Tripitaka often quotes scriptures, while Monkey proposes a pragmatic plan of action. Using examples from the text, compare Tripitaka's theoretical, scriptural knowledge with Monkey's practical, experiential abilities. Who would you say is more enlightened and why? How does your study of this issue inform your notion of tricksters in general?

4. A large part of understanding and appreciating tricksters as characters stems from assuming texts and myths are trustworthy to begin with. Consider the question of the reliability of the narrator or author. While you were reading *Monkey*, did you think to question the narrator or author? For what reasons might it be said that writers can employ trickster techniques? What might they be?

BEYOND THE CLASSROOM

RESEARCH & WRITING

1. Two contemporary novels that draw on the legends of Monkey are Maxine Hong Kingston's *Tripmaster Monkey* and Gerlad Vizenor's *Griever: An American Monkey King in China*. Compare one or both of these novels to *Monkey*. How do these modern writers update the character of Monkey and his story? Discuss whether allegory remains a factor in these contemporary adaptations.

2. Compare Tripitaka's journey to other Western pilgrimage stories, such as Dante's *Divine Comedy* (Book 2), Chaucer's *Canterbury Tales* (Book 2), or Cervantes' *Don Quixote* (p. 262). Why is each set of pilgrims making such a journey? How do the journeys and the journeys' objectives resemble or differ from each other? Discuss how and why each of these pilgrimages focuses more on the eventual destination or on the process of journeying itself. Do the journeys' significance remain culturally specific?

3. Read an excerpt of another Renaissance allegory, such as Edmund Spenser's *The Faerie Queene* or John Bunyan's *Pilgrim's Progress*. How do the heroes of these narratives compare with Monkey? What allegorical challenges does each hero face? Are they similar or dissimilar? Do their responses to these challenges reflect culturally specific belief systems, universal human myths, or both?

4. Research an account of the Native American trickster figure Coyote. Compare Monkey to Coyote in terms of (a) the special powers each possesses, (b) external or internal constraints placed on those powers, (c) the contexts in which those powers are used, and (d) those to whom each trickster is ultimately loyal. In what ways does each disrupt and/or reinforce the established culture of his time?

5. Research the significance of the monkey as an animal in Indian and Asian myth and folklore beyond Wu Chengen's *Monkey* text. Discuss your findings. How does this knowledge better inform your reading of *Monkey*?

Projects

1. Recall one of the trickster stories that you may have heard as a child (for example, Brer Rabbit, Reynard the Fox, Aunt Nancy, or Coyote stories) and write a contemporary version of it. Provide an analysis of the specific elements you modified and why you changed them. What do your changes reveal about the state of the trickster today?

2. *Monkey* continues to be a favorite story to tell and retell, especially in Chinese popular culture. Searching the Internet, find a Web site devoted to *Monkey*. What is its purpose? Who is its author? How do the characters from *Monkey* represented on the Web site resemble or differ from Wu Chengen's account? Why, in your opinion, does the popularity of this story persist?

3. Think of a whistle-blower figure popular in twentieth-century American culture. Find a specific example of this figure from television, cinema, or politics. Discuss the challenges this person faces and how he or she resolves them. How might this person be con-

sidered a trickster? What special powers does this person possess? What kinds of reconciliation does this person bring about?

4. Sketch out plans to stage a scene from *Monkey*. With what cultural knowledge would you need to familiarize yourself before you could do this? Are you more or less aware of these cultural gaps when you approach *Monkey* as a literary work? How do you as a reader fill in the unknown gaps? Write a list of the questions you might have, then find out how you might begin answering them.

WWW   For additional information on Wu Chengen and annotated Web links, see *World Literature Online* at bedfordstmartins.com/worldlit.

FURTHER READING

Campany, Rob. "Demons, Gods, and Pilgrims: The Demonology of the Hsi-yu Chi." 1985.

Erdoes, Richard, and Alfonso Ortiz, eds. *American Indian Trickster Tales*. 1998.

Hyde, Lewis. *Trickster Makes This World: Mischief, Myth, and Art*. 1998.

Hynes, William J., and Doty, William G., eds. *Mythical Trickster Figures: Contours, Contexts, and Criticisms*. 1993.

Lopez, Barry H. *Giving Birth to Thunder, Sleeping with His Daughter: Coyote Builds North America*. 1977.

Wu, Anthony C. "Heroic Verse and Heroic Mission: Dimension of the Epic in the Hsi-yu chi." 1972.

MEDIA RESOURCES

WEB SITES

China-on-Site: The Monkey King — The Journey to the West
www.china-on-site.com/literatu/classic/west
This fascinating site provides a summary and a Chinese "comic strip" version of the famous tale. Click on the frame numbers to view beautiful paintings of scenes from *Monkey*.

Chinese Literature in Translation
www.columbia.edu/itc/eacp/webcourse/chinaworkbook/lit/books.htm
Created for teachers by the Columbia University East Asian Curriculum Project, this site is useful for both students and teachers in that it provides an annotated list of important Chinese titles along with recommended translations. It also includes lessons and workbook pages on Chinese history, geography, culture, and politics. An added bonus is the list of films on tape.

Classical Chinese Novels — Journal to the West
www.chinapage.com/monkey/monkey.html
This site offers an introduction to *Monkey* and an outline of the story in English, an e-text version of the story in Chinese, and several traditional illustrations of the text.

Renditions — A Chinese-English Translation Magazine
Renditions/org/renditions/magazines/m-menu.html
This site contains an index of Chinese authors, including Wu Chengen; it provides biographical information for each as well as bibliographies of works available in English. It also includes links to publishers of Chinese literature.

GENERAL MEDIA RESOURCES

VIDEO

China's Forbidden City
50 min., 1997 (A&E Video)
A&E throws open the doors of this legendary remnant of China's imperial past for an incredible behind-the-scenes tour that takes the viewer to grand palaces, temples, libraries, and gardens. Explore the city's fascinating history, from the tragic demise of the Ming dynasty's last emperor to the story of China's last emperor, Pu Yi, who was only four when communist forces seized control of the grounds. Experts supply insightful commentary, while the stunning photography makes this a memorable journey into China's past.

Empires in Collision
58 min., 1990 (PBS)
From the fifteenth to the eighteenth centuries, Europe underwent a transformation propelled by a revolution of science and technology. While many of the technologies had originated in China, it was in the Western nations that innovation turned into invention and invention into economic, military, and social expansion. The video also documents the Jesuit involvement with China during 1550 to 1700 and the Opium War of 1839.

The Great Wall of China
50 min., 1997 (Video Library Company)
The Great Wall of China is one of the most massive building achievements in history. Winding 6,000 kilometers through undulating mountains, it is said to be visible to the naked eye from space. Yet the true history of this engineering marvel is as mysterious as the mists of the nearby Yellow River Valley. Join modern engineers and historians as they examine one of the world's most awe-inspiring monuments.

Rise of the Dragon
58 min., 1990 (PBS)
This program provides an overview of the political and cultural history of China from 1000 to 1500, highlighting its ancient technological and scientific innovations. It examines why ancient China was so far ahead of the Western world and why it lost its lead to the Western world.

White Gold, Black Market
26 min., 1986 (PBS)
From 1650 onward, the British seized control of the seas and international trade. Opium exports from India to China financed the British East India Company's administration of India and paid for imports of tea, porcelain, and silk. This is the dramatized story of the trading companies' determination to impose their will on China and to control its markets.

WEB SITES

Chinese Literature in Translation
www.columbia.edu/itc.eacp/webcourse/chinaworkbook/lit.books.ht
Created for teachers by the Columbia University East Asian Curriculum Project, this site is useful for both students and teachers in that it provides an annotated list of important Chinese titles along with recommended translations. It also includes lessons and pages on Chinese history, geography, culture, and politics.

Ming China
www.wsu.edu:8080/~dee/MING/MING.HTM
Richard Hooker's (Washington State University) site provides a reasonably complete history of the Ming dynasty and contains links to many other sources on Ming and other Chinese historical periods.

The Ming Dynasty
www.travelchinaguide.com/intro/history/ming.htm
This site gives a brief overview of the history of the Ming dynasty and hotlinks to a site that gives the history of the Great Wall.

The Ming Dynasty's Maritime History
www.ucalgary.ca/applied_history/tutor/eurvoya/ming.html
This site provides an overview and map of explorations that took place during the Ming dynasty and compares it with the European explorations of the era.

Secrets of the Great Wall
www.discovery.com/stories/history/greatwall/ming.html
From the Discovery Channel, this site contains brief information about the historical and cultural milieu of the Ming dynasty and information on the Great Wall.

INDIA:
SPIRITUAL DEVOTION
AND THE COMING
OF THE MUGHALS

Mirabai (p. 921) and *In the Tradition:* Indian Devotional Poetry, p. 929

Though it is not uncommon for religious works to call for a renunciation of worldly concerns and intense dedication to God, the songs of India's devotional poets do this with a special poignancy, passion, and urgency that reaches audiences on many levels. Rooted in an impulse to carve out a space of personal and communal spiritual devotion, the songs of the bhakti movement are especially notable for their rejection of traditional belief systems, attention to the sensual in nature and the body, and use of symbiotic relationships — between union and separation, emptiness and fulfillment, longing and saturation, fear and hope — to explore the nature of humanity's connection with the divine. These songs touch readers across space and time not only because they negotiate eternal questions but also because they address them in a way that speaks to the experience of everyday reality, drawing forth spiritual understanding and connection through the dramatic, lyrical, and sensory use of language and images. Among the most beautiful and passionate of all religious writings, the songs of India's bhakti movement are still performed today.

In order to appreciate the significance of this movement, students need to be familiar with background information (available in the anthology) regarding Sanskrit, the sacred texts of India, and the caste system (especially the role of Brahmins). Draw their attention to references in the poems to formal study or knowledge of traditional writings and rituals, such as those in Basavanna's "What of It That You Have Read So Much?" (p. 949) and Kabir's "Pundit, How Can You Be So Dumb?" (p. 969). Discuss how the authors approach religious authority differently — whether written or practiced — and the implications of their various approaches. Given an understanding of the role the devotional movement played in voicing and creating an alternative path of religious devotion, especially in the rejection of traditional social ties and expectations, ask the class to consider how this movement relates to the European Reformation and other moments of religious protest. How do such movements comment on — and change — cultural ideologies, and what might be their long-term effects on everyday social attitudes and practices? These poets, especially Mirabai, are often quite outspoken and brave in their rejection of accepted norms. Look at the frequent references to practical social realities and duties, such as those in Mirabai's "The Bhil Woman Tasted Them, Plum after Plum" (p. 925), Mahadeviyakka's "Husband Inside" (p. 951), and Chandidasa's "My Mind Is Not on Housework" (p. 965), and examine the ways this movement argues for new priorities to replace more commonly valued obligations.

As you read through and discuss these texts, keep in mind that they are not just poems but also songs whose creation and expression is an act of worship, and that they are a means of building and unifying spiritual communities. Draw attention to the ways spoken language is a means of defining self and world, negotiating everyday challenges, and establishing shared beliefs. Through their songs, how do these authors define not only their own relation to God but also a system of religious belief? Have individual students or groups practice and then perform readings of the works of several authors to elicit a sense of their rhythm and drawing power. Ask several students to provide presentations of the same poem to facilitate a discussion of the significance of oral delivery and its influence on impact and interpretation. To facilitate students' awareness of multiple interpretive possibilities, look at different translations of the same poem and discuss the challenges faced by translators.

References to music and dance are common in devotional poetry. Ask students to take note of these and examine the ways they participate in the speaker's approach to communion with God. While they read, have students also note the regularity of direct address — appeals to God for a release from everyday trials, pleas for spiritual enlightenment or union, and calls to listeners to follow a sometimes difficult path to enlightenment. They should pay particular attention to closing statements, which sometimes proclaim the speaker's personal dedication to her or his God, call for a spiritual commitment, or comment on the meaning of the previous lines. Vidyapati, for example, concludes "O Friend, I Cannot Tell You" (p. 961) with these lines:

> Says Vidyapati:
> How can I possibly believe such nonsense?

As a class, examine the multiple functions of these concluding lines, focusing particularly on why authors identify themselves in this way and how these lines impact listeners' interpretation of the whole.

For their challenges to accepted social expectations, thoughtful exploration of the ties between the material and spiritual world, and boldness of imagery and emotional investment, the bhakti poets offer much to the student of world literature. These writings participate in an exploration of the relationship between the human and the divine addressed by authors across all ages and localities, from *The Descent of Inanna*, to Dante, the poetry of Nezahualcoyotl, and Goethe's Faust. Draw students' attention to the ways these poets, in addressing universal doubts, fears, and hopes regarding non-corporeal life, not only influence the culture of their own time and place but also contribute to a larger cultural conversation.

IN THE CLASSROOM

I. THE ROLE OF CORPOREAL EXISTENCE IN BHAKTI POETRY

Corporeal existence, with its material necessities, social rules and expectations, and physical desires, poses numerous challenges to spiritual belief. The bhakti poets do not demur in confrontation with these realities. On the contrary, these songs are notable for their incorporation of the everyday in contemplation of the divine, for their attention to this world in all its relations to the next world. Imagery drawn from nature, especially when connected to the harvest or human sustenance, from familial or other love relations, and from labor or craft work is common to devotional songs. Partially due to a sympathy between singers and lower or outcast members of society, this concern with the particulars of the everyday testifies to the presence of the divine in all manner of beings, objects, and activities. It serves to explore and demonstrate the integral connection between the moments of any being's reality and her or his participation in the universal.

Discussion

1. Mirabai repeatedly refers to the disapproval she experiences because of her rejection of traditional roles and expectations. Ask the class to draw from her writing a description of the tension she feels between worldly and earthly obligations. Drawing from passages in her poems, analyze her use of imagery to draw conclusions regarding the connection between music, nature, or the body, and worship or devotion to Krishna.

2. Have students come to class ready with references from the poems to nature, whether they point to places, animals, or plants (note especially images of food and the harvest). Using these passages as evidence, explore the role of the natural world in devotional poetry. Why and how is nature or place important to these authors and their belief system? How is it used as a space of connection between this world and the next?

3. Ask students to point to class, occupation, and gender roles described by these poets. Keeping in mind the larger context of the devotional movement, examine what each assigned author has to say about the expectations for these roles and their participation in spiritual concerns. Generate a discussion exploring the ways the texts not only reject traditional expectations but also use them to communicate a specific vision of the relationship between the individual and the divine.

4. As a class, identify passages in these songs that speak to the relationship or obligations of the individual in her or his search for release from earthly existence. Paying special attention to signature lines, look at the ways bhakti poetry calls for an independent spirit, a controversial voice. How do the last few lines of some of these poems contribute to the impact or meaning of the whole?

Connections

1. In *The Souls of Black Folk*, W. E. B. Du Bois (Book 6) describes the Sorrow Songs as "the most beautiful expression of human experience born this side the seas." Emotionally and lyrically powerful, these are songs not only of exile and suffering but also of spiritual strength, hope, and the promise of freedom. Examine Du Bois's analysis of the Sorrow Songs and the works of James Weldon Johnson and Langston Hughes for their exploration of music, nature, and spirituality. What characteristics are shared by these works and the writings of the devotional poets?

2. In Milton's *Paradise Lost* (p. 575), the Garden of Eden may be seen as a physical, earthly expression of God's magnificence and generosity, and Adam and Eve hold a spiritual relationship with their surroundings. Ask the class to characterize Milton's descriptions of the relationship between humanity and nature, before and after the fall. Compare these treatments of the natural world to those of the bhakti poets.

Writing

Ask students to write a short paper in response to one or more of the following:

1. Mirabai writes clearly and often of her defiance of social, especially gendered, expectations. Providing specific references from her poems, compare her treatment of social responsibilities to one or more of the other bhakti poets. In what way do these writers use their songs to express a devotion that defies traditional social ties?

2. Identify several poems calling attention to the significance of worldly concerns, perhaps to the sacrifice of the body in light of spiritual concerns. Use these poems to describe your interpretation of the relationship between physical reality and the spiritual world as represented by one or more of the devotional poets. In this tradition, what is the function of the human body? What is its purpose?

3. In poems like "Go Naked If You Want" (p. 968) and "Pundit, How Can You Be So Dumb" (p. 969), Kabir argues that traditional knowledge and rituals are not needed for true religious devotion. Compare his message in these poems to his observations on the nature of spirituality in "The River and Its Waves Are One Surf" (p. 970) and "I Laugh When I Hear That the Fish in the Water Is Thirsty" (p. 972). Describe in your own words what, according to Kabir, it means to recognize the spiritual and/or practice devotion.

II. PASSION IN DEVOTIONAL POETRY

Perhaps most striking in devotional poetry is its powerful, vivid assertion of emotion, particularly in the exploration of love relationships. Students may be surprised, for example, by the frank sensuality of Jayadeva, the burning desire of Mahadeviyakka, or the urgent longing expressed by Chandidasa. Help them see these expressions of passionate feeling as explorations and testimony of a felt relationship between physical and spiritual being. Ask them to describe and examine parallels between the physical and emotional loves of this world and our understanding of longing and love for the divine.

Discussion

1. Bhakti poets often call for a humbling of one's current existence as a prerequisite for moving beyond it. How do they use the trials of everyday experiences and emotions to introduce audiences to the trials (and rewards) of spiritual belief? How do familiar, sometimes physical, desires teach one about desire for the universal?

2. Focusing particularly on the love between Krishna and Rhadha, discuss the relationship between physical and spiritual love. Why are descriptions of physical longing so often intensely emotional, sensual, or even erotic in these works? What is the status and role of Radha as she is treated by different authors, such as Jayadeva and Vidyapati?

3. What relationships other than that of the love between man and woman are explored in these poems?

4. The songs of the *Tevaram* contain beautiful and complex celebrations of Shiva. As a class, generate a description of the God, analyze the imagery with which he is associated, and examine the function of the many references to heroic deeds. How does the beauty and power of Shiva serve to humble as well as inspire the singer?

Connections

1. In *The Story of the Stone* (Book 4) the young hero, Jia Bao-yu, is the earthly embodiment of a magical jade stone who is brought to earth in order to experience suffering and desire and achieve spiritual enlightenment. In the tale Bao-yu is involved in a complicated love triangle and is challenged by tensions between his social responsibilities and private spiritual devotion. Consider the similarities between the moral and spiritual message of this story and the concerns of the bhakti poets, particularly regarding one's responsibilities to and the illusory nature of this world and the treatment of human relationships.

Writing

Ask students to write a short paper in response to one or more of the following:

1. Pointing to specific lines in her poems, analyze Mirabai's description of her relationship with Krishna. To what kinds of images does she repeatedly return? Why? What advice does she offer for those who offer their love to God?

2. Many of these poems, such as Campantar's "'O God With Matted Hair!' She Cries" (p. 939), contain expressions of overwhelming passion and awe. Drawing from a variety of texts, analyze the tension between what is often a painful desire for union and feelings, or the promise, of fulfillment. How and why are human relationships a particularly fruitful field for demonstrating this tension?

BEYOND THE CLASSROOM

RESEARCH & WRITING

1. Research a spiritual allegory, such as Spencer's *Faerie Queen*, from a culture other than India, and compare its treatment of physical, worldly love relationships to the same in devotional poetry. In what ways does each work speak to its particular social and historic context? In what ways are their spiritual messages or treatment of love similar?

2. Research the ancient sacred texts of India and their influence on spiritual beliefs and practices. Write an essay in which you explore the ways the devotional movement both draws from and rejects this heritage.

FURTHER READING

Archer, W. G. *The Loves of Krishna in Indian Painting and Poetry*. 1957.
Mukta, Parita. *Upholding the Common Life: The Community of Mirabai*. 1994.
Schomer Karine, and W. H. McLeod, eds. *The Saints: Studies in a Devotional Tradition of India*. 1987.

MEDIA RESOURCES

VIDEO

The Taj Mahal: A Love Story
43 min., 1986 (Films for the Humanities & Sciences)
A symbol of passion and despair, the Taj Mahal is the world's most exquisite mausoleum. This program picks up the thread of Mughal history during the reign of Shah Jahan, which marked the culture's peak of refinement. The construction and symbolism of the Taj are attentively described as well as the legendary romance between Shah Jahan and his favorite queen, Mumtaz Mahal. Artisans at work demonstrate age-old methods of painting and stone-cutting, while visits to the immense tombs of Humayun and Akbar set the Taj in the Mughal funerary tradition of sublimating death through architectural beauty.

Spiritual India: A Guide to Jainism, Islam, Buddhism, and Hinduism
50 min., 1999 (Films for the Humanities & Sciences)
In India, religious observances weave countless golden threads into the homespun fabric of daily life. This program provides an overview of four of India's prominent religions: Jainism, Islam, Buddhism, and Hinduism. Stunning footage from all around the subcontinent displays these jewels of India's religious heritage — along with their monuments, shrines, temples, festivals, and sacred rituals — against the backdrop of the nation's intricate history, diverse geography, and rich variety of cultures and languages.

WEB SITES

Basavanna
www.freeindia.org/biographies/sages/basaveshwara/page1.htm
This is an overview of the poet and sage.

Black Peacock
www.goloka.com/docs/gita_govinda/
Paintings of the devotional songs found in the Gita.

Excerpts of the Gita Govinda
www.geocities.com/Athens/Acropolis/5356/Govinda_1.html
This is a beautifully done site that provides access to the poems accompanied by images.

Gita Govinda
ignca.nic.in/gita.htm
This is a thorough page providing background on the Gita with audio files of reading of its poetry.

Indian Saints, Mystics, Philosophers, and Gurus
www.indiayogi.com/content/indsaints/default.asp
This site contains biographical information on such figures as Kabir and Mahadeviyakka.

Kabir
www.boloji.com/kabir/
This site is very interesting and complete; it provides access to biographical information on Kabir and links to many of his poems.

Manas: Indian Religions
www.sscnet.ucla.edu/southasia/Religions/religions.html
This site provides an interesting overview of Indian religions with specific mention of the devotional poets.

Manas: Mirabai
www.sscnet.ucla.edu/southasia/Religions/gurus/Mirabai.html
This site provides a brief biography of Mirabai and a brief bibliography of primary and secondary works on her poetry.

Mirabai
www.tl.infi.net/~ddisse/mirabai.html
This site provides a brief biography of Mirabai and links to several sites that include her poems.

Mirabai Web Site
http://www.chandrakantha.com/biodata/mira.html
Biographical information, additional links, and streaming audio of some of Mirabai's poetry being sung.

Poet Seers: Kabir
poetseers.org/the_poetseers/kabir
This site provides background information on Kabir with links to some of his poems in translation.

Poet Seers: Mirabai
poetseers.org/the_poetseers/mirabai
This is a very good site on Mirabai and contains a biography of the poet as well as many of her poems in translation.

Vidyapati: Love Songs to Krishna
www.wsu.edu:8080/~wldciv/world_civ_reader/world_civ_reader_1/vidyapati.html
This site contains a brief biography of Vidyapati and includes several of his poems.

AUDIO
Songs of Kabir
Purshotamdas Jalota is one of the finest devotional singers in the world of Indian music. Through his many recordings, and through his public performances in a variety of different countries, he has brought the riches of Hinduism's devotional songs to a wide and appreciative audience. His name has come to be virtually synonymous with the bhajan, or religious lyric, which is his chosen specialty; his interpretations of the Hindi songs of poets such as Surdas, Tulsidas, and Kabir are a living channel for the ancient tradition in the modern world.

Songs to Shiva
In the tradition of Yoga, the ultimate experience of transcendence and liberation has most
often been portrayed through the personification and mystical symbolism of Shiva, or
Shambhu, "whose being is peace" and many other names, found here in these ten ancient
songs, or stotra. At once inspiring and terrifying — in meditation on Mt. Kailasa, or
smeared with crematory ashes and wearing a garland of skulls; Shiva is the final truth,
a knowledge of Self that transcends all limiting beliefs and identities; the resolution of
duality — male and female, good and bad, pleasure and pain, life and death. Includes
an illustrated thirty-two-page book with Sanskrit, translation, and transliteration.

GENERAL MEDIA RESOURCES

VIDEO

Akbar the Great, Mogul Emperor of India
54 min., 2000 (Films for the Humanities & Sciences)
A descendant of Genghis Khan and Tamerlane, Akbar the Great succeeded in forging an
empire in India that brought about a splendid period of political stability and religious tolerance. This program blends dramatizations of significant moments in Mughal history
with location footage of intricate architectural landmarks to create a detailed account of
Akbar's reign. Religious and secular customs from both then and now as well as events in
Europe concurrent with the Mughal empire are also documented in order to demonstrate
the historical interplay between East and West and the survival of remnants of Mughal culture in India today.

Indus to Independence: A Journey Through Indian History
34 min., 2000 (Films for the Humanities & Sciences)
India, a rich amalgam of cultures and religions, bears the imprint of many civilizations.
Beginning with the Stone Age, this comprehensive program unfolds India's past, era by era,
covering the Indus Valley civilization, the Vedic Age, the Maurya empire, the Gupta Age,
the southern kingdoms, the Muslim invasion, the Mughal and Maratha empires, the British
Raj, and independence. The impact of India's diverse religions — Hinduism, Buddhism,
Jainism, Islam, and Christianity — is also explored.

The Moguls: In the Gardens of Delight
44 min., 1986 (Films for the Humanities & Sciences)
For devotees of Islam, paradise is said to be a celestial garden. Who created the marvelous
earthly gardens of Kashmir, which stand to this day as a living symbol of Muslim faith?
This program tells the story of the Mughal empire in India, from the victory of Babur at
Panipat through the reign of the syncretic-minded Akbar, who dreamed of integrating
Islam and Hinduism. The intricately designed gardens of Kashmir, with their emblematic
plantings and waterways, and the remarkable Hindu/Islamic architecture of Fatapur Sikri
are featured.

The Taj Mahal: A Love Story
43 min., 1986 (Films for the Humanities & Sciences)
A symbol of passion and despair, the Taj Mahal is the world's most exquisite mausoleum.
This program picks up the thread of Mughal history during the reign of Shah Jahan, which
marked the culture's peak of refinement. The construction and symbolism of the Taj are
attentively described, as well as the legendary romance between Shah Jahan and his favorite
queen, Mumtaz Mahal. Artisans at work demonstrate age-old methods of painting and
stone-cutting, while visits to the immense tombs of Humayun and Akbar set the Taj in the
Mughal funerary tradition of sublimating death through architectural beauty.

The Moguls: Women and Warriors
46 min., 1986 (Films for the Humanities & Sciences)
What was life like for the upper classes of Mughal society, for whom power, wealth, and personal appearance were an obsession? This program appraises the status of empresses, harem favorites, and the Rajput warriors in the Mughal empire over the course of its history. Details of life on the throne, in the boudoir, and in the army's elite forces illustrate a culture both opulent and narcissistic. Prestige is also reflected by the grandeur of the Red Fort at Agra and the Palace of the Winds, the Amber Fort, and the modernistic, sculpture-like Jantar Mantar astronomical observatory in Jaipur, the Pink City of India.

Spiritual India: A Guide to Jainism, Islam, Buddhism, and Hinduism
50 min., 1999 (Films for the Humanities & Sciences)
In India, religious observances weave countless golden threads into the homespun fabric of daily life. This program provides an overview of four of India's prominent religions: Jainism, Islam, Buddhism, and Hinduism. Stunning footage from all around the subcontinent displays these jewels of India's religious heritage — along with their monuments, shrines, temples, festivals, and sacred rituals — against the backdrop of the nation's intricate history, diverse geography, and rich variety of cultures and languages.

WEB SITES

InformationCorner.com: India
www.informationcorner.com/India.asp
This is a very informative site that provides links to audio files of Indian devotional songs.

Manas: The Mughal Empire
www.sscnet.ucla.edu/southasia/History/Mughals/mughals.html
This site out of UCLA contains concise historical and cultural information on the Mughal empire.

The Mughal Empire
www.wikipedia.org/wiki/Mughal_Empire
This site provides an overview of the empire and background on its key rulers.

The Mughal Dynasty
www.islamicart.com/library/empires/india/
The main objectives of this site are to discuss in detail the great dynasty of the Mughals and its lavish patronage of the arts; provide detailed vignettes of the daily life of the Mughal emperors and the members of their entourage; demonstrate the profusion of skills the craftsmen and artists of the Mughals had at their disposal; and explore the remarkable monuments and beautiful artistic objects of the great Mughals.

Virtual Art Exhibit — Mughal Empire
depts.washington.edu/uwch/silkroad/exhibit/mughals/mughals.html
This site provides not only information on the Mughal empire but also a map of the region, selected samples of art of the era, and a timeline comparing India with events in the rest of the world.

AUDIO
Living Biographies of Religious Leaders
8 tapes, 11:25 hrs. (Blackstone Audiobooks)
This program presents the lives of twenty great founders and leading advocates of the world's foremost religions. Here are the historical facts and legends associated with these

forceful personalities who have inspired and influenced humankind through the centuries. Presented here are Jesus Christ, Moses, Isaiah, Zoroaster, Buddha, Confucius, John the Baptist, Paul, Muhammad, Francis of Assisi, John Hus, Luther, Loyola, Calvin, George Fox, Swedenborg, Wesley, Brigham Young, Mary Baker Eddy, and Gandhi.

SAMPLE SYLLABI

Dear Instructor:

Producing syllabi has been a useful exercise to understand the dilemma many of you face as you prepare to use *The Bedford Anthology of World Literature*. Our anthology is very rich in texts, allowing for a huge variety of options. Courses from our book can be organized by historical period, geographical region, theme, and genre. Any syllabus necessarily leaves out a large number of texts, especially considering that any one of the six books could easily be used to structure a sixteen-week course. For those of you with little experience teaching world lit, these choices must appear overwhelming. We've suggested a few ways with thematic and historical options for each of the six books and for Pack A and Pack B—but recognize that there are many other ways to structure the course. If you'd be willing to share your syllabus with other instructors, we'd love to post it on the Web site. Send it to our editor, Alanya Harter, at aharter@bedfordstmartins.com. We think the more syllabi out there, the better.

BOOK 1

HISTORICAL SYLLABUS:
STORIES OF THE AGES

THE AGE OF MYTH AND LEGEND

WEEK 1:

Mesopotamia	*The Descent of Inanna*
	The Epic of Creation

WEEK 2:

Egypt	*Creating the World and Defeating Apophis:*
	A Ritual Hymn. Hymn to Osiris
Greece	Hesiod, from *Theogony*: The Castration of Uranus,
	Kronos Swallows His Children, Prometheus Steals Fire

WEEK 3:

Rome	Ovid, from *Metamorphoses*: The Creation, Four Ages, Orpheus &
	Eurydice, Venus & Adonis
India	*The Rig Veda*: Indra Slays the Dragon Vritra, Hymn to the Horse

WEEK 4:

The Ancient Hebrews	Hebrew Scriptures: Genesis, Exodus, The Song of Songs

THE AGE OF THE EPIC

WEEK 5:
Mesopotamia	*The Epic of Gilgamesh*
India	*The Ramayana*

WEEKS 6–7:
Greece	Homer, *The Odyssey*

THE GOLDEN AGE OF GREECE AND ROME

WEEK 8:	Aeschylus, *The Oresteia* [or: Sophocles, *Oedipus Rex*]
WEEK 9:	Sophocles, *Antigone*
WEEK 10:	Euripides, *Medea* [or Aristophanes, *Lysistrata*]

WEEK 11:
Socrates & Catullus	Plato, *Apology*, from *Phaedo*
	Catullus, selected poems

WEEK 12:
Aeneas & the	Virgil, *The Aeneid*
Founding of Rome	

THE SPIRITUAL PATH IN INDIA

WEEK 13:
Meditation	The Upanishads
	Bhagavad Gita

WEEK 14:
Raising Consciousness	Buddhist Texts. Ashvaghosha, *The Life of Buddha.*
	Sermons & Instructions

CREATING A CIVIL SOCIETY IN CHINA

WEEK 15:
Filial Piety	Confucius (Kongfuzi), *The Analects*

WEEK 16:
Daoism	Laozi (Lao Tzu), *Dao De Jing*
	Zhuangzi (Chuang Tzu), Basic Writings

THEMATIC SYLLABUS:
THEMES IN LITERATURE

The following syllabus is organized around dominant themes and literary genres. This kind of organization allows for substituting different literary texts while preserving the overall plan for a sixteen-week semester. For the most part, the themes are linked to "In the World" sections which provide a variety of contexts for the literature.

CREATING THE WORLD

Week 1:
The Conflict of
Generations

In the World: Creating Cosmogony
Hesiod, *The Castration of Uranus* (Greece)

Week 2:
Patriarchal Order and
the Fall

Genesis (Hebrew)

Week 3:
Masculine Order versus
Feminine Chaos

The Epic of Creation (Mesopotamia)
Creating the World and Defeating Apophis (Egypt)
The Rig Veda: Indra Slays the Dragon Vritra (India)

THE EPIC HERO

Week 4:
The Hero Journey

The Epic of Gilgamesh (Mesopotamia)
Moses, Exodus (Hebrew) [Or Job]

Weeks 5–6:
The Trojan War &
the Journey Home

Homer, *The Odyssey* (Greece)
In the World: Changing Gods: From Religion to Philosophy

Week 7:
From Religion to
Drama

Aeschylus, *The Oresteia* (Greece)

Week 8:
The Making of
a Leader

The Ramayana

GODDESS AND THE FEMALE HERO

Week 9:
The Tradition of
the Goddess

The Descent of Inanna (Mesopotamia)
Euripides, *Medea* (Greece)

WISDOM LITERATURE AND PHILOSOPHY

Week 10:
The Trial of Socrates
(and Job?)

In the World: Heroes and Citizens
Plato, *Apology* & *Phaedo* (Greece)
Optional: Job and Psalms (Hebrew)

Week 11:
Confucius & the
Foundation of
Chinese Civilization

Confucius (Kongfuzi), *The Analects*

THE CREATION OF EMPIRE

WEEK 12:
Rome as Empire
Builder

In the World: War, Rulers, and Empire
Virgil, *The Aeneid* (Rome)

LYRIC POETRY

WEEK 13:
The Mixture of
Sacred and Secular

Egyptian love poems
Sappho, poems (Greece)
The Song of Songs (Hebrew)

WEEK 14:
The Variety of
Poetic Themes

Catullus, poems (Rome)
The Book of Songs (China)

LIVING THE GOOD LIFE

WEEK 15:
The Life of
Consciousness

In the World: The Good Life
Ashvaghosha, *The Life of Buddha* (India)
Buddha's sermons (India)

WEEK 16:
The Daoists & the
Retreat from
Public Life

Laozi (Lao Tzu), *Dao De Jing* (China)
Zhuangzi (Chuang Tzu), Basic Writings (China)

BOOK 2

HISTORICAL SYLLABUS: GEOGRAPHICAL HISTORY

A geographical and historical sequence showing the development of cultural works in relation to geographical proximity and historical events. Sometimes this development is expressed in terms of differences or polarities, as the section titles suggest.

THE NEAR EAST: CHRISTIANITY AND ISLAM

WEEK 1:   The New Testament

WEEK 2:   St. Augustine, *The Confessions*
The Qur'an

WEEK 3:   *The Life of Muhammad. The Life of Charlemagne.*
The Life of Saladin.

INDIA: NORTH AND SOUTH

WEEK 4:   *The Tamil Anthologies*
Kalidasa, *Shakuntala*

CHINA: THE HAN AND TANG DYNASTIES

WEEK 5:	The poetry of Tao Qian. Poets of the Tang dynasty.

ARABIA AND PERSIA: MYSTICISM AND POPULAR LITERATURE

WEEK 6:	Attar, *The Conference of the Birds*; Rumi, poems. *The Thousand and One Nights.*

EUROPE: FROM EPIC TO ROMANCE

WEEK 7:	*Beowulf*
WEEK 8:	*The Song of Roland* *Muslim and Christian at War* (Includes *The Alexiad* of Anna Comnena)
WEEK 9:	Capellanus, *The Art of Courtly Love.* Ibn Hazm, *The Dove's Necklace.* **In the Tradition:** The Courtly Love Lyrics of Muslim Spain and the South of France Marie de France, *The Lay of Chevrefoil*
WEEKS 10–11:	Dante, *Inferno*
WEEK 12:	Boccaccio, *The Decameron* Chaucer, *The Canterbury Tales*
WEEK 13:	*The Origin of Chingis Khan.* Di Carpine, *History of the Mongols.* Marco Polo, *Travels.* Mandeville, *Travels.*

JAPAN: BIRTH OF A CULTURE

WEEK 14:	*Man'yoshu* *Kokinshu*
WEEK 15:	Sei Shonagon, *The Pillow Book* Murasaki Shikibu, *The Tale of Genji* (selections)
WEEK 16:	*The Tale of the Heike* (selections) Zeami Motokiyo, *Atsumori*

THEMATIC SYLLABUS: GREAT THEMES AND MOMENTS IN MEDIEVAL LITERATURE

A diverse handling of the epic genre, a key medieval religious and political conflict, the culture of courtly societies, and the topic of world catastrophe on a comparative basis.

THE EPIC MOMENT

WEEK 1:	Orientation
WEEK 2:	The Germanic epic. *Beowulf.*

WEEK 3:	Persian epic. *The Tragedy of Sohrab and Rostam.*
	Arabian ode. *The Mu'allaqah of Imru'al-Qays.*
WEEK 4:	Poems from *The Tamil Anthologies*
	Kalidasa, *Shakuntala*

CHRISTIANITY AND ISLAM

WEEK 5:	The life of Christ: The New Testament
	St. Augustine, *The Confessions*
WEEK 6:	*The Life of Muhammad*
	The Qur'an
WEEK 7:	*The Life of Charlemagne*
	The Song of Roland
WEEK 8:	The First Crusade (Christian and Byzantine sources)
	Reflections of the Crusaders (Christians and Muslims)

COURTLY LITERATURES OF MEDIEVAL SOCIETY

WEEK 9:	
Tao Qian and poetic style in China	Poets of the Tang dynasty in China
WEEK 10:	*Man'yoshu:* Early poetry of the Japanese Court
	Kokinshu: Later poetry of the Japanese Court
WEEK 11:	Sei Shonagon, *The Pillow Book*, reflections of the Japanese Court
	Murasaki Shikibu, *The Tale of Genji*, Japanese courtly romance
WEEK 12:	The love poetry of Andalusia (Muslim Spain)
	The *troubadours* of the south of France
WEEK 13:	The evolution of medieval story: *The Arabian Nights*
	Chaucer, *The Wife of Bath's Prologue* and *Tale*

VISIONS OF CATASTROPHE AND THE END OF CIVILIZATION

WEEK 14:	Dante, *Inferno* (selections)
WEEK 15:	*The Tale of the Heike*
	Zeami Motoyiko, *Atsumori*
WEEK 16:	*The Origin of Chingis Khan*
	The Histories of Joan of Arc

BOOK 3

HISTORICAL SYLLABUS:
WORLD CULTURAL CONTEXTS

This syllabus follows a masterworks approach to the major texts of world literature in the early modern world. The "In the World" sections add a world cultural context for the major texts within the regional/historical survey.

AFRICA

WEEK 1:
Epic Literature in Mali   *Sunjata*

EUROPE

WEEK 2:
Petrarch and   Petrarch, *Canzoniere*
Lyric Poetry   **In the Tradition:** European Love Lyrics

WEEK 3:
Tales of Love   Marguerite de Navarre, *The Heptameron*

WEEK 4:
Machiavelli in   Machiavelli, *The Prince*
Context   **In the World:** Fashioning the Prince

WEEK 5:
Montaigne's "Of   Montaigne, "Of Cannibals"
Cannibals" in Context   **In the World:** Discovery and Confrontation

WEEK 6:
The Novel   Cervantes, *Don Quixote*

WEEK 7:
Drama: Faustus and   Marlowe, *Doctor Faustus*
the New Learning   **In the World:** Humanism, Learning, and Education

WEEK 8:
The Literary Epic   Milton, *Paradise Lost*
in Context

WEEK 9:
The Literature   **In the World:** Challenging Orthodoxy
of Reform

WEEK 10:
Dramatizing Europe's   Shakespeare, *The Tempest* (This play introduces themes
Encounter with the   important to the next unit on America, thus we present
New World   it after Milton.)

THE AMERICAS

WEEK 11:
Aztec Myth and   The Ancient Mexicans: Myths of Creation, Myth of Quetzalcoatl
Poetry   Poetry of Nezahualcoyotl

WEEK 12:
Cortés's Campaign against the Aztecs — The Conquest of Mexico

WEEK 13:
Reflections on the European Encounter with the New World — Ancient Mexicans: A Defense of Aztec Religion
In the World: Europe Meets America

CHINA

WEEK 14:
The Novel — Wu Chengen, *Monkey*

INDIA

WEEK 15:
Mirabai and Indian Devotional Poetry — Mirabai
In the Tradition: Indian Devotional Poetry: Tamil Poets, Kannada Poets, Jayadeva

WEEK 16:
In the Tradition: Indian Devotional Poetry: Bengali Songs, Kabir

THEMATIC SYLLABUS: THE TEMPEST IN A WORLD HISTORICAL CONTEXT

This syllabus emphasizes a comparative cultural studies approach to the major texts of world literature in the early modern world. Centering upon Shakespeare's *The Tempest*, which introduces the themes of cultural encounter, European contact with the new world, power, knowledge, and love, the course draws upon a variety of themes and genres to place Shakespeare's play in the broad context of world culture. The course begins with a close reading of Shakespeare's play, a showing of one of the film versions or adaptations of the play, and concludes with a re-reading of the play to see what new interpretations have emerged given the enlarged literary and historical context derived from the course readings.

INTRODUCTION: READING THE TEMPEST

WEEK 1:
Dramatizing Europe's Encounter with the New World — Shakespeare, *The Tempest*

WEEK 2:
The Tempest on Film — Peter Greenaway, director. *Prospero's Books* (recommended).
Paul Mazursky, director. *The Tempest*.
Derek Jarman, director. *The Tempest*.
Fred McLeod Wilcox, director. *Forbidden Planet*.

THE RENAISSANCE HERO

WEEK 3:
Africa's epic hero   *The Tempest*
                             Sunjata

WEEK 4:
The European Prince   Machiavelli, *The Prince*
in a Global Context   **In the World:** Fashioning the Prince

DISCOVERY AND CONFRONTATION

WEEK 5:
Montaigne's "Of   Montaigne, "Of Cannibals"
Cannibals" in Context   **In the World:** Discovery and Confrontation

WEEK 6:
Cortés Meets   The Conquest of Mexico
the Aztecs   The Myth of Quetzalcoatl

WEEK 7:
Reflections on the   A Defense of the Aztec Religion
European Encounter   **In the World:** Europe Meets America
with the New World

WEEK 8:
Fictionalizing a   Wu Chengen, *Monkey*
Chinese Traveler
in India

KNOWLEDGE AND POWER

WEEK 9:
European Humanism   Marlowe, *Doctor Faustus*
in a Global Context   **In the World:** Humanism, Learning, and Education

WEEK 10:
Forbidden Knowledge   Milton, *Paradise Lost*

WEEK 11:
The Literature of   **In the World:** Challenging Orthodoxy
Reform in a Global
Context

LOVE

WEEK 12:
Petrarch and European   Petrarch, *Canzoniere*
Love Lyric   **In the Tradition:** European Love Lyrics

WEEK 13:
European Tales   Marguerite de Navarre, *The Heptameron*
of Love

WEEK 14:
Indian Devotional   Mirabai, Poems
Poetry   **In the Tradition:** Indian Devotional Poetry

WEEK 15:
Ironizing Romantic   Cervantes, *Don Quixote*
Love and Power

WEEK 16:
Rereading   Shakespeare, *The Tempest*
The Tempest

PACKAGE A

HISTORICAL SURVEY OF MASTERWORKS FROM THE ANCIENT WORLD THROUGH THE EARLY MODERN PERIOD

This syllabus emphasizes an historical/geographical approach to the major texts of world literature in a variety of genres from the Sumerian epic *Gilgamesh* through Wu Chengen's great novel, *Monkey*.

THE ANCIENT WORLD (Book 1)

MESOPOTAMIA, EGYPT, AND THE NEAR EAST

WEEK 1:   *The Descent of Inanna*
                            The Epic of Gilgamesh

WEEK 2:   Hebrew Scriptures: Genesis, Exodus
                            In the World: Creating Cosmogony

GREECE
WEEK 3:   Homer, *The Iliad*; *The Odyssey*

WEEK 4:   Aeschylus, *The Oresteia*

WEEK 5:   Sophocles, *Oedipus Rex*
                            In the World: Changing Gods: From Religion to Philosophy

ROME
WEEK 6:   Virgil, *The Aeneid*

INDIA
WEEK 7:   *Ramayana*
                            Bhagavad Gita

WEEK 8:   Confucius (Kongfuzi), *Analects*
                            Laozi (Lao Tzu), *Dao De Jing*
                            Zhuangzi (Chuang Tzu), Basic Writings
                            In the World: The Good Life

THE MIDDLE PERIOD (Book 2)

THE NEAR EAST
WEEK 9:   The New Testament
                            The Qur'an

INDIA
WEEK 10:   Kalidasa, *Shakuntala*

CHINA
WEEK 11:   Tao Qian, poems
                In the Tradition: Poets of the Tang Dynasty: Du Fu and Li Bai

JAPAN
WEEK 12:   Lady Murasaki, *The Tale of Genji*
                Zeami, *Atsumori*

ARABIA AND PERSIA
WEEK 13:   Farid ud-Din Attar, from *The Conference of the Birds*
                The Thousand and One Nights

EUROPE
WEEK 14:   Dante, *Inferno*
                Chaucer, *The Wife of Bath's Prologue* and *Tale*

THE EARLY MODERN PERIOD (Book 3)

EUROPE
WEEK 15:   Petrarch, *Canzoniere*
                In the Tradition: European Love Lyrics
                Machiavelli, *The Prince*
                In the World: Fashioning the Prince

WEEK 16:   Shakespeare, *The Tempest*
                In the World: Europe Meets America

CHINA
WEEK 17:   Wu Chengen, *Monkey*

HISTORICAL SURVEY OF MASTERWORKS OF LITERATURE: WORKS AND CIVILIZATIONS

A historical survey introducing the literary and religious masterworks of the great world civilizations. Cultural heritage is envisioned on a world scale: a world literature comes about through conquest, trade, discovery, and the spread of faith and learning.

MESOPOTAMIA AND THE NEAR EAST; GREECE AND ROME

WEEK 1:
Sumerian epic   *The Epic of Gilgamesh*

WEEK 2:   Hebrew Scriptures

WEEK 3:
Greek epic   Homer, *The Odyssey* (selections)

WEEK 4:
Greek tragedy   Sophocles, *Antigone*. Euripides, *Medea*.

WEEK 5:
Roman literary epic   Virgil, *The Aeneid* (selections)

INDIA, CHINA, THE NEAR EAST

WEEK 6:
Indian epic   *The Mahabharata* (selections)

WEEK 7:
Buddhism   Ashvagosa, *The Life of Buddha*. Sermons of Buddha.

WEEK 8:
Confucianism   Confucius (Kongfuzi), *Analects*
Taoism   Laozi (Lao Tzu), *Tao Te Ching*
                               Zhuangzi (Chuang Tzu), Basic Writings

WEEK 9:
Christianity   The New Testament
                               Arabian epic: *The Mu'allaqah of Imru' al-Qays*

WEEK 10:
Islam   *The Life of Muhammad*. The Qur'an (selections).

INDIA, EUROPE, THE NEAR EAST

WEEK 11:
Indian epic drama   Kalidasa, *Shakuntala*

WEEK 12:
Germanic epic   *Beowulf*

WEEK 13:
Japanese literary epic   *The Tale of Genji* (selections)

WEEK 14:
Stories of Arabian   *The Thousand and One Nights*
origin

WEEK 15:
Christian literary epic   Dante, *Inferno* (selections)

AFRICA AND EUROPE

WEEK 16:
West African epic   *Sunjata*
English drama   Shakespeare, *The Tempest* (selections)

PACKAGE A

THEMATIC/GENERIC SYLLABUS:
ANCIENT WORLD TO EARLY MODERN:
HEROES, RULERS, AND LOVERS

This syllabus organizes a course in the great works of the Ancient through the early modern world by genre and by theme. The first seven weeks cover the epic, followed by four weeks on the drama; and five weeks on poetry and fiction. By using the "In the World" sections, units 1 and 2 provide an overlapping discussion of heroic ideals and rulership; unit 3 shifts to a focus on love, generally among courtiers and nobility. Students can compare the way different cultures set up rules and expectations about heroes and heroines, rulers and government, and love. By using different "In the World" sections, one could highlight other themes.

UNIT 1: THE EPIC HERO

WEEK 1:
Mesopotamia   *The Epic of Gilgamesh*

WEEK 2:
Greece   Homer, *The Odyssey*

WEEK 3:
India   Valmiki, *The Ramayana*
                                In the World: Heroes and Citizens. This unit focuses a
                                comparative discussion of the qualities of heroes and citizens
                                in the epics in this unit, and it anticipates and sets up ideas
                                revisited in Weeks 8 and 11.

WEEK 4:
Rome   Virgil, *The Aeneid*

WEEK 5:
Arabia and Africa   Ferdowsi, *Epic of Kings*
                                Sunjata

WEEK 6:
Europe   *Beowulf*
                                Milton, *Paradise Lost*

WEEK 7:
Europe   Milton, *Paradise Lost*
                                Midterm Examination

DRAMA: RULERS AND EMPIRE

WEEK 8:
Greece   Sophocles, *Antigone*
                                In the World: War, Rulers, and Empire. This unit focuses a com-
                                parative discussion on ancient writings about governance and
                                empire, providing a means to compare the various figures in-
                                troduced in the plays and anticipating **In the World:** Fashioning
                                the Prince (Week 11) which offers a view of the ideal ruler in the
                                early modern world.

WEEK 9:
India   Kalidasa, *Shakuntala*

WEEK 10:
Japan/Europe   Zeami, *Atsumori*
                               Shakespeare, *The Tempest*

WEEK 11:
Europe   Shakespeare, *The Tempest*
                               In the World: Fashioning the Prince

LYRIC AND FICTION: LOVERS

WEEK 12:
Egypt, Near East,   Egypt: Ancient Love Poems
and Greece   Hebrew Scriptures: Psalms, The Song of Songs
                               Sappho

WEEK 13:
Rome, Persia,   Catullus
Medieval Europe   Rumi, poems
                               In the Tradition: The Courtly Love Lyrics of Muslim Spain . . .
                               Focusing on love poetry of the middle period, this "In the
                               Tradition" unit focuses a discussion about courtship rituals and
                               love poetry from various traditions; it also anticipates **In the
                               Tradition:** Renaissance Love Lyrics (Week 15) that brings
                               together European love lyrics of the Early Modern period.

WEEK 14:
Japan   *Kokinshu*, Man'yoshu
                               Lady Murasaki, *The Tale of Genji*

WEEK 15:
Europe   Chaucer, *The Wife of Bath's Prologue* and *Tale*
                               In the Tradition: European Love Lyrics

WEEK 16:
Ancient Mexico   The Poetry of Nezahualcoyotl
                               Review

THEMATIC/GENERIC SYLLABUS:
EXPANDING CULTURE

The following syllabus is organized around dominant themes and genres in the
three periods; this kind of organization allows for substituting different literary
texts while preserving the overall plan. Introductory materials and the "In the
World" sections should be included where appropriate.

THE ANCIENT WORLD (7 WEEKS)

CREATION MYTH
WEEK 1:
Creating the World   *Creating the World and Defeating Apophis* (Egypt)
                               Hymn to Aten (Egypt)
                               Genesis (Hebrew)

AGE OF THE EPIC
WEEK 2:
The Earliest Epic and Hero Journey	*The Descent of Inanna* (Mesopotamia) *The Epic of Gilgamesh* (Mesopotamia)

WEEK 3:
The Trojan War & Homer	Homer, *The Odyssey* (Greece)

DRAMA
WEEK 4:
The Roots of Drama & Religion	Job (Hebrew) Aeschylus, *The Oresteia* (Greece) [Or: Sophocles, *Oedipus Rex* or *Antigone*]

HEROES AND PHILOSOPHERS
WEEK 5:
Socrates	Plato, *Apology* & *Phaedo* (Greece) Buddha [Or: Jesus & Christian Scriptures in The Middle Period] Ashvaghosha, *The Life of Buddha* (India)

THE SPIRITUAL PATH AND THE GOOD LIFE
WEEK 6:
The Wisdom of India	Vedic Literature (India) Upanishads (India) & Bhagavad Gita (India)

WEEK 7:
Engaging the World or Retreating: Two Extremes	Confucius (Kongfuzi), *The Analects* (China) Laozi (Lao Tzu), *Dao De Jing* (China) Zhuangzi (Chuang Tzu), Basic Writings (China)

THE MIDDLE PERIOD (4 WEEKS)

CHRISTIANITY AND ISLAM
WEEK 8:
The Story of Jesus & Fighting the Moors	The New Testament *The Song of Roland*

WEEK 9:
The Christian Pilgrimage	Dante, *Inferno* (Europe)

WEEK 10:
The Story of Muhammad & the Islamic World	The Biography of the Prophet The Qur'an

THE COURTS OF CHINA AND JAPAN
WEEK 11:
The Poets of Early China & the Japanese Romance	Poets of the Tang Dynasty (China) Murasaki Shikibu, *The Tale of Genji* (Japan)

THE EARLY MODERN PERIOD (5 WEEKS)

THE REBIRTH OF HUMANISM IN EUROPE

WEEK 12:

The Reformation and the University	Marlowe, *Doctor Faustus* **In the World:** Humanism, Tradition, and Synthesis

WEEK 13:

Politics and Science	Machiavelli, *The Prince* **In the World:** Challenging Orthodoxy

EUROPE MEETS AMERICA

WEEK 14:

European Attitudes	Montaigne, Essays Shakespeare, *The Tempest*

WEEK 15:

The Ancient Mexicans	The Myth of Quetzalcoatl The Conquest of Mexico **In the World:** Europe Meets America

DEVOTIONAL POETRY OF INDIA

WEEK 16:

The Worship of Krishna and Shiva	Kannada Songs to Shiva Kabir & Mirabai, selected poems